THE COMPANION GUIDE TO IRELAND

'A companion of original mind, subtle wit and graceful style.'
Dervla Murphy, *Daily Telegraph*

'The Companion Guide is very good indeed... All Ireland is in this book. May it outlast the country's troubles.'
Eric Newby, *Observer*

'Mr Lehane is my man. He writes agreeably and well, he loves the past and he sees the Anglo-Irish past as clearly as the old Irish past which preceded it and he sees the buildings and scenery with the same imaginative eye.'
Cyril Connolly, *Sunday Times*

'The best guidebooks are like Brendan Lehane's, which leaves you rather taken aback at how much you didn't know. Exploring Ireland with Mr Lehane is like going on a tour with a friend who combines a historian's meticulous scholarship with an ability to tell a gossipy anecdote with wit and point.'
Maureen Vincent, *Catholic Herald*

'As well as being a practical guide it's an exhilarating read... It is a delightful thing: anybody contemplating crossing to Ireland for pleasure shouldn't think of going without consulting it.'
Edward Mace, *Observer*

'An admirable mixture of information, historical and geographical, shrewd dry comment, and lively anecdote. It would make an enjoyable read on its own, whether one visited the country or not.'
Honor Tracy, *Sunday Telegraph*

THE COMPANION GUIDES

*It is the aim of these guides to provide a Companion
in the person of the author; who knows
intimately the places and people of whom he writes, and is able to
communicate this knowledge and affection to his readers.
It is hoped that the text and pictures will aid them
in their preparations and in their travels, and will
help them remember on their return.*

BURGUNDY · THE COUNTRY ROUND PARIS
DEVON · EDINBURGH AND THE BORDERS
FLORENCE · GASCONY AND THE DORDOGNE · GREECE
GREEK ISLANDS · ISTANBUL · KENT AND SUSSEX
LAKE DISTRICT · LONDON
MADRID AND CENTRAL SPAIN
NEW YORK · PARIS · ROME · SOUTH OF SPAIN
SICILY · VENICE

THE COMPANION GUIDE TO

IRELAND

Brendan Lehane

COMPANION GUIDES

First published 1973
Revised edition 1985
Revised edition 2001

ISBN 1 900639 34 3

*The publishers and author have done their best to ensure
the accuracy and currency of all the information in*
The Companion Guide to Ireland.
*However, they can accept no responsibility for any loss, injury,
or inconvenience sustained by any traveller as a result
of information or advice contained in the guide.*

Companion Guides is an imprint of Boydell & Brewer Ltd
PO Box 9, Woodbridge, Suffolk IP12 3DF, UK
and of Boydell & Brewer Inc.
PO Box 41026, Rochester, NY 14604–4126, USA
website: http://www.companionguides.com

A catalogue record for this book is available
from the British Library

Printed in Great Britain by
St Edmundsbury Press Ltd, Bury St Edmunds, Suffolk

For Judy and Hugh Johnson

Contents

Illustrations

Maps and Plans

Acknowledgements

Research on Irish art and architecture has progressed fast in the last few years, and I am extremely grateful to those pioneer authors and scholars who have been generous with their help. Dr Maurice Craig, whose *Dublin 1660–1860* is an essential and delightful source for any work on the capital city and much else in Ireland, read the book both in typescript and proof and did not, I am glad to say, confine his comments to his own special subjects. The Knight of Glin, the Hon. Desmond Guinness, the late Hon. Mrs Guinness (Mariga), and the late Mr Terence de Vere White read the book in proof or typescript; Miss Anne Crookshank read the Dublin chapter and the late Earl of Antrim the Ulster section. Almost all corrections and additions they suggested were made. The formidable revision of the index was made a pleasure by the help and kindness of Joanna Bedford.

A book of this nature must draw on thousands of sources, both written and oral; I have moreover received help and hospitality in all parts of Ireland. In particular I should like to thank John and Miriam de Vere White for their help and kindness in Dublin, and Dervla Murphy for her boundless generosity. It would be impossible to acknowledge more than a fraction of my debts to writers, but I cannot omit mention of works I used repeatedly: the *Shell Guide to Ireland* by Lord Killanin and M.V. Duignan, revised by Peter Harbison, Murray's *Handbook to Ireland* (8th edition, 1912), *Ireland Observed* by Maurice Craig and the Knight of Glin, *The Way that I Went* by R. Lloyd Praeger, *Irish Houses and Castles* by the Hon. Desmond Guinness and William Ryan, *Burke's Guide to Country Houses: Ireland* by Mark Bence-Jones, P.J. Kavanagh's *Voices in Ireland*. I have made full use of the books mentioned in *Further Reading*, and of many more. For some months I received much help from the County Library at Lismore, county Waterford.

I must thank the Irish Tourist Board for much assistance and information, the Northern Ireland Tourist Board for material help, and the Swansea Cork Line for travel on their ferries.

Introduction

Everyone coming to Ireland by sea or air lands near the coast, and this book follows the coast in a clockwise direction, making long circular tours inland from various points. Nothing is as magnificent as the mountains of Kerry or Galway, but Ireland's interior, showing its treasures with greater reluctance, can leave more lasting memories. Both coast and hinterland can be seen by means of buses, trains, motor cruisers or sailing boats, but none of these goes everywhere a car goes. In the directions given, use of a car is assumed.

Though I have tried to show how to get to most sites, some – across fields and tracks, or at the end of a maze of lanes – call for the use of a large-scale map. Asking the way can lead to enlightenment, entertainment or despair and is recommended.

Many houses mentioned in the text open rarely, irregularly or not at all. Some may open in the future. Others, never officially open, seldom turn away a genuinely interested caller. These tend to be away from the main towns and tourist areas. I would not be thanked for giving the names of those whose owners, I know, show callers round and they are considerably less common than they used to be.

1

Dublin

DUBLIN ON THE map is a little like the front half of a lobster seen from above. Its claws curve into the sea to form Dublin Bay, which ends, on the north side, at the peninsula of Howth and on the south at Dun Laoghaire (pronounced, and formerly spelt, Dunleary). The protuberances of Dublin Harbour, in the middle of the bay's shoreline, are the head. If a lobster had a spinal cord it would, in this case, be the Liffey, entering the town on its west side, cutting it in two, and debouching into the harbour itself. Near the river mouth are the sea-ends of two more rivers: the Tolka to the north and the Dodder to the south. These curve in from the west, so that between them they enclose the major part of the city's suburbs. Two canals, the Royal on the north side and the Grand on the south, also start near the Liffey's mouth, and bend west to belt the town more closely. At a glance, Dublin has a symmetrical geography.

Its contents are not so orderly. The south has the larger part of Dublin's historic and architectural distinction and of its antiquity, art, and money. Most of the great maintained showpieces lie on an east–west axis through College Green, 300 yards south of O'Connell Bridge. Most of the best shopping is to its south; and the rich suburbs spread south and south-east again. 'West End' in Dublin, unlike most western cities, equates with humble areas. However, the southern monopoly is not complete. Two of Ireland's finest buildings overlook the river on the north, and there is plenty of interest in the streets and suburbs behind, from the General Post Office, a kind of shrine of Irish patriotism, to the Municipal Gallery, along line upon line of Georgian housing, to the magnificent botanic gardens at Glasnevin.

All the same, time has been harder on the north. Until recently poverty abounded, blotching and rotting dignified Georgian houses that had become slummy tenements. Streets are drearier, shops more gaudy, and the 1916 Rising left uglier scars on the main thorough-fares. Fighting, poverty, neglect and philistinism felled and pocked

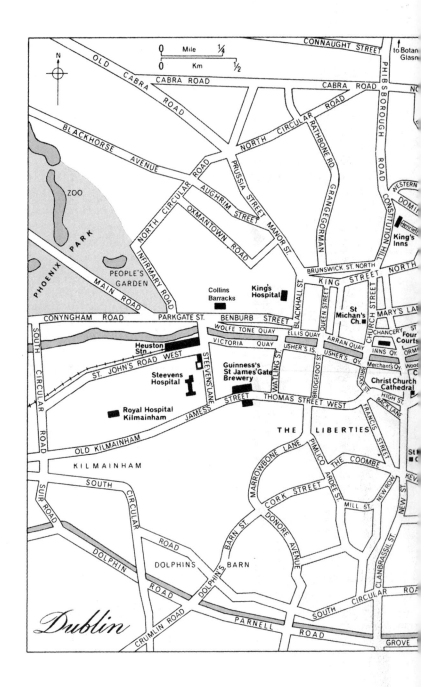

Dublin

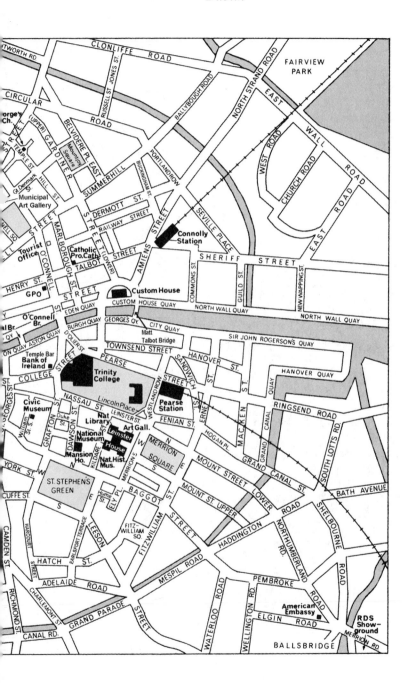

3

much of the eighteenth-century inheritance of north Dublin, and that is the more disastrous since the Irish capital, like Bath or Edinburgh, is essentially an eighteenth-century creation. It was old, of course, before the eighteenth century. Baile-Ath-Cliath, its Gaelic name (pronounced Bawl-aclee), means 'village of the hurdle ford' and dates from prehistory. As in fact does its more usual name. Also Gaelic in origin, Dublin means 'black pool', referring to the peat-stained waters of the Liffey. There were small Gaelic settlements here before the Vikings came, in the area immediately west and south of the Castle, bounded roughly by Thomas Street, the Coombe and Aungier Street and based on the meeting points of ancient roads. But it was a succession of Viking settlers, starting in 841 and involved with native Irish more than is sometimes realised, who began the embankment of what was a vast, swampy estuary (the name Dame Street derives from the original damming of the tidal pool) and made a harbour. The division between Viking and native was not distinct. Vikings from Norway, from Denmark, from England, and fissive Irish groupings would split, war, join, ally, intermarry. Brian Boru beat the Dublin Danes at Clontarf in 1014, but it was a Norse king of Dublin who founded Christ Church Cathedral fourteen years later. And before work was stopped by the construction of Dublin Corporation's massive civic office blocks, there had been much fruitful excavation of an advanced, pre-Norman city between the cathedral and Wood Quay – itself formed by damming at the time. Henry II's Normans took the city in 1170. It was given to Bristol, to people and develop. The Castle was built. The Norsemen moved across the river to settle what became Oxmantown – the town of the east-men or ost-men – around St Michan's church. Walls were built, then rebuilt in part to accommodate expansion; though beyond St Patrick's the Liberties were so-called because they remained without the walls and free from city tax. A century or so of settlement was followed by the ravages of the Black Death, fighting, rebellion, the tendency of new colonists to identify with the Irish and turn against the English who had sent them. The city stagnated till the carbolic policies of the Tudors made Dublin the base for new conquests. The city grew north and south of the river, boasted a university, extended its quays and harbour, raised its mercantile importance.

But a walk round the central area shows the lasting spirit of the eighteenth century, in architecture and town planning; and hundreds of street-names, even after twentieth-century changes, still commemorate the ruling figures of the eighteenth-century Ascendancy.

Dublin

College Green started as a Viking burial ground, Hoggen Green. At its centre are statues of Henry Grattan and Thomas Davis, the latter by Edward Delaney. The Green is flanked by two of the greatest eighteenth-century buildings, the Bank of Ireland on the west and Trinity College, standing in its own 25 acres, on the east. (There is of course a great coming and going of statues in Ireland. That of William III – of whom statues are still being erected in Northern Ireland – was blown up here in 1829, restored, and helped off College Green for good by a land-mine in 1929.)

The **Bank of Ireland** was not built as such, but was started in 1729 by Sir Edward Lovett Pearce, Irish surveyor-general, to house the Irish parliament. Various seventeenth-century parliaments had been held in its predecessor on the site: Chichester House, named after James I's Lord-Deputy, Sir Arthur Chichester. The new parliaments continued the tradition of putty-like subservience to Westminster ('tell us what the pile contains?/Many a head that holds no brains' Swift wrote) but strengthened as the eighteenth century wore on and the Ascendancy's wealth and independence increased. At the height of its power, in the 1780s, it counted orators like Grattan, Flood and Curran among its members and in 1783 achieved some degree of self-government. But real power still lay with the English and their loyal claque. Before two decades were out, the 1798 rebellion, and the fear of French-style revolution or Napoleonic invasion, turned Pitt and the English firmly against independence. By means mostly foul (many Irish titles were created at the time) the Parliament passed the Act of Union in 1800, and so voted its own extinction. Thomas de Quincey, on a visit, described the Lords' last sitting in his autobiographical sketches. Dublin was torn by riots. Grattan's heroic last speech brought him to a duel with the Lord Chancellor, whose hand his bullet smashed. But the Irish Parliament was dead for well over a century, and the building was sold to the Bank of Ireland for £40,000.

The handsome symmetry of the façade belies its own odd history. Pearce designed the main south-facing portico and central colonnade in their present forecourt. (Even in his day the Commons had the large central chamber, while the Lords were kept to the east wing.) Fifty years later, when more space was needed, the sensitive James Gandon designed a discreetly plain convex wall to screen new rooms south-east of the main block. His concern not to detract from Pearce's work still left him free on the east side, where he built a splendid Corinthian portico for the Lords. But when some time later similar development was needed on the west, Gandon was ignored and a

5

committee produced a flamboyant Ionic colonnade that swamped Pearce's structure and left the whole lop-sided. However, after the Bank took over, Francis Johnston toned down the effect of the western colonnade by moving its wall forward *between* the columns, turning them into pilasters. Then he established the balance on the east by applying new columns to Gandon's wall, which he topped with a matching balustrade. The result of several efforts spread over a century is what today looks very like one man's masterpiece.

The British Government stipulated, when the building was sold in 1800, that the interior should be remodelled to preclude any future use as public debating rooms. Only the panelled House of Lords remains much as it was, like a large drawing-room with a fireplace, suitable for the thirty or so peers who deliberated there. It contains a magnificent 1,233-piece chandelier of 1788, two vast Huguenot tapestries of the siege of Derry and the battle of the Boyne, woven in Dublin by 'Jan van Beaver, ye tapestry weaver', fine wood carving, and the 1765 House of Commons mace of silver gilt retrieved at a Belfast auction in 1937. Liveried guides are usually on hand to show visitors round, but most of the rooms are given over to banking activities; a pity, when independence offered a splendid chance of restoring the place to its original use, and plans had already been drawn for doing so, and for extending its grounds north to the quays. As it turned out those in power chose Leinster House.

The stern grey façade of **Trinity College** stands to the east of College Green. Beside its entrance are statues of Burke and Goldsmith, two alumni from a list that includes Congreve, Farquhar (supposedly expelled for a prank), Bishop Berkeley, Swift, Grattan, Emmet, Thomas Davis, Wilde, Synge, Edward Carson, Samuel Beckett and many others. To look at, it could be in Cambridge, with elegant academic buildings round courtyards noisy with students. Being, as it is, at the very centre of the Irish capital, it has played at times a more active part in the nation's affairs, and political debate has often been more partial than at its English equivalents.

The college was founded in 1591 on the site of a dissolved monastery – then, like St Patrick's Cathedral, well outside the walls of the city, which was still concentrated round the Castle. Other proposed colleges were never built. It remained alone, a complete university, despite several plans to fuse it with University College in a newly constituted University of Dublin. Its founder members – among them the future Archbishop Ussher, primate of Ireland (who first dated the creation of Adam to the precise year 4004 BC) – hoped it would be a

Dublin

civilizing influence in popish Ireland, and it remained exclusively
Protestant, with a short break in James II's reign, till 1793. Senior
offices and fellowships were withheld from Catholics till 1873.
Women students, however, were admitted in degrees in 1903, earlier
than in some British universities. Fifty years ago, English students
who failed to get to Oxford or Cambridge often tried for Trinity, as a
more socially approved option than English redbrick. To the Irish, for
some good reasons, it has always had a smack of Ascendancy; though
in its latter years the ban on admission of Catholics was imposed by
the Catholic hierarchy, not the college.

The oldest existing buildings date from the end of the seventeenth
century, a time when Whiggish tutors were resented – and one at least
was murdered – by students of Jacobite sympathy, and the habit
began of defacing King William's statue in College Green, to end
only with the 1929 explosion. A tradition lasted long that 'Trinity
Fellows made up in bad manners for what they lacked in learning'.
As the eighteenth century was set into its rich, Augustan and optimistic mould, both buildings and reputation of the college rose. The
main construction work took place in mid-century, substantially
financed by the Irish Parliament, after which the first courtyard –
Parliament Square – is named. The 300-foot Palladian façade – one of
Dublin's great elevations – dates from 1752 to 1759, a time when the
city, with a population approaching 150,000, was, bar London, the
largest in the British Isles. This west front was the work of the
London architects, Henry Keene and John Sanderson. It houses, on
the upper floor, a hall known as the Regent House. The arch leads by
the porters' lodge towards the clean, grey, slightly forbidding granite
buildings surrounding the two main squares. On the left of Parliament
Square is the **dining-hall**, built in the 1740s by Richard Castle,
second only to Francis Johnston in the number of buildings he
designed for Dublin. Much restored (it started falling down ten years
after erection), it contains portraits of famous Trinity men. Projecting
from the end of this wing is the darkly panelled **chapel**, added
between 1779 and 1790, to the rough designs of Sir William Chambers (at the time heavily occupied with London's Somerset House).
The elegant hundred-foot **campanile** to the front was built in 1853 on
a spot supposed to mark the centre of the medieval priory church. (In
spite of repeated attempts, no undergraduate has reached the top to
plant a trophy.) Opposite and corresponding to the chapel on the right
of the court is the **Examination Hall**, or theatre. Like the chapel, it
was designed by the prolific and fastidious Chambers. It has, like the

7

chapel, good ceiling stucco by Michael Stapleton, whose Adam-like style came into fashion after the more flamboyant work of Robert West. The theatre – with a sixty-light gilt chandelier brought via St Andrew's Church from the Old Parliament House at the time of the Union – makes a lavish setting for the concerts often held here. The 1906 bronze figure to the right of the campanile and not far from a reclining figure by Henry Moore is of W.E.H. Lecky (1838–1903), a scholar of Trinity and author of the masterly *History of Ireland in the Eighteenth Century.* As MP for Trinity from 1895 he opposed home rule, but still comes over as progressive when compared with his contemporary, J.A. Froude. Beyond it, at the far end of the grassed Library Square, are the terraced **Rubrics**, apartments dating from the turn of the seventeenth century and the oldest extant college buildings. Goldsmith had his chambers here. Trinity's greatest treasure is the austere, 270-foot long **library**, to the right of the court. Originally redbrick, it was begun in 1712 to the plans of Thomas Burgh (the first known Irish-trained architect). It opened in 1732, having cost £20,000. Until 1892, when it was closed in, the ground floor was an open arcade, insulating the books from the damp ground below and supporting possibly the largest single-chamber library in the world. Its glory is the interior, lit by a hundred windows. The pinewood barrel-vault by Benjamin Woodward is an early Victorian replacement of, and arguably an improvement on, the original flat plaster ceiling which divided the chamber into two floors. Throughout the interior, whose lofty perspective is emphasised by book-lined recesses and a series of marble busts, there is an economy of decoration (except on the richly carved Corinthian capitals) and an atmosphere of clerical restraint. Trinity is one of the four libraries in these islands entitled, by the Library Act of 1801, to a free copy of every book published in Britain and Ireland.

At the top of the staircase (by Richard Castle) leading up to the library there was until recently an inscribed tablet, and nearby a painting of the battle order at the 1602 Battle of Kinsale. These commemorated the £700 subscribed by the English victors – 'out of the arrears of their pay' – to found the library, in the hopes that what was never to be lastingly achieved by the sword might make steadier progress by the printed word. South of the building is the modern extension, designed by Paul Koralek (who won the commission in an international competition and who later designed the Arts and Social Science building to the south) and opened in 1967 – an annexe of shuttered concrete that has a claim to be the best building of its period in Ireland. Outstanding manuscripts are kept on display in a building beside the new library. They include two of the greatest, but stylistically contrasted, early Celtic manuscripts: the mid-seventh-century Book of Durrow, with its beautiful Irish majuscule text and inspired primitive illuminations; and the famous Book of Kells, compiled a century later, possibly at St Columba's monastery on Iona, showing at its most elaborate the whimsical extravagance of Celtic art. West of this is the neatly square **Provost's House**, separated by a high stone wall from Grafton Street, and built by John Smyth in 1759 following, externally, Lord Burlington's design for General Wade's house in Mayfair (of which Lord Chesterfield said its owner would do best to sell, and buy the house opposite, to be able to see without having to live in it). Closed to the public, it remains as it was originally. One of its rooms, a finely ceilinged saloon, runs the length of the building.

Along the north flank of Library Court is the unlovely Graduates' Memorial Building of 1892. If we pass to the right of the Rubrics we come to New Square, with Benjamin Woodward's **Museum Building** of 1853 to 1857 on the right, now the School of Engineering – a building whose Venetian style, with its outside carvings and spacious domed staircase gave Ruskin, as he said, for the first time the joy of seeing his aesthetic principles carried into practice. On the left, in the square's north-west corner, is Castle's little Doric **Printing House**, a gift to the university from Bishop Stearne of Clogher in 1734. (Bishop Berkeley the philosopher gave a fount of Greek type in the same year.) It still contains, as it did throughout the eighteenth century, the University Press, which until the twentieth century used a picture of the delicate temple-like building as its title-page device.

Beyond the square lie the relieving grass and trees of **College Park**, which we can cross to emerge in Lincoln Place, close to the city's best-preserved Georgian enclave. A right and left turn outside the college's back gate bring us to the north-west corner of **Merrion Square**. Like central Dublin on both sides of the Liffey, this sector owes much to a 1757 Act of the Irish Parliament which set up the 'Commissioners for Making Wide and Convenient Streets', well ahead of other European cities. Their timely work up to 1840, when the Dublin Corporation took over, evokes nostalgia in times of ugly and quick-return development, but it sometimes involved fairly brutal appropriation of crowded buildings along narrow streets. Still, it has left the pleasing spaciousness, sometimes rather windy, of the modern town centre.

Another feature of the residential area that surrounds the square – and an impressive comment on eighteenth-century rationalism – is its shortage of churches. St Stephen's, at the end of Mount Street Upper, brought a magnificent vista to the square's south side, but only in 1824. Growing from empty marshland to be the city's chief residential district in the space of a century (1721–1825) the square did, all that time, without any church at all. It was laid out in 1762 and completed by the end of the century. Most of the tall brick houses, whose small differences in height, style, doorways and wrought-ironwork show the tastes of individual aristocrats and merchants, boast interesting past occupants, and most now house official institutions. Sir William and Lady Wilde (irascible surgeon and antiquary, and histrionic poetess) lived at No. 1, for a time with young Oscar (of whom a statue stands in the central gardens); No. 39 was the British Embassy Chancery until it was burned early in 1972; Sir Jonah Barrington (1760–1834), judge, wit and diarist – who was deprived of office for appropriating money paid into his court, but is still known for his colourful, suspect *Personal Sketches* and *Historic Anecdotes and Secret Memoirs* – lived at No. 42. Daniel O'Connell owned No. 58 in his latter, respectable years. W.B. Yeats, who was born at Sandymount, lived for a while at No. 52; when, in 1922, he became a senator of the Irish Free State, he bought No. 82, staying till 1929 when he took a flat at 42 **Fitzwilliam Square**. AE – George Russell – lived at No. 84. The Duke of Wellington was born – if not at Dangan, county Meath, where he was partly brought up – at No. 24 Upper Merrion Street, which runs from the south-west corner of the square, on 29 April 1769, his father the Earl of Mornington being Professor of Music at Trinity. After the earl's time No. 24 was bought by the first Lord Cloncurry and rented, at the time of the Union, by Lord Castlereagh. The effect the Union had on prices as well as morale is shown by Cloncurry's paying £8,000 for the house and selling it ten years later – but after Union – for £2,500. It now houses the Land Commission. Good Georgian houses continue in the streets to the south, and one of the finest concentrations is in Fitzwilliam Square, built in the 1820s, and now, with doctors thick on the ground, Dublin's Harley Street. It connects with Merrion Square by Fitzwilliam Street, one side of which, despite spirited protest, was maimed in 1965 to make way for a new Electricity Supply Board building.

Facing Merrion Square on the west is Leinster Lawn, at the back of **Leinster House**, seat of the Irish Parliament or *Oireachtas*, which we can visit shortly. Two wings (built much later than Leinster House) flank the lawn, the right-hand of which houses Ireland's **National Gallery**. The statue on the lawn depicts William Dargan, the great Irish Railway King, who used the profits of the 1853 Dublin Exhibition, which he organised on the same site, to found the collection. The statue of Shaw near the entrance is by the Polish Paul Troubetzkoy, and it was the playwright's own favourite. Shaw left the gallery a third of his residual estate in his will. The conversion of *Pygmalion* into *My Fair Lady*, stage show and film, brought windfalls, and there have been more since. Even before this, the gallery housed one of Europe's more important collections, especially in respect of Continental works.

The gallery's distinction is due partly to the stubborn generosity of Sir Hugh Lane, whose nose for art-bargains and old masters of the future, as well as his generosity with an amassed fortune, were put repeatedly at Ireland's disposal, and all too often rejected. In 1903 the governing authority failed to appoint him – obvious and best candidate – curator of the National Museum; and when later, as senator of the new university, he proposed a £350 salary for the new professor of art, the sum was reduced to £100. His sin in official eyes was admiring the Impressionists. When Lane proposed an art gallery spanning the Liffey (where the Metal Bridge now stands) to be designed by Lutyens, he was thwarted at every turn. Yet Lane was offering the finance too, with American support. The architect should be Irish, said officials; (Lutyens in fact had an Irish mother). Dublin's spurning of Lane's love for it at last drove him to give London, then Johannesburg, what he wanted Dublin to possess. He even changed his will in London's favour. Before he died he recanted and added a codicil; but this was not witnessed, and London's National Gallery – legally right but morally equivocal – refused to part with the Lane Collection till arbitration divided the pictures between the two capitals. The Irish half is kept at the Municipal Gallery of Modern Art in Parnell Square.

Besides Shaw's gifts and Lane's work for the gallery, there have been, among many others, important bequests from the Countess of Milltown at the beginning of the twentieth century – two hundred priceless pictures from the Russborough collection – from Evie Hone in 1955, and Sir Chester Beatty in 1960 and again in 1987.

In the important Irish section downstairs there is a good selection of the work of Nathaniel Hone (1831–1917), descendant of a prolifically artistic eighteenth-century family – Nathaniel the Elder's masterly *The*

Conjuror is here to baffle, though not to shock as it did when first shown – and himself much influenced by twenty years spent at Barbizon. Several hundred of his oils and many more watercolours are stored out of sight. His skies and seascapes have great power and drama, and his detail is impeccable – the butcher who came to buy cattle at his home at Portmarnock was told to pick out wanted animals from the latest canvas, which might have been on the lines of his *Cattle at Malahide* here.

Outstanding the century before was James Barry (1741–1806), son of a Catholic bricklayer in Cork, who was taken up by Edmund Burke, and thereafter lived in Rome and England, where he failed to make the impact he hoped and allowed his choler to hamper his career, though he was professor of painting at the Royal Academy for seventeen years from 1782 and decorated the Society of Arts with many huge murals, still in place. His *Self-portrait as Timanthes*, full of fault and failure, has nevertheless a haunting and rather bewildering quality. George Barret (1728–84) is represented by sublime and picturesque landscapes, portraying the country in voguishly romantic mode, as does *The Poachers* of James Arthur O'Connor (1792–1841), much of whose best work is at Westport House, county Mayo. Francis Danby's (1793–1861) cosmic drama, *The Opening of the Sixth Seal*, is a dramatic evocation of apocalypse. The Yeats family gets the ample space it richly deserves. There is a well-known portrait of W.B. Yeats by his father, J.B. Yeats, as well as the *Artist's Wife* and *John O'Leary*, and many dynamic and vividly toned canvases by the poet's brother, Jack B. Yeats. Works by Sir John Lavery, Sir William Orpen, Walter Osborne (an underrated painter, showing Impressionist influence, with a deep feeling for scenes of urban bustle and squalor), Roderic O'Conor, Daniel Maclise, Paul Henry, Mark Shields and many others show both a debt to the Continent and England, but also a wide and buoyant Irish variety.

An impressive collection of English paintings includes works by Gainsborough, Hogarth, Reynolds, Stubbs, Wilson, Turner, Raeburn, Lawrence, Crome, Romney, Constable and others. Many have Irish or Anglo-Irish subjects: some landscapes, portraits of grandees like Lawrence's *Lady Elizabeth Foster* or Francis Wheatley's *Marquess and Marchioness of Antrim* or Reynolds's *Charles Coote, First Earl of Bellamont* looking extraordinarily epicene and unmanly in the full fig of court pink and white silks and tall feathered cap. The display of thirty-one Turner water-colours is limited to the month of January by

Dublin

the terms of a 1900 bequest, but they may be seen in all their coddled freshness on request.

Upstairs, the Italian collection is wonderfully rich in fifteenth- and sixteenth-century paintings – indeed it goes through strongly to the eighteenth century. Caravaggio's *The Taking of Christ* attracts widespread attention, not only because of the vital force that has the characters almost stepping off the canvas, but also because up till 1992 it hung a few hundred yards away, unrecognised, in the Jesuit community in Leeson Street, and is now here on permanent loan.

There are besides Fra Angelico's little *Attempted Martyrdom of Saints Cosmas and Damian*; an unknown painter's *Battle of Anghiari* and *The Taking of Pisa* (both panels on a wedding-chest); Titian's *Ecce Homo* and *Portrait of Baldassare Castiglione*; Tintoretto's *Venice, Queen of the Adriatic*; Perugino's *Pietà*; and works by Giovanni Bellini, Correggio, Palma Vecchio, Veronese, Canaletto, and many others. There are French paintings from all periods, including Gerard David's *Our Lord bidding farewell to his Mother*; Claude's *Juno confiding Io to the care of Argus*; Poussin's *Entombment* and *The Lamentation over the dead Christ*; and ballet sketches by Degas and paintings by Monet, given by Yeats's friend Edward Martyn of Tullira in Galway. The famous *Saint Francis in Ecstasy* by El Greco is in the Spanish section, along with three brilliant Goyas, Murillo's *St Mary Magdalen*, and many others. The Flemish, Dutch and German schools are richly represented by such masterpieces as Geerhardt David's *Christ Saying Farewell to his Mother*; Rubens's *St Dominic*; the younger Brueghel's *Peasant Wedding*; Rembrandt's *Landscape with the rest on the flight to Egypt*, and Vermeer's *Lady writing a letter, with her maid*. There is also an important collection of icons.

The **Natural History Section** of the National Museum is south of Leinster Lawn. It has so far successfully resisted change, gimmick, fad and fashion, and remained a fine, informative, very Victorian collection of specimens preserved by stuffing, drying, pickling or whatever other means suggested itself. It is, it is true, a tiny bit musty, and some of its exhibits would be none the worse for renewing. But, without pretensions to be anything but national, it contains a complete and at the same time digestible representation of Irish ecology. Some creatures are remarkable for their absence. As well as the Romans, the Reformation, and, for a long while, the Industrial Revolution, Ireland has done without moles, weasels, polecats, voles, the greater shrew, two of the four British mice, eight of the fifteen

13

British bats, snakes, nightingales, reed warblers (though one case of breeding is recorded), tawny owls, and a few more. Most flora and fauna that it has nourished are on display here, including (in skeletal form) the Giant Irish Deer, with its eleven-foot antler span, an animal that was not uncommon between twelve and four thousand years ago, after the last Ice Age. The antlers alone weighed about a hundredweight, and were shed and regrown every year. Exclusively Irish animals displayed include the Irish hare and Irish stoat, a smaller, darker version of the British one, and known in Ireland as weasel, though what the British call weasel is not found here. There are particularly good displays of mammals, birds, insects and spiders, and enough specimens of exotic sea creatures – shark, fire fish, sun fish, angel ray, whip ray, blue skate – to deter all but the brave from the tourist sport of sea-fishing.

Leinster House itself faces west to Kildare Street, and its courtyard is flanked by two more repositories, the **National Library** and the National Museum. It was built in 1745, to Richard Castle's plans, for the FitzGerald Earl of Kildare, though the north side of the river was then more fashionable. Castle built it in the manner of a country house – two formal fronts, with a central corridor dividing the house longways, in the harsh, cold stone quarried at Ardbraccan. When the earl, whose country seat was Carton (rebuilt by Castle), was made Duke of Leinster in 1766, the house's name was changed. As Leinster House it was sold in 1815 to the Royal Dublin Society, whose headquarters it remained for a century, during which the great complex of museums and institutes that remain rose around it. The first independent government in 1922 decided to make it the seat of government, and the Royal Dublin Society was evicted to Ballsbridge. Now the Dáil Eireann (or Chamber of Deputies – 148 of them) occupies the Society's old D-shaped lecture hall, and the Seanad (or Senate, of sixty) meets in the attractive north-wing salon, with excellent stucco work on walls and ceiling. Visitors are shown round as much as current business of government allows. The similarity of design between this house and the White House in Washington may stem from the fact that the latter's architect, James Hoban, was born in Carlow in 1762 and trained in Dublin.

To the right of Leinster House on leaving it is the **National Library**, with a rich collection of manuscripts and over half a million books (the reading room can be seen by visitors). Attached to it is the **National College of Art**. On the left is the **National Museum**. Both these flanking buildings were designed in Renaissance style by Sir

Thomas Deane and opened in 1890. Far the most splendid of the museum's displays is in the main hall on the ground floor – a priceless collection of prehistoric Irish antiquities. Of Bronze Age items, the most striking are the gold ornaments – torques, lunulae and fibulae, earrings and necklaces and objects of uncertain purpose that date from as far back as 2000 BC – when immigrant craftsmen, working with gold mined in counties Wicklow, Mayo and elsewhere, produced work that was in demand as far as the Mediterranean. Many of these are arranged by find: Banagher or Gleninsheen or some other site where a hoard was unearthed, usually by someone to whom the possibility of discovering a treasure had not occurred – such as the navvies excavating the West Clare railway in 1854.

The Early Christian period, after St Patrick and others converted the country early in the fifth century, brought Ireland in time to eminence in several branches of the arts and scholarship. Trinity Library possesses some of the best illuminated manuscripts. In the museum the greatest relics include the Ardagh Chalice, a superbly restrained eighth-century silver and copper two-handled cup, decorated with bands, bosses, enamelled beads and gold filigree, in styles which are echoed in other Celtic crafts; the penannular Tara Brooch, of about the same time, of cast silver-gilt studded with glass and amber, and decorated with bird and animal designs in intricate filigree; the Moylough belt-shrine of silvered bronze with enamel appliqué; and the Lough Erne reliquaries. The tradition is continued in later treasures, including the highly decorated brass Shrine of St Patrick's Bell, from the twelfth century; several crosier- and book-shrines, especially those of Lismore, Clonmacnois, and Cormac McCarthy of Cashel (all early twelfth century); the Cross of Cong from the same period, which originally contained one of the alleged pieces of the True Cross; and the later Fiacal Padraig in which, at Killaspugbrone near Sligo, was preserved a tooth of St Patrick, for the edification of the faithful. As a whole, the display rivals and perhaps surpasses all comparable collections in Europe; for Ireland, free of the Romans (Roman items on display were probably pilfered from Britain by third- and fourth-century Irish invaders) preserved and developed its Celtic origins as no other country could. However, it is not the only notable section of the museum. A section dedicated to events leading up to Irish independence will in due course move to the museum's annexe at Collins Barracks, on Benburb Street near the eastern tip of Phoenix Park. However, the upstairs exhibition of objects from the Viking period in Dublin and the rest of Ireland remains, illustrating a more belligerent and outward-looking culture than the Irish, though there are beautiful artefacts shown here too. There is also a small display of manuscripts, mummies and ornaments from ancient Egypt.

Kildare Street, outside, runs from Trinity to St Stephen's Green. At the north – Trinity – end, on the right, is the distinguished building which until 1977 housed the **Kildare Street Club**, in which the principles of the Protestant Ascendancy have been said to survive unmoved by events of the last hundred years. Founded in 1782 in No. 6, near the Shelbourne, it moved for more room in 1860 (during the move the old premises caught fire and three maids were killed) to this Venetian style palace by Deane and Woodward, with its adornment of rather whimsical beasts. The new building is now leased, providing a home for the Alliance Française and the Heraldic Museum. But the club goes on, amalgamated with the **University Club** in St Stephen's Green. No. 39 Kildare Street was home of Lady Morgan (1776–1859), who came to early fame as Sydney Owenson for her rattling wild-Irish novels, then married a learned doctor and became Dublin's leading hostess, a beacon in the drear post-Union days. Her drawing-room has been called 'the foyer of liberation'. Every visitor had to call on her. 'Fifty philosophers passed through my little salon last night', she wrote once. But developers have replaced philosophers and in 1972 the house and several others were demolished.

Molesworth Street is directly opposite Leinster House. It is smart and rich, and retains a few gable-ended houses whose style followed William III from the Netherlands. The site, owned by Robert, first Viscount Molesworth of Swords, was the centre of a development scheme of 1725 and onwards, and the houses are Dublin's oldest this side of the river. The headquarters of the grand masonic lodge of Ireland are at number seventeen, and admit the public to the site of their mysteries and rituals at certain times during the summer. The street was until recently an old-world quarter, with plenty of solicitors, tailors, odd societies, and slightly bijou antique shops, but developers replaced a road of detail and elegance with a uniform range whose proportions go beyond the human and which is almost entirely without interest for the walker. There is perhaps little reason to tear strips off this street for an almost ubiquitous practice. At the far end we meet busy **Dawson Street** which, first laid out in about 1709, boasts mainly late Georgian houses, many rebuilt or converted into shops. The **Royal Hibernian**, one of the best and best-known Dublin hotels, was demolished in the 1980s in favour of a charmless grey replacement. A few doors down on the left is **St Anne's parish church** (Church of Ireland), begun in 1720 to the plans of Isaac Wills, credited also with the design of St Werburgh's church, and still as fashionable as it was in its early years, at the centre of this exclusive parish. Its curved apse and gallery carried on slender pillars keep the elegance which Victorian stained glass and the rebuilding of the west front (by Sir Thomas Deane) did their best to cancel out. Mrs Hemans, author of *The Boy Stood on the Burning Deck* and various religious poems, is buried here: and there are curved shelves on either side of the chancel to hold a weekly twenty-five pence worth of bread for the poor of the parish, bequeathed, at the time of the church's founding, by Theophilus Lord Newtown. Farther down on the left is the home of the **Royal Irish Academy**, originally built for Lord Northland of Dungannon in 1770 and converted in 1852 to its present use. Wolfe Tone, close friend of Northland's son, spent a lot of time here. The academy itself was granted a charter in 1785 to foster the study of 'Science, Polite Literature, and Antiquities', and is still the country's leading academic society. The original building, backed by additions begun in the 1850s, is handsome red brick with stone cornice, string-courses and window-cases. Its library can be visited and contains a priceless collection of ancient manuscripts which include the early ninth-century *Stowe Missal*, the *Book of Ballymote*, the *Speckled Book* (Leabhar Breac) – both of around 1400 – and the early seventeenth-century *Annals of the Four Masters*.

A little farther down on the left is the **Mansion House**, the Lord Mayor's official house since 1715. It was built ten years earlier as a private residence in red brick, then bought by the city; later Victorian stucco and cast-iron work prettified, and so spoiled it. Yeats hated its exterior and wrote at length of his hate. But the interior is closer to the original; and a hall, the Round Room, added hastily in 1821 for George IV's visit, is still, with a ninety-foot diameter, the largest public meeting hall in the city. It was here that the first Dáil Eireann met at the end of 1918, setting up its own administration and bringing British Government to a standstill.

St Stephen's Green opens out at the end of Dawson Street, a fine stretch of ornamental gardens bordered, particularly on the east and south sides, by some good Georgian houses. Its origins as a park go back to Charles I's reign when, with the city population of 9,000 bursting at the walled seams, it was included in a 'green belt', 'wholie kept for the use of citizens and others, to walk & take the open aire'.

Development of its precincts had to wait for the Restoration, which, resolving for a while the squabbles of centuries, encouraged the extension of Dublin's boundaries with less fear of marauding and attack from the mountains. Already, by the late seventeenth century, the Green was fashionable, through the selling of sizeable plots of land around the 27-acre central area, and the prohibition of houses of less than two stories, or built of mud and wattle. During the eighteenth century, several (surviving) mansions of noblemen were built; but the land, thinly treed and without railings, was let out for grazing and put to uncongenial uses, hangings, whippings, riots and the like. The iron balustrade came in 1815, to commemorate Waterloo. In 1880 Lord Ardilaun, a Guinness philanthropist (a happily common combination) had the place converted to its present state, with ornamented lake and gardens, and gave it to the city. It saw havoc in 1916 when a contingent of the Citizen Army, like their comrades in the Post Office, disturbed the peace of a sunny Easter Bank Holiday, barricading themselves in and defending their position with guns. Countess Markievicz, commanding a contingent, gave her first order to kill and was rewarded with the blood of an English soldier. Her bust, by Seamus Murphy, stands in the park. Others include Henry Moore's bronze memorial to W.B. Yeats; Foley's Lord Ardilaun; the poet Mangan by Oliver Sheppard; the patriot Thomas Kettle by Francis Doyle; a German gift of a fountain portraying the three Fates; a stately megalithic memorial, also by Murphy, to the Fenian leader, Jeremiah O'Donovan Rossa; and a bust of Joyce. Van Nost's 1758 equestrian bronze of George II shared the fate of other likenesses of English monarchs, being blown up before the last war. Less predictable was the damaging, in 1969, of Edward Delaney's Wolfe Tone statue opposite the Shelbourne. It is now restored.

Each building has a history, but we must confine ourselves to a few. Walking clockwise round the Green we pass, on the north side (called Beaux' Walk in the eighteenth century) No. 8, built in 1754, now the United Services Club; No. 9, built in 1756, now the Stephen's Green Club, and containing outstanding plasterwork; No. 16, earlier last century the palace of Dublin's Anglican archbishop; and finally the **Shelbourne Hotel**, one of Dublin's best, certainly its most famous. The ingenious bureaucrat Sir William Petty had his home, Kerry House, here in the 1660s (his heirs were the Lansdowne family, one of whose titles was Shelburne). Thackeray, Shelley (who released balloons and leaflets urging the overthrow of authority from his bedroom windows), George Moore and other notables stayed here and Elizabeth Bowen wrote its history. The present building dates from 1865, but Martin Burke opened his hotel in 1824. Beyond the hotel, at the beginning of Merrion Row, is a Huguenot cemetery of 1693, resting-place of many French refugees from Louis XIV's persecution, who brought their invaluable crafts to Dublin at a time, after Ormonde's planning of the modern city, when they were most needed.

The east side of the Green has some dignified Georgian houses, several of them (Nos. 44, 52 and 53) with interior plasterwork by Dublin's master-stuccoist, Michael Stapleton. Hume Street, off this side of the Green, leads the few yards to **Ely** (pronounced Eeligh) **Place**, a fairly unspoiled Georgian cul-de-sac of rich associations. No. 4 was the home of the intractable lawyer, John Philpot Curran (1750–1817), who violently disapproved of his daughter's involvement with the rebel Robert Emmet. George Moore lived in the house a century later, and owned the garden opposite. When he moved in, all the front doors were painted white, by the landlord's orders. Moore, insisting that being an art critic demanded it, painted his green, and a feud began with his neighbours, two sisters. They dumped in his letter-box a torn-up copy of his novel *Esther Waters* labelled 'too filthy to keep'. To retaliate, Moore rattled their railings at night to make the dogs bark. They hired an organ-grinder to play below his window, and he prosecuted the organ-grinder. He threw stones at their cat, which threatened his favourite blackbird in the garden; then bought a trap. They called the RSPCA; but in the end the trap caught the bird.

W.B. Yeats told the story in his *Autobiographies*. He himself frequented No. 8 – Ely House, facing Hume Street – at the turn of the century, then the headquarters of Dublin's Theosophical Society. There, in company with George Russell (AE), Maud Gonne and others, he pursued that mysticism which had its effect on the Anglo-Irish culture of the Celtic Twilight. Stapleton built this house (and Nos. 6 and 15) in 1770 for Henry Loftus, Earl of Ely. It shows strong Adam influence in its mahogany doors, plasterwork, carved chimney pieces, and magnificently flamboyant wrought-iron staircase with the labours of Hercules in gilt bronze inserted at intervals. The place comes to vivid life in the pages of Gogarty's classic (see below) but the days when he sat discussing George Moore's sex life with the then owner Sir Thornley Stoker, brother of Bram, Dracula's creator, amid appropriate period riches, and they were interrupted by the unexplained entry of an elderly naked lady crying 'I like a little

intelligent conversation' are far away. The house is now the headquarters of the Knights of Columbanus, a kind of Catholic
freemasonry. No. 6 was the home of John Fitzgibbon (1749–1802),
Earl of Clare, who as lord chancellor was mainly responsible for the
passing of the Act of Union which brought all hopes of a healthy
independent Ireland to an end. Popular reaction to his policies was
felt at No. 6 when a crowd of six thousand men and women, with *ad
hoc* armaments, chased the chancellor home, stoned the house and
him, and tried to break in; but they were panicked into flight by the
chancellor's sister mixing disguised in the crowd and spreading the
canard that the army was on its way. No. 25 Ely Place was the home
of Oliver St John Gogarty (1878–1957), but was pulled down in
1988 to make way for the Royal Hibernian Academy of Arts gallery.
Not perhaps a very artistic thing to do. Gogarty, surgeon, poet and
author of, besides much else, the autobiographical *As I was going
down Sackville Street*, was a close friend of Joyce and figured as
Malachi Mulligan in *Ulysses*.

Back at St Stephen's Green and continuing down the east side, we
pass, some way along and among other Georgian buildings, the
former St Vincent's hospital, which in 1834 was adapted from
Nos. 54, 55 and 56. Earlsfort Terrace leads away from the Green at
the corner, and down it on the right is the National Concert Hall, a
treasure in a city not abounding in performances of classical music. It
occupies the site of **University College**, Dublin, largest constituent of
the National University of Ireland, now moved to a four hundred acre
estate at Belfield in Donnybrook. Among innumerable other famous
persons, Douglas Hyde (1866–1949), first President of the Irish
Republic, and his co-founder of the Gaelic League, the historian Eoin
MacNeill (1867–1945), the poet Thomas MacDonagh and statesman
Kevin O'Higgins, were at the university here.

Second left off Leeson Street, which also leads from the Green's
south-east corner, is Upper Pembroke Street, in which, between
Nos. 25 and 26, a tunnel leads to the **Tower of Glass**, a studio
founded by Sarah Purser in 1903 for the improvement of ecclesiastical art. Edward Martyn of Tulira overcame his misogyny to co-
operate on the project. To it in part much of the best stained glass
in Irish churches is owed, the work of pupils like Michael Healy,
Evie Hone, Wilhelmina Geddes, Beatrice Elvery (later Lady
Glenavy), and Kitty O'Brien. Sarah Purser died in 1943, but the
studio continues. Its more recent output includes windows for the
new cathedral of Galway. Further on, a bronze image of the poet

Dublin

Patrick Kavanagh sits on a public seat on the Grand Canal towpath, no longer delivering the wry, laconic remarks that characterised him.

We return to St Stephen's Green, on whose south side **Iveagh House**, now the Department of External Affairs, incorporates No. 80 (built by Castle in 1730) and No. 81. They were joined in the 1870s to make one house for the Guinness family. Castle also built No. 85, **Clanwilliam House** (with an elaborate rococo ceiling by the Lafranchini brothers, perhaps their best work, in the upstairs saloon), and it is possible that with this house he introduced the Venetian window – of three lights, the central one arched – into Ireland. Both this and No. 86 – whose handsome grandeur clashes, probably on purpose, with its earlier neighbour – are combined as **Newman House**. They belong to University College and can be seen inside. From a first-floor window of No. 86, its owner, the MP, gambler and rake Buck Whaley, is said to have jumped into a standing coach for a bet. These two houses were formed, in 1853, into the Catholic University, over which Cardinal Newman was first rector. His Neo-Byzantine church adjoins them. Among the university's teachers was Gerard Manley Hopkins, who died in Dublin in 1889 (and is buried in the Jesuit plot at Glasnevin); and James Joyce was a pupil in modern languages – his first published writing appeared in the student magazine. After graduating he left Ireland to spend most of his life in Paris, Trieste and Zurich. (On one return visit, in 1912, he failed to find a publisher for *Dubliners*.) Patrick Pearse and Eamon de Valera were also students here.

Harcourt Street leads off the south-west corner of the Green. Mass conversion into hotels and offices can disguise the excellent Georgian architecture of its terraces. Edward Carson was born at No. 4. No. 17 was the central part of Clonmell House, built for the parvenu rogue and Chief Justice, Jack Scott, 1st Earl of Clonmell. Yeats went as a boy to the Church of Ireland high school at No. 40, one of the best preserved houses. Shaw once lived at No 61. He was born a few streets to the west, at 33 Synge Street. Back in the Green, the only surviving old façade on the west side is that of the **Royal College of Surgeons**, designed in 1806 by Edward Parke (who also planned the dignified Commercial Buildings in Dame Street), but much altered later. It served as headquarters of the St Stephen's Green contingent of the Citizen Army in 1916, and was pocked by bullets. A statue of Robert Emmet by Jerome Connor stands opposite Nos. 124–25, where he was born.

Having walked the four sides of the Green we pass an arch, commemorating those fallen in the Boer War, and come into **Grafton Street**, named after an unmemorable viceroy of the 1720s. It is a busy street, and good shopping centre, preserving in its windings the character of the country lane it used to be before the construction of O'Connell Bridge made it a main north–south highway. The smell of coffee from Bewleys Coffee House (with its few remaining high-backed seats a link with an older Dublin), good bookshop, tobacconist, tailors, handicrafts and old-established department stores all contribute to the street's cachet, something like Bond Street's in London, on an Irish scale. Some lanes and alleys off the street are worth following. Johnston's Court on the left leads past the sequestered Carmelite church of St Teresa. Beyond and parallel to Clarendon Street, at the end of the court, is William Street, in which, to the right, is the massive, granite **Powerscourt Town House**, its stately interior now converted into a series of shops, all forming part of a large shopping centre. The house was built in the early 1770s by Robert Mack for the third Viscount Powerscourt, an opposition leader, who also owned the famous house by Enniskerry in county Wicklow. Its interior preserves good plasterwork by Michael Stapleton, very much in the Adam style.

A little to the south, we come on the **Civic Museum**, built after 1765 for the Society of Artists, and used in 1920 to 1922 as the supreme court of the outlawed Republican government. It houses a collection of Dublin drawings, models and relics of various kinds.

Back in Grafton Street, No. 79 is on the site of Samuel Whyte's Academy, where Sheridan the playwright, the future Duke of Wellington, Robert Emmet and Tom Moore were at school. Over the road is **Duke Street**, with the renovated Bailey restaurant, where once Parnell, and later Arthur Griffith, Gogarty and their friends used to meet regularly in the first-floor smoking room, between five and seven in the evening. Opposite is Davy Byrne's pub. Joyce frequented both, but both were unrecognisably different in his day. A spirit of reverence tended to develop in pubs associated with Joyce or Brendan Behan or Brian Nolan, but the atmospheres congenial to them are seldom found now in the pubs they made famous.

At the top of Grafton Street we return to College Green (passing, on the right, a better view of Trinity's Provost's House than that from the college grounds). Now we turn left and go towards **Dame Street**, and the city's oldest quarters and buildings. Dame Street itself, whose name derives from a dam on the Poddle River, beside the castle, became important in the seventeenth century as the link between the old city and newly founded Trinity College, as well as the harbour beyond. Where before College Green had comprised a pasture on which any citizen could graze his cattle, Dame Street now became the backbone of the city and stayed so till the nineteenth century, when the north–south axis from O'Connell (then Carlisle) Bridge took over. At one time the centre of the city's goldsmiths, it now mixes business and commerce fairly evenly. Beyond the Bank of Ireland, on our right, is the site of Daly's Club House, built in 1791 to house a society of aristocrats and politicians. It was noted for intrigue, high spirits and gambling, detected cheats being thrown from upper windows. But it lost ground to the Kildare Street Club, and closed in 1873. Fragments of the original survive in the present structure.

Anglesea Street is just beyond on the right. Its name recalls the Earls of Anglesey's estates in this area, granted in the seventeenth century and subject, in the eighteenth, of one of the longest Irish legal disputes, when one member of the family was denied his titles by another through unending claims of illegitimacy, bigamy, assault and murder. Characters and episodes probably gave Scott models for the battle for possession of Ellangowan in *Guy Mannering*. The incumbent claimant was finally recognised by an Irish court but not by the English House of Lords, so his titles had to be split between two individuals. Edward Parke's 1799 **Commercial Buildings** stood just beyond, a dignified granite structure in which wholesale commercial business was conducted within easy reach of the quays where, in those days, ships were moored. Of the various narrow streets that lead down towards the river on the right, Fownes Street is named after a philanthropic friend of Swift who persuaded the dean to leave his money to found a lunatic asylum; and **Crow Street** is associated with a theatre that rivalled the Smock Alley theatre to the west, at a time when Ireland's prosperity attracted not only native talent but also the best actors and writers of England as well, including Farquhar, Garrick, the Kembles, Mrs Siddons, and Tate Wilkinson. Thomas Sheridan, R.B.'s father, was the making of Smock Alley, managing it in the mid-century, a time when shouts and missiles from the gallery and invasion of the stage and dressing rooms by bucks who thought actresses fair game at any time make the most fervent modern audience participation look stilted. The Duke of Leinster himself, in a leap from box to stage, was rumoured to have impaled, and virtually castrated, himself on spiked iron bars erected for the players' defence.

But the past seems more shadowy than ever amid the life, vibrancy, pace, youthfulness, style and modish impermanence of the area which incorporates all these streets and buildings between Dame Street and the river, the showplace of the sudden affluence and assurance that overwhelmed Dublin and the rest of Ireland in the 1980s and 1990s. What was till then a rather musty, almost Dickensian maze of lanes teeming with solicitors' offices and businesses that seemed to be tottering dustily into decrepitude has become **Temple Bar**. The name commemorates the Temple family, patrons of Swift, ancestors of Lord Palmerston, who in the seventeenth century owned whatever hereabouts the Angleseas did not, but now, to the Irish, it conjures up an enclave of art galleries, smartly furbished cafés, bars and restaurants, television and music studios, the Irish Film Centre, the Gallery of Photography, shops selling stylish jewellery, clothes, fabrics, with a constant need to change patterns, refresh designs – update, you might be forgiven for thinking, or die. In Eustace Street is the Clarence Hotel, owned and revamped by the pop group U2, where such as Jack Nicholson, Tina Turner or Simon le Bon might occupy the penthouse suite. Not cheap. This is an area where very little is. But it always brims with visitors, native and foreign.

Now the hill rises to the castle and the high ground to which most of medieval Dublin was confined. On the left, just before the Castle Gate, is the imposing domed **City Hall**, with its heavy Corinthian portico, the building of which first brought the architect Thomas Cooley to Dublin from London in 1769. He won the £100 prize for his design (James Gandon came second). It was built, in what a century before had been the Earl of Cork's garden, as the Royal Exchange, to replace the Old Tholsel; but marketing activities followed the city's movement eastwards, and it was left to serve various functions: prison for rebels of the 1798 rising, military depot, corn exchange. In 1852 it was given its present role. The rotunda with twelve support columns is worth a glance from inside. Among several statues the best is by Edward Smyth, of Charles Lucas; another is of the unsung Thomas Drummond, under-secretary for Ireland in the 1830s, a refreshing reformer, inventor and coiner of the maxim 'Property has its duties as well as its rights'. There are ancient charters and regalia but overall the place is cold and unappealing. So, too, was Dublin, when Thomas Wentworth came as Viceroy in 1632 and found that his new home, **Dublin Castle**, was cruelly damp and unkempt. From his study window he used to look at an old horse grazing as best it could in the muddy ooze which was spread so wide there was barely space for 'taking the air'. He rebuilt it with his usual brusque efficiency but five years later a maid left a basket of hot ashes under a wooden staircase and it all burned to a shell. Wentworth wrote to the king that he had lost 'the worst castle in the worst situation in Christendom'. Destruction, with or without intent, had been regular since its first building around 1220. It was the bastion of Englishry from the thirteenth century to 1922, when, after a period during which its prison function was revived, the English moved out. The rebels of 1916 were so awed by its prestige that they did not even try to take it, though at the time of the rising it was not defended. In the past its reputation was as grim as that of the Tower of London, with severed heads of criminals riding its gates. Today, of course, hardly any of the early building survives. It is, in essence, eighteenth century, and it was in the eighteenth century, when feminine Anglo-Irish hearts all over Ireland beat fast in the hopes of an invitation to a ball or presentation to the viceroy, that 'the Castle' meant Ascendancy authority and royal splendour. In its new version it was divided into an upper court, with the viceroy's private and state apartments off, and a lower court, giving on to the Record Tower (now the State Paper Office – the only one of the original Norman corner-towers to survive), and the Chapel Royal, built by Johnston about 1814 (Church of Ireland till 1943; now the Catholic Church of the Most Holy Trinity). The Upper Yard, apart from the grandly porticoed Bedford Tower, containing the Heraldic Museum and Genealogical Office (whose staff, for a fee, help to trace Irish ancestors), and its flanking triumphal arches on the north side, are almost sombrely redbrick and domestic. (It was often noticed that the figure of Justice on the Cork Hill gate faced the viceroy and kept her back to the people.) From a safe in the Bedford Tower, in 1907, just before Edward VII arrived on a state visit, the Irish crown jewels – a misleading term, for these consisted of regalia of vastly less value than the crown jewels proper – were stolen. The theft was followed for years by a trail of rumour, reports of homosexuality in high places, arrests and at least two murders, but the mystery has never been solved nor the jewels found.

Recent years have seen extensive restoration of the Castle, and some rebuilding of the east and south sides of the upper courtyard. An office block has arisen on the east of the lower courtyard. But the state apartments (there are guided tours for the public) are as sumptuous and imposing as they were in their imperial heyday. St Patrick's Hall, at the top of the stairs, has been called the most magnificent room in Ireland. Once used for banquets, state balls, and the investiture of the knights of St Patrick, it is now the setting for the seven-yearly inauguration of presidents and other high-flown happenings. The three huge ceiling paintings by Vincent Waldré date from 1778: their forgotten theme the benefits England showered on Ireland. Waldré's patron was the viceroy, the Marquess of Buckingham, noted by Horace Walpole for his 'many disgusting qualities, as pride, obstinacy, and want of truth, with natural propensity to avarice'. It was here that Buckingham invested himself, in 1783, first grand master of the Knights of St Patrick, a now defunct order whose members' banners still decorate the walls. The Supper Room, with elegant Gothic plasterwork, is situated inside Bermingham Tower, originally of 1411 but rebuilt in 1775. The list of martyrs and rebels confined here is long and distinguished. The State Dining Room was added for George V's visit in 1911. A long gallery leads to the gilded Throne Room, decorated in Buckingham's time; the medallions above the doors may be by Angelica Kauffman. Other rooms contain two fine eighteenth-century plaster ceilings, brought here from Sarah Purser's demolished Mespil House.

Sir Alfred Chester Beatty was an American, naturalised British, resident in Dublin, who combined a successful involvement in African and American mining with an interest, as he put it in *Who's Who*, 'in collecting Oriental manuscripts, specialising particularly in manuscripts of artistic merit from the point of view of miniatures and calligraphy'. The product of these combined horizons is the **Chester Beatty Library and Gallery of Oriental Art**, recently moved from Ballsbridge to a proud site at the Castle, and now best reached from the Ship Street entrance. It contains a magnificent Chinese Library, Japanese prints and manuscripts, and a unique collection of rare Western manuscripts and bindings, ranging from an early ninth-century Italian copy of Bede, to a selection of early printed books, and including some beautiful French and Spanish Books of Hours minutely illustrated. The older and most famous manuscripts include the Chester Beatty papyri, a group of codices found in Egypt and bought in 1931, many of them from the second and third centuries and a hundred or more years older than the earliest vellum manuscripts. Their significance to scholars is chiefly as evidence for the text of the Greek bible. There is also a unique collection of about six hundred Chinese snuff-boxes of various stones including sapphire and garnet, and a collection of Indian, Persian and Middle Eastern manuscripts, paintings, robes, and ornaments.

Dublin

Outside the castle, we can cross Lord Edward Street and continue ahead to Essex Street West to visit, if we are so minded, the **Dublin Viking Adventure**, which brings home in entertaining style some of what we can ascertain, extrapolate or simply guess about Viking ways. A few yards west, **Fishamble Street** curves down to the river. It was in the Charitable Musical Society's Hall here, long since demolished, that Handel's *Messiah* was given its first performance, on 13 April 1742. A plaque marks the site. This was a period of great musical activity in Dublin. Geminiani lived, played and taught in Dame Street for years. Thomas Arne and his son Michael (later an alchemist who tried to concoct gold in a house at Clontarf) gave many concerts – Arne senior's opera *Rosamund* was performed in 1743. But Handel's stay was the high point of these years. Put out by rivalry in London with Bononcini and the public's inability to choose the greater composer, Handel accepted an invitation from the Duke of Devonshire, then viceroy, to visit and compose a new work for Dublin. In six weeks he wrote the *Messiah*. Its performance was triumphant, and often repeated. It was only later that George II began the custom of standing for the *Hallelujah Chorus*, but on this occasion Dr Delany rose at the end of *He was despised* and called emotionally to the soloist, Mrs Cibber: 'Woman, for this, be all thy sins forgiven.' Handel stayed a year and England had to wait nearly two for its first hearing of the new work. Before leaving he was taken to the by now demented Swift, who, on registering who his visitor was, cried out: 'Oh! a German, and a Genius! A Prodigy! Admit him.'

Christ Church Cathedral is the oldest building in Dublin. It is also mother church of the Church of Ireland diocese of Dublin and Glendalough, and one of the two Protestant cathedrals, both originally Catholic, of a mainly Catholic city which lacks one of its own. There have been proposals to hand over Christ Church to the Catholics, but they have always come to grief. Founded by the Dublin Danes, about 1040, it was begun again on something approaching its present scale in 1172, Strongbow and St Laurence O'Toole being sponsors; the basic building was complete fifty years later. Part of the crypt built by the Danes may have been preserved. A lot has changed since the main building period, and the central tower, though it looks perfectly in keeping with the rest, was built about 1600 after one original steeple was burned and another flattened in a storm. Its history reflects that of the town. Lambert Simnel, ten years old and asserted to be son of the Earl of Warwick – and so a claimant to the

27

throne – was crowned here in 1487 as Edward VI, with a golden tiara taken from a statue of the Virgin Mary (a year later, captured in England along with his ambitious backers, he was sent by a wryly merciful Henry VII to work out his days as kitchen-boy). The cathedral adopted Anglicanism in 1551. For a short period under James II it restored the mass, though an Anglican thanksgiving was offered in 1691 after William III's victory at the Boyne. It was used for services and concerts in the eighteenth century, but the urgent need of repairs, as well as the growth of slums, closed its doors in 1829. Massive restoration, costing Henry Roe, a Dublin distiller, a quarter of a million pounds, took place between 1871 and 1878. The architect was George Edmund Street, a prolific and distinguished Gothic Revivalist, and pupil of Sir George Gilbert Scott, who had by this time rebuilt much of England in similar style. Street's work – including the present east wing, west front, flying buttresses, baptistery, and the synod hall across St Michael's Hill, as well as the covered bridge that connects with it – has left more of its stamp on the building than that of any other period. Indeed little of the main structure – the transepts and sagging north nave wall are the exceptions – remains from before.

The interior does preserve some remarkable antiquities. In the south nave arcade is a supposed, much worn effigy of Strongbow, marking his burial place, with another said to be either of Eve, his wife and Dermot MacMurrough's daughter, or of Strongbow's son, whom according to legend he cut in two for being a coward. Just round the corner in the south transept is the magnificent, flamboyant tomb of Robert, 19th Earl of Kildare (1674–1742) and premier earl of Ireland, by Sir Henry Cheere, a popular Westminster sculptor. The statue is perhaps unique in showing the subject prostrate. Eighteenth-century dead are normally shown standing or reclining. In the chapel of St Loo or St Laud in the south-east corner of the cathedral, a bronze, heart-shaped case hangs from a chain, containing St Laurence O'Toole's embalmed heart. (St Laurence mediated between Danes and Normans at the 1170 conquest of Dublin, and died in France.) Most impressive of all is the vaulted crypt, one of the largest in these islands and extending the whole length of the church. Part of the 800-year-old walls are made of lime or mortar mixed with ox-blood and supported by wooden wedges, now supposedly petrified in the damp bog air. In medieval times the crypt was leased to stall-holders who held markets here. As late as the seventeenth century it housed taverns. In haphazard order, remains down here include statues of

Stuart kings, the candlesticks and tabernacle used for mass in James II's reign, and a melodramatic memorial to Nathaniel Sneyd by Thomas Kirk (1781–1845). The synod hall is linked to the main building by a bridge, and now contains **Dublinia**, an interesting presentation of models and tableaux illustrating the city's history.

High Street, over the road, was medieval Dublin's main thoroughfare, and one of the two churches beside it dedicated to St Audoen, now the Protestant one, was built in the twelfth century on the site of a Danish church. (Twice honoured St Audoen, or Ouen, was a seventh-century bishop of Rouen, relics of whom were enshrined at Canterbury; the men of Bristol, granted Dublin by Henry II, introduced him to Ireland.) This church preserves a west door from 1190 and three bells from 1423, the oldest in the country, as well as several early tombs and fragments. But most of its looks are owed to mediocre nineteenth-century restoration. North of the church is St Audoen's Arch, whose lower half, put up in 1240, is all that survives of Dublin's city gates. Above these wall fragments rises Patrick Byrne's **Catholic Church of St Audoen** of 1841 to 1847, whose appearance is much enhanced by its position. On the other side of High Street, in Back Lane, is **Tailors Hall** (in the seventeenth century the Earls of Kildare had a house and the Jesuits, until evicted, a college, in this same street). The hall now gleams from restoration inspired in 1965 by the Irish Georgian Society. It had been closed as unsafe in 1960 and looked ripe for demolition, when an appeal was successfully launched. Built in Queen Anne's reign, it was used by various guilds for formal occasions, possessing as it did Dublin's largest public room. In 1792 the Catholic Convention – or 'Back Lane Parliament' – met here, with Wolfe Tone as secretary, and pressed demands which the following year brought Catholics the vote. In the nineteenth century it was used as school, warehouse, temperance meeting-room, workmen's reading-room, coffee-room. Restored, it became the headquarters of An Taisce, Ireland's equivalent of the English National Trust.

Thomas Street West leads away from Christ Church Place to the west, passing on the left the area of the **Liberties**, a poor and slummy area not long ago, and so called because it was outside the Lord Mayor's jurisdiction. A colony of Huguenot weavers settled here in the seventeenth century, but it stayed poor. Swift, hero of Dublin's underlings, said he should be paid two pounds a year for wear and tear to his hats, caused by acknowledging greetings from residents of the Liberties. At the start of the twentieth century part of the Liberty of St Sepulchre was demolished and replaced with the present blocks of flats by the first Earl of Iveagh, under a Guinness trust. More slum clearance came in recent years. Part of the area, especially Francis Street, is now famous for antique shops. **Guinness's St James's Gate Brewery** is a mile on. The stout it produces is part of the Irish – not to mention British – way of life, but until it was hoisted to multinational status the firm was important to Ireland in other ways – as a model of industrial relations and a notable exporter (to some 120 countries). The brewery, covering sixty acres, and once the biggest in Europe, extends around the site which Arthur Guinness started to rent at £45 a year in 1759, and includes attractive architecture of the end of the eighteenth century, and the tallest windmilltower in these islands. From Arthur's initiative the family – now incorporating the separate titles Iveagh and Moyne and others – has arrived at international status. Its members, however, for long continued to help Dublin in many ways – with grants of land, sports, homes, conservation – both as company and private benefactors.

Beside the brewery, on the south side of James's Street, is the 1769 **Church of St Catherine**, built to John Smyth's designs with a good Roman Doric façade – and until 1967 another candidate for demolition. Saved with the help of the Irish Georgian Society, it is now used as a community centre. The already hanged body of Robert Emmet was beheaded outside it in 1803. But this is taking us beyond the city centre and we return, by the way we came, to Christ Church, turn right just beyond it down Werburgh Street, and pass on the left **St Werburgh's Church**, a sister foundation to the church of the same name in Bristol, its origins going back to Norman times. Its interior is the most elegant of eighteenth-century restorations, designed after a fire in 1754, by John Smyth. After Robert Emmet's rising of 1803, however, castle authorities took a dislike to this vantage point overlooking their fortress, persuaded seven venal architects to declare it unsafe, and pulled down the tall Baroque tower and upper part of the façade. Under the chancel is the family vault of the FitzGeralds, which in 1798 was opened at dead of night to accommodate the body of Lord Edward FitzGerald. Son of the first Duke of Leinster, a former soldier and MP for Athy, he was drawn to Paris by the revolution, and there shed family tradition and joined the revolutionary United Irishmen. After 1796 he moved between Ireland and France on secret missions of dubious importance and little effect, trying to arrange a French invasion of his country to time with the 1798 Rising. On the eve of that he was given away and arrested in nearby Thomas

Street. He and some of his captors were wounded and he died, within a month, at Newgate. Major Henry Sirr, who led his captors, lies buried in the churchyard. So perhaps does Molly Malone – at least a fishmonger of that name appears in eighteenth-century parish records. The sumptuous carved pulpit came from the castle's Chapel Royal; and the viceroy, particularly when Dr Delany was rector, often used the church – his vast pew still remaining in the gallery with a splendid view of the east window and interior.

Werburgh Street is also the site of Dublin's first theatre, founded by the tireless Thomas Wentworth, Earl of Strafford (a tyrant of genius; he would certainly have got trains to run on time had there been any). In 1636 he brought over the playwright James Shirley, whose play *The Royal Master* was first performed here. During one of Wentworth's trips to London, pious Archbishop Ussher closed the theatre down, claiming such licence would bring on the plague. Wentworth reopened it on his return and it did well for four years. No trace of it remains, nor of the house (though there is a wall-tablet on the site) where Swift was born in 1667: No. 7 Hoey's Court, between Werburgh Street and Little Ship Street on the left.

Swift was Dean of **St Patrick's Cathedral** from 1713 to 1745. While, before this, he held the living of Laracor in Meath, he hoped for a bishopric, but Queen Anne, nonplussed by his satires, barred the promotion. Other women were more vulnerable. 'Stella' – his name for Esther Johnson – was a friend from early years who followed him to Laracor, then Dublin, and was close to him – possibly married him in secret – until his death. She kept cool during his stormy affaire with 'Vanessa', Esther Vanhomrigh, which ended with the latter's death at Celbridge; when he himself died in 1745, crazed by pain as he had been for years, he was buried beside Stella in St Patrick's. Both romances live on, one in his *Journal to Stella*, the other in his poem *Cadenus and Vanessa*; so do *Gulliver's Travels*, mostly written here and the only work that earned him money; and satires like *The Tale of a Tub*, the *Battle of the Books*, and the short *Modest Proposal*, in which he dryly urges the fattening, slaughter and sale of starving Irish children to the rich, as joints for eating. But in Ireland his reputation rests on his championship of the Irish against English rule. He was revered for his tireless struggle in the slums and throughout the country, and it was this fight that he most wanted remembered, as his own famous epitaph, '*Ubi saeva indignatio...*', shows. 'He is laid where bitter rage can no more tear his heart. Go, traveller, imitate if you can one who was, to the best of his powers, a defender of liberty.' 'The greatest epitaph in history,' it was called by Yeats, whose own has since been called the same. The odd situation of St Patrick's, on foundations often waterlogged by the Poddle river flowing beneath it, led to a macabre postscript. A flooding in 1835 dislodged flagstones and brought various coffins to view. Swift's and Stella's were opened, and the skulls kept for examination. Sir William Wilde, Oscar's father, traced symptoms of what is known as Menière's syndrome, a disorder of the inner ear causing the pain, giddiness, deafness and vomiting that marked Swift's last years. Stella, however, was 'a perfect model of symmetry and beauty'; and he singles out the teeth 'which for their whiteness and regularity were, in life, the theme of general admiration, are, perhaps, the most perfect ever witnessed in a skull.'

Inundations like that of 1835 happen no more, though there have been more recent leaks from aisles; but they were common – and sometimes rose to six or seven feet in depth – up to 1870, and caused frequent deaths in the lower floors of nearby weavers' slums. But the belief that St Patrick had baptised converts on the site overcame objections of this kind when Archbishops Comyn and Henry de Londres erected what became Ireland's largest church (300 feet long) from 1191 onwards. Another reason for its position was that it escaped the overlordship of Christ Church, with whose dean and chapter de Londres had quarrelled. The rivalry of the two cathedrals, and repeated attempts to turn St Patrick's into a university, continued to the sixteenth century, after which it fell gradually into disrepair. Cromwell's troops stabled horses here (though one sometimes suspects this ubiquitous charge) and James II used it as a barracks. Patching took place from time to time – forty tons of new timber for the roof in 1671, a new Lady Chapel replacing in the 1840s what had become virtually a Huguenot parish church. There were also additions, like George Semple's incongruous granite spire of 1750. Then between 1863 – by which time the roof had fallen again and all but individual chapels were disused – and 1869, Sir Thomas Drew, paid by Sir Benjamin Lee Guinness, carried out almost total rebuilding; and added some touches of his own like the north and south porches, the west window and door, and the buttresses to the nave. But basically the cathedral remains truer to the original Early English and Gothic than Christ Church, keeping also some of the fortifications which had been needed when, being outside the walls, it was often attacked from Wicklow. Drew carried out further repairs in 1900, partly because the Caen stone he used before was not hard-wearing. Again a Guinness, in the person of Lord Iveagh, son of Sir Benjamin, financed the work. The two cathedrals' rivalry had been resolved at the disestablishment of the Church of Ireland in 1869 when St Patrick's was made a national cathedral, standing in relation to Christ Church as Westminster Abbey does to St Paul's.

Like Christ Church its exterior is not outstanding, as compared to others in these islands. The surrounds have improved in recent years. But it is the interior which is of greatest interest, and its length and profuse memorials are impressive. The most obviously striking feature is the Jacobean memorial in black marble and alabaster, still with its original paint, to the wife of the first Earl of Cork (there is a better Cork monument at Youghal), on the left of the entrance. It is the biggest in Ireland. The earl, the most successful adventurer of his time and a great believer in his own importance, first had this erected beside the altar, at a cost then of £1,000. Viceroy Wentworth ordered it moved. The congregation, he said, could not worship without 'crouching to an Earl of Cork and his lady... or to those sea-nymphs his daughters, with coronets upon their heads, their hair dishevelled, down upon their shoulders'. Cork protested but Wentworth won at least this round in their prolonged tussle. On the monument itself, the men portrayed on the top two levels are Lady Cork's distinguished ancestors. She and the Great Earl are below, and eleven of their children below them. The infant is guessed to be Robert Boyle, physicist-to-be.

Swift's and Stella's graves are at the foot of the second column along this side, and against the south nave wall is a fine bust (from 1775, by Patrick Cunningham) of Swift, and his ringing epitaph. An ancient cross in the north-west corner, removed from near the tower, was supposed to mark St Patrick's Well, where the saint once baptised. Opposite the second column in this north aisle is Lady Morgan's monument to Carolan, one of the last of the Irish bards, and farther along a memorial to Samuel Lover, the nineteenth-century novelist. In the north transept, once walled off from the main building and used as the parish church of St Nicholas Without (without, that is, the city walls), are memorials of the Royal Irish Regiment. Founded in Charles II's reign and disbanded in 1922, it had in the period defended the British Empire in most corners of the globe and been target, at Lexington, of the first shots fired in the American War of Independence. Much-married Dame St Leger's memorial in the right-hand corner carries an amusing Elizabethan marital tale. In the other corner is the pulpit used by Swift. In the north choir aisle on the right is Swift's caustic epitaph to Marshal Schomberg, killed at the Boyne, whose family were too mean to record his burial here themselves – 'the fame of his valour was more effective with strangers than his closeness by blood was with his kinsmen'. The choir itself was the chapel of the Order of St Patrick, founded in 1783 by George III to consist of the sovereign and twenty-two knights. Above the stalls are the banners of the knights, an order which, numbering twenty-two knights in the years of the Union, quickly contracted after independence was granted in 1921 and finally ended on the death of the late Duke of Gloucester in 1974. The Lady Chapel at the east end served for 150 years as a Huguenot church; services being a translation from the Anglican form. On the walls of the south choir aisle are four brasses, seldom found in Ireland. A tablet in the south transept commemorates the Rev. Charles Wolfe, known for little but his poem *The Burial of Sir John Moore after Corunna*. But this is only to pick out a few. All the walls are clustered with memorials and epitaphs, amounting to a summary of Anglo-Irish distinction, piety and bombast.

A monument in the south transept commemorates Archbishop Narcissus Marsh, and when we leave the cathedral and turn left we can walk through the close to Marsh's Library, Ireland's oldest public library, built at his order between 1702 and 1707. It is still a public library, available for anyone's use, and from it microfilms of books, from what amounted in the early eighteenth century to the complete gentleman's library, are sent all over the world. The steep-roofed exterior has been often restored; the interior is much as it was – L-shaped, with whitewashed walls and dark ranks of oak shelves, and stalls. In the ground-floor windows is the only Queen Anne glass left in Dublin. Several books are chained to the shelves, a precaution which had never been improved on till electronic tagging arrived. Some of the many treasures are kept on display: notably Swift's personal copy – which he read four times – of Clarendon's *History of the Great Rebellion*. Among the marginal notes in Swift's hand are remarks like (on the Scottish) 'Mad treacherous damnable infernal for ever' and (on Montrose) 'a perfect Hero, wholly un-Scotified'.

North Dublin

The River Liffey cuts Dublin in two. It rises with a westward flow near Sally Gap in the Wicklow Hills, curves round in almost full circle, comes into Dublin by Chapelizod, flows east past the Phoenix Park and then under some dozen bridges within the city to form the harbour and reach the sea at Dublin Bay, taking sixty miles, as someone has pointed out, to cover a distance of ten. Crossing any bridge from south to north we find a different feel in the air. Nowhere is the contrast more marked than over O'Connell Bridge – or the Metal Bridge one move up, sometimes called Ha'penny Bridge because of the toll charged earlier last century – leading from the centres of learning, journalism and finance to the once fine, still broad, somewhat meretricious O'Connell Street.

There are two points of view. One was put by George Moore, quoting Somerville and Ross: 'Few towns are duller out of season than Dublin, but the dullness of its north side neither waxes nor wanes.' Brendan Behan stated the other: the *people* he liked lived mainly on a line between the Custom House and Glasnevin cemetery – 'between birth and death, come to think of it'. There is a lot of room between the extremes, and more good to be said of the north now that, through various agencies, some of the best of its old parts have been brought to the light again.

O'Connell Street was laid out in the late 1740s as Gardiner's Mall, by Luke Gardiner, first Viscount Mountjoy (d. 1755), founder of a family which in less than a century did more than any other to beautify Dublin. He widened the street (which he renamed Sack-ville Street) to 150 feet, let building sites, and planted the 48-foot-wide Mall with trees, planning it as a long residential square. It was one of the earliest components of fashionable north Dublin. After his time the street was extended to the river and gradually became the main north–south thoroughfare it is now. Only two original houses survive. Maurice Craig calls its prevalent style 'neon-classical'.

We can divert along the right-hand quay to the Custom House, a few hundred yards along, passing the skyscraper **Liberty Hall**, the trades union headquarters whose less obtrusive predecessor played a large part in the independence movement. The **Custom House** itself is in fact better appreciated as a unity from across the river. It and the Four Courts are considered by many the finest buildings in Dublin.

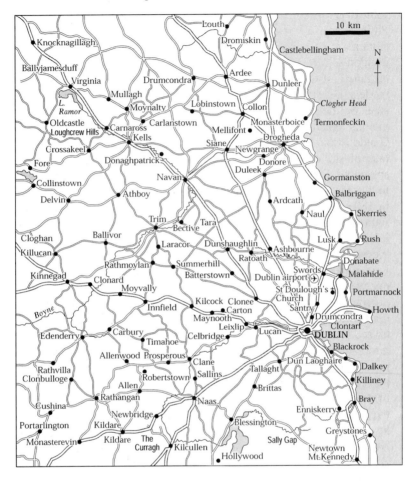

Both were designed by James Gandon, and Maurice Craig finds the Custom House expresses the 'feminine and predominantly horizontal' aspect of Gandon's mind; while the Four Courts upstream is 'masculine in feeling, built on a cubical if not vertical theme'. Gandon, born in England, and pupil of Sir William Chambers, was brought to Ireland in 1781 through friendship with Lord Charlemont, who combined statesmanship with lavish patronage of the arts. Soon

36

Dublin

John Beresford, Chief Commissioner for the Irish Revenue and later Pitt's right-hand man in gerrymandering through the Act of Union, commissioned him to plan the new Custom House, to match London's Somerset House. Gandon rejected the 'meretricious elegance' of the popular Adam style, and looked more to France for models. His style was Palladian with hints of Baroque and Neo-Classical. So the great building rose – in spite of a partly submerged site, vicious hostile demonstrations (Beresford was much hated, and Gandon found 'a good cane sword' a useful escort), and initially a lack of skilled labour – in granite and Portland Stone, in isolated splendour. Finished in 1791, it was described as the greatest building in these islands since the time of Wren; and a friend wrote to Creevey in 1805: 'It is in every respect a noble edifice, in which there is no fault to be found except that old Beresford is sumptuously lodged in it.' Gandon proceeded to adorn Dublin further with the Four Courts, the eastern portico of Parliament House, the King's Inns, and Carlisle Bridge (reconstructed in 1880 and renamed O'Connell Bridge – the one we crossed just now).

But the building is not what it was. In 1921 followers of de Valera marked the Sinn Fein election victory by setting the place on fire. It blazed for five days, and hardly more than the shell survived. So now Ardbraccan stone has replaced Portland, the interior is quite replanned, and the exterior differs in some small but important respects. But many of the sculptures are outstanding – Smyth's statue of 'Commerce' topping the 125-foot dome, the heads round its base, the arms of the Kingdom of Ireland on the end pavilions, and the keystones by the Doric portico on the south side representing the Atlantic and thirteen principal rivers of Ireland. The general impression is one of grandeur. Government business goes on inside and it is not open to the public.

We return to O'Connell Street by Lower Abbey Street, and pass on the left the **Abbey Theatre**, opened in 1966 on the site of the disused Mechanics Institute, which Miss Horniman gave to the Irish National Theatre Society in 1904. It was here, in the original Abbey (which had in its time been both mortuary and pawnbroker's), with Yeats, Lady Gregory, Douglas Hyde, Lennox Robinson and the Fay brothers working together with actors like Sarah Allgood and her sister Maire O'Neill, that the theatre got its international reputation. Synge's *Playboy of the Western World* went on in 1907 and sparked off commotions through the use of the word 'shift' [sic]. (In 1912 the same play, on tour in America, led to arrest of the performers in

37

Philadelphia.) Miss Horniman herself withdrew her backing in 1910 when, through an error, the theatre kept open on the day of Edward VII's death, 7 May. Later, some of Shaw's and most of O'Casey's plays produced violent audience reactions – uproar and salvoes of vegetables on the stage. Then, in 1951, after a performance of *The Plough and the Stars*, which ends with Dublin ablaze after rebellion, the back-stage of the theatre was burned down. The company took a long lease of the Queen's Theatre over the river until 1966, when the new theatre, designed by one of Ireland's best-known architects, Michael Scott, was opened.

No. 32 Abbey Street was the first headquarters of Maud Gonne's Daughters of Erin, a forceful group of female nationalists who, so their enemies said, taught children to answer the catechism question 'what is the origin of evil' with 'England'. We return to O'Connell Street, with its central line of statues (O'Connell himself, by Foley, is near the bridge), its garish cafés and amusement arcades, its two cinemas, shops and stores, and without its **Nelson's Pillar**. The 134-foot column with Kirk's statue on top was blown to bits in 1966 (a less drastic solution to the presence of this tall affront had been suggested in a letter to the *Irish Times* – change eye and arm, and call it Emmet).

It had already survived, what some nearby buildings did not, a bombardment from a British ship in the harbour at the time of the 1916 Easter Rising. The **General Post Office** opposite Abbey Street, to the right, was the rebels' headquarters, and here 37-year-old Patrick Pearse, half-English poet, barrister, journalist, teacher, and chosen president of the Provisional Republican Government, and 47-year-old Scottish-born James Connolly, founder of Irish socialism, and union leader, tried, during the week it lasted, to control that idealist insurrection. They took over the Post Office (a late, massive work of 1815 to 1818 by Francis Johnston) by simply walking in and ordering out the startled staff and customers. With the sun shining brightly, as it is always supposed to do during Irish Easters, Pearse proclaimed a Republic to bemused passers-by. For a day or two Dublin disbelieved. Then troops came, and guns. In four days, 450 Irish and 100 British were dead. Artillery had made rubble of the inside of the Post Office and much else around it (other parts of Dublin suffered too), and the leaders surrendered. Within days General Maxwell, commanding the British, executed, under martial law, Pearse, Connolly (wounded, and fatally ill, he had to sit to be shot) and thirteen others, at Kilmainham Prison. De Valera, condemned, was reprieved, due, it was thought, to his being an American citizen. Despite the agony, O'Casey called 1916 'the year one in Irish history and Irish life'. In 1922 the civil war that followed independence brought more destruction to O'Connell Street. Subsequently, its extensive damage was repaired, but faultily; and it never regained the elegance it had boasted as Sackville Street. Nowadays election, commemorative and other rallies are often held in front of the GPO's still imposing façade.

Henry Street and North Earl Street join O'Connell Street just beyond the GPO. What was to become O'Connell Street was called, when Luke Gardiner bought it in 1714, Drogheda Street. Two nearby lanes were Moore and Off (formerly Of). Together they commemorated the first owner, Henry Moore, Earl of Drogheda. Another curiosity here is a line of London plane trees, in the centre beyond the crossroads. For six months every winter a colony of pied wagtails roosts in them nightly, amid the lights, noise and fumes. They settle at dusk and leave at first light. There have at times been several thousands of them. This, in a species that would normally choose sequestered river banks and country villages, has been going on since 1929. 'In all my birding,' wrote Canon Raven, 'I have come across nothing so bizarre.' (I on the other hand have: a similar community winters in a plane tree near London's Hammersmith tube station.)

Turning right up Cathedral Street and left at Marlborough Street we can visit Dublin's Catholic **Pro-Cathedral**, begun in 1816, a monumental Doric building by John Sweetman. It is very grand outside but in a cramped situation (Church of Ireland interests kept it out of O'Connell Street, for which it was intended). The interior, with its dome and typical apse at the west end, contains some impressive details like the white marble altar, with a small marble canopy on eight pillars by Peter Turnerelli (1774–1839), an Italian born in Dublin. Count John McCormack was once a member of the church's Palestrina Choir, which was endowed by Edward Martyn, who spent fortunes in an attempt to raise the aesthetic standards of Catholic worship in Ireland. It was in this Pro-Cathedral that J.H. Newman made his first profession of the Catholic faith in public, in 1851. 'Ten thousand difficulties do not make one doubt', he had written shortly before. The building adjoins a district known in English days as Monto (from Montgomery, now Foley, Street); then a notorious red-light area, Joyce's 'Nighttown'. What is now Waterford and was then Mecklenburgh Street lies at its centre. Prostitution was done away with in 1925. Before that, up to sixteen hundred girls and women, managed by affluent and often well-known madams, pursued their calling in half a dozen streets, whose names and natures have all been changed.

Tyrone House, opposite, now houses the Government's Education Department, but was built in 1740 by Richard Castle for Sir Marcus Beresford, father of John. One of the first of the aristocracy's town houses, it is heavy, simple and solid, in Irish granite. It was decorated inside with excellent rococo stucco work, on ceilings which still survive, by the Lafranchini brothers. When John Beresford (patron of Gandon at the Custom House) took it over he used parts of the house and outbuildings as torture-chambers to discover plotters and rebels of the 1798 rebellion – work that was said to be congenial to him. In 1835 it was bought by the government, and later a replica was built to balance it, with the domed Central Model Schools (where Shaw was a pupil) in between. Tyrone House's portico and central Venetian window have suffered from later remodelling.

Back in O'Connell Street we turn right, passing the central statue of Father Matthew, nineteenth-century crusader for temperance. At the end of the street stands the **Parnell Monument** and statue, with a long inscription engraved in gold. (With statues of O'Connell, Nelson and Parnell, wrote Yeats, a single Dublin street commemorated three of history's best-known adulterers.) Parnell, formerly Rutland, Square – the city's second oldest after St Stephen's Green – begins beyond the statue. Opposite is the **Rotunda** complex – hospital to the left, and Assembly Rooms on the right. The Round Room, designed by Castle's pupil George Ensor and altered by Gandon in 1786, nowadays houses the Ambassador Cinema, and its interior is changed for the worse. The New Assembly Rooms were built by Richard Johnston (Francis's elder brother) in 1784 to 1786. They now contain the Gate Theatre, founded by Micheal MacLiammoir and Hilton Edwards, who were later subsidised by the fifth Earl of Longford, and presented plays and productions of great distinction, many of them translated from foreign languages. In 1783 the Rotunda witnessed scenes from the great Volunteer Convention, an Anglo-Irish attempt to throw off some of Westminster's control. To it, in expectation of his emergence as some kind of sovereign of Ireland, the flamboyant Frederick Augustus Hervey, Earl of Bristol and Bishop of Derry, drove in state in a coach and six, led by a squadron of dragoons in gold and scarlet attended by liveried lackeys, only to find Lord Charlemont elected above him. The original – and present – purpose of the

Assembly Rooms was to provide funds for the **Maternity Hospital** adjacent, to the left, founded by Bartholomew Mosse, an obscure relation of the great Earl of Cork. Appalled by the squalor in which many Dublin mothers had perforce to produce their babies – the obverse side of the eighteenth-century boom – Mosse in the 1750s commissioned Castle to build a proper hospital, the first of its kind in the two islands. (Even in the hospital, for the first thirty years, the rate of mortality among babies was one in six.) Gem of the hospital is its chapel, a square-shaped riot of Baroque, alive with aerial putti, by the French-Italian stuccoist Barthelemy Cramillion; its bane is the modern red-brick addition on the west side.

There are some imposing houses on the east of **Parnell Square**, erected in the mid eighteenth century, a time when the optimism of the Anglo-Irish brought artistic talents from England, France and Italy to build and decorate rich men's homes. Oliver St John Gogarty, Joyce's 'Buck Mulligan', was born at No. 5. No. 9 was built in the 1750s for the philanthropic Dr Mosse; and No. 11 for the Earl of Ormonde. In the middle of the square is the sunken cross-shaped Garden of Remembrance, designed – rather heavily – by Dáithi P. Hanly in 1966, fiftieth anniversary of the Easter Rising. Beyond that, set back from the north pavement of the square, is **Charlemont House**, now the Hugh Lane Municipal Art Gallery. James Caulfeild, first Earl of Charlemont, had it built. He was a cautious Liberal who, having helped to win some self-government for Ireland in 1782, felt progress had gone far enough and opposed those colleagues – like the florid Earl Bishop of Derry – who wanted more. Charlemont was an eighteenth-century paragon, refined, rational, attractive, kind to everyone.

Macaulay said he 'gave the tone to the society and the age'. He had spent years in Rome, Paris and London (where he was friendly with Burke and Johnson), and settled in his native Ireland more from a sense of duty than desire. But, settled, he took up the causes he felt were right, was a great patron of the arts – architecture, painting, theatre, books – and when in old age he left Dublin for Bath, the streets from Charlemont House to the river were completely thronged. Long before, Charlemont House had earned the title 'the Holland House of Dublin'. It was designed in the 1760s by Sir William Chambers, who also planned the Earl's Casino at Marino. Unpretentious, three stories built of brick faced with granite, it attracted through its owner all the notables of the country and many from outside: 'to see and converse with him,' said Burke, 'would alone induce me to pay a visit to Dublin'.

The porch is an incongruous addition of 1930. Inside, the staircase, some ceilings and isolated details are the only important internal features to survive. But the building still serves an artistic purpose, housing the collection of which Sir Hugh Lane's split legacy forms the nucleus. The collection is representative of Irish, British and Continental artists born less than 110 years ago, though the Lane collection remains regardless of age. Outstanding are Lane's Impressionists (there are seven Constables, including the *Elder Tree*, by way of antecedents). There is Renoir's *Les Parapluies*; a fine group of Corots, including *Landscape* and *The Palace of the Popes at Avignon*; Manet's *Eva Gonzalès* and *A Concert in the Tuileries*; Daumier's *Don Quixote*; Degas' *La Plage*; and several lesser works. There is a wealth of work by Utrillo, Picasso, Bonnard, Piper, John Nash, Jack Yeats – and Rouault's *Christ and Soldier*, which, when first presented by the Friends of the Gallery in 1942 as a gift, was rejected, the Lady Mayoress finding herself 'offended, as a Catholic and a Christian'. A president-to-be of the Royal Hibernian Academy called it 'naive, childish and unintelligent'. A Henry Moore in the small sculpture collection fared no better: 'that figure has got leprosy', said a lady trustee. Fortunately for the gallery, there were second chances. The Rouault was borrowed by that eminently Catholic institution, St Patrick's College, Maynooth, until the gallery came round. Moreover, so ready is the new Ireland to embrace the new, the bizarre and the shocking that *épater le bourgeois*, new Irish style, is beyond the talent of the most provocative artists, and makes such attitudes of the recent past hard to believe.

The Irish collection brings to life great figures from the recent Irish past, the people whose names recur in the political and artistic rebirth of Ireland; and there is a poem by Yeats, *The Municipal Gallery Revisited*, which helps to evoke the period and its luminaries. Here is *George Russell* ('*AE*'), patriarch of the Gaelic Revival, by Casimir Markievicz, husband of the rebel countess; John S. Sargent's delicate *Hugh Lane*; and another *Hugh Lane* by Antonio Mancini; Mancini's *Lady Gregory*; *Katherine Tynan and Douglas Hyde* by John B. Yeats (father of the poet and of artist Jack, who called his father the best portraitist since Goya); William Orpen's *Nathaniel Hone*, and his *Sir John Mahaffy* (the gallery has some of the best work Orpen ever did); one of Orpen himself by his pupil, James Sleator; and several politicians – de Valera, Kevin O'Higgins, Redmond, Cosgrave, Arthur Griffith – by Sir John Lavery (who once taught Churchill how to paint).

No. 18, a couple of doors east of the gallery, is a fine eighteenth-century house, with exquisite plasterwork by Michael Stapleton, containing the Dublin Writers Museum, in which manuscripts, portraits, books and associated bric-a-brac celebrate the city's astonishing contribution to the world of letters. In Great Denmark Street, leading from this north side of the square towards the north-east, is the James Joyce Centre, at No. 18, another display of the tangible properties of a writer's life, in another remarkable Georgian house decorated by the stuccoist Michael Stapleton. A fascinating portrait gallery shows about three hundred of the real characters appearing in *Ulysses*, and besides talks and films and displays there are organised walks to many of the sites most closely linked with the author. The closest of these, to which unfortunately but for obvious reasons the public are not admitted, is the broad, five-bay **Belvedere House**, which has been the Jesuit Belvedere College since 1841. It was built in 1786 (and again decorated by Michael Stapleton, for the second Earl of Belvedere, son of the genial martinet who incarcerated his wife for thirty years because of her adultery with his brother. It has a fine façade, spoiled by twentieth-century alterations, particularly to the windows, and a splendid view downhill to the dome of the Custom House. Inside, the Venus Room, Apollo Room and Diana Room (the school's library, with original bookcases) still keep their magnificent Stapleton plasterwork. This being a Catholic boys' college – attended by James Joyce from 1893 to 1898 and put into *Portrait of the Artist as a Young Man* – the authorities removed Venus herself from the Venus room. But much that is good remains.

Up Temple Street, the next turning to the left, is **St George's Church** by Francis Johnston, with a 200-foot spire imitative of St Martin-in-the-Fields in London. Built in 1802, it is perhaps Johnston's finest work. The broad flat ceiling, without any central support, shows his engineering as well as artistic skill. Below, at the foot of Hill Street, is the old square tower of the church St George's was built to replace. It was here, on 10 April 1806, that the Duke of Wellington married Catherine Pakenham, sister of the second Earl of Longford. It has been called his bravest exploit, so marred by smallpox was the bride he had returned from Indian campaigns to join.

Great Denmark Street leads into Gardiner's Place and that in turn to decayed (but rejuvenating) **Mountjoy Square**, once a model of Georgian near-uniformity partly saved from redevelopment by efforts of, among others, the Irish Georgian Society. The name commemorates Luke Gardiner, third Viscount Mountjoy, grandson of the first viscount, who laid out O'Connell Street. This third viscount pushed the development of Dublin farther east and north, and laid out Mountjoy Square and the long avenue of Gardiner Street in the last decade of the eighteenth century and first two of the nineteenth. On the east side Nos. 25 and 26, built by Charles Thorp, are outstanding. The height of the first-floor windows gives them an imposing elegance. Perhaps the best houses in the square are Nos. 39 – now a Youth Hostel – and 40, by Michael Stapleton. No. 1 Mountjoy Place, off the south-east corner of the square, was built and decorated by Stapleton for himself, and he died here in 1801. The fight against the slummy grubbiness of this quarter of Dublin has been a slow slog. Sean O'Casey and Brendan Behan were born nearby, and lived impressionable years and set their plays in the quarter.

We can follow the faded grandeur out of the north-west corner of the square, along Gardiner Street Upper, then left down **Dorset Street**, named after Lionel Sackville, first Duke of Dorset, who was Lord-Lieutenant when the street was a straggling country lane. Eccles Street is third on the right. At No. 7 (demolished in 1982) lived Leopold Bloom and his Molly, at least in the pages of *Ulysses*. Francis Johnston, and later the Home Ruler Isaac Butt, lived at No. 64, the latter causing distress to his neighbours with early-hours gatherings. Off left is Nelson Street, in a house of which Brendan Behan set his play *The Hostage*. No. 12 Dorset Street was Richard Brinsley Sheridan's birthplace, in 1751; and O'Casey was born, in 1884, in the house now occupied by the Hibernian Bank. St Mary's Place, another right turn off Dorset Street, farther along, leads to **St Mary's Chapel of Ease**, always called the Black Church from the colour of the calp limestone in which it was built in 1830. John Semple designed it with great ingenuity. The principles of his building are severity, a shearing away of Classical ornamentation before Gothic introduced its own. It looks in a sense – what it certainly is not – unfinished Gothic. The ingenuity comes in the basic structure, a revival of simple corbelling techniques used in Ireland a thousand years before, making the church's interior into one enormous parabolic vault, each course of stones overlapping the one beneath. Its solidity was said to be connected with Archbishop Magee's conviction that Protestant congregations were in danger of being massacred and that every church must needs be a fortress too. The church, deconsecrated in 1962, belongs now to the Dublin Corporation. Like others, it owes its survival to the Irish Georgian Society.

Dublin

We return to Dorset Street and cross Dominick Street. No. 20 is the oldest house here, built for himself by the decorator Robert West. It has one of Dublin's best staircases, and its animated plasterwork has been recently restored. St Saviour's Dominican Priory beside it was an early building by J.J. McCarthy, known as Ireland's Pugin in spite of the fact that Pugin himself worked in several parts of Ireland. At this junction, Dorset Street becomes Bolton Street, and the next right turn is **Henrietta Street**, the saddest, because the oldest and once the finest of Georgian streets, built between 1725 and 1794, and now forlorn, slummy and perhaps irredeemable. In its time it was most exclusive, named after the wife of the ducal viceroy who in turn gave his name to Grafton Street. Seven peers lived here in the 1790s; and four successive primates of Ireland had their houses here from 1725 to 1794. Luke Gardiner himself and later his son, Earl of Blessington, lived at No. 10, once Mountjoy House, which like No. 9 was built by Pearce in 1730. Both preserve some good interior work, especially No. 9's staircase and other details. These two and No. 8 together form a convent of the Sisters of Charity of St Vincent de Paul, an order devoted to helping the poor. Nathaniel Clements (1705–77), whose skill as an architect (he built Beauparc, Phoenix Park Lodge, Lodge Park, Kildare and others) is being acknowledged for the first time since his own day, built and lived at No. 7. His extravagance there made his wife, according to Mrs Delany, 'finer than the finest lady in England'.

In 1827 the archiepiscopal houses at the end of the street were demolished to make way for the King's Inns Library. But the real damage was done by a certain Alderman Meade early last century, who bought up most of the houses, stripped their interiors and staircases, and turned them into tenements. The **King's Inns** building itself was based on a late design (1795) of James Gandon; H.A. Baker helped to conceive the great western façade. Francis Johnston added the cupola in 1816, and the two three-bay wings on each side were mid-nineteenth-century extensions. The wings on the Henrietta Street side house, on the north, the restored dining-hall, where training lawyers have to eat a stipulated number of meals; and on the south the Registry of Deeds. The dining-hall is pure Gandon, with stucco figures by Edward Smyth. This is the headquarters of the legal profession's ruling body, which moved here from the site of the Four Courts.

We go back to Bolton Street and bear right where it joins King Street. This ends, half a mile on, opposite the Blue Coat School or

45

King's Hospital, a building rarely noticed because of its inconspicuous placing. Originally founded by Charles II, in 1672, as hospital and school, it became exclusively a school for the sons of 'decayed citizens' of Protestant persuasion. The present building was planned to order by Thomas Ivory in the 1770s but, like Gandon at the King's Inns, he was up against official interference and miserliness. He left the work before the erection of a dome (the present inadequate one was put up in 1894), nor could he build the quadrangle he wanted to at the rear. But the 300-foot façade, with its deep rustication, Ionic columns and elegant balustrades, is very fine, and among the good points inside is a chapel, now lit by an Evie Hone window. The school has lately moved out, and the building has been refurbished by its new owners, the Incorporated Law Society.

We can pass on to the quays, turn left at Ellis Quay, continue through Arran Quay (Edmund Burke was born at No. 12, no longer there; St Paul's church of 1835 to 1840 by Patrick Byrne was one of the first Catholic churches to be built in a conspicuous place) and, before visiting the Four Courts, turn left to see **St Michan's** (pronounced Mikan's) in Church Street. It is one of the oldest of Dublin's churches, first dedicated in 1095 to a Danish saint (after the battle of Clontarf in 1014 Dublin's resident Danes remained, and soon took to Christianity). It was then parish church for the Danish settlement of Ostmanstown or Oxmantown. But most of the fabric dates from 1685 to 1686, the time of the first post-medieval expansion of the town beyond the castle precincts. It was largely restored in 1821, and again in the 1920s after Civil War damage. The interior is pleasingly plain, with some beautiful wood carving, particularly that of seventeen musical instruments, made from one piece of wood, below the organ. The work which is reminiscent of Grinling Gibbons, but not – despite claims to the contrary – by him. The organ dates back to 1724 and was supposedly used by Handel in the 1740s. The fine carved penitents' stool, used for some kind of public trial and confession, is the only one of its kind in Ireland.

The church is famous for its dark and macabre vaults, reached by steps from the outside, and containing extraordinarily well-preserved bodies, probably of the seventeenth century. The misnamed 'Crusader' and a woman and boy, blood vessels visible through their toughened leathery skin, are on display and could till fairly recently be touched (in spite of the fact that, whoever the bodies once were, they had a right in a Christian church to expect the sleep of the just). Their remarkable state is probably due to the moisture-absorbing yellow limestone of the walls. One version has it that a nearby whisky distillery once exploded and provided the embalming spirit. The brothers John and Henry Sheares, executed for rebellion in 1798, are buried here, and the despised third Earl of Leitrim, murdered in Donegal, among other members of the Clements family. What was thought to be the executed patriot Robert Emmet's grave was found, on opening, to be empty.

Facing the river, the 436-foot façade of the **Four Courts** building – another of James Gandon's masterpieces – shows its scarred history to anyone familiar with Gandon's genius. It was begun in 1786, to take over from the previous site in Christ Church Place, and to incorporate the public offices already begun by Thomas Cooley on the west side. In the next sixteen years Gandon erected his great central block with its portico of six Corinthian columns, the vast and distinctive lantern-dome, the radiating extensions containing the original courts of Exchequer, Common Pleas, King's Bench and Chancery, and the two quadrangles and their wings. It was all done against the heaviest odds – economic cutbacks, political attack, sneers against Gandon's Englishness, even a landslide at Portland, which delayed the sending of stone. But Dublin rallied as it neared completion. Gandon's favourite sculptor Edward Smyth did most of the many statues that still beautifully break the skyline, as well as a prodigious number inside. Throughout the nineteenth century the building served its legal purposes while inferior buildings were added to the rear. Then in 1916 it was occupied by rebels, but not for long and without great damage. Disaster came in 1922, when, after the Treaty, Republicans seized the building. Michael Collins ordered a bombardment from the other side of the river, and what had been an acrid debate became the Civil War. Shelling forced the besieged to surrender, but the building was wrecked by land mines they left behind. The contents of the Public Records Office were irreplaceable; and in the rebuilding of the central block and wings, economies and even 'improvements' were incorporated, so that the present building differs from its predecessor in many details, none of them for the better. Meanwhile, the millions of people all over the world who try to trace their Irish ancestry find the search difficult or impossible due to that brief battle.

The return to O'Connell Bridge takes us along the quays. The walk is worth taking, for an intangible quality of Dublin – the busy ensemble of river, bridges, elegant buildings, buses, auction rooms with the variable bric-a-brac of domestic Ireland, chance vistas of spires and domes and towers. Recent years have not improved the interest of the stretch, whatever it has done to the pockets of occupants, for a certain character of picturesque decay has gone. We can make a final detour, left up Capel Street, the centre of the first expansion of Dublin outside the original walls, slummy now, since in many areas north of the river redevelopment of old slums has simply led to new ones forming. **Mary's Abbey** is the second turning left.

The abbey was supposedly founded in the tenth century, but comes into the light in the middle of the twelfth, when it was taken over by the Cistercians, an order grown hardy and expansive after its reformation by St Bernard of Clairvaux. At one time its territory stretched to the river, and its influence much farther. It was here in 1534 that Silken Thomas proclaimed himself a rebel, throwing the sword of state before the assembled council of Ireland, which was accustomed to meet here. (He was caught and beheaded the following year.) Soon after, Henry VIII dissolved the abbey, and by the seventeenth century it was derelict. (Apart from a cluster of buildings round St Michan's, there was still almost nothing north of the river.) In the 1780s its site – most of its stones had already been used for bridge-building – was the home of Ireland's first national bank, and all that survives these vicissitudes are the Chapter House and part of an adjoining passage, topped now by a warehouse which fronts on Meetinghouse Lane. The rib-mouldings of the vault are its isolated treasure.

Farther along Capel Street we can turn first right for **St Mary's**, Dublin's oldest complete church, dating from 1697. Thomas Burgh, architect of Trinity Library, built it when the area was beginning to fill up. The exterior, apart from the east window, is heavy and dull; but inside showed a lighter touch, with good oak panelling and a fine west end, and an organ, which was a rare survival of the work of Renatus Harris, one of the best early eighteenth-century organ builders, and a tablet commemorating the Ormonde family. 'Showed', in the past tense, because this unique and historic church, where both Wolfe Tone (to whose memory the churchyard is dedicated) and the Earl of Charlemont were baptised, where in 1747 John Wesley preached his first Irish sermon from the pulpit, and the poor flocked to hear him – this church, deconsecrated, is now Ryans decorating centre. 'Alas, poor Ireland', Wolfe Tone wrote near the end of his Journal: 'who shall teach thy very Senators wisdom?' Seeing what planners permit these days, and in the church beside his birthplace, he might sigh again.

West Dublin and beyond

A mile and a half west of O'Connell Bridge, just beyond the old Collins Barracks, now converted into a rich home for the National Museum's overspill, the **Phoenix Park** begins, and continues to run close to the Liffey for about three miles. With an area of nearly 1,800 acres – over five times the size of Hyde Park – this is one of Europe's biggest urban parks. Soon after the Anglo-Norman conquest it was granted to Kilmainham Priory's Knights of St John, but the king took it back at the Reformation. From 1661 Charles II's Lord-Lieutenant, the newly created Duke of Ormonde, chose to live in Phoenix Lodge rather than the dank discomforts of Dublin Castle, and though he later built the viceregal lodge at Chapelizod (pronounced to rhyme with gizzard) he carried out the most extensive of his public works in the park, spending £31,000 on a perimeter wall, the planting of beech-mast and mustard, and a full-time ranger to care for his falcons, hounds, beagles, deer and partridges. He also stopped the king granting the park to the Duchess of Cleveland and earned a lifelong enemy at court.

But Lord Chesterfield, viceroy in the 1740s, found the park 'a crude, uncultivated field'. He gave play to his Augustan passion for patterns of trees and well-framed vistas in laying it out at his own expense roughly as it has come down to the present. A philanthropic viceroy, he opened the park to the public, and it soon became a favourite area for robberies and duels, the papers often complaining of the perils of passage. It was also the setting for military reviews and pageants of great splendour. Chesterfield caused to be built the Phoenix Column, which owes its name, as does the park itself, to a semantic error. *Fionn uisg*, though pronounced much like 'phoenix' is in fact Gaelic for the 'clear water' that wells up not far from the pillar. The English took the sound at face value. There are countless similar examples.

From the main gate at the south-east corner a straight road leads through to Castleknock Gate on the north-west. Over to the left is the 205-foot **Wellington Testimonial**, erected after Waterloo with bronze panels on the pedestal commemorating his battles in fine bas-relief. First on the right is the **People's Garden**, spattering its steep lakeside with bright spring and summer colours. Then comes the **Zoo**, thirty acres of it (five less than London's), and one of the prettiest and best-stocked in the world. A *cottage orné* stands at the entrance. It was built by Decimus Burton in 1831, the founding year of the gardens, when the Zoological Society's collection consisted of one wild boar. Nowadays there are most things you can think of, but special pride is felt about the lions. Not only have hundreds of cubs been born and bred here since 1857; they have improved on nature by arriving in bigger, healthier litters of up to five cubs and have at times been exported to Africa. But lions and others are well covered in the zoo's own guide. Beyond, and still to the right, is **Aras an Uachtárain**, the president's official residence. The house was built as his official lodge in 1751 by Nathaniel Clements, who enjoyed the sinecure of park ranger as well as the lucrative post of deputy Paymaster-General. It was expanded to serve as viceroy's home by Francis Johnston in 1815, and given its formal garden by Decimus Burton in 1840 to 1841. Johnston plastered over Clements's original red brick, wings were added for Queen Victoria's visit in 1849, and the interior was more recently adorned with ceilings and mantelpieces salvaged from Sarah Purser's dismantled Mespil House, and Riverstown House, county Cork. A tree by the road here marks the spot where in the evening of 6 May 1882, Lord Frederick Cavendish, newly appointed chief-secretary who had only arrived in Dublin that morning, and his assistant, Thomas H. Burke, were stabbed to death with an amputation knife. Four 'Invincibles' – an extreme wing of the Fenians – were later hanged for the crime. For one of them, Joe Brady, the 'drop' was miscalculated, and Marwood, the executioner, had, in the name of British Justice, to haul on his legs. The killers had been informed on by one of their number, James Carey, who was given a pardon and a one-way ticket to Cape Town. With the tidiness of Jacobean tragedy, Carey was shot dead on the boat, and his own murderer hanged in London.

What was then the under-secretary's residence, now the **Apostolic Nunciature**, is on the right of the main drive, beyond Chesterfield's Phoenix (which was moved off the drive early last century to make way for motor-racing). The **US Ambassador's Residence**, formerly that of the chief secretary, is hidden from view on the left. Beyond and south of the ambassador's house lie the '**Fifteen Acres**' which in fact comprise over a hundred, with paths and copses and a number of playing fields, and turf dust gallops, where racehorses exercise early in the morning. St Mary's Chest Hospital, built in 1766 as a military school, stands on the south side overlooking a steep drop to a picturesque and park-flanked stretch of the river. The hospital's chapel, built in 1771, is by Cooley, and the main building was enlarged by Francis Johnston in 1808 to 1813. Across the river is Chapelizod,

Dublin

whose name obscurely derives from Isoud, or Iseult, or Isolde, sister of the King of Ireland whom Tristan slew, setting in train a sequence of bliss and misery for himself and a recurring theme for writers and composers. Chapelizod, a popular recreation ground in the last century, comes into Joyce's *Finnegan's Wake*. It was here that the Liffey was sublimated in the motherly character of Anna Livia Plurabelle.

We have crossed the river. Palmerston, a mile west of Chapelizod on the Lucan road, gave the Irish branch of the Temple family, and so a nineteenth-century prime minister, their title. But we turn back to Dublin along St Laurence Road and then Sarsfield Road, which leads straight to Kilmainham, passing the 1914–18 **War Memorial Park** on the left, a pleasant enough scene laid out by Lutyens. Just before crossing the South Circular Road we see, on the right, the gaunt pile of **Kilmainham Gaol**, whose list of past inmates – Parnell, William Smith O'Brien, Robert Emmet, Patrick Pearse and many others – reads like a roll-call of Irish patriots. It opened in 1796, built in the shape of Jeremy Bentham's panopticon: long cell-blocks radiating from a controlling centre. Over 100,000 people were confined in it during the 128 years it served as prison. In 1911 it became an army detention centre, and after independence it was used by the government to detain outlawed Republicans. Then for many years it was allowed to decay. Its present museum status is relatively new.

Its most haunting function came in 1916, when fourteen leaders of the Easter Rising were imprisoned and executed here. Despite the horror many Dubliners felt at the barbarities of the rising itself, and the fact that it took place while England was engaged in world war, the speedy sentencing and execution of the men involved shocked them even more, especially when details seeped out: of Joseph Plunkett being allowed to marry ten minutes before he was shot, or Connolly, unable to stand because of leg wounds, being propped in a chair to be gunned down. In its prison days hanging was used 140 times – the punishment was sometimes euphemised as 'the Kilmainham minuet' – and one of the many displays illustrates the history of hanging. The most important exhibition covers various stages in the Irish struggle for independence. The yacht Asgard, in which the nationalist author Erskine Childers was running guns into the country at Howth in 1914, is also here to be inspected. Guided tours of the prison are fascinating and informative.

Over the other side of the South Circular Road is **Kilmainham Royal Hospital**, now, after years of neglect while authorities argued,

51

the Irish Museum of Modern Art, possessing a fine collection of pictures and borrowing on short or long-term loan an even finer. For many years declared unsafe and used as a dump for the national museum's surplus, mainly of old carriages, the hospital, 'for the reception and entertainment of ancient maimed, and infirm officers and soldiers', was built during 1680 to 1684, a little before the Royal Hospital at Chelsea, but after the Invalides at Paris. It supported 400 inmates who had sixpence in the pound docked from their pay. The work was designed by the Irish surveyor, Sir William Robinson, who also designed Marsh's Library. The massive, plain hospital forms a quadrangle round a court, with the main front facing the Liffey to the north. Between massive Corinthian pilasters, and below the arms of Ormonde, the main entrance leads into the magnificent pine-panelled great hall, to the right of which in British times lay the apartments of the army's commander-in-chief. The gem is to the left, on the east side: the chapel, with its charming ceiling of fruit and flower designs, sadly a *papier mâché* copy of the original seventeenth-century plaster which, mounted on oak twigs, crumbled in the nineteenth century. The stained-glass window is supposed to contain fragments from the original Templar-cum-Hospitaller priory dissolved by Henry VIII. This was on an adjacent site, as is Bully's Acre, burial ground for, among others, Murrough and Turlough, Brian Boru's son and grandson, both killed at Clontarf in 1014. The cemetery closed its gates to the dead after five hundred had been buried there within ten cholera-ridden days in 1832.

A few hundred yards east are two of Dublin's oldest hospitals. **Steevens's Hospital** is in fact the fifth oldest in these islands, yielding to three in London and one in Bath, and the first of its kind in Ireland, endowed by the legacy of a professor of physics who died in 1710. His sister, Grizel, known as Madame Steevens – an eccentric lady who through frequent wearing of a veil gave credence to the rumour that a gypsy's curse had transformed her face into a pig's – took charge of the building and got Thomas Burgh to draw designs. These are like a small version of Kilmainham – a court enclosed by arcades on four sides. Building began in 1720 and the hospital opened in 1733. Till her death, aged 92, in 1747, Madame Steevens lived in the rooms to the left of the gate, spending most of her time showing her face at the street window to belie the rumours. The hospital still contains in the board room (the work of Edward Lovett Pearce) the precious library of 4,000 books bequeathed by Edward Worth, an original trustee. Another benefactor was Swift's Stella, who endowed a chaplaincy; and Swift himself was a trustee. Swift also endowed in his will the neighbouring **St Patrick's Hospital**, built just after his death by George Semple and enlarged in 1778 by Cooley. This was intended 'for lunatics and idiots' – Swift wrote:

> *'He gave the little wealth he had*
> *To build a house for fools and mad;*
> *To show by one satiric touch,*
> *No nation wanted it so much.'*

– and is now highly regarded as a psychiatric unit. It is always known as Swift's Hospital, and contains a collection of relics of the dean.

There is some interesting wandering to do in this part. North of Steevens Lane is the handsome Heuston, formerly Kingsbridge, Station, built in 1844 and terminus of the Limerick and Cork line. To the south is the murky terminus and harbour of the Grand Canal. While to the east is the sixty-acre empire of the House of Guinness, a stone's throw from the Liffey water that is blessed daily by a majority of Irishmen, and by those abroad who drink the daily export of nearly a million pints, though sad to say Liffey water is no longer used.

North Dublin suburbs

Dublin's population rose steadily last century from 375,000 at the opening to well over 700,000. The rise has meant an ugly creeping of housing estates, shops and small factories; and the claim that you can walk from the city centre to open country gets a little less true every day. Former country houses – such few as survive – are now pinnacles in suburbia. The only relic of the first Earl of Charlemont's seaside house is surrounded by the bustle of Clontarf, and overlooked by a grandiose redbrick college. This is the famous **Casino** at Marino. It was an odd site even in the eighteenth century when Sir William Chambers designed it, being, though ozone-rich, hardly more than a mile from the earl's town house, now the Municipal Gallery, in Parnell Square. Probably Charlemont was more interested in architectural enterprise than the sensible location of residences, and he had a lifelong association with Chambers – 'the best of men', he called him. The Casino is well worth a visit, a compact, Palladian bid for earthly perfection carried out – with endless plans and counter-plans – between 1758 and 1780 in the grounds of long-vanished Marino House. Utility goes along with aesthetic perfection, for the roof urns are chimneys and the columns hollowed to serve as drains. It is the only building of its kind in Ireland, and cost the builder £60,000.

The outside barely suggests its real size. On the ground floor are a hall, study, bedroom, drawing-room – with magnificent golden sun on the ceiling and fine wood-inlaid floor, remains of sumptuous wall-hangings, gilded pillars, long-mirrors and displays of precious arti-facts; there are more bedrooms upstairs, and in the basement a kitchen, cellars, servants' hall and other service rooms in groined brickwork (used by Republicans around 1920 for practice with small arms). The Casino has recently been fully restored after long neglect.

The suburb of **Clontarf** lies to the east, with Clontarf Castle, built in 1835 on the site of an early Pale Castle, and now a hotel, in the middle. Several street-names round about incorporate the word Kincora, Brian Boru's half-mythical palace by the shores of Lough Derg. Clontarf was Brian's last victory, in which he – with help from some of Dublin's settled Danes – beat the invading Danes who had some assistance from quisling Irish. It began the end of Danish ambitions of outright conquest, but Brian's death finished the national rule of his own family. Probably the main battle took place nearer city than suburb, but the final chase went out to Howth; and Conquer Hill, a turning off the coast road just beyond Clontarf's Yacht Club, is supposed to have seen the issue decided.

East of Clontarf, the **North Bull Wall** protrudes one and three quarter miles into the bay. It was made in 1819, a hundred years after the building of the harbour which revolutionised Irish trade, to save it from silting. Since that year the North Bull itself – a long sandbank that used to trap countless ships driven off course by prevailing winds, and a boon to local peasants who picked the spoils – has grown to three miles and now holds two golf courses, the Royal Dublin and St Anne's, an important bird sanctuary, and splendid beaches. It also has an exceptional variety of wild plants, as well as its own sub-species of house-mouse, *Mus musculus jamesoni*, which has developed a pale coat to blend with the sand. In winter the island is an important sanctuary for something approaching 50,000 birds, breeders in more northerly latitudes.

The coast road continues without excitement past Sutton to **Howth** (pronounced to rhyme with both), a swollen round peninsula with a small harbour and village on the north side and fine views from the encircling road, below and above which seabirds nest with cool contempt for gravity. Guarding the eastern entrance to Ireland, Howth is a symbol of home for the Irish on their travels – 'Delightful to be on the hill of Howth' St Columba sighed in the sixth century, exiled and bidden to convert the Picts of Ireland's eastern colony, Argyll:

> *'Grievous is my errand over the main,*
> *travelling to Alba of the beetling brows.'*

The Dublin road leads straight to village and harbour, passing the demesne of **Howth Castle** on the right. The beautiful gardens, bare rock 150 years ago, are open in spring and summer and are famous for rhododendrons, azaleas, and half a mile of thirty-foot high beech hedges dating from 1710. Two thousand species thrive on this peaty frost-free site, whose original soil was carried up in baskets. The castle is closed to visitors, a break with a tradition that began when the 'pirate' queen, Grace O'Malley, returning to Mayo from a visit to Queen Elizabeth in 1575, was refused admission; she carried off and kept the heir until the owners promised to keep the doors permanently open to needy callers. The resident family is descended in the female line from Sir Almeric Tristram, who in 1177 was granted the property by Henry II. Sir Almeric adopted the name St Lawrence after the saint, in answer to his promise to do so, turned a battle in his favour. The direct male succession was broken in 1909 – and the earldom and barony (Ireland's oldest) of Howth died out then; but the owners are still Gaisford-St Lawrences. The keep of the castle, built in 1564, is incorporated in the present castle, a jumble of styles from different times that includes work by Francis Bindon, the Morrisons, and Lutyens, whose 1910 restoration made it look, according to H.G. Wells, 'as it ought to have looked and never had looked in the past'.

Wells also, in *Joan and Peter*, speaks of the view from the hill – 'one of the most beautiful in the world', with the bay to the south, the lush midlands to the west, and the Mourne mountains sixty miles north; below them, only a mile away, is **Ireland's Eye**, a little island-hump of quartzite, popular with puffins and possessing a restored seventh-century chapel. Immediately below Howth Hill on the north side is the village, and beside that the harbour. The Abbey Tavern is famous for ballad-singing. The ruined abbey church of St Mary looks over the harbour from steep banks, parts of it supposedly dating from 1042, but most from the fourteenth to sixteenth centuries. There is an interesting fifteenth-century St Lawrence tomb in the south-east chantry. The harbour itself was built, like Dun Laoghaire, to receive packet-boats from England in the early nineteenth century, and George IV landed here in 1821 (though a great boon to him, the death of his wife was the official reason for his cancelling his scheduled country tour, so disappointing more than one family that had run up a castle, or at least a ballroom, to receive him). The harbour soon silted up, and has been used since only for fishing and sailing-boats, with one famous exception – the Howth gun-running of 26 July 1914, when Erskine Childers ran in nine hundred rifles from Germany on his yacht *Asgard*, in answer to an open arming of Ulster Protestants by Carson and others. A few months later he had joined British Naval Intelligence, but sided with the Republicans during the Civil War and was finally shot by the Free State government after a court-martial. In due course his son, Protestant like his father, nevertheless became president of the Republic.

Returning to the mainland we turn right to follow the coast north-wards. There is little dramatic in this flank of county Dublin's shoreline. The Irish have built mostly south of the bay and the money and care spent in that direction have prettified it beyond comparison with the north. What we see now is a general flatness, with some patches of development which a dull day makes bleak. But there are good beaches and dunes and after a little way we are passing the long broad peninsula that carries Portmarnock's championship golf-course, and the two-mile Velvet Strand. The next left turn, and a left and right to follow, bring us to **St Doulough's Church**, remarkable for its preservation and one of the oldest still in use – its steep stone roof was built around 1200, though the tower with its stepped battle-ments was added in the fifteenth century. The site was probably that of a seventh-century hermit's hut, and the inclusion of an anchorite's cell and living quarters suggest it housed a community. Various walls and other remains lie about. Opposite is St Doulough's Lodge, where Nathaniel Hone (1831–1917), the greatest Irish landscape painter of his time, lived. He had studied in Paris and spent twenty years at Barbizon, but much of his best work was done on the land and by the sea between here and Malahide.

Malahide is reached by the main road north from St Doulough's, passing on the left the Hill of Feltrim, once seat of the Fagans and dubiously claimed as site of the killing of Ireland's last wolf. Several other places claim the same distinction. **Malahide Castle**, now owned by the Dublin County Council, stands before the village on the right. This was till 1975 the home of the late Baron Talbot de Malahide, by grace of King Edward IV Hereditary Lord Admiral of Malahide and adjacent seas, and a distinguished ex-diplomat in his own right. The family had lived here more than 800 years, with a break in Cromwellian times when a carving of the Virgin Mary took miraculous flight and returned only with the restoration of the king to his palace and the Talbots to their castle. Richard Talbot, Earl of Tyrconnell, lived here, and as James II's Catholic Lord-deputy tried to turn the Protestant tide, until after the Battle of the Boyne he fled, to die in France. The family later won a posthumous link with James Boswell when a Talbot married a descendant of his, and it was here, in the 1930s and 1940s, that caches of his papers were found (later bought and published by Yale) showing that that spunky, tireless, amoral, shrewd biographer richly deserved a biography of his own. The castle has traces of the original moat but little else from before the eighteenth century, the drum tower to the south-east being late nineteenth century. The fifteenth-century church of St Sylvester in the grounds – known as the abbey – was the family vault till 1873. It has a good altar-tomb of Maud Plunket – 'maid, wife and widow in one day' since her first husband fell in battle immediately after their wedding. On the morning of the battle, fourteen Talbots are said to have taken what turned out to be their last breakfast here. In the grounds are the fine and famous Fry Model Railway, and in the well-maintained Botanic Garden an interesting collection includes thousands of plant species from the southern hemisphere.

Malahide is a small seaside resort, close to the Donabate golf-links, one of many on this coast rich in sandbanks. Three miles west is **Swords**, with some interesting antiquities but little hint of its former importance. St Columba founded a monastery here and left in charge St Finan the Leper, so called, the story goes, because he had deliberately contracted the disease from a child as a penance, and went on suffering from it for thirty years. The monastery rose in importance. Brian Boru's body lay here a night on the way to Armagh, and later one of the principal manors of Dublin's archbishop was built here. The five-sided ruin of the manorial castle, with towers at each angle, stands at the north end of the main street, but having been devastated by Edward Bruce in 1316 it has little but the gate-house and west tower of the chapel to show from before. The stepped battlements of the walls are characteristically fifteenth century. Down the road are the Round Tower and steeple of the old abbey church.

The main Swords road takes us directly back to Dublin, passing the airport and cutting through **Santry**, just outside the city boundaries but a suburb in essence. In 1840 Lady Domville built a model village here, a fashionable thing for tidy-minded landlords to do, but it has been swallowed up recently. There is a good church of 1709, containing the tomb of the Lord Santry who died in 1673. A mile and a half farther, in **Drumcondra**, we pass the broad park of **All Hallows College** on the left. The main part of the building was the work of the Neo-Gothicist follower of Pugin, J.J. McCarthy, but **Drumcondra House**, built around 1727 by Sir Edward Lovett Pearce, still stands on the south side. It belonged then to Marmaduke Coghill, one of the trustees of Steevens' Hospital. Later that century it passed to the Earl of Charleville, whose widow remarried, after his death, in the Italianate temple built by Alessandro Galilei (architect of Castletown) and still standing in the park. Coghill, having died, according to the inscription, of 'gout in the stomach', was buried in the church of St John the Baptist nearby; his sumptuous monument, by Scheemakers, shows him haughty in the garb of Chancellor of the Irish Exchequer. The most memorable grave is in the churchyard: to James Gandon, who died in 1824 and to whom Dublin owes the design of her greatest buildings. He was interred in the grave of Francis Grose, his close friend and a pioneering antiquarian. Under Grose's epitaph – he died 'whilst in cheerful conversation with his friends' – is Gandon's: 'Also his Friend James Gandon, Architect, Born in 1742 – Died 1824'. That is all; the rest is said by his surviving buildings.

The main road crosses the River Tolka, and straight away we can turn right along Botanic Avenue to the **National Botanic Gardens** in Glasnevin. This was once an area of high fashion. Steele lived nearby; Addison – who was twice chief secretary in Ireland – has left his name in the riverside elm-walk; and Swift came frequently to visit his friends, Dr and Mrs Delany, resenting the cost of the coach. Their home, Delville, has left no trace; since 1948 the Bon Secours Hospital, on the right and over the river, has smothered the site of the house, the parterre with its orange trees, bowling-green, grotto, temples, rustic bridges, and paddocks of deer and cattle – the model *ferme ornée*, with a shell-house made by Mrs Delany herself, accomplished creator of scores of charming flower pictures using collage of assorted coloured papers, and throughout twenty-five years of happy marriage one of the most delightful and informative diarists of her century.

The Botanic Gardens – forty-seven acres of them – were, to start with, the work of that progressive body, the Dublin Society, which, founded in 1731, combined science and philanthropy in its work for farms, farm-workers, and knowledge in general. The gardens were opened in 1794, shortly before a chair in botany was endowed by the society at Trinity. The director's house, a Lebanon cedar and the ancient yew-avenue commemorating Addison are all that survive from that time. In the nineteenth century the gardens were greatly expanded and most of the present buildings, including the fine early cast-iron conservatories, were put up, the 65-foot high Palm House dating from 1884. The government took direct control in 1877. The gardens can teach and delight. There are beds in which plants are arranged by their scientific families, bringing together unlikely cousins like buttercup, anemone and peony. There are tropical hot-houses with rare ferns, cactuses, lilies, including the seven-foot diameter *Victoria amazonica*, a rich collection of orchids and other exotic plants; pretty herbaceous borders, covered walks and arboreta – containing rich collections of oaks, maples, birches, dwarf conifers – in one of which it is quaint to meet a chubby, affable, marble Socrates on a granite plinth. A small Mexican oak, *Quercus rapanda*, is thought to be the only specimen in these islands. Altogether the gardens, perhaps more compact and digestible than Kew, are one of Dublin's finest offerings.

Having seen them, we can go to Glasnevin, strictly Prospect Cemetery, by turning right at the main gate and right again. The cemetery has its permanent niche in literature as Paddy Dignam's last resting-place in *Ulysses*, but the list of people buried here makes a roll-call of Ireland's great – Curran, O'Connell, O'Donovan Rossa, Parnell, Casement, Arthur Griffith, Collins, Maud Gonne, Constance Markiewicz, Gerard Manley Hopkins (in the Jesuit plot), de Valera, Brendan Behan. O'Donovan Rossa died in New York in 1915, but his body was returned here and buried, Patrick Pearse declaiming an emotive funeral oration that helped rally opinion for the rising the following year. Casement's remains were transferred here from London's Pentonville prison, fifty years after his execution for treason. A state funeral was accorded the remains, which prattle hinted might be blended – owing to the nature of quicklime burials in prisons – with those of Crippen. The Round Tower commemorates O'Connell, through whose efforts this burial place for Catholics was established. His own body was brought back from Genoa, where he died in 1847.

In 1959 the first Irish record of an expansive sub-species of the pigeon family, the collared dove, was made in the cemetery. It had appeared in Britain four years earlier, having swiftly colonised the Continent from Asia before that. It is now resident all over these islands, a success comparable to that of the grey squirrel.

South-east Dublin to Bray

The wealth and prestige of the south-east of inner Dublin – postal district two, with Leinster House at its centre – spreads out in a south-easterly direction. From the city to Dun Laoghaire lies a line of elegant suburbs close to or beside the sea. Ballsbridge, with Sandymount as its shore flank, is the first, and from a Dubliner's point of view the most desirable, with roomy Victorian houses, a leavening of open spaces, broad streets and, for us, some points of great interest. In Pembroke Road, the main through-road, we pass smart hotels, including the Intercontinental, on the site of Trinity College's botanic gardens, and shortly afterwards the rotund American Embassy on the right. Crossing the Dodder (easier than it once was: in 1628 Sir Thomas Molyneux, Chancellor of the Irish Exchequer, lost his son-in-law attempting to ford the river here) we enter Merrion Road. On the right is the arena round which all Dublin seems to revolve in August, the **showground of the Royal Dublin Society** and site of the Annual Dublin Horse Show.

Showing off hunters' paces is the least important (except money-wise) of the society's functions. It is a peculiarly polymorphic body, whose range of activities evolved in pure descent from eighteenth-century beginnings. Progressive landlords and professionals founded it in 1731 'for the improvement of Husbandry, Manufactures and other useful Arts'. They offered prizes for schemes and inventions, circulated books on farming, commerce and industries to those who could benefit, and gave special encouragement to linen, which was of mounting importance since the protective English had banned imports of wool. The king took note and helped the society, and soon the Irish Parliament gave large regular grants. At the turn of the century they had created in embryo the National Library, the National History Museum, the National College of Art, the Glasnevin Botanical Gardens, and endowed lectures and professorships. In 1815, having run through a number of headquarters, they bought Leinster House, whose complex of buildings still houses several of their collections. But the Dail, or Irish Parliament, newly-formed and house-hunting in 1922, evicted them, and they have been based here ever since. They keep up scientific work, mainly agricultural but including cancer research, and publish their proceedings. We can see over the buildings, and the hall where they hold winter concerts; and, if it is May, see their agricultural Spring Show; if August, the Horse Show, one of the world's great equestrian displays.

The road touches the coast at Merrion, and goes on to **Blackrock**. Blackrock College, on the right, is a famous Catholic boys' school founded in 1860, where de Valera was both pupil and master. What is now part of an unbroken line of suburbs was a popular coast and country resort in the eighteenth century, a favourite spot for the new and adventurous sport of bathing. John Scott, Earl of Clonmell and a debauched and venal Lord Chief Justice ('resolve seriously to set about learning my profession' he wrote in his revealing diary, six years after his appointment) had a house here, called Neptune, but an enemy bought land nearby, invited the mob of Dublin to chase and catch well-greased pigs in a Grand Olympic Hunt, and thereby succeeded in destroying Neptune's gardens. The villa still stands. Opposite the far end of Blackrock Park is a remnant of the Villa Frascati. Almost the whole of this eighteenth-century estate is built over. It (along with Carton and Leinster House) belonged to the Duke of Leinster whose wife Emily entrusted the education of the younger of her nineteen children here at Frascati to a tutor, Mr Ogilvie, whom she proceeded to marry on her husband's death and by whom she had four more children. One of the earlier ones was Lord Edward FitzGerald, the aristocratic revolutionary who lived here with his French wife Pamela in the years before the 1798 Rising and his death from wounds received at his arrest. The next right turn but one is Carysfort Avenue, in No. 23 of which Joyce lived for a spell in the 1890s with his parents. Settings of the *Portrait* and *Ulysses* are numerous along this coast, and probably in all his years of exile no area was ever more familiar to him.

A mile or so farther on we reach **Dun Laoghaire**, pronounced and sometimes written Dunleary, but known as Kingstown for a century after 1821, when George IV took unsteady leave of this part of his kingdom from the new harbour. A stone crown on a ball-based obelisk commemorates the event which fifty thousand turned out to see, though they were disappointed by the King's aborting of various prepared speeches, including O'Connell's, by making some hasty promises to his well-beloved people and hurrying for the boat. The harbour was built to the plans of John Rennie, designer of the London Bridge that was removed to America in 1970, and of old Waterloo

Bridge. It has from its inception served the Irish Mail ferries from and to England. Around it are headquarters of seven yacht clubs, including the Royal Irish and the Royal St George.

Rounding Scotsman's Bay, east of Dun Laoghaire, we come to **Sandycove Point**, with its prominent Martello Tower looking over Dublin Bay to the swollen bastion of Howth. That too was Joyce's view. He stayed a short while in 1904 with his elegant medical-student friend, Oliver St John Gogarty, who rented the tower – squat granite relic of British fears of Napoleon – from the War Office for £8 a year. The episode gave Joyce the opening scene of *Ulysses*, in which Gogarty became 'stately plump Buck Mulligan' and Stephen D. felt left out of things. Joyce's final departure was by night, prompted by Gogarty's firing a pistol at a metal pan to wake a third occupant from a noisy dream. In 1962 Sylvia Beech, who first published *Ulysses*, opened the tower as a museum, which it remains, with a few notes, photographs and trinkets that try to evoke the giant. Close by is the Forty Foot, a bathing place formerly for men, and before 8 a.m. for naked men, but allowing admission to both sexes now. 'Forty Foot Gentlemen Only' used to read the sign at the entrance.

Dun Laoghaire leads without break into **Dalkey**, passing on the right modernised, medieval **Bullock Castle**, one of many which guarded the Dublin approaches, and containing a small museum. Bernard Shaw lived in Torca Cottage, on Dalkey Hill, for several years as a boy, and sometimes returned to the place to stay and write. A pretty, palmy, hilly resort, it provides splendid views of the coastline and mountains behind, and of Dalkey Island, with its Martello tower and the ruined church that dates from Danish times. Dublin at last is falling away and the spirit of the resort is taking over. It continues at **Killiney**, with its excellent strand and pleasant Victoria Park, and tall Killiney Hill from which granite used to be quarried, and houses which nowadays change hands – the hands often belong to pop stars or Hollywood actors – for millions of pounds each. From now on the built-up concentration is dissipated, and a few miles on is Bray, one of the strategic gateways to the Wicklow Mountains.

2

Boyne Valley and Meath

T HE DIRECT ROAD from Dublin to Drogheda is the N1, with
some motorway stretches, but we shall keep mostly to the coast.
Beyond Swords, whose suburban sprawl surrounds a fragmentary
five-sided castle of 1200, and – beside the Church of Ireland church –
a restored eleventh-century Round Tower, and the bridge over Broad
Meadow Water, we pass a right turn for Donabate, known for its golf
links, and the little seaside resort of Portraine, whose manor house,
near a modern mental hospital, was for a while home of Swift's
Stella. Returning to the main road (still the N1) we come to
Newbridge House on the left, a handsome, two-storey building of
1737, designed by Richard Castle for Charles Cobbe, later archbishop
of Dublin. For over two centuries it stayed in the same family, several
of whose eldest sons showed talent in securing rich wives, and consequently the means to embellish and extend. There is a rich red
drawing-room with plasterwork possibly by Richard West, an elegant
and airy dining-room, and a fascinating collection of curiosities
assembled by the family since about 1790 from their world-wide
travels as soldiers, sailors, tourists and imperial functionaries. House,
almost all its contents and grounds were bought from the family in
1985 by the county council, and this treasury is open daily.

The next right turn off the N1 brings us to **Lusk**, site of a monastery
founded in the fifth century, in the first wave of evangelism after St
Patrick's mission. The 95-foot Round Tower dates from the last phase
of the monastery, which after several Viking assaults was dissolved in
the tenth century, though a nunnery of Augustinians continued till the
end of the twelfth. The square tower of which the Round Tower seems
a part is a belfry of about 1500, built on to an earlier church replaced in
1847. There are some good tombs and effigies displayed in the tower
(some from other churches in the county), particularly the florid memorial to the Barnewall family, whose Norman ancestor, Sir Michael de
Barneval, landed in Cork in 1172, before Strongbow in Wexford.

Two miles east, outside Rush, is Rogerstown quay from which boats will sail to **Lambay Island**, three miles over the water. (Permission to land must be obtained in advance from the owner, Lord Revelstoke.) The volcanic island, its high cliffs rich in breeding seabirds, has been made a bird sanctuary. There has been a castle here since the fifteenth century, and there was a monastery close on a millennium before that, founded by St Columba. In the aftermath of King William's ousting of James II, some prisoners taken by William's General Ginkel were sent here and died of starvation. Lord Revelstoke's house incorporates the old castle and was designed by Lutyens; it is one of his most subtle works. As elsewhere, Lutyens collaborated with the garden-designer Gertrude Jekyll, founder, with the Irishman William Robinson, of the Surrey School, which shied away from Victorian formalism. Lambay and Howth, a few miles south, are Lutyens's main works in Ireland. The island is valued by naturalists. When Cecil Baring, ancestor of the present owner, bought it in 1902 to celebrate his marriage to an American heiress, his interest in wildlife led him to consult the great botanist Robert Lloyd Praeger who discovered here seventeen species new to British Isles records, and five new to science.

The coast road goes on through Rush, and passes **Kenure**, traditional home of the Palmer family, on the left. George Papworth refaced the eighteenth-century house and added the giant Corinthian portico in 1842, and there was fine plasterwork by Robert West inside, but the house, empty for years, has been allowed to decay. Four miles on, Skerries has a golf-course and holiday camp. Half a mile beyond the town on the left, Cromwell is said to have camped during the Drogheda massacre, at a place still called the Camps. Balbriggan, the next town along the way, was known for the making of stockings for two hundred years; Americans sometimes call them balbriggans to this day. The scant Elizabethan ruins north of the town are of a Barnewall castle. Inland from here, around Naul, the hills and their pretty, cave-rich valleys have yielded several finds of objects from the extensive prehistoric Boyne Valley culture. Keeping to the coast, uniformly sandy from here to the Boyne's mouth, we come to **Gormanston**, home of the Prestons, Viscounts Gormanston, from 1363 to 1947 when the castle was taken over by Franciscans for a college. The only gaps in the Preston ownership – in Cromwellian times and for over a century after William's accession – were caused by their tenacious loyalty to Catholicism. Catholic or no, they did the things Protestant landlords did, hunting included. When the fifteenth

Lord Gormanston died in 1925, it was said spectral foxes entered the family vault as his body lay prepared for burial the next day, and processed round it. This vault is under the roofless sixteenth-century chantry chapel, an extension of the now ruined medieval church. From here on the road leads in from the coast, though Bettystown's horse-races, which take place in high summer on the flat hard sands south of the Boyne's mouth, are worth the detour if you can be there at the right time. This is not so easy. It may be in June, July or August – whenever in fact the tide is out long enough to leave the beach free for a sufficient period.

In eight miles the road reaches the river Boyne, county Louth, and the principal town this side of Ulster. **Drogheda** is three miles from the sea. Rising steeply either side of the river, it has a good harbour, well placed for trade with Liverpool, numerous light industries, among them the making of linen and cotton, breweries and iron foundries, and a violent history that helped shape its present robust character. A ford across the river made it important enough for the Danes, under their pugnacious king Turgesius, to fortify around AD 911, but its foundation was essentially the work of Anglo-Normans. By the end of the eleventh century they had built a 'bridge over the ford' (the Irish for which gave the town its name), and brought it within two centuries to rank among Ireland's four senior towns, with the right – never exploited – to build a university along the lines of Oxford. In the days of the Pale it was a frontier town, facing the rebellious tribes of Ulster; parliaments were often held here as a flourish of authority. The hated Poynings Law, making all Irish laws subject to the English king's approval, was passed here in 1495.

Much went awry in the seventeenth century. In the confused warring that went on after the general rebellion of 1641, one attitude was consistent: that of the Parliamentary English, who saw Catholic Ireland as perverse and hostile. Drogheda, held at first for the Parliamentarians, fell later to the Royalists, and it was Cromwell's first target on his arrival at Dublin in 1649. He came with three convictions – that the 1641 Rising had been the most barbarous massacre the world had seen, that independent Ireland would be a perpetual threat to England, and that God was fully behind him. Taking the town on a third assault he ordered the death of every armed defender. Almost three thousand were massacred – 'a righteous judgment of God upon those barbarous wretches', Cromwell wrote. A hundred who fled to St Peter's steeple for sanctuary were burned inside it, and the few who came off with their lives were transported to Barbados. In 1690

Drogheda again opted for the losing side, sheltering James II before the Battle of the Boyne, but it surrendered to William on the day after the battle and was spared.

Drogheda shared in the eighteenth-century rise and nineteenth-century fall of Irish prosperity. A hundred and more years ago Thackeray, who devoted forty-five minutes to the place, found it 'smoky, dirty, and lively', with many ruined, shuttered houses pointing up the decay. O'Connell spoke there often, lionised by discontented masses. It has remained a moral stronghold of nationalist feeling.

On approach, the town seems like a phalanx of pointed steeples and towers. Within, streets are narrow and houses jostle each other closely. On the south side of the river, off Barrack Street, which leads up from the bridge, is **Millmount**. This is thought to have been a prehistoric burial mound, perhaps on the scale of Newgrange and Knowth up-river. In the twelfth century a motte was built on it, whose adjoining bailey is now partly covered by a museum, formerly army barracks. Views of the country around are dramatic. The cross on top was erected during the holy year of 1950 and, lit up at night, is visible ten miles out to sea.

Crossing central St Mary's river bridge, the harbour, bounded by the nineteenth-century Boyne Viaduct, can be seen over to the right. Drogheda's surviving town-gate, **St Laurence's**, honours Bishop Laurence O'Toole, who after Strongbow's invasion devoted his life to salvaging native Irish rights. The barbican gate is the best of its kind in Ireland, with two tall drum-towers and a curtain wall intact. There are many handsome eighteenth-century houses nearby, some worryingly neglected, as if brash replacements were plotted. Two hundred yards west along St Laurence Street is the pretty eighteenth-century **Tholsel**, or market building, now occupied and well preserved, like hundreds of Ireland's best town houses, by a bank. One of Ireland's greatest native architects, Francis Johnston, best known for his work in Armagh under Archbishop Robinson, designed the tower and spire of St Peter's church, reached through Peter Street to the north. It has interesting monuments and some fine rococo plasterwork inside, and a ghoulish cadaver-tombstone on the Golding grave outside. On the opposite side of West Street is **St Peter's Catholic church**, the memorial church to Saint Oliver Plunkett, seventeenth-century Archbishop of Armagh who was canonised in 1975. Charles II's lenient policy towards Catholics from time to time met violent reactions, in one of which, in 1681, this gentle primate was hauled to Westminster, and tried and hanged on an invented charge. His unlovely head, embalmed, is encased in glass in full public view in the north chapel, far from his body which is decently buried at Downside abbey in England. The head was not always so hygienically preserved. A booklet detailing past damage done by mites, and other depredations, makes gruesome reading.

A short walk along West Street, and a right turn back towards St Mary's bridge, leads to the ruined tower and other slight remains of St Mary d'Urso's Augustinian friary. More graceful is the fifteenth-century tower of St Mary Magdalene's Dominican friary, near Dominic's Bridge to the west.

We shall come shortly to the rich remains and historic and prehistoric events and practices which make Drogheda's river, the Boyne, almost a cross-section of Ireland's past. From the R166 leading northeast from Drogheda direct to Termonfeckin, four miles away, a lane turns right to a private demesne, **Beaulieu**. Its lovely brick-dressed mansion was for long supposed to have been built by Wren, but it was probably the work of a Dutchman, working between 1660 and 1666, and is a uniquely complete survival from that time. The broad eaves show its Dutch inspiration. Behind its rare redbrick demesne wall, this was till 1649 Plunkett property, a family – Lord Dunsany the author was one – who have innumerable associations in the area. **Termonfeckin** is a quiet village, containing till 1613 the summer residence of the archbishops of Armagh, of which nothing remains. A good High Cross is in the graveyard, and nearby is a fifteenth-century tower with stepped battlements, only survivor of the medieval home of the Dowdalls. Three miles up the coast, which is mainly flat and dull (but with the odd resort) as far as Dundalk, Clogher Head makes a relieving promontory with good views of the Mourne Mountains. The road turns inland to Dunleer, where a right turn on to the main road leads after seven miles to **Castlebellingham**, once famous for its ale. Thomas Bellingham, the owner, descendant of a sixteenth-century lord deputy of Ireland, was aide-de-camp to King William at the time of the battle of the Boyne. The original castle was consequently burned down by Jacobites in 1690. Another house rose soon after, at first similar to Beaulieu, later enlarged, and in the early nineteenth century gothicised to its present appearance. At the end of Victoria's reign it was known for extravagance and luxury. A man was employed for no other purpose than to rake gravel in the grounds the moment anybody's footstep disturbed it. The Calvary in the village centre, erected in 1904 by Sir Henry Bellingham in memory of his wife, was the first to be put up in Ireland.

Buried in the churchyard is Dr Thomas Guither, a seventeenth-century physician and Fellow of Trinity, Dublin, to whom has been attributed the introduction of frogs into Ireland. It is an issue over which controversy has flared from time to time. Around 6000 BC, a few thousand years after the ice age ended, the sea severed Ireland from Britain, and rather later Britain from the Continent. The frog, nowadays common in Ireland, may have been ahead of the sea in crossing over to Irish land, and there are remains of it in caves in Sligo, side by side with definitely prehistoric bones, that argue it did. It is also possible, however, that frogs of a later age could have slipped through cracks in the rock, and so become mixed up with earlier remains. Some say frogs came with the Normans. Giraldus Cambrensis, who came with them, denied their presence here before the Normans' arrival. Frogs, he wrote, appeared around Waterford after the Norman landings. His belief tallied with the legend that St Patrick had expelled all noxious creatures, including frogs, toads and snakes, in the fifth century. Expert opinion seems to favour Giraldus on essentials. Dr Guither, who undoubtedly brought spawn from England and let it develop in a Trinity pond, seems unlikely to have been the first introducer.

This central part of county Louth has little to pick out except occasional clusters of antiquities and some pleasing private houses. General views inland and over Dundalk Bay lack height or drama. **Dromiskin**, a couple of miles north of Castlebellingham, breaks the monotony with its stunted Round Tower (much shortened, recapped, and now used as the parish church's belfry), a worn and broken High Cross, and a striking Catholic church. A backwater now, Dromiskin can anyway boast that Patrick founded and Vikings occupied it, and it once contained the relics of St Ronan, whose feats included restoring to life a mother, stoned to death, and the child she had allowed to choke with bread. He also cursed mad king Sweeney (or Suibhne) for entering his church naked and throwing a prayer-book into the lake. The curse condemned the king to lifelong naked wanderings and finally death by spear. Seamus Heaney translated an old version of the story in his *Sweeney Astray*.

A mile away to the west is **Milltown Castle**, a fortified house from Stuart days, private but visible from the road. This westerly road goes through to **Louth**, another centre that history abandoned in the sixteenth century, leaving a few houses and some impressive ruins. St Patrick founded the first church here, entrusting it to St Mochta. The church gave place to an abbey which, being accessible to the coast, was plundered by Norsemen in the ninth century. The abbey was rebuilt at Knock, a mile or so south-west, in 1148 and its name spread so far that the abbot was granted a mitre, usually reserved for bishops. Louth became a county town, but went downhill after the dissolution. There are remains of a Dominican friary of around 1500, and St Mochta's church, stone-roofed, well preserved and neatly enclosed by a wall, of about 1100. Some accounts say the church rose spontaneously and suddenly one night to shelter the saint. Ardpatrick House, a mile east, was once the home of St Oliver Plunkett; and Louth Hall, a colossal pile of nine bays' width attached to a medieval keep, a few miles south, still belongs to his family, the Barons of Louth.

Louth is on the edge of Cuchulain (pronounced Coohullen) country and the hero's admirers can drive a couple of miles north-east to see what is supposed to be the stone, in a field on the right, to which he had himself tied in his last fight in the long wars between Connacht and Ulster. The scene, though its site is little known, has become a symbol of Ireland's struggle to be free, and is depicted in bronze in Dublin's General Post Office, itself a symbol of resistance.

Cuchulain's greatest exploit took place at **Ardee**, a long, large village of over 3,000 inhabitants on a broad main street six miles due south of Louth. Here it was, according to legend, that Connacht's Queen Maeve, jealous of her husband Ailill's magic white-horned bull, arrived with her army to capture the animal's only equal, the brown bull of Cooley. Cooley is now the Carlingford Peninsula and all the men of Ulster would have turned out to resist had they not been laid low by a temporary sickness. Only Cuchulain was fit, a lad of seventeen, who had to smear his chin with blackberry juice to persuade enemies he was of fighting age. The Dee River, wider in the story than it is now (though it is still an excellent salmon river, the fishing free in parts), blocked most of the Connacht men while Cuchulain, a bit like Horatio on his bridge, took them on one at a time, at the ford of Ardee, three hundred yards west of the present bridge. The Cattle Raid of Cooley, or *Táin Bó Cuailgne*, tells how, in the intervals of duelling, Cuchulain kills a hundred men a day with his sling, fells a sewing maid incautiously wearing Maeve's headdress, and destroys an eel, a heifer and a wolf sent against him by the queen of the gods, who thereafter befriends him. He was so agile he could turn round in his skin, putting feet and hands behind and buttocks and calves before him. Maeve, much vexed, and failing to seduce this hero, finally orders Ferdia, a childhood friend of Cuchulain's, to fight. A sad duel of three days begins, and at the end of each

day both friends embrace and tend the other's wounds, till the proph-
esied end arrives. Ferdia is killed, and Cuchulain carries him over the
river he could not cross alive. A large mound now marks his burial
place. At last the Ulster men recover from their epidemic and arrive
to take over from Cuchulain, on whose body there is no spot, not even
'the size of a needle-point' without a wound. He lives to fight again.
But the brown bull has been rustled and carried off to Connacht,
where it kills the white-horned bull, escapes, returns to Cooley, goes
mad, kills all who confront it and finally 'bursts its heart with
bellowing and falls dead'.

Ardee keeps an air of the importance it had after the Anglo-
Norman invasion, when it was for long periods a crucial outpost of
the Pale, though often in Gaelic Irish hands. The larger of the two
castles was built by Roger Pipard, who held the barony of Ardee in
the thirteenth century. Much restored after its violent history, but
giving a good idea of a square keep with projecting towers, it now
houses the courthouse and gaol. Hatch's Castle, a fortified house of
the same period just off the main street, could be mistaken for a
showy terrace-house. The Hatch family, settled in it by Cromwell,
stayed till 1940. Both the Catholic and the pleasing Church of Ireland
churches are thought to be on the sites of religious foundations of
Roger Pipard.

Off a lane a couple of miles south-east of the town, beside a pretty
graveyard with yew and holly trees, is the ruin of an oddly athletic
building, the 'jumping' fourteenth-century church of **Kildemock**.
Little but the wall that jumped still stands, which is strange enough. It
stands moreover at a queer angle that baffles most attempts to trace its
movement. The picturesque story is that the wall sprang of its own
accord to exclude from the church an excommunicated heretic who
had been buried inside. Other verdicts blame a fierce and famous
storm of 1716, but it is hard to see how anything short of an earthquake could have caused such a displacement.

The N2 goes south from Ardee to Collon, passing on the right the
demesne of **Oriel Temple**, a house built by John Foster, speaker of
the Irish parliament in the late eighteenth century, and now the Cistercian Abbey of New Mellifont. Foster, in 1784, during the prosperous
days of Grattan's parliament, introduced a Corn Law which, by
protecting Irish grain against cheaper imports, and subsidising
exports, made Irish tillage for the first time important. This changed
the face of the country, giving to many a means of earning a living
and causing (till the famine of the 1840s broke the system) the

building of corn mills whose hollow shells still dot the countryside. Foster gave the house to his sister and her husband, Lord Massereene, in whose family it stayed till the 1930s. Oriel itself was the name of an ancient Irish kingdom. Nowadays adapted for community needs, the house bears little resemblance to the original, and is rather ugly. Foster's main house, Collon House, still stands in the village, where there is also a good Church of Ireland church of 1813.

Two remarkable monastic sites remain to be seen, before we return to the Boyne. **Monasterboice**, three miles east of Collon, is said to have been founded by St Buithe, a disciple of St Patrick, around AD 500. Like most important early Christian sites its history goes back obscurely into pagan times, as digs have shown. St Buithe gave his name to the Boyne (by a complicated conversion from Irish to English). Nothing is known of him, but legend tells that when in old age he wanted to die, angels sent a ladder for him to climb to his quietus. Being near the coast, the abbey suffered from Danish marauders, and in 968 three hundred of them occupied the place, but were overcome and massacred by the Irish High King's army. A century later the library and Round Tower were burned, but most of the latter still stands, fitted inside with modern staircases leading to a very good all-round view.

In the mid-nineteenth century many scholars came to think that Round Towers, along with anything remotely related in shape, like maypoles, standing stones, and even the Christian cross, were direct descendants of phallic symbols used in an ancient world-wide fertility cult. Dark Ages monks, harried by Vikings, had other things to think of. Their Round Towers were a breakthrough in the art of defence. Entered up a ladder by a door several feet above ground, solidly built and of a shape that deflected missiles, the tower protected its occupants against everything but protracted siege. Which is probably why so many remain. Some deny all this, claiming that a fire started at the bottom would have swept, and on occasion did sweep, up the building as through a chimney. Round Towers, they say, were simply bell-towers. The one in question, topless for a thousand years, is otherwise sound, and its lean from the perpendicular is almost imperceptible.

Monasterboice contains also two church ruins, one thirteenth-century; an earlier sundial eight feet high; and – its proudest feature – three High Crosses, two of which are the best of their kind in Ireland. These richly sculptured pillars are as much Irish landmarks as the Round Towers. The deep relief scenes fitted into panels all over them are thought to have been used for teaching the scriptures to peasants, but at first their purpose was monumental. The circular stays of the typical Celtic cross suggest that the earliest crosses, made of wood, were carried in procession and needed extra support at the joint. These early crosses had at most some abstract or animal carving at the base, but gradually their use changed, and they became visual aids for open-air sermons. Nowadays they provide one of the best accounts of the development of Celtic art, and the Monasterboice crosses represent their peak. Of the two, Muiredach's cross is probably the earlier, dating from the early tenth century, but also the better preserved. One side carries scenes from the New Testament, with the crucifixion in the centre, the other Old Testament scenes and Christ in judgment. The summit is a model of a contemporary church – a gabled building with shingle roof. The west cross is one of the tallest in Ireland (over twenty-one feet high) and of rather later date, though in a worse condition. Only about a quarter of the fifty or so panels are intelligible, and they include scenes from the life of David, and episodes in the life, death and resurrection of Christ. It comes as a surprise that, like the grey interiors of our Gothic cathedrals, these panels were at first brightly painted, and that we see them with the polychrome dimension lost.

A rather complicated drive of three miles south-west leads to **Mellifont**, beside the narrow River Mattock, a monastery whose beautiful remains give no idea of its importance in early Irish church history. Giraldus Cambrensis, the bigoted observer who followed his king to Ireland at the Anglo-Norman conquest, found the Irish 'a filthy people, wallowing in vice'. Since its great expansive years of the sixth and seventh centuries the church had certainly declined, but a few years before Giraldus's visit, St Malachy, archbishop of Armagh and friend of St Bernard of Clairvaux, set in train an effective programme of reform. Using Cistercian monks trained at Clairvaux, and on land provided by the king of Oriel, he founded in 1142 the monastery of Mellifont. He swept away the corruption, immorality and nepotism that had become accepted, and Mellifont's success was closely followed by the founding of daughter establishments all over Ireland, nine of them within ten years. There would in time be twenty Irish Cistercian foundations. Other orders soon followed, but Mellifont marks the beginning of religious reform. Moreover, master-masons and workers sent to Mellifont by Bernard brought new architectural ideas to Ireland.

Among its early patrons was Dervorgilla, on whom blame for the English conquest has often been laid. She retired here incognito after the death of Dermot Macmurrough, her second husband. Muirchertach, High King of Ireland, presented 160 cows and sixty ounces of gold to the monastery, at the same time as he gave the glorious site of Cashel to the Munster church. After the dissolution, the place was made over to Edward Moore, ancestor of the Earls of Drogheda, and a fortified house built, but the bases of walls and columns of the original abbey survive. The tall gatehouse, the restored chapter house (wrongly called St Bernard's chapel) with its exquisitely groined roof and foliated capitals, and the octagonal lavabo of about 1200 still give a melancholy idea of former grandeur. This is one of the most moving sites of Leinster.

Hugh O'Neill submitted here to Mountjoy after the battle of Kinsale had dashed his and Spanish hopes of Irish independence. In the eighteenth century the house was bought by the Balfours of nearby Townley Hall, but they never lived in it. At the end of the nineteenth century it was used for keeping pigs. Residence today is limited to a youth hostel and a farmhouse. The Cistercians themselves occupy New Mellifont and leave the ruins to their memories.

The Balfour home, **Townley Hall**, just south of Mellifont, is generally held to be Francis Johnston's best house in the classical style, with a forbidding cut-stone exterior, and some magnificent features inside, including a cantilevered circular central staircase. Trinity College, Dublin, while owning it, altered it for the worse, sold off Chinese wallpapers and cut down trees. It is now back in private hands. Its demesne runs for a while beside the Boyne, and the road round its eastern end leads to all the sites connected with the river's most famous event, the battle of the Boyne, one of the main turning points in Irish history.

Irish Catholics, who before the Commonwealth owned about three fifths of Irish land, ended that phase with one fifth, 'for fighting', as Swift wrote, 'in defence of their king'. Some of it they got back at the Restoration, but Charles II's reign was a sequence of attempts to please everyone while satisfying few. James's accession in 1685 gave Catholics, still barred from government and administration, hopes of recognition and more of what they considered their own land. Some hopes were fulfilled – even the new viceroy Tyrconnell was a Catholic, and favourable land reform was on the way when the 'glorious revolution' of 1688 tipped James from his throne. Tyrconnell held out for him in Ireland, however, and James planned his come-back from France through Ireland. Early in 1689 he landed with French troops and funds at Kinsale and called a parliament at Dublin which passed various pro-Catholic acts. Protestant opposition massed mainly among the recent Ulster settlers. The English had to act, and what the Irish sometimes call 'the war of the two kings' began when William landed at Carrickfergus, joined his commander-in-chief Marshal Schomberg and marched south. Much hung in the balance, and not only for these islands.

The task of the Jacobites was to keep William away from the prize catch, Dublin. They garrisoned Drogheda and deployed an army of 25,000 men three miles upstream at Oldbridge, on the north face of the hill of Donore. Of James's 25,000 men, 7,000 were French, but the majority were ill-armed Irish irregulars. James himself was a bad general, 'whose weakness, imbecility and bigotry', Sir William Wilde wrote in his florid guide to the Boyne Valley, 'had already lost him a crown'. Wilde, however, and other historians judged James crudely. He was still no match for William who, passing through Ardee, arrived at the Boyne on the 30th of June. Taking the high ground that stretches a mile east from Tullyallen, he looked down on the nakedly exposed camp of the Irish, and began to bombard. In spite of a skin-wound received in a rash reconnoitre, he made plans that the short decisive engagement of the 1st of July fully justified. At dawn that day, he sent 10,000 men three miles west to Rosnaree, burial place of the great Cormac Mac Art, and to Slane, to cross the river and surprise the Jacobite left flank. This was done by 10.30a.m. when he and the remaining forces began crossing the river below Oldbridge. Only the stump of an obelisk, blown apart in the Troubles, marks the stretch. The river, still tidal at this point, was low, but the crossing was difficult and while William nearly lost his horse his general Schomberg, a veteran of the Thirty Years' War, was struck down and killed. There is a memorial to him by the gates of Oldbridge demesne. As soon as William's main army was across, James's centre and right wing broke. They fell back first on Donore, then joined up with the worsted left wing at Duleek, three miles south, where all but James spent the night. That flouted monarch fled to Dublin, then south to Waterford, where he made his escape to France and an old age in exile. His troops dispersed for the time being. It would be more than a year – and two more engagements, at Aughrim and Limerick – before the issue was finally decided, but the Boyne is the battle that caught the imagination; the only battle in which two kings were present until the one trounced the other. Celebrating the Boyne anniversary would in due course become the main date of the Orange Order's calendar. Almost, anyway. In 1752, eleven of the calendar's days were cut out to bring it in line with the Gregorian version. When the Orangemen came to accommodate this change they should have picked the 11th, but plumped, wrongly, for the 12th of July.

Ireland, always a bastion of Catholicism, has often been at odds with the pope. It was with a pope's blessing – Hadrian IV – that the Anglo-Normans occupied Dublin in 1172. After the Boyne battle, Pope Innocent XI had St Peter's illuminated and drank a toast to William, for the battle had indirectly secured Catholic solidarity on the Continent. Irish history is full of paradox. It could perhaps be argued that it was the English who were being exploited when a Scottish king fought a Dutch king on Irish soil for the dominion of England.

Duleek, where the Stuarts as good as quitted their throne, is where the course of the battle has left us. In early days it was the site of a bishopric founded by St Patrick. A later monastery was often pillaged by Norsemen and once by Anglo-Normans. After Clontarf, the body of Brian Boru lay here in state on its way to Armagh. Late in the twelfth century Hugh de Lacy built a manor and castle here and probably founded St Mary's Augustinian priory which prospered till the dissolution, when it was given to the Moores of Mellifont. A ruined keep survives. North-east of it, in the aisle of the church, there are good effigies and tombs, the best being a decorated fifteenth-century Bellew family memorial. There are also two worn High Crosses.

The remnant of a cross of different kind stands in the market place. It was erected by Dame Jennett Dowdall in 1601 in memory of herself and her husband William Bathe of Athcarne, a fortified Elizabethan house still standing three miles south-west of the village. There are several of these crosses in the district, the best of them the so-called white cross with various New Testament carvings, about half a mile north-west of Athcarne.

The Boyne is a running pageant of Irish history, in no chronological order. Upstream from Oldbridge, on both sides of the valley lie the wooded demesnes of Ireland's richest farming country and here, in a loop of the river, three massive prehistoric mounds, bare and fence-bound, preserve the memory of ancient power and wealth. The whole area is called the **Brugh na Bóinne**, or palace of the Boyne, a Stone Age cemetery over two miles in length. Its focal points now are the tumuli of Dowth, Newgrange and Knowth. Apart from these, which crown the ridge north of the river, there are dozens of mounds and tumps in the area. Most have been rifled at some stage, and few if any retain their original shape. Grass grows where stones gleamed white, and over the centuries generations of pasturing cows have flattened the contours.

The River Boyne was always sacred, named after Boann, lover for a day of the Dagda, chief of the ancient gods known as Tuatha de Danann, or people of Danu. She, with a rash disdain for taboos, approached a sacred well shaded by nine magic hazel trees, whose nuts gave the salmon which ate them knowledge of everything in the world. The well's waters rose and forced her back, or possibly – versions vary – drowned her. The flood formed the river Boyne in which the salmon, now scattered, wandered forever, seeking their lost hazel trees. The fish in turn imparted knowledge to those who ate them. Boann's son Aenghus, the god of love, had a magical palace here. Ancient gods killed in battle were buried here, as were kings in later times. Early Christians said that king Cormac mac Art, having switched to Christianity after a long pagan reign, wanted to be buried at the holy Christian site of Rosnaree, a mile upstream. His unregenerate servants placed his coffin down here, among his heathen ancestors. Again the river (a convert too) broke its banks and floated the king to the cemetery he aspired to.

Not much is known of the actual creators of this necropolis. They probably sailed from France – Brittany and parts of Spain preserve related remains – in the third millennium BC, bringing the novelty of settled cereal farming and the custom of building passage-graves. From the Boyne they spread west through the midlands to the neighbourhood of Sligo – a line closely packed with their remains. They paid great attention to their dead, enclosing all kinds of trinkets and valuables (not to be compared with those used in Egyptian funerals) in sometimes colossal tombs. Nothing on the same scale was put up in Ireland till the Normans built their castles. During the Bronze and Iron Ages, these neolithic cities of the dead were used for living in and among; and later again, by Norsemen, for plundering. In recent centuries tons of the stones were carted away for road-building, and sometimes trees were planted on top.

Brugh na Bóinne is Ireland's most visited site, and access is necessarily regimented. You park south of the river, go through the visitors' centre and cross by footbridge to the north bank, where buses take you to Newgrange and Knowth. **Newgrange**'s interior admits only a trickle of people. There are long queues, and in high season it may be necessary to arrive early in the afternoon to get a chance of entry on the same day. The three mounds, and several others in the area, are passage-graves, with one or two central passages lined with stone slabs, some decorated with spiral patterns, leading to a burial chamber on the opposite side. All this was covered with stones to form a mound. Newgrange's diameter is 280 feet and it reaches 44 feet in height. Sir William Wilde noted an estimate that 180,000 tons of stones had been used in its construction. Stones of white quartz were brought from the Wicklow mountains and granite from the Mournes to build a retaining wall up to ten feet high. These dimensions were restored in the 1960s after centuries of neglect and decay. Farther out is an arc of twelve massive standing pillars; traces of others, and the assumption that the arrangement was originally symmetrical, suggests there were thirty-six to start with, forming a circle well over three hundred feet in diameter. The best work is inside the mound, for the benefit of the dead. The enormous greenish stone which partially blocked the entrance has been moved for the sake of visitors. We step into a passage, three feet wide and most of its way high enough to walk along, that leads through sixty-two feet to the main chamber. This magnificent room, corbelled up to an apex over nineteen feet high and ten feet across, is constructed of stones on which the megalith builders lavished their art. The abstract markings include spirals and zigzags, lozenges and coils and triangles and other shapes that surpass the contemporary art of many other countries. The chamber itself has three recesses containing stone troughs that may have been used for the ashes of cremated kings, or possibly for sacrifice. On only four or five days of the year – those falling around the winter solstice on 21 December – are the sun's rays low enough to penetrate the small opening above the entrance, and feebly illuminate, for scarcely a single quarter of an hour, the contained gloom. For the chance to witness this event, dependant on a clear sky, waiting-lists exist for years ahead.

Oddly, **Knowth** had never been methodically explored till 1962, when Dr George Eogan of University College, Dublin, arrived with his team to devote a sequence of ten digging seasons to it. Working inwards from the surround, in which they excavated several smaller tombs, they at last opened up the main passage (114 feet long) and central chamber. The outer tombs were obviously of much later period, perhaps even early Christian. The massive stones along the 114-foot passage – still bearing the colossal weight of the mound after 4,000 years – were covered with the usual doodle-type Celtic motifs. Before the chamber, a stone bore a design of rather human aspect, earning it the name 'guardian of the tomb'. Then on 6 August 1968, the *Irish Times* blazoned the news that, quite by chance and unexpectedly, a second passage had been discovered. This rare addition made it one of the most important neolithic monuments in Europe – a treasury of prehistoric art. It also raised hopes of answers to old questions – the provenance of the first Irish settlers, the source of their manifold skills, the meaning – if any – of their art. Christianity, when it came, so thoroughly eclipsed the previous culture that everything before is the subject of guesswork. Knowth is helping to reconstruct a former age, not only in Ireland but in Europe too. Excavation still goes on, and the interior is not yet shown to the public. Knowth's art, and the scale it is made on, surpass Newgrange's. Both Knowth and Dowth contain traces of items from later times, including early Christian tombs, iron workings, a Dark Ages fort and Norman motte and bailey, and in the case of Dowth a nineteenth-century teahouse erected by the landowner Lord Netterville. Methodical excavations began at Dowth much later than at the other two and will continue for years, during which of course the public will not be admitted.

At **Slane**, a mile or so up the fertile valley, we are at once back in the eighteenth century, or so it seems standing at the crossroads with a neat three-storey Georgian house placed at each corner. But there is much more to Slane, including a good inn well placed for local fishing and lovely countryside. The place's name comes from that of Slanius, ruler of Meath, which once comprised slices of the original four Irish kingdoms. High above the village to the north, a line of evocative ruins tops a hill with a sweeping view of the valley, west to Trim and the central plain, south to the Wicklow Mountains, with the Sugar Loaf in clear blue silhouette, east to the puffing chimneys of Drogheda and the sea beyond, north-east to the hills of Louth. These ruins, of a sixteenth-century Franciscan abbey, are where St Patrick at Easter of 433 AD lit a paschal fire in defiance of the orders of the pagan king Laoghaire of Tara, whom he managed to convert, using clover leaves to explain the one-in-three/three-in-one nature of the Trinity, before serious mischief could be done. Afterwards he founded a church. A worn tomb in the churchyard is said to be that of the man he made bishop, St Erc, a semi-legendary divine from the west who daily, summer and winter, immersed himself in the chill river to recite all the psalms. Up to quite modern times coffins brought here for burial were laid for a while by the old shrine. The steep bulge to the west of the ruins, capped with trees and sometimes cows and bounded by a sheer moat, is what remains of a Norman motte.

The road from Slane to Navan runs parallel with the Boyne and passes some beautiful estates. First, on the left, is the wooded demesne of **Slane Castle**, seat of the Marquess of Conyngham. Up to 1991 you could see the castle from the river, its crenellated corner towers bulging with assurance. Among the best of the crop of pseudo-castles built at the turn of the eighteenth century, it was mainly designed by James Wyatt. The stables were Capability Brown's work, and the lodge-gates Francis Johnston's – he added a few features in time for the visit by George IV in 1821. Newly crowned and, to his great relief, freshly bereaved by the death of his unloved queen, the king made a visit to Ireland the first long engagement of his reign, spending several days here at Slane. For the wife of the owner, the Marquess of Conyngham, was also his new passion and mistress. Lady Conyngham was fat and fifty-four, but George could bring himself to cry when telling friends he had never before known true love. Ten years later, as he slipped towards death, she is supposed to have interrupted her ministrations to remove cartloads of jewelry and other valuables from St James's, but that may have been the malicious gossip mistresses are subject to. More recently the castle grounds saw the likes of Bob Dylan and the Rolling Stones performing at pop concerts. Then in 1991 the castle burned down. Restoration is under way.

On the opposite bank is **Beauparc House**, built in 1755 probably by Nathaniel Clements for Gustavus Lambart. A century later a Miss Lambart of Beauparc danced a jig here in front of Queen Victoria, and after, Salome-like, begged for Mr Gladstone's head on a salver. The Anglo-Irish did not care for that apostle of home rule.

Former Ascendancy demesnes succeed each other along the fertile banks of the Boyne. The sixteenth-century D'Arcy castle ruins and family mausoleum of Dunmoe are farther along on the right, and on the left the belfry of **Ardmulchan Church** on the site of a Norse battle; it is followed on the right by the impressive ruin of Donagh-more with an almost complete Round Tower and more links with the doings of St Patrick. The tower has a striking Romanesque doorway with a crude crucifixion above it. Finally, before Navan, is the demesne of Blackcastle House, from which sprang Mrs Fitzherbert and many a royal wrangle.

Navan is cruelly dissected by the N51 main road. Like some other Irish towns, it unwisely turns its back on the river. At the confluence of the Blackwater and the Boyne, its position in days of water transport was important, and it figures largely in early Pale history and in the war of the 1640s. Cromwell in punitive mood wrecked its abbey. It recovered from the wars, and built up several industries, among them paper, wool and flax. It had again declined until, in the 1970s, a new lead-zinc mining industry restored its bustle and affluence. It is also centrally situated in popular touring country. Until recently its official name, and the official spelling of it, An Uaimh, put people off, but the inhabitants voted to return to the anglicised form, Navan. A mile south-east, at **Athlumney**, is the striking ruin of a seventeenth-century manor, with an earlier square keep abutting on the east of the Boyne. It stands much as it stood in the middle of 1690 after Sir Lancelot Dowdall, its owner, deliberately gutted it. He was loyal to the Stuarts and pinned his hopes on James's victory at the Boyne. When news of defeat came to him he declared that William should never rest under his roof. He thereupon set fire to his house, crossed the river and sat all night on the opposite bank watching the flames. Next day he fled to permanent exile in France and Italy. Four miles south again, grandly overlooking the bank of the Boyne (as many great houses do hereabouts) is one of Richard Castle's last houses, the palatial Bellinter, now a convent of Our Lady of Sion.

There are several more fine houses (and were more) beside or near the ten-mile road north-west from Navan to Kells. **Ardbraccan,** a mile west of the river, by the site where the King of Connacht submitted to King John, was designed in 1776 by James Wyatt, with earlier wings by Richard Castle, who also built the Charter School. The house was used afterwards as the seat of the Church of Ireland bishops of Meath. A mile north is fifteenth-century **Liscartan Castle**, with two square towers linked by a hall beside the river bank. Just west of this is the White Quarry, source of stone for several of Dublin's finest houses. Turning right off the main road at Finnegan's Crossroads a lane leads up to **Donaghpatrick**, where St Patrick built a church sixty feet long, whose medieval successor is now a ruin. Farther along the main road is **Teltown House**, taking its name from the Palace of Tailte, which used to top the hill beside it. In ancient days and up to the twelfth century, Ireland's equivalent of the Olympic games were held here, as part of a Lughnasa festival, held at the beginning of August; parents used this display of the flower of their youth to arrange and negotiate marriages. In 1924 the games were revived in Dublin, changed a bit by the agency of the modern Gaelic movement.

A mile beyond Teltown we can turn right, then left at the crossroads a mile farther on. On the right is **Headfort House**, traditional home of the Taylour family, marquesses of Headfort since 1800. Their ancestor came over with Cromwell and bought the land in 1660. The house, of about 1775, closed to the public, may still admit a student of the Adam brothers writing in advance, for they designed some of the interiors, though they never came to Ireland, and Irishmen supervised the execution of their plans. The outside is plain, the work of George Ensor. The double-cube ballroom has been described as one of Ireland's finest interiors. Much of the building is now taken up by a school. The grounds, sloping down to the Blackwater, and some islands in the river, contain lovely gardens and a remarkable collection of trees.

Then comes **Kells**, famous for a book probably not made there, and a town of great charm and interest for all that. The Book of Kells (now in Trinity Library) certainly comes into its story, but as a tit-bit in a record of 'plague, pestilence and famine, the sword, fire, battle, murder and sudden death', as Wilde puts it. A local king of pagan times was, it is said, the first to 'dig earth so that water might be in wells', not surprising in view of the wealth of inventors reared in the Irish midlands, from the creator of the hangman's 'drop' to him who patented prefabricated telescopic church steeples. Invention may have been the foundation of Kells's prosperity. In the sixth century it became dominant among the abbeys founded by St Columba in Ireland, and when in 807 the mother abbey in Iona was ransacked with much slaughter by Vikings Kells became the chief of the whole Columban family. It was then that the book, probably made on Iona, was brought here. But the move from Scotland was not justified. No sooner had Abbot Cellach and his surviving brothers arrived than the Vikings attacked Kells too. Someone has reckoned that by the twelfth century the town had been burned twenty-one times and plundered seven, the worst onslaught in 996 by Sigtryg Silk-beard, King of the Dublin Norsemen, who later fought and lost at Clontarf.

When the conquering Henry II was recalled from Ireland by the troubles following Becket's murder, he left Hugh de Lacy as viceroy. De Lacy, with half a million acres of Meath to call his own, built castles all over it, one of them at Kells. He also raised walls round the town, bits of which remain. But the stronghold did not last. Baronial and racial struggles over two centuries reduced Kells to a stump of power, finally snuffed out after the dissolution, in 1551. Its charm now is of the eighteenth century, in Francis Johnston's court-house and Catholic church, and the fashionable (in those days) steeple added to the Church of Ireland church's medieval belfry in 1783 by

Thomas Cooley. There are still some remarkable older remains – a good Round Tower over ninety feet high that lacks only its conical cap; it has five instead of the usual four windows at the top, explained by the fact that five main approaches to Kells called for as many lookouts. Beside it but well spaced are three High Crosses and the base of a fourth, the best and oldest of which is the south one, or cross of Patrick and Columba, with a worn inscription to which it owes its name. It is beautifully carved with biblical scenes and patterns, not panelled off as in most later crosses. The animals along the base and human figures all over show a sprightly movement that was seldom improved on. A fifth cross, in the market place, has lost its top in being moved, but though worn consists of an excellent collection of relief sculpture. The late history of the market cross is sombre. Swift is said to have salvaged it and had it put in its present position. Late in the same century, the English commander of the local garrison had local rebels in the '98 hanged from it.

Close to the churchyard is a well-preserved building with stone roof intact, called St Columba's house (or Columcille's house – there were so many dozens of Colums that a few important ones are distinguished by altering the name. Columba is Latin for dove: Columcille means 'dove of the church' and both refer to the Donegal abbot, christened Colum, who left Ireland to found Iona in the sixth century). Built probably in the ninth century, its cleverly designed walls and the barrel vaulting that divides two floors have kept it up for 1,100 years and it is in very good shape still. There are similar buildings at Killaloe and Glendalough. Rather more than a mile west of Kells, the conspicuous hundred-foot tower on the hill of Loyd was ordered by Thomas Taylour, first earl of Bective, in his father's memory.

From Kells we continue along the Blackwater, more or less, through the self-consciously pretty town of Virginia (settled in James I's reign; called after his predecessor the Virgin Queen). Two miles north-east is ruined Cuilcagh (or Quilca) House, home of the playwright Richard Brinsley Sheridan and before him of his feckless, genial grandfather Thomas, author and teacher, whose friend Swift wrote a good part of *Gulliver's Travels* staying here. We can round Lough Ramor and the lakeside lands of former marquesses of Headfort, keep south for the little market-town of Oldcastle, turning left to find our way to the extensive summits of the **Loughcrew Hills**.

Close to the three main peaks of these Loughcrew Hills, or Slieve na Calliagh, is a series of over thirty passage-graves and innumerable ring-forts, mounds, megaliths and miscellaneous earthworks. This is a burial ground of some two thousand years back, and a link in the chain of progress, from the Boyne Valley to Sligo, of early Iron Age conquerors. As always, we know them through their death practices – these were cremated – not as living people; and as usual only the bare outlines even of these have come down, since the graves have been pilfered over the centuries and many, up to this century, poorly excavated by amateurs. Consequently, in spite of some impressive abstract patterns engraved on the massive kerbstones (twenty-seven of them in one cairn on the central peak) and of pottery, beads, pins and pendants extracted and now in museums, it is from the eerie splendour of this necropolis, and its command of spiny hills nearby and the whole central plain beyond, that its awesome force comes. In a quiet and subtle way it is one of Ireland's great sights. Most remains are concentrated – you might trip over them in parts – on the west and middle peaks, Carnbane West and Carnbane East, or Hag's Hills.

South of the hills, over the boundary road, is the demesne of ruinous Loughcrew House, burned down so often – three times in a hundred years – that after the last time, in 1960, it was abandoned. St Oliver Plunkett was born in 1629 in the castle which then occupied the site. The garden has been restored in recent years. To the east, the road leads us back on to the R154, passing close to Ballinlough castle, a nice marriage of Georgian symmetry with the Gothic of battlements, turrets, and round corner-towers, its walled garden and parkland recently resuscitated by virtue of a sizeable grant from Europe. Athboy is twelve miles on. It was here that Tiernan O'Rourke, who had already lost his wife Dervorgilla to Ireland's archetypal traitor, was himself cut down by Hugh de Lacy during a supposed truce and parley. De Lacy's wages came later, in Durrow, county Offaly.

A mile to the town's east the **Hill of Ward** rises to 390 feet, topped by an earthwork of four concentric rings. This used to be the scene of an annual gathering and fair on the feast of Samhain (31 October). In 1168 13,000 horsemen blocked the roads on their way there. In pagan times, the festival (replaced by Hallowe'en in the Christian calendar) marked the waning of the sun's powers and the succession of the gods of darkness, winter, and death. To propitiate the latter, human sacrifice was possibly offered. Plenty of old sources speak of this happening regularly, and plenty more recent ones deny it.

Three miles north-east of Athboy on the N51 is **Rathmore**, with the ruins of St Laurence's church, built early in the fifteenth century by Sir Thomas Plunkett. Among the details to survive are much of the east window, and various sculptured heads, effigies and coats of arms. There is also a later (1519) sculptured cross outside the church.

The main Dublin road R154 leads from Athboy to Trim, another great treasure house of county Meath. For the view it is best approached from the opposite direction but that requires a detour. **Trim** is smaller and perhaps less active and prosperous than Kells but still more obviously impressive. The streets are neat with brightly painted houses and some good Georgian buildings, and the pillar carrying the Duke of Wellington's statue of 1817 – he was for a while MP for Trim – shows through gaps from most angles. The way in along the Dublin road is the finest, with abbey ruins and two castles rising above sedge and meadowland and the narrow river, even if telephone wires and disagreeable buildings obtrude. Most of the town's history revolves around King John's Castle, the largest Anglo-Norman castle in Ireland, whose eleven-foot thick battle-marked walls and towers enclose over three acres. Of course things happened in Trim before it was built. 'Once upon a time (ten thousand years ago) St Patrick being thirsty as he passed …' Thackeray begins a tale about the place which he fails to finish, tired, as many must be, by the continuous popping up of the exemplary patron saint.

Trim came into its own as a stronghold of the Pale. Hugh de Lacy built his main castle here in 1173 but it was knocked down the next year by the Irish resistance. Restored, it soon became the stronghold of a walled town (the 'Sheep Gate' and other remnants still stand between Emmet and Castle Streets). Here came King John in 1210 to scare de Lacy's son, another Hugh, and others back to alliance after the distance from England had lent them the enchanted illusion of independence. John took the castle but handed it back five years later in his humbled, post-Magna Carta mood. Roger Pipard rebuilt it in 1220, as he did the castle at Ardee. Thereafter it received many royal visitors. Prince Henry of Lancaster – later Henry IV – was shut up here by Richard II, shortly before the latter's deposition. In 1536 the castle was seized in Silken Thomas's short campaign against Henry VIII. During the previous century it housed a mint and several parliaments, one of which, trying to make English sheep distinct from Irish goats, enacted that no Englishman was to wear a moustache or a yellow shirt.

In 1415 Trim's second castle, now a magnificently solid ruin on the river's south bank, was built by Sir John Talbot, then Lord Lieutenant of Ireland, before going to immortality in France and the pages of Shakespeare, being finally worsted by Joan of Arc at Orléans. This 'Scourge of France', 'so much feared abroad, that with his name the mothers still their babes', also piously founded Trim's Augustinian Abbey of St Mary, whose older ruined bell-tower, the 125-foot yellow steeple, commands a splendid view. The town, held by the Roman Catholic confederation, had been besieged and taken by Cromwellians in 1649, and by the time of Queen Anne's reign, Talbot's castle was both castle and chronometer. It was vacant and decaying. In 1717, Esther Johnson, Swift's Stella, bought it and sold it to Swift. who sold it in turn, both transactions bringing a profit. It then became a diocesan school (since 1955 Trim is once again seat of a bishop), attended before Eton by the young Duke of Wellington, and by Sir William Rowan Hamilton, inventor of quaternions and Astronomer-Royal. Both Swift and Wellington, as we shall shortly see, have close associations with spots to the south of Trim. About half a mile east is the beautiful ruin of Newtown Trim's thirteenth-century cathedral of SS Peter and Paul, founded in 1206, with some interesting remains, in spite of the fire that devastated it two centuries later.

One of the most distinguished old Catholic families of Ireland, the Barnewalls, Barons Trimleston, had their seat beside a tributary of the Boyne a couple of miles west of Trim. Now ruinous, **Trimleston Castle** housed, in the eighteenth century, the twelfth baron, who returned from years on the Continent with a collection of rare birds and exotic flowers which he bred here. He lived in remarkable style, with a state coach, and a large eagle chained beside the front door. He knew some medicine, treated his tenants for no return, and showed a perhaps premature perception of psychology when he had a woman who complained of depression shut in the dark and threatened with a beating.

Laracor is two miles down the Kilcock road, the R158, from Trim. Here came Swift in 1700, cheated (as he thought) of the deanery of Derry, to spend twelve years interrupted by long visits to London and Dublin. Even at this time he crops up often and hugely in politics and literature. Here he wrote countless tracts, the *Argument to Prove the Inconvenience of abolishing Christianity*, and vindications of his own suspect position as a churchman, and later, having gone over to the Tories, poured forth squibs and vitriol that helped put the Whigs out of office and himself, when they came back after a few years, irredeemably out of favour. Stella – Esther Johnson – came to Laracor as well, and lived in a separate house with her chaperone,

Mrs Dingley. The site of her cottage is marked out by a low wall just north of Laracor, beside the gates of Knightsbrook House. It was to her here that during his absence in London from 1710 to 1712 he sent those letters known as the *Journal to Stella*, a closely observed record of the London life, politics and gossip he was at the hub of.

The church he refurbished with the passion for order that was at the heart of him. On an occasion when none of his sparse flock turned up for the service he looked fixedly at his sole companion, the parish clerk, and began 'Dearly beloved Roger, the Scripture moveth you and me ...' The church was rebuilt in 1857 and deconsecrated in 1979. It is now a rather charming private house. Nothing remains of Swift's own house, or its well-stocked garden, or the avenues of willows he planted by the banks of the little river, or the surrounding wooden huts of the local Irish whom he championed – though rather like a conservationist with wildfowl, keeping them well clear of the house – or of the grander houses of those 'half-score persons' who formed his congregation. In 1713 Swift became Dean of Dublin's St Patrick's, and though he kept the living here till his death he seldom returned.

Two miles on stand the ruins of **Dangan Castle**, the early home and probably birthplace of the Duke of Wellington. Now a long grey shell set beside a copse among pastures and bumpy wastelands (good for boyish battles), the place was inherited from a distant relative by the duke's grandfather, who changed his name from Colley to Wesley out of respect for the donor. (Wellesley was the Duke's change, adding tone and avoiding confusion with perfervid evangelists.) The duke's father, the first Earl of Mornington, was a brilliant musician, liked by everyone, and became first Professor of Music at Trinity. He ruined the family fortune, however, by extending his father's landscaping of the grounds here – with canals, trees, enlargement of the lake (on which among other vessels was a twenty-ton man-of-war), and many ornaments, of which two obelisks on arches still survive. His two sons, Arthur, the great Duke, and Richard, Governor-General of India, redeemed the fortunes; but the house was let, sold about 1797 to an MP who improved it, and let by him to Roger O'Connor, a lawyer, trickster and one-time United Irishman, who insured it for £5,000 suspiciously soon before it was gutted by fire. Today, as for two centuries, this home of a general, statesman, wit and pragmatist placed by some on a plane with Caesar and Napoleon continues to decay (in the most romantic, ivy-clad, crumbly manner), made inaccessible by hedges, plantations and thickets, without so much as a signpost to indicate its presence.

Beyond the southern outskirts of Dangan demesne, **Summerhill** is a pretty eighteenth-century model village of low terraces bordering a spacious rectangle of tree-lined grass. Born here about 1720 to a poor Catholic family, then brought up in Cadiz by his uncle, a Jesuit priest, Ambrosio O'Higgins went fortune-hunting in Peru, rising from pedlar through general to Spanish Viceroy of Peru and Chile. His natural son, Bernardo O'Higgins, led the Chilean revolt of 1810 and became the new Republic's first president. Summerhill House was built in 1731 on a massive scale to the designs of Sir Edward Lovett Pearce, with a ring of Vanbrugh (related to Pearce) in its ornate grandeur. 'The most dramatic of the great Irish Palladian houses,' Mark Bence-Jones called it; 'even in its ruinous state … one of the wonders of Ireland'. It had a massive central block, and symmetrical curved wings leading to towers and pavilions. The Empress Elizabeth of Austria rented it for hunting in the 1870s. None of this could save it. It was twice burned down, the second time in the civil war of 1922, and in 1957 the magnificent ruin was removed. Like a poodle on a throne, a bungalow occupies the site. One of the rusticated, pedimented arches which flanked the original façade still survives.

Before going on towards Dublin we return through Laracor to Tara, if we are to see one of the most famous (if not visually striking) sites of Ireland. The way leads through **Bective**, a beautiful abbey-ruin by an old bridge over the Boyne. Founded in 1147 by Murchad O'Melaghlin, King of Meath, it was entirely rebuilt a century later. The chapter house and parts of the church of this second form still stand. Later it was rebuilt again and adapted as a mansion around 1600. Now the main surviving buildings surround a central cloister with a strong battlemented tower at the south-west angle. Bective was the first daughter house of Mellifont, a distinction that made its abbot automatically a spiritual peer. Wilde reports that Bective was said to have been designed by Greek immigrants before the Anglo-Norman invasion. Elsewhere he tells that there was once a Greek church in Trim. Little supports these attractive claims. Mary Lavin, writer of fine, realistic, often funny, often sad short stories, lived with her husband at the Abbey Farm opposite.

Now we come to **Tara**, once the centre of Irish power, its royal splendours more thoroughly vanished than the creations of Ozymandias, a broad lumpy hilltop affording panoramic views, its rich grass fertilised by millennia of grazing cattle. Discovery of gold remains in 1810 led to a modified gold rush which further hacked the ground about. But Tara remains a symbol of Irish freedom – rebel leaders have always homed to it – and it keeps a few reminders of its past. Its origins are lost altogether, though legends speak of its being founded by Tea, daughter of the king of Spain, when the Milesians arrived. In some accounts the great god Lugh was king of Tara. Though there are neolithic passage tombs and numerous barrows, many of the tangible remains date from the first few centuries AD, and Roman and oriental goods show that Ireland, though always outside the Roman Empire, dealt and traded with (as well as plundered) those inside. It may have been Roman influence which caused the star pattern of long straight roads that led from Tara to other focal points in the land.

At this period Tara rose to its peak of importance. Its kings were priest-kings, and ruled Ireland; and the thrice-yearly *feis* or festival held there involved a ritual marriage between maidens and the king, as nuns later were to marry Christ. King Cormac Mac Art in the third century put up most of the grand wooden buildings where heroic doings of knights and princes were sung and celebrated and which now have rotted to their earthen stumps. (Stone building seems to have come in about the eighth century.) He built roads, and schools for history, war and law, and rooted out rivals for a more or less peaceful forty years. *The Wisdom of Cormac the Wise*, written centuries later, may or may not be derived from him, but it contains a code of breezy pagan living – high marks for victory, tipple, fornication, poetry and intelligent conversation, and low for bad food, petty quarrels and women aspiring to be anything but bedmates. Cormac's army, the Fianna or Fenians, sparked off a colourful cycle of tales about Finn McCool the wise leader, Dermot his romantic, at last treacherous colleague, Oisin (or Ossian) the poet, Grania, Cormac's graceful daughter, who seduced Dermot on the eve of her marriage to Finn, led the latter a chase that covered the country, and left a trail of still-surviving place-names. It was very Iliadic and Arthurian, and quite likely the origin of much of the Round Table romance. In the fifth century, Tara was taken by Niall of the Nine Hostages, a buccaneering princeling who raided (and took hostages from) the coast of Wales and founded the house of O'Neill, which was to rule Ulster for a thousand years. One of his captives, it has been claimed, on a pirate mission to Scotland, was the boy Patrick, who spent some years as a slave before turning evangelist. The O'Neills hung on to the title of High King based on Tara for six centuries until Brian Boru brought an army of such power and prestige from the west that the king gave in without a fight. But Tara's influence declined shortly after Niall. Succession in the old Irish system went to brothers, and cousins, and quickly dissipated central power. When Patrick lit his paschal fire at Slane, and King Laoghaire saw and marched to snuff out the new religion, Tara's stature had become token, and the last feis was held in the mid-sixth century. Laoghaire is said to be buried somewhere here, upright and in full armour, awaiting the armies of the men of Leinster. As an emblem of national unity, Tara lived on, and Tom Moore's 'The harp that once through Tara's halls the soul of music shed ...' gave its glory a fresh lease. O'Connell in 1843 chose the hill for one of his monster meetings, urging repeal of the act of union and restoration of an Irish parliament. *The Times* said a million people were there.

There is a map on the site to show where the various remains are – the Fort of the Synods (mutilated, in spite of a Board of Works ban, at the turn of the century by British Israelites in search of the Ark of the Covenant); the banqueting hall, 250 yards long, where diners were divided up by feudal laws of precedence; Laoghaire's rath; and the vast *rath na rioch*, or fort of the kings, an oval enclosure of about 300 yards diameter, surrounded by a ditch cut eleven feet into the rock, with a statue of St Patrick and a pillarstone close by. This stone, the *lia fail*, has an ancient, very dubious life history. Most national traditions tended to assert rather forced links with Bible lands, to attract a greater aura of sanctity. The Irish have some choice wild claims, one of which may have given rise to the Ark quest above. This pillarstone, the story goes, is the same Jacob's pillow on which the patriarch, flying from Esau's hot temper, slept, and dreamed of a ladder rising to heaven. After 586 BC, when Nebuchadnezzar destroyed the old temple, Israelite refugees carried the stone with them to Ireland, where it was used for coronations and uttered a clairvoyant cry if the claimant was the rightful one. Here accounts diverge.

Scottish legend removes it to Scotland, carried by an Ulster king who went to found the colony of Argyll (or eastern Gael). It passed to Scone, then in 1296 to London, where it rested (until its recent return to Scotland), under the Confessor's chair in Westminster Abbey on which the British monarch is crowned. Yeats's absurd, beloved Maud Gonne favoured this view, and begged him to use his otherworldly contacts to spirit it back to Ireland. Or else it stayed in Ireland on this hill of Tara, with an inscription added to mark the grave of thirty-seven rebels killed in the '98 Rising. Or else, of course, it stayed in Palestine and remains there to this day.

Two neighbouring hills to east and south support, respectively, Skreen castle and church, where Columba's relics were brought in 875 and where stands a small medieval church, and the hillfort of

Rath Maeve. From the last we look down on two demesnes, Killeen on the left and Dunsany on the right. Both belong to different branches of the Plunkett family, Earls of Fingall and Barons Dunsany. They have done so since Henry VII's reign, when Sir Christopher Plunkett, Deputy Governor of Ireland, married the Cusack heiress of both castles, later leaving each one to a different son. The boundary was supposed to have been determined by a race between the sons' wives, each running from her own castle towards the other. In **Dunsany Castle**, till his death in 1957, lived Lord Dunsany, creator in his short stories of Jorkens, an inventive layabout of London clubs. Dunsany discovered and encouraged the young Slane poet Francis Ledwidge, who died in Flanders in 1917. Shortly afterwards, during the Troubles, Dunsany Castle was ransacked by a marauding band. 'Who shall I say called?' the butler is reported to have asked as the looters left. It is a story told of many Irish houses, and probably has to appear once per guidebook. Dunsany, remodelled in the eighteenth century, is majestically solid, multifariously battlemented, windowed, turreted. It has tall interiors, real and *trompe l'oeil* tracery, panelling, fine library, delicate plasterwork and a notable staircase. In the grounds is an early fifteenth-century church ruin, with good monuments. Dunsany church preserves the effigies and tomb of the fifteenth-century church builders, Christopher, Lord Dunsany and his wife, who also ordered the beautifully carved font. During the Penal days, the Protestant Dunsanys kept Killeen in secret trust for their Catholic Fingall cousins who would otherwise have lost their possessions. The Catholic family also resorted at times to another device: nominating one of their number to become token Protestant for as long as necessary to keep the estates intact. Killeen, originally a De Lacy castle of about 1190, is one of the many houses remodelled in the early 1800s by Francis Johnston, but the estate has been sold out of the family. The Fingall earldom has come to the end of its line, and the house at present rots. The Dunsanys stay put. Considering their aptitude for backing wrong horses – Simnel, Warbeck, Charles I, James II – and that in the 1921 Troubles one was arrested because he refused to hand in his gun (needing it to shoot snipe) the achievement is remarkable.

The road back to Dublin leads through Dunshaughlin, with a Johnston court-house. To the east lies **Lagore**, a bog that was once a lake, on which was built a crannog, or lake-island, some fifteen hundred years ago. These structures, fairly safe from attack, but for convenience connected with the mainland by a just-submerged causeway, were common in Ireland. They were built up with stones, faggots, peat and timbers dumped inside a ring of upright stakes or piled stones. This particular crannog, a royal residence, yielded good finds when the Howard Archaeological Mission of 1934 to 1936 uncovered everything from gang-chains for slaves to animal skulls split length-wise to obtain the brains. Most of the material is now in the National Museum in Dublin.

Farther on but just off the main road is Ratoath, birthplace of Richard Pigott, who forged letters sent to *The Times* incriminating Parnell in the Phoenix Park murders; he confessed, and then left for Spain, where he took his own life. A parliamentary commission acquitted Parnell in 1889, and he was cheered when he resumed his seat in the House of Commons. He sued *The Times*, then settled out of court for £5,000. All the same his reputation was harmed, and black-ened soon after by the Kitty O'Shea affair. To the east is **Ashbourne**, where Thomas Ashe, a local schoolmaster, poet and Republican, led a group of insurgents in 1916 to attack the Royal Irish Constabulary barracks, from which they took away arms and ammunition. They went on to ambush an RIC force a mile north of the village, killed eight and wounded more. He was the only 1916 commander to fulfil his mission – the Easter Rising made the impact it did by failure, and the retribution that followed. But a year later Ashe died in Mountjoy prison, during the course of forced feeding following his hunger-strike. Two of his comrades, killed in the action, are commemorated here. The second Baron Ashbourne also lived here till his death in 1942. An eccentric patriot, he insisted on wearing a saffron kilt and on speaking Irish in the House of Lords: one of several who aban-doned an England-orientated, upper-class background – his father was called by Lord Randolph Churchill 'family lawyer of the Tory party' – incurring the disgust of their class and not much more than indifference from their new allies. He died in 1947. From Ashbourne, the straight main road, supposedly built to convey George IV to Slane in 1821, runs twelve miles to Dublin.

3

Middle Ireland: Westmeath, Longford and Roscommon

W HAT THE CENTRAL northern counties of Ireland have in common is wetness. Large parts of the region north and west of Mullingar are more water than land, and the water provides as much swimming, fishing and boating as could keep happy a hundred times the present number of visitors. There are no mountains. But the land is not flat. Old earth movements left it wavy, and here and there gave it small jagged contours. From vantage points like Slane Hill or Slieve Bloom it all looks like a monotonous plain. Below, successions of hill and valley curtail the views. The country is pretty rather than grand. Grass, and masses of purple loose-strife, meadow-sweet, orchids, rushes and other damp-loving flowers dapple the widespread peat-bog, or the huge strips from which all peat has been gouged for power stations or domestic fuel. Lough Ree, a bulge in the River Shannon reaching a width of seven miles, is the central feature. A boat trip down the Shannon from Carrick, or up from Killaloe is a good way of seeing the centre, but we shall keep to land, since movement here is easier, taking Dublin as our starting and finishing point.

The first important town on the R148, after we cross from county Dublin to county Kildare is **Maynooth** (pronounced M'nooth), whose lands and habitations belonged to the FitzGerald family from soon after the Anglo-Norman invasion. The stem of the several boughs of the FitzGerald family tree was Maurice FitzGerald, a companion of Strongbow in the invasion of Ireland who in 1176 built a castle at Maynooth, on land stretching from Naas to the Shannon granted by Strongbow. Well into Tudor times FitzGeralds virtually split power in southern Ireland with the widespread Butlers, earls of Ormond. The FitzGeralds themselves formed two main branches. The FitzGerald earls of Desmond, with cadet branches including the families of the White Knight, Knight of Glin and Knight of Kerry, were the pre-eminent power in Munster until, rebelling once too often, they were eliminated under Queen Elizabeth. The FitzGerald earls of

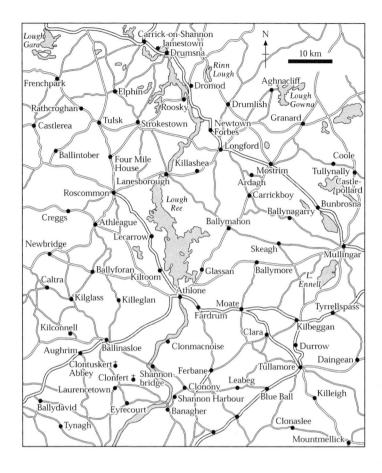

Kildare rose and fell like their western cousins, but unlike them survived to rise again in the eighteenth century with the additional title duke of Leinster. In the earlier centuries they were based at **Maynooth Castle**, whose gatehouse, thirteenth-century keep and great hall, with other fragments, still stand. To Henry VIII the old Anglo-Norman families – FitzGeralds, Butlers and many others – to whom the interests of England had become with time remote and alien, were as dangerous as the native Irish. Finding the Earl of Kildare opposed to his break with the Catholic Church, Henry brought him to London in 1534. The earl's son, Silken Thomas (so called from the silk fringes on his troops' helmets) hearing a false rumour that his father had been executed, raised a rebellion but failed to take Dublin Castle and retired to Maynooth. The king's new deputy, Sir William Skeffington, besieged the castle for a week with the first siege-guns ever used in Ireland, then granted the inmates the 'pardon of Maynooth': a false promise of freedom, followed by exemplary executions. Thomas himself was dispatched to London to lose his head, and six years later Henry assumed the title King of Ireland. The castle was later restored to the Kildare Geraldines (as FitzGeralds are sometimes called) but was finally dismantled in 1647 by Owen Roe O'Neill.

The main feature of the town is **St Patrick's College**, a Roman Catholic seminary refounded in 1795 (there had been a college here in the Middle Ages) by an English parliament anxious to win future priests away from the Republican influences to which Continental training might expose them. Half way through the nineteenth century Maynooth had educated half the priests serving in Ireland, while its Gothic Revival buildings, set elegantly round two huge squares with a chapel boasting Ireland's tallest spire, built late in the century to the design of J.J. McCarthy, give it the august air of an Oxford college. It became a recognised college of the national university in 1908 and, since the 1960s, it accepts lay as well as clerical students. The museum is mainly of ecclesiastical interest, though there are some good paintings, a notable scientific section, and a few of the inventions – including a machine for shoeing horses – of Dr Nicholas Callan (1799–1864). Some vestments are exhibited which were made by ladies-in-waiting to Marie Antoinette and brought across by outlawed French priests who found employment here. There are also the gifts of Empress Elizabeth of Austria, sent in return for a kindness done her by the priests. The first was a large silver statue of St George. It was tactfully remarked to her that England's patron saint might not be an ideal subject for Irish veneration. She promptly sent some superb vestments embroidered with golden shamrocks.

To the east of the town lies the lovely demesne of **Carton**, one of Ireland's greatest houses, wholly recast at the behest of Robert FitzGerald, nineteenth earl of Kildare, in 1739, by the great Richard Castle, the German architect responsible for, among other buildings, Leinster House and Tyrone House in Dublin and Russborough in county Wicklow. Castle died in 1757 and is buried in the Church of Ireland church. He fixed the house firmly in the Palladian pattern of central block, curved colonnades and terminal pavilions, and employed the Lafranchini brothers to execute the superb gilt plaster-work on the coved ceiling of the saloon. Changes, mainly to the park, were carried out under the twentieth earl, who became first duke of Leinster. His request to Capability Brown to do the work brought the riposte that Brown had not finished England yet. The third duke had Sir Richard Morrison around 1815 make the house virtually an insti-tution, turning front into back, replacing the colonnades with straight arcades and packing in rooms wherever he could. It spoiled Castle's work, but pleased Queen Victoria and Prince Albert when they stayed in 1849. The Queen slept in the Chinese bedroom, with its Chinese wallpapers, but the room has suffered since her time, and the bed she slept in has long been sold.

In 1747 the first duke married Emily, one of the daughters of the duke of Richmond whose lifelong exchange of letters with her sisters (one of whom married Tom Conolly of neighbouring Castletown) comprises a treasury of information about the lives of the eighteenth-century aristocracy, and much else. One of Emily's twenty-three chil-dren was Lord Edward FitzGerald, a spoiled and somewhat fatuous figure who, by dint of his looks, birth, amiability and early, agonising and tragic death from a wound received while resisting arrest in 1798, has come down as a famous romantic rebel.

The family ambled through the nineteenth century, weighted with wealth, honours and prestige until in 1887 the wife of the fifth duke gave birth to an heir, Maurice, widely believed to be her lover's and not her husband's child. Maurice's youngest brother, the third son Edward, short of funds, sold or gambled away his very slender chance of inheriting Carton. But inherit he did, after one older brother was killed in the First World War and Maurice died young in 1922. The house was forfeit, forever lost to the FitzGeralds. Much later came a claim that Maurice's coffin had contained nothing but ballast and that he, for a worthwhile reward, had migrated to Canada and changed his identity. In 1967 a man who said he was Maurice's son came forward to claim, but without success, his birthright. Meanwhile Carton passed from hand to hand and role to role, all contents sold, pared down and frequently neglected. Now a company has applied to make it a luxury hotel, a change which would almost inevitably destroy a character redolent of history.

The road we are on, the N4, carries main traffic for Sligo and Galway. There is little to notice on the way and even places of former greatness like Clonard have left nothing more than lumpy contours in the ground. Innfield – often Enfield, from a simple mistake of the Great Western Railway company when it named the station – is close to the restored Royal Canal and its miles of towpath walking. Three miles on, a diversion of five miles can be taken through Longwood to **Castlerickard**, where a decaying pyramid mausoleum engraved with the word 'SWIFTE' marks the grave of the family the dean came from. Donore Castle is a couple of miles west: a mid-fifteenth-century castle built to measurements which qualified the owner for a £10 grant for deterring the frequent native Irish raids into the Pale.

The way back to the main road can take in the Boyne Aqueduct, where the infant river passes under the Royal Canal. A few miles before Kinnegad we pass the site of **Clonard**, once the foremost monastery of Ireland. It was founded about 530 by St Finnian, an ascetic abbot sometimes known as 'tutor of the saints of Ireland'. It was common then for monasteries to double as universities, and Clonard drew students from the Continent as well as Ireland. Brendan the Navigator, Ciaran of Clonmacnois, Columba and Columbanus, the last two apostles of Christianity in, respectively, pagan Scotland and a Europe recently overrun by barbarians, were among those trained here. The ground-plan was that of a rath or hill-fort, and you can still make out, or make up, the way the place was ordered.

The road to the left goes to ruined **Ticroghan Castle**, defended in 1650 by Lady Fitzgarret against the parliamentary army. Like other grass-widows in the civil war, she defended so efficiently that the besiegers were about to go away. But her difficulties were acute. Ammunition was running out, and she had family silver forged into bullets. The Roundheads noticed, deduced, stayed, attacked again, and won.

Just before Kinnegad we enter Westmeath, and twelve miles later reach its capital, **Mullingar**. The twin towers of its modern Catholic cathedral (1936–39) by Ralph Byrne provide 140-foot landmarks, seen for miles across the flat country. There are dull, decent sculptures inside and out by Albert Power, who died in 1945, and striking mosaics by Boris Anrep, and there is an ecclesiastical museum, not always open. There is nothing much to inspire in Mullingar which is kept well-to-do by busy markets where the cattle and other produce of surrounding farms – good hunting country – are sold. But with a pleasant hotel and several farmhouses nearby, it makes a fair base.

The district round Mullingar used to be called 'the country of the waters' and it has welcomed for years that stolid and imperturbable race – the anglers. For the coarse fisher the area is ideal. He wants to fish from a bank, not a boat, and with nearly forty centres of coarse angling and innumerable lakes can find congenial, lonely positions in all directions. A lake to oneself is no rarity. Visiting anglers could be multiplied by tens and still create no sign of a crowd. Pike, perch, rudd, bream, tench and others exist in plenty for all, and of a size that sometimes defeats the English angler, equipped for the rather smaller fish of his home waters. Game fishing exists, too, and most lakes and rivers have been developed and stocked. Those most accessible from Mullingar are Loughs Ennell, Owel and Derravaragh, but every local tourist office can supply details of the many more in the region.

Lough Ennell, four miles south of Mullingar, is of more than angling interest. On its eastern shore is **Belvedere**, a mid-eighteenth-century villa built by Richard Castle for the first Earl of Belvedere, Robert Rochfort. The ivy-covered Neo-Gothic wall near the house, known as the 'jealous wall', was built by the earl to block from view Tudenham, his brother George's house next door. 'Jealous' is a post-humous misnomer, often wrongly explained. The earl simply had a row with George, some time in the 1760s. His jealousy was for the middle brother, Arthur, and began in 1743 when both were living at Gaulston, near Rochfortbridge (five miles south-east). Someone told Robert his wife of seven years, whom he adored, was sleeping with Arthur. She confessed. Robert told her father, Viscount Molesworth, who shrugged and said she was a bastard anyway, born before he married her mother. Robert now sued Arthur and was awarded £20,000 damages. Arthur sailed to England and returned in 1759 to find his brother so far from forgiving that he had Arthur jailed for life, for debts. Meanwhile, in 1743, Robert locked his wife inside Gaulston (burned in 1920 and since demolished), and kept her prisoner. She emerged, cracked and haggard, thirty years later, after he died. Robert during this time had finished Belvedere, been made an earl, and lived the rest of his days active and very popular with society. The line died out with his son (or more likely Arthur's) the second earl, who built Belvedere House in Dublin. When James Joyce was a pupil at the college this became, he made notes towards a book about the family.

A more recent owner of the house was Colonel C. Howard Bury, an Everest climber, who began the quest for the yeti, or abominable snowman, in 1921. He died in 1966, and the fine terraced and walled gardens he cultivated, and long walks through the demesne, are some-times open to the public. South-west of the lake (on which the appearance of the may-fly signals the high fishing season, a good two weeks before it hatches on lakes to the north) is the restored **Lilliput House**, another Rochfort property, visited by Swift and – a study centre now – visitable still down a wooded lane. It is said by some to have provided and, by others, been called after, the name of the island in *Gulliver*. From it can be seen Cormorant Island, on which King Malachy II of Meath and Tara died in 1022. Tudenham House was unroofed in 1957.

Back in Mullingar we can continue north-west, along the Bally-nacarrigy road, and turn right three miles on for Lough Owel and a country of small rounded hills spattered with pretty woods and lakes. Soon Lough Owel comes into view, nearly four miles long and rich in folklore; and we can walk to its edge by the ruins of **Portloman Castle**, named after St Lomman, a colleague of St Patrick, who founded an abbey on whose site, beside the water, ruins still stand. The lake was the scene of the Dane, or Viking, Turgesius's death. It was a time, 845, when Vikings were trying to set up permanent bases in the country. Turgesius arbitrarily 'assumed the sovereignty of all the foreigners in Ireland', kept fleets on Lough Neagh and the Shannon lakes, plundered Clonmacnois and Armagh and, Minoslike, demanded as tribute from Malachy II (or Mael Sechnaill II), king of Meath, and belonging to a branch of the O'Neills, his daughter and fifteen virgins. The Dane here met his Theseus, for Malachy dressed up fifteen men as girls, and these took Turgesius, bound him, and waited by Owel for their king's verdict. Malachy had the trussed pris-oner drowned. But the victory was partial. Soon the Danes were defending their footholds in Ireland, and in doing so building the country's first cities – Dublin, Waterford and the rest.

After we pass Lough Owel, the first road to the left, then first right, diverts us towards Lough Iron and the romantic demesne of long demolished **Baronstown House**. The town of Kilbixy used to be here, with a De Lacy castle and 'twelve burgesses in their scarlet gowns, a mayor or sovereign, with other officers suitable to so great a port'. There was river traffic along the Inny to Lough Ree, and thence to all Ireland. Now, apart from Francis Johnston's Church of Ireland church, there are trees, stones and bog. A mile south, nearer the water, stood **Tristernagh Abbey**, home of the Piers family till Sir William demolished it in 1783. It stood on the site of an Augustinian Priory of 1200, and two tattered arcades still survive. Sir William's son, Sir John Piers, built a cottage here in the early 1800s, surrounded by high walls to keep out law-officers. He had seduced Lady Cloncurry, wife of his close friend, for a bet; and was taken to court and ordered, like

Arthur Rochfort, to pay £20,000. The estates were sold out, and he went bankrupt, but redeemed himself by a later marriage. John Betjeman revived the episode in a series of poems ending with the hauntingly evocative *Tristernagh Today.* The house survived till the Troubles; burned accidentally, say most accounts. Even the estate lake has dried up and an artificial island is no more than a pile of stones in dry ground.

Now we can drive between the two loughs, over the crossroads and the N4 at Bunbrosna, and make for Multyfarnham. Before it, on the right, is **Wilson's Hospital**, an Anglican boys' school from whose steps Lough Derravaragh can best be seen to the north. Designed by John Pentland in 1760, the school looks like a model Palladian country house, with the cupola over the central block, and curved wings linking it with pavilions. On 4 September 1798, it and its grounds were occupied for a night by rebels – seven thousand of them, it was reckoned. But they were a demoralised and undisciplined force, and the second earl of Longford, with a force of Scots and others from Cavan, quickly evicted them, killed a few hundred round and about the hospital, and left others to escape into the night, many drowning in the lake.

Multyfarnham is notable for its Franciscan friary, closed three times – by Henry VIII in 1540, Queen Elizabeth in 1601 and Cromwell in 1651. After each suppression the friars returned, the last time after a thorough restoration in 1973. Beyond, the land slopes down over the old Nugent estate to the site of Donore House and **Lough Derravaragh** (best seen from the top of Knockeyon, 710 feet high, at the south-east end of the lake). The Nugents have been linked with the area since Hugh de Lacy's day, and their old management methods made them part-models for the inhabitants of Castle Rackrent in Maria Edgeworth's novel of that name; though Sir Kit, who fed his Jewish wife on pork and then, in the Westmeath way, locked her up for twenty-five years, was based, not on a Nugent, nor even a Rochfort, but a Maguire of county Fermanagh. But every castle hereabouts has a story that borders on fiction.

Derravaragh is where the four children of Lir (an ocean god, in another version king Lear) were turned into swans by Aoife, sister of their dead mother and now their jealous stepmother. Her servants refused her order to drown them in the lake, so she put them under a magic spell. They were to spend three hundred years on the lake here, three hundred in the strait of Moyle off northern Antrim and a final three hundred in the Atlantic off Belmullet. They kept their beautiful

human voices, and people would come from far away to marvel at
their speech and sad story. When the time was run, they became
human again, but with all the signs of their age and on the point of
death. Monastic scribes made sure of telling that a saint,
Mochaomhog, baptised them in the nick of time. So ran one of 'the
three sorrowful tales of Ireland'.

North-east of Derravaragh is **Tullynally**, formerly Pakenham Hall,
the rambling castellated Irish home of the Pakenham family, whose
forebear fought for Cromwell and was rewarded by him with this and
other estates. The earldom of Longford came late in the eighteenth
century. The present owner, Thomas Pakenham the historian, is heir
to the much publicised, socialist seventh earl, whose predecessor, his
brother Edward, was a well-known theatre manager, playwright, poet
and later senator in Dublin. It was the second earl who from 1803
onwards gave the house most of its present character, employing
Francis Johnston to add another modish Gothic castle to his considerable list, giving the old mansion (itself an advanced one, with a
central heating system designed by Maria Edgeworth's father)
towers, a moat and six hundred feet of battlements. That same earl
rejected the future (at that time insolvent) Duke of Wellington's offer
of marriage to his sister Kitty in 1793. Little but a sense of duty made
the duke marry her, unseen for fourteen years, in 1806, when he
returned from India a hero, and she had meanwhile suffered smallpox
and a nervous breakdown. 'She has grown ugly, by Jove', he whis-
pered to his brother at the wedding. The next earl doubled the
battlements (which had not been entirely for show, the second earl
being fiercely opposed to Catholic emancipation) and put in an
immense kitchen and servants' hall. Sir Richard Morrison designed
these changes. The huge two-storey hall and the library are among the
house's glories, and the grounds and views are superb.

Continuing east through Castlepollard, the road takes us to **Fore
Abbey** in a snug valley under jagged limestone bluffs. The ninth-
century church, with its two-and-a-half-ton cross-inscribed lintel
stone high above the road, marks the foundation in about 630 of St
Fechin's monastery. On the other side of the valley floor are fragments of the cloister, an eastern and a western range, an old tomb, and
a tall tower of the fifteenth century – remains of a Benedictine priory
founded about 1200. There has been considerable restoration here in
the past century. The gateways of the old town of Fore are beside the
road. All the remains repay study, and the whole valley retains a
magical atmosphere. It is alive with miracles. St Fechin built his

monastery on a quaking bog. To get water, he tapped the rock with his crozier, which disappeared, burrowed half a mile through the rock to Lough Lene, a very pretty lake to the south, and returned with a gush of water that ran uphill. The saint had the giant lintel (on a doorway as magnificent, according to Petrie, as any in Greece), which workmen failed to shift, wafted to its present position. An ash tree bore only three branches, symbol of the Trinity.

In the church a stone dated 1616 asks for prayers for Patrick Beglan. Having vowed to live all his life in the tiny anchorite's cell above St Fechin's church, the story goes, he one day could not resist the call of a hunting horn, climbed through the window, fell and broke his neck. He may have been the last of the real hermits. Men acting as hermits were not uncommon in the eighteenth century, and some estate owners had cells built for them, finishing touches to their Arcadian landscapes. Fore was burned after the Dissolution and has happily stayed much as it was since then.

Delvin, a village six miles south-east of Fore, has a castle, Clonyn, on its west side: a square nineteenth-century pile with tall, castellated Round Towers at each corner, a property, like many others in these parts, of the Nugent family. To the village's east is South Hill, where lived Sir Thomas Chapman, father of the illegitimate boy (born in Wales) who became Lawrence of Arabia. The main Chapman seat was Killua castle, five miles north-east, a house built in 1780, Gothicised about 1830, now a romantic ruin in a particularly romantic demesne beside the canal. Delvin was made famous by one of its natives, Brinsley Macnamara, born John Weldon, whose first work, published in 1918, was an uninhibited, unflattering book, *Valley of the Squinting Windows*, about his fellow villagers. It caused outrage. Copies were burned in the village square, the school his father taught at was boycotted. He himself, his life threatened, settled in Dublin. 'Squinting windows' came to describe a category of brutally realistic Irish fiction.

Returning to Castlepollard we turn right and drive north nine miles, passing through Finnea, a charming village on the Inny between Lough Sheelin (a good trout, pike and perch lake which takes in parts of three counties, Westmeath, Cavan and Meath) and Lough Kinale. At Finnea, local Irish in 1646 won a victory over Cromwell. A mile later we turn first left for **Granard**, a small village built along the road like many round here, known for its annual August harp festival. It has at one end a huge and strangely symmetrical mound, seen from miles around and topped by a statue of St

Patrick since 1932, the supposed fifteen-hundredth anniversary of his coming for the second time to Ireland. It was fortified by the Anglo-Normans. From here a diversion can take us through the Black Pigs Race two miles north-west, remains of a massive pre-Norman defensive dyke between Loughs Kinale and Gowna, to Lough Gowna itself, an almost coyly pretty lake with small fir, chestnut and oak-covered hills around and hedgerows packed with honeysuckle, hawthorn and blackberry. Gowna is the source of the River Erne and so starts the massive Lough Erne complex.

South-west of Granard lies **Mostrim**, usually known as Edge-worthstown, in which it is thought Goldsmith went to school. Oscar Wilde's sister died here, staying at the Glebe in 1867 with her aunt's family. She was eight. Oscar, twelve and inconsolable, paid long visits to her grave in the cemetery. The small Georgian mansion built by Richard Lovell Edgeworth still stands, now a nursing home run by the Sisters of Mercy, not improved by extensions. The Edge-worths, whose family vault is in the Church of Ireland church, had come to Ireland in 1585 and to Mostrim in James I's reign. Their first representative was a bishop of Down. Richard Lovell Edge-worth (1744–1817) was an author, inventor, MP and father – by one of four wives – of Maria and twenty-one other children. He wrote on engineering and education (his system, based on Rousseau, has a modern flavour), and invented among countless other things a tele-graph for transmitting horse-racing information (installed at Lord March's house at Reading), a wheel with a barrel inside for making walking faster, a horse-carriage with sails (which frightened the horses), a prototype of caterpillar wheels, a pebble road surface in advance of Macadam, an umbrella to cover haystacks, a method of diverting the Rhone (for which the French gave him land nearby), a semaphore, velocipede, pedometer, the central heating system installed at Tullynally, and a prefabricated spiral of iron for Edge-worthstown's spire. His devoted daughter Maria (1767–1849) – four feet seven inches tall (they tried to stretch her by hanging when young), with a beaky nose and ugly eye-disease – won fame in her time for *Castle Rackrent, The Absentee, Ormond,* and twenty volumes of other writings, as well as her sweetness, kindness to tenants and efforts on their behalf during the famines of the 1840s and her own last years. Scott wrote that he wanted 'in some distant degree to emulate' her 'admirable Irish portraits' and Turgenev said his own writing was inspired by hers. Her novels and diaries paint a vivid portrait of the area. To get to the Pakenhams, as she liked to do, it was necessary to cross 'a vast Serbonian bog; with a bad road, an awkward ferry, and a country so frightful and so overrun with weeds, that it was aptly called by Mrs Greville "the yellow dwarf's country" '.

Ardagh, four miles south-west of Edgeworthstown, is at heart an 1860s Victorian model village based by its then landlords, the Fetherstones, on Swiss models. The big house is supposedly where the boy Goldsmith, sent to school with a guinea and bent on adventure, was directed when he asked for an inn for the night. It was no inn, but Mr Fetherston's private house, and the ensuing confusion is the basis of *She Stoops to Conquer*.

Longford, the county town, has a nineteenth-century Catholic cathedral of St Mel in, as they say, the Italian Renaissance style. Little remains of the castle, besieged unsuccessfully by Owen Roe O'Neill in the Confederation war. There is an ecclesiastical museum at the back of the cathedral, a genealogical centre and a heritage museum in the old post office. The town is a good base for Lough Ree and the countryside around. **Carriglas Manor**, two miles north-east of the capital, is well worth a visit. The property in the seventeenth century of the diocese of Ardagh, then of Trinity College, Dublin, it came in the early 1800s to the Lefroy family who, mercifully leaving alone Gandon's stable court, rebuilt the main house in Tudor Gothic in 1840 (said to be Ireland's first Victorian house, having been completed days after Victoria ascended the throne), blending towers, spindly chimneys, battlements, oriels and gables in heady profusion. As a young man Chief Justice Thomas Lefroy is said to have quickened Jane Austen's pulse, and possibly to have been part-model for d'Arcy in *Pride and Prejudice*. His descendants still inhabit the house, and open it regularly.

The westward N5 leads from Longford to **Richmond Harbour**, terminal of the Royal Canal, where it links with the Shannon. The canal itself was a failure, opening in the 1840s when new railways were rendering water traffic redundant. But Richmond Harbour and Clondra are elegant survivals, and the recent gradual clearance of the canal from here to Dublin has opened up a charming channel for recreational boating.

Returning to the N4 main road going northward from Longford, we pass through Newtown Forbes, with grand, kempt, Gothic **Castle Forbes**, first built in 1619, burned and rebuilt about 1830, seat of the Earl of Granard, on the left overlooking the Shannon. The widow of the original Scottish settler, Sir Arthur Forbes (killed in a duel in

Hamburg while fighting for Gustavus Adolphus), managed to hold off the parliamentary forces in the Civil War, for which the family got its earldom. Eight miles to the right we see bare Carn Hill, county Longford's highest hill (916 feet), two miles north of which, at Ball-inamuck, a statue commemorates General Humbert's defeat in the last encounter of the 1798 Rising.

The flair, energy and good fortune of the young French commander, who having landed with some seven hundred French at Killala a fortnight or so before, had snatched Castlebar, recruited thousands of Irish, and sped across country in an astonishingly bold bid for Dublin itself, were fast running out. New rebels appeared everywhere, muscling their way into towns and mansions. The terri-fied gentry of Longford and Westmeath fled or hid. But peasants could not change overnight into soldiers. They were often brave but untrained, amazed, leaderless and sometimes, when an occupied big house had a well-stocked cellar, drunk. Hours before the confronta-tion here, hundreds of them had been gunned down, stuck like pigs or drowned at Granard and Wilson's Hospital. Here at **Ballinamuck**, on the morning of 8 September, Humbert's few hundreds resisted for half an hour, then surrendered. Humbert reported that he was trapped by 30,000 English. It was more likely 10,000 but still an over-whelming number.

After the engagement, the French troops were locked up in Long-ford, then taken to Tullamore to be put aboard a boat to be sent to Dublin on the Grand Canal, the Royal being then scarcely begun. In courtly fashion, their band was permitted to play the *Marseillaise* to the crowds on the bank. To many of the Irish captives a rougher justice was dispensed. The road north brings us to the Shannon at Roosky. We are in Leitrim now, a county often considered the wettest in Ireland, whatever the records show. It is an endemic, systemic, spreading wetness. Till well after the Second World War it was also the poorest county, many of its people dependant on wages sent back from emigrants to Britain or America. But it is beautiful too, and less interfered with than some counties. Sean O'Faolain said the beauty and the wetness suggested to him a lovely woman always weeping. Beyond Roosky, the pretty Loughs Bofin and Boderg can be seen on the left, divided by the promontory-demesne of ruinous **Derrycarne**, once seat of the Ormsby-Gores. A right turn at Dromod takes us the five miles to Mohill, a pleasant rather labyrinthine town with a bust of the blind harper Turlough O'Carolan in the centre. From here it is a short step south to Lough Rynn and Lough Rynn House, a much gabled, big-windowed Tudor Revival house of 1833, and until recently a home of the Clements family, who included in their number the now extinct line of earls of Leitrim, once owners – mostly absentee – of 90,000 acres spread through four counties. Among the charges levelled at the third earl, murdered near Milford, county Donegal in 1878, was that he exercised droit de seigneur on the prettier brides among his tenantry. The flatness of the demesne is relieved by the lake, extensive woodlands, and walled and terraced gardens.

At riverside **Drumsna** ('drumsnaw', with stress on the second syllable), seven miles west of Mohill, Trollope, on a visit as Post Office inspector in 1843, got matter for his first novel, *The Macdermots of Ballycloran*, a moving story of the decline of a prosperous Catholic family into tragic poverty. He was on a walk from the town, less than two miles along the Mohill road, when sight of a ruinous house sparked off the plot in his mind. Its whereabouts is described in detail in the novel's opening pages, and it is still there, scarcely changed. In the town an obelisk commemorates Robert Strawbridge, born here in 1732, who took Methodism to Maryland. A mile south of the town on the Roscommon side are remains of a huge defensive earthwork, in parts a hundred feet thick, known as the Doon of Drumsna, that cut off the same tongue of land as the navigable Jamestown Cut does now. Some argue that this prehistoric barrier was part of a longer structure designed to keep Ulstermen out of the south, or vice versa. The cut or canal was built in 1848 to avoid a stretch of Shannon rapids, and separated Drumsna from the main river traffic.

Carrick-on-Shannon is Leitrim's capital, incorporated by James I in 1603. It used to have a strongly Protestant reputation. It saw greater days in the early nineteenth century when water transport counted for much. Though the waterways were well advanced in the late eighteenth century, many of the massive locks and waterworks here and elsewhere in Ireland date from the early 1800s, when recurring famines meant cheap labour (the phrase 'famine relief' often enough made exploitation respectable). But before long railways and roads slowly killed these schemes. A hundred years later all the towns we have just been through were crumbling, sleepy and forgotten. Then Carrick, and soon the others, were saved by the growing demand for pleasure boating, of which it has become an important centre. To get the same density of boats as on the Norfolk broads, the Shannon would need nearly 200,000 boats. It has few over a hundredth of that number. The chance to sail, or cruise by motor launch from Carrick, winding down the Shannon, mooring near tiny villages with congenial pubs, hearing tale-telling boatmen and farmers talk and sing local ballads, drifting past castles and villas and hamlets into the rushy paradise of Carnadoe Waters, or on to the sea-like breadth of Lough Ree, is possibly the region's most appealing asset.

From Connemara or Sligo, visitors are not likely to come as far inland as Roscommon, so it is a county neglected by tourists. It lacks the drama of the country and coast to the west, but has quieter attractions, of which one is the quietness itself. We can make first for **Elphin**, south-west of Carrick, where Goldsmith's grandfather was curate and the poet himself, as well as Sir William Wilde, Oscar's father, went to school for a while – both at the diocesan school. Seat of a bishop since St Patrick consecrated it (though no longer), it has preserved little but associations to keep us, and we go on along the Castlerea road and turn left at a crossroads four miles later for **Rathcroghan**, a group of prehistoric ring-forts, megalithic tombs and other graves and monuments, spread over some two square miles of this desolate, windy plateau, on either side of the Tulsk-Ballanagare road. The heart of this complex, south of the Rathcroghan crossroads, is a mound on which it is said the inauguration of the kings of Connacht took place. Here too, it is supposed, was the royal palace, or whatever structure of wood, thatch and skins stood in for a palace. Here presumably the goddess-queen Medb, or Maeve, held court with King Aillil. In a bedroom quarrel (or whatever stood in for a bedroom) these two found that their possessions were exactly equal except for a magnificent white bull belonging to Aillil. Maeve, piqued, asked an Ulster prince for his equally outstanding bull, and offered to sleep with him in return. He refused. She went to war. The account of the *Cattle Raid of Cooley* (Carlingford) constitutes the greatest and most famous of ancient Irish sagas, culminating in the death of Ulster's hero Cuchulain. Near the hill is the Cave of the Cats, a natural fissure which, maybe two thousand years back, was given a dry-built masonry porch. This was no less than an entrance to the Otherworld (Ireland has several others), and home of the Morrigu, war goddess of the Celts. Her spirit went abroad in the form of a hooded crow, a bird that peasants used to regard with some awe. (It looks a little like a carrion crow, to which it is closely related, but with a judge's wig on.) From this cave, birds – and sometimes wild pigs – would issue to deal devastation on the land. North of it is a group of mounds, the king's necropolis, where King Conn – from whom Connacht took its name – is among the buried. One tall monolith marks the grave of the last pagan king of Ireland, Dáithi who, no slouch, conquered Scotland and invaded the Continent and was only brought low by a stroke of lightning on the Alps. Most remains probably belong to the first century AD. Unlike other such sites, where the scope, opulence, coverage and miscellaneous amenities of heritage centre displays can make the subject itself seem poor meat, there is at present little to guide or inform the visitor about the area, most of which is in private ownership.

Isolated points of interest lie some miles away in all directions. Outside **Frenchpark**, six miles north-west, is the ruin of an early eighteenth-century mansion, probably by Castle and once the seat of the Lords de Freyne. In 1846, with famine feelings running high, the owner was hanged in effigy opposite the main door. That sort of thing and much worse was happening throughout the country. Douglas Hyde was born at Castlerea but spent his childhood at the Protestant rectory and is buried in the churchyard. A brilliant Gaelic poet in his youth, whose songs were sung by peasants from Kerry to Donegal, he seemed to lose his poetic genius in Dublin, becoming an academic, the first professor of modern history at University College. More memorably, and with Eoin MacNeill, he founded in 1893 the Gaelic League, of which he was first president. It aimed at the revival of native Irish language and literature and 'the de-anglicising of Ireland'. By 1906 it had three thousand branches, and was a strong influence on later independence movements. In 1938 Hyde was recalled from retirement to be first president of Ireland, one of three Protestants to have held the post so far. The deconsecrated Church of Ireland church is devoted to displays and printed material about him.

Strokestown, ten miles east of Rathcroghan, is an imposing village built along what, at 147 feet, is claimed to be Ireland's broadest avenue, laid out in the 1820s and 1830s between rows of stone houses and inspired by Vienna's Ringstrasse. At the east end is the triple-arched entrance to **Strokestown Park**, the only one of twenty great private houses once standing in the county to survive to the present, home from the reign of Charles II of the Mahon family. Denis Mahon, inheriting the place from a lunatic uncle in 1845, just before the four worst years of famine, offered his tenants free passages to Canada. Soon after, it was put about that the vessels used were 'coffin ships' – and that one had foundered, drowning all on board. It was a lie, but the lie spread. From the altar, the priest said Mahon was 'worse than Cromwell' and one day soon after this Mahon was shot and killed nearby, in his open carriage. The family recovered. In 1914 the woman who had inherited the estate married the heir to Rockingham, bringing together holdings of 30,000 acres and 90,000 acres respectively. The village celebrated, on free liquor. But within nine weeks the new groom was killed in Flanders. And by 1979 the property was sold – to, it luckily happened, a local businessman who wanted house and demesne to tell a deeper story than such survivals usually do, an Irish rather than a limited Ascendancy story. The house is there: its 1694 central block, Castle's Palladian wings of about 1730, the 1819 refurbishment, magnificent details inside and out, the contents as the family are wrongly supposed to have had them, sprightly gardens with a whole spectrum of flower colours, recently given new layout and life. But indoors, near the backdrop of daily gentry life, is a full, moving, highly informative and often shockingly provocative exhibition of the causes, course and effects, in Ireland and elsewhere, of the great famine.

Beyond **Castlerea**, ten miles west of Rathcroghan, and among level fields and rich woods contained between branches of the River Suck is **Clonalis**, ancestral seat of The O'Conor Don, 'The' here signifying head of the family, and 'Don' (meaning brown-haired) one ancient branch of the family as distinct from 'Roe', meaning red-haired, another. The house is Victorian, a blend of Italianate and Norman Shaw's so-called Queen Anne styles. It was built between 1878 and 1880 to replace an early-eighteenth-century house in a situation thought too low and close to the river to be healthy. The interior of the present house, richly furnished, has a warm atmosphere of use, comfort, learning and cultivation. There is a fine library, and an important archive of historic documents, including a family tree tracing the O'Conors back to the old Gaelic kings of Connacht, among whom were several medieval High Kings of all Ireland. Claims are made that this is the oldest recorded family in Europe. The harp that belonged to Turlough O'Carolan is here, and outside is an interesting exhibition of nineteenth-century carriages and farm equipment. The royal coronation stone of Connacht, removed from Rathcroghan, stands beside the front door.

Five miles north-west is **Lough Glinn House**, former seat of the Dillons, once a family with branches and estates over most of these inland counties. They sprang from Henry de Leon, who was granted land here at the Conquest. Catholic, they supported James against Dutch William, fled to France after the Boyne, kept a family regiment in the French army, and were finally reconciled to Ireland by the French Revolution. They thereafter drew rents from about 90,000 acres in Roscommon and Mayo, and sold the lot in 1899. The house, burned in 1904 but rebuilt, is now a convent whose nuns make fine Irish cheeses. From Castlerea we keep to the Roscommon road, and turn left a mile and a half beyond Ballymoe for **Ballintober**, where stand the gatehouses and four polygonal towers of a magnificent castle built by the O'Conors Don at the end of the thirteenth century, probably after they had captured and held Roscommon's Anglo-Norman castle for a few years, and used it as model for their own. Ballintober was, with an interval following Cromwell's confiscation of it, mostly an O'Conor base till the eighteenth century.

The similar castle at **Roscommon**, the county capital, fifteen miles on, was built in 1269 by Robert de Ufford, English justiciar, or administrator: one of many designed by the English to control outlying lands that were literally beyond the Pale. Within a few years the O'Conors took and wrecked it. For four hundred years its ownership alternated between English and Irish. In 1652 it was dismantled by the Cromwellian General Reynolds, and later in the century burned and abandoned by the Irish after the battle of Aughrim. A fine twin-towered gatehouse stands on the east, a subsidiary one on the west, the shell of the state apartments inside, and there is a drum tower at each of the four corners.

At the south end of the town there is the ruin of a Dominican friary dating from 1453 (a few bits are from the first foundation two hundred years earlier). The church contains a fine carved O'Conor tomb. Not far away is a courthouse by Richard Morrison. The museum has a lot of local interest: photographs, cuttings, letters and bric-a-brac.

In the grounds of **Hollywell House**, three miles north of Roscommon is a well sacred to St Brigid. To the special qualities of its waters were attributed, in the middle of the eighteenth century, the beautiful complexions of two daughters of James Gunning of nearby Castle Coote, and by extension the marriages they achieved. Mary, reckoned the most beautiful woman at George II's court, married the Earl of Coventry, but died of consumption in 1760. Elizabeth married, in 1752, the sixth duke of Hamilton, by whom she mothered the future seventh and eighth dukes before marrying, after her first husband's death, the fifth duke of Argyll, who sired on her a further couple of dukes-to-be. 'Double-duchessed', Thackeray called her. Mary's tact was less evident than her beauty. Asked by the king what kind of ceremony would give her greatest pleasure she said, 'A coronation'.

On the road south from Roscommon to Athlone we get several glimpses of **Lough Ree**, a lake best explored by boat from Athlone, Lanesborough, Killaloe or Carrick. We can get down to it at several points, including the Rinndown Peninsula, two miles east of Lecarrow (asking permission at the farm where the road turns sharp right) near the colossal overgrown remains of a medieval town and royal castle, built in 1227 as an outpost for the conquest of Connacht, or at Hodson's Bay, by a smart black and white hotel with chalets, camping, boats, a golf course, and Ireland's main water-skiing centre.

The lake is fifteen miles long, seven wide at its widest, and covers thirty-nine square miles, the fourth largest in the country, its coastline an electroencephalogram of inlets and promontories, distinguished from each other by woods and ruins, reeds and rocks. It is popular for game and coarse fishing. Eels are caught in bulk and exported. Various kinds of duck winter here, particularly tufted duck in the north-east and wigeon and teal in the south-east. Boats should follow buoys carefully, as squalls rise suddenly and there is little protection on the banks and few landmarks when the lake begins to look more like a sea. Among the more interesting of the twenty-six islands is, rather north of central, **Inchcleraun** or Quaker Island with a group of ruined churches in its south-eastern corner, on the site of a sixth century monastery. This was the legendary home of the goddess Ennia, known for eating babies, and scene of the death of the ubiquitous Queen Maeve of Connacht, finally killed, while bathing, by a stone from the sling of Forbaid Prince of Ulster, standing a mile away on the mainland, in revenge for the death of Cuchulain. The island's name is from a Victorian Quaker who settled, pulled down a church to make his house, was cursed, and left soon after. On **Saints Island**, in Inny Bay, there used to be a convent of Poor Clares, built by the Dillon family, and there are still extensive ruins; **Inchbofin** has a few good Romanesque remains; the largest island, **Inchmore**, has a church ruin on the site of St Liobhan's monastery; and **Hare Island**, where St Ciaran founded a monastery before Clonmacnois, possesses a little church adapted as the Dillon mausoleum. Admiralty charts of 1839 (still unsurpassed) show more details of this south-east corner than any other part; for the surveyor had fallen in love with a local farmer's daughter and spent most of his time nearby.

Another legend – this one from folklore – has it that the islands here are for men only, women being ill-advised to step on them, and even female birds keeping clear – a theme repeated elsewhere. In fact every inch of the place has a story to tell. With more space to do so than here, Richard Hayward's *Where the River Shannon Flows* tells many of them, very well, in a book that any river traveller should obtain.

We pass on to **Athlone**, at the lough's southern tip, and virtually a border town between west and east Ireland, sitting as it does astride that geographical and political divider, the Shannon. The town, almost at Ireland's centre, is of importance as a road, rail, canal and river junction, as a big market and boat-building centre, a producer of wool and cotton articles, and the home of a government department. It used to be a crucial garrison centre in the days when it divided Leinster, the plain controllable east, from Connacht, the mountainous undisciplined west, and its military past has left its greatest legacy, the castle, though the fortifications added when invasion by Napoleon was feared have been dismantled. For a hundred years after the Conquest, castles came and went on this site till in 1210 John de Gray, Bishop of Norwich and English Justiciar, put up the present massive keep from where the English tried to control Connacht. In the wars of the 1640s it changed hands many times – and the town itself never fully recovered.

The castle had another day. After the Battle of the Boyne, it was attacked by ten thousand Williamites who failed to take it and a year later by twenty-one thousand. Fifteen hundred Jacobites defended it then. There followed the heaviest bombardment Ireland ever saw. Fifty tons of powder, six hundred bombs, twelve thousand cannon-balls and tons of stone were fired. The main body of Jacobites covered others who succeeded in breaking down the bridge, then plunged in and swam back. The Williamites, prevented from substituting a bridge of boats (they were set on fire) sent forces to cross by a deep ford below the town. This was a brave move but it might have failed had not St Ruth, James's commander, been celebrating what he too early assumed was victory. The Williamites crossed and won, and the Jacobites moved west to Aughrim for the last scene of the campaign.

The castle has been restored since, though its main towers were lowered to take cannons during the Napoleonic scare (there are remains of other cautious defences nearby). It contains a museum of local interest and association, and seems to stand almost outside Athlone, for this like other towns has its focus away from its river. The town proper has decent shops, good hotels, the house (in the Bawn) where John McCormack, the singer, was born in 1884, and another, dated 1628, where the Williamite General Ginkel lived (he became Earl of Athlone after the battle, but the title lapsed, and was later granted to a Prince of Wales), and the Catholic church of saints Peter and Paul, built in 1937, whose twin, green-capped bell-towers and massive dome make a conspicuous landmark. Most of the stained-glass windows were commissioned from Harry Clarke's studios.

About twelve miles by road to the south of Athlone, bordering the Shannon, are some of Ireland's finest ruins, those of the monastery of **Clonmacnois**. To most of us, Clonmacnois appeals more through its setting, history and magically peaceful atmosphere – many say spirituality – than antiquarian value. When St Ciaran founded it in 548, after his education at Clonard and foundation of the monastery on Hare island in Lough Ree, it may not have seemed so quiet. The river would have been a more important highway than it is now, and an esker – a ridge formed by shifting ice in the ice age – brought the old track known as the pilgrims' road from the east, round the north of the Mongan bog (considered wasteland then; valued now for the varied wildlife it nourishes). Ciaran was thirty-three when he came, and died seven months later. King Dermot (a relief at the foot of the Cross of the Scriptures shows him with Ciaran) gave the land, and the place became the chief monastery and place of learning in what was then Connacht. Then the Danes came. The fiercest of them (at least in the way monastic texts depict him), was Turgesius, who burned Clonmacnois in 844 while his wife recited pagan oracles from the high altar. Thirty-five raids and burnings are recorded between 834 and 1163, carried out by Vikings or Irish. Mostly Irish. Still it grew. When the Normans invaded in 1179 they found 105 houses to burn down, and around this time there were twelve churches. One, the Nun's church, some way from the main site, was rebuilt by the penitent, pathetic Dervorgilla, Ireland's Helen of Troy, whose infidelity to her husband brought the Anglo-Normans in. It was probably here that, around 1100, the scribe Maelmuirc wrote *The Book of the Dun Cow*, a collection of old tales and lore, and the oldest extant entirely Gaelic manuscript (said to have been written on the skin of St Ciaran's cow, for loss of which Ciaran's servant was barred burial in the cemetery). In 1135 lightning struck off the top half of O'Rourke's tower. A great storm of 1547 damaged many buildings, and agents of the English Dissolution completed the work in 1553 – 'not a bell, large or small, or an image, or an altar, or a book, or a gem, or even glass in a window, was left which was not carried away'. The see was merged with that of Meath, and later attempts at restoration were obliterated by Cromwell.

Of special interest in a brief walk round are the 600 early monumental grave slabs, entire or partial, many displayed in the visitors' centre. Also kept there for safety is the Cross of the Scriptures, with its finely carved biblical scenes. We pass Fergal O'Rourke's tenth-century, topless Round Tower and cross to the shell of the cathedral, with its good romanesque doorway. Here is buried Ireland's last High King, Rory O'Conor. The stone-vaulted sacristy was later used as a hedge-school where Catholic children were illicitly and secretly educated during the penal years.

The smaller churches that stand about the cathedral include the little church – Temple Kieran – built over the grave of Ciaran himself, and from a corner of which pilgrims still collect sacred earth; Temple Ri or Melaghlin to the north-east, probably the oldest of the churches, with fine east lancet-windows; the late seventeenth-century Temple Doolin, a family chapel of the Dowlings, with the south cross close by, on which stand out a crucifixion scene and other well preserved carvings. A little further away, to the north, but within the graveyard wall, is the still used Church of Ireland Temple Conor, endowed by O'Conors, some of whom were buried within. It was built in 1010 but restored more recently. Temple Finghin, north-east of it, has a small Round Tower as belfry. Beyond the gate in the east wall of the new cemetery stands the beautiful Nun's Church which Dervorgilla restored, but which was burned again a few years later – here, on the chancel arch, is a strangely revealing sheila-na-gig (if 'sheila-of-the-breasts' can be allowed to denote a figure displaying mainly thighs and face). Far over to the west of the cemetery are the sleepy ruins of John de Gray's castle of about 1220, on the site of a former abbot's house, commanding a fine view over flat bog to the Slieve Bloom.

This is the brief inventory. It cannot reproduce – and may even detract from – the beauty of the place, its once famous Catholic university, a glorious and unruly past, and its now quiet prominence beside a reedy bend of the Shannon, with hardly a sign of life apart from inquisitive outsiders like ourselves. This aura of energy spent and gone is characteristic of much of this stretch of the Shannon, between the two large lakes of Ree and Derg. Covering it by boat becomes monotonous, winding round bend after sedgy bend. But glimpsed from the land it evokes something seldom evident in modern, booming Ireland.

Six miles on the road south brings us to **Shannonbridge** ands its power-station, close to which the Tullamore-Ballinasloe road crosses the river by an attractive sixteen-arch bridge. On the west bank a small nineteenth-century fort recalls again the fear of Napoleonic invasion, and there are many more scattered defences. All this is dwarfed by the peat-fired Blackwater power-station, a little way along the eastward R357. Here the Clonmacnois and West Offaly Railway offers informative forty-five minute tours on its narrow-gauge railway. Keeping to this Leinster side of the river we move to **Clonony** where there is an impressive – though, inside, badly defaced – tower and fortified enclosure from the sixteenth century. In 1803 workers looking near the tower for stone for the canal found a lime-stone slab (still there) covering a double grave. The slab has an inscription: 'Hereunder Leys Elizabeth and Mary Bullyn ...' who were second cousins of Anne Boleyn, Henry VIII's wife, and cousins of Queen Elizabeth. Anne herself, who was granddaughter of a Butler and cousin of the Earl of Ossory, may possibly have been born here, possibly at the Butler manor at Carrick-on-Suir. Her family ties with the Butlers contributed to the king's favouring that family at the expense of the FitzGeralds.

The road south leads to **Shannon Harbour**, a subdued village dominated by the massive ruined Grand Canal Company Hotel. From here the canal goes to Dublin Harbour; also a further ten or so miles west to Ballinasloe. We have already touched at many points the Royal Canal whose recently cleared channel lies to the north, from near Longford to Dublin. The Grand has remained navigable, part of the complex of waterways on which some of Ireland's best holidays can be had. It seems an absurd extravagance that two canals, giant undertakings, should co-exist in a land seldom noted for prosperity, but the enthusiasm for building canals in George III's reign was like the acquisition of airlines by semi-bankrupt states in the late twentieth century. Canals could have provided cheap transport had the compa-nies building them not lavished money (£30,000 in the case of the Grand) on hotels that could never hope to be full, or had they provided consistent service within them. The Grand Canal (planned partly by John Smeaton, builder of the Forth and Clyde canals and the great third Eddystone lighthouse) was begun in the 1750s, opened bit by bit from 1783 to 1834, and linked the Shannon not only with the sea at Dublin but with the Barrow and so Waterford as well. The golden age was the first half of the nineteenth century, when hotels and warehouses sprang up and numerous branch lines were built. In

1837 a record 100,695 passengers were carried. Every house in what was then the townlet of Shannon Harbour offered lodging. In all, two million pounds were spent on the canal, and the investment might have paid had not railways come to supersede boats and the Famine to devastate the Irish economy. In the event the harbour villages were left to rot and slowly turn as picturesque as some are now. The canal was used for commercial transport till 1959 (and in the last war carried a quarter of a million tons of turf). In 1960 it was officially closed. But protest and initiative kept it alive for a growing amount of tourist and holiday traffic, and canal cruises run from Tullamore and elsewhere.

At **Banagher**, three miles south-west, Anthony Trollope, on his arrival in 1841 as Post Office surveyor, bought a hunter (and hunted ever after), and started writing novels – 'and since that time who has had a happier life than mine?' Late Georgian houses with bow-front windows testify to the wealth the town once derived (and is now deriving again) from river and canal traffic and from the strategic importance of its bridge, fortified at both ends to resist possible invasion from Napoleon's France. Cuba Court, on the town's east side, brought another link with the pantheon of English novelists. Built about 1730, possibly by Edward Lovett Pearce, it was the home in the nineteenth century of the young Arthur Bell Nicholls; his uncle was a master at the school it then contained. Later, as curate to Patrick Brontë, Nicholls proposed – 'trembling, stirred and overcome' – to Charlotte Brontë, married her in 1854, brought her here for the honeymoon, and made her happy for the last year of her life. Much of his 50-year widowerhood was spent at Hill House here. After the Second World War Cuba Court, described by Maurice Craig as 'perhaps the most splendidly masculine house in the whole country', had its roof removed (to save rates), was allowed to fall into irretrievable ruin and then, inevitably, demolished. Recent development of a marina has put Banagher firmly back on the map. Cloghan Castle, three miles southwest, is well maintained round the core of a medieval keep, stronghold of the local O'Madden sept.

Birr, ten miles away, is one of Ireland's loveliest towns. But since a line between routes must be drawn we leave it for another tour to return, after a westward loop, to Athlone and thence Dublin. We cross the river by the Eyrecourt road bridge, turn right a mile later, and come to **Clonfert** to see the diminutive Church of Ireland cathedral of St Brendan the Navigator, where that roving saint and precursor of Columbus is buried. Rebuilt in 1167 by Conor O'Kelly, the church still displays the tall pedimented west door of that time – perhaps the high point of Irish Romanesque – with its six orders of arches, its fantasy of chevron arches, leaves, animal and human heads, and the odd inward slope of the jambs. Inside, the skeleton of the original building survives, and the fine east window, but with much addition and nineteenth-century restoration. Behind the cathedral is a yew walk and the derelict seventeenth-century bishop's palace, gutted by fire in 1954 when owned by Sir Oswald Mosley. From the grounds there is a glimpse of the westernmost stretch of the canal, leading to Ballinasloe. Following it by road we come after five miles to **Laurencetown**. There is no trace of Belview House in the tousled demesne a mile west of the village, but a handsome triumphal arch, with a sphinx on either side of the pediment, still stands. It was built in 1783 to commemorate the Volunteers' convention of the previous year. There are also two decorative Gothic eyecatchers, built simply to enhance the view.

On the right of the T31, half way between Laurencetown and Balli-nasloe, are the ruins of St Mary's Augustinian abbey of Clontuskert, one of several founded, in this case on the site of a previous monas-tery, by Turlough O'Conor, eleventh-century king of Connacht. It attracted great wealth and was known for its riches in the thirteenth century, its corruption in the fourteenth, a fire and rebuilding in the fifteenth, including construction of the great west door in 1471, evic-tion of the friars in the sixteenth, at the dissolution, their brief return and Cromwell's destruction in the seventeenth and a limited refur-bishment in the twentieth. There is fine carving – of saints, animals, a mermaid with a mirror – round the doorway of 1471.

Attractive **Ballinasloe**, four miles on, has a Catholic church of 1858 partly designed by J.J. McCarthy and Pugin, containing good murals, stained glass, carving and other artifacts from the succeeding hundred years. The fine mental hospital was built in 1838 to Francis Johnston's designs. The gate-lodge is an unworthy modern addition. Some good eighteenth-century houses remain, and every October the town is the setting for Ireland's largest livestock fair, which used also to be the largest horse-fair in Europe. Garbally Court, to the west, is a pleasant late Georgian house, now a school, and once the seat of the Trench family, Earls of Clancarty, who came here in 1632. There is an odd fluted obelisk in the grounds.

We saw the first aftermath of the Boyne at Athlone. **Aughrim**, four miles south-west of Ballinasloe, was the scene of the last but one act in the war. The still considerable Jacobite forces under General St

Ruth lined almost two miles of the raised ground running south-east of the village. On 12 July 1691, Ginkel and the Williamite forces advanced against them and were beaten back several times. Irish hopes were high, when a cannonball struck and killed St Ruth on the slopes of Aughrim Hill. Meanwhile troops in the castle (just north of the village) discovered that large supplies of ammunition did not fit their muskets. Rout followed, and thousands of Irish lay dead. The remainder, under Patrick Sarsfield, moved on in tatters to Limerick. St Ruth's body was probably buried at Kilconnell Friary, four miles north-west, well worth seeing on its own account. The ruins, north of the village street, comprise an elegant tower, a nave, choir and tran-sept with magnificent window tracery, a charming little arcaded cloister, forty-eight feet square, and some graves and memorials including the best Flamboyant tomb in Ireland, and the tomb of the seventh Baron Trimleston, a Catholic aristocrat who 'being trans-planted into Conaght with others by order of the usurper Cromwell, dyed at Moinivae, 1667'. For the baron and innumerable others, 'to Hell or Connacht' must have rung true.

From here to the west the country grows bleak and monotonous, better for sheep than visitors. We return through Ballinasloe to Athlone, and thence by a necessarily zigzag route to Dublin again, delaying entry to the far west for a different and more scenic approach. From Athlone there is a good direct road for Dublin, but we take the Ballymahon road north-east and again skirt Lough Ree. This is Leinster again, and again there are grand houses or their wrecks at every turn. Moydrum Castle, off our way and two miles along the first road to the right, is the romantic ruin of a house designed by Morrison, burned like so many others in 1920. To the right, before we enter **Glassan**, is Waterston House, the work of Richard Castle, now a ruin but with an attractive octagonal-spired dovecote and hermitage in the grounds. Glassan itself begins what is called, with some exag-geration, Goldsmith country. Turning right in the middle of the village, and left a mile on, we arrive at the Pinnacle, one of several claimed centres of Ireland. There is a hill of 337 feet and an obelisk on top, put there in 1769, from which the owner could signal to another of his estates thirty miles away. How anyone can calculate the centre of such an anarchic shape as Ireland's is hard to see, and there are at least three alternative claims – for Birr, the Hill of Uisneach, and an islet in the south-west corner of Lough Ree.

The lane continues to the hamlet of Kilkenny West, Goldsmith's father's parish, and the left fork a quarter of a mile later leads to

Lissoy, or 'Auburn' or 'the Deserted Village' (ostensibly an English village, but with Irish links, though Macaulay wrote correctly that Goldsmith 'had assuredly never seen in his native island such a rural paradise, such a seat of plenty, content and tranquillity, as his Auburn'). The Goldsmiths' ruined house is one of the few authenticated remains in an area subject to promotional inflation. Certainly the poet spent his childhood hereabouts. Born in 1728 near Pallas, east of Ballymahon, he was at schools at Kilkenny West, Elphin, Lissoy, Edgeworthstown (where he heard Carolan the last bard) and Athlone; then at Trinity, Dublin, for four years, which he ran away from but returned to. His family had saved to send this maverick to America, and he is said to have spent the money on the way to Cork harbour. From then on his career lay in Edinburgh, studying medicine, and London, where his fame and friendships were always accompanied by the poverty brought on by rash generosity. It was from London he wrote, 'I sit and sigh for Lissoy fireside and "Johnny Armstrong's Last Goodnight" from Peggy Golden ...' The Three Jolly Pigeons just beyond Lissoy on the right has no material connection with the inn in *She Stoops to Conquer*.

Ballymahon is a pleasant village with a wide main street and modest hotel, a good base for Lough Ree's east side, and the nearest we come to the peninsula of Saints Island. There are some good houses in the district: Georgian Newcastle two miles east, now a hotel, and Castlecor two miles west with its extraordinary ground-plan – an octagonal central block with four projecting wings and a rectangular block in front, copy perhaps of some Baroque Italian model. It is a convent now. We follow the Mullingar road, from which there are two possible diversions. One, to the left beyond Newcastle, leads to Abbeyshrule, beautifully placed at the crossing of the river Inny by the Royal Canal, where there are ivy-covered remains of the 1150 Cistercian abbey, daughter foundation of Mellifont. The second, five miles later, leads right to the **Hill of Uisneach** (pronounced 'ushna'), 602 feet high, from the top of which twenty of Ireland's thirty-two counties are supposedly visible on an exceptionally fine day. Mentioned by Ptolemy as the city of Laberos, and by Giraldus Cambrensis as *umbilicus Hiberniae* or navel of Ireland, this hill, spread with antiquities, is the rival in its place of Tara, Cashel, Rathcroghan and Navan Fort, and as rich in antique association. The Firbolgs, pre-Gaelic invaders, are said to have divided the country into four provinces which met here. In the first century AD Tuathal, High King of the Gaelic race which had conquered the Firbolgs, took an area from each province to create a fifth, Meath (the middle or neck). This centred on an enormous thirty-ton rock, the Cat Stone, on the hill's south-west slope.

The rock, under which the Milesian princess Eriu (who gave her name to Eire) is buried, and its many earthworks, pillar stones and souterrains, bespeak its importance at that time. It was a royal centre, of special significance at Beltane, the May Day festival. St Patrick found time to build a church here, and in 984 Brian Boru occupied the hill to challenge and force terms on the High King, who had invaded his own territory.

Perhaps nothing is as remarkable as the claim that from here came the circle of stones at Stonehenge. Geologists deny it, saying Stonehenge is of rock from Prescelly mountain in Wales. Most other scholars deny it, too, these days. But Geoffrey of Monmouth and after him Giraldus Cambrensis, both of them twelfth century, wrote about it in some detail. According to Geoffrey, African giants originally brought the stones to Ireland and set them up at Killarus, usually thought to be the hill of Uisneach, which is close to a village called Killare. Nobody would ever have moved them again had not Merlin, when the British King Aurelius wanted some suitable setting for his coronation, obligingly taken them to Wiltshire with a team of fifteen thousand soldiers. There they remained in spite of massive Irish resistance. Few would seriously argue for the truth of the tale. But judging by other episodes in Geoffrey's *History*, it is possible that some inscrutable truth lies beneath it.

Mullingar is now nine miles off. From there we retrace our route back to Dublin, or switch to the next route at Innfield.

4

North Kildare, Laois and Offaly

A BOG IS an area from which, for any of several reasons, water has found it difficult to escape. The land becomes waterlogged. Plants able to grow on it do not, when they die, decompose in the normal way. The dark wetness of their remains excludes air, and so oxygen. Without oxygen life is impossible for the myriad bacteria and other life-forms which normally, by feeding on dead remains, do the work of decomposing. Thus plants which grow on the surface of bogs cannot take much nourishment from the dead matter below them. It is unprocessed and indigestible. They must find other food sources. Some make do on almost nothing. Some take what they need from water itself. Sphagnum mosses have masses of fine capillaries which are able to draw rainwater in through all their length and remove vital minerals from it. Other plants – sundews, butterworts, bladderwort – trap and slowly crush insects and draw in their life juices. Each year's dead plants lie in the water, to be covered and crushed by the dead plants of succeeding years, until the packed mass of sodden plant matter – now of a consistency somewhere between woody stems and soil – forms a layer ten, twenty or more feet thick. Sometimes at the base there are numerous stumps and logs, known as bog oak (even though they may be pine); relics of the trees that covered the land before ice movements or clearance by humans began the development of peat. Bog occasionally yields other preserved trophies: caches of stored butter, ancient boats, bodies of animals and humans.

There are two main categories of bog. Blanket bog covers hundreds of hills and the gentler mountain slopes. A paste of iron and other minerals, leached out of soil and spread by rainwater, has blocked up any natural pores in the underlying rock. Where there were dips, bog formation began, creating more dips, more water-traps, more bog. Though many plants, birds and insects have adapted to these conditions, nutriments are scarce – there is so little to replenish them – and survival is often by a hairsbreadth. The commonest plants are rough grasses and sedges. Raised bogs occur on flatter lands, most of them in the interior. The water and vegetation they form on, often fenland, is richer than on the mountainsides, though after a few generations the accumulation of dead matter makes it impossible for the roots of new plants to reach down to these nourishing sources. From that point on, water-fed sphagnum mosses tend to predominate, turning the ground acid and gradually developing into vast broad domes of compacted peat, covering what may be lakes or fenland and rising in parts as high as forty feet. Unlike the blanket bog of mountains, they may when drained make good and fertile farmland.

The bog has always had its uses, providing almost all the fuel burned in Irish hearths. In the past the extraction of peat (called turf by the Irish) was done by each family for their own use and had little effect on the landscape. In the eighteenth and early nineteenth centuries, with population and wealth growing rapidly, the vast extent of unproductive bogs – over a seventh of the country's area – came to seem like a provocation and a challenge. There were plans to turn them into bamboo plantations or vineyards. The Duke of Wellington vexed his mind over the matter but without result. It was left to the twentieth century to realise a valuable resource in a characteristically twentieth century way. In large parts, by means of juggernaut machinery, huge grants from government and huger from Europe, it stripped the boglands bare.

Thus the **Bog of Allen**, an ill-defined area spanning parts of Kildare, Meath and Offaly, is not what it used to be. During the second half of the twentieth century the state's peat board, or Bord na Mona, reduced – as it was set up to do – bogland in many parts to a remnant, giving huge benefits in the process to the Irish economy, in the form of peat sods and briquettes for burning, fuel for several power stations, and a large tonnage of garden peat for export. It long ago became clear, however, that the price of this was the ruination of a precious natural habitat little valued in the past, and a drastic reduction in the populations of, to name a handful, sphagnum mosses, bilberry, cranberry, bog asphodel, bog myrtle, bog bean, bog cotton, the carnivorous plants, many grasses, reeds, sedges, rushes and lichens and huge carpets of heathers and ling whose numberless flowers – wherever there existed some simple natural drainage – coloured miles of late summer countryside with a characteristic purple wash. Insects and birds, in a profusion often unseen in the past, followed. A crisis was registered, and a new council brought into

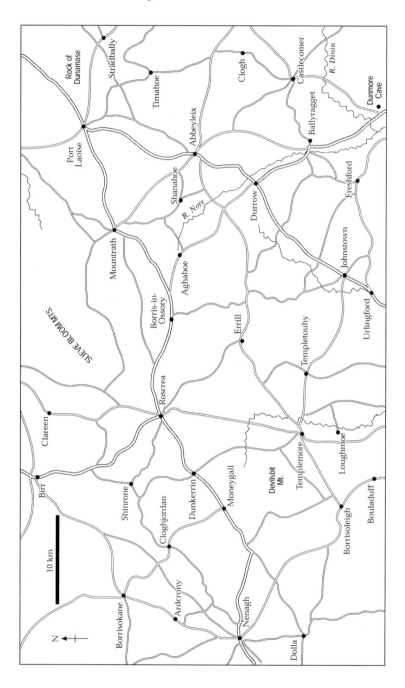

being, set the target of preserving four per cent of Ireland's old boglands. In this modest aim it is probably succeeding. Meanwhile, as we tour, we see large areas of bog – much of it still scheduled for mechanical harvesting – and a great deal of flat lowland scraped bare, though nothing stays bare for long and much that was bog is now farmland, or being developed into it. There is also the occasional giant power-station like Ferbane or Allenwood, and the Peatland Information Centre at nearby Lullymore.

Our present route lies through the north of the Bog of Allen. We have come from Dublin to Innfield on the N4, then turned off left on to the R402. **Carbury Hill**, 470 feet high, is about eight miles on, to the right of the road. It has some prehistoric mounds, the motte of a thirteenth century De Bermingham castle and the ruins of the fortified manor house which succeeded it in the reign of James I. This was built by the Anglo-Norman Colley family. In 1728 Richard Colley was adopted as heir by his sonless cousin Garret Wellesley, owner of Dangan in county Meath, and changed his name to the simpler Wesley. He later became Baron Mornington, his son was raised up the scale to Earl of Mornington, and his grandson was the Duke of Wellington. In his time the name was changed back to Wellesley. On the left of the road is Newbury Hall, a good redbrick house with side pavilions, built in 1760, probably to the plans of Nathaniel Clements.

Being on the outward edge of the early Pale, this area is thick with castles, and there are many in the vicinity of **Edenderry**, a pleasant Georgian town five miles on. The old castle and demesne of the Blundells lie just to the south, and the Grand Canal, on which the town's prosperity was once based, south of that. Two miles west of the town are the remains, fortified in the sixteenth century, of the Franciscan priory of Monasteroris, founded in 1325, again by a De Bermingham. The thick walls are heavily overgrown and there are remains of an early dovecote – a means, in those days, whereby sequestered communities could alter the menu.

Halfway to Tullamore we come to **Daingean**, once a county capital, one which recalls a disappointing phase of Irish history. Native expectations were high when Mary Tudor succeeded her brother Edward VI, restored Catholicism, and absolved some Irish Catholics who had been forced to flee. But her reign showed that religion was no more than a cloak for a persistent English policy of conquest. Married to Philip II of Spain, Mary took her father's policy even further, confiscated two thirds of Irish land in counties Offaly and Laois (pronounced 'leash') and began the plantations which

Elizabeth successfully continued. In honour of which the two counties were renamed King's and Queen's counties (which they remained till independence) with capitals at Philipstown (now Daingean) and Maryborough (now Port Laoise). Philipstown failed to establish itself. It picked up a castle and a court-house, disfigured since but attributed to Gandon, but was superseded as county seat in 1833 by Tullamore.

We can drive on direct to Tullamore, or go by a circular route north of the main road. This takes us to **Tyrrellspass**, a handsome village with a crescent of houses round the green, a spired church with a sumptuous Belvedere monument of 1814 by John Bacon, and at the west end the tower of a Tyrrel Castle. In 1597, in the middle years of the Elizabethan conquest of Ireland, the English met one of a series of reverses when their force of a thousand men, making for a rendezvous with other detachments in the north, was ambushed and cut to pieces by Piers Lacy and a force of Old English Catholics at this pass through bogland. Five miles west is Kilbeggan, terminus of the last completed branch line of the Grand Canal (1834), and home to an eighteenth-century distillery which still operates and can be visited.

On the right, half way to Tullamore on the N52, we pass the ruins of **Durrow Abbey**, a place abundant with stories but short on tangible remains – a beautifully elaborate tenth-century High Cross, a well, various tombstones, and a derelict Protestant church with magnificent west doorway. St Columba of Iona, who should – had not the Scots a predilection for apostles – have been their country's patron saint, founded Durrow in 551, and Bede mentions it – 'a noble monastery in Ireland known in the Scots (Irish) language as Dearmach, the Field of Oaks, because of the oak forest in which it stands'. Here, perhaps, the *Book of Durrow*, now in the library of Trinity College, Dublin, was written around AD 700, the subdued masterpiece of the first phase of Celtic illumination; and here Donal, High King of Ireland, was buried in 758. More dramatically, it saw the death of the dynamic Hugh de Lacy whom we met more than once in the Boyne region. In 1186 he came to build a castle, an outpost of the powerful feudal state he had built up in the centre of the country. To obtain the stone, he pulled down the church – even in settled times a tactless move for a Norman among Irishmen – and as he bent to the work an enraged young man, O'Meey, struck off his head at a blow. Much of his binding of the Pale for the Norman cause was undone, in the instant. De Lacy's motte is still to be seen.

Tullamore, Offaly's county town, is a big – for the area – and busy town with proliferating shops and ugly suburbs. A market town, and centre for distilling and spinning, it nowadays seems to ignore, as it can afford to, the hand that once fed it – the Grand Canal running along its north side (though there are operators of boat-cruise holidays here). Tullamore's nineteenth-century prosperity owed much to the time when it was the canal's terminus and a great distributing centre. Before that it had a short, sorry story. It was planned and built at the initiative of the Bury family of Limerick, Earls of Charleville, in the mid-eighteenth century. In 1790 a great balloon was sent up from Charleville (see below) and, instead of floating over, collapsed amid the new town's buildings which were destroyed (the pub, some say by divine intervention, excepted) in the explosion that followed. Rebuilding started soon and the town's more interesting features – some Regency houses and St Catherine's Church by Francis Johnston half a mile to the east, date from the period. **Charleville Forest**, two miles south-west, is called by Mark Bence-Jones 'the finest and most spectacular early nineteenth century castle in Ireland'. Francis Johnston's Gothic masterpiece, built between 1800 and 1812, packing a dense story-book panoply of towers, parapets and crenellations, it was built for Charles Bury, Earl of Charleville, a genial dilettante who caused a stir by translating Voltaire's mock-heroic and scabrous poem on Joan of Arc, *La Pucelle*, into English. Lately owned, like Belvedere to the north, by Colonel Howard Bury, then neglected for a few years, it is now occupied, and restored in essentials. Both outside and inside preserve a rich concentration of Gothic features – the fireplace in the dining-room is modelled on the west door at Oxford's Magdalen College Chapel, and the gallery ceiling is a replica of the fan-vaulting at Horace Walpole's Strawberry Hill. The demesne includes very fine woods.

Gothic had flourished in Ireland for a long time before Francis Johnston, one of its main Irish practitioners (though he was a master of Palladian classicism as well), designed his remarkable 'pasteboard Gothic' castles in the early 1800s: Slane, Killeen, Glenmore, Pakenham, Charleville and others. In both England and Ireland the strengthened taste for Gothic at this time owed much to the Ossianic Revival and other literary influences. Moreover, the need to grow corn for England during the Napoleonic blockade brought Ireland much of the money that made the new wave of building possible.

South of Tullamore rise the **Slieve Bloom** mountains, an attractive bulge in the prevailing midland flatness, measuring about twelve miles north to south and fourteen west to east, possessing the greatest area of mountain bog in the whole country – now protected by law against further inroads – as well as large capes of conifer plantation on rather too many of its lower slopes. From the highest point, many-masted Arderin, 1,734 feet, you can on a fine day see fifteen counties (they say), but the most attractive features are some of the glens, with their sprightly streams and overhangs of old oaks and birch trees. Three of Ireland's principal rivers – Suir, Barrow and Nore – rise here, but the Silver River above Cadnamstown, Glendine on the south of the ridge and Glenbarrow on the east are perhaps the best attractions of the range. There is a twenty-mile waymarked walk following a partial circuit of the hills. There are chances of seeing a wide variety of plants, though few rarities have been recorded. Over eighty species of bird, from a number of predators down to the tiny goldcrest, are seen; and badger, fox, fallow deer and the rare pine marten are present.

For a circuit of the mountains we can take the N80 out of Tullamore to **Mountmellick**, a once prosperous Quaker settlement, preserving some good Georgian houses. It is tucked into a bend in the river Owenass, a tributary of the young Barrow which begins its journey high above us among the Cones – peaks which dominate this eastern side of the range. Three miles west, at Rosenallis, another Quaker foundation, is a seventeenth-century Quaker cemetery. The ruins of mid-nineteenth-century Brittas House lie to the south-west of the village, but we can take the southerly, mountain road to cross the range; starting with the ascent beside the Gorragh river to the Cut, with a slower drop on the far side bringing us to the neighourhood of **Roundwood House**, a delectable mid-eighteenth-century Palladian villa with a rare Chinese fretwork balcony over the hall. Francis Bindon designed it. In 1970 the Irish Georgian Society bought it, to save it from neglect and rotting. It is run now as a thoroughly congenial and comfortable guesthouse. From here the westward road passes Cardtown House and a steep track up to the Glendine Gap and the Slieve Bloom's highest peak, Arderin. For walks in these parts good large-scale maps are indispensible. We can continue along Moll Joy's Hill (misnamed from a certain Poll Joyce, who kept a shebeen hereabouts) through Nealstown and Boheraphuca and subsequent left and right turns, to glimpse Leap Castle, an impressive ruined fifteenth-century keep of the local O'Carrolls, much altered later and finally blown up during the civil war in 1922. It preserves macabre memories of earlier times – a dungeon was found full of bones a hundred years ago – and sightings of a ghoulish sheep-sized greyish animal with black holes for eyes and a transparent lower half were often reported. It was one of the houses claimed to be Ireland's most haunted. Six miles north, on the R421, is Kinnitty, with the Tudor-revival Castle Bernard, now a forestry property, in its afforested demesne just beyond. The road we have been on, and its continuation through Cadamstown back to Clonaslee, and the Mountrath road from Kinnitty up the Camcor river, and several other ways in this sector of the mountains, offer views of fine scenery. But we now drive ten miles west from Kinnitty to the ancient and remarkable town of Birr.

The centre of **Birr** is Emmet – formerly Duke's – Square. In the middle is a tall Doric column with no statue on top. From 1747 it bore the figure of the Duke of Cumberland, who more justly earned the name of 'Butcher' than the £25,000 a year awarded him after Culloden. Erection of the statue, signifying the final, ruthless destruction of an ancient Gaelic clan system, in what is claimed the very centre of Ireland (a stone known as the *Umbilicus Hiberniae*, or Ireland's navel, is to be seen in the grounds of the little Greek temple which serves as a heritage centre) displayed a certain want of tact. In the twenties of the last century, the statue was 'found unsafe', and removed, taking with it the one sore spot in a small town of unmatched charm, lovely buildings, and an attractive asymmetry.

Birr, founded by St Brendan (of Birr, as opposed to the sailor saint of Clonfert) suffered from customary Danish ravages (we are only ten miles from the Shannon, which was their approach), then rose to importance as an Anglo-Norman outpost. This importance is shown by the claim that, when plague struck the place in 1447, seven hundred clerics died of it. The local Irish royal family was O'Carroll, 'a hospitable, fierce, yellow-haired race', one of whom fought with Brian Boru at Clontarf. Their hospitality was sorely tried by the English, who expropriated their lands, first under Henry II and again in the Marian plantations of Laois and Offaly.

Plantation – the policy of setting up enclaves of English among the unruly Irish – got fresh impetus after the Battle of Kinsale (1601) and the Flight of the Earls into exile. In 1620 a thousand acres of Birr were allotted to Sir Laurence Parsons, who with his brother William had arrived in Ireland in 1590 and risen to choice status as receiver-general of crown lands. He built or rebuilt the castle in the 1620s. His family has remained ever since. They were on Parliament's side in the Civil War, and on William's in the Revolution.

This pattern of adherence caused them to lose their castle more than once and brought a charge of high treason under James II, but they ended the century in full possession of their heads and acres. Laurence did well by the town. Among other things he promoted the manufacture of window and table glass by a Huguenot family at Clonoghill Castle, whose ruins are at Syngefield on the Kinnitty Road. Little survives from the four years' (1623–26) operation of the factory, and what does is highly valued. Parsons was also a martinet: anyone lighting a domestic fire in anything but a stone fireplace was banished by his command, and women serving beer got three days in the stocks.

It was another Sir Laurence Parsons (later second earl of Rosse) who despite his ancestor's precautions planned the castle's rebuilding after a fire in 1832. But the most famous of the family was the third earl, William Parsons (1800–67). Leaving Oxford with a mathematical first he became MP for King's County (now Offaly) before inheriting his father's title in 1841. Having already improved the techniques of casting reflectors for telescopes he constructed his own – in 1843, at the sixth attempt – of an alloy of copper and tin. Weighing four tons, it remained the world's largest for seventy-five years. With it he revealed that some nebulae of stars have a spiral structure rather like Catherine wheels. A whorl of lime trees was planted in 1995 to commemorate this disclosure. The telescope is now in the Science Museum in London, with a working model to scale. The fourth earl continued his father's observations though he moved away from the giant telescope, and another son, Sir Charles Parsons, developed the steam turbine that made ships like *Dreadnought* and *Mauretania* faster than all competitors.

The walls and cylinder – fifty-six feet long – of the telescope stand in the centre of **Birr Castle's** park. (The observer would look into the side of the tube near its upper end.) The grounds themselves (open to the public) are perhaps the best kept in Ireland, with magnificent trees, especially magnolias and maples, shrubs and two century-old box hedges, reputedly the tallest in the world at thirty-four feet. They benefit from the family's sponsorship of several nineteenth-century plant-finding expeditions. The late sixth earl, a champion of tree conservation, laid out many of the flowerbeds, making excellent use of the waterfalls from the Little Brosna River that flows through the estate. Lack of space prevents the opening of the castle (and a good private collection of pictures) to visitors, but it makes an impressive sight outside. Rebuilt in Gothic style with castellated front in the early nineteenth century, it incorporates a small part of the eighteenth-century castle.

Birr's charm lies in its unity, not – apart from the castle – in highlights. Almost the whole of it was laid out in the eighteenth and early nineteenth centuries, a reminder, as with many Irish towns, of the first great age of new-town planning. Opposite the castle gates, Oxmantown Mall, with uneven, Georgian houses on the left and a line of chestnuts on the right, leads to the delightful Church of Ireland St Brendan's Church. At the end, Emmet Street, with doorway fanlights to match the best of Dublin, leads to Emmet Square, in which, besides the column already referred to, is the tourist office, in an upper room of which Melba sang; and Dooley's Hotel, once burned down by tippling guests from the Galway Hunt, who were thereafter known as the 'Blazers'. John's Place, with a monument to the third earl and John's Mall lead off to the left, and from the Place a right turn runs up to St Brendan's Roman Catholic Church, with its fine tower and 124-foot spire designed by Bernard Mullen in 1817. Next door is a little-known work by Pugin, the Convent of Mercy.

South of the castle, the road leads south-west to Borrisokane, a small town of under a thousand inhabitants, then on again to Nenagh. The route runs close to Lough Derg, a beautiful widening of the Shannon, which is described elsewhere. To the south of Nenagh are the Silvermines Mountains, where silver, zinc and lead are mined, and behind them the Slieve Felim. **Nenagh** is the handsome county town of the north of Tipperary, which is divided into two ridings for administration. It is dominated by the cylindrical keep of a Butler castle built soon after the Anglo-Norman invasion (the Butlers were granted Ormond, an area which corresponds roughly with county Tipperary). Though a Bishop of Killaloe castellated it 'after the manner of Windsor' around 1860, it remains the finest of its kind in Ireland. There are also a good nineteenth-century courthouse and town hall, and the remains of a friary of 1250, while the old gaol building houses the 'heritage centre' and the old governor's house a museum. At this time enmity between Irish and English was reflected in the Franciscan order, and Nenagh Friary came to lead the Irish camp. It was destroyed, naturally, by the Cromwellians.

The road to Thurles takes us over the pass between the Devil's Bit Mountain and the Slieve Felim. The former's name is owed to a story that the Devil, as he flew south over Ireland, furious that the country was yielding him no souls (a Promised Race complex must be observed in any study of the Irish) took a bite out of a mountain –

there is a remarkable cleft – and dropped it on the plain in front of him. The expectoration is the Rock of Cashel. Unfortunately Cashel is limestone, the other old red sandstone.

By turning right three miles after Borrisoleigh and keeping straight on for eight miles we can visit **Holy Cross Abbey** before entering Thurles and beginning the return journey to Dublin. Castle keeps and ruined abbeys of various kinds are such a familiar sight in Ireland that those of exceptional interest – Holy Cross, Mellifont, Jerpoint and others – are in danger of being passed by. Holy Cross, on the banks of the Suir among trees and meadows, is one of the country's best preserved, and certainly among its most beautiful remains. Founded in 1168, it passed soon under the wing of the Cistercians and grew grand and prosperous. Its swift rise was due in part – and its name entirely – to two pieces of the True Cross, given by Pope Pascal II to the founder's father. Such fragments benefitted the churches that contained them, as lions do Longleat. Holy Cross grew rich as a place of pilgrimage and in the fifteenth century the buildings were remodelled. Even after the Dissolution it was kept intact with Butler protection. It has a typical Cistercian form (cruciform shape, aisled nave, low central tower and an east chapel in each transept). Its treasures include beautiful fifteenth-century sedilia or stone seats, in the presbytery or east end; the east window with its tracery network; some scattered carvings, including a delightful owl, on nave capitals and walls (owls often symbolised evil, as preferring dark to light); a mural painting in the north transept; and a magnificently carved stone shrine, which may have been made to contain the Cross fragments, in the south transept. In 1977 a substantial and harmonious restoration of the abbey was completed, including a re-roofing of the nave for use as a parish church.

Thurles (pronounced Thur-lez), three miles north-east, is a marketing centre on the Suir in the midst of the rich farmlands of north Tipperary. It also manufactures sugar, the beet for which is being developed as another bog enterprise. A Butler town, it has a ruined tower at each end of its broad main street, one of which guards the river bridge. Beyond the east tower is the gleaming Roman Catholic Cathedral, built by J.J. McCarthy around 1870, with a façade on the model of that at Pisa. Inside, the tabernacle was originally designed in the early 1600s for the Gesu, Rome's gaudiest church. At Hayes's Commercial Hotel in Liberty Square, the GAA, or Gaelic Athletic Association, was founded in 1884 by Michael Cusack (1847–1906) – 'Citizen Cusack' he liked to be called – a teacher grown rich from the proceeds of his crammer college in Dublin. He was quickly ousted by more political, nationalistic interests. For most of its existence it barred from membership anyone who so much as watched 'imported games' (English, that is to say). But its strengthening effect on Irish pride and nationalism is incalculable.

Two miles north of Thurles and among fine woods is the grand moated folly of **Brittas Castle**, planned by W.V. Morrison to be a replica of Roscommon castle, or something on the same scale, but aborted by a fatal fall of stone on the head of the nineteenth-century owner, Mr Langley. Though it is private, permission to view may be given by the owner, and the barbican tower, moat and unfinished walls, and a park rich in trees are well worth seeing. The demesne is on the right of the road to Templemore. Nearly four miles further on, a road right leads a mile or so to **Loughmoe Court**, vast ruin of a seventeenth-century fortified mansion, once seat of the Purcells and now a national monument. **Templemore** is a small town described by George Borrow, whose father was stationed here in 1816, in *Lavengro*. The enormous and lovely park, former demesne of the Carden family, has become a town park, with lake, sports grounds and good walks among the trees. Carden's Folly is a tower four miles west, in what was the demesne of ruined Barnane Castle, just south of the summit of Devil's Bit. This was home of John Carden, squire, JP and deputy lord lieutenant, who in 1854 made a farcical attempt to abduct one Eleanor Arbuthnot, who had scorned his advances, from her home, Rathronan, near Clonmel. He got two years in gaol. The folly gives magnificent views over Offaly and the Suir Valley. From Templemore we take the road north and after a straight drive of eleven miles, with the Devil's Bit to the left and Slieve Bloom straight ahead, arrive at **Roscrea**, a town of ancient and modern importance, and a good alternative base for exploring the Slieve Bloom.

A fortress at Roscrea, guarding the pass between steep mountain ranges, was of first importance to the Normans, who built one in 1212 and replaced it with a better in 1280. From this, and castles at Clonmacnois and Athlone, they could keep a watchful eye on the Shannon approaches, and occasionally cross the river for a show of force. The second castle, built by Edmund Butler, father of the first Earl of Ormonde, in 1280, survives as the town's best ruin, with a solid gate-tower and crumbling drum towers along its massive curtain wall. Inside the bailey is a handsome, three-storey Queen Anne house, home of the Damer family in the eighteenth century, a barracks in the nineteenth, and an unloved dump in the twentieth, until the Irish Georgian Society leased and restored it. Open to the public as a so-called heritage centre, and housing permanent and visiting exhibitions, it possesses a beautiful carved staircase and many other details. On the east side of the town is the stump of a Round Tower, with a High Cross and Romanesque doorway. These are on the site of one of St Cronan's seventh-century monasteries. The surviving twelfth-century remains were scarred and separated by the laying of the Dublin road. In the valley on the south side of the town is a slender mellowed tower, remnant of a fifteenth-century friary, demolished around 1800 and serving now as gate-tower – an unhappy contrast – to the Roman Catholic Gothic Revival Church. The town entices by its ruins, its informality, and the many signs of buildings of great age hidden behind more recent façades and terraces.

St Cronan's first monastery was at the end of a peninsula (roscre) in what was, till drained in the eighteenth century, a shallow lake amid Mona Incha bog. To get to it from Roscrea, drive a mile east along the main road, then first right and first left. After a mile the remains of the abbey, surrounded by trees and a low wall, rise high above the flat meadows. There are an exquisite Romanesque church with fine west door, a cross, some gravestones – mainly of the twelfth century. As elsewhere in Ireland, bog air used to preserve dead bodies more or less intact, and a smaller island nearby was hallowed on this account, even regarded as an earthly paradise. Giraldus Cambrensis got the story charmingly wrong. It was impossible to die on the island, he thought; a mixed blessing, since some people grew so old that they wanted to die, and 'have to be transported by boat to the larger island. As soon as they touch its ground, they give up the ghost.' He described another of Mona Incha's features: 'No woman or animal of the female sex could ever enter the island without dying immediately. This has been proved many times. A remarkable thing about the birds there is that while the males settle on the bushes everywhere throughout the island, the females fly over and leave their mates there and avoid the island like a plague.'

A couple of miles south, scattered over the Timoney Hills, is an enigmatic collection of three hundred standing stones, each about three feet high, whose arrangement baffles archaeologists. One unlikely suggestion is that each represents a body, in the place it lay, after some ancient battle. We carry on along the main Dublin road to **Borris-in-Ossory**, once an important coaching stage, where the ruins of a Fitzpatrick castle stand. The 1969 Catholic church is striking.

From here we can continue straight on to **Mountrath**, a town built about a triangular green in the eighteenth century that shows little sign of its former monastic, and later linen-manufacturing importance.

Four miles north of Mountrath by the L147 is **Ballyfin**, which Mark Bence-Jones calls 'the grandest and most lavishly appointed early Classical house in Ireland'. It was built for the Coote family in the 1820s on the site of a house which had belonged to one of the Duke of Wellington's brothers, mainly by the Morrisons, father and son. Its heavy, solid, Roman exterior is matched by a grand use of scagliola columns, elaborate plasterwork and coffered ceilings inside. It was sold in the 1920s to the Patrician Brothers, who made it into a college and sometimes open it to the public. From it, a road runs six miles east to **Port Laoise**, county town of Laois (formerly Maryborough, county town of Queen's County). It has a few points of architectural interest. Gandon designed the obelisk spire on the Church of Ireland church. Sir Richard Morrison, his pupil, designed the courthouse, at the back of which is the grotesquely rusticated old prison. The Pain brothers did the modern prison in 1830. Francis Johnston probably built a mental hospital opposite. For all these talents, the town is unexciting.

An alternative route from Borris is to turn right a mile out of the town and come, after four miles, to **Aghaboe**, whose customarily turbulent history before and after the Normans is not at all reflected in the ivy-covered fourteenth-century friary ruins near the parish church. Turning first left after the village, right two miles later and right again at Shanahoe brings us to the Durrow–Abbeyleix road, at which we turn left. On the right is the large and finely wooded demesne of **Abbey Leix House**. The De Vesci family, who owned it till 1995, became lords of Kildare after the break-up of Strongbow's original fief of Leinster in 1243. They lost much of their power soon afterwards by identifying overmuch with the Irish, becoming degenerate as contemporary England saw it, but survived in the area for seven centuries – 'improving' landlords who often promoted the Irish cause. The square house, built by James Wyatt in 1773–74, and refaced in the nineteenth century, contains good original plasterwork. The gardens are supposedly modelled on the fantastic estate of Alupka, beside the Black Sea, which once belonged to a Vorontsov, Russian ancestor of the De Vescis. Farther on, **Abbeyleix**, laid out as a model village in the eighteenth century, preserves its charm, with good modest Georgian houses, a market house in the centre of the very broad main street and a crescent of terrace houses behind. The church, with spire by John Semple, was rebuilt by Thomas M. Wyatt, one of myriad architectural kinsmen of the great James, in 1865.

To reach **Timahoe** we follow the Carlow road, R430, and take the second turning left after two miles. On the south side of this tiny village is a very tall Round Tower, almost 100 feet high, the shaft of which is two feet out of true. It has walls four feet thick and a splendid Romanesque doorway, seventeen feet up. A monastery was founded here around 650 by St Mochua, a semi-mythical saint whose distinction was to heal others – Colman Elo of loss of memory, Fintan of leprosy – and to keep, among other pets, a fly, which walked along lines of scripture as he read and halted to keep his place when he broke off to expound. In 1970, genealogists were moved to discover that Richard Milhous, great-great-grandfather of US president Richard Nixon, was born at Timahoe. That was in time for the president's obligatory Irish visit.

Stradbally is straight on to the north-east, built along a single mile-long street. It was principal seat of the O'Mores, an Irish sept (a grouping of relations rather broader than a family), who like the O'Connors in Offaly remained unsubdued till the end of the sixteenth century. Long before, the first Tudor confiscations had given their Stradbally lands to Captain Francis Cosby, who turned the friary here into a castle. His descendants still live in the grand hall west of the town. Little ancient remains in Stradbally, but it does boast the Irish Steam Museum, a collection of engines, cars (including racing), tricycles, fire-engines and other objects in the pageant of steam power, many of which on the first weekend in August participate in an annual and famous steam rally that attracts thousands.

Two miles east of the town is Ballykilcavan, where it has been said the young gardener William Robinson, after a quarrel with his Walsh-Kemmis employers in the late 1850s, deliberately opened all the greenhouse windows on a freezing night, and so destroyed all the contents. He quickly departed for England, to usher in the revolution away from Victorian formality to the relaxed and natural ease of the modern herbaceous border. Three miles west of Stradbally, north of the Port Laoise road, is the **Rock of Dunamase**, a massive outcrop, 200 feet high, of limestone in a limestone plain; and first reported by Ptolemy under the name of Dunum. At no stage of its history was its advantage ignored. Gael fought Gael for it, and lost it to the Anglo-Normans (it went to Strongbow as part of Dermot McMurrough's daughter's dowry). In 1479 the O'Mores retrieved and held it till

Mary I's reign and the plantation of Laois. It was in O'More hands again when the Earl of Essex, during his pointless, ignominious campaign of 1599 marched from Athy to relieve Port Laoise. He decided against occupying it, and instead made his way from Port Laoise towards Kilkenny, but paid dearly for his neglect in the Pass of the Plumes, on the R427 three miles south-west. Here, ambushed by Owen O'More, he lost hundreds of men before escaping to Wicklow. Cromwellian detachments, more decisive, stormed Dunamase in 1650, took it from Confederate troops and destroyed the buildings. The ruins – of a rectangular thirteenth-century keep and other buildings – are what they left. But the place, from a distance, still looks impregnable.

We can continue north-west to the main Dublin road, turn right on to it, and left a mile after towards Portarlington. The road crosses the Great Heath of Maryborough, and two miles from the main road we pass on the right the church of **Coolbanagher**, designed by Gandon, and one of the most graceful Georgian churches in the country, recently restored. Within is the fine mausoleum of the Dawson-Damer family, earls of Portarlington, also Gandon's work. Branching right just farther on we can glimpse **Emo Court**. Built in the first instance to Gandon's designs just before 1800, for the first Earl of Portarlington, but not completed till sixty years later, it is set in fine grounds with good trees, including an avenue of wellingtonias. The first earl was Gandon's first patron. Sold to Jesuits for a novitiate college in 1939, Emo has now reverted to private hands and a sympathetic restorer who opens house and gardens to the public. **Portarlington**, a few miles on, beside the Barrow and close to the Grand Canal, is a pretty seventeenth-century foundation with good eighteenth-century houses. Under William III, the Marquis de Ruvigny, Earl of Galway, settled many Huguenots here (a little earlier nearby Mountmellick and some other towns were settled as Quaker colonies). Though the 1851 church of St Paul replaced the French church of 1696, the graveyard still contains many stones inscribed in French, some not much more than a hundred years old, and until 1861 services were held in French. There is a lovely market-house of about 1800 in the centre and many rather earlier houses. Ireland's first turf power-station is north of the town, but we go east, keeping quite close to the canal, seeing Lea Castle on the left after two miles – a towered, thirteenth-century keep of the FitzGeralds, destroyed by Cromwell – and carrying along the straight road. **Monasterevin**, with its handsome houses of merchants enriched by canal trade, was for a while the home of Gerard Manley Hopkins. South of it is **Moore Abbey**, a magnificent and rare example of mid-eighteenth-century Gothic architecture. The original house was built by Adam, first Viscount Loftus, lord chancellor of Ireland from 1619 to 1639, who lived here until Wentworth's spiteful legislation forced him to pay a large sum of money to his daughter-in-law, a relation of the lord deputy, in settlement of a very dubious claim. He is said to have held court in the present, much altered, great hall. His own daughter married Charles Moore, later Earl of Drogheda, whose heirs reconstructed the property. Nineteenth-century changes imposed a heavier kind of Tudor Gothic and made the place notoriously cold. When a particularly heavy portmanteau belonging to a guest, the Earl of Clonmell, fell and burst open on the stairs, it was found to be full of coal. This century the Moores let the house to the singer Count (a papal title) John McCormack, who died in Dublin in 1945. It was sold soon after, to become a hospital run by the Sisters of Charity of Jesus and Mary.

The Dublin road, N7, now leads straight to Kildare. To the north a group of hills (including Grange Hill, 745 feet, with the **Chair of Kildare**, a limestone outcrop, on top) comprises the last high ground before the seemingly endless Bog of Allen beyond. From the top, views are good; from bog-level, trees, borders and the occasional Peat Board kiln interrupt all countryside panoramas. On the southern side there are signs of great wealth in the houses and wealthy demesnes.

Kildare is a town whose history could detain us far longer than its relics. The ninth-century scholar and grammarian Sedulius Scotus studied here, Vikings plundered, Dermot MacMurrough ravaged, Giraldus Cambrensis admired and Confederates bombarded the town. More important, perhaps, St Brigid founded in 480 the first monastery here and died here about 520. There is far more to Brigid than a Christian saint with quaint attributes. In the Irish hagiography she ranks second only to St Patrick, which is explained in part by her previous prominent place in pagan lore. In this previous manifestation she was a threefold goddess, daughter of the Dagda, chief of the Celtic gods, and with similarities to Brizo, the moon goddess of Delos. As such she was revered in Gaul, Brittany, and Britain (as Bride, Brigantia, Brit and other names). Her influence was far too great for fifth-century Christians to deny her existence; and pagan threads were woven into the advancing Christian pattern. Her Christian image constantly harked back to her pagan. At Kildare, unlike other foundations, there were both monks and nuns, and suspicions that, though segregated by a screen in church, they mixed freely in private. One folk-tale even has Brigid proposing to Patrick, and securing from him women's leap-year rights. Also at Kildare a flame burned constantly, from its foundation to the Dissolution, without a break; pagan Brigid was goddess of fire. Moreover, the Irish plainly transferred attributes of the Virgin Mary to Brigid, often known as 'the Mary of the Gael', and Mary herself is seen by some to have descended, in some senses, from pre-Christian deities. Irish devotion to Brigid appears to be due to the antiquity of her worship, and to the need for a feminine leavening in the stern patriarchy of the early Christian Trinity.

The Church of Ireland **Cathedral of St Brigid** embraces a hotch-potch of periods in its stones. It was begun in 1229, devastated in the sixteenth century, and given a new chancel in the 1680s. Then it fell into decay until G.E. Street's restoration in 1875, which has given its stamp to the whole building. There are a few good early memorials, notably the sixteenth-century tomb of Bishop Wellesley with its fine-cut carvings. A fine Round Tower of 106 feet, whiskered with grass, stands without (the battlemented top is nineteenth century and wrong; it should, like others, be a cone). On the far side of the village square is a fifteenth-century tower. The flawed but romantic rebel Lord Edward FitzGerald lived some years next door in Kildare Lodge, long since demolished.

One signposted mile south-east of the town is **Tully House**, seat of the National Stud. A Scotsman, William Hall-Walker, began to breed thoroughbreds here in 1900. His stallion boxes, still here, rise to elegant lantern roofs, so that the moon and stars may exercise their powers on the animals. Keeping or disposing of a new-born foal depended on its astrological birth-chart. To this day mares are played tranquil music in their stalls. The charming Japanese gardens were laid out by Tassa Eida and his son between 1906 and 1910 (Powerscourt's Japanese Garden was laid out at the same time) with a symbolism – representing the soul's journey through mortal life to eternity – much to Hall-Walker's taste. The Irish National Stud took over the estate after the Second World War. Visitors may see the horse museum, where among other displays stands the skeleton of Arkle, one of the world's great steeplechasers, put down after breaking a bone in 1970 – a household word in his day; also on view are the foaling unit, stallion boxes and the various amenities of the visitors' centre.

The **Curragh**, stretching east from Kildare, is the largest area (5,000 acres) of unfenced common land in the country. St Brigid's flocks pastured here. The military centre, on the east side, has been famous since 1646; but curragh means racecourse, and there has been one here, north of the Dublin road, for two thousand years. As the headquarters of Irish horse-racing it is surrounded by training stables and grand houses; horse country, with large fields and impeccable fencing to show the richness, both of land and owners. The course, in recent times, has had a distinctly social aura round it; in English days it was necessary to be an officer or member of a good Dublin social club to attend. In 1969, at the Irish Derby held there in early July, the Duke of Devonshire said approvingly, 'It's the last racecourse in the world where the waiters wear white gloves – it's got more *chic* than Ascot.'

The Curragh has seen other sport beside racing. Towards the east, beyond the camp on the Kilcullen road is Donnelly's Hollow, a dent in the plain where bare-fist prize-fights used to take place. Dan Donnelly was the champion of the early nineteenth century – he won his greatest battle, against an English champion, in 1815 – and his supposed giant footprints are marked across the area. In 1914 General Gough and sixty cavalry officers at the Curragh barracks resigned their commissions to avoid being ordered to Ulster to fire on Edward Carson's newly formed Ulster Volunteers, a completely illegal group, formed to resist by all possible means the introduction of home rule into Ireland. Their decision has gone down as the Curragh Mutiny.

Of many interesting private houses in the area, two may be mentioned. Beyond, and to the east of, the Curragh, but this side of Kilcullen, is early-eighteenth-century **Castlemartin**, which housed General Sir Ralph Dundas during the 1798 rebellion. His promise of safe passage to a peasant army of thousands of rebels at Gibbet Rath on the Curragh was not circulated to his men. The rebels surrendered, and some three hundred and fifty were promptly massacred. Castle-martin was more recently inherited by Lord Gowrie who sold it to Tony O'Reilly, one of an expanding breed of phenomenally successful Irish businessmen. A former rugby international and hero, twenty-nine times capped, he has been one of the world's highest paid business executives, ran Heinz, Waterford Wedgwood, then Independent Newspapers with publications world-wide, is worth untold hundreds of millions and has here a thousand acres of prime Kildare. Georgian **Harristown House**, two miles east of Kilcullen, formerly home of the Huguenot banking family of La Touche, has a stranger story. In 1858 John Ruskin, nearly forty and losing his faith, was persuaded by Mrs La Touche to teach drawing to her nine-year-old daughter Rose. They offered him a cottage in the grounds. Rose charmed him, called him St Crumpet, chivvied him on his religious lapses. When she was seventeen he proposed. She put him off. Mad with love, he offered to work as a farm-hand, sleeping in a shed, till she was of age. The parents heard of the failure of his marriage and the alleged cause of it: his impotence. Mrs La Touche, against him now, pointed out that if he was impotent he was no good for her daughter, and if he was not, then his divorce was invalid. Meanwhile Rose fell ill, and became iller still each of the few times he saw her. He was in torment, she dying. She died, here at Harristown, in 1875. He for twenty-five more years continued to tell the world, with beautiful lucidity and reason, what was good and bad in art and architecture.

From Kildare the R415 (and from Kilcullen a cross-country route) leads us past the **Hill of Allen**. The legendary Finn McCool had his stronghold here. Finn's Fianna (the word means band of soldiers, and appears in the name of, among other groups, one of the Republic's two leading political parties) served the welfare of Ireland, not individual kings. Their ethic anticipated chivalry. Each recruit swore never to cheat or harm a woman, never to turn down a call for help, never to flee before fewer than ten attackers. He must be able to leap a tree as high as himself and pass under a branch as low as his knee while running at full speed. The Fianna punished all wickedness and dishonour and were themselves above reproach (exceptions included Dermot, who eloped with Finn's bride Grania on the eve of the wedding). Their life was war – they even repelled the invasion of Dáire Donn, king of the world, at Ventry in Kerry – and when there was no war they hunted, sometimes including all the provinces of Ireland in a single chase of boar or deer. Their stronghold, with its halls, couches, golden vats and goblets, armoury and smithies, is marked, rather unworthily, by an eye-catcher obelisk erected in 1859.

At Kilmeage, a right turn goes to **Robertstown** on the Grand Canal, a rather sleepy canal town with its former huge hotel built to accommodate 'express' passengers and a steeply humped bridge over the water. Here and elsewhere there are good walks along the towpaths. Here alone is a splendid Grand Canal festival held in early August, pioneered by the priest and other locals who thought their town should not be allowed to die without resistance. Some of the things offered are the Irish Georgian Society's Annual Cricket Match, played to the rules of 1744, a tour of Kildare period houses, lectures, dances, fishing competitions, and period style, candlelight suppers in the Canal Hotel itself (built at a cost of £7,452; opened in 1803).

There is also a permanent exhibition of items connected with the canal.

We go on to Clane, by a road whose straightness is only possible on bogland or desert, through **Prosperous**, a village created – two hundred houses in three years, besides factories and machinery – and named in hopes of wealth to come from its cotton and linen mills in the late eighteenth century. But money ran out, and last hopes were dashed by the 1798 rebellion. Clane, three miles on, has the remains of a Franciscan friary to the south-east. If we turn left and continue for a mile we reach on the right the entrance to **Clongoweswood** Jesuit boarding college, founded in 1814 in what had been Castle Browne, home of the Wogan-Browne family. On the north of the demesne, two miles from the college, is the gatehouse of ruined Rathcoffey Castle, seat of the heirs of Sir John de Wogan, Edward I's Justiciar from 1295, who in seventeen years of office settled many wrangles among the, by now, unreliable Anglo-Normans and made the Pale not only self-supporting but also a source of royal revenue, much needed for Scottish wars. The new college chapel is rich in Irish art – many stained glass windows by Evie Hone and Michael Healy, and paintings by Sean Keating and others. By contrast to the park, the inside of the school is dark and sombre – easy to people with figures from James Joyce's *Portrait of the Artist*. Joyce was seven when he came. Primed by a father whose advice was 'Mix with gentlemen', he was at first teased, perhaps bullied. Asked his age, he replied 'Half past six', and was thereafter known as that. But he enjoyed the school more than the *Portrait* suggests. He played cricket well, won cups for hurdling and walking, and developed a phenomenally methodical mind. 'If that fellow was dropped in the middle of the Sahara,' his father wrote, 'he'd sit, be God, and make a map of it.'

The road south from Clane runs close to Dublin's river Liffey for two miles, passing Blackhall, once home of the Wolfe family, one of whom gave Theobald Wolfe Tone his first two names. The Tones were tenants on the estate. The next turn left leads to **Bodenstown**, in whose Church of Ireland churchyard Tone was buried after his arrest and suicide in 1798. Here, each year, leading Republicans, nationalists and other admirers come on annual pilgrimage.

Six miles due south of Clane (a turn right, half-way, leads to the 400-foot-long Leinster Aqueduct, a stately construction for the canal to cross a lovely stretch of the Liffey) is Kildare's county town, **Naas**, with its famous racecourse a mile to the east and Goff's Kildare Paddocks a couple of miles further on. A mile to its west is the evocative ruin of **Jigginstown**. Here Lord Deputy Wentworth, later Earl of Strafford, planned his finest house, fit to lodge the king, Charles I. He brought over workmen from his Yorkshire home, and planned a lavish hall with floor of marble (in which he was an expert), and columns of black Kilkenny marble. But from building at Jigginstown he was recalled to England to try to patch (he alone could) the king's splitting kingdom. Instead, attacked by hostile court factions, many of them Anglo-Irish offended by his rule, he went as Charles's sacrifice to the scaffold. Had Wentworth, a loyal servant of Charles, been allowed to continue in Ireland, he might have settled it – in his ruthless, tactless way he had already made it richer than ever before and established some semblance of justice in the midst of anarchy – and so deferred the apocalyptic alternative of Cromwell. Half-finished Jigginstown fell back into ruin. In the 1650s all its lead and iron had been stripped for ammunition. Now the huge vaulted cellars, and gaunt skeleton of brick walls, 380 feet by 80 feet, with their broad windows, cleared by the Irish Georgian Society and other volunteers, have been accepted into state care.

There is more zigzagging before the return to Dublin if we are to see a concentration of grand things in and near Celbridge. To do this, we take the R407 north from Naas to Sallins. We turn right in the village on to the minor road for Celbridge. Six miles on there are impressive views of **Lyons House** on the right, against a background of hills. The house was built for £200,000, for Valentine Lawless, Baron Cloncurry (whose wife Sir John Piers seduced for a bet, and so kindled a famous court case). It stayed in the family till 1962 when, line and title dying out, it was transformed into an agricultural college. On Lyons Hill behind, an important Iron Age hill-fort with a wondrous view from the top, O'Connell fought a duel and killed his man in 1815. Later that year he was challenged by Robert Peel, young and in his 'Orange Peel' phase, and accepted. But O'Connell's wife had him arrested and bound over, to prevent more blood-spilling.

Closer to the road and beside the Liffey is **Lodge Park**, designed probably by Nathaniel Clements in 1775 to 1777, and, if it was, the last work he did. Its design is unusual – a plain central block with two pavilions, instead of the normal one, on each side. It is privately owned. Farther on is Killadoon, also possibly built by Clements for his family in the 1770s.

After joining the main R403 road to Dublin we come into **Celbridge** past Celbridge Abbey, once owned by Bartholomew Vanhomrigh. He was a Dutchman who came to Ireland with King

William as Commissary General to the army. He provisioned the troops before and after the battle of the Boyne, grew rich on commissions, and bought the abbey. General Ginkel became godfather to his son. His daughter Hester, on his death in 1709, moved with her mother to London. There she met and fell in love with Swift, and a little later followed him, as would Esther Johnson, to Ireland. He came to see her often at Celbridge. He called her Vanessa, and Esther Johnson Stella. With the years, his visits tailed off and in 1723 he may have married Stella, secretly – though many authorities doubt this. Vanessa heard the rumour, and wrote to Stella asking for confirmation. Swift, according to an unreliable source, got the letter, rode over, abused, raged, stormed and left. A little later Vanessa died here; not before changing her will and leaving her considerable fortune to Bishop Berkeley instead of Swift. The present house, rich in delightful Gothic detail, was largely built in the late eighteenth century by Henry Grattan's uncle. The order of St John of God, who now own the place, have introduced everything imaginable to tempt tourists. The place is not improved. Swift, who could despise the common man even while fighting for his rights, would have galloped off once more.

Another to make his fortune from the Glorious Revolution that brought William III to the throne in place of James II was William Conolly, a pub-keeper's son. He acted as agent for beneficiaries of the settlement and took thick slices of their cakes. In 1715 he crowned his ascent in society by being appointed Speaker of the House of Commons, and acted as Lord Justice many times after that. He died in 1729 and his wife ordered the grandiose monument in the Death House, a plain mausoleum in Celbridge's old Church of Ireland churchyard. 'He made a modest but splendid use of his great riches', reads the epitaph. Splendid, but hardly modest, is **Castletown**, the house he built in 1722 in a large park north-east of the village – the largest and one of the most beautiful private houses ever built in Ireland.

The main façade, sixty feet tall, is in severe Palladian style, like a broad Venetian Grand Canal palace bounded by two pavilions. Each of these is joined to the central block by semi-circular colonnades, a popular device that created the longest possible frontage – about 400 feet in this case – and hid utilitarian, farmwork areas beside the house. One pavilion housed the kitchens, the other the horses. A balustrade tops house and colonnades, and the windows of the central course have alternating curved and straight-sided pediments. Broad steps lead to the front door.

The upshot of recent researches is that Alessandro Galilei designed the house (he later did the façade of St John in Lateran in Rome) but that Edward Lovett Pearce, who at first interpreted his plans on the spot, later took a more creative hand. Working for Speaker Conolly was Pearce's first big chance, and probably led him to obtain the commission for the Parliament building in Dublin. His main work is to be seen in the pavilions, and, inside, in the austerely architectural entrance hall and the long gallery. Around 1760 Chambers had an indirect hand in the design of the dining-room and two drawing-rooms downstairs. Numerous craftsmen and masons were employed, among them the Lafranchini brothers (possibly only one), Simon Vierpyl, and Reynolds's 'little delicate deformed' pupil, Thomas Reily, who painted the designs in the gallery. The festoons of delicate plasterwork by the Lafranchinis by the main staircase – more free and rococo than their previous work – are as aerial and elegant as any of their kind; but art's prestige was not what it is. Tom Conolly, the owner, who inherited the house from the Speaker's widow, writes grudgingly in 1765 of amounts paid to 'Frankiney stucco man'.

In parts of the house, however, there survives a buoyantly amateurish spirit, the legacy of Tom's wife, Lady Louisa. The Print Room, the only one of its kind in Ireland, is her and her sister Sarah's work, done during a winter of the 1770s. There is a natural evolution from this to the gallery, with its painted festoons and garlands and symbols, its Etruscan and Arcadian panels, its niches, bookcases, busts, Venetian chandeliers (the wrong blue, Lady Louisa rightly complained), its deeply compartmented ceiling and, for such large dimensions, a general air of lived-in comfort. It was, in fact, in Tom's time, the room where most things went on – dancing, eating, card-playing, theatricals and the eternal airing of politics by men and gossip by women. From Lady Louisa's and other letters comes a vivid picture of the primeval distinction between the functions of men and women of society.

Society was a thing old William Conolly could never feel quite part of, though his aspirations and success in getting as near as possible are evident. They stand out in the portraits. The Speaker himself was childless. His nephew William married an earl's daughter and had five daughters and one son. The son, Tom, married the amiable Louisa, daughter of the second Duke of Richmond, himself a grandson of Charles II. Of her sisters one became Lady Holland (of Holland Park), another the Duchess of Leinster (living over the road from Castletown at Carton) and another, Sarah, came near to marrying George III, failing which she married first a rustic baronet, then the humbler George Napier, and by him mothered three generals. With Napier she lived in Celbridge, at Oakly Park – a fine house of 1724, probably designed by Thomas Burgh. Tom's own sisters by their marriages connected him with just about every titled family in Ireland and a good many in England.

The Speaker lived to see none of this, nor, mercifully for him, the second demise of his male line soon after. Tom and Louisa were childless, in their turn. The estate went through their adopted niece to her Pakenham son, who changed his name to Conolly. Family succession lasted to 1965, when the estate was sold to a man bent on redevelopment. For want of other sponsors, Desmond Guinness, founder and first president of the Irish Georgian Society, borrowed £93,000, bought the house, and leased it to the society, whose headquarters it was for some years. When they took it over it was empty. Lead was being stripped from the roof. Now it is probably grander than in Tom Conolly's time. It has concerts, lectures, dances, and seminars, and shares with Carton in June a Festival of Great Irish Houses.

There are two curiosities in the demesne, one of which can be seen through the north-west vista from the long gallery. This is Conolly's Folly, the obelisk that the Speaker's widow had Richard Castle design in 1740. It was an eye-catcher, to which the family sometimes went out for tea. With its bold pillar surmounting a complex of arches it has been called the only piece of real architecture in Ireland, but that on a narrow and academic definition. The other feature is the Wonderful Barn that ends the north-east vista and comprises four domes, one atop the other, with a spiral staircase outside. It was probably used for storing grain.

The return to Dublin can take us through **Leixlip**, with its splendid medieval castle, adorned with Gothic detail in the eighteenth century, privately owned and bordering a fine reach of the Liffey or, more directly, through **Lucan**, with the beautiful demesne surrounding Lucan House, now the Italian embassy, on the left. The Jacobite hero Patrick Sarsfield was born hereabouts, and took the name Lucan as title of his short-lived earldom. It later went to the Binghams, after the daughter of the owner, the lushly named Agmondisham Vesey MP, kinsman of the Abbey Leix De Vescis, married into the family. A couple of miles on, we are back in the built-up purlieus of Dublin.

5

Wicklow Hills

FOR THE LONDONER, it is as if the Lake District began at Golders Green. A dozen miles south of O'Connell Bridge you can be amid mountains, in furzy, heathery country, waiting for bent rustic figures to whistle their dogs to clear a way for your car among sheep or cattle. The population is confined to a few villages and, except for the highest highlands, where there is no habitation at all, scattered cottages and farmhouses. To reach such dramatic country again it is necessary to cross Ireland to the west coast or go north to the Mourne mountains and Antrim beyond. The Wicklow Mountains form the biggest of the few granite outcrops in the country, indeed in what one tends to call, but to avoid offence should not, the British Isles. As elsewhere in Ireland, the sculpting of this landscape goes back half a billion years. The tectonic plate on which America lies had floated away from the European, forming a first Atlantic ocean, and now floated back, taking hundreds of millions of years each way. The long-drawn, cosmically mighty impact of this reunion pressed the Ordovician sea-bed rock into rucks and rumples of slatey, shaley mountain thousands of feet high. Then molten larva burst from below, forcing the peaks and ranges higher still, cooling and settling as hard granite below the breakable slate and shale. The rest of time, to the present, wore away parts of this vulnerable surface rock and left the granite exposed. The consistency and nature of the rocks, and the work of rain and particularly ice, rubbed the granite – by now forming the main summits – relatively smooth but left peripheral slates sharper and spikier. Sharply profiled glens incised into the main mass are a common and beautiful feature of the foothills. Ice made its impressions too, right up to its recent departure (about twelve thousand years ago). It scraped out valleys, dug long lakes. The colder, more persistent lower ice held meltwaters high up the mountainsides, where their agitations excavated deep corries, and their eventual escape carved thin spillways at the ends of these cavities, creating the

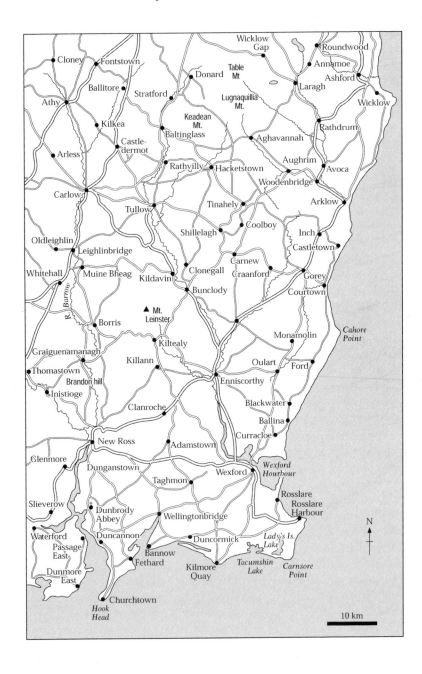

Wicklow
Gap
Roundwood
Cloney
Fontstown
Annamoe
Donard
Table
Mt
Ashford
Ballitore
Stratford
Laragh
Athy
Lugnaquillia
Mt.
Wicklow
Keadean
Mt.
Kilkea
Rathdrum
Baltinglass
Castle-
dermot
Aghavannah
Arless
Aughrim
Rathvilly
Hacketstown
Avoca
Woodenbridge
Carlow
Arklow
Tullow
Tinahely
Coolboy
Shillelagh
Inch
Oldleighlin
Castletown
Leighlinbridge
Carnew
Whitehall
Muine Bheag
Clonegall
Gorey
Kildavin
Craanford
Courtown
Bunclody
R. Barrow
Mt.
Borris
Leinster
Cahore
Point
Kiltealy
Monamolin
Graiguenamanagh
Killann
Oulart
Ford
Thomastown
Brandon hill
Enniscorthy
Inistioge
Clanroche
Blackwater
Ballina
New Ross
Curracloe
Glenmore
Adamstown
Dunganstown
Wexford
Hourbour
Taghmon
Wexford
Slieverow
Rosslare
Dunbrody
Rosslare
Abbey
Wellingtonbridge
Harbour
Waterford
Duncannon
N
Passage
Duncormick
Lady's Is.
East
Lake
Dunmore
Bannow
Tacumshin
Carnsore
East
Fethard
Kilmore
Lake
Point
Quay
Churchtown
Hook
Head
10 km

otherwise inexplicable 'dry gaps' of, say, the Glen of the Downs and the Scalp. These features are all more typical of the east of the range than of its west.

There are plenty of decent roads, but the mountains are God's gift to the hiker. The views are rewards of toil (and nowhere needs this be acute) and best appreciated as such. It was the Wicklow Mountains, said Edward Lear, that decided him to be 'a painter of topographical landscapes'. The hiker has youth hostels well placed hereabouts. The folklore is colourful – even though W. M. Thackeray thought it all 'abominably stupid and stale'. The history is rich, too, for rugged highlands made an ideal base and retreat for fighters against the English. O'Tooles, O'Byrnes, MacMurroughs and O'Dwyers lured, trounced, evaded and infuriated the coloniser over centuries. Some of the best roads date from the '98, when the British built them and a chain of barracks to contain the rebels on their own ground.

We can start from Dublin by the road south-west through Tallaght – site of St Maelruan's seventh-century monastery, and of the four-teenth-century country palace of Dublin's archbishops. **Blessington** is a long broad village founded in about 1682 by another Dublin arch-bishop, Michael Boyle. It lies beside the seven-mile-long Lacken, often known as the Poulaphouca, Reservoir, formed in 1940 by flooding for hydro-electric works. The lake is part of the Liffey's course from its source near Sally Gap. A lakeside road has been built all round. In the village a granite drinking fountain with lion's head bears the inscription: 'the water supplied at the cost of a kind and generous LANDLORD for the benefit of his attached and loyal tenants'. It was put there in 1865 as a tribute to the Marquess of Downshire, who owned the village as well as large tracts of county Down. What was the family's home here is now the centrally sited Downshire House hotel.

Russborough House stands a couple of miles further on, designed by Richard Castle in the 1740s for Joseph Leeson, first Earl of Miltown. Leeson was a great grand-tourer, and filled the house with a rich collection of paintings which went to Ireland's National Gallery at the end of the nineteenth century, when his family and title expired. The house competes with Carton for the distinction of being Castle's best extant work, combining his heavy faults with all his virtues. Its frontage is the longest in Ireland – 700 feet in all – with a central block, long seven-bay wings joined to it by curved colonnades, and two further wings attached by plain walls with a Baroque gateway in the centre of each. Inside it has fine stucco work ascribed to the

Lafranchini brothers, an unusual spacious landing lit by a large lantern, and a host of other attractions. The late owner, Sir Alfred Beit, a South African mining millionaire, before his death formed a foundation to manage the house and its collections and to open them regularly to the public. The paintings, by Vermeer, Rubens, Goya, Velazquez and others, form one of the finest private collections in these islands, and there is a splendid collection of Irish silver, much of it from the time – the eighteenth century – when Ireland's silversmiths were the equal of any in Europe. In 1974 callers with guns removed several invaluable paintings, which were later recovered. Partaking in the raid was Rose Dugdale, from a wealthy upper class English family – a stratum which has supplied the IRA with several of its keenest recruits. Four miles further along the main road we pass Hollywood, and a left turn that leads to the Wicklow Gap. This road has broad sweeping views, wild and desolate at first, sweeter as it reaches the Gap, cut between Tonelagee (the easy ascent of which affords stunning panoramas) and Table Mountain, before descending, among frequent sightings of stream and waterfall, on Glendalough. However on this occasion at least we are neglecting this beautiful route in favour of another.

Half a mile south of Hollywood a left turn takes us into the Hollywood Glen, a three-mile hanging valley that well illustrates the effects of the ice-blanket. A mile down on the left are remains of St Kevin's Church, on the site perhaps of the saint's first oratory, set in a 'holy wood'. From here he moved east to Glendalough. A 1914 statue of him crowns a nearby summit. West of the church, and closer to the N81 road from which we broke away, is one of the many circles of granite stones known as Piper's Stones – fourteen boulders (the dancers) and one set away from them. One legend is that the group were dancing to the piper's tunes on a Sunday, and were petrified for their sacrilege.

At Donard, we turn left and keep straight on beside the Leagh River, a tributary of the Slaney, to the end of the Glen of Imaal, lying at the feet of Table, Lugnaquillia and Keadeen Mountains. Here stands Leitrim Barracks, erected in 1798 to cope with the tactics of the rebel leader Michael Dwyer, in whose honour a cottage at **Derrynamuck**, two miles south-south-west, has been reconstructed in traditional style to contain a small folk museum – in as remote a spot as any fugitive would choose. The '98 was sustained longest by Wicklow and Wexford guerrillas, and Dwyer kept the English preoccupied with only a small group of men. When he was eventually surrounded by British troops, a comrade, Samuel McAllister, deliberately attracted their attention – and was shot dead – to allow Dwyer to escape. Captured later, Dwyer was sent to Australia, imprisoned briefly by Captain Bligh of the Bounty, at this time governor of New South Wales, and died a respected freeman in 1825. Returning down the glen we turn left at the main road and reach the busy market town of Baltinglass after five miles, passing on the right the high and charming village of Stratford, built to order by Edward Stratford in the eighteenth century. In the nineteenth, its linen factory employed up to a thousand men. The Stratford family, earls of Aldborough, laid out or enlarged and improved several villages in the area.

Baltinglass is beautifully set on the Slaney River, which, after its mountain origins, adopts here a more gradual descent on its long journey to Wexford harbour. The Cistercian Abbey of Vallis Salutis, founded about 1150 by Dermot MacMurrough, who later instigated the Anglo-Norman invasion, stands in ruins to the north, on the river's left bank. Inside the part of the nave and chancel walled off to make the Protestant church (the square tower is later, and the cloisters much reconstructed) is the splendid empire-style mausoleum of the Stratford family, Lords of Baltinglass. The original Norman Viscounts Baltinglass, FitzEustaces, forfeited their title in 1586, having joined the Munster rising sparked by the Elizabethan conquest. They were upheld by a conviction that Mary Queen of Scots was the rightful monarch. The Stratfords were granted the lapsed title.

At the top of the hill to the north-east is **Rathcoran**, an Iron Age hill-fort in which are three older passage-graves, from which various implements, utensils, and fragments of bone were taken in a 1934 excavation. The countryside hereabouts is spattered with prehistoric remains.

We cross the bridge and stay with the main road for three miles, then turn off left and keep going eastwards, with Lugnaquillia on the left, to Rathdangan and **Aghavannagh Barracks**, where there is a junction with the old Military Road to Glenmalure. The youth hostel, a good base for climbing the mountain to the north (Lugnaquillia, 3,039 feet, is the highest mountain in eastern Ireland, third in Ireland), was originally another of the chain of forts erected by the British in the 1790s. Later Parnell used it as a shooting lodge – convenient for his home at Avondale – and afterwards it was the country home of John Redmond, the moderate leader of the Irish party at Westminster.

Another superb approach to Lugnaquillia is to take the old Military Road to Glenmalure, turning left after four miles at Drumgoff Bridge and going up the valley till the road peters out, at Baravore Ford, beside a high waterfall. This was the setting of J.M. Synge's play *The Shadow of the Glen*, in which a disenchanted peasant wife makes off with a beguiling tramp from her dismal home, husband, loneliness, bog and mist. There were protests at the slight to Irish moral rectitude at the play's first performance at the Abbey in 1903. Among others, Yeats's beloved Maud Gonne walked out. But years later, when she had refused Yeats repeatedly, and he had rather wildly proposed to her daughter Iseult and had been refused by her too, Maud bought the house here at Baravore and Iseult came with her young husband, the stormy and perfervid novelist Francis Stuart, to live here. They soon moved to Laragh Castle, eight miles north of Drumgoff bridge. Then Stuart, oppressed in his turn by endless bog and mist, went to teach in Germany, to which he was in some ways sympathetic, and spent the Second World War there. He told a German agent, being sent to contact the IRA, to use Laragh as sanctuary, which the German did. Lonely Iseult fell in love with him but was sent to gaol before love could run its course. The agent was discovered and interned in gaol as well.

Back at Aghavannagh, we take the southerly road for Aughrim, accompanying the Ow River on its chattering descent. Just before Aughrim the Derry River joins the Ow, to make the Aughrim River, and the village of that name is prettily set below the junction. Crossing its bridge we keep to the river's right bank for a mile and a bit, then cross back on the road to Woodenbridge.

Croghan Mountain, on the right, has for long been linked with gold. As far back as 2000 BC, soon after workers in the Middle East had learned to melt and mould metal ores, prospectors arrived in Ireland to search for them, and their success is seen in the fact that most more recent local copper mines had already been worked in prehistoric times. Around Croghan they came on gold and began to create the kind of ornament – crescent-shaped lunulae, sun-discs, cups, torques and so on – displayed in considerable numbers in the National Museum, but the metal was not found without much laborious panning. It seemed for ever impossible to trace the motherlode from which the gold came, but that did not stop occasional goldrushes, notably in 1796 when a nugget weighing over twenty-one ounces was discovered. Perhaps a quarter of a million pounds' worth was yielded in the years that followed, but it was slow work. There have been excitements since, but it is unlikely any substantial seam exists. As Praeger says, 'if digging ever produces wealth for this island, it is from peat'. The destruction of many ancient remains was carried out in the hope of uncovering gold ornaments, but very few have ever been found.

We now arrive at Woodenbridge and the **Vale of Avoca**, which imposes its name on the river Aughrim from here to its estuary at Arklow. Though waters meet here, Tom Moore's lyric *Meeting of the Waters* is supposedly four miles up the Avoca Valley at the confluence of Avonbeg and Avonmore. The delight of this wooded valley, with high, nineteenth-century Gothic Castle Howard like a crusader's castle above it, is spoiled only by the scars of past and present copper pyrites mines and the prettifying of the spot that is meant to have inspired Moore. Even in 1836 John Barrow, with experience of the Arctic, China and Africa for comparison, stated coolly, 'I think more has been made of it than either the waters or their meeting deserve', and preferred, as many do, Woodenbridge. There has always been needless controversy about the spot the poet meant: needless, since Moore wrote to an inquirer, 'the fact is, I wrote the song at neither place,' and could not for sure remember which confluence suggested 'There is not in the wide world a valley so sweet ...'

The R752 takes us northward towards Rathdrum, but two miles before it, a right turn brings us to **Avondale**, the lovely, square 1779 Georgian home of Charles Stewart Parnell. Last century it served for many years as a college of forestry. Still the forestry board's property, its parkland and woods, with their many walks, are well kept. Parnell was born here to a Protestant, landowning family. Their land included lead mines, whose sole visible remains are a scatter of ruined smelting houses, along with slag heaps and miners' cottages, in nearby valleys. Parnell started as his background might suggest. At 28 he was high sheriff of the county. Then he went into politics determined to embarrass the English into granting home rule. He formulated the technique of boycotting, and in spite of being once gaoled for seven months by Gladstone made his Irish party of eighty-six indispensable to the Liberals. He survived several ruthless attacks and an incriminating forgery published by *The Times*, to become uncrowned king of Ireland and Gladstone's close ally, till the disclosure of his adultery with Kitty O'Shea antagonised Irish Catholics and English non-conformists and lost him leadership of the Irish MPs. He campaigned to retrieve it, certain he was Ireland's only hope, then died, aged 45. During most of the latter years Avondale was deeply mortgaged to cover his legal expenses.

From Rathdrum a main road leads north-north-west to Laragh up the beautiful Clara valley, and so to **Glendalough**, one of Ireland's most romantic, evocative sights – as long as the mists that frightened off Synge's heroine and Francis Stuart allow it to be seen. (We would have reached here from the opposite direction had we crossed the mountains by the Wicklow Gap.) The two lakes, which the second part of the word Glendalough means, were scooped out by ice which left a trough much deeper than the water's final outlet. At one stage ice blocked the water in the middle, and a lateral stream and bank were formed, the bank remaining as a broad delta to divide the two lakes. The beauty of this steep wooded valley ringed by mountains is most striking. It combined with remoteness to attract Kevin, future saint, to build his solitary cell here in 545, just before St Ciaran founded Clonmacnois, St Brendan Clonfert, and St Comgall Bangor. Kevin, like most of his contemporary saints, had an impressive empathy with the animal world. The story goes that once, as he sat in his cell (remains by the upper lake, across the bridge near his 'bed' and first church), reading attentively and resting his arm on the window sill, a blackbird came and, taking his hand to be a nest, laid its eggs there. When the saint at last noticed, he was so moved that he kept his open hand in the same position till the young hatched. After his day the place grew in size and sanctity. There were the usual Viking raids but the eastern range of buildings – the cathedral, the barrel-vaulted St Kevin's Kitchen with its belfry, the still almost perfect 110-foot Round Tower (its top is a reconstruction) and several others that survive continued to go up. After the Anglo-Norman invasion the monastery of Glendalough had a chequered history till the Tudor-Stuart conquest of Wicklow finally closed it, and decay began, though some buildings were in use, legally and otherwise, till the nineteenth century. Barrow noted in 1835 that burials of local Catholics took place here regularly. As elsewhere, penal laws were no match for peasant persistence. Thackeray as usual found reason to be sceptical. 'There are seven churches,' he wrote (as there are, in the lower range), 'whereof the clergy must have been the smallest persons, and have had the smallest benefices and the littlest congregations ever known.'

We return to Laragh and turn left on the R755 towards Dublin. High on the right, two miles on, is **Castlekevin**, the motte-and-bailey remains of a 1214 Norman castle, in the centre of what used to be

O'Toole territory and was in recent times owned by the Synges, the playwright's family. For centuries a thorn in the flesh of English ambition, it was finally occupied by the Lord Deputy in 1597 and dismantled, to become soon after the ruin it remains. We pass through Annamoe, where the young Laurence Sterne fell into the mill-race, and then through Roundwood, a centre for anglers beside the Vartry reservoir. There are two smaller lakes in the district, Lough Dan and to the north-west Lough Tay in its circular corrie. This is on the steep road up to **Sally Gap**, with its daunting views. By the top end of the lake is Luggala (pronounced Luggla), where the house-parties given by Lady Oranmore and Browne for the likes of John Huston, Woodrow Wyatt, Brendan Behan, Claud Cockburn and other luminaries have been described in the memoirs of some of them. 'Cyril Connolly was there one year in his red waistcoat,' wrote Behan, 'and I sang rebel ballads for him the whole evening.' Burned down in 1956, the house was rebuilt exactly as before.

Our road lies north from Roundwood. Ten miles on we reach **Enniskerry**, passing on the way the Great Sugar Loaf mountain, which in spite of appearances is not a volcanic mountain but a stack of quartzite, once covered with slate but now exposed by denudation and weathered into the characteristic quartzite cone. Enniskerry is pretty enough, and it contains the strikingly luxuriant garden of Dargle Cottage, brilliantly conceived by Sir Basil Goulding beside a precipitous stretch of the Dargle. Still, the village is more notable for proximity to **Powerscourt**, home of the Wingfield family from James I's reign to 1961, when Viscount Powerscourt sold it. The house, rich in plasterwork, marble mantels and inlaid floors, and complete with its original furniture, Waterford chandeliers and Wingfield portraits, was accidentally burned down in 1974. It was to have opened to the public for the first time the following year. Every Irish mansion which survived the Troubles and other depredations is a priceless part of the country's inheritance, but Powerscourt, designed by Castle around 1730 and the prominent focus of a fine estate, was specially valuable. Still, the terraces remain, and the magnificent arboretum, lake and prospect of the Sugar Loaf mountain. The terraces were begun in 1745 but the main work dates from the middle of the nineteenth century. Mainly responsible was Daniel Robertson, whose taste – this in the 1840s – was directed both at landscaping and sherry, which he drank as, from a wheelbarrow, he directed the efforts of a hundred men.

Powerscourt was almost the last house to be landscaped in the grand manner, before taste and economics dictated the swing to high

Victorian horticultural gardening. The raw materials could hardly be bettered – the steep slope below the house, a natural lake, and the Wicklow Hills with their rapid colour-changes beyond. The lake was formalised into the present Triton Pool, and work on the terraces began in 1843. From the upper perron, floored with pebbles from Bray beach, and with statues from the Palais Royal which used to breathe fire, five terraces descend to the lake, and a grille with winged horses – a family emblem – on either side. That is the simple plan, and it is combined with richly varied detail – the bronze Amorini on the perron, the Vine Gate, the Bamberg Gate (in *trompe l'oeil* perspective) and other wrought-iron gates, the two Pegasi, unusually cast in zinc. Below is a magnificent tree collection – including a 30-foot aromatic *Drimys winteri*, relation of the magnolia, monkey puzzles, a eucalyptus grown to 100 feet in forty years, and a Sitka spruce claimed – like one at Curraghmore – to be Ireland's tallest tree. There is also a Japanese garden of 1908, and many other items of curiosity. A drive, or a four-mile walk through woods, south of the house, brings us to the lovely 400-foot drop of Powerscourt waterfall – the tallest in these islands – in a deer park. In preparation for a visit by George IV a reservoir was dug at the top to keep the water falling, but the king never arrived. Unlike other Wicklow cataracts, this costs money to see, but it is the only Wicklow scene Edward Lear painted successfully and is worth the fee.

We can now make our way back to Dublin by the R117, through the picturesque Scalp. Or we can follow the Glencree River valley west into the hills again, turning right and north at the old reformatory of **Glencree**. Not long ago a centre for promoting mutual knowledge among children of the Republic and of Northern Ireland, the building, like others spaced over the hills, began as a barracks in 1798, becoming a Catholic boys' reformatory in 1859. Beside it is a cemetery, for the bodies of Germans whose ships foundered or planes crashed in or near Ireland during the two world wars. Over a mile west is the source of Dublin's river Dodder, which flows north-west before swinging round through the city's southern suburbs to the sea. Its upper valley is one of the more beautiful and sequestered in the area – it was part of Synge's favourite walk from Dublin. Four miles along the road from Glencree to Dublin we pass on the left **Montpelier Hill**, on top of which is Speaker Conolly's ruined sporting lodge, built in 1720. (Conolly also owned the Elizabethan Rathfarnham Castle to the north.) On shallow evidence, the lodge is associated with the Hell-Fire Club that was supposed to meet here, and to have at last gutted the place in an effort to ascertain what the members' destination after this life might be like. The club met regularly in the Eagle Tavern by Dublin Castle. In spite of hints of black magic and debauchery, its activities for all we know were confined to heroic intoxication, the relation of improper stories and a few harmless rituals.

We enter Dublin through **Rathfarnham**, whose castle to the right was built in the 1580s by Archbishop Loftus, who was to become first provost of Trinity college. From 1770 to 1771 his descendant, the Earl of Ely, had Chambers as consultant architect for modernisation. The Georgian version became a byword for sybaritic luxury. Like many of Dublin's suburban grand houses it has been kept in a fair state by clerical incumbents, in this case the Jesuits. It has recently been undergoing fundamental refurbishment, and preserves beautiful decorations by Angelica Kauffman and others. A mile south of the castle, down Whitechurch Road, is the **Hermitage**, an eighteenth-century house by an unknown architect, with strong nationalist links. Here Robert Emmet courted Sarah Curran, whose father lived in the now ruined priory over the road. In 1910 Patrick Pearse moved his College of St Enda here, building chalets in the grounds when the house overflowed. The enterprise was bankrupt by the time Pearse was executed for his part in the 1916 Easter Rising. House and grounds were bequeathed to the nation by Pearse's sister. His memory is hallowed by Irish Republicans, and the place has something of the aura of a shrine. It is regularly open as a Pearse museum, and there are nice riverside and garden walks in the surrounding demesne.

6

The South-East: Wicklow, Wexford and Carlow

U RBAN DUBLIN CREEPS round the coast, through pretty, two-castled Dalkey on its cliff-top, where pop-singers, Hollywood film-stars and best-selling authors have taken to buying for millions of pounds seaside villas which fetched only hundreds forty years ago, through Killiney, whose adjacent bay has been compared with that of Naples and is well seen from Sorrento Point or the top of Killiney Hill, to Bray. Two roads run southwards from Bray in roughly parallel courses between the sea and the mountains. The faster, main N11 mounts the Wicklow foothills from time to time and traverses some pretty valleys and passes. The coast road is minor, slower (especially in season), and mostly duller, but it takes you past miles of good beach, and some attractive headlands and fishing villages. Both get you round the Wicklow Mountains to the undulating, greener, gentler contours of county Wexford. To bird-watchers the coastline of this south-eastern corner of Ireland offers as much spectacle and interest as anywhere in the two islands, especially in winter. The climate attracts too, with the lowest year-round rainfall and highest temperatures – an average 62 degrees Fahrenheit in July – in the country.

Both roads lead to **Bray**, nine miles south of the city centre, a town which emerged out of the vast railway investment of the mid-nineteenth century. William Dargan, the 'Railway King' who constructed the first (Dublin to Dun Laoghaire) and many later Irish railways, lost his last fortune trying to turn Bray into Ireland's Brighton. It has all the trappings, recreations, vivaciousness and vulgarity of a seaside resort, besides some fine villas and terraces and a striking Neo-Tudor town hall (by Sir Thomas Deane and Son) and there are splendid cliff and shore walks round triple-peaked Bray Head south of the town, and a couple of miles beyond to Greystones. Inland and southward looms the Little Sugar Loaf Mountain, conical quartz neighbour of the Great Sugar Loaf, the view of which it obscures from Bray. The main road runs between the two peaks and continues in a fine sweep through the oak-cloaked Glen of the Downs. The minor road goes more haltingly. A mile after Bray it passes the demesne of **Kilruddery House,** held within the lovely valley formed by the Little Sugar Loaf and Bray Head. The land has been owned for four centuries by the Brabazon family, earls of Meath since the early seventeenth century.

The tenth earl had Richard Morrison design him a Tudor-revival mansion here, whose roof is alive with pinnacles, willowy chimneys, turrets and curved and stepped gables and which remains massive even after the postwar removal of a large rotted chunk. It contains a forty-foot high great hall and impressive plasterwork in different styles. Outside is a rare and remarkable survival from the seventeenth century: a formal garden, complete with lake, twin canals, curved banks, cliffs of cut hedge, along with sumptuous statuary of later dates, much of it contained within a fine domed conservatory of 1852. Four miles on, Delgany Church of Ireland church has a majestic monument of 1790 to David La Touche, descended from one of hundreds of Huguenot officers in King William's victorious army, who had become Dublin's first banker. The church was built, also at La Touche's expense, in 1789, in Gothic-revival style. His palatial house, Bellevue (the name survives), and a 200-metre long, curling glazed garden passage linking greenhouses were all demolished in the 1950s.

Nine miles further, a minor road leads from Ashford up the pictur-esque defile of the Devil's Glen, thickly wooded with oaks and conifers, down which the river Vartry tumbles, at one point down a hundred-foot fall, from its mountain reservoir. There are good walks along the river and in the woods. Just beyond Ashford, lying on both sides of the river, are **Mount Usher Gardens,** famous for rare exotic herbs, trees and shrubs obtained from different parts of the world since 1868 by generations of the Walpole family. The eucalyptus specimens are said to be the finest in Europe, and the nineteenth-century weirs and water-courses were designed by an engineer member of the family.

Wicklow is three miles beyond, a small county town of eccentric, easy-going charm, grown beside the mouth of the River Vartry which for its last two miles, after descending from the mountains, has widened into the Broad Lough, divided from the sea by a strip of sand and grass known as the Murrough and rich in bird-life. Whooper and Bewick's swans as well as mute, and a huge flock of greylag geese are among many species making their winter homes here. Like most coastal settlements Wicklow was founded by the Vikings (hence the 'wick' of the name), though centuries before that St Patrick tried unsuccessfully to convert the local chief to Christianity. (A recalcitrant pagan knocked all the teeth out of one of the saint's holy companions.) During the Middle Ages O'Byrnes and O'Tooles plagued the English settlement here, exacting 'black rents' from English townsmen till the sixteenth century, and once burning the town to the ground. The tower of the good eighteenth-century Church of Ireland church is surmounted by a dome, and there is an older Romanesque doorway in the south porch. **Wicklow Gaol**, behind the court-house on the square, has been converted into a museum on 'heritage centre' lines, with a number of set scenes complete with static human figures, representing such themes as old prison conditions, the 1798 rebellion, prison reform and the impact of the transportation of convicts on themselves and on Australia. The gaunt ruins of Black Castle stand on a rocky outcrop near the harbour. It was built by the Norman Maurice FitzGerald, and left to decay after Cromwell's troops besieged and took it from Confederates in 1649.

The coast road from here to Arklow passes a succession of good sandy beaches, including the long, popular, sandy arc of Brittas Bay. The river Avoca reaches a sedate maturity after its picturesque tumble down the Wicklow Mountains, and at its mouth is the busy town of Arklow. A couple of miles before this, high above the left bank, stands **Shelton Abbey**, built in 1770 to the Gothic-revival designs of Sir Richard Morrison for the Howard family, later earls of Wicklow, and well into the twentieth century a byword for stately grandeur, with fine woods, a famous collection of subtropical plants and a two-mile drive hemmed by rhododendrons. It was too expensive to maintain, and since the war has been in turn a hotel, a forestry school and an open prison, the majesty of the demesne ravaged by commercial forestry and other developments. The mining which has defaced parts of the valley helped to make Arklow the busy, prosperous little town it is. Forestry, too, helps to answer a need, since the Republic, though producing ten times more timber than when it achieved independence, is well behind both its own requirements and the percentage produce of other European countries.

Arklow itself has an old and continuing boat-building tradition, and a Maritime Museum in the old technical college which reflects various marine matters. A few wall fragments remain of the thirteenth-century castle erected by Theobald Butler, ancestor of one of the two most powerful clans in Ireland over the next four centuries. (The other was the FitzGeralds.) It was one of the country's four main Butler fortresses, but in 1315 Edward Bruce, brother of Robert the Bruce, king of the Scots, sacked it during his abortive campaign to secure Ireland for his own. This was a spur to the Irish who for years after that would make destructive sorties from their mountain fast-nesses to reclaim their ancestral lands. Arklow was only preserved by the English at heavy cost to life and money. Like Wicklow, it was occupied by Confederates, and eventually taken and brought into line by Cromwell.

It saw a further critical scene, when in 1798 Father Michael Murphy, who had raised the Wexford rebellion by killing a British soldier, pitted his brave medley, armed mainly with pitchforks, against Arklow's defences, hoping to link up with their Dublin coun-terparts beyond. His monument stands in the square. As a priest, Murphy was neither typical nor a success. The Catholic hierarchy roundly condemned the rebellion, and two and a half hours saw the death of Murphy and the end of Wexford hopes. Days later came the hour-long battle of Vinegar Hill, which merely cleared up the remains. There is a good Roman Catholic church of 1840, by Patrick Byrne, while some windows of the 1900 Church of Ireland church contain stained glass by Harry Clarke. But there is now no sign of the sea-girt rock reported by Giraldus 'from which the tide ebbs on one side while it flows on the other'. *Pace* the chronicler, who was curious about tides (Wicklow Harbour 'fills up when the tide is ebbing from all other places'), there is very little tidal movement on this coast at all. We go on south by the main road to Gorey passing on the left 833-foot Tara Hill (not the famous Tara), prominent in its flat surrounds.

Gorey, too, was assaulted by insurgents on their way to Arklow, and gave way. It was built early in the seventeenth century, its streets on a grid pattern characteristic of the time. St Michael's grand Roman Catholic church and the Loreto convent were built between 1839 and 1842 by the opinionated, fastidious Augustus Welby Pugin, devoted with a fanatical purism to the revival of medi-eval Gothic styles of the late thirteenth and early fourteenth centuries (especially in the English Houses of Parliament, in the rebuilding of which he was assistant to Sir Charles Barry) to super-sede what he saw as the debased, loose, voguish Gothic. He was influenced here by the remains of Dunbrody abbey beside Waterford Harbour.

159

South-east lies the best part of this Leinster coastline, with several resorts, much sand and relatively few people. (One slight climatic hazard can be the cool east wind; the prevailing south-westerly, from which the dunes protect, is usually mild.) We are now well into county Wexford, whose interior is often called the Garden of Ireland – a name that, while sticking in the throat, gives a correct impression. It is delightfully undramatic, restful, fertile country, with enough hills and rivers to give variety. Its coast is unlike any other Irish coast, fairly flat and sandy, with occasional broad inlets. The south-facing section has peculiar fascination, but this eastern part is best for bathing. Out to sea, the Glassgorman and other sandbanks and gravel ridges, deposited by the glacial flow on what was then land, have been a fatal hazard for shipping, and are well lined with lightships. The first seaside village we reach is **Courtown,** a pleasant resort with a fine beach and harbour that balks fishermen by frequently silting up. Ardamine, two miles south, on the same stretch as Courtown, is notable, but not the only local village to make the claim to be the landing place of Ladhra, a companion and possibly brother of Cesair, Noah's granddaughter, and the first man on Irish soil. The flood did for him, according to some ancient records. Others suggest too many women. One, an oar in the buttock.

The coast continues, marked here and there by little villages. Cahore is quiet, in a lovely area of woods and low hills, with the beaches of the Point close by. Blackwater is amazing, not as a competitor for, but a frequent winner of the Tidy Towns competition; tidy it is, of course, but startling too in the luminous colour scheme of its houses, and central religious grotto. Curracloe is a quieter village of thatched and whitewashed cottages, with dunes and wonderfully sandy bay stretching north and south for miles.

Beyond that, off to the left of the Wexford road (the R742) and situated north of **Wexford** Harbour, is a broad expanse of mud-flat and sand-dune with the unpromising name of Wexford Slobs (there are more on the harbour's southern side). In a bird-rich coastline, this Wexford Wildfowl Reserve is exceptional. Winter brings ten thousand Greenland white-fronted geese and high numbers of Brent geese and Bewick's swans. There are wigeon, mallard and other ducks, black-tailed godwits, golden plovers, curlew and many other waders and there are rafts of common scoter out at sea, as well as a large year-round population of pinioned birds easily seen from roomy hides. For the birds, the main appeal is in the population of molluscs and crustaceans inhabiting the shifting tidal world of shoal, reef and sandbank, as well as, for some, the grain planted on the neighbouring fields.

We cross the bridge over Wexford harbour and enter the town, whose ancient, labyrinthine character is preserved in and off the narrow, winding Main Street running through its middle, and whose eighteenth-century opera house has brought it worldwide fame. The harbour is partly filled with sediment from the Slaney River, whose estuary it forms, and almost blocked from the sea by a long bar of sand and gravel. (Large boats have to use the artificial harbour of Rosslare to the south.) But neither feature could stop the flat-bottomed boats of Norsemen, who created a trading port (Wexford is Norse for 'fjord by the sandbank'), nor the English allies of Dermot MacMurrough, who here began the campaign that created Ireland's main preoccupation for seven centuries.

The Danes, or Norsemen, appeared in 850 and having conquered stayed for three hundred years. They went down well with the locals, forming treaties, establishing regular merchant shipping lines between Wexford Harbour and Britain, France and beyond, hauling in sea-fish, building a timber city with lanes leading down to wharves and an earthen wall that later broke the first Norman advance. They erected several churches after their conversion in 1035, and even had the men of Leinster on their side at Clontarf, against Boru.

Robert FitzStephen, heading the Norman influx, arrived at Wexford in May 1169, and a few days later the Danes surrendered. In 1172 Henry II made the town over to Strongbow, and the king himself spent Lent at Selskar Abbey, continuing his penance for the murder of Becket. Strongbow settled the place with his own countryfolk. By some quirk of history the language of these English speakers was retained by the inhabitants of the barony of Forth till recent times, mixed with a little of the Irish that was spoken all around. It was hardly understood by either Irish or English and eventually died out at the end of last century. After Strongbow, the place continued to prosper. The Normans made permanent settlements on Danish foundations, and were followed by the Cistercians, who founded abbeys like Dunbrody and Tintern in the county. New walls and gates went up round Wexford in the fourteenth century and all was well until Cromwell's visit. Early in his progress through southern Ireland, and fresh from his Drogheda bloodbath, the future Protector took Wexford – the Confederates' naval base – by storm, and massacred 1,500 defenders and every visible priest in the streets. That left a population of under 400. Cromwell's supposed headquarters are inside the present Woolworth's.

Wexford's sufferings were not over. In 1798 the United Irishmen made their poorly planned, uncoordinated bid for independence. Revolution had been in the air for years, imported from America and France, and a few concessions to Catholics had increased the appetite for more. But the south-east was not reckoned by the government a grave threat to peace. On 26 May, however, fuelled by news of risings elsewhere, of torture, massacre of prisoners at Carlow and repeated provocation by army patrols, Father John Murphy of Boulavogue, ten miles north of Wexford, led a ramshackle force, which quickly grew to a thousand or more, to the top of nearby Oulart Hill. The provoked military ravaged the country and stormed the hill. They were unexpectedly defeated and many killed. The peasant army moved out to the town of Enniscorthy, ten miles west. Again they beat the government troops, burned the town to the ground, and camped on the neighbouring Vinegar Hill. But they had little idea of what to do with success. The weather was beautiful and the hillside was coated with carpets brought from neighbouring houses. There was a lot of drunkenness, and much slaughter of cattle and sheep (men later carried raw wheat grains in their pockets to stave off starvation, and it was said sprouting wheat often marked the graves of rebels speedily buried in shallow graves). Both sides were at times barbarously cruel to their opponents. To Vinegar Hill a loyalist delegation came from Wexford to ask the untrained cohorts to spare their town. This seems to have given the indecisive leaders (who would have done better to move north and link with other rebels near Dublin) the contrary idea of attacking it. Thousands of pikemen and gunmen moved off to Three Rocks, an outcrop of the long ridge of the Forth mountain three miles west of Wexford. Government troops fled, and the rebels soon swarmed into the defenceless town, where they stayed for several weeks, appointing a rich but radical Protestant landlord, Bagenal Harvey, as their commander-in-chief. In spite of his efforts to prevent it, there was a lot of plunder, brawling and drunken swagger. But events elsewhere in the county turned the tables on the rebels. Before they left, in the middle of June, they rounded up a hundred or more Protestants by the wooden bridge that then linked the town with the north bank, shot or piked them and tipped the bodies off their pike-ends into the river. Then they made once more for the main rebel camp on Vinegar Hill, outside Enniscorthy, for the final confrontation. Retribution followed. Wexford saw another scene like the last – more spiking on pikes, and government troops kicking the severed heads of rebel leaders about the quays, official hangings and beheadings.

In the nineteenth century the harbour was silted further, and trade and traffic ebbed away. The early 1900s saw the end of the old oyster trade – three to five shillings a hundred and rows of eating houses that served them – when a European virus destroyed the twenty miles of beds along the coast. More recently, however, Wexford, with generous Guinness subsidies, pulled itself up by its festival. Disdaining high summer, Wexford waits till the end of October to put on a programme of lesser known operas with world-class soloists, Irish TV's orchestra, and the splendid local chorus, as well as a full complement of films, recitals, exhibitions and so on. The eighteenth-century theatre is not large, nor indeed is the town, and a very special intimacy is created between those who perform and those who watch during this charming week. For walking round, Wexford has a more historic atmosphere than most Irish cities. Much even of the old Norse arrangement survives in the low alleys leading from the long curving main street to the quay (till 1800 they used to lead straight to wharves). The dull quay is still magnificently situated on the Slaney estuary. It has a monument to Commodore John Barry, founder of the American navy, who was born at Ballysampson, some miles south-west. Behind, among the narrow streets and old-fashioned shops, some special monuments stand out. **Selskar** (Holy Sepulchre) **Abbey**, by the West Gate and near remains of the fifteenth-century wall at the town's north-west end beyond Cornmarket and Abbey Street, is where Henry II did penance and Strongbow's daughter (by his first marriage) married Raymond le Gros, his FitzGerald lieutenant. The West Gate itself now houses a heritage centre. The Bull Ring, coming south along Main Street, has an excellent 1700 Flemish-gabled house, and the site of the Old Rectory, now part of White's Hotel, where the archdeacon, father of 'Speranza', Oscar Wilde's poet-mother, lived, and where she was born. The pikeman monument commemorates the 1798 Rising and is by Oliver Sheppard (1864–1941), a sculptor who elsewhere pioneered *art nouveau* styles in Ireland. Bull-baiting took place till 1792. Pugin designed the church of St Peter's Roman Catholic College in Summerhill Road, and his pupil, Robert Pierce, the 'twin churches', both in the upper south-west part of the town. Walks – the Tourist Office lays on very good guided ones – are helped by the system of explanatory plaques arranged at points of interest round the town. Two miles west of Wexford on the Enniscorthy road is the impressive National Heritage Park at **Ferrycarrig**, a collection of replicas of Irish homes from mesolithic to medieval times.

From here, or from Wexford itself, we move towards the south coast of the county, a stretch with a peculiar character of its own, where the scenery of lagoons and sandbanks, sea-birds and Norman ghosts make equal claims on our attention. First we drive three miles south-west of Wexford to take in **Johnstown Castle**, which is a spirited 1840ish package of theatrical Gothic, designed by Daniel Robertson of Kilkenny, who was responsible also for Powerscourt gardens and several other houses in the area. Set among gardens, lakes, greenhouses and a marvellous collection of trees, and close to the estate farmyard which now houses a sensible and instructive Museum of Agriculture and Rural Life, the castle and demesne form an agricultural college and research institute – an enlightened way of extending the life of an ostentatious Ascendancy pile. Two miles south-south-east stands the mellow ruin of Rathmacknee Castle, one of Wexford's best fifteenth-century remains, with five stories and well-preserved stepped battlements.

We can now make for the coast at **Rosslare** – a developed resort with a good eighteen-hole golf-course. Bernard Shaw could be 'lost in dreams there; one cannot work in a place of such infinite peace'. Five miles south-east, is the quite distinct and rapidly expanding Rosslare Harbour, which receives ferry-boats from Fishguard, Pembroke and Le Havre. Or we can bypass Rosslare and head south for **Lady's Island**, passing through Tagoat, where is the county's genealogical centre and a Yola farmstead, Yola being a name of Fleming settlers who followed the Normans to this area. Lady's Island, attractively set on a deep lagoon and reached by a causeway, is the site of a ruined Augustinian abbey, St Mary's, built like the ruined Lambert Castle close by in the mid-thirteenth century. During a search by troops in Penal times, it is said that a crucifix and statue were discovered and thrown into the lake. Recovered years later, they were restored and make the place a scene of annual pilgrimage (15 August). Not far away, in summer, is a colony of rare and raucous roseate terns.

Three miles south, **Carnsore Point**, an isolated granite outlier from the Leinster chain, makes a secure south-east bastion for the country against the conflicting currents beyond. This mixing of waters, from the south-west Gulf Stream and northerly Labrador Current, makes this one of the richest sea-fishing areas of these islands. Currents make it also one of the most dangerous. But sea-fishing trips from several bases within a few miles are under supervision and quite safe. There are chances at appropriate times to see huge numbers of birds on passage between the Mediterranean, or further, and such northerly breeding-grounds as Iceland and Greenland. On the landward side is a virtual jungle of fern, gorse and various shrubs. From here to the west the miles of wild fuchsia and escallonia are one of the greatest surprises for the British traveller. Even more startling is that, biologically, these fuchsia flowers by the million are a waste. In our latitudes the plant reproduces only vegetatively – by shoots, chance cuttings and so on – never by seed. St Vogue's, or Vauk's, Well and church ruins to the north of the point recall (very little else does) a sixth-century hermit who was reputed to have sailed to Brittany on a stone and died there. The stone is pointed out here. It must have sailed back.

We return past Lady's Island, and then turn left twice to reach **Tacumshane**, which boasts a complete windmill. It was built in 1846, of the kind known as tower-mill, with the thatched cap on top revolving to suit the wind direction. Used in earnest till 1936, it was restored in 1952 and is preserved by the State but no longer worked.

Tacumshin Lake, another lagoon cut off from the sea by a long shingle banks topped by sand, is to the west, rich in waders and wild-fowl, as is most of the Wexford coast, second only to county Cork in its importance for birds. We go north and turn left on the R736 to round the lake, passing at its head Bargy Castle, a solid, happy blend of stepped crenellation, Georgian sash windows, arches, bartizans, internal secret passages and winding staircases. Now a hotel, this was once the family home of Bagenal Harvey who, after his part in the '98, and his escape to Saltee Island, was caught, hanged in Wexford and buried at last in Mayglass Church, two miles north-west. The left turn after the castle takes us straight to **Kilmore Quay**, a long and very pretty village in which all the cottages are thatched and whitewashed. From the harbour, with its healthful kelpy smell, there is a pleasing view over the shallow flats that stretch miles to the east. From the harbour, too, fishing-boats go out, for bass and conger eel and lobsters; and a trip can usually be hired to the **Great Saltee Island**, providing the wind is not strong and northerly. (It is important to check whether landing will be allowed.)

The island is the final appearance of a mostly submerged ridge reaching out from Forlorn Point, by the quay. Privately owned by 'Prince Michael the First' (who having achieved his boyhood desire of buying the place, had himself crowned on a limestone throne near the house he inhabits during part of the summer), Great Saltee is one of Ireland's most thriving bird sanctuaries. Here among the wild hyacinths, the sea-campion, sea-pink and scurry-grass dwell, during the nesting period of late spring and early summer, hundreds of thousands of birds. Herring, great and lesser black-backed gulls and kittiwakes keep mainly towards the rocky scarp on the island's south side. There are besides those relatives of the extinct great auk (of which the last Irish specimen was caught at Waterford Harbour in 1846), the puffin with its technicolor bill, the razorbill with a monochrome substitute, and the white and dark brown guillemot with its sinuous neck. Cormorants are there, too, and the superficially gull-like fulmar petrel whose range seems oddly but steadily to expand, unlike that of the peregrine falcon, which used to lord it here but is seldom seen now. In June eggs almost block progress and the noisy birds can be aggressive. By the end of July they have gone to the sea, and the trip is hardly worth taking. In Saltee most of the handful of Irish records of the nightingale have been made, but none in recent years. The success story is that of gannets, whose numbers have risen from a handful in the 1930s to over a thousand pairs.

We take the minor north road out of Kilmore Quay, turn left after two miles, left again at Duncormick through a land rich in castle ruins to reach **Bannow** on the extreme west of Ballyteige Bay. At Bannow, mounds and sandy humps and the scant ruins of thirteenth-century St Mary's Church mark a lost Norman city, already covered by drifting sands in the seventeenth century. (MPs representing a church and a chimney were still returned to the Irish Parliament till 1798, when £15,000 compensation was paid to the landowner, the earl of Ely.) Beyond is the peninsula of misnamed Bannow Island, an island proper in Norman times; and it was here that the Norman Conquest began. Dermot MacMurrough, whose snatching of the willing, mature (she was forty-four at the time) Dervorgilla from Tiernan O'Rourke in 1152 had led to the loss of most of his Leinster lands, had meanwhile busied himself finding allies to help him recover them. From Henry II of England and France he obtained a letter inviting English knights to help him. The letter had the desired effect of rallying Richard FitzGilbert de Clare, Earl of Pembroke and better known as 'Strongbow' and others to his cause. Strongbow was bribed with an offer of MacMurrough's daughter Eva in marriage and the right of succession to his Leinster territory. In May 1169, Strongbow's advance guard under Robert FitzStephen arrived at Bannow Island. Days later they held Wexford, and shortly after MacMurrough was secure in his Leinster estates, based on Ferns. In the old cemetery beside Bannow Church is said to be Princess Eva's grave.

We follow Bannow Bay round, across Wellingtonbridge, and turn off first left to **Clonmines**, another town that died. In Norse times it had its own mint, for which silver and lead were mined on the opposite riverbank. William the Marshall, Strongbow's son-in-law, fortified it and gave it a Charter of Liberty. It was destroyed at the end of the fourteenth century but, rebuilt soon after, it grew rich again. By 1684 the sands had blocked its access to the sea and silted its harbour. As a thoroughfare it was at an end. But the ruins of three churches and four castles, and its place by the bay, make it an evocative sight. Reverting to the main road we turn off left to round the Hook Peninsula. **Tintern Abbey**, two miles along on the right, was a daughter foundation of its Wye Valley namesake, and was founded by William the Marshall in gratitude for a safe crossing. Granted to the Colclough family after the Dissolution, it remained their home for four centuries. In the 1950s they gave it to the state, which has cleared away most of the residential additions and restored some of the earlier parts.

Beyond Fethard the road leads to **Baginbun Head**, where the headland itself is marked off by a large ditch and ramparts – the defences of the second contingent of Norman invaders under Raymond le Gros. They numbered less than a hundred and set themselves to collect a large herd of cows. Soon a force of three thousand Irish and Norse approached to send them whence they came (though in old accounts three thousand often means simply a large, unspecifiable number). The Normans stampeded the cattle into the attackers and followed up with a charge. Such prisoners as were taken had their limbs broken before being thrown over the cliffs, and the Normans waited confidently for the arrival of Strongbow himself at Passage East, in Waterford. We can continue down the Hook, which was one of two alternative approaches to Waterford for Cromwell when he arrived in 1649. The other was by the west side of Waterford Harbour on which stands, a mile south of Passage East, a village called Crooke. Either way, Cromwell vowed to take the city, and his words 'By Hook or by Crook' are with us still. (But Cromwell may have been playing on an older use of the phrase.) Near **Hook Head** is the graceful, crenellated fifteenth-century and later castle of Slade, with its fine tapered tower, assigned by Cromwell to the Loftus family, later Earls of Ely. The drive up the western coast takes us through Duncannon, where the refugee James II, after the rout of the Boyne, took ship for Kinsale to spend his last years at St Germain. The little fortified town was soon after taken by the officer destined to become first Duke of Marlborough. The handsome, often rebuilt and recently restored late Tudor fort on the headland stands on the site of an Iron Age fortification.

Two miles beyond Duncannon, at **Ballyhack**, there is a year-round ferry service across the narrows of Waterford Harbour to Passage East, cutting the journey to Waterford (should you be going that way) from forty to ten miles. Three miles further north, opposite the point where the River Suir spills into Waterford Harbour, and right beside a creek on its eastern side, is the magnificent ruin of **Dunbrody** – a large Cistercian abbey built in the early thirteenth century on land granted by one of the first Norman arrivals, Hervey de Montmorency, in 1178. One of its names, St Mary of Refuge, recalls its mother abbey in Dublin and its old sanctuary rights for malefactors, stipulated by the founder. It appears relatively plain, in the ascetic Cistercian tradition, with an aisled nave (and its graceful Early English arches), six transept chapels and a low central tower (added, as such towers usually were, in the fifteenth century), and austere cloister buildings. Above all it provides a superb view, especially from the road, and those treasured accompaniments of Irish remains – ivy overgrowth, grass-topped walls, jackdaws above and sheep grazing below – all enhance the effect.

From here, for many miles, our journey is close to the Barrow, one of four major rivers of the south-east. The Barrow is navigable and connects, just above Athy, with the Grand Canal extension, so that it would be possible to get from here to Limerick or Leitrim in the same boat. That requires time and a penchant for uneventful water travel. All the same, to keep to roads that skirt these rivers is almost a guarantee of good scenery, and a lot of the more interesting sights of the country will be met this way – a legacy of the days when forest covered the uplands and valleys were the only means of travel. Most of our travels from now on in the southern hinterland will be based on rivers, from the Slaney in the east to the Lee that recedes almost to the west coast. For the present we follow, more or less, the Barrow and make along the main road for New Ross. Five miles before getting there we can turn right to see the **Kennedy Memorial Park** on the southern slope of Sliabh Coillte. John F. Kennedy's great-grandfather Patrick lived at a farmhouse in Dunganstown, on the left of the main road. It was Patrick's son who emigrated to Boston. The original house has gone, but there is a later one in its place. The park was sponsored by the Irish in America. Trees were given by countries around the world, and the mountain slopes are being converted into a magnificent arboretum containing five hundred species of tree and shrub. The low grey-stone timber-roofed building in the centre offers fine views and displays, including a bronze map showing the gardens and arboreta of Ireland, and an interesting display of the woods and grains of some 136 different tree species. Signposted off the R733, on the last run into New Ross, is the delightful seven-acre garden of Kilmokea Country Manor, on what used to be an island on the River Barrow. Warm tidal water keeps the place relatively frost-free, and crinodendron, myrtle and drimys are among the hundreds of thriving species.

The best thing about **New Ross** is its old aura – the tall thin Dutch-type houses of irregular height on the waterfront, the twisting lanes and old steps and cobbled path up the hill, flanked by terraces of charming cottages. It owes its origins to William the Marshall and his wife Isabella de Clare, daughter and more importantly heir of Strongbow by his wife Eve or Aoife, daughter of the Leinster king Dermot MacMurrough. William's lively abilities in this area matched those of Hugh de Lacy in Meath, with as lasting results. He built the large parish church of St Mary's at the top of the hill, in Early English style, and so paved the way for the import of English Gothic that was the making of Cashel and other cathedrals. Later the town's walls were erected, with everyone compelled to take part in the building. This was the apogee of the Anglo-Norman occupation. By the end of the thirteenth century they were far flung over the land, but too thinly. In the following century the Irish had learned enough of Norman ways to strike back effectively: by 1400, after a short-lived settlement by Richard II, last medieval king to land in Ireland, English territory had shrunk to the Pale and had to wait for the Tudors to expand again. One of the chief leaders in this Gaelic resurgence, Art MacMurrough, devastated the town at Richard's coming in 1398, and later regained possession of it, and most of Leinster, earning the title 'most fierce rebel'. He died here in 1418, after token submission to a much weakened English monarchy. In 1649, having supported the Confederacy against Ormonde, the town yielded to Cromwell at his crossing of the river by a bridge of boats, preferring not to go the dreadful way of Drogheda and Wexford.

New Ross did not, however, escape the impact of the '98, and here took place the biggest battle of the whole rebellion. Bagenal Harvey, the local landlord appointed leader of the Wexford insurgents, led thousands of rebels in a wild attempt to carry New Ross. They burned and advanced steadily while the garrisons hailed them with cannon shot. Then the government cavalry charged and spread disorder. The initial cohesion of the rebels, once lost, was never restored. Women and children helped them and the tales of bravery and sacrifice are legion. But in the end two thousand rebels were dead, and hardly more than two hundred soldiers, and the net was closing for its final catch at Vinegar Hill. At the end of the battle some rebels fled along the Wexford road and gave the news to comrades holding some two hundred Protestant men, women and children, mainly taken in Wexford town, in the barn at Scullabogue, just south of Carrickbyrne Hill Wood. In panic, an order was given to set fire to the barn. Those who tried to break out were piked back inside. The screams of the burning were heard over a mile away. No prisoners survived. There are good views of the country from the town's heights, but of most interest is the ruin of the original **St Mary's Abbey** with the early nineteenth-century Church of Ireland church occupying the nave. There are some ghoulish graves and memorials in the crypt and church. The elegant Tholsel, with its domed cupola, in the lower part of the town, was built in 1749. Damaged in 1798, it was rebuilt in 1806 to the old plan.

On the river, the Galley Cruising Restaurant provides meals on board during up-river journeys. By road, keeping to the right or east bank of the river described by Spenser, who knew it well, as 'the goodly Barrow, which doth hoord Great heapes of Salmons in his deep bosome', we make our way north, through a delightful valley. Woods hang high on either side. There are rare flowers – a cousin of the bluebell, the nettle-leaved bell-flower – among the woods, and the lovely pink trumpeting lily, meadow saffron, in damp fields. The first flowers in spring, the second autumn. After eight miles, with conical Mount Brandon looming on the left, we come to **St Mullins**, and the attractive but scanty remains of a monastery founded by St Moling, on a shelf raised above the river. Moling, who died in 697, is often associated with foxes and kept one as a pet. His monastery was to include the burial place of the MacMurrough kings of Leinster. The remains include a Round Tower's stump, a carved High Cross and some rudimentary church ruins, but, in spite of their paucity, their position by the river and the still-used surround of the graveyard leave a lasting impression.

For several miles the Blackstairs Mountains can be seen on the right, rising to 2,610 feet at Mount Leinster, on whose north slopes (goes a by no means unique claim) the last Irish wolf was killed near Myshall, in 1786. This range is an exposed continuation of the granite of the Wicklow Mountains, as is the heathery Mount Brandon on the other side. Sheltering beneath the latter, on a lovely stretch of the river, is the little town of **Graiguenamanagh** ('Granary of the Monks'), founded by William the Marshall, with picturesque streets (the mountain road west to Inistiogue makes a good diversion). The Cistercian **Abbey of Vallis Sancti Salvatoris**, or Duiske Abbey, recently well restored, has much of beauty and interest including the early fourteenth-century effigy of a mail-clad knight. The fall of the central tower in 1774, and subsequent spread of rubble, has raised the floor several feet above its original level. The abbey was a copy of, and partly colonised by monks from, Strata Florida in Cardiganshire, Wales, but colonised from Stanley in Wiltshire (of which no trace remains). Almost the whole of the town is set in the purlieus of the original abbey, the largest Cistercian foundation in Ireland and dating from 1207. We can cross here to the west bank and reach Borris, five miles north, by way of **Ullard**, where there are the scant remains of seventh-century St Fiachra's monastery and later buildings, which include a good Romanesque doorway and worn tenth-century High Cross. Fiachra went to France from Ireland and died there in 670. His name is forever associated with haemorrhoids and syphilis, which he allegedly cured, taxis which in French are named after him because the hotel that first hired them out had him as patron, and gardens, because his hermitage at Meaux was admired for its vegetables.

Borris, with its steep, wide and handsome main street and excellent views of the mountains, is beside the impressively set demesne of the Kavanaghs, descendants of Art MacMurrough and the Kings of Leinster. Heavy, foursquare, battlemented **Borris House**, built in the eighteenth century, was restored by Sir Richard Morrison and his son William Vitruvius in about 1820 in the Tudor Gothic style they are much linked with. Long before, in 1778, the Kavanagh family guarded Mrs Kavanagh's sister Eleanor Butler after her first scandalous attempt to elope with Sarah Ponsonby. Eleanor escaped after three weeks and tramped twelve miles south-west to Woodstock, where Sarah secreted her in her room until Eleanor's father conceded defeat and sent a carriage to take them to Waterford, whence they sailed to Wales and a fifty-year lifetime of seclusion (neither ever spent a night away from home), mutual devotion and fame as the Ladies of Llangollen. A later owner of the house, Arthur MacMurrough Kavanagh, despite being born with stumps instead of arms and legs, contrived to ride, shoot, marry, sire seven children including the present owner's great-grandfather, serve with reforming zeal as an MP, and travel adventurously in remote parts of Asia. Four centuries earlier, Eileen Kavanagh eloped with her lover Cormac O'Daly, giving rise to the love-song Eileen Aroon. Muine Bheag (pronounced Mooni beg) or **Bagenalstown** (the Irish name was adopted by a vote in the 1950s) is seven miles on, with the Bagenal family's former demesne of Dunleckny, which they were granted in the sixteenth century, to the north-east. The present house (opened by appointment), Tudor-Gothic in style, was built about 1850 to Daniel Robertson's design. Walter Bagenal laid out the town in the eighteenth century. He had great ambitions for its architectural splendour and intended it to be called Versailles, but removal of the old coach route left it much as it is, and with a name he would scarcely have approved. There is a good early nineteenth-century Greek-revival courthouse. On the Barrow's west bank, just south of Leighlinbridge is **Dinn Righ**, a rath that marks an ancient seat of the Kings of Leinster; it was the site of an apocalyptic pre-Gaelic battle. On the opposite bank in the village are the ruins of twelfth-century **Black Castle**, which was built by Hugh de Lacy in 1180 and destroyed progressively – by Rory Og O'More in 1577, Cromwell in 1649, and some more natural cause in 1892.

Three miles west is the small, sequestered and delightfully casual village of **Old Leighlin**. The Church of Ireland **Cathedral of St Laserian** is a relic of the days when it was the diocesan church. Much of the building dates from the thirteenth century. Its overgrown churchyard creates a strong feel of the past, with often-recurring names on the tombstones – Nolan, Bryan, Murphy (and a stone over a '98 victim, that reads simply 'the love is true that I.O.U.'), many of them in the clear and legible lettering of what became a distinct school of tombstone cutters in north Wexford in the early nineteenth century. Inside, the church has some interesting fragments from an earlier building.

Since St Mullins we have been in the wedge-shaped county of Carlow, and now, halfway up its western border (at this point the river) we come to its namesake county town. In the maze of old Anglo-Irish snobberies, a Carlow address was much superior to a Wexford one. The novelist Molly Keane (M. J. Farrell) was brought up in Wexford, acutely conscious of her address's low rating. It made no difference that her home was almost on the border. **Carlow's** name is odd in that it has no apparent significance – 'four lakes' or 'quadruple lake' in a part where there is no lake at all. There may have been once. The town is busy with the smaller industries – mainly sugar beet (since the first Irish factory opened here in 1926). Its boast is

William the Marshall's castle, Ireland's earliest four-tower keep, of which only a curtain wall and two drum towers survive. Nothing done to it by Art MacMurrough (in 1405), Rory O'More (in 1577), Cromwell's Ireton or the '98 rebels compared with the achievement of a certain Dr Middleton, who, in 1814, deciding it would function well as a lunatic asylum if only the walls were not quite so thick, used a charge of dynamite to reduce them and so blew away all but what still stands. The striking Neo-Gothic Roman Catholic cathedral and St Mary's Church of Ireland church both date from the early nineteenth century; as does the fine central classical courthouse by William Vitruvius Morrison – perhaps the finest of all Irish courthouses. In the cathedral is a statue by John Hogan of the founder, Bishop Doyle of Kildare and Leighlin (known as JKL), heroic champion of Catholic rights and pride, to whom the eighteenth century was 'the bad century' – a concept difficult for many Protestants to sympathise with – and who tore down, sometimes with his own hands, the cabins and flimsy churches his flock were expected to live and worship in. As a boy he saw the 1798 massacres here, and as an old man lived at the double-bow-fronted house Braganza close by. The gravel pits at Graigue on the west bank are where, after a vain assault on the town in May 1798, over four hundred insurgents from the surrounding countryside were buried in quicklime after being shot, bayonetted, burned or drowned. The place was known as the 'croppy hole'.

Two miles east of Carlow (leave by the R726 and find it on the right after a mile), in the demesne of Browne's Hill House, a very fine three-storey building of 1765, is the outstanding dolmen of **Browne's Hill**, the largest in Ireland and perhaps in Europe. (Permission to view should be asked of the farmer.) Its capstone, which measures twenty feet square by five feet thick, and could weigh as much as a hundred tons, is supported by smaller stones at each end. It could be up to five thousand years old. The incredible achievement of lifting the capstone was obscured by the builders, who probably covered the whole edifice, with its royal corpse underneath, with earth or stones, and possibly a gleaming coat of crystalline quartzite on top. Though modern archaeologists confess their ignorance of the practices surrounding dolmens, people in the past were full of theories. Folklore (and Yeats's 'Faery Song') hold them to be the beds in which Dermot and Grania, Conchobar's daughter, slept when pursued by Finn McCool after eloping from Tara. No less mythical are old assertions that dolmens were tables on which the Druids laid out human sacrifices in order to apply their knives.

We are about to stray from the south-east, Carlow being halfway between Wexford and Dublin on the inland route west of Wicklow. The river borders have flattened out now for we are coming to the level county of Kildare.

The bustling town of **Athy** (pronounced Athigh; 'Why is the county of Kildare like the leg of a fellow's breeches?' 'Because it has Athy in it.' Blame James Joyce, in *Portrait*, for that), has a good Georgian market-house and late sixteenth-century White's Castle defending the bridgehead (private, with lace curtains at its windows). It has seen a good deal of warfare due to its position on the border between Kildare and Laois. What is not so usual for an Irish town is the existence of a fairly modern Roman Catholic church, built in 1963 to 1965, that evokes a good deal of admiration. Five-sided, and with a hyperbolic roof, it owes something to cinema architecture, but is bright, spacious, and still one of the best modern churches in the country. In 1307 Edward Bruce, after defeating a Butler-commanded army three miles north at Ardscull, sacked the town on his journey south. In the square here early in 1798 the authorities first introduced the wooden 'triangle', a frame to which stripped suspects were tied and flogged.

From Athy we drive almost due east, seven miles or so, to glimpse the monastic remains of **Moone**. They stand in private farm ground, but access is public. Chief among them is tall, thin Moone High Cross, of the tenth century, and probably one of the earliest erected. Its well preserved figures are superbly primitive, and the Twelve Apostles, Sacrifice of Isaac, Daniel in the Lions' Den and the Flight into Egypt look like the polished conceptions of a tidy-minded child. Moone Abbey House nearby is an elegant eighteenth-century Palladian house with central block and side pavilions. It was raised a storey early last century.

A couple of miles south, on the right of the N9, is the demesne of the long demolished eighteenth-century Belan House, home of the Earls of Aldborough, with two plaintive obelisks and the remains of a rotunda temple to commemorate its lost grandeur. The next right turn brings us to the grand demesne, with meadows and streams, of **Kilkea Castle**, an impressive medieval fortress reconstructed, after a fire, in 1849. Until 1960 the property (and after the sale of Carton in 1949 the seat) of the Duke of Leinster, it is now a luxurious hotel. It also has a ghost, that of Gerald, eleventh Earl of Kildare, the pathetic half-brother of Silken Thomas (who lost his head in 1537). Gerald, aged 10 in 1535, when the Geraldines were all but eliminated by

Henry VIII, was brought up abroad. For a time he served under Cosimo de Medici. Later he was restored to his estates but never regained any of his family's former power. Every seventh year this 'friendly' (the hotel claims) ghost rides a white charger into his former study. Kilkea House, to the south, was the birthplace of Sir Ernest Shackleton, who accompanied Scott and led later expeditions to the Antarctic. One of Shackleton's ancestors had founded the Quaker school at the early-eighteenth-century Quaker village of Ballitore, a few miles north, where the boy Edmund Burke was a pupil. The meeting-house is now a Quaker museum. Three miles south-east of Kilkea is **Castledermot**, a straggly village with remains, at its south end, of a monastery founded by St Dermot or Diarmuid, in the more modern churchyard. Dermot is associated with a movement which, after the great expansive efforts of the early Irish church had lapsed, tried to revive the vigour, discipline and scholar-ship once again. The Culdees, or Friends of God, began to make themselves felt in the last part of the eighth century. They banished abuses and took over the running of the church with military thor-oughness. The writings they concerned themselves with were ascetic rather than aesthetic, and many that have come down are the rules and records of the harshest regime in Church history – prescriptions of beatings, genuflexions by the hundred, long recitations by heart in awkward postures, spending nights on nettles, or beside dead bodies. But through their agency a cultural revival came also. The Book of Kells may owe its existence to their vigour, though not to their crafts-manship. All that is known of Dermot is that he was one of them and that, having founded the monastery about 800, he died in 823. The Culdees spread from the south, the way we have come, and moved on to the rest of the country. The monastery remains include a good sixty-six foot high Round Tower, two High Crosses and the base of a third, and the doorway which alone survives from a Romanesque church (and from which the modern church's door is copied). Nearby are the impressive remains of a Franciscan friary.

We now drive south-east along the R418 and pass on the right after four miles the old demesne and ruins of Duckett's Grove, a huge, free-ranging fantasy of Victorian Gothic, burned in 1933 but still part-used. Six miles further, **Tullow**, with its narrow main street and pretty bridge over the Slaney (which replaces, for us, the Barrow, left to its higher stages in the surrounds of Slieve Bloom). The town's themes are the familiar ones of the south-east – Butler dominion, Cromwellian massacre and '98 troubles (Father John Murphy, its most enterprising leader, was hanged here) – but very little survives. There are good walks, and the river splashes prettily down some rapids beside the bridge. Five miles south of the town, off the Bunclody road, is **Altamont**, an eighteenth-century house with nineteenth-century Gothic wings, whose fine gardens are sometimes open to the public. We now go east, for a last look at county Wicklow, but a quiet corner of it resting against the southern slopes of the Wicklow Mountains. We reach **Shillelagh** in ten miles. The area round about is known for its oak forests, and the roof timbers of Westminster Hall are supposed to have been sent as a gift from here by the king of Leinster. The region grew so many oaks that it gave its name to a stick more essential to an Irishman than an umbrella to an Englishman. 'An Irishman cannot walk or wander, sport or fight, buy or sell comfortably without an oak stick in his hands.' The shillelagh was used as a walking-stick, for fighting, for hurling, for urging on cattle. But in the eighteenth-century English landlords found they could sell them, at ten pounds a thousand, as pipe-staves to London dealers. They did, and got their short-lived quick return, and now the blackthorn cudgel, a substitute and nothing to do with the real thing, is sold to credulous tourists as if it were. **Coolattin**, the handsome, unpretentious house within the neighbouring demesne, was built in 1801 to 1804 for the Earl Fitzwilliam, a former lord lieutenant of Ireland. It stayed in the family until 1977 when the last earl died and the title became extinct. Family and name are supposed to stem from an illegitimate son of William the Conqueror, but authorities rubbish the claim. Their wealth was more firmly based. In the 1880s they owned over ninety thousand acres in Ireland and twenty-four thousand acres in England, the income totalling almost £140,000 a year. It was a distantly related branch of the family which owned some of the most delectable parts of Dublin and is commemorated in the names of streets and squares there.

Up the valley of the Derry, which winds north-east between regular shaped green hills, is Tinahely, and, just across the river, **Fairwood**, the name given by Thomas Wentworth, Earl of Strafford, in 1639, when he was building a grand house for himself amid 'the daintiliest and plentifullyest watered country I ever saw'. He planned a park with 1,500 deer, and 'a breed of horses' and an ironworks to give local labour. 'Black Tom's cellars' are the remains of what was only a beginning anyway. We can return to the Slaney through Carnew. **Clonegal**, a lovely village where the Derry joins the Slaney, has a long arched bridge over the sedgy broadening of the river, and pretty houses in a tree-lined main street. The massive pile of Huntington Castle stands high in its demesne to the west of the village, and is occupied still by descendants of the family which built its nucleus in 1625. Of an agreeable mishmash of styles, the house has been recently restored. The owner, an ordained Church of Ireland parson, has added the Egyptian goddess Isis to the objects of his devotion, and dedicated the cellars to the Fellowship of Isis. Visits must be arranged beforehand.

Bunclody (alias Newtownbarry), with its enormous square, is at the meeting of the Clody and the Slaney and makes a good base for exploring the bosomy landscape of the Blackstairs Mountains. The last lap of the 2,610-foot Mount Leinster is closed to cars, but the walk is easy and the view broader than almost anywhere in Ireland. On Sundays many locals go up for the walk and view, and pick whortleberries that abound among the heather.

Ferns, eight miles south-east of Bunclody, was the capital of Dermot MacMurrough's elastic twelfth-century kingdom. Worsted for years by his northern rivals, he here, backed by the first contingents of Normans, received O'Connor's and O'Rourke's confirmation of his kingship over all Leinster; and here he died two years later in 1171, rotting alive, it has been said, according to his deserts, in the priory he had built, having opened Ireland to the full measure of foreign conquest. The former capital has become a market village. The thirteenth-century castle preserves only one and a half drum towers and a wall. It was dismantled by Sir Charles Coote in 1641. There is a fine chapel, however, and Round Tower beside it. The Cathedral of St Aodan, or Maedog, dates from 1817, but contains interesting earlier fragments. To the east are the remains of MacMurrough's Augustinian Friary with graceful lancet windows and a belfry that is curiously square below and becomes a Round Tower above. It is on the site of the early monastery founded by Maedog, who achieved sanctity by, *inter alia*, lying naked on the cold stone to recite from memory all the psalms each day of his life. Renunciation also figures at the end of Ferns's history, for it was here in the nineteenth century that Father Cullen founded the Pioneer Total Abstinence Association, so paving the way for the temperance movement that spread widely in Ireland last century, and is still strong.

Eight miles south-south-west and lying in the middle of the Wexford farmlands is **Enniscorthy**, a thriving market centre on a steep slope with unusual (for Ireland) irregular streets and a river, the Slaney, that is both tidal and navigable from here to the sea. A statue

177

of Father John Murphy and other figures by Oliver Sheppard stands in the market place. It was he who started the rising, striking dead a looting British soldier, eight miles away; and beside the town, on **Vinegar Hill**, the interlude was all but ended, when on 21 June 1798, General Lake with thirteen thousand men stormed the rebel encampment which had held the town over three weeks, and killed and scattered their force. There is a good view of the town from the hill. Below, the castle and Church of Ireland cathedral of St Aidan are worth examining more closely. Raymond le Gros built the castle but it was rebuilt in 1586; shortly afterwards Edmund Spenser leased it for a while. It comes down to us, splendidly solid and little affected by Cromwell or Lake, but restored and modernised in 1900, and now houses the tourist office and fascinating county museum. The Roman Catholic Cathedral was designed by A.W. Pugin in 1840 and is one of the best examples of Gothic Revival style, with a narrow elevated look inside and out, and a characteristic attention to fine points of detail. Augustus Welby Pugin, son of Augustus Charles, did other work in this area and as far afield as Adare in Limerick, but it brought him little satisfaction. Of the cathedral nave he complains in a letter: 'the new bishop has blocked up the tower and stuck altars under the tower! ... it could hardly have been worse if it had fallen into the hands of Hottentots.' Two miles south, at Borodale House, Admiral Lord Beatty was born in 1871.

From Enniscorthy we can return to Wexford to complete the circle, close to some lovely stretches of the Slaney; or drive straight across to New Ross, thence to follow roughly the course of the Nore into the heart of county Kilkenny.

1 *St Patrick's Cathedral, Dublin, whose most famous dean was Jonathan Swift*
2 *Killiney Bay, south of Dublin, compared for its languid beauty with the Bay of Naples*
3 *The Cross of the Scriptures at Clonmacnois vividly depicts biblical and historical scenes*
4 *Glendalough, where the aggressively celibate St Kevin built his cell in the year 545*
5 *Interior of Westport House, County Mayo, dating from 1731 but much enlarged later*
6 *The Rock of Cashel, with its cathedral, Round Tower and Romanesque Cormac's Chapel*
7 *Jerpoint Abbey, County Kilkenny, a Cistercian foundation*
8 *Ancestral home of the Butlers, massive Kilkenny Castle*
9 *Dun Aenghus, a semi-circular prehistoric fortress on the southern cliffs of Inishmore*

7

Kilkenny and South-East Tipperary, Waterford and Coastline

COUNTY KILKENNY IS on the fringe of Leinster, and
Tipperary is in Munster. Somewhere here, people stop regarding
Dublin as the big city and think of Cork or Limerick instead. Except
for the Wicklow Mountains and some smaller rocky outcrops, rural
Leinster is a rich green province of large estates and farms and the
houses and demesnes that have traditionally gone with them. Much of
Munster, but by no means all, is mountain and moorland with a
rugged rocky coastline that is, to us anyway, one of its chief attractions. The farming country of Tipperary's Golden Vale, and of large
parts of Limerick beyond, is as rich as any in Ireland, but every fertile
stretch is hemmed in by mountains. Here in county Kilkenny, we are
firmly in prosperous, comfortable Leinster. The county owes much of
its wealth and fertility to rivers which often, by their channels or
catchment areas, dictate the limits of Irish counties. Ireland's longest
river, the Shannon, spends its life dividing counties from one another.
Wexford is bisected by the Slaney, Meath by the Boyne, Tipperary by
the Suir. The central artery of Kilkenny is the Nore. Old abbeys,
castles, great houses, the ruins of other great abbeys, castles and
mansions, and the stoneless memories of still others line its banks.
Kilkenny city looms over it. It laps pretty villages like Inistioge and
Thomastown. There are flat green water-meadows, ancient bridges,
willows, alders, herons; and concurrent roads on which traffic races
hectically and incongruously from somewhere to somewhere else.

It is the Nore we follow from New Ross, at this stage spilling prettily down a valley flanked with wooded gorges. In ten miles we come
to **Inistioge** (pronounced Inisteeg), and just before can look left and
up to the wooded surrounds of **Woodstock**, once one of the grandest
houses in Kilkenny but burned in the Civil War. The spruce village,
with a handsome tree-lined green and river walk, juxtaposed
churches, the remains of two towers in the Church of Ireland churchyard, is perhaps too pretty for its own good, a favourite location for

179

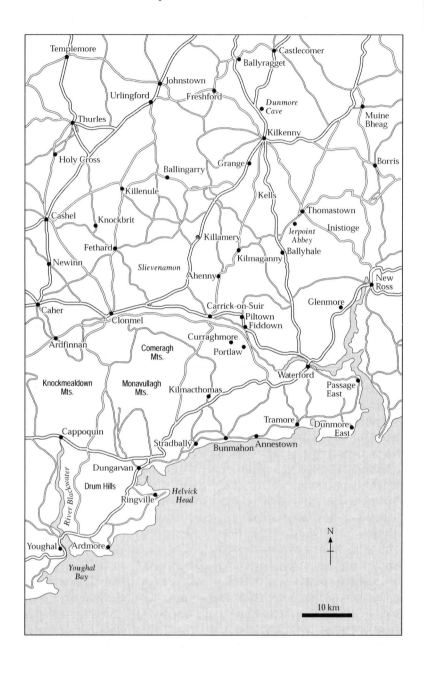

film directors, Dubliners wanting second homes and promotional tourist authorities. But Woodstock deserved more attention than the twentieth century was giving it. 'Never did my imagination paint Paradise itself so full of Nature's sweets', wrote a visiting parson in 1796. He would be shocked to return. The house is a gaping wreck, burned out in 1922. But right at the end of the twentieth century those parts of the woodland which had not been replanted were scrutinised by sensitive experts. An eighteenth-century (and later) treasure was laid open. An avenue of noble firs, a kilometre long, and another of monkey-puzzle trees emerged from a tangled coat of scrub. Huge specimens of sequoia, cypress, Himalayan hemlock, Japanese thuja, and rarities like Hartweg's pine and a bladdernut tree emerged. The grand complexities of the original gardens were exposed: remains of conservatory, greenhouses, a steam bath-house, rockeries and so on. The house is still a ghost. It was built about 1745 by Francis Bindon, and was at its historic liveliest for a few weeks in 1778. The inhabitants, Sir William and Lady Betty Fownes, had her orphaned cousin, Sarah Ponsonby, aged 23, living here. One night she disappeared. She had in fact climbed out of a downstairs window, dressed as a man and carrying a pistol. An older woman, Eleanor Butler, was missing too, from her home, Kilkenny Castle. Searchers found them both at Waterford, ready to take ship to Wales. Sarah was brought back to Woodstock, Eleanor to cousins at Borris House (where we saw her). A few weeks of menaces, letters, pleas, sulks, a certain wary curiosity about the nature of their mutual affection, on the parts of parents and guardians and – from Eleanor and Sarah – tungsten stubbornness, won them freedom. They sailed to Wales and lived happily ever after, the famously retiring Ladies of Llangollen. A graceful monument by Flaxman to Mary Tighe, Sarah's cousin and a poetess held in repute by the Victorians, stands in the mausoleum behind the Church of Ireland parish church near the demesne gates. The fine old ten-arched bridge marks the approximate tidal limit of the river.

By turning left two miles on where the main road to Thomastown crosses the river, we can pass **Dysart Castle**, a crumbling keep in the middle of a field, once home of the Berkeley family. The philosopher-bishop George Berkeley was born here in 1685. He was educated at Kilkenny College and wrote a surviving description of the Dunmore cave, both of which places we are approaching. **Thomastown** itself is pretty but reduced in status. Fragments of town walls and the remains of the thirteenth-century parish church founded by the Norman seneschal of Leinster, Thomas (whence the village name) FitzAnthony, recall its better times. But instead of crossing its mellowed bridge we turn left and cover the two miles to the much grander riverside ruin of **Jerpoint Abbey**, founded in 1180, a daughter house of Mellifont. The usual Irish stepped battlements are conspicuous from all angles. Like other Cistercian foundations, it owes its situation to the order's rejection of town for country, and a lonely site where monks could work and pray in peace, and their need for good sheep pasture nearby, for they traded in wool. Like others, too, it has an austerity of design in contrast with the buildings of other orders, but this – as at Boyle, Mellifont, Holy Cross and Kilcooly – stands out grandly in the rustic setting. Most of the present buildings date from the fifteenth-century rebuilding, when the central tower was erected, though there has been partial restoration in the nineteenth century and more recently. Much of Jerpoint's interest lies in its details, the effigy tomb of Felix O'Dullany, twelfth-century Bishop of Ossory, with a serpent in his crozier, among a collection north of the chancel; and the later effigies of two knights in coats of mail; the Walshe and Butler tombs in the south transept; but especially the carvings of the cloister, each one different and done with a skill and vigour that could make them convincing relief illustrations for characters in Chaucer's tales.

Two miles north-west of Jerpoint is massive, solid Mount Juliet, built after 1750 by the Butler Earl of Carrick, home of the McCalmonts and their famous stud until the 1990s, now an expensive hotel, some of its character lost, much of its richly wooded demesne ironed into a dull green 18-hole championship golf course (designed by Jack Nicklaus) interwoven with smoothly tarmacked drives. A couple of miles south of Jerpoint, in the valley of the Little Arrigle River, there are two virtually invisible curiosities. Some years ago the rock round Kiltorcan House, near Knocktopher, was quarried for road-building, and it was possible to walk along the quarry edges picking out fossils of the oldest known plant life of Ireland. They date from the Carboniferous Age, which elsewhere left us our legacy of coal. Here a gradual accumulation of plants and sand under an ancient shallow lake has left a wealth of clear sandstone fossils of primitive plants like club-mosses, horsetails and ferns, some of which grew several feet high. They are still plentiful, but require a careful search – and permission to make it. Around Ballyhale, half a mile away, the people are supposed to be descended from Welsh settlers of the early centuries AD – 'a clan of Welshes', says Thackeray, who 'maintain themselves in their occupancy of the farms in Tipperary fashion, by simply putting a ball into the body of every man who would come to take a farm over any one of them'.

Knocktopher, a mile north on the N9, has a Romanesque doorway, a tower, a fine fifteenth-century tomb with twin effigies, and wall and window remains of a medieval church, while in private grounds on the west of the village are ruins of an old Carmelite friary, part of it absorbed into a private house. Were we to take the road west to Kilmaganny we should pass two remarkable houses but the first, Mount Morres, a palatial mid-eighteenth-century mansion with a nine-bay front by Francis Bindon, is a substantial ruin; and Rossenara, built by the architect of the White House, James Hoban, and home in the twentieth century of the American novelist Richard Condon, stands invisible among its woods, and powerfully proofed against intruders. The De Montmorencys of Mount Morres have a curious distinction. The surname – their 'ancient and original name' – was 'resumed', by Royal Licence, in 1815. They had been merely Morres before. The change fitted a fashion for medievalising names, Gothicising buildings, holding tournaments and so on. But not everyone was happy. G. E. Cokayne, the great authority on genealogy, wrote of 'this cock-and-bull pedigree, or genealogical nightmare which, for sheer topsy-turvydom, has never been surpassed ...' and continued for pages. Even dressing up in fancy surnames, it seems, has its rules.

Two miles north of Knocktopher, west of the main road, the N10, is the site of Flood Hall, long since demolished, birthplace in 1732 of the nationalist orator Henry Flood. The second turn left beyond this, at Stonyford, brings us to **Kells**, nothing to do with the famous Kells in Meath, but the charmed site of a fortified Augustinian priory whose buildings enclosed five acres in the thirteenth century, and, though long since ruined, still do. The need for fortification is seen in the fact that the place was burned by a Bermingham, taken by Edward Bruce and burned by the first Earl of Desmond in the space of a hundred years – the last being occasioned by Kells's owner calling the earl an Irish poet. (Times changed: the earl's grandson was famous for his Irish poetry.) Most of the surviving remains are fifteenth-century towers with connecting walls round the long perimeter, and church – especially cloister – buildings, containing good tombs. Two miles south is Kilree, where a topless, 98-foot tall Round Tower, ruined medieval church and High Cross with very worn carvings are all that remains of a monastery of which nothing is known.

Callan, five miles west of Kells, has a richer history and associations than its ruins suggest. A few interesting details survive in the fifteenth-century Augustinian friary – above all the finely carved sedilia in the choir. But we need to go to Jerpoint or Kilcooly to see the work of Callan stonemasons of that period. The tree-topped mound to the left of the Kilkenny road, overlooking the river, is the remains of a castle built by William the Marshall, about 1217. Later it was acquired by a branch of the pervasive Butlers and remained theirs till Cromwell sacked the fort in 1650. A battle fought here in 1407 between Butlers and an alliance of Norman and native Irish forces left eight hundred of the latter dead. (An Irish diarist, Amhlaoibh O Suilleabhain, living here 400 years later, in the mid-nineteenth century, describes more peaceable gatherings: a thousand young men and women dancing on the hillside, and twenty thousand horsemen gathered at a political rally.) North-west of the town is **West Court**, and the restored thatched farmhouse, containing a museum, where Edmund Rice was born in 1762. In 1802 he opened in Waterford the first Irish Christian Brothers school. Today the order educates Catholic boys around the world, and Rice is a candidate for canonisation.

We follow the N76 for Kilkenny, passing after about four miles a sign to the woodland walks of Desart Court, site of a Palladian house of the 1730s which was home for two centuries of the Cuffe family, earls of Desart, most records of whom are favourable and even endearing. The last countess but one fought vigorously to raise living standards, building a model village, mills, factories, public library, hospital, theatre and so on, at the edge of Kilkenny, being made a senator in the newly independent Irish parliament, and having her house burned down for her pains, in 1923. A few miles on, we reach **Kilkenny**, county capital, and the only true Irish city not on the coast. It was important soon after the Anglo-Normans came, even before. Castle (founded by William the Marshall), cathedral and various monastic foundations testify to that. Parliaments met here, and the Statute of Kilkenny of 1366 is still famous for trying what was actually to take another three centuries to bring about: to keep the English English, or more accurately perhaps the Anglo-Normans Anglo-Norman, and stop the rot of 'Gaelicisation'. The English must not marry the Irish or entertain Irish shanachies (story-tellers), or sell them horses or arms; must speak English, stick to English personal names, ride in the English style (i.e. with a saddle), eschew the game of hurling, and use English bows and arrows; and they must keep the Irish from their churches. This all seemed quite reasonable to the assembled bishops and archbishops who 'all being present at the said parliament did fulminate sentence of excommunications against those contravening the aforesaid statutes'. Their spirit lived on. In 1844 the town was still officially divided into the distinct corporations of Irishtown, to the north, around St Canice's, and Hightown, by the castle – a pattern repeated in many other cities and one of the perennial grievances of the native population.

In 1391 Edmund Butler, third earl of Ormonde, bought the castle. In a century during which the English government had neglected Ireland for more pressing troubles in France and Scotland, the FitzGeralds of Desmond (roughly, modern county Cork) and the Butlers had tussled for top status, wealth, land and influence. The Butlers had started well – with royal favour (the name comes from the privilege, as 'chief butler of Ireland', of setting duty on wine imports) and a grant of 750,000 acres of north Munster, with a first headquarters at Nenagh in north Tipperary. They were particularly good at producing male heirs, and from now till the end of the seventeenth century Butlers of various branches occupied, influenced and flavoured life for miles around. Direct succession did lapse in 1515, but Piers Butler, with a feeble claim but a will to make up for it, introduced a fresh and sparky line. He had the ear of Henry VIII – his grandson was brought up at Windsor with young Edward VI – and in the course of a century this new flowering of Butlers stayed loyal to the crown, disdained (unlike many 'old English') Irish ways and dismantled the power of the Geraldines.

Loyalty survived the Stuarts, and in 1642 was rewarded with a marquisate and a dukedom. Forced to withdraw when the king's fortunes were lost, the future first duke nevertheless brought over an army from France in 1650, though he soon had to withdraw. He came back to his dukedom at the Restoration, was twice viceroy, and retains a vital place in Irish history. His son backed the winning side at the Boyne, but later intrigued with Spain over the projected invasion of England in 1714. He was impeached and died in exile in 1745, and his successors, though restored to estates and some titles, never repeated the impact of their ancestors.

Most of the places we have seen over the last thirty miles were once Butler property. Butler history abounds in stone in **St Canice's Cathedral** in the form of tombs, one of the earliest topped with the effigy of a mail-clad crusader knight. The place is rich in epitaphs from the sixteenth century and later – 'a vertuous mother, and her New-borne Sonne/ (Parted) here meet, and end where they begun ...'

begins a touching tribute of 1631; and the eighteenth century is well represented by rounded heroic couplets. Peter Scheemakers did the memorial to Archbishop Cox's wife in the south transept, which is crowded with good work. The Cox memorial was erected in the archbishop's lifetime with a blank left for an inscription when he came to die. This was taken as an invitation to impiety by young clerics, and a premature epitaph appeared – ' ...This well-known truth, by every tongue confest,/ That by this blank thy life is best express'd.' The Archbishop is chiefly remembered for the building of Castletown Cox, Davis Ducart's masterpiece in county Kilkenny.

St Canice or Kenneth, who founded a monastery here in 577, gave his name to town and cathedral. The latter is primarily thirteenth century, though it incorporates parts of an earlier Romanesque church, whose coneless Round Tower adjoins the building, and has been vastly altered by later events and restorations. It suffered more than most at the Dissolution through a fanatically iconoclastic bishop, who was nevertheless outdone in their day by Cromwell's men. The bishop of that time recorded that the troops had 'utterly defaced, and ruined' the building. They had 'thrown down all the roof of it, taken away five great goodly bells, broken down all the windows, and carried away every bit of the glass, and all the doors of it, that hogs might come and root, and the dogs gnaw the bones of the dead'. They also stabled their horses inside. The reconstruction carried out a century later by Bishop Pococke might have been better had he not used plans drawn by a man who had never seen the cathedral. Subsequent restoration has not been faithful to the original, but the cathedral retains much of its restrained Gothic beauty. It is a pity that the rather stubby central tower should be lower than the original; but the details of quatrefoil clerestory windows, the gallery over the west doors, and the rich collection of memorials and tombs are all of great interest, the tomb of Piers Butler and his wife Margaret being probably the best. North of the cathedral is the plain eighteenth-century Bishop's Palace and cathedral library of 1679, with a precious collection of seventeenth- and eighteenth-century books.

Between cathedral and castle runs the main street, changing its name from Parliament to High Street halfway, and then, close to the river, the Parade. Behind Parliament Street to the left is the Franciscan friary, a scant ruin close to Smithwick's Brewery. On the right of Parliament Street, the Dominican 'Black Abbey' of 1226 was reroofed and restored to use in 1840. Rothe House, on the right, well restored and housing the offices and library of the worthy and vigorous Kilkenny Archaeological Society, as well as Kilkenny's genealogical centre, is a Tudor merchant's house of 1594 comprising three blocks (built successively to house John Rothe's family as it expanded to twelve children) with cobbled courtyards between. It is one of several surviving Tudor houses within the medieval nucleus; Kilkenny possesses more than any other Irish town. The Rothes themselves got the worst of the seventeenth century, opposing first Cromwell, then William. They left to distinguish themselves in France.

Nearly opposite is the courthouse of 1794, much influenced by Gandon's work. Kyteler's Inn, now a restaurant and an almost complete reconstruction, was one of many coaching inns in the same street; it was the home in the early fourteenth century of Dame Alice Kyteler, a lady of four husbands who, accused of sacrificing cocks and having communion with the Devil in the cause of witchcraft, fled to England leaving behind a maid, Petronella, to be burned at the stake. The case is well-documented, and an intriguing example of medieval judicial practice. The Tholsel, or Exchange – now the City Hall – is an arcaded building of 1761. In the municipal offices, behind the Great Council Chamber upstairs, are some interesting old documents including a thirteenth-century minute book, the *Liber Primus*. The city calls for exploratory walks, for it has fine terraces of Georgian and earlier houses, almshouses, churches and various medieval monastic remains. Near John's Bridge on the left of Rose Inn Street, is Shee's Almshouse, founded 1582 and home now of the Tourist Office and an impressive model of medieval Kilkenny. We may cross the bridge to glimpse Kilkenny College off John Street on the right. Founded by the Great Duke in 1666, it included Swift, Bishop Berkeley, Congreve, Farquhar, Earl Beatty, and many others among its pupils. The college in fact moved from the building in 1990, for more practical premises. The present building dates from 1782.

The place round which history revolved was, of course, the **Castle**. Strongbow built the first castle in 1172, and this was followed by William the Marshall's sturdier structure of about 1200. To Marshall the town, like many we have seen already, owes its existence. The third Earl of Ormonde bought it in 1391 and from then on it was the chief Butler seat. Marshall's castle remained till the seventeenth century but now only three of his drum towers and the north wall survive. The first duke remodelled it after the Restoration, under the French influence he had been exposed to during exile (the west gateway remains from his work, Ireland's earliest piece of properly classical architecture). When his son was attainted and left the country, it fell into decay, and owes its present state to a major reconstruction by William Robertson in the early 1800s, followed by smaller operations. The civil war of 1922 saw the castle captured by each side in turn, and then tragically neglected. Soon after, all the contents were sold off and the place surrendered to dry rot. Among others, Evelyn Waugh thought of buying it, but eventually, in the 1960s, the sixth Marquess of Ormonde gave the castle to the city and the park to the nation. In 1967 the castle was the centre of a massive rally, to which Butlers came from all parts of the world. There is an interesting exhibition of Butler portraits in the gallery, but no match for the fine paintings collected by successive marquesses and now scattered.

At the old Kilkenny Private Theatre opposite the castle, Gay's opera *Polly* was given its first performance and later Tom Moore acted and met his future wife, sixteen-year-old Bessy Dyke. Nearby are the classical castle stable-buildings, Gibbsian in character, now skilfully converted into the Kilkenny Design Centre, where Irish crafts of many kinds – silver, linen, wool, copper, pottery, etc. – are exhibited and sold.

We now move on from manmade beauties, north along the N77 and soon turning right for Castlecomer, along the valley of the river Dinin. On the left, Jenkinstown Wood, with walks and picnic places, site of a manic sprawl of stagey, early-nineteenth-century Gothick, now in ruins, and its spacious demesne, is followed by a locale of natural gloom, the vast and sultry depths of **Dunmore Cave**. This is seven miles north of Kilkenny, at the edge of hilly country abounding in ring-forts and giants' graves. A few years ago one could imagine oneself, were it not for the single iron supporting rail down the steep, long and slippery slope, in unexplored country. Now, lights, paths, viewing-platforms and a car park have removed not only the discomforts but also something of the macabre appeal. As usual with large caves, this is set in limestone, whose soluble calcium carbonate makes it subject to hollowing. It has, as Mr Thomas Molyneux observed in 1709, a 'dreadful Romantick appearance'. Two English visitors of forty years later wrote: 'when you enter the Mouth, a sudden Chilness seizes all parts of the body, and a Dimness surrounded our lights, as if the Place were filled with a thick fog … In several Places were Skulls and human Bones, as it were set in the Crystalline substance.' The cave opens on the left of the descent into an enormous chamber with various evocative rock formations, and then continues through a narrow channel to more subterranean spaces. In earliest days, there was supposed to be a monstrous enchanted wild cat living in the entrance, a match for any fighter that challenged it. This probably stemmed from the presence of real wild cats which were still found in Ireland in the nineteenth century. Later it was used for living in, most likely as a refuge in times of war. The Englishman's reference to bones may well link with an entry in the *Annals of the Four Masters* for the year 928: 'Godfrey, grandson of Imhar, with the foreigners of Ath Cliath [Dublin] demolished and plundered Dearc Fearna [Dunmore], where one thousand people were killed in this year.' In 1999 a guide found a cache of silver jewellery and coins in the cave, which suggested some of the victims had taken their valuables with them.

The land rises to the north to make the dull Kilkenny coalfield, an isolated stretch among the limestone, which has over the ages been mainly stripped of its coal deposits. The town of **Castlecomer** was planned, with its surviving wide streets, by the Wandesford family after they had settled in 1635. It suffered in the '98 and, though pretty, has little left of interest. The Wandesfords exploited the local mines, and smokeless anthracite was produced till the last of them closed down in the 1970s. We turn left in the town for **Ballyragget**, six miles away. The tower here, still roofed, is of a castle built by a Butler of the sixteenth century. Half a mile beyond the village we turn off left to reach **Freshford** in five miles. Here the eighteenth-century Church of Ireland parish church incorporates a fine Romanesque doorway from the monastery first founded by St Lachtan in the seventh century. The appearance of inward lean of the pillars is an obvious characteristic of these Romanesque doorways, but so are the four or five richly carved orders which this lacks. Also unusual is the figured frieze at the top of each outer pilaster. Eight miles west, after turning right in Freshford, we come to Urlingford, and four miles south, to the left of the R690, to the remains of the small Cistercian Abbey of **Kilcooly**. It is, characteristically, in a lovely setting of trees at the foot of the Slieve Ardagh Hills and beside a lake. Founded about 1180, with monks from Jerpoint, by Donal O'Brien, King of Thomond (an area that comprised more or less county Clare, north of the Shannon estuary), it was destroyed in the mid-fifteenth century and partly rebuilt and enlarged soon after. Inside are several curiosities – the tomb of Piers Butler of Clonamicklon, and his parents and son, with an excellent effigy of a mail-clad knight, and merry-looking apostle figures on the side, exquisitely carved by masons from Callan, whose work occurs also at Jerpoint and Kilkenny; several other tombs; and some intriguing carvings in the south transept, including a Crucifixion, a St Christopher, and a mermaid pointing invitingly at two fishes. Mermaids are often represented with St Christopher, symbolising the snares in store for the honest traveller. In this carving the dubiously sensual mermaid is trying to entice the fish, which have represented Christians since early churchmen found the initials of the Greek for 'Jesus Christ, son of God' formed the Greek word for fish – *ichthus*. Outside the abbey is a rounded, corbelled dovecote, doubly useful to farming Cistercians who thereby could have fresh meat in late winter when there was no other available, and could use the lime to improve their soils.

A main road leads direct from Urlingford to Cashel, the romantic, much visited capital of the Kings of Munster, its rock standing prominent for miles in the plain where the Devil spewed it out. But we can turn off to the right four miles before to make a tortuous way to **Longfield House**, the home, open to the public, of a man who did as much as anyone in the nineteenth century to open up the country, Charles Bianconi, entrepreneur of the once famous Bianconi cars. Born in Lombardy in 1786 he came to Dublin at the turn of the century as a travelling salesman in cheap prints which he framed himself. By 1815 he had dropped the prints and simply sold travel. His horse-drawn side-cars, starting with the short run between Clonmel and Cahir, soon linked up with the rapidly growing canal services, and before he died covered four thousand miles. By that time, however, the railways were well established, the canals declining, and his virtual monopoly of the Irish road transport system had ceased. The cost to passengers was twopence a mile. The house was built about 1770 by Richard Long, British ambassador to an Indian prince. The last of the Longs was murdered, in the 1820s, supposedly while sitting on the garden lavatory. Bianconi's descendants lived in it till 1968. The last of them in 1962 wrote a book here about her ancestor by the light of an oil-lamp, neither electricity nor central heating being then installed. Following her death, and after a period as a hotel, it reverted to private ownership.

Cashel, in one sense, is a sharp fold of limestone standing a hundred feet above the plain that surrounds it. King Cormac had his Munster capital here in the fourth century, and it became a Christian centre in the fifth, when its king was converted by St Patrick. The saint is said to have spiked his crozier by accident through the king's foot during the baptism, which the monarch took to be a

partial re-enactment of the Crucifixion and necessary to the ceremony. Brian Boru was crowned King of Munster here in 977, but
maintained his court at Kincora beside Lough Derg, and in 1101 the
O'Briens gave the land to the Church. Here in 1127 Cormac MacCarthy, King of Desmond, began to build the little Romanesque church
now known as Cormac's Chapel. A cathedral was begun beside this
in 1169 and here, two years later, the assembled clergy of Ireland
did homage first to Strongbow, then to Henry II himself. Within
another hundred years the cathedral was pulled down to make way
for that whose shell now dominates the rock – one of the few still
standing in Ireland whose dimensions match those of Gothic cathedrals in Britain or on the Continent.

In the late fifteenth century, Garret More, the 'Great' Earl of
Kildare and most influential leader in the country, rebelled against the
administration of Sir Edward Poynings, Henry VII's stern viceroy,
whose 'Law' once more curtailed native liberties, this time to enact
legislation not approved in advance by the English king. In the course
of his campaign he set fire to Cashel Cathedral, without dire result.
Arrested, he explained to the king: 'he thought the archbishop was in
it'. 'All Ireland cannot rule this man!' shouted a priest who stood by.
'Then he shall rule all Ireland,' is said to have been Henry's epigram-
matic reply. As it was, Kildare was freed and for the future exercised
his influence in the king's favour. More serious damage was done in
1647 by the parliamentarian General Murrough O'Brien, Earl of
Inchiquin. When he had done with the place, according to an eye-
witness, the altar, steps, chapels, sacristies, seats and numerous
passages were piled with the dead. After Inchiquin's assault, the
cathedral fell into disuse. It was restored later in the century, but in
the eighteenth, at the instance of Archbishop Agar, ancestor of the
Earls of Normanton, who disliked having to climb the hill, the lead
roof was removed and the see transferred to St John the Baptist's
church in the town. A hundred years later a storm brought down some
parts of the buildings which, in 1869, some time after the horse had
bolted, were handed over to be preserved by the State.

The entrance to the enclosure is to the left of the fifteenth-century
Hall of Vicars Choral, laymen endowed with church lands who
helped in chanting the services. A High Cross of the eleventh century,
on a carved plinth of the same date (and so not the Munster kings'
coronation stone, though the mound on which it stands may be the
site) has a worn full-length Crucifixion on one side and St Patrick on
the other, unlike the complex contents of other crosses. The cathedral

is of a simple cruciform pattern, with side chapels on the east of both transepts; the choir is twice as long as the simple aisle-less nave. There are some interesting details – a cross-legged sheila-na-gig (making one incline more to the belief that these curiously obscene little carvings are warnings against lechery than that they carry on some pre-Christian fertility cult), some coats of arms, beasts of the Apocalypse, apostles, several other rather cryptic reliefs, and the tomb of Myler McGrath, Cashel's bishop under Queen Elizabeth, and a notorious pluralist and denominational turncoat. On the north-east corner, adjoining the cathedral, is a Round Tower, ninety-two feet high and restored to its original state after damage by lightning in 1965. The west end of the nave leads, through a splendid door, into the archbishops' castle, a fourteenth-century addition, with thick walls riddled with passages, whose windows give good views of the country around. On the other, south-east side, cramped between the cathedral and south transept, is the Rock's main treasure, **Cormac's chapel**.

It is one thing to abstract the features common to Irish Romanesque architecture – the transient style that flourished through the twelfth century before it gave way to Gothic in the next: the high, steeply pitched roofs, the arched windows and doorways with their four, five or more elaborately carved orders. Or to trace, as is possible, the connection of these features with buildings at Ratisbon, Cologne, and other Rhineland centres where Irish monks had been established since the seventh century or earlier. But it is quite another to pick out the qualities that give the style its individual genius. There seems to be an unsystematic, almost perverse whimsy about essentially Celtic Irish creations, be they book illuminations, jewellery or churches. They are the products more of instinct than of evolved style and as such have died away without greatly influencing the styles that came after. Celtic artists seem to have gone about their creation with a confident and unreflective intuition. That the western nave arches are off-centre to the chancel, the south tower less massive than the north, the details of design and decoration sited without regard for symmetry – almost with the simple purpose of filling up blank spaces – in every way enhances the building. Even if some of the irregularities resulted from changing needs during the course of building, the way they have been carried out are evidence enough of some wayward inspiration. At the same time this skill in conception goes with a thorough mastery of technique. For a heavy stone roof to have remained at such an acute angle for nearly nine hundred years shows that; and the barrel vault and corbelling bear it out. It is sad that other examples of the style survive only in arches and doorways, the body having long ago crumbled. At Cashel, almost alone, one can look on the complete work of art.

The most memorable views of Cashel can be from below, looking from any direction at this outcrop of nature and human inspiration, warmly set in its Tipperary green. Below, too, there are other sights to see in the town. There are ruins of a Dominican priory – other orders followed as Cashel became an ecclesiastical capital; fragments of the fourteenth-century city wall; fifteenth-century Grant's Castle, now a hotel; the elegant late-eighteenth-century Church of Ireland cathedral with a later west front and spire by Richard Morrison, and the chapter house with its valuable library and exhibitions; the Catholic parish church of St John, built in 1795 (one of the earliest to take advantage of the slow lifting of the Penal Laws) on the site of a thirteenth-century Franciscan friary, its interior a mass of showy decoration; and the beautiful redbrick-fronted Cashel Palace, designed by Sir Edward Lovett Pearce. Oddly, the rear of the building is entirely of stone. It has a fine interior, with the original pine-panelled hall and staircase, and the larger downstairs rooms redecorated in the early nineteenth century, after damage during the 1798 rebellion, with Regency cornices and dadoes. Formerly the Archbishop's Palace, the building was sold by the church in 1962 and restored as a hotel. West of the town are the picturesque ruins of Hore Abbey, originally Benedictine, altered in 1266 for the Cistercians. It is best seen from the Rock.

Five miles along the N8, the main road going south from Cashel, on the right, is Rockwell College, a Roman Catholic boys' boarding school the nucleus of which is a house built about 1830. It belonged to the Roe family, who had an earlier house on the site, to which the Rev. Nicholas Herbert, rector of Carrick-on-Suir, ordered by his bishop to spend more time at his additional living of Knockgrafton, four miles to the south of Rockwell, brought his family, including diarist daughter Dorothea, in about 1784 on a first ill-fated social visit. (The rectory he built at Knockgrafton is still there, with a floor added since.) Dorothea fell in love with John Roe, who showed great interest, then didn't, then seemed to, then … His erratic attentions became the main theme of her diary for twenty years after which, believing he had betrayed her, she went mad and lived out her last years as an old maid, embittered and alone. But she kept an account, neither published nor known of till 1929, delightful in its perceptions, humour and intimacy, of the everyday doings and routines of her class at that time. We see huge luxury, huge indulgence, endless dances, teas, dinners, 'syllabubs', flirtings, practical jokes, the torture of young women – legs and arms stretched with ropes, bodies wrapped tightly in greasy brown paper – all to enhance their power of trapping still-free squires and lordlings – occasional horrors of war, rebellion, epidemic disease, duelling, murder (the staff at the rectory were one night 'horribly butchered'). Relating many of the big-house families to each other, the *Retrospections* of Dorothea Herbert (still in print) adds a dimension to our feel for the region's past.

To the west of the main road the woods and rich pastures of the Golden Vale and the Glen of Aherlow stretch away between the Galty Mountains and Slieve Felim, and Cahir and the Suir valley lie a few miles on. But on this route we shall drive due east, veer south-east and reach the Suir at a later stage of its course, which we shall follow to Waterford Harbour – the estuary it shares with its sister rivers the Nore and Barrow. Where the road bends right, five miles from Cashel, we pass within a mile of **Knockbrit**, the birthplace (in 1789) of Marguerite Power. Her squalid, squandering father was a vicious Catholic turned Castle agent, whose function was to indict his former friends. He married her to a local wastrel, Captain Farmer, whose physical cruelty drove her – not yet sixteen – to leave him after three months. In 1809 she went to England and later (after her first husband died in a debtor's gaol) married the Earl of Blessington. From then on her repressed talents were released. Before the earl's death in 1829 the couple drained his fortune in Continental travel and as cynosures of society. After, living in London with the Comte d'Orsay (estranged husband of her stepdaughter), she wrote essays, articles, memoirs and novels to pay the heavy costs of entertaining all and patronising many of the artistic and social talents of her day. When the two of them could pay no longer they left for Paris, hoping Napoleon III, whom they had helped, would reward the count with office. He did not, and the count died bankrupt, and she of apoplexy in 1849.

On our left, the land is for miles scattered with raths, mounds and other prehistoric remains. In front rises the 2,368-foot sandstone hill of **Slievenamon** – Mount of the Women of Finn. Finn McCool, a close parallel and perhaps precursor in Celtic myth of King Arthur in English, used to exercise his little band of choice warriors, the Fenians (a bit like Arthur's Round Table Knights) on the hill. And here, faced with the necessity of choosing a wife, he did it ostensibly by competitive examination. All the girls who wanted him were to run up the hill, he sitting on top, and the first to reach him would win.

In secret he knew whom he wanted, and carried Grania, daughter of Cormac Mac Art, to the top the night before; and so they were betrothed. Later came a disastrous sequel. Finn's close friend Dermot had a beauty spot on his cheek, seeing which any woman fell in love with him. Grania saw and fell. The story of their fatal elopement is told elsewhere.

Fethard is a quiet charming place that turns its back on progress, preserving four fifteenth-century tower-houses, an Augustinian friary of 1306 and a massive section of town wall, restored in 1993, close to its reedy river. Survival of much of this is due to the town's acceptance of very favourable terms offered by Cromwell in 1650. Essentially a Butler town, it faded with them to an agreeable retirement.

A good diversion can be made two and a half miles east to sixteenth-century Knockkelly Castle, the finest of many ruins round here, set on a hill and looking a little like a walled town in southern France – but privately owned and not open to the public. But views from here and further along the road, of the Galty Mountains, Knockmealdowns, Comeraghs and Slievenamon and the plain they rise from, are magnificent.

Risings of the last two centuries before British rule ended can easily confuse the visitor unfamiliar with Irish names and history. (It is extraordinary how little of Irish history is taught in British schools, when it is considered that hardly a single well-known Englishman of the last two centuries did not owe some of his experience, wealth, blood or position to Irish connections or services.) A short-lived one took place in this neighbourhood. In 1848, hundreds of thousands were starving, and still the abundant corn and wheat harvest (only potatoes had failed) was being sent to England to be marketed and fill the pockets of landlords who lived there anyway. The Young Ireland party, ancestor of most subsequent forces for the complete and violent secession of Ireland, directed at the time by a hitherto peaceable landlord called William Smith O'Brien, raised their standard in tragi-comic isolation. Such action as there was took place mainly within a few miles of where we are. On 26 July, with two comrades (most had deserted; a feature of many Irish risings has been that, on the morrow of the call to arms, honest rebels have been loath to inconvenience their employers, and so returned to work), O'Brien advanced to Mullinahone (ten miles east of Fethard) police barracks and called on the occupants to surrender. The constables were cooking breakfast. They asked him kindly to collect more men, to make their surrender less dishonourable to them. He went, and returned to find them fled, with the arms, to a stronger place. The only real action took place on 5 August between thirty-five rebels and a garrison of police, in the garden of the Widow McCormack, one mile outside Ballingarry (twelve miles north-east of Fethard: the house still stands). The widow cried, O'Brien parleyed with the police, stones were thrown, and shots were fired. A few insurgents fell, the rest hid or fled. O'Brien faced the enemy – 'An O'Brien never turned his back on an enemy' – then fled too. Picked up later, his death sentence at Clonmel was commuted to exile in Tasmania, from which he returned years later to die in Wales.

The Suir has grown to full size, with islands and excellent riverside walks, and a spot where Lady Blessington used to bathe, where we rejoin it at **Clonmel**, capital of the South Riding of Tipperary. (A riding is from the Norse for third; Tipperary has but two, with Nenagh the northern capital.) This is one of the largest inland towns in Ireland with a population over eleven thousand, several flourishing industries, an agreeable bustle, fine buildings and beautiful surrounds. Laurence Sterne was born here, in Mary Street, though he spent only a few boyhood years in Ireland, where his father was an army officer. George Borrow lived here for a few months as a boy, attending the grammar school and learning Irish. In 1844 and 1845 Trollope, then a post office inspector, lodged in Anne Street. And Carlo Bianconi's famous coaches began in 1815 from the coach-house at the still existing Hearn's Hotel, named after his assistant. Founded by a De Burgo in the early thirteenth century, the town passed to the Desmond FitzGeralds, then the Ormondes. The Confederates met here in 1647, and three years later Cromwell arrived on his westerly progress. Under Hugh O'Neill, Owen Roe's nephew, the garrison – 'the stoutest enemy this army had ever met with in Ireland' according to the Ironsides – first repulsed Cromwell, killing 1,500 of his men. The inmates escaped that night, and next day the town had to surrender. The operation was carried out with such skill that Cromwell, thinking the town still strong, conceded more generous terms than he allowed others.

O'Connell Street, the main thoroughfare, runs east-west and parallel to the river, near which old warehouses have become smart apartment blocks in recent years. At one end is the West Gate, built in 1831 on the site of the medieval one, which divided the Norman part of the town from Irishtown; and at the other the restored Main Guard, which began (in 1674) as the Court of the Palatinate of Ormonde, later became Tholsel and assize court, and was spoiled last century by a row of shops built into its open ground-floor gallery. (A palatinate was an administrative area in which much power was delegated from central to local authority because governing from afar was unusually difficult. Ormonde, Ireland's last, was abolished as such in 1716.) The Town Hall, farther on, is modern; beyond that, to the right is the Court House by Sir Richard Morrison, where William Smith O'Brien was sentenced in 1848. Old St Mary's parish church, handsome and restored, with bits dating from the thirteenth century, stands beside remains of the medieval town walls. It has good windows, tombs of former local grandees, and other details. The Franciscan friary in Abbey Street incorporates interesting parts and details of earlier churches, and possesses an attractive Butler double effigy in the Franciscan churchyard. Clonmel is headquarters of the Tipperary foxhounds, and well known for its greyhound racing, which being a popular national institution deserves some attention here.

Dogs have always been important in Ireland. In Roman times the vast fast Irish wolfhound was exported to the empire and used in the games at Rome: 'all Rome viewed them with wonder and thought they must have been brought hither in iron cages'. In those days they were usually white, and sometimes dyed; blue was a favourite colour, and a white body with purple ears is on record. St Patrick is said to have escaped from boy-slavery in Ireland among a cargo of dogs bound for the Continent. As long as Ireland was beset with wolves, till the eighteenth century, these agile giants (Edmund Campion in 1571 said they were bigger than colts) were bred intensively to catch them, and pedigree specimens were sold all over the world. Then they declined. Export and inactivity did for them in the nineteenth century. But in 1863 an English breeder reconstituted the strain and managed to restore it to fame and the international status it still enjoys. Not among the Irish, however, who respect its memory – it appeared on the sixpenny piece and as the stamp of Belleek China – but enthuse nowadays about that sleek racer, the greyhound. Hundreds of pounds are nightly won and lost on betting, and a large proportion of farmers keep and train the dogs to enter them for the stakes. Every year Ireland exports 7,000 greyhounds. Here at Clonmel, the Irish Coursing Club has its headquarters by the stadium east of the town in Davis Road. The National Coursing meeting is held nearby early in February.

Like most fertile valleys in Ireland, the Suir was thronged with the estates of the Anglo-Irish: Knocklofty (Earls of Donoughmore); Rathronan House (Gough); Mandeville at Castle Anner, Le Poer at

Gurteen Le Poer, Bagwells at Marlfield, many more. Some are flattened, some ruinous, a few still private homes, very few homes of the
original family. Sometimes you glimpse them between trees, or
standing clear like turreted and battlemented Gurteen Le Poer, across
the Suir five miles east of Clonmel.

Knocklofty, sitting in its noble demesne five miles west of the
town, is a hotel, its broad eighteenth-century yellow-stoned front,
Palladian wings and domed portico welcoming well-heeled tourists
and expense-account businessmen where once they greeted the Hely-
Hutchinsons, Earls of Donoughmore, whose line owed its prosperity
to the unblushing venality and subservience to government of an
eighteenth-century ancestor who according to his contemporary
Henry Flood 'received more for ruining one kingdom than Admiral
Hawke had received for saving three'. The last family occupants, the
seventh earl and his wife, both into their seventies, were kidnapped
by the IRA, but civilly treated and soon released. Unfortunately,
adaptations and additions caused by the new commercialism mars the
look of the place, and interiors are tasteless and vapid. But the riverside park is fine.

Two miles east of Clonmel the road forks and we can turn left on to
the N76, and three miles later left again towards the foothills of
Slievenamon to see **Kilcash** Castle, beside the village of the same
name, once a Butler stronghold, in ruins since 1800, beside an old
church. It is a common enough kind of site, yet rich in history and
association, and with fine views. The church has a Romanesque south
doorway and was for a while in the hands of the Knights Hospitaller,
an order dedicated to the liberation and guarding of the Holy Land,
through funds collected from estates it owned in Europe. Various
metal objects were stolen from it in 1848 to be forged into bullets for
O'Brien's Young Ireland rising. In the castle, James, Earl of Castle-
haven, whom we meet all over the south fighting for the Catholic
Confederates in the 1640s, wrote his memoirs. Buried in the Butler
mausoleum in the church is Margaret Butler, widow of the Jacobite
Viscount Iveagh. She, after the Boyne, protected hunted Catholics
from the English and earned the tribute 'the spot where that lady
waited, who shamed all women for grace ...' in a famous Gaelic
poem. But her successors chose to be Protestant.

Returning to the T13 we follow the course of the River Suir eastward, with the wooded slopes of the Comeraghs on the right. Just
before Kilsheelan the castellated towers and gables of Gurteen le Poer
rise romantically from a beautiful and bosky demesne. This is the

ancestral home of the De la Poers (formerly Power; in 1863 they, like many others, reverted to the Norman form of their name, moved by the same passion for medievalism which inspired the courtly, chivalric echoes of this 1868 house). Much of the family's vast territory in county Waterford went, through marriage in 1717, to the Beresfords, later Marquesses of Waterford.

Two miles before Carrick we pass on the right the site of Coolnamuck. A story tells that a family which once owned it, having lost their money through extravagance, packed into their coach and drove it over the cliffs at Tramore. **Carrick-on-Suir** is a pleasant, prosperous town of busy narrow streets, a dominant 1784 clock-tower, and handsome old buildings on the quays beside the fast-flowing Suir, here crossed by a seven-arched bridge of the fifteenth century. By far its greatest treasure is the well-preserved Butler manor house, built in the years following 1568 beside an older Butler keep overlooking the river. This older castle has been claimed, but so have other sites, as the birthplace of Anne Boleyn, whose grandfather was a Butler. The manor was built by the tenth Earl of Ormonde – 'Black Tom' – to entertain her daughter, Queen Elizabeth, but she never came. It is one of the loveliest Tudor remains in the country, and contains Ireland's earliest stucco work, with many armorials and busts of the expected queen. It has been well restored, and now houses a museum, but its contents are scant. Dorothea Herbert, the parson's daughter we met at Knockgrafton near Cahir, and whose family's main house was just west of the town (perhaps within the bounds of the modern chemical plant) paints a charming though often callous picture of Protestant provincial life at the end of the eighteenth century.

A diversion from Carrick takes us due north by the R697. In three miles (one mile beyond Whitechurch, with its Church of Ireland church in an ancient enclosure), we pass on the right the entrance to **Castletown House** (often called Castletown Cox, from the name of the first owner, to distinguish it from others). Like its Kildare namesake, it is one of the finest houses in the country, designed in 1767 by Davis Ducart, a Sardinian whose other work survives in county Cork, the city of Limerick, and additions to Florence Court in Fermanagh. Arcaded wings on either side of the main block lead to domed pavilions set forward from the house, and the whole is rich in detail. There is good plasterwork inside, but the house – built for the Archbishop of Cashel of the time – is closed to the public.

Farther along the same road we come to **Ahenny**, on the left, where among the broken gravestones and trees of the churchyard are two very fine High Crosses and the base of a third. The worn carvings are still in the main quite recognisable – animals, monks, some on horseback, a procession of monks carrying a dead body, Daniel in the lions' den, and a typical selection of abstract motifs. These crosses, and several others in the district, belong to the earliest period of cross-building, and may date from the eighth century. The south cross in particular has a wide area of interlacing coils spaced with raised bosses which very much recalls the twisted silver, gold or bronze work with inset gems to be found on Irish metal bowls, ornaments and so on, of the time. There are less distinguished crosses at Killamery, six miles north-north-west, Kilkieran, a mile south, and Tibberaghny, beside the Suir between Carrick and Fiddown. A wide variety of prehistoric objects in the locality and for several miles around point to continual occupation from earliest times.

South of the Suir and on the right of Carrick as we return rise the joined ranges of the **Comeragh Mountains** and beyond them the Monavullaghs that together form a beautiful range of cliff-edged old red sandstone. The action of ice and snow in the glacial period is well seen on the eastern side of the mountains, where it has in its descent clawed out precipices from the heads of glens, piling up moraine below, and so formed huge deep tarns. **Coomshingaun**, a mile from the main Carrick-Dungarvan road and six hundred feet above it, is the most spectacular of these. A rough path leads up to it from the point where the valley stream reaches the road, through furzy fields in which the little popping sounds in summer are gorse pods bursting to scatter their seeds. The tarn itself, of unknown depth (and associated in local folklore with irresistible currents, evil spirits and the like) is half a mile long broadening at the far end as the surrounding cliffs rise spectacularly to a thousand feet over the water. There is a fairly demanding walk along the south side, up a gully that leads off to the left and round the cliffs above the head of the lake. From here the highest point of the Comeraghs is a mile west. One can return down the more gentle slope of the north side, and so back to the road.

Returning to Carrick we cover the four miles east to **Piltown**. This was the site of an important battle in 1462 between the Ormonde Butlers and Desmond FitzGeralds, one of many clashes between these two dominant families. The pretext was different sympathies in the English Wars of the Roses – Butlers supporting Lancastrians and Desmond York. Thomas, Earl of Desmond, won the battle, after which, the Four Masters recorded, 'there were four hundred and ten of the slain of his people interred, besides the number who were devoured by the dogs and birds of prey'. Desmond emerged, for a while, the most powerful man in Ireland.

East of Piltown is the large demesne of **Bessborough House**, which after being burned down in the Civil War in 1923 was taken over by the Oblate Fathers, rebuilt, sold, and in 1981 opened as the agricultural college it remains. Built originally in 1744 by Francis Bindon, it was till last century the seat of the Ponsonbys, Earls of Bessborough – a family that gave the world two remarkable women: Lady Caroline Lamb, daughter of the third earl, who married Lord Melbourne and had a traumatic affaire with Byron in 1813; and Sarah Ponsonby, the first earl's great-niece, who betook herself with Lady Eleanor Butler to Plas Newydd, in Llangollen, Wales, to live together happily ever after. The fourth Earl of Bessborough was Lord Lieutenant during the Great Famine in 1846. The sham castle in the grounds was being erected as a memorial to a Ponsonby presumed killed in the Napoleonic wars. He returned unexpectedly and building was stopped midway. Belline House, north-west of Bessborough, for long housed the Ponsonby agent; also, Caroline Lamb, brought here by her husband in 1812 to try to get Byron off her mind.

Two miles farther towards Waterford, **Fiddown Chapel** is set prettily in an overgrown churchyard beside the road. On the other side is a lovely stretch of the river with a long island dividing the stream. The chapel is the mausoleum of the Ponsonby family, adapted from the chancel of a thirteenth-century church. Restored by the Irish Georgian Society, it boasts some splendid Bessborough monuments of the early eighteenth century, cleanly classical memorials set against the white background of this sequestered gem. Across the long bridge is the beautifully set village of **Portlaw**. It was founded in the early nineteenth century as a model village for their cotton mill workers by the Quaker family of Malcolmson. The village with its tanneries does not detain us, but the beautiful adjacent demesne of **Curraghmore**, seat of the Beresford family, Marquesses of Waterford, is not to be missed. The house itself is mainly eighteenth century but built around a central tower that dates from the twelfth, when Robert Le Poer was granted the surrounding lands by Henry II and made a governor of Ireland jointly with Hugh de Lacy. The Powers, as they became, held most of county Waterford till 1717 (in Cromwell's time the fifth Lord Le Poer survived changes of government by going mad). Then the only surviving daughter of the family, Catherine, married Sir Marcus Beresford of a county Derry family. It was he who had Curraghmore built as it is, as well as Tyrone House in Dublin. His son (one of thirteen, besides at least two illegitimate sons, one of whom became a general and the other an admiral) was made first Marquess of Waterford, and his descendants – for generations distinguished in the horse-racing world – still live in the house.

Other descendants of Sir Marcus had their effect. His son John became Commissioner of the Irish Revenue, an architect of the 1800 Act of Union and one of the most hated men in Ireland. Between 1822 and 1885 two successive Beresfords were Archbishops of Armagh and Primates of Ireland. Later, family fame came more from forms of puerility euphemised as eccentric: riding a pig along Piccadilly, stealing the whipping-block from Eton, painting a policeman green. However the Beresfords who did these things also distinguished themselves in the navy, army and in horsemanship.

The house has a long entrance courtyard flanked by low wings. With the tower straight ahead, it has a smack of Blenheim about it, and its architectural ancestry can be traced to Vanbrugh. The actual designer was John Roberts of Waterford. His inspiration is said to have come from Vanbrugh's other palace, Seaton Delaval, in Northumberland. Inside, James Wyatt decorated many of the rooms in the 1780s, and there is earlier plasterwork by the Lafranchinis, while Angelica Kauffman or her husband, Antonio Zucchi, did the ceiling roundels in the dining-room. There is also a magnificent collection of pictures, including Reynolds, Gainsborough and Lawrence, and Astley's portrait of the whole family – eleven of them – painted in about 1760; possibly the largest family portrait in Ireland.

The formal gardens, supposedly laid out to the plans of Versailles, are beautifully set among a vast demesne of woods and with the dramatic background of the Comeraghs. Among the trees is that far from unique specimen, the tallest tree in Ireland – a Sitka spruce of 156 feet. On the right is a shell-house, the shells put up by Lady Catherine in 261 days of 1754. And inside is a charming statue of her by John van Nost.

Ten miles east of Portlaw lies the city of **Waterford**. We can go north or south of the river, though the northern route allows us to see the broken tower and walls, overlooking the river and Waterford's port, of Granny Castle, two miles west of the town itself. Originally a Le Poer castle, later an Ormonde, it was reduced to its present state by Cromwell, but the thirteenth-century leftovers, with an isolated oriel window, make a romantic ruin.

Waterford is a great meeting-place of historical paths and the undisputed centre of commerce in south-east Ireland. It does not give of its best to those who keep to the main through-roads. Behind the wide streets are narrow ones, hedged with old buildings and historical links that, if they were not a microcosm of Irish history, might suggest a Continental town – so used does one get in Ireland to spacious city layouts. Its first foundation was in 914, by the Vikings, who came, according to the chronicles, in 'immense floods and countless sea-vomitings of ships and boats and fleets so that there was not a harbour nor a land-post nor a dun nor a fastness in all Munster without floods of Danes and pirates'. They walled the town, and, after a century, had settled, turned Christian, and come to depend on the Irish as the Irish did on them. In 1096, the Norse bishop of Waterford was consecrated by the Archbishop of Canterbury, but within seventy-five years the settlement's security was dashed by the Anglo-Normans' arrival. Their advance guard had already opened up parts of Wexford when Strongbow, Earl of Pembroke, landed at Passage East, in Waterford Harbour, pushed on to the city and after a day of bloody fighting made the town his own. He promptly claimed the fee due to him – Eva, the daughter of Dermot MacMurrough, who had persuaded him to come – and was married to her in 1170 in the surviving, though heavily restored, Reginald's Tower. He then began his effective march north. Three years later Henry II arrived at Waterford before a triumphal progress through his new possessions. In 1487 the town opposed the Yorkist pretender, Lambert Simnel, after Henry VII had come to the English throne. Simnel was crowned Edward VI in Dublin, a boy of 10, who cannot be supposed to have been the main force behind his own elevation. In his successful progress through Ireland, Waterford – the only town against him – managed to survive a six-week siege. In the event, Simnel fought and lost in England, and was deposed to the rank of kitchen servant. A second siege of twelve days followed in 1495, during Perkin Warbeck's abortive rising. For its double resistance, the king rewarded Waterford with the motto *Urbs intacta manet* (the city remains safe).

It remained vainly loyal after Cromwell came in 1649. At first, its stubborn resistance to his siege broke the reputation for instant conquest that Cromwell had earned. Ireton took almost all the rest of Munster before he finally broke into Waterford in August, 1650, giving honourable terms to its citizens. James II, fleeing, passed through the town in 1690, but it yielded to the Williamites soon after. It later shielded a Huguenot influx from France, but in the eighteenth century its significance was small – the elegant cathedral city of a county known for its wealth and the beauty of its Anglo-Irish demesnes.

It also began to manufacture glass, one of many towns to do so. The best period was from the late seventeen-eighties to the early years of the nineteenth century, and examples of its work then, displayed in museums and halls in various parts of Ireland, have an exquisite, minutely opaque quality far removed from the modern products. The factory closed in 1861. Its modern successor employs 1,500 workers at Kilbarry, two miles west of the city on the Cork road. A visit is repaid by the almost medieval sight of busy, bare-armed craftsmen deftly shaping, blowing, swinging and appraising all manner of glass forms against a background of glowing furnaces, constant noise and bustle. All stages, from fashioning the molten glass to the cutting and polishing, are seen, and it is possible to examine magnificent specimens of finished glass, old and new.

A tour of the town could begin at **Reginald's Tower**, built in the twelfth or thirteenth century at the north-east corner of the town walls. The museum within contains a remarkable collection of town charters from Tudor times on, with the signatures of the sovereigns and illuminated miniatures depicting them above the curvy script. These are in the room where Strongbow's marriage allegedly took place. There is a tavern beside the tower which incorporates bits of the city wall.

The **quays**, described in the eighteenth century as the best in Europe, stretch nearly a mile along the Suir. Moored ships, wharves, cranes and railway trucks are flanked by many good buildings. Opposite are precipitous heights with a golf-course and parkland on top, giving good views of the town. Among the many narrow streets that lead off the quays, and close to Reginald's Tower, is the **French Church**, whose central tower, nave and chancel remain. On the site of a Franciscan friary of 1240, it was used later – for a century – by Huguenots. Next door is the Waterford Heritage Museum, with a rich collection of Viking and Norman artifacts unearthed during excavations for the foundations of new building in the late 1980s. Nearby, in Bailey's New Street, is the Church of Ireland **Christ Church Cathedral**, built in the 1770s to replace a medieval cathedral by John Roberts, whose work is scattered in Waterford as that of the Pain brothers is in Cork. It was later twice damaged by fire and restored in 1891 by Sir Thomas Drew, who also reconstructed St Patrick's Cathedral, Dublin. The cathedral, with its strange stepped steeple at the west end, basks in the background supplied by the 1741 Bishop's Palace and deanery. The spacious interior contains a good selection of plaques, monuments and *memento mori*s, of which the most imposing is that of James Rice, six times mayor of the town during the difficult York – Lancaster struggles. His scrawny figure lies atop the decorated sarcophagus with worms coiling in and out of his ribs and a frog at his vitals. (Frogs have an odd connection with Waterford. Giraldus reports that they were unknown in Ireland till the Conquest because 'the mud does not contain the seeds from which green frogs are born'. Then one was found near the city. 'The English, and more so the Irish, regarded it with great wonder till the King of Ossory, a man of great wisdom, with a great shaking of his head and sorrow in his heart, said "that reptile brings very bad news to Ireland" ', which was taken to foretell the complete conquest.) There is also a collection of old books and signatures – of Wentworth, the Great Earl of Cork, Archbishop Ussher and others – on display. At the entrance is a memorial tablet to an English lieutenant who in 1799 'volunteered his service in Ireland To repel an Invading enemy and suppress rebellion'. It makes an odd but familiar antithesis to the gravestones of Catholic fighters within a mile of the cathedral, likewise praised for fighting on the other side.

The 1792 **Catholic Cathedral** stands in Barronstrand Street. It too, most curiously, was built by Roberts, supposedly with funds collected as alms on the steps, but it is in contrast to Christ Church's restrained decoration, with heavy pillars, oppressive expanse of ceiling, and a later, dull Corinthian facade. It was built in its humble setting in Penal times, on land granted by a Protestant corporation. The west front long remained incomplete for want of funds, and its design cannot be blamed on Roberts.

In O'Connell Street, running parallel to the quays, is the fine old **Chamber of Commerce**, once a private house, again by Roberts. It has a beautiful oval, cantilevered staircase and excellent plasterwork within. The **Mall**, leading south-west from Reginald's Tower, has some exceptional Georgian houses, with their essentially Irish fanlights above the doors. Beyond them is Roberts's City Hall, of 1782, containing the Victorian Theatre Royal, a magnificent old Waterford chandelier and dinner service, other relics and some rather fustian portraits of Waterford and national notables. Among the relics are some connected with Thomas Francis Meagher, a Young Irelander, and participant in O'Brien's 1848 rising who, condemned to death, escaped to America to win military honours and become Governor of Montana. In the public park opposite is the stolid Court House of 1849, by Terence O'Reilly. It replaces one by James Gandon, who also built the local gaol.

Before driving out of town to the east, and so beginning the round of the Waterford coastline, it might be worth making the five-mile excursion west to **Mount Congreve**, an early eighteenth-century house (recently extensively refaced and remodelled) near Kilmeadan on the N25. The gardens and woods, overlooking the Suir, are – in good times – open to the public. At present and for some time past the place has been plagued with industrial and various other disputes. The hundred acres of gardens (including the old walled garden) are well known for their spring bulbs, rare rhododendrons, azaleas and other shrubs and trees. Nearby on the other, south side of the N25 is Whitfield Court, a charming mid-nineteenth-century house with fine terraced gardens (private), doubling in recent years as a school for instruction in polo, the sport of kings.

To the east of Waterford, keeping south of the river, the road leads to Passage East. A diversion to the left leads to Cheekpoint, a hill of 436 feet with excellent views of the town, the various mountain ranges, Dunbrody Abbey to the east and to the south Waterford Harbour – triple estuary of the Suir, Barrow and Nore. Passage East is a precipitous little fishing village, most of its gaily painted houses set low and with steep climbs all round. It seems almost too cosy for its romantic name. It was here that Strongbow landed, content with the work of his advance parties, to claim, like a fairy prince in this one respect, the hand of a princess and rights to a kingdom; and here that Henry II followed him, to confirm himself at the top of the feudal tree. Crooke, a mile south, is possibly what gave rise to Cromwell's 'By Hook or by Crooke', and was duly occupied by Ireton in 1649. Another mile on, we pass **Geneva Barracks**, where in 1783 the government, pleased with the influence on the economy of German immigrants in Limerick, and Huguenots and Quakers elsewhere, encouraged Swiss Huguenots to settle, planning a new city and university. The plan aborted, and the place is famous for a different episode. The Croppy Boy, a '98 rebel, came here to confess, but the supposed priest was an army captain in a cassock, who arrested the boy and had him hanged. **Woodstown** farther on has a broad shallow sand-beach, a regency villa once rented by Jacqueline Kennedy, and, like other parts of this delectable coast, is often free from crowds, which are rather more in evidence at **Dunmore East**, an anglers' resort with sandy cove, delightfully set but become self-conscious from the attentions of visitors. From the hill behind is an amazing view, neatly combining geology with aesthetics, of the estuary. The road from here to Tramore is set back from the sea, the land between being an undulating duney strip indented with deep bays, stretching out to Brownstown Head, one of the cusps of Tramore Bay.

Tramore itself has been a more popular, brasher resort since Georgian days, when George III and his son the Prince Regent made the seaside popular for the first time (a little later Coleridge and the Lake poets took to climbing mountains, so redeeming them from centuries of dark superstition). People came from as far as Dublin then, and now from still farther. The length of the beach, which after half a mile of promenade goes on for miles along a salt-marsh spit that almost cuts off the inner part of the bay, usually prevents it from becoming too crowded, even during its September festival. It has a race-course, caravan park, amusement arcade, seafood bars, putting green, and other resort trappings. At the points of Tramore Bay a series of five tall enigmatic stacks are in fact warnings – or land-based buoys – erected in Napoleon's time to distinguish the shallow bay from the navigable Waterford Harbour. The central of the western ones, from the painted iron statue of a sailor on it, is known as the Metal Man, and the girl who hops three times round the base of his pedestal, always keeping one foot off the ground, will marry in a year. The walk here is magnificent, with good views of the coastal cliffs and the sight, in early summer, of large colonies of sea-birds.

This type of coastal scenery accompanies us for the twenty miles or so to Dungarvan. There are some rare plants hereabouts and a great wealth of common ones, and villages and hamlets nestle at the outlets of several rivers. One such is **Annestown**, another **Bunmahon**, which has the usual good beach and small population – both of natives and trippers. It also has an Irish Language College. There are plenty of quiet coves for good bathing from rocks. In this neighbourhood there are a number of disused copper mines, which were worked in the nineteenth century to a depth of 800 feet below sea level. Most of the labour came from Cornwall, 'the Irish having no great taste for it', according to a contemporary. Irishmen were more easily found to work in the diving bells, rates of pay being much better. **Kilmacthomas**, five miles inland from here, was the birthplace in 1797 of Tyrone Power, actor and comedian. Among his great-grandsons were his namesake film-star, and the director Tyrone Guthrie, who lived till his death in 1971 at Annaghmakerrig in county Monaghan.

Two changes come over the coast along this stretch. The high soft grass of Wexford and East Waterford is giving way gradually to heath and moorland, a wetter climate creating and maintaining the bog. The climate is the second change. West of the Monavullagh Mountains, that tail down to the sea east of Dungarvan, rainfall rises. It is, of course, by a gradual scale that Dublin's annual twenty inches or so – a good ten less than Bath's – rise to the forty, sixty, or even eighty sometimes falling on the top of west coast mountains. Here, anyway, a jump in that scale is noticeable. The compensation is the warmth of Irish rain – a dowsing to the skin hardly ever means a chill – and the clarity of light, that with its bluish tinge in the distance makes outlines starker and colours bolder. Rain means, besides, cloud. One should make a mental note to bear clouds in mind when first one steps on Irish soil, simply for the endless and beautiful variations they work on the landscape.

Stradbally, four miles on, has another pleasant cove, and one of the last of the larger beaches before we cross the southern foothills of the Monavullaghs and cover the last straight stretch beside Dungarvan Harbour to **Dungarvan** itself, capital of the old barony of Decies. In recent years it has grown and become animated. Grattan Square in the centre boasts handsome buildings and displays illuminated advertisements that might have their inspiration in Piccadilly Circus. Busy shopping streets radiate from it. The Old Market House contains a museum, which vividly records the wreck of the sailing-ship Moresby, storm-smashed on nearby rocks in 1895. Castle Street, beside it, leads to the remains of Dungarvan Castle, built for the future King John in 1185. The town is divided by the River Colligan, which till the nineteenth century had to be crossed by ferry or on foot. The crossing was then known as the 'Dungarvan Prospect' because of the sight of the local women hoisting their skirts to step through the shallow water. At a cost of £80,000, the Duke of Devonshire had a causeway laid and the two parts – Abbeyside, with thirteenth-century friary remains (from which there are superb views of the coastal headlands) to the east, and the town proper, with the castle, to the west – were united. Much of the castle's stone was incorporated in the British barracks, from which, in the nervy famine times of 1846, Royal Dragoons issued onto the square to fire on a crowd that was complaining of the danger of harbour work. Two were killed. In 1921 the barracks itself was destroyed. The vast estuary, with its mud-flats stretching to **Helvick Head** on the south, may seem a pretentious outlet for a river once crossed by barefoot ladies. A glance at a physical map shows the reason. Two major valleys run west to east through the long mountain ranges of Cork, and in glacial times the vast ice-flows which occupied them must have continued east, and straight to the sea. Later, when the ice melted, the Rivers Lee and Blackwater found the effects of glaciation had opened up shorter cuts to the sea. Now both, instead of staying on the obvious limestone course, turned right, through new clefts in the old red sandstone, and left Dungarvan harbour and Youghal Bay to be spread with silt.

Of interest to dog-fanciers is a memorial, at the junction of main roads three miles north-west of the town, to Master McGrath (McGrath is an old Waterford family; the abbey-side castle was theirs), a greyhound beaten only once in thirty-seven public appearances, who won the Waterloo Cup in 1868, 1869 and 1871. The obelisk, with relief profile of the champion, is said to be the only roadside monument to a dog in Ireland. It is a diversion from which we revert to the coast road south from Dungarvan, round the harbour, then through Ring, or An Rinn, noted for its Irish college, and, diverting again, to Helvick Head, for the astonishing view of the cliff-edged south Waterford coastline. There is in fact little but views, mainly of beautiful broad sweeps down to the sea, to take our attention as we keep to the coast, rounding the low outcrop of the Drumhills, to reach **Ardmore**, a village of great charm (as holiday-makers know too well) twelve miles to the south-west. Here the ruins are among the best, certainly the best placed, of any in Ireland, but the site itself has possibly increased importance as having had a Christian settlement before the evangelising of St Patrick in other parts of the country. Though early manuscript sources point clearly to Patrick's pioneer work being elsewhere, it was probably to the south and east of the country, where contacts with Europe were strongest (and possibly to the west, from Spain), that Christianity first came. Here St Declan was the pioneer. He arrived, after studying in Wales. Old annals say that, finding the place an island and not suitable to his purposes, he pushed the sea back and made it a headland instead. (Nowadays the sea is reclaiming its old ground, due perhaps to the spiritual climate.) The stone on which he sailed still lies on the beach, and at the annual pattern in July (which in 1847 drew fourteen thousand people and still attracts crowds of cure-seekers) pilgrims used to be obliged to crawl under it. This was held to cure rheumatism, though it is arguable that rheumatism would have to have gone before the feat was performed. Declan's activity in converting locals was so successful that later on there was resistance here to St Patrick's more Rome-influenced administration.

Of the three main buildings on the site, the **Round Tower**, with subtly tapering walls, a landmark for miles around but seen best from the field above, is perhaps the finest in Ireland, and may also be the latest. Its cap is a recent restoration. **St Declan's House**, a steep-gabled building, is supposed to be his own oratory, though unlikely to be of so early a date. A stone-lined trough dug into the floor is called the Saint's Grave. Most detail of interest is to be found in the **Cathedral**, whose Romanesque nave is probably eleventh-century work, the chancel – with outstanding carved capitals – being two hundred years later. The purpose of the arcading along the north walls of both is not known, but it may have had frescoes on it. There are two ogham stones inside, while on the exterior west wall some figures representing the Judgment of Solomon, the Temptation and other themes may be much earlier than the church itself. Half a mile to the east a few other church remains exist, and here also is the site of a castle occupied by Perkin Warbeck on his second attempt to force his claim to the throne. The castle was in 1649 defended by Catholic Confederates against a besieging force under the Cromwellian Lord Broghill. Forty of the defenders occupied the Round Tower, and two days were enough to force the garrison's surrender. Of the total of 240 prisoners, 117 were hanged on the spot.

Broghill's father was the first 'Great' Earl of Cork whose old haunts and territory we are approaching as we drive nine miles west, crossing the Blackwater to enter county Cork and the city of Youghal. Though most parts of Ireland have felt the effect of each architect, or vandal, of national history, each part seems to identify itself particularly with certain persons or phases. East and north Cork, having no monopoly of the period, is stamped deeply with the mark of Elizabethans and those Irish on whom they ruthlessly forced subjection. The Great Earl, Spenser, Raleigh are with us now for miles, haunting every valley, lake and castle.

d, South-West Tipperary,
East Cork

Y OUGHAL IS BESIDE an easily accessible harbour, the
gateway to the River Blackwater. This fact has, in the past,
given it greater importance than it enjoys today. Founded in the thirteenth century by Anglo-Normans and included in the barony of
Imokilly, Youghal changed hands a number of times before passing
to the Desmond (west Cork and east Kerry, roughly speaking)
FitzGeralds, whose family catastrophes followed close on those of
their Kildare cousins. The policies of Elizabeth were in the main
based on hopes of peaceful expansion among the 'old English', by
now as Irish – and Catholic – as the Irish. But her religion prevented
peace, especially after the Pope barred her from Heaven's gates in
1570. Chief among the reactions she sparked was the Munster rebellion begun in 1579, in the course of which the fifteenth and last
'Rebel' Earl of Desmond thoroughly sacked the town of Youghal
before moving on to the great reverse at Smerwick. Raleigh was one
of the queen's commanders in Munster, and when Elizabeth saw her
only hope of lasting success was to plant the area with English colonists he was granted 42,000 acres around Lismore in 1586. In the
main the land came from the FitzGeralds, and stretched down-river
to Youghal, where Raleigh lived at, and may have built, Myrtle
Grove. But it was for brief spells only, most of his time going on
countering Irish rebellion, his Sherborne estate, scanning the
Orinoco, Spain-baiting and playing the dice for royal favour. With
that denied by the immanence of James's accession, he sold his
estates in 1602 at a fraction of their market value to a younger man
who, arriving earlier in the country with only £27, had found a job
conveyancing confiscated lands. This was Richard Boyle, later to
become first and 'Great' Earl of Cork. He paid £1,500 for Raleigh's
acres.

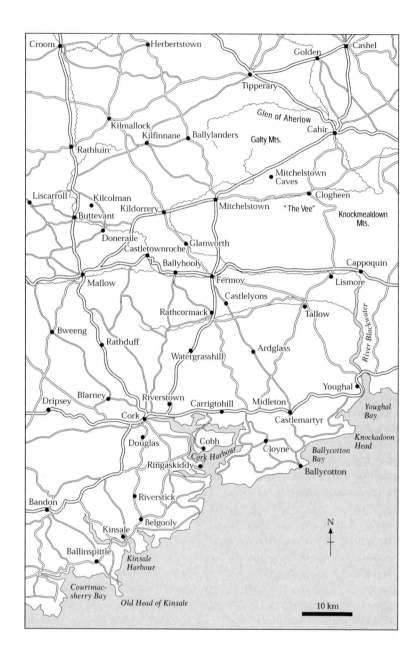

Croom   Herbertstown   Golden   Cashel

Tipperary

Glen of Aherlow

Kilmallock

Kilfinnane   Ballylanders   Galty Mts.   Cahir

Rathluirc

Liscarroll   Kilcolman   Mitchelstown Caves   Clogheen

Kildorrery

Buttevant   Mitchelstown   "The Vee"   Knockmealdown Mts.

Doneraile

Castletownroche   Glanworth   Cappoquin

Ballyhooly   Fermoy   Lismore

Mallow   Castlelyons

Rathcormack   Tallow

Bweeng   Rathduff   Ardglass   River Blackwater

Watergrasshill

Youghal

Blarney   Riverstown   Carrigtohill   Midleton   Youghal Bay

Dripsey   Cork   Castlemartyr   Knockadoon Head

Douglas   Cobh   Cloyne   Ballycotton Bay

Ringaskiddy   Cork Harbour   Ballycotton

Bandon   Riverstick

Belgooly   N

Kinsale

Ballinspittle   Kinsale Harbour

Courtmac-sherry Bay   Old Head of Kinsale   10 km

Meanwhile Edmund Spenser, who had a rough obverse to his poetic side, had accompanied and found nothing distasteful in the repressive expedition of 1580. He, too, acquired land – about 4,000 acres of it – and in 1588 began to live at Kilcolman Castle, near Doneraile. He married Boyle's cousin (and wrote for her his *Epithalamium*) and became friendly with Raleigh when they both lived in Cork. Each showed the other his current writing, Spenser his *Faerie Queene* and Raleigh short poems intended to win back the queen's good opinion. In the event, Raleigh failed to rediscover royal favour, spent fifteen years in the Tower and ended after a short and disastrous period of freedom on the scaffold. Spenser was chased from Kilcolman in 1598 by insurgents of the O'Neill rising, and died in poverty in England soon after (though he was still rightful owner of the demesne and his grandson later sold it). Only Boyle, the canniest of the three, kept in with the king, amassed great wealth, on top of Raleigh's old property, and lived to help Wentworth to his grave. He divided his land into estates which he leased to English settlers. He built houses, castles, bridges; put up factories of various kinds, many of which flourished, and embellished his own dwellings with works of art both inside and out. He cut down the great primeval forests of his area as fuel for his ironworks. He was also an astute speculator and a swindler.

Youghal today is a fine resort with a harbour and broad sandy beaches, and a pleasing town, rich in good building, beside the picturesque estuary of the Blackwater, and with a long gently curving main street over the middle of which rises the Georgian Clock Gate tower erected in 1771. Early last century the buildings flanking it served as a gaol. North Main Street, on the side we come in, has some houses of interest – Tynte's Castle, fifteenth century (one Robert Tynte married Spenser's widow), altered and used now as a warehouse; Uniacke or Red House, a rare Irish survival of the Dutch Renaissance style, built between 1706 and 1715, painted pink; and a terrace of almshouses built in 1634 by the Great Earl for six Protestant widows, and still fulfilling the same purpose. Parallel with the street is another long one to the east which gives on to quays and warehouses. The finest assembly of buildings is to the west, landward side of North Main Street – the Church of St Mary, New College House and **Myrtle Grove**. The last was owned and inhabited for a while by Raleigh and may be where he entertained Spenser. The house is private. Some say the first potato was planted here by Raleigh, but Killua in county Westmeath has a better claim. What is known is that, on the first try, Raleigh ate the plant's berry, which is disgusting. He ordered it to be rooted out, and the gardener discovered the nutritious tuber, ever since an Irish national dish. It is said that when he sat in the garden here smoking Ireland's first pipe of tobacco, a maid dowsed him with water, thinking he was on fire. In fact the time, place and agent of introduction of tobacco into Europe is much argued over.

New College House is on the site of the medieval college which the Great Earl acquired with the rest and which he put under the care of his brother, the Bishop of Cork. This family connection enabled ninety-five per cent of the college revenues – some £1,000 a year – to reach the earl's pocket. When the reforming Wentworth learned this, in spite of having married his niece to Cork's son, he called him to account. The earl was forced to pay £15,000. Archbishop Laud wrote to Wentworth gleefully: 'No physic is better than a vomit.' But Cork wrote in his diary 'God never forgive the Lord Deputy'; he had the satisfaction a few years later of knowing his own complaints had helped bring Wentworth to the scaffold.

The church is a mixture of styles, from the little that survived Desmond's assault to the giant restoration of the 1850s. Its great appeal is in details. One is the tomb considered to be that of the Countess of Desmond, wife of the twelfth earl who, the story goes, died aged 140 when she fell from a cherry tree at Dromana, up the river. She had danced with Henry VII in London a hundred years before and once visited Elizabeth at her court, walking all the way. The greatest monument is the one erected by himself to the Great Earl. In colourful Italian style, it bears carvings of himself, his two wives (the second in ermine, because he was a peer by her time), and mother, and small figures of nine of his sixteen children. These do not include the natural scientist Robert, who appears, however, in the similar chantry in St Patrick's Cathedral, Dublin.

We start inland by recrossing the river and keeping close to its east side, either by the main road or the longer lanes that at times run alongside the water. Approaching Cappoquin we pass the demesne of **Dromana** to the left, in which the Methuselah Countess of Desmond was born. This was for centuries a FitzGerald stronghold. In 1676 it came by marriage into the Villiers family, which during that century supplied four kings with favourites – the first and second Dukes of Buckingham, the Duchess of Cleveland, who bore Charles II three Fitzroy dukes, and Elizabeth Villiers, William III's mistress, later Countess of Orkney. In 1802 the Villiers heiress married Henry Stuart, son of the Marquess of Bute, and the Villiers-Stuarts own the place to this day, though a large part of the beautiful waterside demesne has been taken over by the State for forestry.

Henry Stuart's son, in 1826, made himself a local hero by ousting the Beresford MP for Waterford, having entertained Daniel O'Connell at the house during the campaign. He was later created Lord Stuart de Decies. He built the exotic gate, in Brighton Regency style, with its onion domes and minarets, across the main entrance to the estate off the Cappoquin road. **Affane**, east of the gate, was in 1564 the scene of one of the last episodes in the age-old Butler-FitzGerald feud. The Geraldines lost and their leader was carried wounded by the Butlers off the field. 'Where is the great Earl of Desmond now?' jeered the Butlers. 'In his proper place, on the necks of the Butlers,' the earl replied.

Raleigh planted cherry trees at Affane, and in Charles II's reign one Valentine Greatraks lived in the castle that preceded the surviving but ruinous Georgian house. He claimed to cure scrofula and other ills by stroking and hypnotism, and the king was one of his patients. Reversing a cliché, an Irishman has called the Rhine Germany's Blackwater. It is full of beauty and history and curiosity, and we shall return to it on the return journey, later in the chapter. Meanwhile we go on through the village of Cappoquin, where the big house preserves memorials of Lord Keane, who conquered Kabul in 1839, and died before the subsequent rout and massacre of the British in the Khyber Pass; then turn right, and make for the mountains. After five miles we reach **Mount Melleray Monastery**. Expelled from Brittany in 1832, a community of Trappists, members of a strict reformist branch of Cistercians who take a vow of silence, were given six hundred bleak and stoney acres here by the Keanes of Cappoquin. They settled, planted 17,000 trees to ward off wind, and slowly cultivated the hard land. In the 1920s they built their Gothic abbey church, using stone from the remains of Mitchelstown Castle. Thackeray was glad to give the place a miss – 'as for seeing shoes made or fields tilled by reverend amateurs, we can find cobblers and ploughboys to do the work better'. The established farmlands and the hospitality of today's monks might have changed his tune.

A few miles beyond we join the main road over the **Knockmealdowns**, once known for the eagles and wolves that inhabited them, now more for the magnificent views to north and south to be had from the pass and angular section of main road known as the Vee. Claims have been made that the last wolf in Ireland was killed here in 1770 (though another claim is made for a Carlow catch in 1786). Whenever it was, it long outlived England's last survivor of the species (around 1600) and Scotland's (1743). In Norse and earlier days wolves had been common; and a belief grew up that they had inherited the souls of men who rejected St Patrick's teaching. Giraldus tells of a travelling priest coming on a wolf one evening in the wilderness; after it had 'said some things about God that seemed reasonable' it confirmed the man-wolf theory by peeling its skin to reveal, temporarily, human form – a possible transference from German werewolf lore. (Giraldus also explained the fact that Irish wolves whelp in December as 'a symbol of the evils of treachery and plunder which here blossom before their season'.) Cultivation and wolfhounds gradually did for wolves, and though Cromwell's depredations gave them a last brief respite, Ireland's eighteenth-century recovery finished them off. Naturally the Great Earl and others like him preferred to hunt deer, for the meat.

On the left, just before the Vee proper, is **Bay Lough**, a glacial tarn of unknown depth, surrounded by rhododendrons and, metaphorically, by rumours of undercurrents and monsters. It is said to be the influence of Petticoat Loose, a haunting harridan, that caused the road to be built zigzag instead of straight along the old track. The rhododendron, ponticum variety, the only one to grow wild on such a scale, a pestilent colonist that eliminates native plants, nevertheless pays its rent with a staggering display of colour in late spring, making it hard to believe that the plant was unknown in these islands before George Ill's day. Missing this view, but presumably appreciating the broad one to the north from the north slope of Sugarloaf Hill (on the other side of the road from the lake), are the earthly remains of Samuel Grubb, a Quaker who owned Castlegrace House on the Tar River below. He was buried upright, as he wished, in a kind of beehive cairn in 1921. In this position he followed the example of King Cormac at Tara, the King of Leinster at Tountinna and some others. There is also an orthodox grave on top of the hill, that of Henry Eeles, an early pioneer of electricity. Five miles south, off the Lismore Road, Castle Dodard is a frisky folly of a castle or château, a B-and-B of the upper order, with conical roofs and battlements, full of character outside and in (where age, quality and decorative value distinguish practically all the multifarious contents taken, sent, given and bought from all corners of the world).

However, we descend northward into county Tipperary and the pretty village of Clogheen, and turn left towards Ballyporeen, visited in 1984 by President Ronald Reagan, in honour of an

O'Regan or O'Reagan ancestor. Here a right turn brings us after nearly three miles to **Mitchelstown Caves**. Straight ahead is the splendid line of sandstone gullies and escarpments making the south face of the almost roadless Galty Mountains, which are best climbed from the west, east or north. The caves themselves are the best in Ireland, and divided into two groups, the Old and New. The Old have been known for centuries. James FitzThomas, who claimed to be the Earl of Desmond and was known by Irishmen as the Sugan, or 'straw' earl, sheltered here in the bitter aftermath of the last Munster rising in 1601. Betrayed by the last White Knight, he was taken to the Tower to end both his life and, after a century of decline, the line of Munster Geraldines. Undoubtedly the so-called Old Caves have hidden others than him. The use of caves in prehistoric times is well attested by the bones of animals brought in to eat. (Other Irish caves have yielded remains of Arctic lemming, bear, African wild cat, spotted hyena, and other species rare or undocumented for Europe. Though the Old Caves contain the longest chamber of all, 390 feet long and 40 feet high, they are not so remarkable as the New, which were discovered in 1833, and which comprise the normal guided tour. These have spectacular subterranean scenery, a series of chambers that extend nearly a mile and a half, and most evocative formations. All the chambers have been given names which detract from their impact, since the reality never lives up to the fiction.

Burncourt, two miles north of the caves, is the burned out (whence the name) case of a many-gabled, fortified house of 1640. Sir Richard Everard, its builder and a Catholic Confederate, was involved in preparing the defence of Limerick when news came to his wife that Cromwellians were approaching the house. Sooner than let them take it, the story goes, she set fire to it, almost new as it was. When Limerick was taken the following year Sir Richard was hanged by Ireton. Now, with its four square towers at each corner of the central block, its twenty-six gables, and the holes along the top of the walls to take supports for defensive galleries, it still shows clearly the original concept, better than similar remains in the country. A couple of miles south, the raw stumps of Shanbally Castle, built by John Nash in 1812 and knocked down after a fire in 1958, commemorate a massive Gothic Revival complex of battlements, towers round, square and octagonal, and machicolations. North of Burncourt we come to the main Mitchelstown–Cahir road, and turn right, reaching Cahir after about eight miles.

Cahir ('Fort'), a very pretty town, possesses a vast central castle, on a rock-island in the Suir. The **Castle** is the last of a series, as the town's name and literary clues point to the existence of a fortress here at least as early as the third century. The present one, part restored in 1840, was built in the twelfth century but mainly shows the sturdy defences of a fifteenth-century or later reconstruction. It was a Butler base, but of the branch of the family which did not, like the main line, join the king's men and turn Protestant when required, so that Essex besieged it in 1599 and in one of his few successes captured the place after a few days. Cromwell took it in February, 1650, without any trouble, before going to break the stronger back of Clonmel. To the inmates' lack of last-ditch defiance is owed the unusual completeness both of keep and exterior walls. It is a majestic shell, well restored and clinically maintained; and very short on content and suitable atmosphere.

In 1788 the Butler title, Baron Caher, went, on the deaths of two successive childless holders, sideways and downwards to the young son of a local beggarwoman. Higher bred relations, hoping thereby to bring the succession closer to themselves, kidnapped the boy and his sister and sent them to France, to be kept in squalid obscurity and ignorant of their entitlement. Luckily, a lady of means, Mrs Jefferys of Blarney Castle, found out, and had the children sought and brought back to their rightful inheritance. Not forgetting her own interests, she arranged a marriage between the heir to the title and her daughter. The old beggarwoman ended her days as dowager, in the castle.

The town is well supplied with Georgian houses, beside the river, along the sides of the main square. Its Gothic Revival Church of Ireland church was built in 1817 to designs by Nash, who also designed, for the tenth baron (son of the beggarwoman), the riverside *cottage orné*, a romantic little retreat a mile south in the Butler demesne that has now become Cahir Park. Known as Swiss Cottage, it can be seen inside and out, and its details – thatch gently sculpted round dormer windows, wallpaper showing scenes of the Bosphorus, a wooden spiral staircase, well-wrought rustic furniture – display all the cosily picturesque aspirations of leisured Georgians.

Leaving Cahir by the Tipperary road (on the right beyond the turn are the ruins of thirteenth-century Augustinian Cahir Abbey), we come after three miles to a signpost pointing left to the Glen of Aherlow, a long fertile valley spread between the Galtees and Slieve-namuck to the north. It is not the most dramatic scenery hereabouts, in spite of its reputation, though there is a drive, with views like a geography lesson, over the Slievenamuck range on the north. The glen and the Golden Vale which its eastern end joins are rich farm-lands, with fat dark hedges marking the green pastures like a chessboard. Together with the plains to the north they make the country's main dairying area. Pig rearing goes on as a subsidiary, and sugar beet is grown. It is all good hunting and shooting country and as so often in Ireland there are facilities for visitors who want to join in.

Farming activities make **Tipperary** itself, a few miles north, important as a market town, but it might disappoint anyone deserting Leicester Square for the visit. Long and straggling, hiding its river, the Ara, behind its back streets, as so many Irish towns do, it harbours a history of spasmodic resistance from the time of King John, who built a castle here, to the various tenant agitations of the nineteenth century. Republican sentiment remains strong to this day. In the late 1880s the so-called Plan of Campaign urged tenants to resist unrea-sonable rent rises. Those who were evicted would be supported from a common fund. In Tipperary 152 tenants were so evicted by their landlord, Arthur Smith-Barry. The surprise response was the building of New Tipperary on land outside the town. Smith-Barry appealed to Catholic Archbishop Croke of Cashel, who called him 'an aggressive busybody'. But the scheme soon exhausted its funds and collapsed. Much of the new town was bulldozed. Two streets remain. Smith-Barry was later ennobled. If not distinguished, the town has provided the seeds of distinction elsewhere. Hazlitt's grandfather, the fathers of Eugene O'Neill and Ned Kelly the Australian bushranger, and John O'Leary the Fenian were all born here or nearby. There is a good statue of the patriot and novelist Charles Kickham outside the Allied Irish Bank and another, at the junction of Main and O'Brien streets, of the Maid of Erin, commemorating the four 'Manchester Martyrs', publicly hanged in 1867, on questionable evidence, for the murder of a policeman.

The road east leads to Golden, passing **Thomastown Castle**, a superb ivy-clad ruin in Wagnerian mould, allowed to deteriorate since the 1870s and not easily reached across privately owned fields. Built, with a famous formal garden added, in the eighteenth century, it was Gothicised and painted celestial blue by Richard Morrison in the 1820s, for the Mathew family, Earls of Llandaff. Father Mathew, who led a brave and effective campaign against liquor in the nineteenth century, was born here. He was against gambling too. 'Horse-sense is something a horse has that prevents him betting on people' is attrib-uted to him. Farther on the same road is the ruined Augustinian **St**

Edmund's Priory of Athassel, which grew so wealthy after its foundation in 1205 that a town – of which nothing but wall fragments remain – grew round it. The priory's ruins are still most impressive, with interesting details like the doorway to the choir, the chapter house and refectory on a vaulted basement, and the vaulted gatehouse.

This is a detour, however, and our way lies west-south-west from Tipperary along the north side of Slievenamuck, turning left after six miles to go over the west end of the hills and see **Moor Abbey** below their southern slopes. Strictly a Franciscan friary, it was built in 1471, burned the next year, and served thereafter more as a fortress than a place of worship, with the friars harbouring outlaws during the Munster conquest and thereby risking, and at least once incurring, death at the hands of the English troops. North Cork and adjoining areas saw much action both in the Anglo-Irish War of 1918–21, and again in the Civil War that followed the signing of the Anglo-Irish Treaty. (Soloheadbeg, or Solohod, four miles north of Tipperary, is where the first shots of this guerrilla war were fired.) During the former, the abbey was often used as a cover by insurgents, and the Royal Irish Constabulary made several attempts to blow the place up. We move south from Galbally, the nearby village, close to the higher reaches of the Aherlow, through the eastern pass between the Ballyhoura and Galtys, and come down on Mitchelstown. The Kilworth Mountains, forming the western end of the Knockmealdowns, are straight ahead, and the Nagles in the distance to the right. This is county Cork, and we are well within the south-western system of old red sandstone ranges running mainly east-west, with limestone valleys – in this case that of the Blackwater – lying between.

Mitchelstown is situated in what was the major part of the territory of the FitzGerald Earls of Desmond – well over half a million acres of Kerry and Cork – until 1586, when following the defeat of the rebel fifteenth earl it was forfeited to the crown and made over to Edmund FitzGibbon the eleventh White Knight. It was he who smirched this ancient title (given by Edward III on the battlefield of Halidon Hill in 1333) by betraying the so-called Sugan Earl of Desmond in 1601 in his hiding-place, the Mitchelstown caves. By this treachery he incurred what was taken to be a family curse, a lasting shortage of male heirs among his descendants. His own son died the day before he did, in 1608. His granddaughter brought the estates, through marriage, to the Fenton family; and her daughter, by marriage, to the King family who, enormously rich, soon contrived an earldom which continues today but not without many sideways inheritances and losses of fortune. The town, now a marketing and dairy centre in the midst of rich farmland, was built to a neat right-angled plan. The old demesne, enclosed by over six miles of wall, still mostly standing, lies to the west. On the site on which the old medieval castle, the late-seventeenth-century house, the early-eighteenth-century house, the Palladian mansion of the late eighteenth century, and the Gothick castle of 1823 all succeeded each other, there is now one huge industrial twentieth-century creamery. Tankers noisily rumble to and from it under the mature avenue that runs through College Square, with its handsome eighteenth-century terraces including **Kingston College**, a 1780 foundation for 'decayed Protestant gentlefolk' fallen on hard times which still affords each of twelve gentlemen and eighteen ladies a rent-free house, garden and small annuity. This was the achievement of Robert, second earl, a man with a dark and a light side. He wisely employed Arthur Young as his agent and unwisely sacked him two years later on false suspicion of flirting with the countess. He employed young Mary Wollstonecraft, later a feminist firebrand and mother of Mary Shelley, as governess to his children. She was sacked by the countess on the same kind of suspicion. (Much later, his son employed an undercook called Claridge who went on to London to found the famous hotel.) But with cotton, soap and tobacco factories, linen works, wool and flour mills, churches, school library, and the planting of half a million mulberry trees for making silk (there is still an area called the Mulberries), Robert, his wife and later his son made their town one of the most prosperous in Europe. On the other hand he invented, so it is said, the pitch-cap for scalding the scalps of captive rebels, and together with his son murdered the seducer of his daughter.

This son, the third earl, found his father's Palladian house 'too large', as he put it, 'to hang on a watch-chain, too small to live in' and pulled it down to make way for a Gothic castle that was near to being Ireland's largest residence. Designed by G.R. Pain, this was erected at a cost exceeding £100,000 for a visit of George IV. The king, detained by good living in Dublin, failed to arrive, and the earl – and in due course his heir – lost both reason and fortune. Mitchelstown returned to the news in the 1880s. Agricultural depression reduced the estate's income. There was already a huge mortgage. As part of the Plan of Campaign, tenants insisted on paying lower rents or none at all. There were huge meetings, demonstrations, a torchlight procession with nationalist airs played by a local band, a riot –

followed by evictions (very few, most quickly reinstated). Hundreds of police and troops were imported to control things. A few years later, in 1887, there were more disturbances at the castle gates. William O'Brien, John Dillon and other agitators were present, and Wilfrid Scawen Blunt, fiery Henry Labouchère and other liberals from England. In a clash between police and rioters three of the latter were killed. Three crosses on the pavement commemorate them. There were arrests and imprisonments, Blunt himself being briefly incarcerated. 'Remember Mitchelstown' became a famous catch-phrase. In 1914, days before the outbreak of war, a prearranged party for all the local gentry was held in an atmosphere of brave gaiety. Ten years later the vast castle with its towers and turrets was gone, burned by Republicans in the civil war that followed independence; the stone sold to the monks of Mount Melleray to build a church with. The old demesne now comprised fourteen farms, playing fields, golf course and soon the dairy; and modern Mitchelstown seems forgetful of its heady past.

To the right of the road that accompanies the River Funshion west, the countryside is enchanting, and it goes on being so beyond Kildor-rery, which is as far as we go with it now. Any direction is good to go in; we are tied by the need to keep more or less to one at a time but will return to the neighbourhood later. It is a good area to stay in, its rich spread of trees concealing lanes and bohreens (the stone-sided tracks built for the moving of cattle), rivers that coil and dip into limestone tunnels, small clearings for farms and graveyards, a wealth of wild flowers and birds, herons lazily stream-spotting from the air, or standing still and priestlike in the water, waiting to strike. Spenser lived a short way to the west, a little disgruntled, using the lore of the people he despised as the matter for his *Faerie Queene*. In our times Elizabeth Bowen lived just outside **Kildorrery** to which we have come. **Bowen's Court** was the name of the house and of the sad, scholarly, loving book she wrote about it. It was a high, austere, hip-roofed building of 1776, built by a descendant of the first Bowen settler, an atheist Welshman who came over with Cromwell. That first unsociable Bowen kept hawks, one of which Cromwell is supposed to have strangled in a rage, then compensated him with the land. Like Mitchelstown, the Georgian house cost too much, and nineteenth-century Bowens never had enough money to enjoy to the full its size and splendour, the ballroom, the park with its beeches and limes. Elizabeth Bowen, brought up here, came back to live in 1952. Her husband died that same year and it was too much for her. She sold it to a progressive neighbour and the neighbour pulled it down. 'It was a clean end. Bowen's Court never lived to be a ruin,' she wrote, though she had not foreseen the end; and in an access of melodrama, standing by the meadows and trees, in view of the blue Galtees, one can see what she means, a rounded inevitability.

The first Bowens had their land at the expense of Anglo-Norman Roches, whose name lives on in Castletownroche, seven miles south of Kildorrery, and near the meeting of Spenser's Awbeg River with the east-flowing Blackwater. Two miles before the town, on the right, are the extensive and luxuriant gardens of **Annes Grove** – the name is from the Groves, early owners, and the Annesleys who inherited and continue to own it. They rise, at times steeply, from the west bank of the Awbeg. There are rare rhododendrons, camellias, magnolias and other shrubs and trees, and long woodland, garden and riverside walks, mostly planned or planted before and just after the First World War, many of the plants acquired from the classic eastern explorations of the day. The handsome early-nineteenth-century house is at the top (you pass it on the way in) as is a fine and more formal walled garden.

In 1649 the Lord Roche of the time, attainted as a royalist, fled from his seat at Castletownroche and his wife – a familiar pattern in Ireland, as in England – defended their castle, now **Castle Widenham**, against Cromwell. She was captured and hanged on the dubious charge that she had shot a man who was not named. The family never recovered its fortunes, and the last of the line worked as a stable-boy, refusing wages from pride. (Sir Boyle Roche, who possibly had a claim to the defunct title, was a distantly related eighteenth-century politician, famous for perpetrating Irish bulls. 'For posterity?' he once iterated in parliament; 'And what pray has posterity ever done for me?') Much of the huge Roche territory went to the Boyle family. Subsequent owners of the castle added a house to the keep and early in the nineteenth century topped it with battlements. The estate is privately owned, and has fine gardens, sometimes opened to the public.

We follow the river on the east side, near its passage through a steep limestone gorge to its well-set meeting with the Blackwater. Caves in the gorge have yielded bones of Irish elk and reindeer, now in Dublin's National Museum. On the bigger river's south bank stand the handsome remains of the thirteenth-century Augustinian abbey of Bridgetown. We turn east with the road to **Ballyhooly**, where stands another Roche castle, restored in the nineteenth century by the Earl of

Listowel, impressively seen from the road against the thickness of trees lining the river. The Listowels' main house was Convamore, a mile north-west; they sometimes ferried guests downstream in boats for lavish castle parties. The house was built by the Pain brothers in 1833 and burned down in 1921. Yet another Roche Castle, this one decayed and ivy-covered, stands at **Glanworth** four miles to the north, reached by a road leading to the left just beyond Ballyhooly. The village is pretty, with an ancient thirteen-arch bridge and ruined Dominican friary. If we continue the detour by taking the direct Fermoy road from Glanworth we pass a magnificent gallery-grave on the left at **Labbacallee**. The name means 'Grave of the Old Woman', and at the excavation in 1934 a headless female skeleton was found in the inner chamber at the far end from the road, while the skull was in the larger chamber near the road. This is the most elaborate and largest of several hundred known wedge-shaped gallery tombs in the country, and measures twenty-five feet in length, five feet wide and nine feet at the highest point of its sloping three-slabbed roof. It probably dates from the second half of the third millennium BC and is of a type which, with variations, is found mainly in the south-western counties. Two interesting details are the hole clipped out of the corner of the large upright slab that separates the two chambers – thought to have been an escape route for the buried lady's spirit – and the west-east axis (characteristic of these tombs) hinting perhaps at sun-worship. The whole was originally covered with earth. Excavation discovered other skeletons – male – in the outer chamber, which may, or may not, say something of the society of the day.

When we rejoin the Ballyhooly-Fermoy road, the gates of **Castle Hyde**, with sphinxes above the arches, are on the right, on the river-side. A handsome, three-storeyed (above a basement) house, with wings, built about 1801, it has a staircase up to its cliff-top garden, where the ruined Condon tower commands impressive views. But the house is not open to the public, and we continue east to **Fermoy**, a town once noted for the British garrison that occupied the barracks, and which – a rare event in Ireland – faces its river – the Blackwater – on whose southern bank it mostly lies. Till 1791 there was only a village here. It was a time when most Irish towns were owned by landlords, the inhabitants being no more than tenants. Then John Anderson, ex-Glasgow labourer made rich by a fishing venture and richer (to the tune of £20,000) by dealing in provisions in Cork, bought most of the now urban land. Restless, kind and canny, he started building: houses, square, theatre, market-house, hotel, livery stable (for Dublin-Cork travellers), bank, brewery, flour and paper mills, and – most important, having induced the government to quarter troops here – a barracks. Trade with the soldiers was the key to prosperity and bustling Fermoy had in 1800 twice its present population, all comparatively well off. He also held to the belief that 'Irish Papists were as well entitled as Protestants to live all the days of their lives', and encouraged them to build a chapel. The town held its position through the nineteenth century, always a military centre, with the kind of social life bound to thrive round officers and their ladies. Since the British left, the bustle has subsided. The barracks are in ruins, and an elegant market-house on the south side of the central square and several nice Georgian houses within and close to the town are scant evidence of its former character.

Five miles south of Fermoy is the village of Rathcormack, and a mile south of that, across the River Bride, stands **Kilshannig** House, which, when finished in 1765, must have been one of Ireland's most beautiful mansions. Built by Davis Ducart, the Sardinian designer of Castletown in county Kilkenny (for whose domed wings those at Kilshannig, now greatly reduced, served as models) and of the Limerick Customs House, it has magnificent interior plasterwork by the Lafranchini brothers.

At **Castle Lyons**, two miles north-east of Rathcormack, are the spindly, ivy-covered ruins of a sixteenth-century Barrymore castle, built on the site of the original stronghold of the Lehane or O Liathain family, local pre-Norman chiefs (Lehane and Lyons, like Leane, Lyne and Lane, are often, where they occur hereabouts, anglicised forms of the original name). Their land, extending over much of east Cork, was granted to the Barrys after the conquest. At the end of the sixteenth century, the estate, about 80,000 acres, was acquired by the future Earl of Cork, who gave it to his daughter on her marriage to the Earl of Barrymore, to help her 'to buy gloves and pins'. Subsequent Earls of Barrymore restored the building, which became a fashionable mansion of the Ascendancy, till a fire of 1771 left it much as it is now. Within fifty years the Barry line went out in a blaze of dissipation and debt. The village also contains extensive ruins of an early fourteenth-century Carmelite friary, but a more curious ruin is that of the Church of Ireland church to the north-west. It stands among the trees and overgrowth of its churchyard, its windows cemented to prevent pilfering that sometimes follows abandonment by a dwindled Protestant congregation. To the east is the mausoleum of the Barrymores, a charming Palladian building of brick and stone, erected around 1750 to house the superb monument, by David Sheehan, to the first earl. Building, sculpture, plaster- and ironwork were restored in 1975 by the Irish Georgian Society.

Returning to Fermoy, we drive east along the north shore of the Blackwater, here broader and faster and best in Ireland for salmon, through a richly wooded valley, to **Lismore** and catch glimpses of several hoary castles against the long, bosomy backdrop of the Knockmealdowns. Beyond Ballyduff and set in thick woods we pass the elaborate nineteenth-century Gothic gates and castle-bridge of Ballysaggartmore, whose owner, running into debt on their construction, had nothing left for the house he planned to replace the old one. That still stands, ruined and rambling. Lismore has little better to show than the first fairytale view of its castle from the bridge (mid-eighteenth century; Thomas Ivory's earliest work) which we cross before entering the town – for the town gives away little of its former status. In the eighth century it was one of the best-known monastic centres of the country, founded by St Carthach or Carthage. He brought both loyal followers and leprosy patients to Lismore, whose prestige soon rose. A century later it was said to have counted the future King Alfred among its students, and there are now claims that over twenty calendared saints were buried here. Henry II called soon after his arrival in Ireland, and the future King John picked the riverside site for a castle. This was later handed over to the church authorities, and so came into the possession (as he saw it) of the volatile Bishop Myler McGrath, now in a Protestant phase – he found sect-changes easy – who sold a long lease on it in 1589 to Sir Walter Raleigh.

The poet-knight-adventurer was more concerned to regain the queen's lost regard than to exploit the vast areas of tillage, pasture, woods, minerals and fishing that he acquired. He did not stay long in the country, returned to England, offended the queen by making a maid-of-honour – whom he had to marry – pregnant, spent four years in the Tower, explored Trinidad and the Orinoco, and won long-sung victories against the Spanish on their own ground. Unwisely, he did not ingratiate himself with the young heir, James VI of Scotland. Others did, and poisoned the prince's ear against him. He was forced to sell his Irish estates for a song and languished in the Tower from 1603 to his last disastrous expedition to Guiana and subsequent execution in 1618.

The ultimate beneficiary of his sale, in 1627, was Richard Boyle, future Earl of Cork, who also combined Tudor virtues and vices. To him and Raleigh are owed many existing features of the area – the castles, towns, the division of the land, and the great number of Dorset families who settled at the time and whose descendants, Allen, Coppinger, Mead, Russell, Stout, are still found hereabouts. The earl lived to become the richest man in Ireland and to see the beginning of the Confederate War, in which his son Roger defended the castle against the Catholics. The earl died in 1643. Another son, Robert, born at Lismore, soon went to England, where he became a founder member of the Royal Society, author of 'Boyle's law' and the claimed founder of modern chemistry. The last Lismore Boyle, fourth Earl of Cork but better known as third Earl of Burlington, was the Palladian architect whose collaboration with Gibbs produced what is now the Royal Academy's headquarters in London. At his death in 1753, Lismore Castle passed, by the marriage of his daughter, to the Dukes of Devonshire, with whom it has remained. Survivals from Cork's time include the gatehouse, the toy-like riding-house (next to the avenue of pollarded yews planted by the earl's son), the north-west Round Tower and the walls of the upper garden; but the basic work of the period – four gabled ranges round a courtyard – was 'ruinated' by 1654, according to the *Civil Survey*. As it stands today the castle is owed mainly to the enthusiasm of the sixth Duke of Devonshire and the skill of his one-time gardener, Joseph Paxton, designer of the Crystal Palace. Paxton's great river-front dates from the early 1850s, as does most of the interior, for which Pugin designed much of the furniture and chimney-pieces, as well as the great banqueting hall, a sort of miniature House of Lords. Apart from that the interior is modest and a little disappointing, but the outside still makes it the most grandiose castle in Ireland, what the duke himself called 'this quasi-feudal, ultra-regal fortress'.

Lord Charles Cavendish, a younger brother of the tenth duke, married in 1932 Adele Astaire, the dancer Fred's dancing sister, and they held the castle until his death, when it reverted to the duke. Lord Charles was buried in the graveyard of the Church of Ireland Cathedral of St Carthage. This medieval church, reroofed by the Great Earl, had its tall delicate spire added by G.R. Pain in 1827 – one of the prettiest in the country. It incorporates a splendid Tudor McGrath monument, Gothic vaulting, and some eloquent memorials, not least to that Richard Musgrave who, 'as a Landlord, and a Master, A Husband, and a Father, A Magistrate, and a Christian, Left behind him few equals, and no Superior ...' though he did advocate flogging, burning and the like for rebels and was felt by his friend Jonah

Barrington to take leave of his senses during any discussion of 'politics, religion, martial law, his wife, the Pope, the Pretender, the Jesuits, Napper Tandy and the whipping-post'. In the 1840s his son introduced steamers onto the river, which they plied till 1914. Most of the riverside houses downstream from Lismore have big crumbling jetties.

We return to the river by a scenic route that brings us opposite the most impressive side of Dromana, then over the bridge that crosses the river Bride. Six miles west beside the Bride, **Tallow** has Ireland's largest annual horse-fair. The name means Iron Hill, and the Earl of Cork exploited its minerals, making guns and cannons for export and bringing great prosperity to the area. Iron-ore mine shafts abound, and in his day the forges glowed in every village. But all this meant the baring of the land, for thousands of trees were destroyed for charcoal, as well as for shipbuilding, and pipestaves and hogsheads to be sent to France and Spain.

Keeping to the Blackwater, we pass the Pains' hauntingly Gothic Strancally Castle, and the ruined keep beside it where a medieval FitzGerald was given to cutting his guests' throats and dropping their bodies in the river so as to acquire their lands. Six miles on is the decaying Georgian (1795–97) eleven-bay-fronted Ballynatray House, magnificently set in its deer-park by the river, with the ruined abbey of Molana on a causewayed island in the demesne. Strongbow's lieutenant Raymond le Gros is said to be buried on the island, and a later owner placed a funeral urn to mark the fact. (Below the abbey is Ireland's only sprat-weir, a wattle contraption for catching sea fish – the river being tidal well above this point.) The Holroyd-Smyths, who owned the house until 1969, were descended from Richard Smyth, who built the original house and married the Great Earl of Cork's sister Mary. Last century the family kept the captain's barge from a Napoleonic man-of-war, which had been wrecked off the coast, as a state barge complete with musicians; and a Smyth daughter married the brother of King Ferdinand II of Naples, infuriating the King and condemning herself and her husband, after long diplomatic wrangles, to a life of exile and poverty.

The direct road from Youghal to Cork passes through Castlemartyr, ten miles west. The beautiful demesne here had an exacting share of Tudor-Stuart history. It was captured twice for the queen in the Munster invasion, acquired by Raleigh, passed to Boyle, taken by FitzGeralds (the original owners) in the Civil War, enlarged by Boyle's son, the Earl of Orrery, and reduced to ruins in 1688. The gaunt fifteenth-century keep and walls still stand. **Castlemartyr House**, built by the Earl of Shannon, one of Boyle's great-grandsons, in the eighteenth century, now belongs to the Carmelites, but visits may be arranged. It has a magnificent double-cube saloon, with plasterwork by Robert West added in the 1760s by the second Earl of Shannon. His father had constructed the impressive watercourse which still snakes through the demesne and round the town.

A road leads south from the village to **Ballycotton Bay**, to which we could have come direct from Youghal by the picturesque coast-road, taking in Knockadoon Head. **Shanagarry**, set a mile back from the sea, has a famous modern pottery. Beside the village is Shanagarry House, with a ruined castle where the Penn family lived after Charles II had given them the land in place of an earlier Cromwellian grant at Macroom. William Penn came in 1666 to sort out estate affairs for his father, the admiral whose bickering with rivals had squashed Cromwell's West Indies ambitions. While staying here, William, a Quaker since Oxford days, attended a proscribed Quaker meeting in Cork. He was imprisoned, but soon released, and returned to England to preach, go to gaol again, and finally to leave for the American colony which he named Pennsylvania in his father's honour.

A mile west of Shanagarry is the Ballymaloe House Hotel, an eighteenth-century mansion incorporating seventeenth-century bits and a medieval keep, with one of Ireland's best restaurants, run by Myrtle Allen and overlooked by several of Jack Yeats's paintings. To the east is **Ballycotton** village, a charming, busy and popular resort with good beaches and a pretty harbour, and a base for deep-sea fishing. Shark, skate, conger, cod, ling and pollock are the species most sought, and a number of Irish records have been established here, though the headquarters of shark fishing is at Kinsale, west of Cork.

Quieter interest is to be had at **Cloyne**, a pretty village with a small Church of Ireland cathedral, on the way west across this broad peninsula. St Colman, around 600, began the religious tradition here. Colman was such a common name, one story tells, that when once St Carthage, directing a party of monks working beside a river, called 'Into the water, Colman', twelve jumped. This one, a poet some of whose lines survive, was a late vocation, persuaded to take orders by St Brendan the Navigator. Of the medieval church buildings, a ruined oratory and Round Tower remain. In 1734 George Berkeley, the philosopher, was made Bishop of Cloyne. Earlier, with a government grant promised and a legacy from Swift's 'Vanessa', he crossed to Rhode Island bent on 'converting the savage Americans to Christianity'. He founded a college in Bermuda, but the grant never came and he retired to eighteen years of happy home life and philosophy. Though the village had twice as many people as it has now, and the diocese stretched to Limerick's hills, he had time for writing, reading, and publishing issues of *The Querist*, in which he advocated economic independence for Ireland. He had earlier, in Sydney Smith's words, 'destroyed this world in one volume octavo' by proposing that things exist only through being perceived. He wrote at Cloyne on the universal benefits to be had from tar water, founded a spinning school and a workhouse, taught improved farming methods, and when the area was swept by a dysentery plague acted the doctor and made large grants to the poor. St Colman's cathedral (the see is now incorporated with that of Cork) is basically thirteenth century but with the mark of most subsequent styles. It has a fine alabaster effigy of Berkeley, above his tomb. He lived in a large house beside the cathedral, but it burned down in 1870.

We rejoin the main Cork road at **Midleton**, where in 1825 the Pain brothers built the Church of Ireland church on the site of a Cistercian monastery. Midleton College, rebuilt in 1829, was founded by William III's mistress, Elizabeth Villiers, in 1696 (Swift deplored the king's taste: she 'squinted like a dragon'). The guilt-ridden king, after the Boyne, and the death of his wife, gave her the most valuable grant of land in Ireland – nearly 100,000 acres that had been James II's personal estates; and she, in an attempt to make herself popular, founded the college. The grant was later revoked. The town contains a thriving distillery making whiskey but also vodka and gin, complete with heritage centre, a 1789 market-house and a good Church of Ireland church.

West of Midleton the road leads straight and wide into Cork, but it is worth diverting left at Carrigtohill. We pass the beautiful and almost insular demesne of **Fota**, formerly belonging to the Smith-Barry family, a cadet branch of the Barrymores. Most of the present house was designed by the Morrisons, father and son, in the early nineteenth century, who disguised the eighteenth-century hunting-lodge, which still remains the heart of the building, in stuccoed Regency simplicity. Its interiors are very rich and elaborate: a long scagliola-pillared hall, ornate plasterwork above the staircase (a comparatively small one, being confined within the original house), good furniture and a fine collection of paintings by James Barry, Daniel Maclise, James Arthur O'Connor, Thomas Roberts and others. The sheltered, balmy climate allows the gardens, in part reclaimed from the sea, to support many rare subtropical species, among the finest in these islands. A century ago over a hundred thousand plants were bedded in the borders. Such gardening, like the stove house, peach house, melon house and vinery, is of the past. But the magnificent arboretum remains, and a wildlife park has been opened in the grounds. The acres of mud-flats around are a great attraction to wildfowl. (Cork harbour as a whole furnishes a winter home to about five thousand wildfowl and twenty thousand waders.) After six miles we reach **Cobh**, on Great Island in the middle of vast Cork harbour. Cobh, pronounced Cove, was in English days known as Queenstown. 'To give the people the satisfaction of calling the place Queenstown,' wrote benign Victoria on her visit in 1849, 'in honour of its being the first spot on which I set foot on Irish ground, I stepped on shore amidst a roar of cannon and enthusiastic shouts of the people.' The mayor had requested the queen to stay on board since preparations were not complete. She refused the delay, and all went well. It was till recently Cork's main harbour, and in the eighteenth century lighters and small vessels would take cargoes and passengers hence to the canals of Cork city. It remained in British hands till 1937. From here in 1838 the *Sirius* sailed to make the first Atlantic steamer crossing. Impressive from afar, St Colman's is a Pugin-Ashlin cathedral of 1869 onwards. The town has little to offer; but the island is lovely. Nearly a mile north of Cobh is the churchyard of Clonmel, which harbours the remains of the poet Charles Wolfe, James Verling, sometime surgeon to Napoleon, and many who went down with the *Lusitania* in 1915, in a plainly marked communal grave maintained by the Cunard Line. Cobh also boasted the world's oldest yacht club, the Royal Cork, founded in 1720, until it moved its clubhouse across the water to Crosshaven.

There is no way back but the way we came to rejoin the main Cork road. Six miles further on we pass on the right Dunkathel, or Dunkettle, a handsome house (in a region where rich Cork merchants built many such) of the 1780s, with fine interior plasterwork, friezes and frescoes of the nineteenth century. The next right turn on to the Fermoy road brings us after a couple of miles to **Riverstown**, a house built early in the eighteenth century for Bishop Jemmet Browne of Cork. One room was used for storing potatoes up to a few years ago when the Irish Georgian Society discovered within it some glorious stucco work done by the Lafranchini brothers in 1745. The society restored it with the owner's encouragement. The public are admitted, and several other items of interest have subsequently been unearthed in both house and garden.

9

West Cork, North Cork and the Cork Coast
(Cork to Kenmare)

D UBLINERS ARE SUPPOSED to say that when a Cork man
starts smiling at you, it's too late to look for the knife in your
back; that Cork is a soft town with a sting in its tail; or that Cork
people have a sense of inferiority, which sends them to Dublin or
London or the USA as soon as they are free, to pass the time singing
praises of their native city. A lot of past travellers have found it ugly,
gloomy, a 'magazine of nastiness'. Thackeray was irked by the popu-
lace – 'could they do nothing but stare, swagger and be idle in the
streets?'; blown from a concert hall by the blare of a dragoon band;
affronted by shabbiness and waste. He published an article in *The
Cornhill* that vented his feelings and in answer a Cork potter patented
a chamber-pot with an open-mouthed Thackeray decorating the bowl.
The line was a grand success and the pots are now prized rarities.
(Gladstone was later to receive the same treatment.)

But for every word of abuse there has been more praise. Arthur
Young found it pleasant, like a Dutch town with its streets inter-
sected by canals. Wesley thought it 'one of the pleasantest and most
ancient cities in the kingdom'. Thackeray himself found the people,
even the beggars, cleverer and better-read than most Englishmen.
This, according to Padraic Colum, is the city that gives Ireland her
journalists, schoolmasters and civil servants. Away from the over-
whelmingly English influence of the Pale (though curiously, older
architecture shows more English influence than any other part of
Ireland) Cork developed in a highly individual way. It consisted at
first of islands scattered between the north and south banks of the
Lee, the channels serving as thoroughfares. Many of them, converted
into roads, still do. The way Corkonians speak English, with a lilting
sing-song not far removed from the Welsh way, and the un-English
uses they put English to, indicate the singularity of what lies
beneath. For in Cork city and the south-western part of the country –
in spite of the familiar list of English invasions, of plantations, of

sporting Anglo-Irish landlords – the highlights of the past are quite different from those of eastern Ireland. Conquerors were more fully absorbed into existing ways. Rebels were welcomed. Perkin Warbeck was here acclaimed King of England and provided with men and gold by the mayor, so losing the city its charter and himself in due course his head. The Desmond FitzGeralds, grabbing land from old Irish McCarthys, soon became Irish enough to worry their English lieges. Ignoring the Reformation, they stayed Catholic, and in 1579 the fifteenth FitzGerald earl rebelled against Queen Elizabeth, sacked Youghal, and tried to join with Spanish and Italian forces in Kerry. The subsequent Munster plantation was not as successful as that of Connacht. The Irish kept rallying, but they kept backing losers too: Charles I, the boy Charles II on his way to ten years' exile, the enemies of Cromwell, James II when his cause was lost. All the same it took a five-day bombardment and the destruction of the city walls by King William's commander (the future Duke of Marlborough) and his five thousand troops after the battle of the Boyne, to bring the citizens to heel. All this time, and especially after Cromwell's successes brought in a new Protestant merchant elite, Cork prospered. In the eighteenth century, despite Munster Whiteboys – guerrillas campaigning for redress from enclosure, rack-rents, tithes and forced labour – the city prospered even more. It was Munster's chief processor and exporter – to Britain, the Continent and America north and south, of agricultural produce. The flat marshy lands around it were gradually reclaimed and population multiplied. By the nineteenth century, however, Irish trade and commerce was facing east, and Cork lost out. Worse, it and its dependant port Queenstown or Cove (now restored to the Irish spelling Cobh) formed the main funnel through which passed hundreds of thousands of weary, disenchanted, sick and often dying emigrants on their way to America. Depression of more than one kind afflicted Cork, and the migration, though vastly reduced, continued into the twentieth century, even to the 1970s.

The same century allotted Cork and Munster a copious share of violent political action. One mayor of the city, Thomas MacCurtain, was murdered in 1920 by (so a jury found) a gang of constabulary. It was in Cork that the Black and Tans, ex-army roughs recruited in England to beat nationalist Ireland into submission, most ably fulfilled their Gestapo roles; they were seen, wrote Lord Longford, 'strutting down the streets of Cork, crazy with drink and nerves, lashing passers-by across the face with riding-whips stolen from the

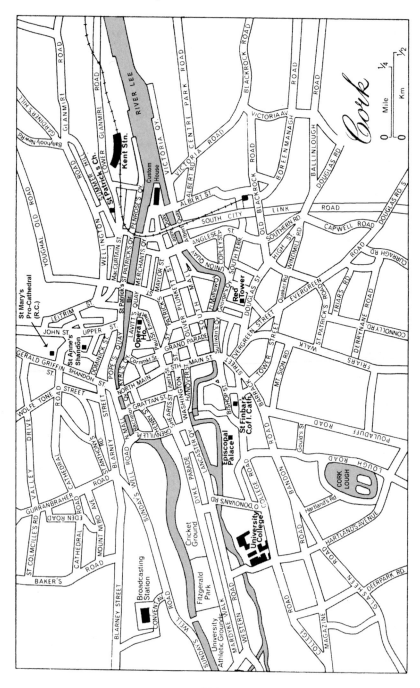

shops'. They smashed windows and looted, thugged and raped, and most of what they did was exonerated by leaders who thought brutish reprisal the only way of countering rebellion. The next lord mayor, Terence MacSwiney – poet, playwright, revolutionary propagandist – was imprisoned, went on hunger strike, and died in Brixton after seventy-five days – until recently the longest prison abstinence on record. Both Free Staters and Republicans were based in turn on the city in the Civil War of 1922–23. The uncompromising Volunteers operated from camps in the surrounding hills, and on a narrow lane near Clonakilty the Free State commander-in-chief Michael Collins was killed in an ambush.

Its native writers best express Cork's essence, whether or not they talk explicitly of it. None were better than Sean O'Faolain (pronounced rather like O'Fwelaun; an Irishing of Whelan) and Frank O'Connor (pseudonym for Michael O'Donovan), born within three years and a mile of each other, both rising from humble origins by way of humble jobs to dominate the Irish literary scene – no mean achievement – in the mid-twentieth century. Young O'Faolain was a commercial traveller in America, then fought in the hills for the Republicans before getting an academic training and writing novels, biographies and neat, wry short stories. His life epitomises Cork obstinacy. Having fought for an enlightened Republic in 1922 he saw the movement's leaders create a society of 'the most blatant inequalities, the clear absence of equal opportunities for all, a large and flourishing and privileged minority, a bourgeois class utterly devoid of moral courage, an indescribably repressive and obscurantist church, and the most constant and shameless inroads on personal freedom of thought and expression'. Both Church and State attacked his work and banned some of his writing. The words quoted were written in 1966, anniversary of the 1916 Rising and execution of those 'whom we are now about to honour fifty years after we have forgotten what they meant to create'.

If O'Faolain is the cussed stubbornness of Cork, O'Connor is the rugged, twinkling-eyed humanity. His autobiography, *An Only Son*, paints the Cork of the 1900s – poverty, wit, songs in grimy Blarney Lane, musty priests, nuns saintly and spiteful, wasting disease, a drunken father, incorruptible mother, cramped cabins to live in and wide-eyed glimpses of the teacup gentry in large terrace-houses in Sunday's Well; and the confused loyalties of the Civil War, during which it was occupied first by Republicans, from whom Michael Collins and his Free State army reclaimed it. Nothing better shows the muddle of those times than his description of the war's outbreak, issues misunderstood, orders miscarried, front lines ignored as fighters on both sides went to Mass or mother-visiting. Suddenly, for him, the comedy was cut, when he, imprisoned and not sorry for a rest, saw a fellow prisoner dying, his arms pierced by an enemy bayonet. A story-teller, rooted to his city and province yet universal like Chekhov or de Maupassant, he is as integral to Cork as Dickens to London.

Cork is lively and bustling, Ireland's third largest town (with the same population as Bath), and very much its own place. It was founded beside water and marsh ('marsh' is what corcagh means) – along the Lee's southern shore – and expanded on to a cluster of islands the river held at this point. Many of its central roads were, even up to a century or two ago, bridged waterways. Its seaward outlet faces south to Spain and France rather than east to the old enemy, and it is the nearest major Irish harbour to America. It has a long industrial tradition (Fords put their first European factory here, in 1917) and brewing, distilling and the manufacture of sausages and dairy products are still carried on. It has excellent shops, and good wide streets due to its having had, like Dublin, a Wide Streets Commission in the early nineteenth century; and its situation, where, as Spenser wrote, 'the spreading Lee, that like an island fayre, Encloseth Corke with his divided flood' is one of the most charming in Ireland. But war, flood (in 1789 the houses were nine feet deep in water, which carried many of them away) and depression wiped away much that was oldest and best, and few buildings are more than two centuries old. In Black and Tan times three million pounds' worth of the city's centre was burned. One consequence of this is that the whole of the eastern side of the main street, St Patrick's, consists of newer, taller, brasher buildings than those of the western.

Though the town has almost none of Dublin's Georgian grandeur it is crammed in unlikely places with domestic architectural curiosities. Nowhere is this more true than north of the river, in the area round **St Anne's**, **Shandon**, reached from the river by a lovely steep hill with wide steps on either side. The 1722 church, like London's St Mary le Bow, is best known for its bells, acclaimed in the lines of Father Prout – 'With thy bells of Shandon, That sound so grand on The pleasant waters of the river Lee.' 'Father Prout' was the invention of a nine-teenth-century expelled Jesuit satirist, Francis Sylvester Mahony, and his 'sermons' are a comical collection of gossip, banter, Irish bulls, knotted logic, and the fear of God. His doggerel verse trails on in a stream of wit and ready use of many living and some dead languages. He lived and died in Cork and was buried in the graveyard here. An oddity of the elegant pepper-pot church tower is that two sides are made of red sandstone and two of white limestone. The gilded salmon acting as weathervane atop the tower is eleven feet in length. Around the church are various good buildings including the Greencoat school, the arcaded Skiddy's Almshouse of the early eighteenth century and the Butter Exchange, now housing the Shandon Craft Centre, of a hundred years later. West of the church is the unimpressive **St Mary's Pro-Cathedral**, started in 1808, with some interior work by G.R. Pain; and, half a mile north, the much more inspired and modern **Church of the Assumption**, designed and with statues by Seamus Murphy. The Catholic Church has been in the twentieth century a bold patron of the plastic arts as Murphy's work all about county Cork, as well as that of Evie Hone, Maimie Jellett, Michael Healy, Harry Clarke and many others, testifies. Some stained glass by Hone and Healy is to be seen in the chapel of Collins Barracks, half a mile east of St Anne's.

George Richard and James Pain, whose work we come on all over Ireland, were sons of an English architect and pupils of John Nash, who brought them to Ireland to help with the construction of Lough Cutra Castle. G.R. Pain's work is specially prominent in Cork. Like Nash, he was adaptable in style, equally at ease in the Gothic Revival that came in the train of the Romantic Movement, and the new emphasis on Greek styles that accompanied the virtual closure of Italy to English travellers during the Napoleonic war and the subsequent Greek War of Independence. He was a lesser architect than Nash, and nothing like as prolific, but his work abounds here. One of the best examples is **St Patrick's Church** of 1836 on MacCurtain Street – with a good pillared portico and roof lantern, let down by the predictable flamboyance of the heavy, marbled interior. Over to the west of this north bank of the Lee is Sunday's Well and, high above it, the old city gaol, which now houses a museum.

On the central, nearly water-bound area of the city a few scattered points of interest lie behind the main thoroughfares. On the north side, beside Lavitt's Quay, west of St Patrick's Bridge, is the modern **Opera House**, opened in 1965 to replace the one burned down in 1955. Michael Scott built it. Its fare is light – usually a summer season of plays, and music (the jollier operettas) kept for the winter. A little to the west is **Coal Quay**, and off it the old Cornmarket, with its flea-market – a treasury of tat in an eighteenth-century arcaded market house. This is a lively, colourful, arty shopping area. Nearby in Emmet Place, next to the Opera House, is the **Crawford Munic-ipal Art Gallery**, recently extended, on the site of the town's original custom house. The exhibition includes some minor old masters and interesting Irish work – notably by James Barry (1741–1806), a seaman, then artist-protégé of Edmund Burke, who instilled in him an ambition that outstripped his abilities, so that his patchy treatment of great themes, and a temper that got him expelled from the Royal Academy, led to his death in poverty; Sir William Orpen (1878–1931), an anglicised product of county Dublin who, made known and knighted by his official drawings of the First World War, grew bitter as his realistic school faded from the scene; and Sir John Lavery (1856–1951), born in Belfast but trained among the Glasgow school, who suffered the same public fate as Orpen. There are also works by Leo Whelan and James Sleator, younger artists in line of descent from Orpen, as well as by Jack Yeats, the poet's brother, including a good pastel self-portrait; and sculpture by, among others, John Hogan. A short walk south-west of the Art School is Pugin's Catholic Church of St Peter and St Paul, a good specimen of Gothic Revival. South-west again, between Grand Parade and South Main Street, is the Church of Ireland **Christ Church**, built in 1720 to replace a church destroyed in John Churchill's (later Duke of Marlborough) siege of 1690, after the Boyne. Much of the pleasant, plain interior is the work of G.R. Pain. In the church which stood here before, Edmund Spenser is supposed to have married the Earl of Cork's kinswoman, Elizabeth Boyle, 'the soverayne beauty which I do admyre' of his *Amoretti*.

South Mall, leading off the south end of Grand Parade, is the city's financial centre, flanked by smart bank buildings. Near the junction of the two streets is the headquarters of the Cork Film Festival, that unlikely event in the film-world calendar when the sun, tantrums, Martinis and nymphets of the South of France give place to the blarney, threatening damp, Guinness and hospitality of the Irish scene, creating, as the London *Times* said, the best film festival. It takes place in late September, and offers the most perceptively chosen selection of current world cinema. South of South Mall, off Father Mathew Quay, is the Capuchin Church of the Holy Trinity, an ornate G.R. Pain structure with a light and fanciful west front and a pleas-antly plain interior. Father Theobald Mathew (1790–1856), the 'apostle of temperance', was first superior of the convent attached to the church. 'Here goes, in the name of God,' he is said to have said in 1838, as he signed his name at the head of the list of total abstainers (a stone's throw from the premises of Beamish and other brewers and distillers). A landmark statue of him, known simply as 'the Statue' stands where St Patrick's Street meets Merchants' Quay.

South of Holy Trinity, across the bridge and east of Mary Street, is one of Cork's few medieval remains, the **Red Tower** of a fourteenth-century Augustinian abbey, probably on the site where the city was conceived. From the top of the tower Churchill is said to have watched the progress of his siege in 1690. Half a mile west is the prominent landmark of **St Finbar's Cathedral** (Church of Ireland), whose spires make impressive skyline silhouettes from many angles around. When its early Georgian predecessor was pulled down in 1864 the new design was opened to competition. William Burges, a lover of French Gothic, won. He also built additions to Cardiff Castle and Castell Coch whose florid medievalism foreshadowed Holly-wood's, and designed Hertford College, Connecticut. Burges' gaining the contract over his nearest rival, William Barre, made the awarding committee, according to a friend of Barre's, 'guilty of the despicable fraud they did unblushingly commit', but the result is lustrous, exuberant, high-Victorian homage to medieval French Gothic, with a deal of dazzling detail in the internal painting, bright ceiling mosaics, stonework and woodwork. A brass marking the grave of the first woman Freemason, Elizabeth Aldworth, will be explained when we visit Doneraile.

Half a mile west of the cathedral are the grounds of **University College**, a constituent college of the National University. The original 'Queen's colleges' of Dublin, Cork and Galway were founded in 1845, in response to the demand for Catholic higher education. Being undenominational, they did not satisfy the Catholics, who called them the Godless Colleges and, forming the vast majority, wanted exclusive seats of learning. In 1851 the abortive 'Catholic University' was founded under Cardinal Newman, in Dublin. Disraeli, in 1880, tried to satisfy the Catholics with his 'Royal University', an examining but non-teaching compromise, and finally in 1908 the National University was founded, with princely endowments from the British government. The Cork college was by then well developed, with moderately successful buildings of the mid-nineteenth century by Sir Thomas Deane's firm. Macaulay thought them worth a place in Oxford High Street. Various collections, to be seen on application, are housed in the faculty buildings, and the college grounds are delightful. The front of the Pain brothers' Doric-porticoed county gaol of 1818, now incorporated in the college (its function changed, it

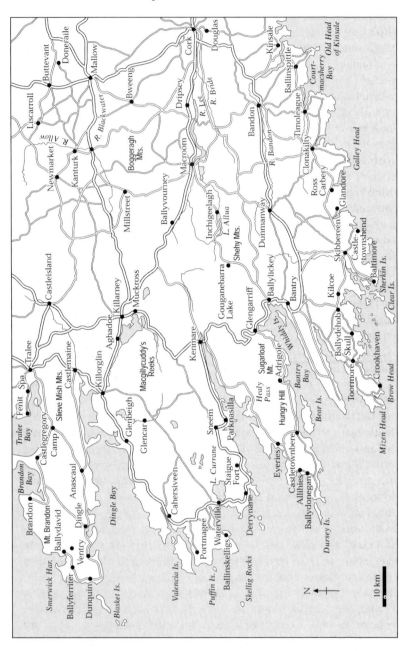

need hardly be said) is a fine example of the Greek Revival. An aspect of the Church of Ireland's attempt, spurred by Gladstone's Disestablishment in 1869 and the mounting wealth and influence of Catholics, to show its true and unique descent from the primitive Irish church, was to patronise the revival of the Irish Romanesque style which had come to its peak (at Roscrea, Cashel and elsewhere) in the twelfth century. The **Honan Collegiate Chapel** is a late (1916) example of this revival. Its plan is that of St Cronan's, Roscrea, and into it is fitted the work of those considered best in contemporary Irish craftsmanship: stained glass (by Sarah Purser and Harry Clarke), statues, ironwork, stonework, carpets, banners and vestments, cross, monstrance and altar cruets. Together they make a showpiece for the movement. But the general effect is one of self-conscious artiness, lacking the spontaneous vitality of, say, Cormac's Chapel at Cashel. North of the university, along the river, is the **Mardyke**, a no longer fashionable elm walk made along a former causeway, with Fitzgerald Park, its fine ornamental gardens and lake, and a good museum of local interest, at the promenade's west end.

Three miles east of the city, just south of the river, stands **Black-rock Castle**, whose imposing present form – seen magnificently on the road into Cork from the east – is owed to the brothers Pain, but which stands on the site of a fort erected by Lord Mountjoy after the Battle of Kinsale. It is a restaurant now.

A castle of different, better known appeal is **Blarney**, five miles north-west of the town which, though a crowded tourist haunt, is worth a visit for the beauty of its position and the good presentation of its complex interior. It stands south-west of the somewhat commer-cialised village of the same name that houses the Muskerry Hunt kennels and a woollen mill of 1750. 'Blarney', of course, has come to mean a special brand of Irish talk which persuades, deceives even, without actually offending the dupe. The origin of the meaning is supposedly in the procrastination of the then Lord of Blarney, a MacCarthy, when Elizabeth's governors were trying to wean him from dangerous Irish practices. Day to day he made promises 'with fair words and soft speech', till Elizabeth broke out with the words 'this is all Blarney; what he says he never means', and Tudor vocabu-lary was further enriched. The other Blarney tradition of kissing the Blarney Stone at the top of the tower – 'a stone that whoever kisses, O he never misses to grow eloquent' (wrote Prout) is nowadays very commercialised. There is a story that an early MacCarthy, having helped Edward Bruce in his campaign to win the English crown, was rewarded with a piece of the stone of Scone, and fixed it on the battlements. A more explicit tale claims that an old woman, saved from drowning by a king of Munster, rewarded him with a spell: that if he would kiss a stone on the castle's topmost wall he would gain a speech that would win all to him. The best thing about the keep's summit is the view from it. Eighteenth-century Richard Millikin, a popular Anglo-Irish poet, made up a song that quaintly caught its attraction, 'the groves of Blarney, they look so charming, Down by the purling of sweet silent streams ...', a faintly bawdy, beautifully worded poem that James Stephens said he would sooner have written than anything else in an Irish anthology. The castle itself was built in 1446 by Cormac MacCarthy, whose family, once Kings of south Munster, repeatedly gained and lost their dominance of Muskerry (West Cork) from and to the English, till their departure with the 'Wild Geese' after the Boyne. The tall, stout tower and keep with good machicolations (open-bottomed projections from the battlements, through which stones and possibly boiling oil could be dropped on a besieging enemy) and some well-preserved rooms on a thick base of solid granite give a good picture of the fortified house of the time, and the setting within. The ruin attached to the keep is of an eighteenth-century addition. The large occupied house in the demesne is of 1874 and in unrelieved Scottish baronial style, burgeoning with bartizans, round corner-towers, cone-turrets, stepped gables and heavy multiple chimneys.

Inner Cork

Cork city is the gateway to southern Ireland's most dramatic scenery – the mountainous, deeply indented western coast. Many visitors go straight from the city or harbour to the sea. Well they might; but the result is that the great beauty and interest of inner Cork is less known than it might be. Deferring an Atlantic tour, we can drive north from Cork to Mallow, between the Nagles and the Boggeragh Mountains, up the valley of the Martin, to see more of the area begun in the last chapter. The N20 road, well clear of Cork, is pretty. We cross a deep glen by a seven-arched viaduct and climb slowly to the 'Red Forge' at Sluggary crossroads, passing through more level country. At Rathduff crossroads, which we cross, two pubs compete for the position of halfway house between Cork and Mallow. Megalithic forts and tombs abound in the area, and that familiar Irish sight, a nipple-like tomb-silhouette on a bosomy hill, comes often into view. Another regular feature, here as elsewhere, is the grand estate gate that leads at best to a modest house, more often to nothing. The burning of the houses of the great explains some, but the destruction was not confined to this century's Troubles. The great houses began to decline at the Union, when landlords increasingly grew conspicuous by their absence; but even that does not explain the large number of gates leading almost nowhere. Many are no more than specious symbols of coveted status. Five miles this side of Mallow we pass, on the right, **Mourne Abbey**, a vast area enclosed by defensive walls and towers built in 1216 by the Knights Hospitallers. In its heyday it was a complete little town, with Mayor and Corporation. But this, and Castle Barrett, a short way beyond and on the left, were stage by stage reduced by the Dissolution, the Parliamentarians and King William, and little is left to see.

Mallow itself, a town of just over 5,000, has a long and winding main street which abuts, at its east end, on the castle demesne. It keeps a sneering distance from the Blackwater, which we crossed on entering, in the hydrophobic way of most inland Irish towns. But water has played a decisive role in Mallow's history. Founded by Desmond Geraldines in the thirteenth century, the town was granted in 1584 to Sir Thomas Norreys, Lord President of Munster, whose tenure was cut short by the Munster rising of 1598. He had time, however, to build a fortified house in the new, graceful, frail-looking style that succeeded the sturdy functional keeps of Norman and Tudor times. The style (seen also at Kanturk and Liscarroll) was not in fact premature, since not even the former stone masses could withstand assault from the new cannons of the period; and it was fire, not shot, which reduced the house to its present skeletal aspect in the Williamite wars. Meanwhile the demesne had passed by marriage to the Jephson family, who moved into a stable block when their house was gutted. The block was enlarged and adapted for living in after 1837 (a new entrance, based on the 1837 plans and using stones ready cut at that time, had to wait till 1954), and is now a smart, unpretentious, ten-gabled, Tudor-revival residence. It is the Jephson family's still. The white deer in the park are supposed to descend from two white harts, the gift of Queen Elizabeth to her god-child Elizabeth Norreys, whose marriage to Sir John Jephson brought the estate to the family which owns it still.

It is hard to imagine, in the days of the six-county border, the Orange order thriving in this south-western province. In fact such associations prospered all over the country, and the Moyallow Loyal Protestant Society, founded in the wake of the 1745 Jacobite rising to maintain loyalty to the Hanoverian kings and provide if necessary a militia to fight for them, grew rich on its unspent funds. An ancestor of Elizabeth Bowen was one of its presidents, and the minute-book preserved in her family speaks of festive dinners, the wearing of Orange cockades and medals, loyal toasts and speeches, and rewards offered for the arrest of felons. This last was specially helpful in maintaining Mallow's eighteenth-century reputation as the prime spa of Ireland, often known as the Irish Bath. Its warm springs, promoted by Dr Rogers of Cork, became famous as a cure for consumption, and society of all ages gathered to take the cure. Arthur Young and Charles Wesley came, and so did the young blades of the time, those 'Rakes of Mallow' from whom the early-morning Cork coach was named: 'Beaving, belling, dancing, drinking, Breaking windows, damning, sinking, Ever raking, never thinking, Live the Rakes of Mallow.' It lost ground towards the end of the eighteenth century to the Hot Wells of Bristol, but Sir Walter Scott came in the early 1800s. Nowadays only the original Spa House, which is private, and three little spouts on the Fermoy road, remain from its prosperous days. In 1814 Thomas Davis, founder-member of the Young Irelanders, was born at what is now 72 Thomas Davis Street.

Either side of Mallow, the Blackwater is flecked with the demesnes and houses, some entire, some ruinous, of old settler families: Fairy Hill, Woodfort, ruined Dromaneen, Waterloo and Longueville (now a hotel) to the west; Bearforest, Rook Forest and Ballymacmoy to the east. Six miles north-west, beside Cecilstown, is the curious relic of the Perceval family home, Lohort Castle. Sir Philip Perceval secured over 100,000 acres of north Cork in the early seventeenth century. His descendant, the second Earl of Egmont, restored Lohort's fifteenth century MacCarthy tower-house. (He thought gunpowder would prove a passing phase, put more faith in bows and arrows, and equipped the castle with weapons for a hundred horse. He was also a vigorous advocate of British occupation of the Falkland Islands: 'the key to the whole Pacific Ocean'.) He afforested the demesne in the shape of an octagon, more apparent now from the map than on the ground. His son became Prime Minister and was assassinated in 1812. The Egmont title went astray, to cousins, nephews and so to dormancy, though it was successfully reclaimed by a Canadian Perceval in 1939. The family abandoned Lohort, which was badly burned in 1922, but the tower is still occupied.

Eight miles north-north-east of Mallow, **Doneraile Court**, a handsome house of 1725 in strict Queen Anne style, but later altered, was the home of (besides many other St Legers) Arthur St Leger, first Viscount Doneraile, whose daughter Elizabeth (later Lady Aldworth), having fallen asleep in her chair one afternoon, woke to find herself unwittingly (or according to another version deliberately hid in a large clock in order to be) in earshot of a secret meeting of Freemasons hosted by her father. The members, on discovering her, and in order to protect their secrets, enrolled her: until modern times the first and one of only three women Masons. She is buried in Cork's St Finbar's Cathedral. The son of a later viscount founded in 1776 the famous stakes at Doncaster. Another local legacy came from a running match held in 1752 from Buttevant to Doneraile church. To guide them the runners kept Doneraile's spire in sight – whence the word steeplechase. In 1969, the St Leger title and line having died out, the Irish Georgian Society tried to preserve the contents and open the house to the public, but they were balked by the trustees. All the contents were sold and the Land Commission took over the estate. Decay and vandalism took their toll. But in 1975 the Commission leased the house, with its stately Ionic Grand Gates, ilex trees and heron-haunted fishponds, to the Society, which with its usual flair and energy recruited armies of volunteers to restore the buildings. Provided with large paintings and suitable furniture, it is now open to the public, but the gardens with lake, canal 170 yards long, shady groves, cascades, labyrinth, deer park and picturesque wilderness are long since vanished.

The Court and small village were part of Edmund Spenser's land, granted him after the Desmond Rebellion. He, Raleigh and Sir Philip Sidney all walked here, 'among the cooly shade of the green alders'. Spenser's home was **Kilcolman Castle**, four miles north of Doneraile, delightfully set in cornfields by a reedy lane and marsh on which seagulls breed in spring. The castle is half a mile from the road. All that remains is a stumpy tower overgrown with ivy, but the view is of a spreading lonely plateau in a mountain-ringed basin. Spenser came to Ireland in 1580 as Lord Deputy Grey's secretary. Grey's mission was to suppress the risings in Ulster and Munster, which he tackled so ruthlessly that he was recalled in 1582. Spenser stayed on, but his feelings for the Irish were much as his master's. In 1588 he came to Kilcolman to live on land forfeited by the Earl of Desmond. He returned the hostile feelings of the natives, and one side of his character is starkly revealed in his *View of the Present State of*

Ireland, in which he advocates a policy of elimination akin to Hitler's. (Even the English government refused its publication.) The other facet, the poet's, found fulfilment in a long friendship with Raleigh and a steady output of cantos of *The Faerie Queene*, begun in England, and written mainly at the castle. He also met and married Elizabeth Boyle, and wrote some of his best work for her. In the Munster rising of 1598 unpopular Spenser was besieged at Kilcolman by a ragged mob. He and his family escaped but the castle was burned down. In England at Christmas he addressed the queen: 'Out of the ashes of disolacion and wastnes of this your wretched Realms of Ireland, vouchsafe, most mightie Empresse, our Dred soveraigne, to receive the voices of a few most unhappie Ghostes.' But the queen was deaf to his pleas, and he died destitute in 1599. In Cromwell's time, a grandson, Peregrine Spenser, who had reoccupied the land, was threatened with transplantation to Connacht. Cromwell himself intervened to save him, for the sake, not of *The Faerie Queene*, but the *View of the Present State*.

Two miles west of the castle is **Buttevant**, a town that lies at the northern end of what was the territory of the Barry family, whose earliest title, granted in 1273, was the Viscountcy of Buttevant. It is built along a wide main street, where a famous horse-fair takes place every 12 July. A mile south, beside the river Awbeg, are the ruins of Ballybeg, or the Augustinian Abbey of St Thomas, dating from the thirteenth century, with a belfry tower, cloister walls, and a well-preserved circular dovecote in a field close by. The town itself has a Franciscan friary of 1251, also dedicated to St Thomas, with a rather sinister crypt and sub-crypt below, where bones were in evidence within living memory. They are said to be the Confederate victims of a Parliamentary army led by the renegade Irishman, Murrough O'Brien. Ruined Buttevant Castle was a good example of the Gothic Revival of the early nineteenth century.

Eight miles west-north-west of Buttevant is **Liscarroll**, with one of the three largest Irish medieval castles, built by the Barrys in the thir-teenth century. Its massive, thirty-foot-high curtain walls – recently restored – are flanked by two sturdy drum towers and four square ones, reduced to their present ruinous state in 1642, again by Murrough O'Brien. This whole area figured largely in the fighting of the more recent Civil War of 1922. It also appears in Spenser's work, and several of its more musical names were borrowed by him. From here a series of minor roads lead west-south-west ten miles to **Newmarket**, in the shadow of the desolate Mullaghareirk Mountains to the west. The place is remarkable for little but a link with an often told tale of love. John Philpot Curran (1750–1817) was born and lived here – at The Priory – for several years. He studied law, made a name securing the conviction of the Lord Doneraile mentioned above for horse-whipping a Catholic priest, and rose with Grattan to champion Irish Ireland in the Dublin Parliament. He defended several United Irishmen, and fought the Union – the 'annihilation of Ireland'. But he had a dark side. Unknown to him, his daughter Sarah loved and was loved by Robert Emmet, the callow, ineffectual rebel of 1803. Curran learned of the affair and expelled Sarah from his house. After the rising he refused to defend Emmet in court. The young lover was both hanged and beheaded. The Cork city family which gave Sarah refuge kept the news of his execution from her. She later married an Englishman but died abroad in 1808 – of a broken heart, as Tom Moore had it in his poem.

Kanturk, a few miles south-east, is prettily sited at the meeting of the Allow and Dalua Rivers, both in Spenser's *Faerie Queene*. The surrounding country is rich in castles, many dating from the Munster plantations, that can be glimpsed in any drive round local lanes. Far the most magnificent is the shell of early-seventeenth-century MacDonagh's Court, or **Kanturk Castle**, a mile south of the village. It was no fire or bombardment that reduced it to its present hollow state but the wariness of MacDonagh MacCarthy's neighbours, who, suspicious of the purpose of the magnificent rectangular house, heavily fortified with four corner towers, complained to the government. The government, equally disconcerted, ordered an end to the building in 1615. MacCarthy in fury smashed the glass tiles that were ready for the roof, and left the place as it appears now, with empty mullioned windows, brackets for the machicolation, holes for beams, fireplaces, but no floors, no roof, and no history of habitation.

From here we continue south to the main Mallow-Killarney road, the N72, turn right on to it and along the Blackwater valley, past Dromagh Castle on the right, and turn left after four miles. Seven more miles bring us alongside the demesne of **Drishane Castle**, a large and rambling eighteenth-century house whose every wall was in the early 1800s sprinkled with battlements. It is a convent now. The original fifteenth-century square MacCarthy keep stands on a mound nearby, much restored. **Millstreet**, to the south, is a busy village which draws many to the events held within the largest show-jumping ring outside Dublin. It nestles among mountains, and the southward road we now follow to Macroom runs between the Boggeragh and

Derrynasaggart ranges, rising from fringes of bog and stone-fenced fields. Musheramore, 2,118 feet, the tallest peak in the Boggeraghs, remains in view as we go. Both mountain chains are full of folklore, supernatural explanations of the standing stones and dolmens that are found across their bleak humps. Leprechauns are not tied to specific places in Ireland but are found all over, though they tend to patronise the prettiest of ruined castles. There is as much chance of meeting one here as elsewhere in the country, and the drill for an encounter needs stating. They are very small people and go around singly. By a confusion of their name, which means 'little people', with the Irish word for shoe, 'brog' or brogue (which by association came to be a name for the Irish accent), they were always taken to be obsessive shoe-makers. A leprechaun, if seen at all, is always making shoes for the fairies and taking sips of mountain dew, which is a brand of whiskey. It will be a moonlit evening, and he should be approached without a sound, grasped firmly in the hand, fixedly gazed on, and asked where are the crocks of gold. He will try to talk his way out of the question, using immense cunning. If he cannot escape he will give the information. Leprechaun history goes far back into Irish prehistory. Races, once dominant, then superseded by conquering immigrants, were mentally relegated to a low supernatural status. Leprechauns were in better days the conquering Tuatha de Danaan, and ruled all Ireland.

Macroom is a market town, not long ago the capital of Irish-speaking West Cork, made to look bigger than it is by the ribbon development along its main road. Amid the general ugliness of the place, only the gateway of the ruined castle, with a longer than usual pedigree of ownership, delays us. In the fifteenth century it was a stronghold of the MacCarthys. In 1649 a force preparing to join the Catholic resurgence of Hugh O'Neill was attacked here and beaten by Lord Broghill. Their leader, Bishop MacEgan, one of several prelates who took military command at the time, was captured, and ordered to tell his garrison at nearby Carrigadrohid to surrender. He refused, and was hanged above the river there. Admiral Penn, the Quaker's father, was granted the land in 1654 at Cromwell's settlement, then deprived of it and compensated with that at Shanagarry by Charles II. The castle subsequently passed through the hands of several families and was modernised by the Earl of Bantry in the nineteenth century. To little purpose: it was burned in 1922. Frank O'Connor sat in the grounds, then an IRA base, in the last stages of the civil war, chatting with Erskine Childers, who was soon to cross Ireland in an adventurous bid to escape the Free Staters, be caught in Wicklow and shot by a firing squad. 'You know they will kill you if they catch you, Mr Childers', said someone on this lawn. 'Oh, why does everyone tell me that?' he snapped irritably. An Englishman, veteran of the Boer and Great Wars, he knew, said O'Connor, that 'in a family row it is always the outsider who gets the blame'. The castle's park is now public, with parts given over to sports and recreation.

Drives either side of Macroom show the town is the boundary between the lush, well-farmed east Lee valley and the craggy, mountain-ringed, boggy west. A round tour that shows off some of the best of the latter begins from Macroom, along the Killarney road, turns left at Ballyvourney, zigzags through hard mountain roads south-west to Gouganebarra Lake, source of the Lee, and follows the Lee back to Macroom. This detour begins up the beautiful valley of the Sullane, and passes, three miles from Macroom, fifteenth-century **Carriga-phouca Castle**. This is named from the existence of a *puca* or goblin, a more recent introduction to Irish lore than the leprechaun, and probably coming over with the Danes (from whom the English 'Puck' came too). The castle's foundation is a clear example of a *roche moutonnée* or sheep-back, a rock-mound rounded at the end which faced the glacier's flow. **Ballyvourney**, a few miles farther along this twisting road with its sheep and rock bluffs, is well inside the Muskerry Gaeltacht, or Irish-speaking area. Nearby is the site of a sixth-century nunnery founded by St Gobnat, a still popular saint whose patterns on 11 February and Whit Sunday attract enormous crowds. She was a beekeeper, and is so represented in the statue of 1951 by Seamus Murphy outside the graveyard. The main remains comprise St Gobnat's House and medieval church, St Gobnat's Grave and Well. All these fit into a Round, walked by people who still come throughout the year for cures. Gobnat was adept at healing her nuns and kept the plague from Ballyvourney. Trinkets and little offerings are much in evidence.

A further climb of nearly four miles leads to a good view across to the MacGillicuddy Reeks above Killarney. But we leave Killarney for a later tour, and drive south-west to reach, after some difficult driving, the source of the river Lee and sequestered treasure of West Cork, **Lake Gouganebarra**, in a corrie magnificently set under the sheer heights of the Shehy Mountains. It was on an island of this lake that St Finbar (a well-connected saint who having allegedly crossed the sea to Britain on horseback travelled with St David to Rome), founded an oratory and drowned a monster that St Patrick, in his eviction of reptiles, had overlooked. Finbar went on to work in Cork, but his island remained a sanctuary and the present raised courtyard, save for the 1900 memorial church, inspired – if that is the word – by Cormac's Chapel at Cashel, was built around 1700. The pilgrimage to the site was at its height in the eighteenth century, when Thomas Crofton Croker came and saw, along with the devotion of crowds at prayer in and around the little cells and diseased bathers in the narrow well, a great trade in whiskey and porter, and on the shore the dancing of jigs, an inexorable increase in drunkenness, and brawls breaking out with fists and cudgels. On the mainland lived Teig Buckley and his wife Ansty, whom Eric Cross immortalised in *The Tailor and Ansty*. The holly trees on the island were probably planted for the protective powers of their red berries, which like those of rowan and hawthorn have had a religious significance since prehistoric times. A National Forest Park, opened in 1966, lies to the north of the lake and there are beautiful walks in it, and fine views over Kerry and the western sea from the mountain tops.

The scenic main road east leads back to Macroom, passing long Lough Allua. A still more attractive minor road leads along the south side of the lake. Beside this southern road, less than a mile before it recrosses the Lee, a plaque stands bearing the inscription 'Altar of Penal Times. Mass was said here 1640–1800'. There were thousands of such sites all over Ireland. **Carrignacurra Castle**, a mile east of Inchigeelagh, was an O'Leary property, forfeited by the family, which joined the losing side in the 1641 war. From here the views grow less dramatic, as the road draws near the widening of the Lee above Macroom known as the Gearagh, a swamp of three miles' length, with channels of the river alternating with strips of alder and reedy flats. Below Macroom the river widens again, this time from the giant dams erected for hydro-electric purposes. The road that keeps north of the river, the R618, passes **Carrigadrohid**, where a castle protrudes into the river beside the bridge. It was here in 1650 that Bishop MacEgan, staunchly refusing to order his own side to capitulate to Broghill and the Cromwellians, was hanged after the stronghold was taken. The road continues through the pretty valley, edged with forested hills, closely following the river for the remaining eighteen miles to Cork.

Cork to Kenmare by coast

The south-west of Ireland is warm, warmer than anywhere else in
Ireland, not only in the climatic sense but also like a seat well sat in.
The list of the famous who have been here is inexhaustible. Among
those who have recorded their experiences are Tennyson, Macaulay,
Thackeray, Scott, Fox, Maria Edgeworth, Alfred Austin, Queen
Victoria. More recently Benjamin Britten, Sir Arnold Bax, Françoise
Sagan, Charlie Chaplin, Sir Alec Guinness, Sir Bernard Lovell of
Jodrell Bank, Gore Vidal and many others have owned land here, and
here General de Gaulle came in 1969 at the end of his presidency.
What draws people is the complexity of features that make beautiful
landscape, a climate where subtropical vegetation thrives, an indented
coastline that makes a thousand miles of what, were it straight, would
be a hundred, and in which soft sand alternates with rugged cliff,
dune, and rock; a series of sandstone mountain ranges, some with
rounded surfaces that look as if you could slide down them, others
jagged like Gothic castles built by mad Ludwig of Bavaria, all of
them changing their aspect as the light and clouds alter unceasingly;
several hundred islands of all shapes, sizes, and states of cultivation;
remains from every stage of the least interrupted historical sequence
in Europe; a kind people whose instinct for entertainment is unri-
valled. And all of it – except for a few square miles round Killarney –
is more thinly peopled, either by native or visitor, than any comparable area in Europe.

We approach the far west by the coast road. From Cork we drive
due south to **Kinsale**, a historic harbour town, one of the prettiest in
Ireland, that grew popular as bathing did in the late eighteenth
century and owes much of its charm to that time. Before that, it had
had the varied record, common to a west Munster seaport, of exposure both to trade and attack from French and Spanish. The famous
Battle of Kinsale took place in 1601. Hugh O'Neill, descendant of the
great O'Neill kings, had rebelled in 1595 to defend Ulster and the rest
of Ireland against Elizabeth's systematic encroachments. His great
victory at the Yellow Ford brought over Lord Mountjoy and a
vigorous punishment of the Irish. O'Neill pinned all on the arrival of
Spanish allies, who came eventually, not to the north where he needed
them, but here to the estuary of the Bandon beside Kinsale, where
they secured themselves against Mountjoy's blockade. Forced
marches from the north brought O'Neill's army to the scene. Unable
to link with the Spanish he had to fight the English alone, and was

routed. He escaped, carried on fitful resistance for two years, then submitted. Four years later he and others of the Ulster Irish left Ireland for foreign service in what came to be known as the Flight of the Earls. Thus the effects of the battle were to smash the old Irish order for good, to make Ireland temporarily docile and ready for the uprootings of James I's plantation policy, and to make England – an aim from which all her Irish policy inevitably followed – secure from back-door attacks by Catholic Europe. Nearly fifty years later the town saw another frustrated sea-venture. After Charles I's execution in 1649, loyal Ormonde had Charles II proclaimed here, as in all the Munster coast-towns. Prince Rupert entered the harbour to prepare the way for the young king's arrival, with sixteen black-draped ships. But he was blockaded by Parliamentary ships, while young Charles was unable to make the journey for want of funds. Rupert slipped the line and made Lisbon, and within a year elements in Kinsale negotiated with Cromwell and gave up the town quietly. Still later, in 1690, James II sailed out of Ireland and history from Kinsale. In his wake came John Churchill, Marlborough-to-be, and destroyed the walls. Decline set in. From being the only port where the king's ships could be repaired, it lost trade and naval importance to Cork. Its revival came from peacetime activities and is now in full swing, as weekend crowds, including many yachtsmen, deep-sea anglers and gourmets here for the restaurants, show. It contains some interesting buildings, including the old Dutch-gabled courthouse of 1706, boasting Ireland's oldest Venetian window and now a museum; the newly restored Southwell Gift Houses of 1682; the sixteenth-century tower house of Desmond Castle, used in Napoleonic times for French prisoners of war; and the curious, much restored thirteenth-century Church of St Multose, with a roofless south transept of 1550; as well as quaint Georgian houses with their bow windows, curved walls and some pretty shaped gables – mostly within the main nucleus of labyrinthine streets.

All the coastline is delightful on both sides of the harbour and there is a good drive through Scilly down the east side, through Summer Cove and past **Charles Fort**, a monster built in 1677 by Sir William Robinson, often added to and continually occupied by the British till 1922. It was then burned. But we now continue westward from Kinsale, crossing the Bandon River after two miles and making south for the **Old Head of Kinsale**, a magnificent headland – made rather less magnificent recently by supplanting rough dairy farmland with a smooth golf course, and anarchic growths of native plants with trim, alien, suburban shrubberies. There is a ruined castle at the headland's neck and a Napoleonic Wars watchtower on its summit. The castle belonged to the De Courcy family, Barons Kingsale, premier barons of Ireland who are said to have once had the right to stand with their hats on in the presence of royalty. Ten miles south of the Head, in 1915, the *Lusitania* was torpedoed by the Germans and more than 1,500 were drowned. For weeks, bodies were washed up on the shore (Edith Somerville recorded six at Castletownshend).

Ballinspittle boasts the prehistoric ring-fort of Ballycatteen and a grotto in which the plaster statue of the Virgin Mary was thought by local women to have waved its arms. Pilgrims flocked in coachloads. Many still come. From here, the coast road goes west, passing several lanes leading left to the beaches and flats, the curlews and oyster-catchers, of Courtmacsherry Bay. We cross a creek cutting in from the bay and soon after the road from Bandon joins ours from the right. There is little to draw us to Bandon, unless it be the rather grandiose hilltop pile of Kilbrittain, a mile or so up this road, recently restored from the dereliction it had sunk into since being burned during the 1920s; or the Church of Ireland church in the town itself – the oldest such church built as such (after the Reformation, that is) – or the fishing, or the riverside demesne of **Castle Bernard** west of the town, now a golf course and displaying little of its Ascendancy past. The old house, situated beside an ancient O'Mahony castle, belonged to the Bernard family, earls of Bandon, and there are woeful accounts of the events of the day in June 1921, when the IRA arrived at dawn, kidnapped the aged earl (he was later released), poured petrol over floors and walls and fired a sumptuous collection of furniture and old masters. Fifteen local big houses were burned on the same night, including Inishannon, home of Moreton Frewen, lover of Lily Langtry, Texan cattle-puncher, adventurer, sportsman and uncle by marriage of Winston Churchill, who often stayed.

Back at the coast road, we continue beside the estuary of the river Argideen. **Timoleague** is an ancient, languid village dozing beside the estuary with its low-tide spread of mud-flats. Over the wash the thin tower of a large Franciscan friary of 1312 stands out, with other remains from the time when, in 1642, Lord Forbes and an English army burned it out. **Clonakilty** is six miles west, through lanes thickly hedged with wild flowers and a prospect of hills to north and south. (The promontory of the Seven Heads, like all headlands and promontories along this coast, offers magnificent views to the walker. The less exposed coast is spattered with sandy resorts.) Clonakilty is a pleasant market town, founded by the Earl of Cork (a glance at names on shops shows how lastingly successful the plantations were; English and Scottish names are sometimes as common as Irish). He established spinning and weaving here, and as late as 1839 there were four hundred looms in the area. Emmet Square is handsome, restrained and Georgian.

Three miles west a signpost points to Sam's Cross, and Woodfield, the former a hamlet with a dominant population of Collinses, the latter nearby and the birthplace of Michael Collins (1890–1922). There is a memorial to him by Seamus Murphy at **Sam's Cross**. Collins had a genius for organising guerrilla warfare, and it was largely this that made the British position untenable in 1921. In that year, he and Arthur Griffith were sent to London for the thorny nego-tiations with two masters of the art, Lloyd George and Lord Birkenhead. They returned with less than some of their fellows were prepared to accept. Ranks divided, and the more disgruntled, including de Valera, took to the hills. The Civil War followed. In August, 1922, Collins himself was ambushed and killed at Bealnabla (fourteen miles north of Clonakilty, near the Lee). The war made little difference. Within a few years de Valera himself was proscribing those who continued to champion the cause he had himself fought for.

The road continues, and lanes with attractive sea views to the left, often festooned with crimson fuchsia, which is as common here as hawthorn or hazel in England (it has had since the 1780s to grow to such profusion; at that time an English sailor brought it to England from Chile and his wife sold it to a nurseryman in Hammersmith). Galley Head promontory is privately owned and at present sternly forbidden to the traveller, as are the ruins of Castle Freke, former Gothicised home of the Barons Carbury, and Derry House, both of them by the coast-road leading into Ross Carbery. **Derry House** (burned in 1921), was the home of Charlotte Payne-Townshend, later Mrs Bernard Shaw. Shaw's first visit was in 1905, when he spent the time revising *Captain Brassbound's Conversion*. Charlotte, he wrote, stayed behind, 'doing a round of Bandons and Castletowns and King-stons and other Irish peers and their castles. I fled to England.'

Ross Carbery is a thin village set on a broad inlet among many trees, possessing a small, heavily restored, medieval cathedral, St Fachtna's, with a very fine spire. Several houses have *trompe l'oeil* figures painted on outside walls. A minor road from Ross to Glandore takes us past **Coppinger's Court**, a ruined fortified house of the seventeenth century. Set stark and unlikely among gentle hills, with an unusual ground-plan, tall gables and elaborate machicolations, it was attacked and reduced to more or less its present state in the 1640s. **Glandore** is a lovely, quiet fishing village, refurbished by a progressive landlord, James Redmond Barry, in the 1830s. He and a neighbour, William Thompson, were early socialists, founding cooperatives for industry and fishing, and establishing schools. Thompson earned a footnote in Marx's *Das Kapital*, and some of Barry's planning and building is still evident. Swift stayed a while in 1723 in Rock Cottage, outside Unionhall, a hamlet on the far side of the estuary. Myross, the promontory between here and Castle Haven, was called by Daniel Corkery (whose talk and writings – especially *The Hidden Ireland* – strongly influenced Frank O'Connor) 'one of the most secret places in Ireland, without traffic, almost without pulse of life'. Turning left soon after, we come to **Castletownshend**.

This long village, its main street steeply descending to the water, is where the prolific partnership of Edith Somerville and Martin Ross (pen-name of Edith's cousin Violet Martin, from Galway) brought forth, during the dozen or so years before and after 1900, the *Irish RM*, or Resident Magistrate, books, the still reprinted stories of the West Carbery Hunt – of which Edith was for a time master – and all matters and people attendant on it. Since they failed to show the Irishman always in a serious, patriotic and noble light, they have found more favour in England and further afield than in modern Ireland. The collaboration was a remarkable blending of the wit, acuity and narrative skill of each author, done as they teased out ideas with such sympathy and humour that neither could ever say which one had invented what. *The Real Charlotte* is a deeper and greater work, still set in Ascendancy Ireland but with far larger emotional scope. Edith, born in Corfu and educated in Paris and London, was of an old Castletownshend family. Her ancestor Thomas built the big family house at the top of the Mall, Drishane, in 1790, and with the profits from trade with the West Indies several other extant houses and quayside buildings. It was mostly at Drishane that the books were composed. There too that Edith's brother, Admiral Boyle Somerville, was shot dead at the door in 1936 for – as a note left by the never-traced murderers said – helping unemployed local boys to join the Royal Navy. But it was Richard Townshend, a mostly Cromwellian soldier (his loyalty strayed from time to time) who after years of campaigning in Munster acquired the waterside estate to which his name was attached. The present castle is a charmingly mellowed Victorian, dormer-gabled home, squashed between castellated towers, set back from the shore, still in Townshend hands and serving as a guesthouse. Finely set above it, its tower peering over the trees, is the Church of Ireland church of St Barrahane, where Edith played the organ (she was also an accomplished artist) and in whose churchyard she and Violet are buried. Violet died in 1915, Edith in 1949, at Tally Ho, a house near the top of the Mall. Edith, an ardent spiritualist, kept in touch with Violet after the latter's death in 1915, worried her publishers by insisting her current work was the result of transcendental collaboration and must be attributed to them both, and once claimed Martin had teased her by saying she had fallen (in the hereafter) for Tennyson, who sat her on his knee. Edith also believed that dogs, unlike horses, had an afterlife and could be communicated with. In 1923 Edith, to the vicar's consternation, had an altar erected in gratitude for Violet's ethereal protection during the Troubles. A little before, she recorded a local woman's comment on the end of the Troubles: 'The Black and Tans are gone and the soldiers are gone and now the polis is going and the boys can fight in peace.'

A mile south of the village the lane slopes steeply down to Toberbarrahane, where exiguous church ruins stand in a cemetery used by Townshends, Somervilles and others before the nineteenth century. Beside them, a thirty-foot cube of tangled ivy conceals the ruins of an ancient O'Driscoll castle. Just beyond is **Galleon Point**, off which an engagement between Spanish and English took place in 1601 at the time of Kinsale. The Spanish garrisoned the headland and there is supposed to be a Spanish graveyard here. (Boyle Somerville, also a spiritualist, once had it pointed out to him by 'a Spanish ghost'.) The road continues past a succession of bays and precipitous headlands with pretty beaches, with too many holiday chalets, though not as many as there would be without some legal controls on building near the sea (which are at present in question). Rounding Toe Head we get a view of the westward coast, rock islands, and – recognisable from its lighthouse tower – Fastnet Rock.

Lough Hyne (the 'h' is not pronounced), south-south-west of Skibbereen, is a charming rarity: an inland salt-water lake with a long narrow inlet from the sea which slows the tide so much that it takes three hours to rise and nine in its imperceptible fall. Streams from the pretty wooded slopes around reduce the salinity of the water. All these unusual conditions make for a rich supply of plankton and a high tally of rare plants and fish, the subject of continuing research. Recently married in 1919, young Julian Huxley came here to study the bristle-worm *Sabella*, only seen at extra-low water. Three miles to the west, **Baltimore** is an attractive fishing village built round its harbour, with a ruined sixteenth-century O'Driscoll castle above. It was here that Algerian privateers burst into Irish history in 1631 to massacre some inhabitants and take others as slaves to Africa. Spanish Island, opposite the harbour, recalls again the Spanish expedition of 1601 that ended in the rout of Kinsale. South-west of it lies Sherkin Island, whose ruined Franciscan friary of 1460 can be seen from the mainland. Sherkin offers good beaches and walks, but **Clear Island** has better. Both islands are reached by boat from Baltimore, Clear Island from Skull as well. In 1958 a small amateur group set up the Cape Clear Bird Observatory. In season there is never any difficulty on any island in seeing the best-known sea-species – the various gulls, kittiwakes, guillemots, puffins, razorbills, skuas, cormorants and others. But the setting up of new observatories in Britain and Ireland showed the local existence of far more sea and land birds than had been suspected. Some are strays and casuals, some have always lived on the sea, out of sight until regular manning of telescopes began. Cape Clear was a pioneer in sea-bird watching, and has become known for its sooty, Cary's, and great shearwaters (of which 5,000 were once seen in a single day) – considered rare off these coasts till the regular watch began. Actual rarities seen here include the black-browed albatross, little shearwater and Wilson's petrel.

These and the other islands, and farther out lighthouse-bearing Fastnet Rock, of weather-forecast fame, are the unsubmerged heights of what was once a long old red sandstone peninsula. From here on our route is a succession of five such exposed strips which together comprise Ireland's most dramatic scenery. To reach the first, we must drive north-east along the R595 to Skibbereen, keeping close to the estuary of the river Ilen. On the way we pass **Creagh**, a conspicuous Regency house whose very fine gardens, stretching to the water's edge, with many rarities and wonderful views with the sea or mountains for background, are open to the public. **Skibbereen** is a busy market town, famous for a warning in its former local paper towards the end of the nineteenth century, following some Russian sabre-rattling, that the *Skibbereen Eagle* would from now be keeping a close eye on the Tsar. We cross the Ilen River bridge and head west along the N71. Views improve wherever the road draws near the sea, especially when it overlooks Roaring Water Bay with its hosts of islands and solitary Fastnet in the distance. A couple of miles off to the left and cut off from land by high tides is Kilcoe Castle, an elaborate old MacCarthy fortress beside a ruined church, which withstood the English for two years after Kinsale. It is a private home now. Inland is wild scrub, sometimes dramatically wild, rising on the right to the shapely peak of Mount Gabriel, from the top of which is seen the best view of the peninsula. The two shining spheres on the mountain top are integral to an international system for tracking aircraft. Skull (meaning school; monks from Ross Carbery founded one here in the tenth century) is a small town with the brightly painted façades of most of the local towns, and a Church of Ireland church with medieval fragments. J.M. Synge's grandfather was rector here, a man who, in his own words, dedicated his life 'to waging war against Popery in its thousand forms of wickedness'. His church is long since disused. This was until independence traditionally loyalist country, with a dominant Protestant population. Today's incomers – from England, France, Germany, rich, famous, grateful for a peaceful pace – are less obtrusive. There are plenty of them.

The road west passes by Toormore Bay, with its castle, capes, coves and beaches set round an aquamarine sea. At its western end is the opening to the two miles of Crook Haven, said to be the safest harbour in these islands. Mizen Head, with its clearly marked layers of sandstone rock piled into angular cliffs that jut into the Atlantic, its sequestered signal station, redundant now and converted into a visitor centre, and tall rock-stacks covered in a fidgetty coating of guillemots, is one of three lofty headlands that terminate the peninsula. Three Castle Head, named after three ancient Mahony fortresses, rises to the north; Brow Head to the south, across the broad, sand-fringed blue of Barley Cove. Of the varied (and seasonal) bird populations, gannets are commonly seen, plunging like missiles, folding their black-tipped wings just before entering the water. Choughs get rarer by the year. There are innumerable ducks, waders and gulls in the area.

The road back along the north side is of different character, a ruggeder scene of small stone-bordered fields, with harvests carefully tended in patches that anywhere else might be ignored. Poverty has gone now, but until well after the Second World War it had been familiar here for a century and a half. Unexplained slumps in fish populations, loss of foreign markets due to war or new competition, infertility of local land and of course famine were chief causes. Emigration alleviated a problem made more acute by the fissive system of inheritance and primitive farming methods, which still included ploughing with the plough attached to a horse's tail, plucking sheep instead of shearing, and burning corn to divide straw from grain, so destroying useful winter fodder and bedding for cattle. You would have seen some of these things not much more than a generation ago.

'Were such a bay lying upon English shore, it would be the world's wonder,' Thackeray wrote about Bantry Bay. The beauty remains, and even the huge tanks on Whiddy Island, opposite the town, there for storage of oil off-loaded by huge tankers, are discreetly buried, with little more than their dome-tops visible. **Bantry**'s market square is huge, and very bleak when empty, but the town serves well as a market and amenity base for the magical area it is set amid. In the past, not all visitors were tourists. In 1689 a French fleet sailed in to help James II's supporters, but turned back after an indecisive battle. In 1796 the French came again, this time with Wolfe Tone on board the *Indomptable*. For years Tone had been in Paris planning Ireland's break from England and lobbying for support. Out of forty-three ships that left Brest only sixteen got through the channel storms – Tone's diary on board records every variant of wind in hope, gloom and insouciance – 'Je m'en fiche, if ever they hang me, they are welcome to embowel me if they please'. Wind and fog kept them six days in the bay, unable to land. In the end they had to turn back, and it was two years before the next attempt.

There is a permanent exhibition about the aborted Tone invasion in the courtyard of **Bantry House**, a good eighteenth-century house set in a commanding position at the town's west end. The nucleus of the house dates to before 1740, but it was given much of its present shape, appearance, decoration and most of its important contents, by Richard White, second Earl of Bantry, around 1845. His father had been given the title for organising the defences against Tone and the French. The second earl travelled in Europe to amass a collection of paintings, Gobelin tapestries, Russian icons, furniture, Savonnerie and Aubusson carpets, tiling, fireplaces and trinkets (some from Versailles), which are on view to the public or contained in that part of the house functioning as a very special hotel. The owner, Egerton Shelswell-White, is a direct descendant of the earls, and he maintains an endearing character of quirky amateurishness about the place. The garden, laid out in the Italian style with terraces, seasoned stone steps and statuary, gives beautiful views over the bay to the Beara peninsula. The house is open to the public – was, in fact, the first in Ireland to be opened at regular times.

After a beautiful drive of some ten miles round the head of the bay (halfway along a right turn leads to Gouganebarra, described elsewhere) we come to **Glengarriff**. The village, with its mellow climate, dense vegetation, fine walks and abundance of comfortable hotels within and around, is something of a rest-cure fantasy, marred by the customary excess of bungalows and chalets. It is the climate, frost-free, that makes for the abundance of flowers, some found nowhere else in these islands. But **Ilnacullin Island**, also known as Garinish, is more of a miracle than that. When John Annan Bryce, a Belfast-born MP, took it over it was almost solid rock. Every spadeful of earth was brought by boat before the gardens could be shaped, in 1910, to the designs of Harold Peto (1854–1933), whose architect's training led him always to use the stone of statuary and masonry in what he thought a just proportion with the plants. State-owned now, it is is one of the most beautiful gardens in the area, with exotic shrubberies, rock gardens, Japanese gardens, prominent Italian porch, Italian gardens round a lily pond, and some beautiful vistas of the bay and Caha mountains. It was on this island that Shaw, as Bryce's guest, wrote much of his *St Joan* in 1923.

From here on one soon grows accustomed to luxuriant growth: fuchsia up to twenty-five feet, escallonia with its pink trumpets against thick shiny green foliage, tree-ferns, eucalyptus with its shimmering banana leaves, mountain ash, oak, holly, yew, Chilean myrtle, *Clethra arborea*, and the famous strawberry tree, *Arbutus unedo*, which grows mainly at Glengarriff and Killarney. The last, otherwise found wild in Europe mainly among the mountains of Spain and on the west coast of France, is made distinct by its flowers (cream, like lily of the valley, and appearing September to October), its leathery glossy leaves, and its prickly scarlet berries, last year's fruit appearing at the same time as this year's flowers. Its specific name, *unedo*, is Latin for 'I eat one'; no more – only its looks are like the strawberry. Less obvious than these plants, but also more or less confined to these parts of Cork and Kerry, are the two rock-loving saxifrages, the delicate pink and ineptly named London Pride, and Kidney-leaved Saxifrage (*Saxifraga hirsuta*); Irish Spurge with little yellow flowers in early summer and long leaves up to three inches; pale pink Irish Heath, common on moorland in spring; Greater Butterwort with yellow-green leaves and deep blue flowers, enormous compared to their slender stems, on bogs in May – 'the most beautiful member of the Irish flora' wrote Dr Scully, who earlier this century compiled a *Flora of County Kerry* (the Butter-wort is notable also for its feeding on small insects which are trapped on the sticky leaves, digested by a discharge of a kind of gastric juice, and absorbed into the system); July-flowering Blue-eyed Grass with delicate star-shaped flowers at the tips of grassy stems – a botanical problem is that it is found elsewhere mainly in Western America; and the rare fern found at Killarney, *Trichomanes radians*. For most of the flowers, late spring is the best time to arrive. The late-autumn-blooming strawberry tree is an exception.

The **Beara** peninsula is as beautiful as the Dingle, far to the north, but it is perhaps the least known of the western peninsulas. It is ruggeder and till now lonelier than the others. Its fate is being argued. One faction, led and supported by conservationists, tourists, and many German, Dutch and English settlers, is for keeping things much as they are. The other, including a number of influential locals, wants the god Development: roads, houses, hotels and industry to match Ireland's economic surge of the 1980s and 1990s. Having fouled up your own countries, these Irish seem to be saying, you want to stop us fouling up ours, and that is for us to decide. Unfortunately a great deal of fouling has happened already and it would be nice to see it stop.

The drive round Beara takes us from Glengarriff along the south coast, between the island-streaked bay and the Sugarloaf and Caha Mountains and other curiously geometrical formations of old red sandstone, resulting from tectonic clash and upheaval some 300 million years ago, beside bog and well-walled oases of grass reserved for some farmstead's few cows. At Adrigole a road branches right to cross the mountains steeply and with frequent hairpin bends at **Healy Pass**, above which stands a huge figure of Christ. The road was begun as relief work in Famine times – fourpence for a twelve-hour day; but a high death-rate and slow progress brought it to a halt. It was begun again in 1928, at the instance of Bantry-born Tim Healy (1855–1931), the most vituperative of those who voted against Parnell, and from 1922–28 first governor-general of the Free State, and opened in 1931. It makes a memorable scenic route passing on the northern descent the dark, islanded, sheer-sided lake of Glanmore. But we continue west from Adrigole, past Hungry Hill (2,251 feet), highest hill of the Caha range and source of the title of Daphne du Maurier's novel, six-mile-long Bear Island and the haven that it forms – till 1937 an anchorage of the British Atlantic fleet. **Castletown Bearhaven** is a long, straggling town and a port much used by fishing trawlers whose catches are processed here. Two miles south-west, through a picture-book Gothic gate-lodge, past the burned-out (in 1921) shell of the 1838 home of the Puxleys, is the dramatic ruin, well set beside the straits of Bear Haven, of old **Dunboy Castle**, once seat of the O'Sullivans, the most numerous of the local families. It was here in 1602 that Sir George Carew with an English force, after a siege, took and butchered the last Spanish-Irish garrison to hold out after the Battle of Kinsale. Within a year Owen Roe O'Neill had capitulated, and the rising was over. By the mid-eighteenth century the Puxley family had succeeded the O'Sullivans (who remained, and still do, in large numbers) in ownership of much of the peninsula. The two families feuded and occasionally murdered one another. The stirring story is told in the novel *The Two Chiefs of Dunboy* by the historian of eighteenth-century Ireland J.A. Froude, who wrote it while staying in Lord Lansdowne's house, Derreen, in the 1860s. We shall reach the house shortly. Rather later than this Henry Puxley, by now vastly rich owner of the local copper mines, built the huge house whose shell remains, with its steep roofs, gangling chimneys, Gothic arches and oriel windows. Using pseudonyms, Daphne du Maurier told a dramatic story of the family and mines in her novel *Hungry Hill*, though the actual mines were at Allihies, to which we come after driving through lovely scenery and past the excellent beach of Bally-donegan near the peninsula's end.

The copper workings are still in evidence at **Allihies**, and were recently worked again for a short time. The workers were imported from Cornwall, and there are still remains of the village they built. We drive along a zigzag coast road with splendid sheer drops of rock beside it. The Ring of Kerry makes the north view, with foam-splashed islands and outcrops on the Kenmare River estuary in between, and often (in a climate where in parts an eighty-inch annual rainfall is not uncommon) the addition of a complete rainbow. At **Eyeries** there is a pillar seventeen feet high with ogham inscriptions. Though this is the tallest in the country, over three hundred more exist, many of them, like this, staying *in situ*. They serve in general as gravestones, and signs usually record the buried person's name. The script is formed of twenty letters, representing the vowels of the Latin alphabet by notches, and consonants by strokes (slanting or straight). The edge of the stone is used as a line, and the strokes and dots go along it, up and down. Transliterated, the words are usually found to be Irish. Though they used to be considered proof of a literate society stretching far back into prehistory they are now thought to have been invented in the fourth century in this part of Ireland, from which they spread in a small way to other parts of the country, Wales and Cornwall.

Halfway back we cross, without noticeable difference between one side and the other, the Cork-Kerry border and five miles later reach the demesne of **Derreen House**, the gardens of which open to the public from April to September. The demesne belongs to descendants, through the Marquesses of Lansdowne, of Sir William Petty, described in the next chapter. It is well worth visiting for the substantial collection of trees, rhododendrons (*Sinogrande* and other big-leaved varieties), myrtles, conifers, arbutus, and prolific New Zealand tree ferns, as well as exceptional species like *Embothrium longifolium* and the largest *Cryptomeria elegans* in these islands. The setting, beside Kilmakillogue Harbour and under the conical thousand-foot peak of Knockatee, is unsurpassed anywhere. The house itself was rebuilt after destruction during the Troubles. Its predecessor was rented in 1867 and 1868 by the historian J.A. Froude, and it was here that he wrote most of his *The English in Ireland*, in which he was at pains to show Celts and 'Papists' in sub-Anglo-Saxon colours.

A few miles farther, a lane leads right from the village of Cloonee. The walk up this, past the three Cloonee Loughs – extensions of the river of the same name and in the shadow of Caha Mountain – is one of innumerable superb stretches in these hills, which are much loved by climbers. Beyond the lane, our road takes us the remaining eight miles to Kenmare, along one of the most striking stretches of the whole journey.

10

Kerry, Limerick Coast Road

'THERE THE SHE-WOLF littered, and some half-naked savages, who could not speak a word of English, made themselves burrows in the mud and lived on roots and sour milk ... scarcely any village, built by an enterprising band of New Englanders far from the dwellings of their countrymen in the midst of the hunting-grounds of the Red Indians, was more completely out of the pale of civilization than Kenmare.' This is Macaulay, describing – and fiercely exaggerating – what had to be overcome by the inventor, anatomist, economist, surveyor and man of several other parts, Sir William Petty (1623–87), to make profitable sense of the country hereabouts. It had been granted to him by Henry Cromwell as reward for his *Down Survey* of Ireland, the first scientific map of the country, made to facilitate and regulate the massive forfeitures and regrants of land as a result of the Cromwellian conquest. (Sadly, it was destroyed in a Dublin Castle fire in 1711, and only copies and a few county records survive.) In his new estate, he turned his energy to the setting up of iron-works, lead-mines, sea-fisheries and other industries, and in 1670 to the founding of **Kenmare**, then called Nedeen or Neidin, itself. He also proposed to solve 'the Irish problem': ensure that the soldiers awarded land in the west of Ireland should find there good Protestant English girls to marry – and so father good Protestant children, thus ending the constant reversion to papism which had dogged previous settlements. The design was to be achieved by exporting 20,000 doughty maidens culled from the streets of Manchester and elsewhere. Though this never took off, and few of his local enterprises survived his death, his great-grandson, the second Earl of Shelburne, short-lived British prime minister (in 1782) and first Marquess of Lansdowne, took what was for the time considerable trouble with his estate, by now approaching 150,000 acres. For him, agriculture was the key to Irish recovery, and he set up an Agricultural Society to spur on his own and others' tenants. The reward of industry was a moral medal, showing on one side barefoot children leaving a smoky, crumbling cabin, and on the other a prospering farm with well-stacked sheaves of corn. He also had his agent build roads and bridges, plant trees, drain bogs, promote fishing, and develop the town then renamed Kenmare. A quay, a market-house, courthouse, bridewell, spinning factory and inn were built, and the town prospered. Some houses from the time still stand, but none of the major buildings. Nowadays Kenmare is a busy, handsome town expending most of its energies on the tourist industry, for only ten miles north is that fantastic assemblage of lake, mountain, wildness and tamed demesne that has assumed the name of the small town to its east, Killarney.

Killarney is best approached from Kenmare. The road climbs steeply till the formidable silhouette of MacGillycuddy's Reeks comes into view on the left, with the Gap of Dunloe towards the east. Four miles beyond the sharp right turn the road makes, there is a parking place on the left. This is known as **Ladies' View**, and it introduces the two salient points about Killarney. The first is that the region is one of the most beautiful parts of Ireland, as everybody says (though it does have rivals). The second is that more tourist amenities are provided than anywhere else in the country, for the simple reason that Killarney draws more tourists than anywhere else. In the season it seethes with people, and with hotels and bars and sweetly smiling guides and souvenir shops. Many visitors, having once seen the sights, swear never to return, and some keep well away in the first place. Some of the best sights necessitate walks, and the longer the walk, of course, the thinner the crowd. The rest must be seen with the world and his mistress – and one area with an affable cicerone whose automatic chanting of made-up legend detracts from beauties best seen in silence. These resident experts suffer not at all from the reticence of Arthur Young, writing in 1776 – 'there have been so many descriptions of Killarney written by gentlemen who have resided some time there, that for a passing traveller to attempt the like would be in vain.' He, however, got the better of his fine feelings and went on to write fourteen pages of mauve-to-purple prose.

Killarney town is very commercial, very spoilt and of little interest save for 1842–55 St Mary's Roman Catholic cathedral, the best among sixty or so churches designed by Pugin in Ireland, constructed between 1842 and 1855 – a period prolonged by the diversion of funds in the late 1840s to famine relief. In part inspired by the derelict cathedral of Ardfert to the north, it was Pugin's most

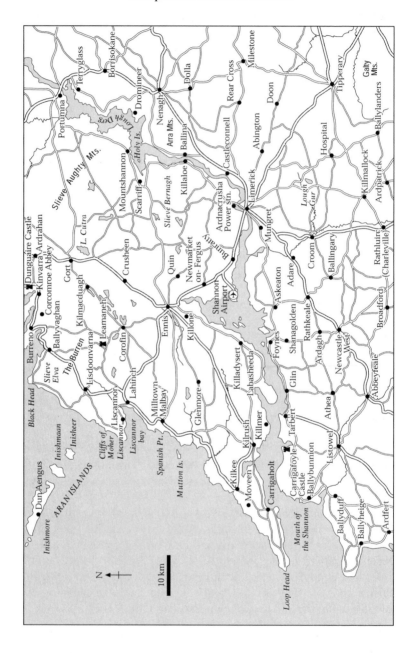

cherished undertaking, but he was dead of overwork before it was completed. The slender simplicity of the interior is his finest memorial. His disciple and successor J.J. McCarthy took over. The spire was added around 1910.

What is normally understood by the word Killarney is the series of three lakes lying a mile to the south-west of the town and the mountainsides to west and south of them. The arrangement is easily seen from Ladies View. The mountains to the left, or north, are MacGillycuddy's Reeks with Ireland's highest peak, Carrauntoohill (3,314 feet), in their midst; their eastern section, topped by Purple Mountain (2,739 feet), is cut off from the western by a glacial overflow channel, the Gap of Dunloe. Of the three lakes the Upper Lake, two and a half miles long, is immediately below Ladies View. A broad two-and-a-half-mile river known as the Long Range connects Upper Lake with Muckross Lake to the north-east, smallest of the three and only a few feet lower than the Upper Lake. Muckross Lake is on the same level as Lough Leane or Lower Lake, biggest of the three, from which a narrow peninsula, with part of the Muckross demesne on it, separates it. **Lough Leane** contains over thirty islands, including Inisfallen with its old abbey and the peninsular Ross Island. On the right of the road we shall shortly descend rise Torc Mountain and the Mangerton range, with Lough Guitane beyond. The main historic spots are along the eastern bank of the lough: Kenmare demesne, Flesk Priory, Ross Castle (and offshore the Abbey of Inisfallen), the ruins of Muckross Abbey and the present house and demesne of Muckross. The main botanical interest is beside the Upper Lake, but there are fine tree collections on the Muckross estate and Governor's Rock, near Ross Castle; and tree ferns, thorn-apples, bamboos and succulent mesembryanthemums are seen in many gardens. Geological interest is everywhere, the whole lake complex having been scooped out by glacial action from limestone remnants lying within the valleys of the old red sandstone mountains. The dramatic scenery of course spreads over the whole area – and to west and south many miles beyond. Away from the main circuit of the Gap of Dunloe and the lakes, it becomes proportionally less crowded and some of the finest walks are to be had around and on the north side of Mangerton, between the splendid sixty-foot tumble of Torc Cascade and Lough Guitane, or on the slopes flanking Cummenduff Glen, south-west of the southern approach to the Gap of Dunloe.

Short of walking, the best policy for central sightseeing might be to fall in with the wishes of official Killarney and travel by jaunting car and boat. The round trip can take most of a day, and prices should always be agreed beforehand. Cars are not allowed between the main road and lakeside, and though they are technically allowed through the Gap of Dunloe there is emphatic opposition by the jaunting car 'jarveys' to any attempt at passage before the evening. Starting from Killarney the best way is westward by the R562, north of Lough Leane, through Aghadoe (from which there is a marvellous view of the whole region), and then left to Dunloe Castle. Near the castle is one of the finest collections of ogham stones. The road goes south from here to Kate Kearney's Cottage (not the original), she having been one of the 'mountain dew women tribe', or sellers of poteen, who used to solicit tourist trade. From here, unless you are in a jaunting car already, safely lethargic horses or traps may be hired for the trip through the Gap, with its three lakes and steepening craggy sides to the climactic view at the head. If a boat has not been arranged, return from here can be made back through the Gap. If it has, the way lies on down the southern slope past the entrance to the Black Valley (which leads up to the heart of the Reeks), and round to the head of **Upper Lake**.

The water journey goes close to pretty islands with exotic plants, through the Long Range fringed with arbutus and royal fern and a profusion of rare mosses and liverworts, passing the pointed Eagle's Nest on the left. Last century cannons or bugles sounded here to produce a roaring echo. Tennyson heard it in 1848 and the same evening wrote one of his best poems – '... The long light shakes across the lakes, And the wild cataract leaps in glory. Blow, bugle, blow, set the wild echoes flying ...', and Benjamin Britten, who owned a cottage not far away, composed his *Serenade for Tenor, Horn and Strings* to the words. Tennyson's cataract may have been the Torc Cascade, which falls above **Muckross Lake**, entered here beside lush Dinish Island, with its bamboo, eucalyptus, magnolia and other subtropical plants. There are red deer in the woods around the lakes and in the eighteenth century one attraction of Killarney to the gentry was hunting them down from the hills and into the water, where the chase continued by boat.

The real Colleen Bawn, a girl called Ellen Hanley, murdered in 1819 by her husband on the River Shannon, had nothing to do with so-called Colleen Bawn Rock on Muckross Lake, except through a delicate transplantation in Gerald Griffin's novel, *The Collegians*. The boat goes on into Lough Leane and crosses two miles of open water to Ross Castle. The sights on the east shore of the lake are to be seen on foot – by far the best of them the lovely remains of Muckross Franciscan Friary, late fifteenth century, ruined by Cromwellians, with a magnificent yew in the cloister. Muckross House is a Victorian mansion (1843) in Tudor style, now made into a museum, with lovely grounds which, together with ten thousand acres around, was presented to the nation to be Ireland's first National Park by the previous American owners. An earlier house on the site was the scene in 1794 of the death of Rudolf Erich Raspe, narrator of the comically exaggerated, still read memoirs of Baron Munchausen. Raspe himself was a good scholar and a better charlatan and swindler, often on the run. He came here, pretending to be a mining expert, to escape some fearful come-uppance in Scotland, but died of scarlet fever and was buried in a pauper's grave. Fifteenth-century **Ross Castle** was the last place in Munster to be taken by the army Cromwell left behind, in 1652, placed with a good view across the lake. Some of the lakeside walks go through to Kenmare demesne, site now of luxury hotels, previously the home of the Browne family, Earls of Kenmare. It was Sir Valentine Browne who in Elizabeth's reign bought this and surrounding land stretching into county Cork. The house of his descendant the fourth Earl of Kenmare, a redbrick monster of opulence, built in 1872 on a site supposedly chosen by Queen Victoria (for whose visit a royal barge was sailed from London) and in place of an eighteenth-century house a little to the south-east, was gutted in 1913. A replacement to this, known now as Killarney House, was made from the old stable block, and was home of Viscount Castlerosse, later sixth Earl, and doyen of gossip columnists when he worked for Lord Beaverbrook on the *Daily Express* and *Evening Standard*. It was he who designed the picturesque golf-course with the help of golfer and writer Henry Longhurst.

Killarney can be marred by weather. Mangerton in 1903 took 141 inches of rain. Though Killarney town itself and much of the lake area averages between forty to sixty, a point just to the north got an average of eighty-seven inches for each of seventeen years. Back in the 1780s Charles James Fox arrived in heavy rain. His host Lord Kenmare reassured him: it was only a shower. It continued raining, Fox vexed, the earl sanguine. After five days Fox had to leave, without seeing the views. Three years later they met in London. 'Ah, my lord,' said the Fox, 'and tell me, is the *shower* yet over?' Queen Victoria, on the other hand, was put out by the heat. In spite of the scenery reminding her 'of *Scotland*, it was *so* fine' she makes constant mention of 'the great heat', 'it was overpoweringly hot' and at Killarney House (where they celebrated Albert's last birthday, she much worried over his health) though 'all the windows were open, there was not a breath of air, and the heat was intense'. (She also found 'that peculiar shriek' of the Irish a drawback.)

For the day or days spent in Killarney we will have done well to have stayed nights at or near Kenmare, or on the other side of the Iveragh Peninsula near Killorglin or Glenbeigh. Another tour from Kenmare is the coastal **Ring of Kerry**, which we can follow clockwise by driving west from the town. This way takes us past houses of Riviera design, and a few castles, some of each kind converted into hotels. Beside the sea at **Parknasilla**, thirteen miles from Kenmare, stands the Great Southern, a luxury hotel in what used to be the demesne and home – his actual residence is a staff house now, marked with a plaque – of Limerick's one-time Church of Ireland bishop, Dr Charles Graves, grandfather of the poet Robert. Parkland, gardens, cultivated surrounds, islanded bay and backdrop of mountains to north and south make this an elysian setting. Shaw wrote parts of *St Joan* in a private sitting-room in the hotel.

Sneem is a pretty village with houses in colours that make them look like toys, an interesting garden of sculpture and an Italianate church of 1865. A boat can be hired to make the trip to Garinish Island, at the mouth of the creek, where many rarities from the southern hemisphere were planted by Lord Dunraven around the turn of the nineteenth century; but the island is private and permission has to be sought first. (It is not to be confused with Ilnacullen, also known as Garinish, off Glengarriff in county Cork.) Beyond, the road goes inland through a bleak slatey plateau, and returns to the sea and a series of delightful bays and coves. A signposted side road leads three miles to **Staigue Fort**, the most perfectly preserved, though not the biggest, of its kind in the country, set in a commanding amphitheatre among the hills. The skill of the workers who built this vast free-stone fortress with its inward-sloping, eighteen-foot high, thirteen-foot thick walls, points to the Early Christian period for its construction. Some recent theories put it as much as a thousand years earlier, and till more excavations are done the truth will not be known. A fibula found in the walls of Dun Aengus, a similar fortress on the Aran Islands, gave a carbon-14 reading of about 100 BC though work at Leacanbuaile supports the first argument. If true, it could have been built under the threat of Norse invasions, which ravaged the coastline from around 800. In a field on the left, close to the turning to Staigue Fort, stands a line of derelict and wholly unappealing buildings whose demolition, desired by many locals, cannot at present be effected because ownership is uncertain. They were put up in 1913 or 1914 by the Hon. Albinia Brodrick, who – daughter of viscount Midleton and sister of a senior British cabinet minister – appalled her family, friends and class by settling here and espousing the cause of the IRA The buildings were to be an IRA hospital. When she died in 1955 she left her estate, including the buildings, to 'Republicans', far too vaguely defined for the beneficiaries to be identified. Lawyers have not yet sorted the matter out.

Derrynane, farther on, is one of the country's best beaches, close to the island (at low tide linked to the mainland) on which St Finan Cam is said to have founded a monastery, a few remains of which still stand. But the presiding spirit of the demesne and house is Daniel O'Connell (1775–1847), whose ancestral home it was. He inherited it from a bachelor uncle and made additions, which date from 1825 to 1844, including the chapel. Now owned by the Commissioners of Public Works, the house has been restored and opened as a memorial to 'the Liberator'. O'Connell was a prophet in his own land of Munster, where he was on the court circuit for twenty years, enjoying the dual role of crusader and histrionic performer – 'the great comedian of the Irish race' said Yeats, contrasting him with Parnell, the 'great tragedian'. But the greatest battles of the man who brought Ireland from Penal days – when in theory at least a Catholic could not own land, or vote, or educate his children at home or abroad, or carry a sword as gentlemen did, or own a horse worth over £10, or take part in his country's lawmaking – to Emancipation, were fought far from here, many at Westminster, of which he said, 'I can drive a coach and horses through any act of Parliament.' In fact O'Connell was a landlord here, and behaved like one: hunting, shooting and amassing debts however great his lawyer's earnings. The house is open to the public.

Beyond Caherdaniel the road rises over the Pass of Coomakista, revealing for the first time a view of the **Skellig Islands**, then drops to the little resort of Waterville, standing between the sea and three-mile-long Lough Currane, which makes it popular with anglers. The whole peninsula, like Dingle to the north, is littered with ogham stones, oratories and neolithic graves; and on Church Island in the lake are the sparse ruins of another of St Finan Cam's sixth-century foundations. The saint was credited with introducing wheat into the country, as St Declan of Ardmore was with rye. Curiously, recent research suggests that the building on the end of the island supposed

271

to have been Finan's cell is a kiln for drying grain and of much later date. A grand inland road turns right off the coast road beyond Waterville, rising along the River Inny with the looming prospect of the MacGillicuddy's Reeks ahead. But we stay near the sea, and turn left a mile later, descending on Irish-speaking **Ballinskelligs**, a sweet village with a good beach and that familiar occurrence, the burned-out big house. Rounding the north end of the bay the road climbs to a pass near which one of the finest views in Ireland can be obtained. In one sweep it takes in the western half of Dingle Peninsula with each of the Blaskets looking far less then eighteen miles away; the flat field-patchwork of **Valentia Island**, with bosomy swellings at each end; Portmagee and its new bridge; around to the west the almost Gothic architecture of the Skelligs – tiny sharp peaks building up to the great central one in a foamy base; the tip of Puffin Island near at hand; and far to the south the curved back of Beara Peninsula.

From the eastern harbour on Valentia Island (reached now by the Portmagee Bridge) as well as Ballinskelligs and Waterville, boats can be hired to go to the **Skelligs**. It is a trip that cannot be counted on till the day since everything depends on the weather being calm. If this were oftener, the Skelligs would be almost as much a place of pilgrimage as Cashel or the Giant's Causeway, but the Atlantic swell, rising and falling up to twenty feet at the little harbour, makes it otherwise. As it is, weeks and sometimes months can pass without a decent chance of access – which is why so many of these south-west coastal islands have had their populations removed in the twentieth century. Little Skellig is often called, wrongly, the most southerly breeding haunt of gannets in these islands (there is a small colony on Bull Rock at the tip of Beara Peninsula), but its population of about 18,000 of the birds makes it the second biggest in the northern hemisphere, St Kilda in the Hebrides having more than twice as many. Besides these goose-sized birds, with their six-foot wing-spans and hundred-foot headlong plunges into the sea for fish, there are predictable quantities of other sea birds – guillemots, kittiwakes, razorbills, puffins, and so on, on this and the other islands. No landing is allowed on the little Skellig, but excursion boats take you close and slowly by, to see, hear and smell the noisy, crowded, reeking, tight-packed home life of these balletic aeronauts, where the main hazards during a young bird's early stumbles to and from the water come from the aggressive pecks of the adults it has to pass on the way. Skellig Michael, patronised by the Archangel as rocky heights often are, is the site of the best preserved early Irish monastery, founded in the seventh or eighth century by most determined ascetics. The bare rock rises to a peak seven hundred feet above the water, with a further, sheer, ninety-fathom drop underwater; and mist often blots out the mainland altogether. The lighthouse, now automatically operated, is a hundred and thirty feet up. While they were here, in the nineteenth and twentieth centuries, the keepers and their families had to be as self-sufficient as the monks had been. They did of course add potatoes to the daily fare. Higher up comes Christ's Saddle, where the rock forks into two peaks. The main monastic ruins are on the southwest branch, at about five hundred and fifty feet above sea-level. They comprise six beehive huts or clochans (circular corbelled drywalled living-quarters, each probably shared by two monks and all but one extraordinarily well preserved), two circular oratories, some worn primitive High Crosses, and a ruinous church dedicated to St Michael. A wall bounds the monastery and its graveyards from a precipitous drop to the sea. Though earth had to be brought from the mainland, and little but grass and sea-pink seem content with the setting, the monks may have had a happier time than the confinement suggests. Birds could be caught and eaten, and the sea is rich in fish. Herbs were grown and the monastery faced the sun while being well sheltered from winds. A harder time was had by pilgrims and penitents of later years, who not only had to risk the wrath of laws which tried to suppress pilgrimages, but also mounted by cruder steps (which survive) than the present Lighthouse Road. Then, having as part of their tour of the stations of the cross seen the old buildings, they were required to return to the 'saddle', climb the other, higher, north-eastern peak, squeeze through 'the Needle's Eye' to ascend the 'stone of Pain', a smooth sloping rock; finally sitting astride a spindle of rock two foot wide and ten foot long projecting into space and seven hundred feet above the ocean, and work their way to the outer end, kiss an engraved cross and recite the Lord's prayer. And then of course come back. Backwards.

Valentia Island's chief claim to fame is as the eastern terminal of the first transatlantic telegraph cable. Several attempts were made from 1857 onwards, but each time the cable broke, or water penetrated the insulation. In August, 1858, verbal messages could at last be passed from Valentia to Newfoundland, but the line, which was erratic, broke down in October. It was not till 1866 that, with improved cables, the Anglo-American Telegraph Company established a permanent link. Other stations followed, at Ballinskelligs (1874) and Waterville (1885). Ten years later telegraphs were a commonplace across the floors of all the great oceans. The cable went from near the south-east corner of the island and was in use till the 1960s. On the north coast is Glanleam, seat of Lord Monteagle and previously of the Knights of Kerry. The nineteenth Knight (1805–80) succeeded by profuse plantings of windbreak shrubs (one fuchsia was reported in 1905 to have a ninety-five yard circumference) in culti-vating many South American introductions: embothriums, drimys, myrtles, escallonias and others; and the garden remains a fine one. **Caherciveen**, the town we come to next, was so remote from Irish postal services that it was reported in 1818 to have better contact with America than with Dublin, and Dublin newspapers and letters some-times arrived via New York. As the century progressed the contact between the Irish peasantry and Irish America grew rapidly through forced emigration, and more than one American politician came to western Ireland to meet the people and make speeches, knowing their appreciation would be transmitted to his American constituents with far more effect than his election propaganda. Nowadays, though the biggest town on the peninsula, it has only two thousand inhabitants, and contains little of note. O'Connell's ruined birthplace, Carhan House, is a mile to the east beside a bridge and commemorative garden, but the most interesting local sights are to the north-west, across the bridge over the Valentia River. Near the MacCarthy castle of Ballycarbery are two stone ring-forts related to that on the penin-sula's southern side at Staigue. Of the two the better preserved, **Leacanbuaile**, has been dated by means of small iron, bone and stone artifacts to the ninth or tenth century AD. Both forts are placed to cover approach from the sea, though in this terrain of many humps and hills a stealthy progress might still have been possible. Yet the forts, in some ways anticipating the Norman motte-and-bailey, were obviously intended for the protection of a small number – the chief-tain's family – within its walls, and could hardly have been part of any grand strategy.

The northern road of the Ring of Kerry is less spectacular than the southern, in spite of good views of Dingle Peninsula. **Kells Bay**, between the two ranges of Knockadober (the initial K is pronounced locally) and Teermoyle Mountain, contains a pretty harbour village. Rossbeigh has a magnificent strand along a dune-backed bar that stretches nearly three miles into Dingle Bay (Françoise Sagan had a holiday chalet in the area). **Glenbeigh** is a charming town to which come many anglers, golfers, and refugees from Killarney. Here, too, are the gutted (in 1922) ruins of E.W. Godwin's Winn's Castle, or

Glenbeigh Towers, built in 1867, in very ungarnished Gothic style, for Rowland Winn. He sued the architect (who had damaged his reputation by eloping with Ellen Terry) on the grounds of leaks and costs. His harsh policy to his tenants resulted in a series of evictions and fights during the Plan of Campaign of 1887. His heir, a cousin, having married three times, turned Muslim, and made the pilgrimage to Mecca, returning to insist on being known as 'Al Hadji'. In 1925 he claimed to the Press he had been offered the throne of Albania three times (rather a lot of people were) – 'but there is no salary attached to it'. Only a corner of the building survives. Three miles beyond Glenbeigh the road crosses the River Caragh, and a turn to the right leads to the beautiful Glencar, whose lower half is occupied by Lough Caragh under the great natural fortress of MacGillicuddy's Reeks, to which we are giving too little attention. There are good drives among them, with wonderful views, fishing, legends and associations. But they are perhaps best left mainly to the walker and rock-climber, who has plenty of scope up there but will bring his own book – than which I know none better than Richard Mersey's *The Hills of Cork and Kerry* – clothes, boots and maps.

Killorglin is five miles on, beside the broad River Laune, which is the outflow from Killarney's lakes and noted for its trout and salmon, a town of little distinction save when turned upside down every August by Puck Fair, which centres on its square. For three days a goat, King Puck, which may not appreciate the privilege, is hoisted on to a platform high above the square, and looks down, plentifully fed, its horns bedecked with ribbons and rosettes, on the cattle, sheep and horse-fair taking place below. Shops and bars stay open day and night and there are many more dealings in stout and whiskey than livestock. On the third day the goat is led round the town and released in the hills from which it came. Though one explanation gives it that goats, like the geese on the Roman Capitol, warned the town's inhabitants of the approach of Cromwell's army by running into its streets, and so saved it, the fair possibly has much older origins. It could date far back to pagan times, and the Festival of Lughnare, which celebrated the first fruits of the harvest. There are a few other festivals in Ireland which seem to be related, and to hark back to the same origins. The anthropologist Margaret Murray linked it with an ancient religious cult of Alexander the Great.

Dingle Peninsula

To round the spreading flats of Castlemaine Harbour we drive north-east to the town of Castlemaine, and turn left towards the southern edge of the Dingle Peninsula. Two miles north of the road the plain begins its slow rise to the rounded heights of the Slieve Mish range – the Mountains of Phantoms. These are the beginning of a continuous chain, the spine of the Dingle Peninsula, that stretches thirty miles out to sea and holds, at its tip, the western-most habitations of Europe. In some respects richer than other south-western peninsulas – its impressively rugged landscape, a mostly unprettified, natural look (which in parts is rapidly going), a wealth of ancient remains and associations – it is curiously short of trees. From the road skirting the giant silted harbour there are good views of MacGillycuddy's Reeks. Also, less obvious, there are natterjack toads. These are of interest here because the northern side of Castlemaine Harbour (and since 1968 Castlegregory over the other side of the Dingle Peninsula) are almost their only known habitats in the country. They, along with all other amphibians and reptiles, are meant to have been banished by St Patrick (though there are common lizards, common newts and common frogs). More factually, they may represent an interesting connection between Ireland and Spain. A hundred and fifty years ago the discovery of a natterjack (which has a narrow yellow line down its back, and shorter legs than the common toad) led to long correspondence in nature magazines. Continued patchily for years, it ended in 1846 with the decision that *Bufo calamita* had been introduced within the previous few centuries, thus vindicating the national saint. They may have been brought by boat and landed nearby – may even like the frog have been intentionally introduced. They are nevertheless only one of many species common to Ireland and the west and south-west coasts of Europe, known as the Lusitanian flora and fauna. These include the spotted or Kerry Slug, confined otherwise to Spain and Portugal; two beetles known only in France; four Spanish species of woodlouse; and some earthworms, false scorpions and various molluscs. More apparent are some of the plants – arbutus, and some of the saxifrages and heaths mentioned elsewhere.

Of equal interest is the human link with Spain. It is often said that the people of Dingle and Galway have sallower complexions than their compatriots, a result of the flourishing trade that used to be carried on with Spain, mainly from this west coast; and also perhaps of survivors from the Armada and other forces sent by Spain – to Smerwick, for instance – to provide an anti-English foothold in the country. Farther back in time the links become mythical, but perhaps to some degree true. Scota and her son Goidel, descendants of Fenius Farsa, a Scythian prince – from these three came the whole race of, and three alternative names for, Gael – were supposed to have reached Ireland directly from a long stay in Spain. The look of the place, especially of farms, religious grottoes, statues and other signs can reinforce the fancy.

We keep going along the peninsula's south coast-road. Castle-maine Harbour is on the left, winter home of several thousand Brent geese and even greater flocks of wigeon. The harbour is bounded by the two-mile sandspit of Inch, reaching out into the bay and supplying a broad sandy beach along its western edge. We turn inland with the road for **Anascaul**, a lively village, one of whose pubs, the 'South Pole Inn' used to be the home of Thomas Crean, who was with Scott in the Antarctic. The Dingle road leads away to the left. A narrower lane leads three miles south-west to the coastal ruin of Minard Castle, built by a Knight of Kerry in the fifteenth century. Several ogham stones survive at Ballintaggart, a mile or so south-east of Dingle town. The enclosure used to be reserved for the burial of suicides and unbaptised infants. **Dingle** itself is ten miles on. The town spreads up from the fishing-boat harbour, from which a considerable fleet puts out to gather its harvest of mackerel, bass, plaice, codling and the rest. Elizabethan campaigns and Cromwellian ravages wiped out all the town's antiquities, though there is an interesting Desmond tomb of 1540 in the Church of Ireland church. The town attracts the young, especially those with leanings to the mystical alternative. Shop windows display zodiac signs, mantras, moon, ads for B-and-Bs with yoga and healing. There are plenty of restaurants and craft shops, and a craft centre. In a stage-Irish way, the most famous house in the town no longer exists and its fame accrued from something that didn't happen. In 1792, James Rice, a papal count in the Irish Brigade of the French army, planned to rescue Marie Antoinette from captivity. She was to be brought to Dingle and there lodged in the count's house, beside the modern Catholic presbytery. The queen agreed till she learned her husband and children were not to come with her; and in the event stayed to lose her head.

Continuing west, we pass through **Ventry** and by the broad bay known as Ventry Harbour with its sandy beaches. It was here that

Daire Donn, the King of the World (all but Ireland), swept with his monstrous forces and advanced up the slope beyond. Finn MacCool, that Gaelic Arthur, and his men fell on the invaders. The clangour, prowess and gallantry of epic Irish battle went on three days and nights (they generally did) till Finn, waist deep in blood, fought his way to the king and slew him and his remnant bodyguard. The king's 'grave' is still there, under a ridge that may conceal a souterrain, or artificially built cave. It is claimed locally that Ventry was the last Norse foothold in Ireland and that the story symbolises their final departure. But the area is so remarkably rich in remains of various ages that a dozen explanations could be made to fit.

The great wealth of megalithic tombs and other memorials in the area records its apparent importance from as far back as the second millennium BC, a period in which Ireland in general grew wealthy through trade with places as distant as the Middle East. But more abundantly scattered over the area, especially west of Dingle, are the beehive huts, or clochans, which probably date from the sixth, seventh and eighth centuries. Many of these are visible from the road beyond Ventry, though the first main sight, about two miles on, is of Dunbeg promontory fort (which can be visited) hanging dramatically over the sea down to the left. Its inner buildings are defended by four massive earth banks and a stone wall, with an underground exit. The road has begun its rising loop round Mount Eagle and the western end of the peninsula, and about two miles further on passes the so-called village of clochans at Fahan, in Glenfahan. Many of these stone huts stand no more than three or four feet high, and people could only crouch or lie within them. None of them is mortared. This seems to date them roughly to the sixth, seventh and eighth centuries, before which most buildings were of wood and after of mortared stone. They may have been used as individual cells by monks in the earliest monasteries. Remains of over four hundred have been recorded in this area.

The road rounds Slea Head and reaches one of the best views along this dramatic corniche: of the **Blasket Islands**, a bit like recumbent reptiles in the lowering sun, the nearest and largest of them lying just over a mile out to sea. With fieldglasses it is possible to make out fat-tailed sheep grazing round derelict – and some restored – stone cottages. People lived here, on and off, over two thousand years. A hundred years ago Great Blasket was known as the 'next parish to America'. Life was elemental. There were up to a hundred and fifty people, a thousand sheep and thirty cows, but no bulls – cows were taken by delicate curragh to the mainland for mating. There was no church, no pub, no shop; though there was a king, and one old woman's house served as the dail or talking place. New houses were built from local rock and furniture from driftwood, but few were needed as the population seldom rose. When a cargo of tea was washed ashore from a wreck, the leaves, being unknown, were used as a dye. In the evenings the people told each other variations of ancient stories. Three of them wrote books about themselves and the island's ways, and *Twenty Years A-growing* by Maurice O'Sullivan, *The Islandman* by Tomas O Crohan and *An Old Woman's Reflections* by Peig Sayers brought their authors justified fame. After the Second World War a visitor noted that the village was 'a wilderness of nettles and weeds, with hens scratching in dung and midden heaps, and cows and donkeys browsing here and there, both in and out of doorways'. By 1953 the population was shrunken and depressed; no young people stayed long. The government decided to bring the remaining villagers to the mainland and resettle them, but most went to relatives in Springfield, Connecticut, and many of the men manned police forces thereabouts. There are regular sailings to these mesmeric ghost-islands in summer, weather allowing.

Three miles beyond Slea Head, past country where ravens and choughs may be seen, and a mile or so inland, among prettily patterned stone-walled fields, lies the hamlet of **Dunquin**. The guesthouse was owned till his death in 1971 by Kruger Kavanagh, a restless village native who during spells abroad held a commission in the American Army, counted gangsters, boxers, and politicians among his friends, was Metro-Goldwyn-Mayer's publicity manager and bodyguard to de Valera. Then he came back to Dunquin and ran a guesthouse for fifty years, delighting to gawp at the braggings of Dubliners who assumed the likes of him had never strayed from the west coast. Kruger (the adopted name indicated where much Catholic Irish sympathy lay in the Boer War) taught Gaelic, to his and the government's mutual benefit. The remote possibility of making Gaelic the country's first language was still being pursued energetically. Here and in the other Gaelic-speaking areas, known as the Gaeltacht, in Kerry, Cork, Mayo, Donegal and elsewhere, there still exist Gaelic summer-schools where soil-tillers turn temporary professor to impart their mother-tongue. Gaelic contains charm, beauty, and a rich literature: the language, Arland Ussher wrote, of a race 'which has tired the sun with quips, hyperboles, cajoleries, endearments, lamentations, blessings, cursings, tirades – and all very often in the same breath'.

Beyond Dunquin is the Blaskets Heritage Centre, worth visiting particularly by those prevented from seeing the real thing by rough seas, time or disinclination. Then comes the flat open country that leads to Sybil Point, **Smerwick Harbour** and miles of picturesque coastline. Several tiny villages – Ballyrannig, Ballydavid, Smerwick – lie round the harbour, a natural inlet about two miles long and a mile wide. Fishing is a main means of livelihood, and to this end the building of curraghs is continued: light boats made of tarred canvas stretched tightly round a wooden frame. Being light and slender they speedily skim the tops of the waves, and their rounded bottoms make them difficult to capsize (though bad weather can hold up fishing for as long as weeks, even in summer). On shore they are carefully tethered, to avoid strong winds hoisting them seaward.

Smerwick was the beautiful setting of an ugly event during the Desmond rebellion. In 1579 a Papal Nuncio and eighty Spaniards built a fort here, with the aim of linking with the rebels. In 1580 they were reinforced by six hundred Italians, and fortified themselves within the ancient Dun an Oir (or Fort of Gold, near which two years earlier a ship of Frobisher's, carrying from America what he believed to be gold but was in fact pyrites, was wrecked). A vastly superior naval force under Admiral Winter (Raleigh's and Spenser's presence is disputed) sped to the scene, bombarded, took and massacred, using their full repertoire of tortures, though the garrison had surrendered. The treatment, typical of the times, became well known because of the foreigners involved. 'Many years passed,' wrote Kingsley with Aryan satisfaction – he described the affair in *Westward Ho!* – 'before a Spaniard set foot again in Ireland.' On the western side of this neck of land leading to the Three Sisters rocks is Ferriter's Castle, whose last owner, Pearce Ferriter, soldier and poet, was the last Kerry commander to submit to the Cromwellians. He was hanged at Killarney in 1653.

Nowadays the pace of life has accelerated. A couple of generations ago more people went to church by pony-drawn trap than by car. Pound notes accumulated under mattresses and other old habits persisted. Brendan Behan told of a police check-up at a Ballyferriter bar. It was no raid. The sergeant first telephoned to give an hour's notice of arrival. Before he was due the bar's occupants were ushered out politely, for it was after hours, and asked to take their bottles and glasses a little way up the hill. The sergeant came, drank a friendly pint and withdrew, in full knowledge of the facts but satisfied by the display of deference. Variations on this ritual were common in many parts of Ireland. Now, though they have not vanished, they are fewer. This western tip of Europe, haunt of birds, saintly ascetics, peasants wringing hard lives from rain, wind and scarcity, seems a little demeaned by a snow-shower of white bungalows. The people, still charming, are a mite more conscious of the clock, the need to drive children to school, themselves to jobs. Computer and mobile phone wreak their will here as much as elsewhere. It is of course their home, but for us to decide whether or not to come back. It is not so easy now to endorse Cyril Connolly's comment: 'The whole landscape is expectant and devotional like Iona or Delphi.'

Five miles east of Ballyferriter is a remarkable survival from Early Christian times, the **Gallarus Oratory**, or church. A rectangular building about twelve by eighteen feet, and sixteen feet high, it is the most perfect of its kind, better than the two on Skellig Michael. Built by corbelling – making each stone course of smaller measurement than the one beneath so that the courses overlap and eventually meet at the top – it shows the limitations of a method that was ideal for circular buildings; for here the roof definitely sags (after eleven hundred years or so). At Kilmalkedar, a mile away, is a ruined twelfth-century church with a good Romanesque doorway, the first building to have been strongly influenced by Cormac's Chapel at Cashel. It contains an ogham stone, no rarity in these parts.

East of Ballydavid rises Ireland's second highest peak, **Mount Brandon** (3,127 feet), and a steep and stony track, the Saint's Road, follows a zigzag course to the top. The saint in question, Brandon, or Brendan, was one of the more daring of those holy Irish stalwarts who left their land in the sixth and seventh centuries to find God and the Promised Land, which they took to be located on earth. True or not, the life story compiled by monks of later centuries is a colourful one. He was born in 484, in circumstances oddly akin to those of Christ's birth, with prophecies, cows, a star and a wise man all playing prominent parts. His boyhood and youth included a due mixture of study, pilgrimage, vicious asceticism, and miracles. Once ordained, he founded monasteries throughout Connacht and Munster, then took himself to lonely meditation atop Mount Brandon, where a pile of stones is claimed to be the remains of his oratory. Anyone enjoying the sunset view from this summit is likely to be moved. St Brendan, his vision enhanced perhaps by a diet of berries and stream water, resolved to sail the Atlantic and find the Promised Land. The account of his subsequent seven years of navigating mentions no identifiable names, of course, but describes places that can seem to resemble parts of Iceland, Greenland, the Azores and Bahamas, and the eastern seaboard of the United States. It became a medieval best-seller, in Latin, and was translated into Irish, English, Welsh, Scots Gaelic, Breton, French, Saxon and Flemish. The question whether St Brendan discovered North America before Columbus and Leif Eriksson will be decided perhaps only if an Irish equivalent of the Vinland map is unearthed. One sceptical interpretation of the text had the whole journey confined to a circuit of Galway Bay. Some make real or mythical islands like Hy-Brasil, and St Brendan's Island (marked on maps till the nineteenth century, and the object of Portuguese exploration till the eighteenth) his western limit. But he stays the patron saint of seamen and travellers. Brandon Mountain, where he conceived his project, partakes in his prestige. Till the eighteenth century it was second only to Croagh Patrick as an Irish place of pilgrimage, one of the four holy places which serious penitents were required to visit. The saint died in 578 AD at Annaghdown in Galway, and was buried at Clonfert.

The mountain itself and the glens around are ideal country for walking. Each climb to a higher level peels away the view of the nearest hill or valley to reveal those beyond, fields present patterns of brown, green and steel-blue, specked with the white of sheep, little and large basins of land have gathered lakes over the millennia, and along the coast black rocks are flecked with white as rollers break and the thunder of waves rumbles in subterranean channels. But the mountain falls as a steep cliff to the sea, and to proceed it is necessary to return to Dingle, then travel north-east, over the **Connor Pass**, to the edge of Brandon Bay and Castlegregory. From Connor Pass on a fine day there is a view not only of the southern Kerry peninsulas but also of the Clare coast and Aran Islands to the north. The eastern shore of Brandon Bay comprises the longest sandy beach in Ireland – twelve uninterrupted miles.

Old tales cling to **Castlegregory** but the village itself is no more than a pleasant resort with fine bathing and good fishing. A flat sandy promontory stretching a mile to the north points to the Magharee Islands, on one of which are the remains of St Seanach's sixth-century monastery. The road continues eastward, flanking the south side of Tralee Bay. Near Camp is the Glen of Galt, with spring waters that cure madness, but there is nothing more to arrest attention before crossing the trickle which by some geographical hyperbole was given the name of River Lee (Tralee is named from it). It was here, at Scota's Glen, that the Scythian Fenius Farsa, having refused to join the persecution of Jews in Egypt and fled to Spain, brought his daughter Scota, her husband Milesius, and their son Goidel, and so established the race that has been known at different stages as the Fenians, the Scots, the Milesians and the Goidels (or Gaels). Here too that Scota was buried after her death in battle with the former dominant race, the Tuatha de Danaan. A mile beyond lies the chief town of county Kerry, Tralee.

Tralee used to be the chief demesne of the Earls of Desmond, and thirteen of them were buried in the now ruined, almost vanished, Dominican friary. It was near here that Gerald, the fifteenth earl, brought the line to an end. For twenty years, through surprise attacks, leagues and intrigues with neighbouring malcontents, tactical mind-changing, natural inconstancy, cunning and terror, he had frustrated Queen Elizabeth's colonial ambitions in Munster. His sacking of Youghal at the end of 1579 brought down a landslide of Tudor vengeance, culminating in the slaughter at Smerwick. In 1582 his titles and lands – 600,000 acres of them – were forfeited by attainder. He wandered with a withered band of followers and at last was betrayed to English soldiers close to the river **Glenageenty**, in the wooded foothills of Stack's Mountains, five miles east of Tralee. To prevent his rescue, they cut off his head, later spiked on London Bridge. An engraved stone marks the spot where he was killed, placed there after four hundred years to the day: 11 November 1983. Gerald's son James was carefully reared in London as a Protestant and had the title restored. But he proved a cipher and died without heir, bringing the Desmond era (though others for a while claimed the title) to an end.

The Tralee estates came to the Denny family, whose seat was for a while the town castle, destroyed with most of the rest of the town in 1643; and in part to the Blennerhassetts, whose seat, Ballyseedy, three miles east of the town, is an eighteenth-century mansion extravagantly adorned with Victorian battlements and other Gothic parafernalia. A rare survivor of twentieth-century destruction, it is now a rather grand hotel. The big, bustling, colourful town has a port, served by ships' canal, and too much road traffic for its capacity. Most of the best of Tralee, including the classical courthouse by W.V. Morrison, and some impressive merchants' houses in the centre, is Georgian; there is an 1870 Catholic Church of St John by J.J. McCarthy, with Ireland's tallest spire, an 1861 Dominican church by E.W. Pugin and George Ashlin; and little else of interest. It is the biggest town on the south-west coast.

A left turn off the Ardfert road north-west of the town leads through the little village of Spa, whose iron-rich spring, guaranteed to 'raise the spirits' and give 'a voracious appetite', attracted visitors in the eighteenth century and later. **Fenit**, on the corner of land projecting into Tralee Bay, is a lively fishing port. It was St Brendan's birthplace, and from here he sailed on his great westward journey. The coast here is flat and duney, with white sands stretching for miles to the north.

It was at an old rath near **Banna Strand** that, on Good Friday of 1916, Sir Roger Casement was arrested, having just landed from a German submarine. His part in the Easter Rising was short and muddled, in spite of months of planning in hospitable Germany. Three months after his arrest he was hanged in London, but his name, like those of the executed Dublin insurgents, was soon to be a rallying cry, and it was to gratify repeated requests that Harold Wilson allowed the return of his body to Dublin in 1966. There is a simple likeness of him in relief close to the landing-point.

The most impressive artifact of this area is on the site of one of St Brendan's foundations – the hoary, graceful ruins of medieval **Ardfert Cathedral**, with fine east window and Romanesque west doorway, this latter probably of the twelfth century. It was wrecked by Cromwellians in 1641. North-west of the choir is the grave of Anne, daughter of Sir William Petty of Kenmare. Her marriage to the first Earl of Kerry in 1692 founded the Petty-FitzMaurice family, which produced the still extant line of the Marquesses of Lansdowne, which has numbered one prime minister and one viceroy of India. The grave was incorporated in the family vault of the Crosbies, Earls of Glandore, Tudor settlers, who owned the demesne into the twentieth century. A Round Tower, 120 feet high, stood opposite the cathedral's west doorway till 1771, when it fell. To the north-west are ruins of Romanesque Temple-na-Hoe, with lovely flower decoration inside the south window; and fifteenth-century Temple na Griffin, with worn sculpted griffins inside. In the demesne of Ardfert House, a relic to the east of the village, are the ruins of a Franciscan friary of 1253, founded by Thomas FitzMaurice, first Lord of Kerry.

We have come to the least picturesque part of county Kerry, though the coast road is attractive in parts. At Ballyheige are the ruins of a house reconstructed in 1809 in grandiose Gothic by Sir Richard Morrison for a branch of the Crosbie family. The original eighteenth-century house is said to have been built with the silver from a wrecked East Indiaman. The later one was burned down by Republican forces in 1922. Near Ballyduff is Rattoo Round Tower, beside the remains of an Augustinian abbey, and some miles to the north, over the estuary of the River Feale, is the resort of Ballybunion. Crowds of tourists, mainly Irish, descend in summer on its hotels, amusement places, championship golf-course and beaches. To the north, as the road bends round with the coast to the east, good views of Clare are revealed. Of several castle remains on this part of the coast, the most impressive is **Carrigafoyle**, reached by a narrow causeway from the land. Till Cromwell's time it belonged to the O'Connor family and for a while during the Desmond rising harboured a rebel garrison till the English took it and hanged the defenders. It was again taken and finally mutilated by Cromwell's troops. There are good views from the top. Herbert Kitchener, future Lord Kitchener of Khartoum, was born at Crotter House, near **Ballylongford**, in 1850. His father, an army colonel, was very unpopular locally and once, for threatening some of his tenants with eviction, was publicly horsewhipped at Tralee races by his unstable neighbour the Knight of Glin. On the estuary shore north of the town are the lovely remains of sixteenth-century Lislaughtin Friary. Sir William Pelham, who led the English troops in 1580, and was at the time Lord Justice of Ireland, had sworn to make this strip of coast, as far as Limerick 'as bare a country as ever Spaniard set foot in', and even today the success of his mission seems to have been lasting in parts. But beyond Tarbert (to the north-west of which there is a regular car ferry service to county Clare) the scenery grows all the time prettier, as the river channel narrows.

Six miles on, behind extensive walls to the right of the road, is **Glin Castle**, an enchanting pasteboard Gothic mansion built between 1790 and 1812 in the vicinity of a castle and former house inhabited by the same family since the thirteenth century. From the three-storey, bow-fronted main block a long low wing spreads out, in a rather unbalanced way, to the west. Turrets and battlements were added in the nineteenth century, along with delightfully theatrical round-towered entrance gates. The FitzGerald Knights of Glin, the Knights of Kerry, and the White Knights, appear to have been the only enduring hereditary knights in British history. They are thought to have shared with the Earls of Desmond an ancestor, Lord of Decies and Desmond and a count palatine in the thirteenth century, who bestowed the honours on his three sons. From time to time their status was confirmed by the monarch, so that however untidily they fit into the hierarchy of rank they would, but for providence, have been there to stay. As it was, the White Knights died out in the seventeenth century, the knighthood of Kerry was subsumed into a baronetcy in the nineteenth century, and the present, twenty-ninth Knight of Glin is last of his line, having fathered daughters but no sons. Remote and part-Gaelicised in the far west, earlier Knights of Glin took part in most of the rebellions against Tudor rule and stayed Catholic and from an English point of view unreliable until the eighteenth century. Glin has seen battle, ambush, intrigue and the threat in 1600, unful-filled, of firing the then Knight's six-year-old son from a cannon. Then, in common with other families of the west, they were drawn by the lure of English ways to send sons to Winchester and suchlike institutions, marry English, renounce their religion, bards and stone fortresses, and import architects and decorators to provide suitable accommodation. Glin Castle, with its remarkable plasterwork and a fine double-staircase resembling work by Wyatt, is the result. The present Knight is a distinguished scholar of Georgian art and architec-ture and President of the Irish Georgian Society. In the village is the stump of the old castle, destroyed by Sir George Carew after a siege in 1600. Glin Castle is open to the public, and bed and breakfast, in majestic style, are available.

The town of **Foynes** is eight miles farther on, under a hill topped by a Celtic cross memorial to Edmond Spring-Rice, son of the first Baron Monteagle (an 1830s Chancellor of the Exchequer) and father of the second. They lived at Mount Trenchard, a Georgian house, now a convent, still overlooking the estuary a mile or two west of the town. Between the mainland and Foynes Island, is the strip of water once used for the descent of the first transatlantic seaplanes. An excellent museum takes in the terminal building and other facilities then in use. **Shanagolden** is four miles inland, to the south. (The ruined castle of Shanid, two miles south-south-west of it, was built around 1200 by Thomas FitzMaurice, son of the founder of the whole FitzGerald family.) The Angkor-like smothered remains of the thir-teenth-century Augustinian nunnery of Old Abbey two miles east of Shanagolden illustrate well those two food sources of self-sufficient orders, the fishpond and the dovecote. Withdrawn from the river and on the edge of the level plain of west county Limerick (well seen from the hills west of Shanagolden) the road goes on from Foynes to **Askeaton**, whose bridge over the River Deal is its focal point. The castle, another Desmond fortress, was the final refuge of Garrett, the last Earl of Desmond, before his fatal wanderings in the Glenageenty valley. Besieged in 1579, he held out, while the English under Sir Nicholas Malby sacked the Franciscan friary, with its Desmond tombs, nearby. Next year, with the earl gone, the garrison surrendered, having first in a pacifying gesture set fire to the castle themselves. In the seventeenth-century wars it was taken by Confederates in 1642, and held by them till Cromwellians took it and finally reduced it to its present state – all but a brick building by the keep, added in the eighteenth century for the use of the local Hell Fire Club. From the evidence of the few records, this never attained the excesses of its English counterpart. Most of the big local families were represented, and a Mrs Celinda Blennerhassett, from a local gentry family, was herself not ashamed to belong along with her husband. The friary remains, restored after Malby's time but finally evacuated at the approach of the Cromwellians, include a beautiful cloister. In the Church of Ireland graveyard is buried Aubrey de Vere (1814–1902), the ruin of whose family house, **Curragh Chase** (burned down in 1941), stands five miles away in a romantic setting of lakes, woods and hills by a lane leading from the Limerick road. It was his poet father, Aubrey (1788–1846), a friend of Wordsworth and married to Mary Spring-Rice, who adopted the surname – he was a Hunt till he succeeded to a baronetcy in 1818. The younger Aubrey, best known for his *The Foray of Queen Maeve*, was in his turn a friend of Tennyson (who came here in 1848), wrote a deal of literary criticism, and under the influences of medievalism, Irish religious history and the Oxford Movement, became a Catholic in 1851.

Dromore Castle, to the left of the main road three miles beyond the Curragh Chase turning, was built in a hotch-potch style of Gothic with Irish-Romanesque accretions, known quaintly as 'archaeological Gothic', for the Earl of Limerick between 1867 and 1870. Its architect was E.W. Godwin, a friend of Whistler and father, by his mistress Ellen Terry, of Edward Gordon Craig. Inhabited till 1950, then offered for sale, the house – magnificent of its kind – found no takers. With a roof on, according to the destructive Irish law, it was liable for rates; without it, it was free. The roof came off in 1954, and now the building rots in the damp atmosphere. It still makes a most impressive profile.

There are several more ancient castles in the area, which from Norse times has guarded the vulnerable back door to Ireland, the Shannon. One of these, **Carrigogunnel**, stands prominent for miles around on a mound of basalt, five miles beyond Dromore. Originally built by the O'Briens of Thomond in the fifteenth century, it was blown up by General Ginkel in 1691, in the closing phase of William III's conquest. North of Dromore is Shannongrove House, close to the river, built around 1709 for the Bury family, later Earls of Charleville, and the earliest eighteenth-century house in the county. Flanked by symmetrical wings, it is an elegant example of the Dutch Palladian style. Privately owned, it has superb wood-panelling inside. Just to the east, off Mellon Point, occurs the greatest tidal range in Ireland. The mean spring tide is 18.3 feet. The last stretch of the Limerick road takes us through the small village of **Mungret**, where in the sixth century a monastery was founded by St Nessan, about whom nothing is known save the date of his death, 551. The remains of later buildings include a crenellated tower, two churches, a castle, and the nave and choir of the late medieval abbey, sufficient signs of its prestige in early times. From here the road leads four miles north-east to Limerick City.

11

Limerick City, Inner Limerick and Lower Shannon

MUNSTER WAS, WITH Connacht, Ulster and Leinster, one of the four rather mutable kingdoms of ancient Ireland (with Meath a short-lived fifth); but in pre-Christian times it was divided into two sub-kingdoms: Desmond in the south and Thomond (pronounced 'toemond') in the north. Desmond in due course went to the Norman FitzGeralds. Thomond took in parts of the counties Tipperary and Limerick and most of Clare, and was O'Brien territory long after the Norman invasion. When, early in the tenth century, the Danes built the country's main ports, **Limerick** was one of them. Strategically placed on an island in the Shannon, with easy access to the sea and far into the interior of Ireland, it was highly prized. In the late tenth century Brian Boru, heir of the old local Gaelic rulers, the Dal Cais, managed to oust the Danish intruders. Based first on Kincora, near Killaloe, he made himself king of Munster, and the whole of Ireland his field of action. He gave much to the church and monasteries – the main seats of learning – but his main concern seems to have been the acquisition of land and power. Piety, virtue and patriotism were added to his reputation by tame recorders after his death, which occurred at Clontarf, north of Dublin, in 1014, while he was crushing an alliance of Leinstermen and Danes. After him, the O'Brien kingship of Thomond came to settle at Limerick, and it was one of Brian's descendants, Donal Mor O'Brien, who inflicted the first reverse on the Anglo-Normans, at Thurles in 1174.

As the English presence withdrew to the Pale – the securer regions of the eastern half of Ireland – O'Briens lost some power in disputes with other local families. In 1543, accepting Henry VIII's offer of 'surrender and regrant', one branch of them turned Protestant and became earls and marquesses of Thomond and barons Inchiquin, unlike the other senior family branch which stayed Catholic and decamped to France with James II. The present Baron Inchiquin is that rare peer, a descendant in unbroken male line from Gaels ruling before the Normans came. He lives at Dromoland, which we shall visit shortly, and where his ancestors have lived for more than three centuries.

The Normans built Limerick's first walls; stout ones, on the island known as King's Island, to the north of the main modern town. They had no wish to mix with the Irish, whom, following the precepts of Giraldus Cambrensis, they believed to be 'a filthy people, wallowing in vice'. 'Moreover,' he wrote, 'and this is surely a detestable thing, and contrary not only to the Faith but to any feeling of honour – men in many places in Ireland, I shall not say marry, but rather debauch, the wives of their dead brothers.' Still, the newcomers needed the Irish for menial tasks, and the Irish took to queueing outside the town gates for work, and building their living-quarters nearby, and in this way, as in many other Irish cities, two towns grew up – Englishtown on King's Island and Irishtown just across the Abbey River to the south – and as such the two areas remained known. As Old English and Irish drew closer together, walls were built round both districts.

It was this combined walled town that the governor, Hugh O'Neill, defended for six months against the troops of Ireton, Cromwell's general and son-in-law who, having taken the place in 1651, and ordered the Irish inhabitants to leave the city within six months, and forbidden the soldiers who were to replace them to marry any but Protestant wives, died of the plague that often gripped a besieged city, in a house in Nicholas Street. (He was buried in Westminster Abbey, but bundled off to Tyburn after the Restoration.) A more notable siege came in 1690, after the Boyne. William III assumed James II was done for, as indeed did James, who fled to the Continent. But his general, Patrick Sarsfield, thought otherwise, and picked Limerick as a base for further fighting. His commander, the Earl of Tyrconnel, retired to France, as did Sarsfield's French comrade, General Lauzun, saying the city 'could be taken with roasted apples'.

William arrived with an army of twenty-six thousand, and waited for his artillery to come up. With inside information, Sarsfield broke through the English lines at night and skilfully managed to capture William's convoy of supplies at Ballyneety, six miles south-east of the city. Since the cannon were no use to him, he filled the barrels with powder, buried the mouths in the earth and fired them, destroying the lot. He returned to withstand three weeks of William's assaults, during which the city walls were badly breached. In September, however,the siege was raised and William returned to England. James created Sarsfield earl of Lucan. But it was a temporary success. A year later the Irish cause was finally shattered at Athlone, Aughrim, here at Limerick and at Galway.

When Limerick was attacked again in 1691, Sarsfield held out for a month, then capitulated on what seemed generous terms. Catholics were to enjoy the rights they had held under Charles II, and the Irish army was to be allowed to depart unmolested to France. The treaty was signed on the stone still sited by Thomond Bridge, west of King's Island. The Irish departed – fourteen thousand of them – in what is known as the Flight of the Wild Geese, the second mass emigration in a century of capable, mostly ill-led pawns on the board of English and French hostilities – to form the Irish Brigade of the French Army and fight with more often and against the English in several wars for a hundred years and more. Sarsfield himself was killed in 1693 at the battle of Landen in Belgium, again fighting William.

But the rest of the treaty was soon nullified by the Protestant English parliament. Instead of codified rights, the Catholics got Penal Laws – barring them from parliament, government office, the law, the army, the navy, juries, owning weapons, being educated abroad, teaching, voting, buying land, inheriting it by bequest of or marriage to a Protestant, or taking long leases (some landowners got over this by turning Protestant, or entrusting their lands to Protestant friends or relations, who seldom reneged).

Three sieges in forty years, each ending with storming, burning and looting, had smashed the city. The new laws brought resentment, reprisals, revenge and fear. For sixty years Limerick's gates were locked every night. Then in the mid eighteenth century the city was declared to be a fortress no longer. Edmund Sexten Pery, of an established Limerick family, and a gifted administrator (he was later Speaker of the Irish House of Commons for fourteen years) led moves to bring down the old city walls, build new roads, quays, docks, bridge, barracks, custom house, courthouse, theatre; and develop a large area of houses and shops south of Irishtown, on a neat grid pattern of wide streets, which is still called Newtown Pery or, inaccurately, the 'west end'. 'You could not in many parts of it help thinking yourself in London, so like are some of the streets and general contour of the houses', wrote Rev. James Hall in 1813. There was a new gaol, too, built by William Blackburn, a friend of the reformer John Howard. The town became as smart as any in the British Isles. Later, the Grand Canal linked it with Dublin, and crops, cattle, pigs, eggs and other agricultural products were conveyed up the Shannon for export to England. This profitable trade continued till the 1840s, when famine came and the Irish poor died in the streets or sailed to a new life in a new world. The old commerce recovered, but until Ireland's 'Celtic Tiger' boom came at the end of the twentieth century, religion and poverty were leading players in Limerick. It is said to have more churches than any other city, and is still is noted for its high (over 90 per cent) Catholic population, for the strength of its Catholic Arch Confraternity, and for the powerful, fire-and-brimstone, widely influential rhetoric of the Redemptorist Order, which has been settled here since the mid nineteenth century.

There was bitter fighting in the Anglo-Irish war and Robert Graves, posted here, wrote that 'it looked like a war-ravaged town. The main streets were pitted with holes like shell-craters and many of the bigger houses seemed on the point of collapse.' (He also affirmed that 'everyone died of drink in Limerick except the Plymouth Brethren, who died of religious melancholia'.)

The reason for the well-known five-line verse being called a limerick is obscure. The word is first recorded in this sense in 1898, long after Edward Lear made the form popular and even longer after books of the things had been published. The form, more or less, is found in Shakespeare, Ben Jonson, even Aristophanes. Also in France: and a thin theory suggests that returning descendants of Sarsfield's fellow exiles brought it back to Limerick, whose name it assumed. Others say that in Lear's time people took to inventing these verses, each person adding one line in turn. To give the next person time to think, they recited between each attempt – for no known reason – an old river song: '… Oh won't you come up, come all the way up, Come all the way up to Limerick?'

All three parts of Limerick contain mainly buildings from the eighteenth century onward, though each maintains the flavour of a different period. Islanded **English Town**, the oldest sector, has the narrow curving streets of the medieval city and contains at its north end, by James Pain's Thomond Bridge, **King John's Castle**, built in 1210, in British times a barracks, recently restored from a ruinous state. It still makes, as first intended, an impressive sight from across the river. The Potato Market, 1810 county courthouse and St Mary's Church of Ireland Cathedral are all on Merchant's Quay, on the southwest of the island. The fine and fascinating **St Mary's Cathedral**, originally built on the site of his own royal palace by Donal Mor O'Brien in 1179 – he later built the rock-top cathedral at Cashel – is an amalgam of styles, with Romanesque restored west doorway and Irish-battlemented tower, 120 feet high, and a great variety of window designs. Donal Mor's grave is here in the chancel, outshone by a splendid monument to the Great Earl of Thomond, who died in 1624; this was rebuilt in 1678 after destruction by Cromwellians, but with the original effigies. In the choir the seat ends are decorated with twenty-three misericords, probably of around 1500, the only examples from that period in an Irish church. They include some splendid allegorical beasts, among them a lioness, symbol of the Resurrection because she was thought to bring forth lifeless cubs which on the third day she breathed on to waken them. The O'Brien chapel on the north aisle does not contain the body of Murrough 'of the Burnings' O'Brien, though he was buried here in 1674. The morning after, the good citizens, mindful of his actions at Cashel twenty years before, snatched the body and threw it into the Shannon. Hard by, in Bridge Street, the Gerald Griffin Memorial Schools incorporates the old city courthouse, in which John Scanlon, perpetrator of the murder which inspired Griffin's *The Collegians*, was sentenced to be publicly hanged.

A footbridge close by leads to Rutland Street and the beautiful **Custom House** of 1765 to 1769, designed by the Sardinian Davis Ducart (interchangeable with Dukart and Duckart) and the finest of Limerick's old buildings. It now contains the **Hunt Collection**, a collection of artworks privately assembled by John Hunt and his wife Gertrude and left by them to the Irish nation. Limerick-born, historian of medieval art, archaeologist, Hunt lived beside Lough Gur till his death in 1976 and was the moving spirit behind the Bunratty 'folk-park' and the re-creation of ancient dwellings at Craggaunowen, both in county Clare. Reverently arranged on three floors, the collection comprises about two thousand artifacts of the highest distinction and artistry, originating from all over Europe and the Middle East, from ancient times to the present. There is a bronze horse by Leonardo, paintings by Picasso, Renoir, Yeats, Stone Age flints, Greek and Roman sculptures, Charles I's personal seal, Mary Queen of Scots' personal cross, a coin held for over a thousand years at least to be one of the thirty pieces of silver for which Christ was betrayed.

A walk along the Abbey River takes us past Mathew Bridge to Baal's Bridge (which succeeded one washed away by a high tide of 1775) where we can turn right down Broad Street, then John Street, to John's Square, with some houses of 1751 by Francis Bindon. The Catholic cathedral here is Gothic Revival of the 1850s, by P.C. Hardwick, who worked at Adare.

Newtown Pery, to the south and west, is – in the way of the open plan towns of Georgian times – a little windswept and exposed, handsome, perhaps heartless, but home to the city's main shops and businesses. Its axis is O'Connell Street, with a famous statue of O'Connell by John Hogan. Much good Georgian has gone since the Second World War. Much remains that is exceptionally good on The Crescent, Henry Street and other roads.

Inner Limerick County

Of several trips of interest round Limerick, one is through the rich farming and horse-breeding area that makes up the Plain of Limerick. It used to be known for sheep-rearing and cider, till more profitable uses were found for the land. We take the N20 south-west from Limerick and after eleven miles reach **Adare**, a pretty model village on the River Maigue with many thatched and tiled cottages built in the mid nineteenth century for Edwin, third Earl of Dunraven. His family, the Quins, claimed they could trace their line to pre-Norman Celtic forbears. An Oxford Movement convert to Catholicism, the earl was antiquarian, archaeologist – with particular interest in Irish matters – and a popular and improving landlord. For some of the rebuilding of the manor, and restoration of the Trinitarian monastery, he used the versatile architect P.C. Hardwick, member of an architectural dynasty about as long-lasting as that of the Wyatts, even the Scotts, who in London designed the Great Hall of Euston Station and the vertiginous Great Western Hotel at Paddington.

As we approach the village from Limerick, the old riverside castle of the Kildare FitzGeralds, and later the Desmond FitzGeralds, stands across the fields to our left, ruinous as the Cromwellians left it, backed by woods and the lovely languishing ruins of the Franciscan friary, containing several FitzGerald tombs. We cross the 600-year-old bridge over the River Maigue, well known to fishers of salmon and trout. On the right is the Augustinian friary of 1315, with its gracefully slender tower rising above what has been since 1807 the Church of Ireland church, generously lighted through the old tracery of its windows, and a cloister with memorials to the Wyndham Quins. Beyond comes the 1792 Dunraven Arms, then, at the centre of the village, the Trinitarian monastery with its more thickset tower. Since 1811 the buildings have provided Adare with its Catholic parish church – the only medieval building in Ireland still used for Catholic services. This was enlarged and refurbished by P.C. Hardwick in

1854. Trinitarians, who had no other house in Ireland, were founded to ransom Crusade hostages taken by the Moors.

Nearby is a tourist centre with the usual presentations and merchandise. Further down the road, beyond the fork and to the left, are some pleasing, eye-catching but modest arts and crafts cottages designed by Detmar Blow, who knew well and worked for Wyndham relations of the Dunravens in England: a socialist who could never stray far from the upper classes, who insisted that masters and servants in his own English house should eat at the same table – until the great embarrassment of both forced him to change. The Adare demesne is to the left of the road we have come along and contains Adare Manor, an excellent piece of Victorian Tudor-Gothic, now a ritzy hotel. It contains a fine gallery, 132 feet long, with elaborate wood carving upstairs, designed like much else here by A.W. Pugin. The good garden front is by Hardwick. Beyond it is a large, handsome and geometrical box garden with steps leading down to the river. The fourth earl, who died in 1926, ran a successful stud as well as being a war correspondent, competing in the Americas Cup in 1893 and 1895 (and protesting vigorously, like others later, at the way it was run) and establishing a Turkish cigarette factory here at Adare. It was due to his energies that the Wyndham Land Act of 1903 was passed which, enabling tenants to buy the land they farmed, greatly advanced the yielding of Ireland's great estates to the Irish.

Croom is a few miles to the south, up the Maigue from Adare, in unpretentious countryside thick with old keeps. The village was the meeting place of a group of local eighteenth-century poets, and puts on an annual literary festival. It has a few fragments of a castle built by Gerald FitzMaurice, brother of the progenitor of the Kildare FitzGeralds. **Monaster**, two miles east, contains the fragmentary ruins of a Cistercian abbey, daughter-foundation of Mellifont, and founded in 1148 by Turlough O'Brien in honour of his victory over the Norse at nearby Rathmore (two miles east again). There are some good Romanesque details in the remains, and the old mill by the bridge is a reminder of the Spartan self-sufficiency of this order, which usually chose to settle in the remotest places. The 863-foot Knockfeerina Hill, seen to the south-west from the Croom–Monaster road, is the other-world seat of the Celtic god Donn Firinne. When the cairn on top was removed by Ordnance Survey researchers in the last century, it was replaced by the local inhabitants.

Rathkeale, four miles west of Adare, has good Georgian houses along its main street, and the ruins of a Desmond FitzGerald castle burned down by a punitive force including Raleigh and Spenser in 1580, and of a thirteenth-century Augustinian priory, as well as J.J. McCarthy's Gothic Revival Catholic church. The reason why the region hereabouts is still sometimes known as the Palatinate is to be found a mile west, on the T28, at Castle Matrix (formerly Mattress, a winsome corruption of the original Matres, signifying pagan goddesses). Now refurbished with much flair by its American-Irish owner and open to the public, the castle was for centuries home of the Southwell family, one of whom, the first Baron Southwell, a valiant Williamite, in 1709 gave a home to some twelve hundred German Lutherans evicted from the Rhenish Palatinate. Others were settled in Wexford, Cork and Dublin. It was a government scheme, aimed in part at spreading foreign skills and crafts; partly at strengthening Protestantism in diehard Catholic areas. Its success was qualified. Most of the newcomers had left within ten years, while others kept to themselves, went on speaking German for more than a hundred years, then gradually intermarried with the Irish and became Catholic. But horticulture and agriculture were improved; and two Palatines from **Ballingrane**, two miles north of Rathkeale, Philip Embury and Barbara Heck (born Ruttle – her family's home still stands), were converted by John Wesley's preaching here and went on to introduce Methodism to America. A wall-plaque in Ballingrane's Embury and Heck Memorial church tells that Embury emigrated in 1766, preached the first Methodist sermon in America the same year – to a congregation of five, four of them from this village – and two years later dedicated the first Methodist church in America. Several common local names – Switzer, Delmege, Teskey, Twiss – have come down from palatine immigrants. Castle Matrix contains interesting furnishings and a wealth of fascinating documents relating to the Wild Geese.

Five miles further west on the N20 is **Newcastle West**. An eastern counterpart is sought in vain. We are required to believe that the name comes from a shortening of the address 'Newcastle, West Limerick'. It is the county's largest town outside Limerick itself. Here are remains, partly incorporated in a more recent building, of a large, mainly fifteenth-century Desmond castle. Two halls, a circular keep, a tower-house, and part of the curtain wall survive. Two Desmond earls, the third – sometimes described as the fourth, known as magician, mathematician and poet – and eighth, died here. The castle was granted at the plantation of Munster, in 1591, to Sir William Courtenay (whose second wife was Francis Drake's widow), ancestor of the Earls of Devon, who continued to own much of the town well into the nineteenth century. In 1641 it was besieged and taken by Confederate Catholics, who burned it.

The R522 southward takes us to Drumcolligher, whence the R515 leads us eastward, with the Ballyhoura Mountains ahead, to **Rathluirc**, previously known as Charleville, which name it was given by the Great Earl of Cork's son, Lord Broghill, in honour of Charles II. It was here in 1922 that Frank O'Connor, unsoldierly recruit to the Republican forces in the Civil War, was captured for the first time. He and his comrades were arrested and lodged in a farmhouse. But captivity was short-lived. A Republican armoured car moved up and battered the house with shells. Captors and captives changed roles, with much waving of white handkerchiefs, and O'Connor was preserved for more confused campaigning. Eamon de Valera, whose uncompromising, pious and reactionary policies helped mould early independent Ireland, began his education at Rathluirc's Christian Brothers' college. He had been born in 1882 at Bruree, six miles north, son of a local woman and a Spaniard from New York. His birthplace can be visited on application and the schoolhouse he attended there is now a museum dedicated to him.

From Rathluirc we move south along the Buttevant road but turn off left after four miles to go along the north side of the mountains. At Ardpatrick, where there are a few remains of an early monastery, we can turn right to glimpse, after three miles, the demesne of **Castle Oliver**. The eighteenth-century house and the landscaping done by Silver Oliver, MP and High Sheriff, using the bosky mountainside and innumerable artificial streams and waterfalls to achieve a fashionable 'picturesque' effect, was found by Arthur Young to be 'in an exceedingly good taste'. The house was rebuilt in impressive Scottish baronial style later, but the memory of Marie Gilbert, born here in 1818, lives on under the assumed name of Lola Montez. Her dancing won her a world reputation on the stages of London, St Petersburg, Warsaw, Berlin and Paris – and the title Countess of Landsfeld, given her by Ludwig I of Bavaria, whose mistress she was until the 1848 revolution.

Above the house rises the highest peak of the Ballyhoura range, Mount Seefin, on which Oisin (pronounced Usheen), son of Finn MacCool, is supposed to be buried. Oisin was the quiet one of the Finn cycle. A poet (long after, James Macpherson created what he claimed to be Oisin's poetry in his Ossianic forgeries), he fell in love with the Princess Niamh, who carried him over the sea to the Land of Youth, set in the western sea. He stayed there what seemed to him three years but was in reality three hundred, so pleasantly did the time pass. When he returned, Finn and the companions of his youth were gone, the country peopled by a race that was mean and diminutive compared with his heroic contemporaries. Christianity had arrived, and he spent long hours arguing the merits of the pagan life with St Patrick. He died unrepentant but, like Virgil, was made by Christians the epitome of pagan virtue, lacking only the grace that Christianity is said to give.

Kilmallock lies seven miles north-north-west. Its remains – two of the old town gates, a solitary tower of King's Castle, the fifteenth-century church of Saints Peter and Paul, and the beautiful ruins of the thirteenth-century Dominican friary beside the river – tell little of its past history or appearance, described in the eighteenth century as 'a greater show of magnificence than any other town in the Kingdom'. Originally it was the creation of the FitzGibbon family, the White Knights. These came to an end with the twelfth of the line, who betrayed the Sugan Earl of Desmond in his cave sanctuary at Mitchelstown, fifteen miles south-east. His memorial is in the Dominican friary which, founded in 1291, expanded during the next two centuries. During his lifetime Kilmallock had risen to its highest importance, with massive walls, four gates and castles, and a crop of gabled fortified houses. Then with the revolt of the fifteenth earl in 1579 it attracted the batteries of the English and was partly burned. But it recovered. Here the rebel earl's son was brought from imprisonment in the Tower, Elizabeth thinking to attract the loyalty of the people away from the rebellious Sugan Earl, his cousin. For a day the plan worked – he was lavishly received by the townsfolk. Next day he went to church, the Protestant Church, and the people turned against him for his heresy. In desperation the English, when they captured the Sugan Earl in 1600, brought him here and at swordpoint in the church forced him to swear allegiance to the queen. He was then lodged in the Tower till his death in 1608. The town suffered badly in the Confederate War of 1641 and steadily declined, though it could still, in the eighteenth century, be called 'the Baalbek of Ireland'. Since then much of what remained has been broken up for new buildings. A mile to the south-west, in the demesne of Gothic Ash Hill Towers, the Republican army of 1922 had its temporary front-line headquarters. The house was built, with its deep stable court before a three-storeyed main block, with round, battlemented corner-towers (now gone) in 1781. There is good plasterwork inside. The rear façade was reconstructed in the early nineteenth century by the Pain brothers in fashionable Gothic style.

Hospital, eleven miles north-east, was one of John Betjeman's favourite towns in Ireland – simply for its name. (On the subject of names, that of 'Black and Tans' came from the nickname of a nearby pack of foxhounds, the Scarteen, five miles south-east.) The village's name actually came from the Knights Hospitaller, who owned it from 1215, and it preserves a thirteenth-century church in which are some interesting old De Marisco memorials. West of the town rises the hill of Knockainy (537 feet), otherworld seat of Aine or Anu, a Munster goddess of prosperity and abundance. It was she who gave its scent to the meadowsweet. Up to the last century this deity, always friendly to men (and sometimes more than friendly, as many claims of descent from her – including that of the fourth Earl of Desmond – testify) was propitiated here by a magic ritual on St John's eve. Villagers would carry bunches of burning hay on poles to the top of the hill, then disperse among the fields waving the torches over cattle and crops. Her putative son, Earl Gerald, was received into the fairy world after his death, and taken to Lough Gur, which he still circles on horseback every seventh year. It is not, however, for a sight of the earl that we move now to the Lough, a few miles north-west, but to see the centre of an area richer than most in prehistoric remains.

Lough Gur is county Limerick's only lake, set among limestone hills. Drainage in the nineteenth century greatly reduced its size, for the two ruined castles beside it used to be on islands. Drainage also exposed some remains of crannogs, or lake-dwellings of prehistoric times. (These artificial islands were made by piling up peat, faggots, timber and stones inside a ring of stones or stakes. They sometimes continued in use till the Middle Ages.) This is among the places where people first tilled the soil of Ireland between 3000 BC and 2000 BC – choosing the area thickest with elm trees in the knowledge, perhaps, that this would make the richest soil. Their skills were numerous – they kept cattle, sheep and pigs, spun cloth, hunted birds, adorned themselves, felled trees and in their place planted cereals. They also made axes, some to be sent as far as southern England. Of their elaborate burial methods numerous remains are in the hills around – stone circles, cairns, ring-forts, standing stones, megalithic tombs – and even though they do not compare with possibly contemporary structures in the Boyne Valley, they do constitute one of the most important archaeological sites in Ireland. The country's largest stone circle is at **Grange**, between the lake and the Kilmallock–Limerick road. A hundred boulders form a circle more than fifty yards in diameter. There are altogether twenty-eight monuments under state care, and innumerable more that are not. Various exhibitions, explanations, amenities and a shop have been provided at the north-western corner of the lake. All the same the irregular profusion of humps and tumps and rocky outcrops rising from the bog is fascinating in itself; and there are other treasures, like the spiny-flowered golden dock, hardly found elsewhere in Ireland, and the rare hornwort growing in the lake. The neighbouring bogs have yielded many remains of the so-called Irish elk, or great deer, a close but giant relation of the fallow deer. This it seems lived and died – and attained bigger dimensions in Ireland than anywhere else – before the bogs were formed, for its remains always underlie the bog. It may have died out before men reached the country. Splendid specimens are in the Natural History Museum in Dublin and elsewhere. On May Day the magician third earl of Desmond rises from his watery grave in full armour and gallops over the surface of the lake on his silver-shod horse. He will be relieved of this duty only when this annual or in some accounts septennial ride has worn down the horse's shoes. From Lough Gur, the R512 leads twelve miles back to Limerick.

Lower Shannon

Ardnacrusha Power Station, three miles north of Limerick, was constructed in 1925 as the first major step in developing the country's natural resources after independence. A German firm, Siemens, was brought in to do the work, a step which provoked some anger among Unionists, with their English loyalties. The scheme transformed the Lower Shannon between Limerick and Lough Derg, and indirectly all the rest of the river. In the sixteen-mile stretch between Killaloe and Limerick the river used to fall, by a series of weirs and rapids, a total of 100 feet. To harness the potential electric power a canal was built from O'Brien's Bridge to a loop in the river north of Limerick; a weir was made just below the canal intake to control flow to the river and create a reservoir; and a power station was built at Ardnacrusha to convert the single 100-foot fall of water which had now been contrived beside it. The result is that turbines of over 38,000 horsepower are now driven by the water. A side effect of the removal of 252 million cubic feet of earth and 39 million cubic feet of rock has been the flooding of a large area of the valley below Killaloe. Navigation there is now an expert business because of church towers and gables lurking under the surface. Ardnacrusha can be seen by the public by previous arrangement, and our drive to Killaloe brings us close to the newly shaped river at several points of its western bank.

Killaloe is a pretty town in a pretty situation, with Slieve Bernagh rising steeply behind it and the neck of Lough Derg bending away to its north. Much of its energy is devoted to tourism and aquatic activities on the lake. St Molua, or Lua – whence Killaloe, the church of Lua – founded a church here about 600. Nothing of him is known, but a stone oratory he is supposed to have built stood till recently on Friar's Island, a place of pilgrimage below the town until in 1929 the Shannon Scheme flooding made the building's removal necessary, stone by stone. It is now beside the Catholic church. (Submerged along with Friar's Island are the hoof-marks on rock which were made by St Patrick's horse as, helping his master escape from pursuing pagan enemies, it leaped about two hundred yards across the river.) The Church of Ireland cathedral occupies the site of Molua's successor St Flannan's monastery. A pleasant light church, it contains a good Romanesque doorway, blocked off now in the south wall, and said to have been the entrance to King Murchad O'Brien's tomb of 1120, round which the first cathedral was built about 1185. It also has a bilingual stone with ogham and runic inscriptions, a rare combination, which may be a memorial to a Danish convert. In the churchyard is St Flannan's Oratory, which is the nave of a Romanesque church, containing some early gravestones and sculptures. Nobody knows for sure where the Palace of Kincora, Brian Boru's stronghold, stood, though it was in or near Killaloe. Claims are made for the easily defended site of the Catholic church, and for the neighbourhood of Beal Boru, an early ring-fort on the lake's west bank a mile and a half north of Killaloe. A rectangular timber house with a central hearth was discovered in a 1961 excavation. It was in this region, living 'in the wild huts of the desert, and on the hard knotty wet roots', that Brian and his brother Mahon and their people, the Dalcassians, who occupied about half modern Clare, began the expulsion of the Norse, killing them progressively 'in twos and threes, and in fives and scores and in hundreds', before moving on to the national scene.

For a few miles north of Killaloe the shore road keeps close to the water, then breaks away to return on the north side of Scariff Bay. The scenery along this road, especially on the southern half of the lake, is magnificent, but there are sights which can only be seen from the water (cruises operate from Killaloe and Portumna). One of these, **Holy Island** in Scariff Bay, has on it extensive remains of a monastery originally founded by St Caimin in the seventh century, destroyed by the Norse and rebuilt on the orders of Brian Boru. The pattern associated with it till the 1830s – a religious festival, in which pilgrims seek indulgences – was one of the longest in the country, beginning with seven circuits of the edge of the island (about seven miles) and continuing with visits to the main sites, each of which was circled seven times, ending with the well, from which water was drunk. It was suppressed, like several others, allegedly because of the fighting and fornication that came to be connected with it. The remains include a Round Tower and several ancient churches. The largest island of the lake, Illaunmore, also has a few church remains, and it comes into view if we follow any of the lanes leading to the water from the main road after Mountshannon. One of these lanes leads to Williamstown, scene of an ugly episode in the Civil War when the Republicans landed, burned the house, took four Irish Free Staters prisoners to the bridge at Killaloe and there shot them.

The novelist Edna O'Brien was born at Drewsborough House, just north of Tuamgraney, a mile or so south of Scarriff. Five miles west of Scarriff by the R461 is **Feakle**, where Brian Merriman, author of *The Midnight Court*, was farmer and hedge-school teacher towards the end of the eighteenth century. The poem is a cheeky but far from obscene skit, still in print, on the reputed indifference of Irishmen to the pleasures of sex. As we return to the lakeside and go north the scene gets less dramatic with the levelling out of the mountains into Ireland's vast central plain. But there is interest, not least natural, for the shores abound in rare plants that include *Inula salicina*, willow-leaved Inula, a fen-plant a bit like a small sunflower, found nowhere else in these islands (flowers July–August); *Lathyrus palustris*, marsh pea (June–August), with pale purple flowers; *Teucrium scordium*, water germander (July–September), with its mauve flower – both these last in the soggy parts of the bog – and several others.

Portumna, at the head of the lake, is a pleasant, prosperous market town, grown because of its bridge across a river which often unbridgeably separates west from east. Boat tours of the lake and river can be arranged here. The vast demesne of Portumna Castle, now a forest park with the obligatory golf-course but also extensive woods sheltering deer and other wildlife, lies at the west end of the broad main street. The semi-fortified 1618 house whose ruins, under a rim of battlements and rounded, pinnacled gables, loom over the lake, was built by Burkes who had once been lords of the whole province of Connacht. Ulick Burke in the time of Henry VIII accepted the king as overlord, gave up his old ways – including the piling of heads of beaten enemies into mounds and covering them with earth – and was made earl of Clanricarde. The family tended to support the sovereign thereafter: the wrong one in the case of James II, but a switch to the Church of Ireland in 1699 put them back into line. The house, thought by Mark Bence-Jones to be probably the finest of its period, was accidentally burned in 1826 and has remained a shell ever since. A Gothic replacement was built at the other end of the park in 1862. This was burned in 1922. Meanwhile, the fifteenth earl, also second marquess, earned himself a bad name. Succeeding in 1874, he never visited his 56,000 acre estate here, preferring rooms in Albany, Piccadilly, where he was noted for his ragged clothes and solitary habits. Nevertheless, he opposed all the government's land reforms, and when tenants withheld their rents in 1886 evicted 186 of them, replacing them by what were called 'emergency men'. Some of these, along with the agent, were murdered. Police and military moved in. Clanricarde remained absent and unrepentant till his death in 1916, when both titles were extinguished. The second house was burned down in 1922. Seven years later, Lord Harewood, who as great nephew had inherited the property, and his wife, the Princess Royal, arrived to restore it. But they found the stable deliberately burned when they came, and felt perhaps that Ireland at the time was no place for English blood with a royal ingredient. The state took over the property in 1948. The ruin is a ruin still.

We drive down the east side of the lough, keeping always near the water. The best views come later on, seen from raised ground, where the Arra Mountains and Slieve Bernagh approach each other, and create the lake by constricting the water-flow. (The mountains are hard red sandstone; limestone has worn away to make the passage and the lough's bed, whose irregularity is caused by this limestone's continued decomposition by water.) The lake's latent powers, now exploited by the Ardnacrusha scheme, were seen over a century ago by a scientist who noted that its level could rise a couple of inches in a day and had been known to rise a foot. A foot would mean 36 million tons of water acquired in a single day – and an average winter would bring 400 million tons.

Terryglass, a pretty lakeside village with ruined abbey and castle (on private ground) can be our first stopping-point. Founded soon after Patrick's time by one of the many St Colums, the abbey became a centre of learning and produced, about 1150, the *Book of Leinster*, now in Trinity College, Dublin, an important collection of history tales and poems in Middle Irish including the saga of the *Brown Bull of Cooley*. A few years later the abbey was the victim of an attack by Galway Irish, and the monks left it for ever, taking their possessions to Lorrha, four miles north-east – and still rich in medieval and later remains. From the keep of Terryglass's Norman castle, probably built by Butlers, the last of the O'Kennedys, local chiefs, was thrown to his death in the water below. Before, and for many years after this, a banshee wailed and waved her arms on the battlements. The Catholic church contains what is said to be a fragment of the True Cross.

On the right two miles on is Drominagh House, and the castle of the same name on the foreshore. The high hill in view miles to the left is Knockshigowna, 689 feet high, the otherworld seat of the Munster fairies. In the ensuing miles we pass castles whose history is lost, and see the dark range of the Slieve Aughty, the lake looking like a pretty fjord where Ree, a few miles above, seems a bleak ocean; Illaunmore, with its fragmentary monastic remains and large new houses of managing directors able to persuade the Land Commission they are not defacing the scenery; the fishing, boating and snipe-shooting resort of Dromineer with its O'Kennedy castle and church; and **Garrykennedy** with its old harbour and ivy-covered ruin and twenty white-washed cottages and bar.

Ahead, the Arra Mountains rise steeply and soon we pass – quite close if we take the mountain road – **Tountinna**, the highest of them (1,517 feet), with the Graves of the Leinster Men north-east of its summit. The earthworks themselves are Bronze Age chamber tombs – a series of slate slabs – but the place is central to an earlier and a later legend. The first tells how Cesair, great-granddaughter of Noah, came to Ireland – being a place where no sin had been committed since nobody had yet lived here – to avoid the impending flood. She brought with her three men and fifty women. 'In spite of her, for a woman, commendable astuteness', says Giraldus Cambrensis, she failed to escape disaster. One of the men died, and Fintan, of the two survivors, tired doubtless of an unending round of masculine duty, fled to Tountinna. The peak escaped the flood and all the others were drowned, but Fintan was soon joined by other refugees and the race's future assured. Then in Brian Boru's time the King of Leinster, lured hither by Boru's wife's promise of her daughter in marriage, was killed in an ambush prepared by her. Boru, furious, beat his wife, who ran away to the Danes to cause him more mischief. From a distance the mountain, like many in Ireland, looks as if it would be nice to slide down. Good views of Killaloe come into sight and we descend on the small village of Ballina, opposite the town, then continue southwards keeping close to the river bank. Castleconnell has no reason to thank the Shannon Scheme, for it used to be internationally famous for its salmon fishing (salmon do in fact still inhabit the river and a jump has been built for them at the new weir) and for the nearby Doonass falls and rapids, which re-routing the current and flooding have deprived of their force. In the eighteenth century the place was also known as a spa with a medicinal sulphur well. From here to Limerick several historic demesnes lie between road and river. Ruined Hermitage is the first, in a wooded demesne that was formerly Lord Massy's. **Mount Shannon** used to be the home of the Earls of Clare. Its fine Georgian house was enlarged by John Fitzgibbon, then converted to classical style and given its huge pedimented portico by his son. The father was Attorney-General and Lord Chancellor in the Parliament before Union and later became first earl. A vigorous reactionary, he largely engineered the Parliament of 1799 into voting itself out of existence for the sake of complete union with Britain. He was known as 'Black Jack'. The house was burned down in 1922. The return to Limerick is five miles along the main road.

12

Clare and South Galway

C OUNTY CLARE IS a peninsula on the grand scale, cut off on three of its four sides by Lough Derg, the Shannon estuary, and the Atlantic. It is linked with the rest of Munster by only half a dozen bridges, all of which are in the neighbourhood of Limerick and Killaloe. In many ways it seems more a part of Connacht (in ancient times it was) to which it is joined along forty miles of its north side. It has much of the bleak ruggedness of its northern neighbours, and its population is thinly scattered. But in truth it fits no pattern. It is too mutable for that. Its eastern half is mountainy, with old red sandstone poking through a worn mantle of limestone. The county's centre, north to south, is all carboniferous limestone, lower, middle and upper, the middle providing a connected tangle of turloughs: basins of porous limestone that can fill with water and be drained dry in a night and never allow plants to creep far down their dry banks without welling up again and submerging them. The north of the county consists of the Burren, a unique desert of huge limestone slabs, with floral rarities that have botanists at critical times swarming all over it. Towards the coastal west, beyond a broad bed of coal, the county subsides in a featureless plain of weathered millstone grit, an underlay often associated with gloomy landscape. Inland, by and large, Clare is not a county that photographs well. Its coast can be spectacular, though, and none of it is short of interest. The county is famous for music-making, in pubs and the like. It has nourished and cherished many effective patriots. O'Connell and de Valera both represented Clare in parliament.

Cut off as it was, Clare stayed poor. Till well into the twentieth century most of the inhabitants had seen neither car nor train. They used the swing-plough, cut meadows with scythes and corn with sickles and spoke Irish universally, as they had done for centuries. Much of the soil is poor. The ruthless felling of trees, which happened periodically from the arrival of mesolithic man to Cromwellian times and after, created bog where there had been pasture. Atlantic gales have never allowed trees to grow in the western part of the county. A visitor used to farms in Leinster or lowland England or America may still marvel at the midget stone-bordered fields.

But none of this is apparent as we enter the county. Cromwell's agents reserved a five-mile strip round the coast for Protestant settlers. In the event, they claimed only about one mile's width and kept to the Shannon estuary. The result is a much richer look on the southern edge of the county; and between Limerick and Ennis – a busy thoroughfare – the estates are richest of all. The creation of Shannon Airport in 1947 shot wealth into the region, brought by employment and tourists who were offered entertaining package deals for their one-, two- or three-day stops. Nine miles from Limerick on the main Ennis road we reach the best-known ingredient of these tours, **Bunratty Castle**. The building that survives in part was fifteenth-century work, and may have started as O'Brien property. It was so grand for its time that the Papal Nuncio Rinuccini, arriving to bolster the Catholics in the civil war of the 1640s, could write home, 'In Italy there is nothing like the palace and grounds of the Lord Thomond'; but the war finished it, the massive keep and little else remaining. After the Second World War it was well restored, beautifully furnished with pieces from the fifteenth and sixteenth centuries, opened to the public and given by its owner Lord Gort to the nation, for whom it has since been held in trust. It is also used in the evenings for old-time banquets, based as nearly on medieval conventions as today's jet travellers would happily countenance.

Beside the castle is the Bunratty Folk Park, a fascinating reconstruction of several traditional kinds of Irish cottage and cabin with authentic trimmings. 'Traditional Irish Nights' are held here, in which simple food is followed by folk dances, singing and story-telling. A daytime visit is more informative, giving an intriguing glance at a way of life that has only recently quite disappeared. R.A.S. Macalister, one of the greatest Irish archaeologists, wrote in the 1920s that Ireland 'has rendered to Anthropology the unique, inestimable, indispensable service of carrying a primitive European *Precivilisation* down into late historic times and there holding it up for observation and instruction'. Modern Ireland has let go of this legacy, but the folk park still manages to employ mature women who greet visitors to the cottage interiors, tend the peat fire and talk, if asked, with authority, warmth and charm, about the vanished way of life in which they grew up, the barefoot walks to school, the punitive removals to the Board school in Limerick, the closeness of America, the monotony of food and endlessness of work.

Four miles north-east, at Sixmilebridge, is **Mount Ievers**, an enchanting and graceful early-eighteenth-century mansion, like a doll's house, the height of its three storeys accentuated by the fact that each is slightly narrower than the one below. Bricks for one façade (the other is of stone) were shipped from the Netherlands. Unfortunately the house has shut its doors to the public.

Keeping to the R462, on which Sixmilebridge is situated, we continue north and after three miles fork left in the Quin direction. The second right turn after the fork brings us to **Craggaunowen**, where, around a fortified sixteenth-century house, is set an intriguing exhibition of replicas of prehistoric dwellings and other structures, including a Bronze Age crannog set in the lake and a ring-fort. The leather boat, or curragh, used by the adventurous author Tim Severin in 1976 and 1977 to follow what he believed to be St Brendan the Navigator's Atlantic route is preserved here. There are smaller exhibits in the house. The development was the work of John Hunt, donor to Limerick City of the Hunt Collection. From here the road to Quin takes us on through the lake-spattered plain past **Knappogue**, a medieval tower extended by a low castellated Victorian Gothic range. This is highly commercialised, aims at Shannon coach-trippers, and like Bunratty provides what are called medieval banquets in the evenings. **Quin Abbey** is one of the best-preserved Franciscan friaries in Ireland, built early in the fifteenth century (within the four walls of a De Clare castle of 1280) and in use from then till the early nineteenth century, in spite of the suppression of the order in 1541. The last friar died in 1820 and was buried in the north-east corner of the cloister. Good views of surrounding castles are to be had from the slender tower which tapers beautifully in four stages, a characteristic device of Irish building. About fifty of the castles hereabouts were the property of the Macnamaras, including nearby Danganbrack.

About three miles south of Quin and across the Ennis–Limerick railway (during the construction of which in 1854 several hundred prehistoric gold objects were unearthed) is **Dromoland Castle**, and its lovely sweeping demesne. Till 1962 this attractive Gothic pile, by James Pain, was the home of Sir Donough Edward Foster O'Brien, Baron Inchiquin, The O'Brien of Thomond, a direct descendant of Brian Boru and one of many O'Briens still owning land in the old Thomond kingdom. It is now a luxury hotel, with old masters in the public rooms. Old masters in a different sense, the O'Briens keep now to a house on the estate. From here the N18 runs north to Ennis, passing on the right, a mile before the town, the lovely 1195 Augustinian friary of Clare Castle.

Ennis itself is Clare's county town, beside the river Fergus and with a population around 16,000. Remote from the great central axis of Irish life and power, it nevertheless looms large in political history. It was here that Parnell made the masterly speech that introduced boycotting to the land struggle – 'by isolating him [the evictor] from his kind as if he were a leper of old, you must show him your detestation of the crime he had committed' – a speech that helped Gladstone to put Parnell temporarily away in gaol. Here, Eamonn de Valera made many speeches, for Clare was the county that kept him in power through all his years as a member of the Dáil, 1917 to 1959, and which O'Connell also represented for some years. Huddles of shops in alleys and covered-in arcades and narrow streets give the place character. But there is not so much of abiding importance in the town – some good Georgian houses, a decent courthouse of 1854, a statue of O'Connell in unlikely Roman costume, scant ruins of a Franciscan friary with two interesting tombs beside the bridge (it was with the friary, founded in the thirteenth century under O'Brien patronage, that Ennis had its beginnings), a nineteenth-century Catholic pro-cathedral, and, over the river, in what was (when it was needed) a Presbyterian chapel, the De Valera Museum and Library. In 1800 Harriet Smithson was born in Ennis, to a theatre manager and his wife. She became an actress, had success in London and Paris, married Berlioz, became ill and so shrewish he left her, and died in Paris after some years spent paralysed and poor. There is a memorial in the pro-cathedral to her childhood guardian Father James Barrett.

We are on the brink of fine country, the best of it to the west and north. We can hurry first round the south-western corner, which is worth the drive, and for those looking for beaches, resorts and pretty countryside and views a good area to stay in. Three miles out of the town, on the left of the coast-road, the R473, is Francis Bindon's New Hall, a good red-brick, bow-fronted house of 1745, in whose grounds is the ruined Augustinian nunnery of **Killone**, beautifully sited by a lake. Founded by Donal O'Brien around 1190, it was for years ruled by his granddaughter Slaney. It preserves good Romanesque east windows and, below the chancel, a vaulted crypt. Farther on, the estuary of the Fergus comes into view, spotted with islands, on many of which are monastic remains. Beyond Killadysert the road bends gradually right and passes through Labasheeda, Knock and Killimer, from which a regular car ferry carries traffic over the Shannon to Tarbert in Limerick. On the beach at Money Point, a mile west, where now a coal-fired power station generates electricity, the rock-weighted, drowned body of sixteen-year-old Ellen or Eily Hanley, the real 'Colleen Bawn' (or 'white maiden'), was washed up in 1819. She was buried in Killimer churchyard. Regretting his secret marriage to a girl socially below him, and dreading the shame of introducing her to his parents, it seems that John Scanlon, from Ballycahane House near Croom, took her out on a boat and drowned her, or had a servant do it for him. It was assumed at his trial that because of his background, and hers, and since Daniel O'Connell defended him, he would be acquitted, but he was publicly hanged, as was the servant, caught later. The story was made famous by Gerald Griffin's novel, a play and an opera.

Kilrush, five miles farther on, is the largest town of this corner of Clare, with a new marina for sailing and fishing boats. Just over the water, and reached by boat from Cappagh Pier – a mile away by road, or by the creek south-west of the town – is **Scattery Island**, on which stand remains of the principal monastery founded by St Senan in the early sixth century. Senan was, like many of his holy colleagues, a misogynist (St Brendan thrashed a girl who wanted 'to play her game' with him; St Kevin threw his succubus into the lake at Glendalough), and sternly exiled the virgin Canair who tried to follow him to Scattery, though Tom Moore thought he might, given time, have yielded to persuasion. Right on the path of the intruding Danes, the monastery suffered in the ninth and tenth centuries, but it grew rich in medieval times. The island is dotted with church ruins, some as early as the ninth century. Most impressive is the Angel's Church on the island's summit, incorporating vast undressed boulders in its lower walls.

On a fine day the humped promontory of Dingle to the south-west comes into view on the final westward stretch of the road to Loop Head. The main road inland is a dull one, through a flat, treeless region of peat bog and rushy swamps. The coastal lane is much better, and brings us to **Carrigaholt**, where there is a college of Irish language and an O'Brien (and before them MacMahon) castle, recently restored. Here the last O'Brien Viscount Clare to live in Ireland drilled his Dragoons to save his country for James II; and, having lost, set sail with his troops – one of Sarsfield's Wild Geese – to win renown in the Irish brigades of the French army, a tradition continued by successive Viscounts Clare and Counts of Thomond.

The last lap to **Loop Head** must be covered by the inland road. The view from the Head itself, a plateau of sea-pink enclosed by steep 200-foot cliffs, takes in a vast circuit – MacGillicuddy's Reeks to the south, with Kerry Head near at hand and Dingle's Mount Brandon beyond, and to the north the Aran Islands, and the Twelve Bens of Connemara. From here to Kilkee it is possible to walk, keeping more or less to the cliff-top, for fifteen miles along a varied, indented coast-line with strange rock forms to entertain along the way. Ross Bridges, three miles up the coast, are the most spectacular of these, but just before the turn to these the village church of **Moneen** preserves an interesting relic of the campaign of 'souperism', in which many Prot-estant groups tried to convert Catholic victims of the Famine with offers of soup. In Penal days the local landlord refused to have a Catholic church on his land. An ark on wheels was constructed and kept on the beach below high-water mark and so legally beyond his clutches. Here an altar was kept and services held. The ark is still preserved in the church.

Twelve miles more brings us to **Kilkee**, a village resort with a good crescent of sandy beach in the arms of a cliff-bordered bay. Here and for several miles northward, interest lies along the coast. A short walk to the west leads to the peculiar outcrop of the Duggerna Rocks, neatly patterned strata of shale with what is called the Amphitheatre beyond them. There are other marine curiosities, odd rock formations and puffing-holes, and the only thing to watch out for is the rising tide, which isolates parts of the shoreline. Kilkee has been known as a resort from Victorian times, and Tennyson came here twice. A good way to see the coastline is by hired boat, in calm weather. In bad weather the coast can be a great danger to shipping, and there have been several disastrous wrecks in the vicinity.

From here we pass on north-east, keeping as near to the coastline, which becomes more beautiful, as the roads allow. Several side lanes lead down to broad sandy beaches. Spanish Point, about twenty miles beyond Kilkee, recalls the many Armada vessels wrecked along this shore. Most of the Spaniards who survived the wrecks – at Mutton Island to the south-west a thousand men are supposed to have gone down – were caught and executed by Turlough O'Brien on the orders of Sir Richard Bingham, Elizabeth's unscrupulous Governor of Connacht. Indeed the only vessels which can possibly cope with the elements on this part of the coast are curraghs, which require great skill in those who sail them in pursuit of fish or, in the past, of articles to smuggle into the country. In the eighteenth century smuggling was the major source of welfare to the inhabitants. About four-fifths of Irish sheep fleeces, it was thought, were carried to France in exchange for wine, spirits, tobacco, tea and fabrics. The caves that pit the coast provided useful warehouses for this contraband, and many land-owners who took the goods in place of rent were happy to turn a blind eye on their provenance. Much the same sort of curraghs were used as those seen beside the sea now, securely tethered against the winds that could easily lift the weight of wood and tarred canvas they consist of. Farther north these tender vessels have been often used for catching the basking shark, a fish – not a man-eater – of up to forty feet in length whose liver alone can fill seven or eight barrels.

We round Liscannor Bay and enter a region where in spite of human incursions nature predominates. In the curve of the bay are some small villages – Lahinch, a resort with a mile-long beach and one of Ireland's best golf-courses, and Liscannor, where John Holland (1841–1914), inventor of the submarine, was born. (The inspiration for his work, carried out in New Jersey, was the hope that an American navy might one day be able to sink British warships.) The ruinous, early-nineteenth-century Gothick Birchfield House, with its rather Moorish features, was the home of Cornelius O'Brien, MP, who laid out the walk above the Moher Cliffs – they being, it was said, the only local feature that he did not build himself. He also prompted his tenants to erect and pay for the urn-topped column half a mile north-west, complete with its fulsome engraved tribute. As we continue west, then bend north with the coast, the road rises and the inland hills appear more varied. But the great drama is on the seaward side. The **Cliffs of Moher** are one of the grandest natural sights in Ireland: a series of jutting headlands, stretching in all along about five miles, with sheer and clearly strati-fied faces dropping to the constant slick of spume edging the Atlantic at their feet. At the southern end, the view, of the cliffs themselves and over the Aran Islands to Connemara, is magnificent. A tower built as a tea-house by Cornelius O'Brien is restored now, as misplaced as the mock-Tudor cafe that stood beside Stonehenge years ago. Below, the layers of sandstone topped by a bed of dark shale curve out here and there to spindly stacks, some as high as two hundred feet, living out their last centuries against the Atlantic onslaught. The best views (if we have to exclude those from the sea itself) both of cliffs and sea-birds are to be had from O'Brien's Tower, though the cliffs rise to their highest point of 668 feet at the northern end, and a walk taken from either, the Doolin or the

Liscannor end, protected from the drop by a fence of tombstone-like slabs, is well rewarded.

Doolin, four miles north, is a charming fishing village internationally known for the folk music played in its pubs. Augustus John stayed in a cottage here, belonging to his friend Francis Macnamara whose daughter Caitlin, later Dylan Thomas's wife, was brought up in the family home, now a hotel, at Ennistimon. The party called down priestly wrath by bathing naked. Black and Tans later burned the cottage down. The ferry to the Aran Islands leaves from the quay at Fisherstreet, down the lane. From Doolin the main road, R478, runs inland to Lisdoonvarna. This southern part of the Burren is dismal country, based on millstone grit and coal measures, thought dismal, too, by prehistoric folk, who consigned their remains to the limestone uplands to the north. But **Lisdoonvarna's** fame rests on the more recent (eighteenth-century) discovery of curative, if repellent, sulphurated waters flowing from the surrounding heights. These are alleged to combine with altitude, the heat caused by sun hitting the bare limestone to the north, and the moisture brought from the Atlantic, to bring relief to sufferers from rheumatism and related maladies. But the place's benefits are not confined to the sick. It long ago became a tradition for local bachelor farmers to book into the hotels at the end of the harvest for a period of relaxation. Unmarried girls moved in, too, attended by their mothers or other guardians, and matches were made. Match-makers were professionals during the nineteenth and earlier centuries – some later – and always did good business at fairs and gatherings. Their main function was diplomatic, reconciling the conflicting interests of two families, but they needed also to be able to read and draw up a contract. The September throng has possibly increased rather than diminished in recent years due to a dramatic addition of city dwellers and, so they say, American women in search of spouses. The beneficent effects of the town's waters, moreover, are more sought after than ever.

North and north-east of the town lies the Burren. Lisdoonvarna with its many hotels is a good base. **The Burren** can seem monotonous at first casual sighting: a high (several plateaux of 1,000 feet and more) expanse of grey limestone pavements with gently sloping sides and a few valleys, bounded by Galway Bay to the north and the Atlantic to the west. Many speak of a lunar likeness. It put Augustus John in mind of 'an immobilised rough sea'. Shaw wrote of 'a region of stone-capped hills and granite fields' – he was wrong about the rock, of course. 'Desolate country' was Thackeray's verdict; and it is true that over most of the Burren there are no trees, no soil, no obvious water – 'savage land', Cromwell's surveyors told him, 'yielding neither water enough to drown a man, nor a tree to hang him, nor soil enough to bury'. A closer look across the whole area shows limestone, the shape-changing conjuror of our geological constituents, at its creative acme, forging, besides the clints – the flat pavements – and grikes – the deep cracks at the joints of these – an exciting statuary of gorges, caves, tunnels, channels, pillars, rock gruyeres, benches and tables. Within the clefts, chinks and runnels, and sometimes spreading thickly over the flat surfaces where some slight but sufficient patina of soil has settled, there is not simply a varied flora but one that is highly unusual and yet, locally, strong and teeming. It includes both alpine plants more often thriving in more northerly latitudes or high on mountainsides, and alongside them Mediterranean plants whose needs are generally reckoned quite different.

How all this comes about is by no means clear, but somehow a combination of the Burren's evolution, thin peat, a climate kept frost-less by very moist sea-winds, and most effective drainage through the porous limestone has brought about this cosmopolitan floral society. There are the little Spring Gentians with intense blue five-petalled flowers in spring and early summer; or, among the twenty-two separate species of orchid found here, the Irish Close-flowered Orchid, with its light pink flowers that are never fully open, another spring bloom often thought the Burren's main treasure; Hoary Rockrose, a dwarf with bright yellow flowers found in early summer; purple-berried Burnet Rose; Vernal Sandwort with narrow leaves and five white petals, a later summer flower; Dark-red Helleborine, a midsummer orchid with small elliptical leaves and a white-ringed red flower; the tall (up to three feet) Shrubby Cinquefoil with bright yellow flowers, blooming both in June and August; Bloody Cranes-bill; Mountain Avens; Bearberry and several unusual Saxifrages. Maidenhair Fern with its fan-shaped leaflets is common, too, in the vertical fissures. The range of many of these plants stretches far to the north, in some cases through Galway to Mayo. But the Burren sees them at their most varied and profuse. The best time to visit is generally reckoned late May and early June.

Flowers are not the only interest in the Burren. The high clear plateaux have an eerie quality with scattered houses, stony tracks, mazes of grey stone walls, streams and little lakes that come and go with heavy rains, and the rounded hills, some topped by prehistoric cairns. The caves that riddle the rock include, on Slieve Elva's east side, the Polnagollum complex, Ireland's longest known cave system, prized by potholers, which has been surveyed for over seven miles. Many of these caves have been inhabited in the past both by animals and, later, men. Remains found in large quantities have included those of the African wild cat which, till the discovery, was not known to have existed in Europe, and the Arctic lemming, as well as wolves, bears, reindeer and the giant Irish elk. To see all the Burren has to offer, a lengthy stay is necessary. A quick tour should include the whole of the coast road from Lisdoonvarna through Doolin, then northwards, round Black Head to Ballyvaghan. Corkscrew Hill, south of Ballyvaghan, leads to the Burren's centre, and any of the lanes to right or left can be taken for the uplands. Prehistoric remains – galley-graves, portal dolmens, cairns, ring-forts – are abundant in this hinter-land, but their copious survival probably means that nobody has since wanted to pull them down for other building or to make way for the plough.

To the south-east is an area of lakes, or turloughs, many of which empty right out in dry weather as the porous limestone absorbs the water. This lowland region, centring on Corrofin, makes a green and pleasant change from the upland karsts. To reach it from Lisdoon-varna we pass through **Kilfenora**, where there is a Burren Centre aspiring to show the nature of the region's geology and wildlife by means of displays and videos. The western part of the twelfth-century cathedral here serves as Church of Ireland church; the rest is roofless. Early remains include altar-tombs and effigies, and in the churchyard is a superb High Cross engraved with figures of bishops, a two-headed bird and so on. There are four other crosses, much more worn. A mile east the road goes near a vast circular limestone cashel surrounded by a broad *cheval de frise*, a broad strip of up-ended stones to fell assaulting cavalry. After three more miles we pass the haunting, beautifully proportioned ruin of **Leamaneagh Castle**. This consists of a fine four-storey house of 1643 grafted on to a five-storey tower of about 1480. The castle was the home during the Cromwellian campaign of Conor O'Brien, till he was killed in battle. To save it from confiscation, and for her young son, his famously wilful wife Maire Ruadh (said to have hanged erring maidservants by their hair) offered to marry a Cromwellian officer, and an obedient cavalryman, Cooper, was ordered to comply – a situation that came about more than once. She later kicked poor Cooper out of a high window to his death. The son, Sir Donough O'Brien, abandoned the

Companion Guide to Ireland

house to decay and went to live at Dromoland. **Corrofin**, in nice bumpy turlough country, and among innumerable castle ruins of O'Briens and others, is six miles farther on. The Church of Ireland church has become the Clare Heritage Centre. We approach the area again soon (at Lough Cutra) and meanwhile resume our coastal journey at Ballyvaghan.

The eastward road rounds Moneen Mountain and bends left towards the village of Burren. Near the bend, a track leads up to the ruins of the typically sequestered Cistercian abbey of **Corcomroe**, founded about 1180 by that tireless patron of the church, Donal Mor O'Brien, and a century later placed under the rule of Furness Abbey in Lancashire. Dissolved in 1554, the community continued its discreet existence well into the seventeenth century. There are some good effigies, decorated column capitals, lancet windows and grave-stones, many of them of the Burke family, which figures large in the histories of Clare and of Galway, whose border we shall shortly cross. If we continue east on the N67 and turn left a mile before Kinvarra we come to Duras or **Durrus House**, on the west of Kinvarra Bay. Now a youth hostel, this was in the last years of the nineteenth century a shooting-lodge belonging to the affable Count Florimond de Basterot, scion of a noble French family which had fled to Ireland at the Revolution. He kept up literary links with his homeland and possibly brought here de Maupassant, Maurice Barrès and other friends. Here, too, came his Irish guests, Edward Martyn, his cousin from nearby Tulira, and Yeats and Lady Gregory, and it was in the garden that in 1897 the idea of a national theatre – what became the Abbey – was first broached. 'Where, but for that conversation at Florimond de Basterot's,' Yeats mused later, 'had been the genius of Synge?' That idea and others mellowed at Coole, to which we shall come shortly. The ineptly named Celtic Twilight glows bright in this region of Galway, but it is far from being its only theme.

Beyond Kinvarra on the left, a narrow-necked promontory in the bay contains the compact, restored castle of **Dunguaire** (or Dungory), privately owned but open at set times and offering 'medi-eval' banquets. The castle dates to the sixteenth century but is supposedly on the site of seventh-century King Guaire of Connacht's royal palace. A more modern owner was the late Christabel Lady Ampthill, whose divorce case in the 1920s, in which unorthodox use of a sponge in the bath was mooted, suggested she had been blessed with a virgin birth. From Kinvarra a road leads south about seven miles to **Kilmacduagh**. The same King Guaire had a kinsman,

316

Colman MacDuagh, and when Colman was proved by displays of magic to have saintly leanings, the king granted him land to found a monastery, with lovely views across to the Burren hills. The present cathedral ruins are fifteenth century with earlier work incorporated. O'Heyne's Abbey to the north-west contains good thirteenth-century Romanesque work; and there are other remains including a fine 112-foot Round Tower. The saint, however, thought the place too good for him and in old age moved away to Oughtmama near Corcomroe, where he died. Lough Cutra is five miles east, across the main Gort-Ennis road. Half a mile up the west shore of this beautifully wooded lake stands **Lough Cutra Castle**, originally built for the second Lord Gort by the Pain brothers to designs of John Nash, who seems to have based them on his own Wyatt-designed Norris Castle at Cowes, Isle of Wight. This was the start of the Pains' prolific building careers in Ireland. The third Lord Gort, at the time of the Famine, cancelled rents and gave large sums to help the needy, but his generosity ruined him – as it did a number of his class whose virtual extinction meant they had no voice, and were given too little credit, in subsequent historical assessments. The estate was bought by Lord Gough, later field-marshal and the conqueror both of the Chinese in the Opium War and the Sikhs before the annexation of the Punjab. A hundred years later the seventh Lord Gort (who a little later also bought and developed Bunratty) bought the property back and restored it, then sold it on.

Gort, a few miles north along the main road, is an unremarkable town with a broad main street and triangular marketplace, amid flat country. Thackeray, in a bad mood, thought it 'looked as if it wondered how the deuce it got itself in the midst of such a desolate country, and seemed to bore itself there considerably. It had nothing to do and no society.' A very special species of society was on its way. In 1852 Augusta Persse, of a branch of an old Northumberland (Percy) family which had settled in Ireland in Cromwell's time, was born at nearby Roxborough House (on the Loughrea road, but burned down in the Civil War), her family home. When she was twenty-nine she married Sir William Gregory, a diplomat, of **Coole Park**, three miles north of Gort, and with him travelled to London, Italy and India. She had a son by him but he, thirty-five years her senior, died a few years later. As her son grew up she turned her untrained eye to literature, and especially the myth and folklore that were still the currency of the cottages hereabouts. Then she met Yeats and found herself precipitated into the literary activity of the 1890s, partly as a

317

patroness – for she was a wealthy widow – and in part as writer – 'Her literary style', wrote Yeats condescendingly, 'became in my ears the best written by a woman.' She travelled much round the locality collecting folklore for her books and plays in Irish, and Kiltartan, the hamlet almost at her gates, gave its name to the local dialect she reproduced, for which Synge would later be much in her debt. Here at Coole she entertained the cultural stars of the day. Today the house is vanished, but the tree stands where distinguished visitors – Douglas Hyde, Shaw, Yeats, AE, Violet Martin and many others – carved their initials. Yeats himself, who in later years remembered the place 'better than any spot on earth', recalled the art treasures, the Indian artifacts, the signed photographs of Tennyson, Browning, Thackeray, Mark Twain with which it had been crammed. Many of the paintings had been bought in Europe by an eighteenth-century Gregory who, when young, fell in love with a schoolgirl but was debarred from marrying her. He had kept her in a little house on the demesne disguised as a boy till his father died; then they married. The guests were not only literary. Lady Gregory's favourite nephew was Hugh Lane, who often stayed. Here, too, her other nephew, John Shawe-Taylor, (from Castle Taylor, nine miles north, demolished since the war) decided to organise a conference which led directly to Land Purchase (the rights of tenants to buy the land on which they lived, with money lent by the British government). Nowadays the estate, partly given over to forestry, shows no sign of its past activities. Only a few initials on a railed-in copper beech tree recall its greatest years. The house was demolished, for no good reason – a builder wanted the stone – in 1941. 'Here, traveller, scholar, poet, take your stand/When all these rooms and passages are gone', wrote Yeats in 1927. In the refurbished stable block, however, is a visitors' centre with well-arranged displays and films illustrating local wildlife and geology.

Swans on Coole Lough, south-west of what was then the house, inspired Yeats's *The Wild Swans of Coole*.Yeats associations are all around. Four miles east of Coole is a solitary sixteenth-century castle keep, beside a bridge over the river Cloon, amid low woods and slight hills. This is **Thoor Ballylee** (Thoor means tower; added by Yeats to avoid confusion with rambling roomy Ascendancy castles with long drives and deer parks) which Yeats bought for £35 in 1917 and had restored 'for my wife George' around 1920. Their wedding followed speedily his rejection as suitor by Iseult, daughter of Maud Gonne, in a year considered astrologically favourable to his marriage. In 1922 Republicans came at midnight to blow up the bridge beside the tower.

'They forbade us to leave the house,' Yeats wrote, 'but were otherwise polite, even saying at last "Good-night, thank you," as though we had given them the bridge.' The resulting rubble blocked the river and their kitchen flooded to a depth of two feet. When movement was possible, 'Ford cars passed the house from time to time with coffins standing on end between the seats, and sometimes at night we heard an explosion, and once by day saw the smoke made by the burning of a great neighbouring house'. He gave up the place in 1929 but it has been restored as a Yeats Museum. **Tullira Castle**, to the right of the Galway road eight miles north of Gort, was the ancestral home of Edward Martyn, also active in the cultural revival. Signs of his lavish patronage of the arts, especially Catholic church decoration, are evident at nearby Laban and at **Loughrea**, eleven miles east, in both of which are stained glass windows by graduates of Sarah Purser's 'Tower of Glass' – A.E. Childe, Michael Healy, Evie Hone and Sarah Purser herself. St Brendan's Catholic cathedral at Loughrea was Martyn's particular interest, and shows the best results of a movement he and others fostered to raise the standard of Catholic church architecture and ornament. The outside, erected between 1898 and 1903, is workaday. The interior is brilliant. Tullira itself, in a mock-Tudor style that replaced a Georgian house in 1882, was loathed by Yeats – 'those pillars, that stair, and varnished roof with their mechanical ornament, were among the worst inventions of the Gothic Revival', but here he nevertheless, in mystical mood, made his first 'invocation of the moon' and saw in a vision as a reward 'a naked woman of incredible beauty standing upon a pedestal'. Martyn hated the house, too, which his mother had had rebuilt around its central medieval tower by George Ashlin; but he was content to go on living there, among his Impressionists, planning the Catholic artistic renaissance, eating enormously (but only once a day, so thinking himself an ascetic), hating women, worshipping Degas whom he had once known, and arguing whenever possible with his irascible and inventive friend George Moore.

A right turn at Ardrahan leads the nine miles to Craughwell, and the kennels of the Galway Blazers hunt. Four miles north of Craughwell is **Athenry** (Ath-en-rye), once principal seat of the Berminghams and preserving several medieval ruins: patches of the town walls and five towers, the massively forbidding keep of the Bermingham castle of about 1238, with its basement vault carried on three pillars, and graceful ruins of a Dominican priory, with window tracery from two centuries culminating in the fine north transept window. From here the main road west leads straight to Galway city, though a diversion after three miles leads to Clarinbridge, famous for its September Galway Oyster Festival which has opened at Paddy Burke's Inn since 1954. The miles of Galway Bay oyster beds stretch from Oranmore in the north-east corner of the bay all down the east side to Kinvarra.

Two miles south-west of Clarinbridge, on the south bank of the Kilcolgan's estuary, is the demesne and substantial overgrown ruin of Tyrone House, built in a robust Palladian style in 1779 by Christopher French St. George. Resisting absenteeism and the appeal of Dublin or London, the St Georges stayed put. Though they hunted and raced fervently, and sired occasional children on local girls, they were by the standards of the age very generous to their many tenants. Gossip gave them a different reputation, of good English stock reverting to peasant barbarism, and it was this version which Violet Martin heard when in 1912 she visited the house, by then empty. 'If I dared to work up that subject ...' she wrote to Edith Somerville. The result was one of their best novels, *The Big House of Inver*. In 1972 the Irish Georgian Society bought the ruin.

13

Galway North and West

'A S IN THE body naturall the crisis of the disease is often made by throwing the peccant humor into the extreame parts, soe here the barbarities of Ireland under which it so long laboured, and with which it was soe miserably infected, are all accumulated.' So John Dunton of Galway wrote in a letter to England in 1698. Fifty years earlier Connacht had been lumped by Cromwell with Hell as a suitable destination for Irishmen. It had had a bad reputation for centuries before this. Though Henry II had acknowledged Irish ownership by the Treaty of Windsor in 1175, his barons had broken his word for him and crossed the Shannon, which till then divided the independent Celts from Anglo-Norman conquerors. The stony flats and marshes of Leitrim and Roscommon were left to the Irish. The rest of Connacht became the spoil of Normans, Welsh and Flemings. From them came some of the most common names of the Galway-Mayo bulge – Athy, Bodkin, Blake, Browne, D'Arcy, ffont, ffrench, Joyce, Kirwan, Lynch, Martin, Morris and Skerrett.

These thirteen 'tribes of Galway' found it hard to maintain their tenure. They had the O'Flaherties and other Irish clans to contend with. Over the west gate of **Galway City** was engraved a prayer: 'From the fury of the O'Flaherties, Good Lord deliver us.' And to preserve the exclusive nature of the city at least a law was passed in 1518: 'no man of this towne shall oste or receive into their housses at Christemas, Easter, nor no feast alles, any of the Burkes, MacWilliams, the Kellies, nor no cepte elles, without license of the mayor and council, on payn to forfeit 5 pounds, that neither o' nor Mac shalle strutte ne swaggere thro the streetes of Galway'. (As lately as the 1940s William Joyce, 'Lord Haw-Haw', thought he might mitigate the penalty for his high treason by reminding his judges that he had helped suppress the Irish of Galway in Black and Tan times.)

Trade prospered in competition with Limerick, and there was a great deal of mercantile contact with Spain (Columbus, before his

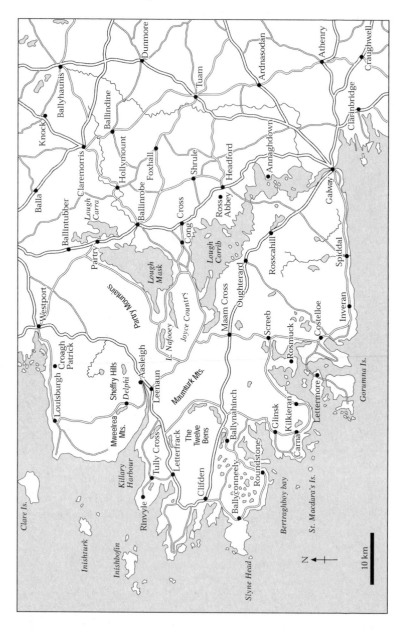

Atlantic journey, is supposed to have come here to check on reports of St Brendan's Island). Wine imports and beef, pork, butter and wool exports made Galway one of the greatest commercial towns in the British Isles, till in the 1641 Civil War the citizens made the mistake of backing the king and the Catholic Church. Eleven years later, Cromwell's General Coote took Parliament's revenge, and razed much of the recently rebuilt town to the ground. It was after the citizens' second disaster – capture after backing King James – in the same century that Dunton wrote the verdict above. Galway never fully recovered – not till recently at least. In the eighteenth and nineteenth centuries its population remained static, even went down a little. The coming of the railway ensured Dublin's primacy as nerve-centre of the network. After 1912, however, Galway's population rose by over half in fifty or so years. More recently it has been called the fastest growing town in Europe: a busy county town with thriving maritime and tourist trade, and rapidly expanding industry. Green Connemara marble is exported all over the world from here. And Galway remains what it always has been: key to the west, between the sea and the longitudinal barrier of Loughs Corrib and Mask.

Not long after the Second World War the city council was only just prevented from flattening the old central parts of the city, between Eyre Square and the river, for redevelopment. Today this area of narrow lanes, alleys and idiosyncrasy buzzes with life: all colour and busily patronised shops, cafes, bars and restaurants. (Kennys in High Street is one of the world's great bookshops.) Lynch's Castle, in Shop Street, is a sixteenth-century town house now containing a bank.

Lynch is a distinguished name in these parts. In the 170 years before Coote's victory a total of eighty-four mayors had been of that name and it still figures all over the place. One mayor, Stephen Lynch FitzStephen, made himself a legend in 1493 when, finding no one willing to hang his son, who had confessed to the murder of a visiting Spaniard, he did the job himself. The scene of the hanging is indicated by a memorial beside the churchyard of Church of Ireland **St Nicholas's Collegiate Church**, the town's most interesting antiquity. Founded in the early fourteenth century (an Aran man who died in 1590 supposedly aged 220 was said to remember a time when the church did not exist), it has since been much altered and restored, but remains the largest medieval church in Ireland. The curious pyramid-shaped spire was added in 1683 and the parapet restored in 1883. Inside, the simplicity of the cruciform design is pointed up by a number of interesting memorials. In Bowling Green nearby is the tiny terraced house, sometimes open to the public, that served as home to Nora Barnacle, future wife of James Joyce.

On the west bank of the pretty Corrib River is the **Catholic Cathedral** of Our Lady Assumed into Heaven and St Nicholas, built between 1959 and 1965 under the dynamic aegis of the late Bishop of Galway, Dr Browne. Built to the design of John J. Robinson, it stands stiffly to attention, displaying an odd assortment of features, many of them Spanish in character. You long to tell it to stand easy. Its essentially simple cruciform shape, worked in limestone and topped by a heavy copper dome, is clumsily rooted to the ground by a cluster of buildings attached at the south side, which ineptly break the line. The interior is vast and light but the separate parts, made from stone, marbles, wood and other materials of impeccable quality, eye each other surlily across the empty spaces. Altogether a very uncomfortable architectural dodo. Over the west branch of the river is University College, designed in buoyant redbrick Victorian Tudor by Joseph B. Keane and finished in 1849; one of the three 'godless colleges', so named by O'Connell because they were to be free of religious exclusivity and patronage. It was clearly, though by no means exactly, modelled on Christ Church, Oxford, though English links end there. This is the academic hub of Irish language studies and promotion.

Down river on the west side is the area known as the Claddagh, once a pattern of rows of low-built cottages. Up to their demolition in 1934, they housed an Irish-speaking community numbering some three thousand, all fishermen and their families, the women famous for their black gowns and deep red petticoats. On the city side of the river is the Spanish Arch, part of the old city walls, its name commemorating the heavy trade once carried on between Galway and Spain. Nearby a plinth displays the stylised image of a galleon with an inscription to the effect that around 1477 Columbus, contemplating his greatest voyage, found here 'sure signs of land beyond the Atlantic', presumably from far-travelled fishermen. There is no proof that he came, or – as is said sometimes – that he attended a final mass in the church of St Nicholas (then Roman Catholic) before embarking for the West. It is not, though, impossible.

Galway extends its bounds, constantly and uglily, to east, west and north. Westward, the coast is an ever-lengthening resort area, with promenades, good beaches, and all the relevant trappings. From the harbour, and from Rossaveal twenty miles west of the city, and Doolin in county Clare, there are regular sailings to the **Aran Islands**, and it is possible to make the round trip in a day, though a great deal more time is needed to see even one of the three with any thoroughness. There are also flights from Inverin, a few miles short of Rossaveal. Weather is important. Winds can make a normal two and a half hour sailing last six hours. Jokes about island weather (if you can't see them from the mainland it's raining; if you can, it's going to rain – and so on) are not fair since the islands get less rain than the mainland, where there are mountains to precipitate it. The islands have got themselves into the paradoxical situation of being world-renowned for their pure Gaelic culture (though Liam O'Flaherty, Aran-born novelist, said that many islanders descend from the ruggedest of Cromwell's troops, put there to be out of the way, and that 'they still speak English with a cockney accent'). As a result, visitors stream in and out, films are made and books written about the islands, and the lives of the inhabitants are based as much as main-landers' on television, cars, the internet, foreign holidays and supermarket shopping. Despite the Irish television channel, it is not easy in such circumstances to maintain the old language or the old ways in their natural form. The playwright Synge could describe an islander as shut inside 'a world of individual conceits and theories'. Not that that world was sweet and lovely. Living meant a tireless exploitation of nature. The sea drowned young fishermen and carried away others to American homes. There was cruelty to animals and a perhaps necessary callousness to human suffering. Nowadays health, education, homes and comforts are unrecognisably improved. There are cousins in Manhattan and Kilburn, and there is as much worldly wisdom here as in any other spot. But still Aran retains an outwardly timeless appearance; and the curraghs that convey some goods and people between the three islands, and the rawhide sandals worn by some islanders, *look* primeval even if there is no sensible alternative to them.

Geologically the islands are the summits of a reef that stretches out from the limestone surface of Clare and the Burren (only five miles from the tip of the eastern island, Inisheer). Inishmore presents a sheer wall of rock, sometimes 400 feet high, to the ocean at the south-west, but on the north-east all three main islands tilt down gradually to the sea. In the past, the land surface was as grey and featureless as that of the Burren. Gradually, and over centuries, by stopping up the joints of the limestone with splinters and spreading sand and seaweed over the bare rock, islanders have created a soil that provides them and their stock with grass, potatoes and cereals. Loose rocks have been gathered to build the walls that make a pretty patchwork of the whole area. In the past, especially in early Christian times, they were used for buildings on the grand scale.

All three islands abound in remains of churches, High Crosses, Round Towers and other monastic buildings. Plentiful ruins of another sort survive in the shape of prehistoric forts – of a period unknown but possibly, like Staigue Fort, from the first centuries AD, before St Patrick's mission. Legends connect them with the original colonisation of Ireland. **Dun Aenghus** on **Inishmore** was called by Dr Petrie 'the most magnificent barbaric monument in Europe'. It stands above a 250-foot vertical drop (an old rockslide, some have claimed, reduced the oval form of the fort to its present horseshoe shape) amid three lines of ramparts, the outer of which encloses eleven acres. Additional defence was given by thousands of outward-pointing sharp stones – the *chevaux-de-frise* – on the landward side. There are three other forts, one on the cliff-edge, two inland, the walls of both of these forming full circles. In the late fifth century, St Enda lived on Inishmore, founding a monastery, maintaining a strict discipline – weeding, ditch-digging and other chores all to be done by hand, without implement – and teaching several acolytes who would in later years wield great influence in Ireland's rapid cultural and religious expansion. Some of these are recalled by St Ciaran's church, St Brecan's church, Temple MacDuagh and other ancient ecclesiastical remains.

Both Inishmaan ('middle island') and Inisheer ('east island', the smallest of the three) have forts and monastic remains also, preserved in a slightly more sequestered atmosphere. (Neither has a police force on it.) **Inishmaan** ('middle island') is the least developed. Synge had a thatched cottage here and set his *Riders to the Sea* on the island and the coast about it. Dun Conor, an oval fort, has been much but impressively restored. A story attaches to the strip of water between the two bigger islands. Pope Gregory the Great, who sent the officious Augustine on his mission to convert Britain, was known to be a great sympathiser with the Celts even while his official position made it necessary for him to bring their errant church into line with Roman practice. That and his obsessive playing with words ('*Non Angli sed Angeli*' was one of his better puns) endeared him to the Irish, who called him the Goldenmouth, and in time an Irishman – or son of one. The story developed that before his death the Pope ordered his coffined body to be lowered into the Tiber. This was done, and river and sea bore it round Western Europe to these islands, where finally he was buried. The strip of water is known as Gregory's Sound.

Lough Corrib, due north of Galway, is the second largest lake in Ireland. In parts as much as 150 feet deep, it contains innumerable islands, many of them of antiquarian interest. This aspect of the local scene was covered with gusto and great scholarship by Oscar Wilde's eccentric father, Sir William, who with his wife 'Speranza' made up a team almost as picturesque as their son. Wilde's book, *Lough Corrib, Its Shores and Islands*, is still an excellent detailed guide, though written for an age used to the pace of walking and trap rather than cars, and it serves well on the lake cruises which can be taken from Galway. Here we shall keep to the road and round both lakes – Corrib and Mask – meeting Wilde halfway at his house near Cong. Most noticeable in the trip is the way the lakes divide the flat barren eastern part of the county from the mountainous miles of Connemara and the west, to which we shall shortly come.

The long straight N84 leads north up the east side of the lake and after seven miles a turn to the left leads by a roundabout route to **Annaghdown**, where there are evocative lakeside ruins of a Franciscan church, friary and a Norman castle. St Brendan, tired at last by his Atlantic and other travels, died here, in the nunnery he himself had earlier founded, in the arms of his sister Brig, who was its head. The lane leads back to the main road which five miles farther comes to Headford. A mile north-west of the town is **Ross Abbey**, in fact a Franciscan friary refounded in 1498, a time when the neglect of the Church by bishops – often illegitimate sons of great families – put the weight of religious continuity on this and other mendicant orders. They responded with several new foundations and vigorous preaching and many continued long after the official dissolution of the monasteries. Ross, which was wrecked by Cromwell's troops, still shows plainly the characteristic plan of Franciscan houses, being the best preserved friary in Ireland. On the shore a few miles to the south-west are several demesnes and good houses, beside a pretty stretch of the lake. The area is also rich in medieval castle ruins and particularly in prehistoric remains. From Headford the R333 to the east passes Knockma Hill, one of the many hills in the country that were seats of gods and fairies – this one remains the abode of Finbarra, present king of the fairies. It then goes on to **Tuam**, see of the united Church of Ireland diocese of Tuam, Killala and Achonry, whose bishop claims the largest area and the smallest community of any in the British Isles. The Church of Ireland cathedral dates back in part to the twelfth century but was totally restored and in parts spoiled during a nineteenth-century restoration by Sir Thomas Deane. It still preserves a superb Romanesque chancel arch, the widest in the country, and sumptuously Baroque Italian choir stalls of 1740. The Catholic cathedral, outside the town, is duller work of Gothic Revival style. Two miles east is Bermingham House, once seat of the Lords Athenry and from the early nineteenth century home of the Denis family, one of whom, John Denis, founded the 'Galway Blazers'. A descendant, Molly, Lady Cusack-Smith, who might have and possibly did grace the pages of Molly Keane's novels, a Paris couturière in the 1920s and lifelong cigar-smoker, lived here throughout the second half of the twentieth century, hostess of biannual hunt-balls. The kennels of the Bermingham and North Galway hunt are still here.

Crossing the flat country westwards we return through Tuam and continue to Shrule, with its ruined abbey and castle beside the Black River, where in 1641 a party of some seventy Parliamentarians, offered safe conduct after surrendering Castlebar to the Catholic Confederacy, were handed by the Earl of Mayo into the keeping of Edmund Bourke, a cousin, who had sixty-five of them shot, piked or drowned. Further west the R334 brings us quickly to Cross, where a turn left puts us on the Cong road that runs between Loughs Mask and Corrib. The two lakes are connected by subterranean channels through the limestone rock and in the Famine a canal was dug, at great cost, in the Famine Relief programme, to link them for boat traffic. The water, which was to debouch into the Corrib at Cong did nothing of the sort, since the porous rock allowed it to sink through; and the virtually dry canal, complete with virginal locks, remains, running beside a minor road to the north of the town, as a memorial to improvidence. A mile before Cong an unsignposted lane leads to the (still private) house that Sir William Wilde built and in which he and his family spent long periods. It is a plain gabled house with magnificent views over the lake and its islands, called Moytura, after the prehistoric battlefield Wilde supposed he had identified all round this area. Scholars today doubt his findings and some reject them. Some say there were two battles, of which the one here was the first. But his ingenuity in fitting physical remains of mounds, circles and cairns – with which this 'Plain of Moytura' is littered – to literary accounts, was admirable. The battle, if and wherever it took place, was supposed to have been between the Firbolgs, the fourth wave of invaders of Ireland, and the Tuatha de Danaan, or people of the goddess Danu, who arrived after them and here defeated them. The

Tuatha were supposed to be the last colonial wave before the Milesians – otherwise known as Gaels – came to displace them and
thoroughly settle the country. From the chiefs of the Firbolgs and
Tuatha derived many of the shadier gods and spirits, banished in
many cases to remote hills and valleys by the introduced Gaelic gods.

Most of the interest of Cong is contained in the demesne of
Ashford Castle. This large baronial pile in its magnificent grounds
was built for Sir Arthur Edward Guinness, son of the brewer-philan-
thropist Sir Benjamin Lee Guiness and himself created Lord Ardilaun
in 1880. The house is now a hotel, one of the grandest in the country,
as is its restaurant. Beside the demesne gates are the beautiful and
recently restored ruins of Cong Abbey, an early-twelfth-century foundation of which part of the chancel and the conventual buildings
remain. The cloister is mainly a reconstruction of the 1860s. From
Cong can be made the circuit of Lough Mask, with its constant views,
on the eastern side, of the Partry Mountains to the west. On the left,
four miles along the Ballinrobe road is the lakeside **Lough Mask
House**, surrounded by the former estates of Lord Erne, who employed
Captain Boycott as his agent. In 1879, in spite of threats to his life if
he refused to reduce rents by more than the ten per cent already
offered, almost all his tenants paid up. The following year a demand,
backed by Land League agitators, was made for a twenty-five per cent
reduction of rents. Boycott offered twenty per cent. Most tenants paid;
and on those who did not Boycott served notice of eviction. A few
days before, at Ennis, Parnell had proposed a way of dealing with any
evictor: isolate him 'as if he was a leper of old'. Overnight Boycott
became a harassed, hustled outpost of the Ascendancy. His crops were
neglected, walls destroyed, animals scattered – one night the tails of
all his cattle were cut off – his mail and laundry withheld. No shop in
Ballinrobe would sell to him or his wife. But he stood his ground and,
when his stand was publicised, found support in many quarters. Fifty
volunteers were dispatched by Orange landlords in Monaghan to help
him gather crops, on which the issue mainly turned. Seven thousand
police and troops were posted to keep order. The Irish did nothing.
When the crop was in, the volunteers went away, but the Boycotts
departed too. In the event neither side had won, neither lost. Within a
year the agitation died down and Boycott returned – to threats and
abuse at first, but gradually normality. In 1886 he moved to a job in
Suffolk, but came for holidays to Achill Island.

Ballinrobe's Catholic parish church has nine good stained glass
windows by Harry Clarke, one of the most remarkable of the Tower

of Glass graduates. A right turn off the main Castlebar road, just out
of the town, leads us round Lough Carra with its clear blue-green
waters, where pike has been caught under ice in winter, to the impressive lakeside ruin of **Moore Hall**, empty and sealed among forestry
walks. The Moores were a family of eccentric distinction. In 1798
John Moore was proclaimed first president of the Republic of
Connacht on the arrival of French ships to back up the rising of
United Irishmen (which had already, over much of the land, been
effectively crushed). George Moore (1852–1933) the novelist, friend
and occasional enemy of Yeats, Edward Martyn, Lady Gregory and
most other cultural lights either side of the turn of the century and of
the Irish Sea, about whom nobody said a good word but everyone told
a story more interesting than the last, spent much of his time here in
middle age, and described the local scene, but more particularly the
progress of the Irish literary revival, in his *Ave, Salve, Vale* trilogy and
in his novel *The Lake*. His novel *Esther Waters* ranks with the twentieth-century's greatest. Among many other things, Moore thought
himself a gourmet, and was always sending back dishes in restaurants. At Moore Hall, he sacked six cooks in succession. The last
protested and returned with a policeman. Moore dragged the baffled
constable into the dining-room and put him the judicial question: 'Is
there a law in this country to compel me to eat this abominable
omelette?' At his death, his ashes were placed here, under a lake-
island cairn. The house was burned in 1923.

At the north tip of Lough Carra stands **Ballintubber Abbey**, from
1795 till early this century a possession of the Moores. It was recently
thoroughly restored after a turbulent history that included, after its
foundation in 1216 by the O'Conor King of Connacht, burning,
deroofing by Cromwellians, the subsequent collapse of the tower, and
an unbroken tradition of masses held, even during Penal times, for
over seven hundred and fifty years. The recent work has left it light,
simple and spacious inside, preserving some good Romanesque
details of the early thirteenth century, and a few interesting tombs.
Outside, the excavations carried out between 1963 and 1966 show
well the transition from Romanesque to Gothic styles that was taking
place at the time of its construction. Of the extensive fifteenth-
century reconstruction the west doorway (which was removed in the
nineteenth century and replaced in the twentieth) is one of the most
graceful remains.

Driving south down the Galway road and turning right at the
village of Partry and left a mile later we come on to the road that

leads down the west side of Lough Mask, in country that is in every way different from that to the east. Limestone has given way abruptly to massive beds of Ordovician rock, with small stretches of earlier volcanic rocks. The valleys and tarns of the Partry Mountains, often hemmed in by cliffs 1,000 feet high, are the results of glacial action and can be appreciated by hard walking, especially up the valley of the Owenbrin; but the drive itself is magnificent, with new vistas opening at each bend of the road. This is **Joyce Country**, an unoffi-cial title, like Connemara, coming from a Welsh family that settled here in the thirteenth century, from whom many of today's inhabitants are descended. At the junction by Lough Nafooey we turn right. Vivid in the angled light of the early or late sun are the 'lazy beds', the relict ridges on the lower but often dauntingly steep slopes across the lake in which peasants grew their potatoes in harder times.

We soon cross the pass through another line of mountains and descend on the broad and beautiful valley of Joyce's River. Four miles down the valley road we cross the river, and passing Leckavrea Mountain on the right come on Maam Cross, a good centre for the lakes and mountain country. **Oughterard**, ten miles east along the N59 is a bigger pleasant town much given over to the tourist and angling trade. At peak mayfly time children get a day off school to sell them to trout-fishers. Local fishermen will for an agreed price convey visitors to Inchagoill, 'the island of the stranger', where two churches, one of them restored, possessing a fine Romanesque west doorway, survive of an ancient monastery. Two miles down the Galway road is a left turn to Aughnanure Castle, which opens in summer; an O'Flaherty stronghold of 1500 with a dark six-storey restored keep in a broad bawn beside a romantic stream. Five miles ahead, on the left, is Ross Lake with **Ross House**, built in 1777, beside it, ancestral home of the Martins of Ross, who were in their time among the greatest landowners of Connacht. Violet Martin, 'Martin Ross' of the *Irish RM* stories, was born in Ross House in 1862. By her time the family had lost its money. The house was soon let, and after fifteen years – as Violet wrote to Edith – had 'lost every shrub, and the melon grove rears a pit of nettles with great care'. She loved but disparaged the three-storey, worn but mellowed house with its Venetian window at the front and urns around the roof. 'It is said that a man is never in love till he is in love with a plain woman; and in spite of draughts, of exhausting flights of stairs, of chimneys that are the despair of sweeps, it has held the affections of five generations of Martins.' When she made money she spent it on preserving the house, but it was sold in 1924, nine years after her death. She had lived through the last, benighted years of the Ascendancy, and she wrote of the vain attempts to preserve gentility among the big houses roundabout, and how a Miss O'Flaherty nearby used to dress up as a maid to tell people her mistress was out, not wishing them to know there was no real maid to tell them.

Galway to Westport, Connemara

West of Galway the coast road leads straight between dribbles of bungalows for eight or nine miles. The few breaks remind picturesquely of a harder era: cramped patterns of granite walls on uneven granite foundations, sparse pasture between them, shallow ponds and lakes with reeds and flags, a cow and calves, all tightly fitted. There are good beaches here and there, and Spiddal, twelve miles along, is a popular seaside resort, with an Irish college, for this is part of the Gaeltacht. When the road eventually bends right and north over twenty miles from Galway, long stony promontories lead down towards a maze of islands stretching for miles to the west. The shore here is dotted with beaches which out of season are all but private, so many there are for so few visitors (a number of famous Irish come here as an escape from crush and bother). From Costelloe a lane to the left crosses to Lettermore Island and hence to the largest of the islands, **Gorumna**. The big islands are all joined by bridges. Teeranea on Gorumna has a museum of old artifacts and ways.

As we continue north there are views of the Twelve Bens which make the heart of Connemara. Four miles west of Screeb, the road passes a turning to **Rosmuck**, on a peninsula, and just past the turning a track leads a quarter of a mile to Patrick Pearse's white thatched cottage, built by him in 1910, lonely on a small rise. It was here that this Irish patriot son of an English monumental sculptor came for long spells to learn Irish, and then to translate local Irish poetry into English, to write both plays and poems in Irish, and to make 'a little Gaelic kingdom of our own'. The cottage has been much restored to house mementoes of him. A few miles on, the road bends again and follows the coast beside Kilkieran Bay. Behind, the mountains rise up from the plain like a gigantic fortress, rather as MacGillycuddy's Reeks do from the west, or the Wicklow Hills in the east. In common with Wicklow, the whole of south Connemara is granite, the result of volcanic eruptions in the Caledonian period, while the mountains to the north are covered in quartzite, whose hard weathering gives them their jagged, sometimes conical shapes. Gleaming schists, worn down by glaciation, fill the valleys between, or carry on the mountain ranges to the north. The region we are covering now is a strange plain of rock-strewn bog and lake, with a peculiar beauty not usually associated with the name Connemara, but quite as much a part of it. (Connemara is in fact an unofficial name, anciently one of the divisions of Connacht – Conmacnamara – meaning perhaps 'sea-coast belonging to Conmac', and now a term loosely applied to west Galway.)

Kilkieran, a pretty harbour village where Irish is very much the first language, is a centre of the seaweed industry. Lobsters, oysters and scallops make a profitable business on the west coast of Ireland, but this vegetable harvest from the sea was also of vital importance. The weed, cut at low tide, by men and women alike, is used to enrich the stony land, so making possible crops of potatoes, corn and hay. From Kilkieran the weed is also exported to Scotland for culinary and cosmetic uses, but this is a more recent development. All aspects of cultivation are hard here, for the use of mechanical ploughs is impossible in such stony soils, and it is difficult – amid the signs of hard hand industry, among people who make English sound a foreign language and who still take more seriously than most their age-old saint cults and patterns – to remember that Galway a few miles back is a town of thriving up-to-the-minute business and international trade. One of the old religious festivals takes place on 16 July at St Macdara's Island, one and a half miles south-west of the peninsula, where there is an ancient stone church and other remains associated with the saint. Until recently it was the custom for passing sailing boats to dip their sails three times when passing the island.

The next main promontory off Connemara, circled by the R341 road, lies between Bertraghboy Bay and Clifden. The scenery near the road is similar to what we have seen, but the views of the distant hills are grandly different. **Roundstone** is one of the nicest resorts in Connemara, with pretty white-washed two-storey houses in a line beside a deep sheltered inlet of sea. It was built in the 1820s by Alexander Nimmo, a Scottish engineer responsible for the building of many Irish harbours and the reclamation of much Irish bogland. Numbers of Scottish fishermen settled here. Above Roundstone rises the serrated ridge of Errisbeg, and from its summit (987 feet) can be had perhaps the best panoramic view of the whole region – the extraordinary complex of rocky lakes below, the main range of the

Twelve Bens, thousands of islands great and small out to sea, and to the south the coasts of Clare and Kerry, and the Aran Islands standing out against the Cliffs of Moher.

Errisbeg and the country round about is widely known for its rare flora, including species usually found in America and seldom elsewhere in the British Isles. There are several orchids including the Green-winged Orchid, *Orchis morio*, which has declined elsewhere in recent years. There is the carnivorous Long-leaved Sundew, *Drosera intermedia*, the slender Pipewort, *Eriocaulon septangulare*, at lake edges, once reckoned a recent introduction from America, where it is very common, but found from pollen samples to have been resident here for six thousand years. And many many more. Three varieties of heath – Irish (miscalled Mediterranean), Mackay's and St Dabeoc's, with its long purple bells – are abundant here. In addition there are plants that have spread from the limestone of the Burren. Several more common flowers – Purple Loosestrife is an example – are notable for their profusion. Continuing round to the south and west of the promontory we cross the stretch of road described as 'brandy and soda' because of the fresh invigorating wind that blows in from the sea. Dog's Bay, south of Errisbeg, is one of the most delightful beaches for miles, with its white sand and sheltered position. Beyond Ballyconneely, where a bulge of lake-speckled land stretches out to Slyne Head, past the wan remains of Bunowen Castle and some fine beaches, the **Derrygimlagh Bog** opens out to the east. It was here, on a terrain of peat, ponds, sedge and rock that few pilots would have chosen for a safe touchdown, that John William Alcock with his co-pilot, Arthur Whitton Brown, crash-landed in June 1919, after the first transatlantic flight, begun from Newfoundland sixteen hours twenty-seven minutes before. (Both were knighted, and Alcock was killed in a plane accident, in the same year.) A simple stone model of an aeroplane's nosecone, a mile's walk from the road, along a track, marks the spot where they came down. A few yards away an inscription on a dilapidated wall commemorates the use of this site, from 1907 to 1922, by Guglielmo Marconi as the first transatlantic commercial wireless station.

A few miles farther on we enter **Clifden**, known as the capital of Connemara, a pleasant resort well protected from Atlantic gales at the head of its own creek, famous for the weaving of tweeds and for its lobster fishery. It is a good base for both sea and land sides of Connemara, and in August the Connemara Pony Show is held here. The roofless castle, a mile or so to the west, was a Gothic construction for

John d'Arcy who laid out the town in 1812, when the attractions of the west began to be realised by the outside world. Westport, Roundstone and Letterfrack were built in the same period, often for immigrant populations. The D'Arcys were one of the old 'tribes of Galway', but it was another of these, the Martins, whose influence extended furthest, and amounted at times to that of a feudal royal family, a notion they cherished. One Martin boasted to the Prince Regent that the Long Walk at Windsor was badly named. His own drive was thirty miles long, as in a sense it was, for the road from Galway to Ballynahinch, his residence, was almost entirely flanked by estates he owned.

North of Clifden the so-called Sky Road leads off to the left, along the north coast of Streamstown Bay, passing Omey island and its sparse monastic remains, to which at low tide it is possible both to walk and to drive. Cleggan Bay cuts into the north-west coast of the peninsula, with Cleggan at its head, from which ferries cross to the inhabited island of **Inishbofin**. This boasts sandy beaches, good walks, two hotels, several early Christian remains and an interesting early connection with the seventh-century clash in Britain between the pious, effective but quirky Celtic church and the disciplined conformism of Rome. At the Synod of Whitby in 664, Irish St Colman, Abbot of Lindisfarne, off the Northumberland coast, was worsted by the sly, bellicose arguments of Bishop Wilfrid. Colman retired to Inishbofin with a group of his Irish and English monks, and founded a monastery. Here, according to Bede, the Irish grew perverse in their habits, took little part in the farm work and expected to benefit from the Englishmen's exertions. Rows flared up, and eventually Colman moved with the English to Mayo (a hamlet now, with a few ruins, south of Balla in county Mayo) where the new foundation gained wide fame and praise. It was still famous in the time of Alcuin, who wrote to the monks from the court of Charlemagne, in an early instance of Ascendancy sentiment, 'Let your light shine among that barbarous nation like a star in the western skies.'

Returning to Clifden, we can take the N59 eastward. After seven miles we reach **Ballynahinch Castle**, a rather ugly and much restored eighteenth-century house, beside the lake of the same name. One of many distinctions is that in 1923 Ballynahinch had the highest number of rainy days ever recorded in these islands – 309. A medieval O'Flaherty demesne, the original castle was confiscated by the ruthless and unloved Sir Richard Bingham, President of Connacht in Elizabeth's reign. Best known of the Martins who ruled here was

Colonel Richard Martin (1754–1834), who was mainly responsible
for the founding of the RSPCA. Maria Edgeworth wrote that as 'King
of Connemara' he had ruled over his people 'with absolute power,
with laws of his own and setting all other laws at defiance'. His early
days were known for innumerable duels. Later he discovered a fond-
ness for animals and introduced a bill to protect them in Parliament.
'Hairtrigger Dick', his early nickname, was dropped for 'Humanity
Martin', and the more pious tag has stuck. He was wildly extravagant
and died a debtor in Boulogne. Later, the Famine finished off the
family fortunes, and the house went through several owners –
including from 1926 Prince Ranjitsinhji of Nawanagar, an international cricketer who once scored three separate centuries for three
separate teams in one day. ('Gentlemen,' he was once introduced at a
Dublin dinner, 'he might have fished the Ganges; but he prefers the
river at Ballynahinch.') In 1945 the house became a hotel, which it
remains.

Continuing east on the N59 for six miles beyond Ballynahinch a
left turn leads up the valley between the Twelve Bens and the Maum-
turk Mountains. The Bens are formed of grey quartzite, almost bare
of vegetation apart from forestry on lower slopes, and with rock so
firm that, in Praeger's view, they were 'evidently created for the
climber'. Ten miles through this valley, with Lough Inagh and the
hills from which Connemara marble is quarried on the left, and countless waterfalls on both sides, we reach the N59 again and turn left
towards Letterfrack. We are soon passing Kylemore Lake, 'clothed
purple and silver under windows lit by the southern sun', as Gogarty
wrote in bittersweet mood in 1922, when his and others' houses were
being burned and ransacked by the IRA. Beyond the lake, on the
right, is the extraordinary lush demesne of **Kylemore Castle**, since
the First World War a convent of Benedictine nuns. (Visitors are
welcome to the grounds, and there is a large carpark, shop and cafe-
teria.) The castle and the Gothic church to its east were built by a
Liverpool millionaire, Mitchell Henry, in the late nineteenth century.
He spent thousands of pounds reclaiming adjacent land from the bog.
Now, with bog become a rarity, and the pretty mauve-flowered
Ponticum rhododendron which has replaced miles of it recognised as
an appalling scourge of other forms of wildlife, the need grows for a
reverse reclamation.

Three miles on, in and among roads crimson-fringed with fuchsia
in the summer, we can call into the Connemara National Park Centre,
with displays and videos and walks in the 3,000 acres that belong to it

helpful in the understanding of the region's ecology. At Letterfrack, a Quaker settlement of the early nineteenth century, we turn right, and after another three miles branch left at Tully Cross. Beyond the little village of Renvyle, on the right, is **Renvyle House Hotel**, seat of the Blake family till 1883, when it was turned into a hotel. Later it was bought by Oliver St John Gogarty (1878–1957), the doctor turned writer whose racy *As I was Going down Sackville Street* provides a sensitive and amusing picture of the extraordinary maze of cultural Dublin in the twenties. Here at Renvyle he entertained Yeats (who disliked the house, or rather sensed that he himself was disliked by its dormant spirits), Shaw and Augustus John, who called it the most beautiful landscape in the world and did several paintings here. Then in 1922 the house – 'the long, long house in the ultimate land of the undiscovered West' – was burned by republicans. 'They say it took a week to burn. Blue china fused like solder.' In the same month the houses of thirty-seven other senators were burned, many of them with priceless treasures inside. Gogarty rebuilt the house in 1930 and reopened it as a hotel, which, in different hands, upgraded, expanded and changed utterly, it is today. The surrounding beauty remains, and fine sandy beaches, and out to sea a scatter of islands. A mile and a half west is ruined Renvyle Castle, home successively of Joyces and O'Flahertys, and once stormed by the autocratic Grace O'Malley. The ruin of a church, a holy well and an interesting dolmen are close by.

Returning to Tully Cross, we turn left and drive east towards Leenaun, with first the sea at our left, and later Lough Fee lapping the roadside at the right. The first left turn here takes us down a steep narrow lane to a tiny village close to the outlet of Killary Harbour. This is in fact the drowned valley of the Erriff River, deep (up to eighty feet in its middle passage) enough for the British Channel Fleet that used sometimes to be stationed here, and which was visited by Edward VII and his queen, who landed at Bundorragha, five miles east on the opposite shore. A later visitor was the ascetic philosopher Ludwig Wittgenstein, who came to the unremarkable settlement we have reached, to live here alone and unravel the problem of numbers. Rather like St Kevin, he would stand so long in deep meditation, according to Bertrand Russell, that the seagulls came to settle on him. (At first he adored Russell, then came to detect a glib facility in his thought; and ingeniously condemned him, along with Wells, as suffering from 'loss of problem'.) He lived in a cottage on a site now occupied by the youth hostel. Returning to Lough Fee, we continue east, rejoin the N59 and come to **Leenaun**, at the inner end of Killary harbour. This is a good centre for local exploration, beautifully set, with an informative centre, a good exhibition with demonstrations of old ways of processing sheep's wool, and plenty of accommodation nearby. It remains very conscious of its use as location for the film of John B. Keane's chilling play *The Field*, describing one hideous consequence of the obsessive attachment of the rural Irish to their land. A couple of miles east, at the extreme head of the harbour, we cross over the Erriff, a noted salmon river, beside the picturesque Aasleagh waterfall, and enter county Mayo.

10 *King John's Castle at the north end of Englishtown, the oldest part of the city of Limerick*
11 *The Cliffs of Moher, some five miles of jutting headlands along the coast of County Clare*
12 *Flat-topped Ben Bulben, rich in associations with the legendary Dermot and with Yeats*
13 *Bantry House, with garden terraces behind and the Bay stretching out to the Atlantic in front*
14 *Lismore Castle, rising above the County Waterford Blackwater*
15 *The quartzite cone of Mount Errigal dominates the wild interior of County Donegal*
16 *Tudor-revival Queen's University, Belfast, designed by Charles Lanyon*
17 *The Giant's Causeway, on the north coast of County Antrim*
18 *Mussenden Temple, built by the Earl Bishop of Derry close to the cliff-edge as his library*

14

Mayo and West Sligo

J UST BEFORE THE Aasleagh Falls we cross into county Mayo. 'Mayo, God help us' was a common extension of the name of this wild, boggy and inhospitable county, back in the times of want, cabins and congested districts, before tourism, industry, affluence and bungalow bliss touched the region with their wands. Wildness survives in large parts, but most of it can be seen from positions of comfort. From the Aasleagh Falls the R335 hugs the north shore of Killary harbour for as long as it can. After about four miles, the side of Mweelrea Mountain rising from the water prevents further progress, and the road bends right to climb the picturesque valley of the River Bundorragha to Delphi, where there is a hotel (with the fishing along several miles of river and lake) and an adventure centre. The name was given by a young Marquess of Sligo to what was then his fishing lodge, following his grand tour of classical lands (enthusiasm led to his being imprisoned for a short time for bribing British sailors to convey antiquities in their ships during war-time). The mountain country around, with its peaks, woods and loughs, is very beautiful. Further along our road lies the majestically dark long lake of Dulough with a wall of mountain on its far side. Some of the views in the vicinity surpass the best of Connemara. One tough walk on to the mountain can begin along a track north of the lake (large-scale map essential).

Two roadside Celtic crosses on our road refer to a Famine march from Louisburgh which failed to earn poor relief for its participants, some of whom died hereabouts. 'To the hungry poor who walked here in 1849', reads one inscription, 'and walk the third world today.' A few miles north, with conical Croagh Patrick in view on the right, we come to Louisburgh, where there is a centre devoted to Queen Grace O'Malley, and the choice of turning left or right. Left leads to Killadoon, and a cul-de-sac about ten miles in length, cut off from southerly progress by (once again) the steep-sided mass of Mweelrea.

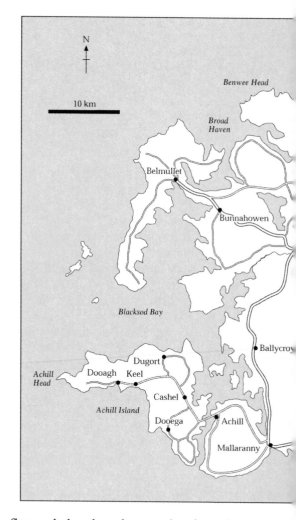

There are some very flat sandy beaches, dunes and rock-pools along the way. From Roonah quay, due west of Louisburgh, the ferry crosses to **Clare Island**, inhabited, with flat pastures and good beaches to east and south, and highlands reaching 1,520 feet to the west, within its four-mile length and two-mile breadth. It possesses busy farms, a hotel, a ruined castle of Grace O'Malley's and abbey buildings which according to tradition contain her grave. This was the local pirate-queen, or 'Queen of Clew Bay', born 1530, died 1603, twice-married, a great plunderer, a calculating chieftain who through

340

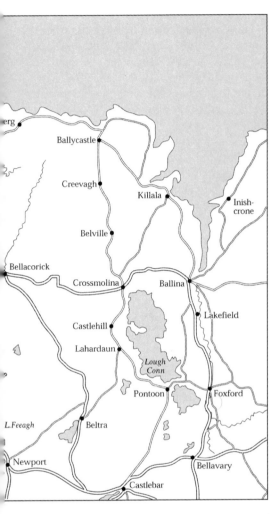

sons, in-laws and allies came to control, for a while, many of the fortresses of the Connacht seaboard; a provincial Celtic heroine who fought the English, once visited Queen Elizabeth in London and refused gifts from her on the grounds that she was a monarch of equal status. She crops up often in the places we are about to visit.

Rejoining the R335 at Louisburgh, we continue eastward. **Croagh Patrick**, which they call the Reek locally, is four miles on. It is not, at 2,510 feet, the highest but it is one of the most famous and holiest of Irish mountains; and Clew Bay, beside which the road now runs, affords one of the loveliest stretches of coastal scenery, speckled with islands and surrounded by tall mountains. From here the descending eastward slant of the islands, or drumlins as these still somewhat baffling glacier deposits are called, appears to indicate the westward direction of the ice that left them behind. On the left, after seven miles, down by the sea, are the fine ruins, behind battlemented walls, of Murrisk, an Augustinian friary of 1457, from which the pilgrimage to the mountain top traditionally begins. Patrick's conversion of Ireland took place in the middle of the fifth century – there is dispute over the dates – and he is supposed one year to have withdrawn here to spend the forty days and nights of Lent in fasting and prayer. During that time he managed to summon together all noxious beasts of the island, 'venomous and monstrous creatures' which stung men and 'not seldom rent and devoured their members' and were often seen 'flying in the air and walking on the earth, loathsome and horrible to behold'. These he persuaded to precipitate themselves to their death down the sheer southern edge of the mountain. The result, if such it is, is that Ireland lacks many of the amphibians and reptiles common in Britain, and certainly has no snakes. (Enviably to many gardeners, it lacks moles too.) The story reflects the attempts of early monks to raise their own saints to apostolic rank, for St Paul was credited with similar achievements in Cyprus and Malta, though the story goes back to Greek myth for its origins. Nevertheless it was widely believed, and the sagacious Bede held that even when introduced to Ireland snakes would no sooner touch land than die. Moreover, people in England bitten by snakes had often been cured by drinking water 'in which scrapings from the leaves of books from Ireland have been steeped'. 'When Patrick drove out the snakes,' wrote James Connolly, the 1916 Rising leader, on a different tack, 'they swam the western ocean and turned into Irish Americans.' The sanctity of the mountain has caused it to remain a place of pilgrimage for centuries, and every year on the last Sunday of July, thousands of fasting Catholics throng the roads and the hillside, and climb to the top where services are held. Hardly any do the climb barefoot any more, nor have plenary indulgences been granted since 1958, but there are still those who circle the church at the summit on their bare knees. Given decent visibility, the panoramic view from the top might well undermine an atheist's certainties.

Westport, six miles east and screened from the bay by the demesne of Westport House, is the prettiest town in the county, laid out at a time of growth and hope in the late eighteenth century by

Peter Browne, second Earl of Altamont. He was one of the few land-lords Arthur Young praised without stint, for his standards in both agriculture and linen manufacture. He built a first-rate harbour, enor-mous warehouses and houses in the town which were let to weavers, while they were given looms and the money to buy yarn. (James Wyatt may have designed the town, though he never came here.) The Mall, with its central canal (Actually the straitjacketed river Carrowbeg) and avenue of lime-trees, survives elegantly, and the town makes a humming regional centre, with good shops and restau-rants. The warehouses survive, too, but long converted to shops or apartments. For, from its peak in the 1830s, when the harbour was a vital link in Atlantic trade, the town crashed in ten years, a victim of famine, the railway, and the competition brought by England's indus-trial revolution. (The grandiose statue of St Patrick in the centre of the Octagon replaced one of George Glendinning, a banker, who helped the town in the 1840s. It was pulled down, and the inscription obliter-ated, in 1922, by men who liked neither the English nor the thought that some of the gentry served Ireland better than others.)

The town's grandest sight is **Westport House**. Underneath are the dungeons of the O'Malley castle that used to stand on the site. The Browne family settled here in 1685, and as Marquesses of Sligo and Earls of Altamont, own it still. They boast descent from Grace O'Malley, which is more of a blessing to them now than it would ever have been in the past. On the death of the present marquess, who has three daughters and no son, the titles will go sideways to England. Some years back the terms of the trust made it seem the estate would as well. The marquess could make no arrangement for inheritance by his daughters while there was the possibility of a son, and the law ruled that neither a vasectomy nor old age, when it came, would preclude that. Vasectomy was deemed reversible, and castration, which was not, was not to his taste. Inheritance by the daughters was at last assured by a Castlebar solicitor pointing out that a private bill in the Dáil could break the trust.

It was for the Brownes that Richard Castle built the original house in 1731, whose classical east front remains as he designed it. Later, around 1780, Thomas Ivory (designer of Dublin's Blue Coat School) doubled the size of the house and, leaving the east front as it was, added the strangely plain west front and pedimented south front. Inside, the house is rich in the decoration of, among others, Wyatt – the dining-room is one of his masterpieces. There is a lavish, in parts crowded collection of paintings including family portraits by Kneller,

Reynolds and Opie and some beautiful landscapes by one of the best, and in his time, least appreciated of Irish artists, James Arthur O'Connor (1792–1841), who spent two years pioneering the Irish landscape picture in this part of Ireland before travelling the Continent and dying, in poverty and still obscure, in London. There are also good collections of silver and Waterford glass. The house and its lovely setting of park, lake and woods, is open to the public and with its shops, camping grounds and many other amenities for children and adults has become an important tourist centre.

At Aghagower, five miles south-east of the town, there are fifteenth-century church remains and a remarkable Round Tower, lacking its conical top. Possibly lightning removed it. The main inland road from Westport, the N60, is not specially rewarding, running past lake-spattered flatlands (the region to the right is known as the Plains of Mayo) but **Castlebar**, Mayo's rather shabby county town twelve miles east-north-east, has tales to tell. Founded in James I's reign, it was the scene of an Irish victory in the Civil War of the 1640s (followed by a treacherous butchery of the English at Shrule), and of a French victory in 1798. Humbert and his 700 French troops, having landed at Killala, and been joined by untrained Irish rebels, put to flight General Lake's garrison and took 1,200 prisoners with such ease that the interlude became known as the Castlebar Races. Later, in 1879, Michael Davitt founded the Land League in the town's Imperial Hotel. Hatred of landlords was fierce here. Till the late nineteenth century the mainly absentee Binghams owned the town and much of its surrounds, but they were so seldom present that when Castlebar Castle was burned down (for a second time) during the 1798 Rising nobody bothered to rebuild it. When needed, a smaller house nearby was used. The Irish line began with Sir Richard, Queen Elizabeth's vicious Governor of Connacht. The earldom came in 1795: 'no wonder', wrote Horace Walpole, 'Lady Camden, the Vice-Queen, is, as you know, Lady Lucan's niece.' The third earl, who was later to order the charge of the Light Brigade, came to Castlebar determined to improve a vast estate which was untouched by new methods of farming and a serious drain on his finances. He sacked his agent, St. Clair O'Malley, who was incompetent but liked, and related to half the town. Since too many people lived on the land for any profit to come from it, the earl evicted those who failed to pay their rents. He evicted thousands. On land cleared of tenants at Ballinrobe, a racecourse was constructed. He brought in Scots farm managers, Protestant and much disliked by the Irish. He tried to revive a personal medieval manorial court until the Lord Chancellor told him it was no longer recognised. And when the Famine came and people were dying of disease and starvation, even more in Mayo than elsewhere in Ireland, he went on evicting, earning himself the name 'Exterminator'. He died in 1888, covered in honours. His son succeeded as fourth earl, brimming with all the humanity his father had lacked. He helped his tenants buy land, started up local industry, moved to improve Catholics' education, and was to be seen daily walking the Mall with his close friend the Catholic priest.

Possessed of a vastly reduced estate in these parts, the seventh earl was different again. He is reckoned to have murdered his children's nanny in London in 1974, thinking she was his wife, and then taken his own life, though no body was ever found and there were innumerable claimed sightings of him afterwards. He was declared officially dead in 1999. His disappearance is said, mischievously, to have given remaining tenants the perfect pretext for withholding their rents. The Mall with its trees, the eighteenth-century Linen Hall, the Methodist church and some handsome houses are fine. The later house, with its view over the river, is gone, burned in the Troubles, but for gate piers and other fragments.

Within the precincts of the Church of Ireland church, whose thick black railings and padlocks suggest a state of siege, is a plinth-based statue of Major-General Sir Charles O'Malley, in full, classically robed fig above a stained inscription testifying to his distinction beside Wellington at Waterloo, in the Peninsula campaign and so on. On the other side of the road a memorial to the 1798 rising shows a rebel kneeling before a priest. A few yards away lies the body of John Moore of Moore Hall, who was declared first president of an Irish Republic by an invading French force in 1798, and died awaiting transportation in 1799. So an Irish native turned Ascendancy grandee, an Ascendancy grandee turned Irish rebel, and an Irish native set on the destruction of the Ascendancy are all freely commemorated within a few yards of each other, close to a stream of heedless traffic, in the county town of a country which does not always live comfortably with the complex interweavings of its cultural fabric.

Turlough, four miles north-east, has a plump Round Tower, eighteenth-century church remains, a mansion – Turlough Park – built in 1865 in the same laterally striped Victorian Gothic as Keble College, Oxford, and close to the ruins of its eighteenth-century predecessor. In this was born George Robert FitzGerald, descended from the

Geraldines on one side and nephew of the florid Earl of Bristol on the other. He married the sister of Tom Conolly of Castletown, but her life became hell and she soon left him. His father could not escape so easily. George kept a pet bear, and after a quarrel locked his father to the bear (muzzled) in close confinement for several months. He ruled his territory in feudal state, kept a private army, and fortified the local rath with guns from a Dutch shipwreck. He also fought over seventy duels and hunted at night by the light of torches. Then in the 1780s he was astounded not to be chosen as Colonel of the Mayo Volunteers. In pique, he captured the man chosen and murdered him. This time he was arrested by troops sent for the purpose, tried in Castlebar, and sentenced to death. His forthcoming execution became one of the season's events and people flocked to watch. On the day, he drank a bottle of port, swaggered out of the prison (under a gate with the solemn inscription 'Without Beware. Within Amend'), climbed the gallows ladder, made a defiant speech, sprang off – and snapped the rope. During the hours it took to fetch a new one his mood changed to gloomy penitence. He was buried at Turlough.

Knock is easily reached on a round drive from Castlebar. The N60 takes us through Balla, with the stump of a Round Tower, and four miles north of the unremarkable village of Mayo, which gave the county its name and to which St Colman came from the island of Inishbofin. Some ruins of the abbey he founded remain. The N60 continues through the rich farmland of the Plains of Mayo to the prosperous town of Claremorris, close to which Claremount, an eighteenth-century Palladian mansion, once home of Browne relations of the Marquess of Sligo, has been swallowed up within later convent buildings. Uniquely, the banshee said to be heard here heralds good things, not bad. From here the N17 leads north to **Knock**, a town nobody had heard much of till 1879. In August of that year the Virgin Mary was seen beside the south wall of the church. She was seen again, several times. Vatican approval was given to the belief that miracles were occurring. Today the Basilica of Our Lady Queen of Ireland accommodates twelve thousand people. There are numerous other places of worship and other facilities, and always the coexistence of commercialism and deep faith in the cures claimed. There is also a small museum. From here the R323 goes north-west to Kiltamagh, pronounced 'Kulchimah' and source of the word 'kulchie': denoting one characterised by degrees of cunning and greed not to be found in decent folk like Dubliners –

so Dubliners might say. The R324 takes us back to Balla, and the N60 to Castlebar.

Newport is a small village ten miles west of Castlebar, in a valley at the north-east corner of Clew Bay. The 1914 Catholic parish church, with Romanesque Revival details much loved at that period, contains one of Harry Clarke's best windows at the east end, with typically glowing colours and a mass of ghoulish detail in the portrayal of Judgement Day. Taking the N59 north, then bending west round the coast, we turn left towards the sea for the remains of the Dominican priory of Burrishoole, founded in 1486, with good windows among its extensive remains; then, returning to the main road turn left again after three miles down a lane leading down to Rockfleet, or Carrigahooley Castle, the only ruin that can be positively associated with Grace O'Malley, the stay of all rebellions in the west, earning the title 'Queen of Clew Bay' by her expert strategy, large private army, and efficient fleet. **Carrigahooley** she came to possess by marrying her second husband, Sir Richard Burke, on a trial basis for a year, at the end of which, having filled the place with her own followers and got herself an heir, she dismissed him. From here she waged war with Sir Richard Bingham and his troops for a while, but later came to an agreement with him and travelled to London to meet the queen. She seems to have ended her days loyal, and possessing at most a third of her former empire.

To the north of the road we are on lies the loneliest stretch of all Ireland – the Nephin Beg range which, except for the picturesque road from Newport up the east side of Lough Feeagh, comprises over two hundred square miles without road or house. In the centre is **Nephin Beg** itself, 2,065 feet high. At the east end of the range, and cut off from it by a road, is conical Nephin, 2,646 feet high and commanding magnificent views of the wildest and least peopled county in Ireland, with the great Bog of Erris stretching away to the north. A circuit of the range takes us through magnificently desolate country which, though less needs to be said of it because of its want of people and outstanding features, is in some people's eyes the most inspiring part of Ireland.

We continue west to Mallaranny, or Mulrany, a pretty resort festooned with rhododendron and fuchsia, whose Mulrany Bay Hotel, vacant for some years, is a reminder of the day when big middle-class families came, complete with nannies and maids, mainly to the Great Southern Hotel and rentable houses round about, for the children's summer holidays. In his time the Beatle John Lennon stayed, and bought an island in the bay. A path runs down through neglected hotel gardens to a good broad causewayed beach. In summer the Curraun Hills to the west are carpeted with juniper, crowberry and Irish heath.

The largest of Irish islands is **Achill**, a mere twenty yards off the mainland, or rather the peninsula, of Corraun, and reached by the bridge over Achill Sound. Before the bridge was built there were no foxes on the island; after, the islanders had to construct fences to protect their poultry. Nowadays the island is kept affluent by tourism and fishing, but till this century it was one of the most remote and backward parts of the country. Even in the early 1900s, oats and potatoes were grown in tiny plots barely able to support the population of 4,000, who relied largely on remittances sent by emigrants to their families. Not so long ago the target of fishermen was the basking shark. From April to July the harmless creatures, which can be as long as forty feet, were caught in nets stretched across the shoreline at Keem Bay, then speared by fishermen in curraghs. Later they were cut up for the extraction of oil.

The road from Achill Sound brings us round Mount Minawn, on whose western, sea side the Cathedral Rocks, cut into the Menawn Cliffs, form a splendid work of natural architecture. Trawmore Sand takes over, the longest of many fine beaches on the island. Keel is the principal resort. Two miles on, the pub at Dooagh contains photographs of Don Allum and his boat the QE3. In 1982 he landed here after becoming the first person to row the Atlantic in both directions. To the west the road continues past Corrymore House Hotel (which once belonged to Captain Boycott, and later, from 1924 to 1929, to the American artist Robert Henri) to the delightful, protected Keem Strand, situated under Croaghaun, whose seaward cliffs, over 2,000 feet, are among the highest in Europe. They are best seen from the sea, but there are breathtaking views from the summit, reached by walking past Lough Acorrymore, behind Corrymore House. It was in the waters below them that the Children of Lir, turned into swans, lived out one part of their long exile.

At Doogort on the north coast, a colony of Protestants was settled in 1834 by a Church of Ireland clergyman, the Rev. E. Nangle, of the Church Missionary Society. His battles with the Catholic establishment became a national issue, as anything that can be seen as an attempt to poach souls in Ireland always has been. Nangle himself was obviously a kindly, energetic soul but he was the servant of an uppish society convinced of its moral superiority. Untold bigotry and a deal of violence was evinced from either side. The colony lasted but it never achieved its purpose, and Achill remains as strongly Catholic as other regions hereabouts.

On the slopes of Slievemore above Doogort and among the hills farther west are to be found the remains of booley-houses, some of the few to have survived at all (there are several more in Sligo). Some were still used in living memory. They were summer milking-houses for the cattle to which whole families would migrate for the season, living in temporary huts round about. The system probably goes back to prehistory. The freedom, away from home, was condemned by Spenser as leading to 'mischeives and villanyes'.

Returning to Mulrany, we drive north on the long road to Belmullet, with delightful coastal views to the left and mountains to the right. A detour to the left eight miles before Bangor could bring us to Gweesalia, in the Gaelic-speaking area between Blacksod Bay and Tullaghan Bay, supposedly where J.M. Synge set the action of his *Playboy of the Western World*. Just before Bangor, main town of the great Bog of Erris, we cross the Owenmore River, an anglers' favourite, and in the village turn left to cover the last twelve miles to Belmullet. (A turn to the right, along the Ballina road, would bring us after nine miles to the Bellacorick power station, run on peat – black expanses abound in the landscape, where the peat has been scraped away for fuel – and anxious to endear themselves to the public with an interesting rail tour, taking in an impressive wind-farm of twenty-one mills.)

Belmullet, nothing much in itself, occupies the narrow isthmus between the mainland and the Mullet Peninsula. It has always been a vulnerable area, and when the famines of the 1840s struck, its inhabitants were reported by a Commissioner to be 'the lowest and most degraded he had ever met with, even among the Ashantees and wild Indians'. Tourism, a golf course and fishing help it along today. To the west of the town lie the sea-beleaguered wilds of the Mullet, forming the two bays of Blacksod and Broad Haven. Apart from the scenery there is little noteworthy, and the scenery is bare enough, there being hardly any trees. Five miles south-west, near the shore are the ruins of a church, once part of a fourteenth-century priory known as Cross Abbey, and offshore from this is Inishglora, an island monastery founded by St Brendan, the preserving air of which was said to save corpses from corruption and even to allow their nails and hair to continue growing. 'Every one there recognises his father and grandfather for a long time after death; and no meat will putrefy on it', wrote the fifteenth-century author of the Book of Ballymote. At the south-western tip of the peninsula are further ruins, of St Derivla's church and St Derivla's Grave; while several islands out to sea – Inishkea North, Inishkea South and Duvillaun More – retain monastic remains.

Returning to Belmullet and along the main road, we break off left after three miles and follow the R314 towards scenery that is by contrast most dramatic. **Benwee Head**, off to the left, has magnificent cliffs over 800 feet high and the view from the top gives geographic views over hundreds of miles of coast and out to the Stags of Broadhaven, seven rocks two miles offshore, rising to 300 feet. There are other sheer headlands, difficult to get at, farther east. Beyond Belderg the road approaches the sea and there follow several tiny harbour villages – Portacloy, Porturlin and Belderg – and some cliff-bound bays, many with large caves and smooth sandy strands facing the Arctic Circle. Five miles short of Ballycastle is the car park and striking, pyramidal visitors' centre of **Ceide Fields**. Several feet below the rain-swept, heathery country round about, part of a past age has been preserved in peat. Settlers of about five thousand years ago, it seems, cut down trees, marked off fields with stone walls and planted their crops – all with great efficiency. But their work brought its own destruction. Trees suck up and use water fallen as rain and return it to the atmosphere by evaporation. When the trees went, over hundreds of years, the ground became wetter. Dead vegetation failed to rot, amassing in the patchy, peaty wetness which is bog, and burying the site. Painstaking twentieth-century work traced the outline of the old walls. You can push a long pole down through several feet of bog as if it were time, and tap the structures of five thousand years ago. Some of the old fields are exposed, unchanged in shape. Archaeology has since disclosed a deal of new information, not only about this site but others in the area, which is also as rich as any in Ireland in megalithic tombs. A visit to the centre is richly rewarding for its displays related not just to the ancient settlements, but to the geology and botany of the area.

Ballycastle, a seaside resort, lies at the head of a long bay which has excellent beaches. Turning left here we carry on round the coast and can, after six miles, turn left again to see Kilcummin Head, at the end of an untarred track. A hilltop memorial on this inhospitable shore marks the landing place of General Humbert's French army that arrived in 1798 to join the Irish insurgents. From here the French made their way to an easy victory at Castlebar, then a decisive defeat at Ballinamuck. A few miles farther on the main road enters **Killala**, where at the time of the invasion the Protestant bishop was kept captive by the French in his own house, and afterwards wrote of the extreme courtesy of his warders. The small, gracefully spired Church of Ireland cathedral here (the diocese is linked with Tuam and Achonry) was built about 1680 on the site of a medieval church. One original doorway, on the south wall, survives. The pews are really a series of stalls all round. A mile south-east of the town are the unusually complete remains of the 1455 Franciscan friary of Moyne, which survived a turbulent history during Sir Richard Bingham's Elizabethan conquest of Connacht. Bartragh, the long low island opposite the shore here, belongs to the English golf champion Nick Faldo. It has a private golf course. Another friary, **Rosserk**, is beside the river Moy three miles on. It was founded in 1441 by the Joyces, and it, too, suffered under Bingham. Compactly set in a field beside the water, its church, cloister, refectory and dormitory buildings are among the best preserved in Ireland.

Ballina (pronounced with stress on the last syllable), though not the county town, is Mayo's biggest, well situated, with its own harbour, by the salmon-rich Moy with some rich and pleasant demesnes to the north. (The land is good round here; good land was seldom missed by Anglo-Irish settlers.) Former president Mary Robinson was born here. Apart from the Catholic cathedral and a broken-down fifteenth-century Augustinian friary beside it, there is little to fascinate in the town, though it is a good base. One good trip may be taken round **Lough Conn**. The road near the south-eastern corner of the lake leads to a height from which, with no need of walking, the lake and its gaunt rocky surrounds, with conical Nephin in the background, can be seen. Three miles south-east is the neat town of **Foxford**, on the Moy, famous for its summer run of salmon grilse, and more so for its woollen factory, begun in the nineteenth century and still run by the Sisters of Charity. It was the birthplace of Admiral William Brown (1777–1857), like Ambrosio O'Higgins a notable Irish exile to South America; he founded the Argentine navy. Twenty flat and often boggy miles east, beyond Swinford, lies a town with a past of greater interest than its present. In *Death of an Irish Town*, John Healy tells the strange beginning and what seemed to him, writing in the 1960s, the end of Charlestown, on the border of Mayo and Sligo. It was founded out of spite. In the 1840s it was nothing but bog, belonging to Lord Dillon, whose estates were managed by Charles Strickland. Just over in Sligo, on land belonging to the Knox family, was Bellahy, an important little town with a market and a public weighbridge. Insulted one day by Lord Knox, Strickland offered the public big inducements to build houses, to his plan, and at great expense, on the shifting Mayo bog. This worked. Then, to knock out Bellahy altogether, he erected a public scales. Knox sued him. He put up the scales elsewhere and was sued again; and elsewhere again and was sued again. Next time Knox bowed out. The scales stand in the public square. The clever arrangement of original Charlestown is still visible. Like many western towns, it nearly died after the war, when Healy wrote. It has recovered, helped by the closeness of Knock International Airport. Bellahy is insignificant.

Returning to Foxford and the southern end of Lough Conn, we cross the bridge at Pontoon, where the limestone bed of Lough Conn to the north touches on the granite bed of smaller Lough Cullin, each rock base having a characteristic effect on the plants and scenery. On the hillside just west of the hotel on the far side of Pontoon Bridge is a large granite block, delicately poised. Many stories accrued to this, as to similar phenomena in the district, connecting it with the magic powers of druids. Unfortunately this one does not rock, as others do, making ideal if hazardous nut-crackers. It was simply shifted by glacial ice and brought to rest by chance at this point. The country and lakes are rich in wildfowl and this is a favourite haunt of shooting and fishing men (there is hardly any hunting in the whole of Connacht apart from two Galway hunts and the Sligo harriers). Lough Conn earlier this century yielded Ireland's record pike – a fifty-three-pounder. From the western road the lake is hidden by intervening demesnes most of the way, but there are tracks leading here and there to the shore. Crossmolina at the north-west corner is a small pretty town, and the circuit is completed by turning right and reaching Ballina again, this time from the west.

We now take the main N59 to the north-east out of the town, but soon turn left into the coast road, R297, rather more scenic than the shorter inland route. Four miles on, still beside the Moy estuary, rich in bird life, we leave county Mayo and enter county Sligo. Enniscrone is a popular seaside resort, eight miles from Ballina. Two and a half miles beyond it, close to the shore, is ruined Castle Firbis, or Lecan Castle, one of many keeps hereabouts that belonged to the chief local families – MacFirbis, MacSweeney and O'Dowd. The building hardly survives at all, but in its day belonged to the family at the end of whose line came Duald MacFirbis, last and one of the greatest hereditary Irish genealogists or shanachies. His book of *Genealogies* was compiled in St Nicholas's College, Galway, and he wrote a history of the Irish – *Chronicon Scotorum*. His family had been prominent for centuries in this field.

Dromore West, nine miles on, is a pretty village beside the Dunneill River with the ruins of a medieval church used as a Protestant church in the eighteenth century. Farther on the Ox Mountains close in on the road from the south. In their foothills, two miles due south of Skreen and reached by a lane, is **Lough Achree**, known as Ireland's youngest lake. A volcano formed it in 1490. To the left of our road, lanes reach to good beaches and headlands. We carry on along the south of Ballysadare Bay and at Ballysadare turn left to Sligo.

15

Sligo, Leitrim, Fermanagh

T HE PREHISTORIC MYTHS of Ireland are endlessly complicated. As with Greek and Roman myths, attempts to tally
different versions lead to the marriage of one hero to his great-grand-
mother and his, maybe, siring his great-aunt. Despair confronts the
literal mind that goes further and tries to explain the stories of individuals in terms of the movements and histories of peoples. Yet it
seems that some history does underlie some myth, and there are
eminent scholars in Dublin and elsewhere busy showing which and
why. The process has been full of dispute because the status of Celtic
myth has been afflicted with excess of sentimentality (Tom Moore,
etc.), forgery (James Macpherson, etc.), racial and cultural bias (a
certain brand of nineteenth-century Protestant cleric, etc., and more
recently partisan scholars) and a tendency to hallow those from whom
you would like to be descended. When we are confidently told as
much about Fir Bolg, Fomorians and Tuatha de Danann as is known,
say, about the Minoans, the Sligo region will figure large in the
account. Every stage of prehistory is represented here, in both mythical and archaeological manifestations. Every expedition from Sligo
town takes us back one, two or three thousand years, or even farther,
to the dawn of Irish civilisation. Sligo is the western end of an almost
unbroken chain of prehistoric traces stretching westward from the
royal cemetery on the Boyne. Four miles west of the town is a landmark that impressively reminds us of this antiquity, and to that pile of
40,000 tons of stone, heaped over the tomb of Queen Maeve and
breaking the smooth line of Knocknarea Mountain, we shall go after a
brief glimpse at **Sligo** city itself.

Only a few buildings take notice of the Garavogue River, running
to the north of the town's centre between Lough Gill and the harbour.
The town is, as a result, less attractive than it might be – its main
purpose, from the visitor's point of view, being to serve as a base for
sights and beaches in the area. Though the town was fortified early in

the thirteenth century by the Anglo-Norman Maurice FitzGerald, forefather of the earls of Kildare, who received it and the surrounding lands as a grant, nothing much survived the subsequent assaults on walls and often repaired castles by dispossessed Gaels, notably the overlord O'Donnells. Control passed to the De Burgos, then the royal family of O'Conor, until Tudors and Cromwellians asserted English power. The oldest building is the Dominican friary, known as the **Abbey**, whose ruins go back to 1253 but which was virtually rebuilt in the early fifteenth century. It possesses some fine memorials, including that to the O'Conor Sligo and Lady Eleanor Butler, his wife, who died in 1623, and another of 1616 in the nave, the altar tomb of the O'Creans. The cloisters to the north are in good condition, with good carving on the pillars. A quarter of a mile west, in what could be taken as the ecclesiastical headquarters of the town, are the dull Catholic cathedral and Church of Ireland parish church, since 1962 also a cathedral. The one is a copy of a church in Rome, the other an 1812 reworking of a church by Richard Castle – one of the few he did, smothering it under Gothic decoration.

The road due west out of Sligo leads to **Knocknarea,** close to a succession of delightful sandy strands which have attracted Irish and other holiday-makers since the eighteenth century, when sea-bathing first became a popular pastime. Strandhill is the best known of these – tides and currents can be dangerous, and there have been drownings in modern times. Near the north-west tip of the peninsula is Killaspugbrone, a ruin on the site of a church founded by St Patrick's disciple, Bishop Bronus. The patron saint allegedly dropped a tooth here one day, which was preserved in the beautiful casket known as the Fiacal Padraig now displayed, albeit toothless, in the National Museum. The straightforward ascent to the summit (1,078 feet) of Knocknarea is best made from the eastern side. From its flat top the complexity of inlets and promontories around Sligo Harbour, with Inishmurray out to sea twelve miles north, appear like a colourful map. The great hump of Maeve's Grave is seen to be a vast pile of loose stones, the perimeter of which is about two hundred yards. Maeve was the tangled synthesis of a Connacht queen and a Celtic goddess (the same as Mab in British folklore) and the mound is likely to pre-date the Celtic invasions, which makes the name probably misleading. There are, besides, rival claimants for her remains, notably Knockma. Nothing is certain about the matter, but experts are inclined to account it a Bronze Age grave and leave further details to excavation, if ever that takes place. Technical problems and costs

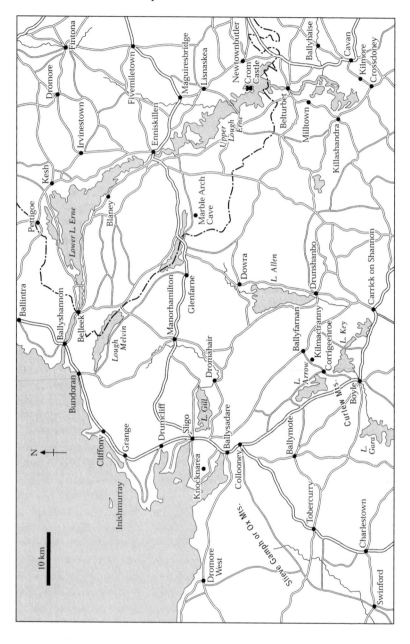

would be immense – 40,000 tons of chippings to be removed by hand. On the other hand, it is much less likely than a generation ago that locals would sabotage any attempt to disturb their queen protector.

Excavation has, however, gone on in the vast megalithic cemetery of Carrowmore, two miles east of the hill, which can be reached after a circuit of Knocknarea and a walk in the extraordinary Glen of Knocknarea (south of the mountain, and through an iron gate just south of the lane that leads off the main road and circles the southern slopes). **Carrowmore** is second only to Carnac in Brittany as a mega-lithic graveyard, and far the biggest in Ireland, spreading over a mile and a half. Time, pilferers, amateur archaeologists and gravel extrac-tion have reduced the number of identifiable graves by hundreds, and much of the wall prehistoric man erected round the site twentieth-century man removed. Originally these dolmens and passage tombs, a few of which are visible from the road, were the actual chambers containing the dead, and were covered with earth and stones to make uniform humps over the whole area. Now in most cases only the heavy capstones and their supporting boulders remain. Their place in the scheme of prehistory is obscure, being at the end of a line of related graves that came to Ireland from Brittany, reached their peak in the Boyne Valley and then spread westward. Discoveries in the Boyne Valley threatened to upset fragile preconceptions, but where archaeology is timid, myth feels no restraint. Carrowmore is supposed to be the burial ground of the dead from the great battle of Northern Moytura, in which the Tuatha de Danaan defeated the Fomorians for all time. There is of course a large, Europe-funded visitors' centre.

The local trip from Sligo on its east side is to **Lough Gill**, which opens out, two and a half miles upstream, from Sligo's Garavogue River. The lake is one of Ireland's prettiest, its surrounding wooded hills stretching to where the naked concave shapes of the limestone mountains take over to the north. What it shares with Killarney (to which it is often unnecessarily compared) is a vegetation on some of its islands that includes arbutus, yew and whitebeam, and on shore, among other rare flowers, the Bird's-nest Orchis and the Yellow Bird's-nest. On a clockwise circuit of the lake we can turn right two miles out of the town and see the peninsula which makes up the demesne of Hazelwood House, a heavy square house with curving arcades on either side leading to pavilions. Richard Castle built it, less inspired than he was at Leinster House or Russborough. It was about to be pulled down when the town council saved it to become the psychiatric wing of St Columba's Hospital. They spoiled it with numerous accretions. The next owner, an Italian fibre-manufacturing firm, restored the house but their and subsequent factory buildings destroyed the demesne. At present the house is empty and unused.

Three miles farther along the main road, lanes lead left to Colgagh Lough, north-east of which is the Magheraghanrush or Deerpark monument, on top of a hill with wonderful views over Lough Gill. The monument is a court cairn, the oldest type of megalithic tomb, and incorporates an unroofed court, probably used for ritual purposes. The whole is oval in shape and about 180 feet long with a burial chamber each side of the central court. The fact that three pairs of uprights had lintels in place led for a long time to confusion with Stonehenge, and to the name of the 'Irish Stonehenge'; more recent research has placed it more accurately. The whole site has suffered much from farmers, who used the stones to build stone walls round their fields. Three miles farther along the main road splendid, well restored, lakeside Parkes Castle, built early in the seventeenth century, comes into view. A water bus goes from here to and from Innisfree. Beyond the castle the road bends to the right, and leads away from the lake to **Dromahair**, chief seat in Anglo-Norman times of the O'Rourke kings of Breifne. From their castle, while her husband, Tiernan O'Rourke, was on a pilgrimage to St Patrick's Purgatory in Lough Derg, Dervorgilla eloped with Dermot MacMurrough, king of Leinster, and so began the fateful sequence of events that led to the Anglo-Norman Conquest. Most of the O'Rourke castle was demolished to provide stone for the fortified house built by Sir William Villiers, half-brother of Charles I's favourite, the Duke of Buckingham, in 1626. He was also given 11,000 acres. The house too is now ruinous.

Extensive remains of Creevelea Friary, founded for Franciscans by the O'Rourkes in 1508 and containing many of their tombs and some pillar-carvings of St Francis, one showing him preaching to birds on a tree, are beside the river half a mile downstream of the town. A right turn beyond Dromahair brings us after two miles to a crossroads, where a bohreen (or lane) to the right leads to the lake's edge and a sight of Yeats's little Innisfree, or 'Heather island' – in fact the lake's most insignificant isle, and looking a little cramped and overgrown for a bee-loud glade and bean-rows. Years ago Yeats's sister Lucy predicted future signs: 'Do not eat the beans' or 'The cabin is private' – that kind of thing. The main road continues for a mile, bends right through the glacial channel of Slish Gap, and then keeps to the lake for two miles before breaking away to return to Sligo. To the left, Dooney Rock, again known for Yeats's use of it, provides excellent views, from its top, of the whole scene.

Southern Sligo, Northern Leitrim

Innumerable lakes and rivers feed the Shannon River at its northern end. The technical source of the river, the Shannon Pot, is about twenty-five miles east of Sligo. About fifteen miles south-west of the town, a lower stretch of the river is fed from a group of lakes lying amidst beautiful scenery. On our way there we drive south, past the eastern end of Ballysadare Bay. Just before Collooney, beside the old road, is a sumptuous monument to Bartholomew Teeling, a French officer who during the battle here in 1798 successfully stormed a British artillery post, thus deciding the outcome. Captured later, he was hanged in Dublin.

Beyond Collooney we turn right on to the N17. Collooney Pass, where the limestone and (hereabouts) quartzite ridge of the Ox Mountains sink almost to sea level before rising again to the north-east under different names, has always been of great strategic importance; nowadays two rivers, three main roads and the railway share it. A mile east (off the N4 road to Boyle) is the demesne of **Markree**, an eighteenth-century house with Gothic enlargements and alterations of 1803 by Francis Johnston. The domed tower of the old observatory, for years Europe's largest telescope, still stands. (The telescope is in Hong Kong.) The gateway has a fifty-foot tower, designed for telegraphic links with other big houses. In 1860 that prolific apostle of 'muscular Christianity', Charles Kingsley, stayed at the house with his friend Joshua Cooper (it is still in the same family). There had been a spate of evictions in South Sligo before his arrival. 'It is a land of ruins and of the dead', he wrote, and 'it moves me to tears.' But not for long, there being so many salmon in the river: 'I had magnificent sport this morning. There is nothing like it. The excitement is maddening.' The park is lit with standard gas lamps, as there used to be a gasworks on the demesne. The house has been consistently inhabited by the Cooper family from Cromwellian times, except that is for a few postwar years when it was too costly to run as a home. Use as a set for the film version of J.G. Farrell's *Troubles* began its redemption, then conversion to a stylish hotel by the present Cooper generation. It is said that Victorian Mrs Alexander, writing the lines 'the rich man in his castle, the poor man at his gate … The purple-headed mountain, The river running by …' in the hymn *All Things Bright and Beautiful*, had Markree, where she had stayed, in mind. Four miles south-east is Coopershill, originally a Cooper seat, this one ungarnished Georgian in fine grounds, also offering accommodation.

We keep to the western road, then branch left on the R293 and come to **Ballymote**, where in 1917 Constance Markievicz, released from a British gaol, received a minutes-long ovation on her return home. (She was born at Lissadell, north-west of Sligo.) The large castle here, built in 1300 by Richard de Burgo, Earl of Ulster, has declined since the Cromwellian campaign into a pleasing ivy-covered ruin. In the ruined Franciscan friary was written the *Book of Bally-mote*, the largest of all Irish codices, preserved in the Royal Irish Academy and containing numerous highly contrived historical works, including the *Book of Invasions*. Four miles west of Ballymote is Temple House, a massive pile built for the Perceval family in 1820 and enlarged from time to time to its present tally of ninety bedrooms; it offers bed and breakfast in lovely old-world, rather melancholy rooms, set amid enchanting parkland, whose owner, allergic to perfumes, asks his guests to desist from the use of them.

A few miles beyond Ballymote, left of the R295, is the 1,168-foot rounded limestone cone of **Keshcorran**. Halfway up its west face is a row of caves, which were used as habitations in prehistoric times – bones include reindeer, Arctic lemming, bears and wolves – all now extinct in the country but common apparently in the Bronze Age – snails, fishes and birds. It was in one of these caves that King Cormac Mac Art, the real architect of Tara, was supposed to have been reared by a she-wolf, which had carried him off from his sleeping mother (as, among others, Romulus and Remus, founders of Rome, were also reared – it is not only New Testament stories that are suspiciously echoed in Irish myth). The Bricklieve Mountains, with **Carrowkeel** among them, are connected to Keshcorran on the east by a low broad neck. Its broad flat summit has a jagged edge cut by hillside gorges, and on many of the platforms between these gorges are old stone cairns – most of them as prominent over the surrounding country as their builders, working between 3000 and 2000 BC, obviously intended. The total collection – fourteen chambered cairns, two dolmens and many more circles of low stones – has been claimed to have formed a prehistoric village, the only one of its kind in the country. Many of the remains, excavated earlier in the twentieth century, had remained untouched down the centuries and so yielded a wealth of Bronze Age objects and several clues as to the old methods of burial. Trinkets continued to be found long after the experts had departed. East of the mountains, and beyond the main N4 road, is charming Lough Arrow, with its many islands and multitudes of brown trout, perch, pike and so on. Back on the main road we can now cross the Curlew Mountains, and pass the spot where Red Hugh O'Donnell, Hugh O'Neill's spirited lieutenant in the 1599 Rebellion, inflicted his last victory in the war, against Sir Conyers Clifford's advancing army.

Boyle is well situated on a hillside, most of the town being at the foot, but the square at the top contains a good Georgian courthouse. Within this, Count G.N. Plunkett, father of the executed 1916 revolutionary Joseph Mary Plunkett, was in February, 1917, declared MP for North Roscommon, the first Sinn Feiner to be so; the victory, first of many, marked both the end of Redmond's moderate Home Rule Party and the revival of militant politics. But the town has greater treasure. Boyle Abbey, beside the River Boyle and east of the town, was founded by Cistercians here as a daughter of Mellifont in 1161, as usual for Cistercians in a remote and unpeopled place. The town later grew round it and took its name from the abbey. Though badly mutilated in the 1650s by Commonwealth troops, its imposing ruins spread over a wide area and well preserve the basic plan and much of the walls of the abbey cloister and conventual buildings. Of special interest are the eight Norman arches on the south side, probably remnants of an earlier church, and many fine details in capitals, pillars and windows. Among those buried here was Edward King (1612–37), Milton's fellow student, whose early death by drowning off the Welsh coast was the inspiration of *Lycidas*. Impressively restored in recent years from a state of dereliction, King House was the King family home during most of the eighteenth century. Towards 1800 the first earl of Kingston was laying out Rockingham on the south shore of Lough Key, and in the nineteenth century King House was demoted to use as a barracks. Unusually for its time, it was built of brick. It now houses exhibitions and displays, many of them centred on the King family.

For people cruising from Carrick-on-Shannon, Boyle is the western upstream limit for their wandering, and makes an ideal base for exploring Lough Key, the most beautiful of local lakes. But the Boyle River, though unnavigable, goes on west to **Lough Gara**, which makes a pretty detour here. Excavations in the lake some years ago yielded evidence of several crannogs – prehistoric lake-dwellings

– with many intricately worked artifacts. Coolavin, on the western shore of the lake, was in the eighteenth century all that was left of the estates of the MacDermot family, rulers of huge tracts for over a thousand years but dispossessed by Cromwell and the Penal Laws. Arthur Young in 1780 called at the house of the MacDermot, who making the best of his affairs called himself 'Prince of Coolavin' and 'though he has not even £100 a year will not permit his children to sit down in his presence'. The present gabled house was built in 1898.

From Boyle we drive east and after two miles turn left into the **Rockingham** demesne. The mansion was built originally in the seventeenth century by the Kings, one of whom later became the first Earl of Kingston, living at Mitchelstown in Cork. The most striking view from the site of the house, now replaced by a grimly institutional complex of amenities, is of Lough Key, almost fragile in its prettiness, studded with wooded islands, with the Curlew Mountains (from which are seen the best views of the lake) rising on the left and further ranges farther north; it conjures up the blades and beauties, the gaiety, boats and lacy parasols of another age. Castle Island, opposite, was a possession of the MacDermots before their lands dwindled to Coolavin. It still has a castle, but it is crumbling and dangerous. Yeats wanted to make it a Castle of Heroes, a sanctuary to which those who had proved their devotion to Ireland might come and plan Ireland's spiritual rebirth. To the left is Trinity Island, with a ruined abbey in which was composed in the sixteenth century the valuable *Annals of Lough Key*. Rockingham demesne has become a forest park, and the house has disappeared. It had a hectic history. Nash rebuilt it in 1810 for the first Viscount Lorton, brother of the Earl of Kingston. Sacheverell Sitwell called this building one of the two finest Nash houses in Ireland (the other being Caledon). But Lorton, jealous of the size of his brother's house at Mitchelstown, had the two-storey house spoiled by the addition of a third in 1820. In 1863 the place was accidentally burned down. Rebuilt to its later plan, it survived intact till 1957 and was known for lavish hospitality. Then it was burned again. For a few years its gutted ghost lorded it over the water, and the demesne, the little round battlemented fishing house, the many Gothic follies, Soane's Tiara Lodge, and the ruined church, all added to the unreal quality of the place. Finally the authorities, declaring it beyond repair, demolished it.

From the lakeside and the large wooded demesne, we return to the main N4 road and drive on east, and may then fork left – about four miles east of Boyle – to follow the lake, more or less, round its eastern and northern shores. If, before this, we continue a little further along the main Carrick road we reach, on the left, but cannot enter, Woodbrook, the modest gentry house in which, during the 1930s, young David Thomson went to coach the Kirkwood daughters and stayed, on and off, ten years. His *Woodbrook* published in 1974 beautifully, romantically and at times sadly evokes the pleasures, and some of the cares, of rural Anglo-Irish life, and a lot of its history besides. A mile or so before the entrance to the Woodbrook drive, and on the right-hand side of the road, a lane leads to Ardcarne, with a handsome Church of Ireland church possessing an Evie Hone window and, outside, a striking bronze kneeling figure commemorating the great famine. Returning to the road along the east of Lough Key, we come to the crossroads of Corrigeenroe and turn right. After two miles and two sharp bends we can divert to the left and visit **Moytura** (two miles north of the village of Kilmactranny) where some scattered cairns may mark the site of the second, half-legendary battle of Moytura, in which the Tuatha de Danann, precursors of the Milesians and the Celts themselves, pushed the unsavoury sea-spirits the Fomorians out of their way and out of history. A mile or so west, close to the lake, are Ballindoon's abbey ruins.

From Moytura we return through Kilmactranny, turn left, pass Lough Skean on the right, turn right at the T-junction, continue through Ballyfarnan, leaving it by the Keadew road; and a mile farther come to the fourteenth-century ruined church of **Kilronan** beside Lough Meelagh. Turlough O'Carolan (1670–1738) was buried here after his death in Alderford House, then a MacDermot property. Born blind, he was, as Goldsmith wrote, 'the last and the greatest' of the old bards, coming at the end of a court tradition that had lasted since the Celtic migrations and before. A bard was a kind of local poet laureate, hired to sing praises, generally of the old Irish aristocracy. Carolan was at once an excellent poet, singer, player and composer – the music of *The Star-spangled Banner* is his. He was also a great drinker, used to whole bottles of whiskey, and it was from this he is supposed to have sickened. On his deathbed he called for a cup, but could not drink; and then he kissed the cup, saying two such old friends could not part without kissing, and died. Later in the eighteenth century his skull was displayed in the church, and then it was lost. Kilronan Castle is big, nineteenth century, possessing baronial features, and somehow dull.

Beyond Keadew the R285 goes east towards Lough Allen. Rising up on the left is Arigna, where coal was mined from the surface in a fitful way for centuries, up to 1990. The product was poor and government backing could not make it compete with the price of American low-quality coal. We can drive round the southern end of the lake, through the anglers' resort of **Drumshanbo**, scene of a festival known as An Tostal, introduced nationwide by the government in 1953 to spread some cheer in the economic gloom. It survives here alone. We go on beside the lake's east shore under Slieve Anierin, which contains not only coal but bands of iron underlying it. This, too, has been exploited in the past, but the last attempt, in 1765, to smelt iron with pit-coal ended soon after for want of capital. Following the lake, we are also following the Shannon, which can be traced a few miles north-east of Dowra to what is known as its source, the Shannon Pot, though in fact this is itself supplied from a small lough a mile to the north-east, while the Owenmore River to the south collects the waters from higher up the mountains and more properly deserves the name of source. Nevertheless it is to the Pot that most of the credit and legends attach.

At the head of the R207, four miles farther on, we turn left – leaving the Six Counties border to the right till later – and make our way the ten miles or so to **Manorhamilton**. This town, beautifully and strategically set on a high plateau, with main roads running to all four compass points and more, is what strategic centres have often become nowadays, a very good base for the tourist, with fine scenery, a plethora of ancient remains, and easy access to the sea and five other counties. To the north is the ruined seventeenth-century fortified house of Sir Frederick Hamilton, granted large confiscated estates by Charles I. (From here onwards Scottish names figure increasingly in past and present events.) We can drive a magnificent circuit through the Glenade valley and along the southern shore of Lough Melvin, returning by the R282; then continue west through the delightful valley of Glencar with the almost sculptured forms of its limestone mountains on either side, towards the western end, and the lake itself with several spindly waterfalls dropping into it from the opposite side. Yeats brings them into his poem *The Stolen Child*, in which the thief is a faery. Faeries cannot cross water, so steal children to use as vessels; male children in particular – hence a practice of representing boys in pictures as girls. Elsewhere Yeats noted the old belief that Glencar fish observe the county boundary which cuts across the lake. No Sligo fish would even think of swimming into Leitrim, nor a Leitrim one into Sligo.

Near the west end of the lake the road bends round to the south and returns to Sligo.

Sligo to Ballyshannon

Clear of Sligo, the northbound R291 swings westward to reach Rosses Point five miles on. In the almost boundless flatness of land and sea west of Sligo, this supplies a long and loved sandy beach and a championship golf course. As a boy, Yeats was sometimes at 'Elsinore', a family house by the harbour, neglected now. A shallow channel in the middle of which stands a metal man on a drum divides the Point from Coney Island, 'set on a storm-bitten green', which on its other side and at low tide can be reached on foot from Strandhill.

Another road going north from Sligo, the N15, brings us after five miles to **Drumcliff**, whose churchyard is on the site of a monastery supposedly founded by St Columba in atonement for the battle and carnage he caused earlier by refusing, when accused of plagiarism, to abide by the High King's verdict. The battle took place on the slopes of Ben Bulben to the north, and the High King was worsted. Seeing with horror what he had caused, Columba settled at Iona in Scotland, and began to convert the natives. The stump of a Round Tower and a good High Cross remain of the medieval monastery. W.B. Yeats is buried in the Church of Ireland churchyard under the epitaph he wrote himself, and in the midst of countryside richly represented in his work. He died in France in 1939 and was buried there; his remains were brought back in 1948, and placed where he had directed: 'under bare Ben Bulben's head'. His great-grandfather had been rector here a hundred years earlier. The epitaph – 'Cast a cold eye on life, on death. Horseman, pass by!' – was inspired by annoyance at reading Rilke's ideas on death.

Shapely Ben Bulben occurs in several early myths, and it was here that the most romantic of ancient tales found its resolution. Finn McCool's pursuit of Grania, his old love, and Dermot, the young warrior with whom she eloped, is marked up and down the country by cairns, hills and valleys that bear their names. At last they were overtly reconciled. Then Finn ordered Dermot to catch the wild mountain boar that lived on Ben Bulben, and when he had done so told him to measure its skin with his bare feet. Dermot, like Greek Achilles, had one vulnerable point and it, too, was his heel. When he had measured out the skin one way, Finn told him to check it the other way, and this was against the boar's bristles. A bristle, as Finn intended, pierced his heel. Finn vindictively mocked the dying man. Begged to bring water, he fetched it from a spring and let it trickle through his fingers as he carried it.

A left turn just beyond the bridge takes us four miles along the north of Drumcliff Bay to **Lissadell House**, built in classical style in the 1830s and with magnificent views across the water to Knocknarea and the Ox Mountains behind. It is the home of the Gore-Booths, whose ancestor, Captain Paul Gore, came to Ireland with Essex. There had been buildings here – a castle, an earlier house – for centuries, and a famous poet Muireadhach O Dalaigh, living here in the thirteenth century, murdered a steward. One of his poems complains about his master's anger: it was after all only a servant. Not only Anglo-Normans were caste-minded. A descendant of Paul's, Sir Nathaniel Gore, married in the early 1700s Letitia Booth, a lady of high spirits who forced her coachman at pistol point to drive her round the chasms and promontories to the west of the house. She still haunts the place. Sir Robert Gore-Booth built the present house in 1834, in Grecian style (designed by Francis Goodwin, who also did the Gothic gates at Markree, and various civic buildings in the north of England). After the Famine, Gore-Booth was accused of having sent hundreds of tenants to America in an old boat that sank. Many such reports were made up about Anglo-Irish families. Documentary records speak only of his strenuous efforts and crippling expenditure of £40,000 on his tenants' behalf. His son, Sir Henry, was a distinguished Arctic explorer, and Henry's two daughters rose to high fame in different realms – Eva (1870–1926) as poetess, and Constance (1884–1927), who as Countess Markievicz helped engineer the 1916 Rising and, after imprisonment in England, became the first female British MP, and later Minister of Labour in the proscribed Dáil's first cabinet of 1919. Sarah Purser painted them here in a portrait (still in the house) that brought her first success. Yeats visited them in 1894 – 'the light of evening, Lissadell,/Great windows open to the south;/ Two girls in silk kimonos,/Both beautiful, one a gazelle ...' The house, among other features remarkable for its hundred-foot-long columnar gallery, is open to the public, and holds many mementoes, and even more ghosts of the family. The tour round it is enhanced by the guide, sometimes a present member of the family and full of reminiscence among an agreeable clutter of Anglo-Irish effects.

After glimpsing the old Gore castle ruin at Ardtermon Strand and haunted Knocklane, at the western tip of this peninsula, we can drive north-east to rejoin the main road at Grange. The island of Inishmurray is a couple of miles out – fishing boats can be got at Mullaghmore or Rosses Point – on which is a very well preserved sixth-century monastery founded by St Molaise. Till 1948 the island was inhabited by up to a hundred people. They buried men and women in separate graveyards, and poured three drops of spring water on the sea to ensure a calm journey. A mile before Grange a lane leads left to Streedagh Point and the strand where three ships of the Armada were wrecked – 'I numbered,' wrote Sir Geoffrey Fenton to Lord Burleigh, 'in one strand less than five miles in length eleven hundred dead corpses.' The English descended and caught such survivors as they could and hanged them beside nearby Staad Abbey, whose ruins stand. Some escaped and one, Don Francesco Cuellar, wrote his subsequent adventures, which have more than once been published in English. Turning left at Grange we drive six miles to Cliffoney, where a left turn leads to **Classiebawn**, a Neo-Gothic house belonging, till he was murdered by the IRA in a boat off the coast, to Earl Mountbatten, one-time viceroy of India and a cousin of the Queen, who inherited it from his wife. It belonged in the nineteenth century, with the rest of the 6,000-acre peninsula, to Lord Palmerston, the prime minister, who as a necessarily absentee landlord had a bad reputation for evictions, though he built several Catholic schools. He did not in fact live to see the castle's completion.

Bundoran, seven miles on, is a popular seaside resort with good beaches and views. It is just inside Donegal. Four miles beyond is **Ballyshannon**, setting of a famous August traditional music festival. The town has always been important as the western bridgehead across the River Erne. In 1597 it saw battle between Red Hugh O'Donnell, Lord of Tyrconnell, in league with the rebel Hugh O'Neill, against Essex, and Sir Conyers Clifford, Governor of Connacht, leading an English force. The English, attempting to take the castle (now reduced almost to nothing) were thrown back and made a perilous escape across the rapids, losing many men. In the narrow lane called the Mall a plaque marks the birthplace of William Allingham (1824–89), a good poet and friend of Tennyson, Browning and Rossetti. A revealing diarist, he is buried in the Church of Ireland cemetery, where the stone wall built to deflect wind also eliminated fine views. Other natives of Ballyshannon include Mary Wollstonecraft's mother, Elizabeth Dixon, born into a genteel family involved in the wine trade; and Hazel Corscadden, who remained here till three, later married a Captain Blair, and used to bring her three children on holiday to Rossnowlagh, five miles up the coast. The middle child, Tony, became British Prime Minister in 1996. Off the Rossnowlagh road north-west of the town are the scant remains of the Cistercian abbey of Assaroe. A colony of Boyle abbey, beside a watermill, it stands in the glen Lugnanore, in which there is a dank cave and, close by, a mass rock. The site is made more of than the remains warrant.

Lough Erne and Fermanagh

From Ballyshannon the N3 goes south-south-east, keeping to the right of Assaroe Lake and the power station, which since 1952 has exploited the force of the reservoir then created by damming. After four miles, we cross the Northern Ireland border, enter county Fermanagh, and find ourselves in **Belleek**, a small village with a large china factory. The original nineteenth-century Belleek porcelain, first produced in 1863, was made from feldspar then dug at nearby Castle Caldwell, whose owner was promoting the enterprise. It was often superbly designed and had a rare and elusive glaze. Modern produce, though successfully exported, is less enticing, though the tour round the factory seeing every phase of the making can be of great interest.

We are close to the north-west shore of Lower Lough Erne. Our road has a UK number, A47, and will take us to Enniskillen, chief city of county Fermanagh. The first six miles bring us to the demesne of **Castle Caldwell**, one of many large estates bordering the lake and now given over to forestry, and a park which the public, and particularly naturalists, can enjoy, for nature trails are laid out among labelled trees. There are hides from which to observe the plentiful wildfowl. (The Common Scoter, which breeds only in a few places in Scotland and two in northern Ireland, does so here.) The castle itself was built by a Plantation settler, Francis Blennerhasset, but passed soon to the Caldwells. The ageing Sir James Caldwell in 1778, who two years before had sped Arthur Young on his way in a stately six-oared barge, colours flying and band playing, wrote to his son, 'you will have a place universally allowed to be the most beautiful in England or Ireland'. He once removed two hundred of his men from harvesting to re-enact, for Lord Shelburne's benefit, Captain Cook's encounter with New Zealand 'savages'. All wore costumes made specially by tailors. In the event, Lord Shelburne failed to arrive, and the harvest was lost. Early this century the property became encumbered and passed, via an insurance company, to the government. The castle is now in ruins. Four miles beyond the demesne the road divides and the right fork carries on over a bridge across long, thin **Boa Island**. A mile from the bridge a notice points right to Caldragh

Cemetery, at the bottom of a field near the lake. It contains two carved squat stone figures, triangular faces and formalised bodies at back and front, that evoke glib associations with Polynesian more than Celtic art. Their double faces suggest a common source with the Roman god Janus. But they are mysteries, and may be pre-Christian; nobody feels sure about them, or about superficially similar figures on White Island.

When the island road rejoins the main road we almost double back, following the main road to Pettigo and then turning right, crossing the border, and driving to **Lough Derg**, a wild stretch of water amid low brown mountains, with no road or path round much of its shore. (An eighteenth-century parson of Pettigo called the region 'Siberia'.) At the end of our road is a quay from which ferries take up to 30,000 pilgrims – cabinet ministers, coal miners, it makes no difference – in June, July and August to the island – now encumbered with Neo-Byzantine buildings – from which St Patrick once descended to Purgatory. The legend is older but was first recorded by an English monk who described the descent of a Norman knight, Owen, through a cave on the island, across the fields of punishment to the earthly paradise. Penitential pilgrims, locked in the cave for a night and day, would see Hell and Purgatory. The legend and site grew in popularity, being mentioned in the same breath as Santiago de Compostela, and pilgrims flocked from all over Europe. Because of the heretical nature of the pilgrimage, the Borgia Pope Alexander VI ordered the cave's destruction. This was carried out in 1497. It was soon flourishing again; a new cave-mouth was opened and continued to attract thousands even when specifically prohibited by English and Irish laws, and even after the second cave was destroyed. To this day it is the most revered, and most punishing, pilgrimage in the country, 'such as no man', wrote William Carleton, 'with flesh and blood capable of suffering ... could readily forget'. Participants fast for three days – toast and black tea allowed – and go without sleep two days and the night in between, being in duty bound to wake nodders and dozers. Rain or hail, nobody catches cold (they say). Sun and heat are worse, and the second morning is anyway worst of all. But for days afterwards great mental clarity and elation are experienced by many.

From here we return to the lake road and continue east, and then south, to Kesh. A minor road from here keeps close to the lake and passes after two miles the ruins (two storeys and a square turret) of Crevinish Castle, built by Thomas Blennerhasset before 1618. Two miles on it passes near **White Island** (to which boat-trips go from

Enniskillen or Castle Archdale, where boats of various kinds may also be hired), which contains, socketed into the walls of its roofless twelfth-century Romanesque church, eight grotesque squat figures with rather more details than the Boa Island figures above. (There are plans to remove them to a museum, because of damage by the weather, and replace them with casts.) Some of the things these figures are carrying point to them being Christian, of perhaps the ninth or tenth centuries, with the exception of an obvious Sheila-na-gig, a symbol of some fertility cult. Some other pagan suggestions and the crudeness of the work appear to have decided builders of the later church to use them as masonry, from which role the church's ruin at last released them. White Island is part of the demesne of Castle Archdale, to the right of the main road and a bit farther on. The pleasant Georgian house of 1773, now fallen into ruin, was built near a Plantation castle of 1615, fragments of which still survive its 1689 destruction. The thousand acres of demesne contain a usual run of public amenities and a very modern caravan park.

To the east and south-east is lush, largely Protestant, countryside with clean-cut towns and big estates owned by families still prospering after four hundred years of settlement. Irvinestown has on the surface an old-English cosiness. Mrs Delany's husband Patrick was vicar in the 1730s, and built the Delany clock-tower. South of the town, Irvine or Necarne Castle grew from normal seventeenth-century castle proportions to Gothic grandiosity in the nineteenth. It pays for its insolence by being neglected and boarded up within a hundred and seventy acres of rolling parkland, home of the Ulster Lakeland Equestrian Park. The spruce town of Ballinamallard, five miles south, has boasted of being a hundred per cent loyalist.

Commanding as it does the land-gap between Upper and Lower Lough Erne, **Enniskillen**, like Ballyshannon, is in a strategic position to control Ulster–Connacht traffic. It has been a Protestant stronghold – though now with a predominantly Catholic population – ever since the Tudor and Stuart plantations ousted the Maguires, then lords of most of Fermanagh. Weapons found here and at other Erne fords show it saw innumerable battles before English and Scottish settlement. The castle, off Wellington Road at the town's west end, and home now to a heritage centre and military museum, incorporates bits of the original Maguire fortress, and of the construction made by the first Protestant settler, Sir William Cole. He was granted the place in 1612 and with twenty families defended it against the Irish rebels in 1641. Like Derry, it became almost a frontier post of loyalist sentiment, and resisted an attack of King James's troops in 1689. Later, the townsmen organised themselves into a regiment which was chosen as his personal guard by King William at the Boyne. This led to the formation of two regiments, the Royal Inniskilling Dragoon Guards and the Royal Inniskilling Fusiliers – a double distinction shared by no other British city. In the eighteenth century the Cole family became Earls of Enniskillen, with their seat at Florence Court (below). In spite of the hideous political crimes of recent years, the prettily situated town remains buoyant and busy, but is not rich in items of striking interest. The Church of Ireland cathedral of 1840 incorporates a tower of 1637; the Convent of Mercy contains windows by Michael Healy, Sarah Purser, and Beatrice Glenavy. To the east of the town, beyond East Bridge, is the war memorial beside which, at the Remembrance Day service in 1987, eleven citizens, including a young girl, were blown to bits by a terrorist bomb. Beyond, on top of the pretty park of Fort Hill (from which there are superb views) is a conspicuous memorial column to Sir Galbraith Lowry Cole (1772–1842), brother of the second Earl of Enniskillen and Governor of Cape Colony. On the hill north-west of the town is Portora Royal School, built in 1777 to house a school founded by the Cole family in Charles I's reign, in 1626. The hymn writer, M.F. Lyte ('Abide with Me'), and two rather more magical word-spinners, Oscar Wilde and Samuel Beckett, were educated here.

Within a few miles of the city are an ancient and holy island, two of Ireland's finest houses, and a great deal else of beauty and interest. Two miles north-north-west of Enniskillen, in lower Lough Erne, is **Devenish Island**, to which cruises run from the town. The remains of the monastery first founded by St Molaise (who is said to have exiled St Columba to Scotland for causing the Battle of Culdreimne, with instructions to convert as many souls as were killed in the battle), include an almost perfect Round Tower (with sculptured heads on a cornice beneath the cap), an ancient house and church, and fifteenth-century St Mary's Abbey. **Castle Coole** is two miles south-east of the town. It dates, like much of the best of Irish building, to the last years of the eighteenth century when Armar Lowry-Corry, first Earl of Belmore, paid £54,000 altogether to have it erected to the meticulously detailed plans of James Wyatt, whose best work some consider this to be. As with other places associated with his name in Ireland, there is nothing to show that he came here to supervise the work. No expense was spared. Portland stone came by chartered brig from

Portland Bill to Ballyshannon, where a special quay had to be built to take it. Thence it was carried by ox-cart. The finest English and continental craftsmen were imported for adornments, including the plasterer Joseph Rose, sculptor Sir Richard Westmacott and marble-worker Dominico Bartoli. When construction was at its height in 1791, no less than twenty-five stonecutters, twenty-six stonemasons, ten stone sawyers, seventeen carpenters and eighty-three labourers were being employed. When it was complete, keeping the house's 116 rooms warm required six cartloads of peat a day. The earl died in 1802, heavily in debt, but he was not unusual in this; Arthur Young and others often note the grandiose pretensions of the Anglo-Irish gentry who, able to enjoy the service of far more poorly paid servants than the English, wanted the setting to match. The result is superb, from the magnificent 280-foot long façade, with its Doric colonnades and elegant pavilions, to the restrained decoration of the interior, in which everything, including the iron stoves in the beautiful circular saloon, share the pervasive spirit of Wyatt in classical, as opposed to Neo-Gothic mood. The gardens, which after years of neglect have recently been cleared and replanted, have one rare distinction: on the lake is the only breeding colony of greylag geese, outside Scotland, in the British Isles. Oddly, the contents remain the property of the family. The house itself and grounds are owned by the National Trust and open to the public.

There are several other places worth visiting or glimpsing on this side of Upper Lough Erne – Tempo Manor (once home of Bryan, last of the Maguires and a compulsive duellist who spat at strangers for the joy of a challenge), possessing a famous garden sometimes open to the public; and Georgian **Brookeborough**, once the home of Lord Alanbrooke, Chief of the Imperial General Staff during the Second World War, and of Lord Brookeborough, Prime Minister of Northern Ireland from 1943 to 1963, a reactionary Unionist who advanced the Orange Order in influence, officially ignored Catholics, and as minister of agriculture, in the 1930s, set what he intended to be an example by sacking all Catholic workers from his vast estates. Fifteen miles south of Lisnaskea, on a broad tongue of land protruding into the lake, is **Crom Castle**, the splendid Tudor-revival home and demesne of the Crichtons, Earls of Erne, *(see* Chapter 20). In the highlands to the east, as to the west of the lake, are large numbers of prehistoric remains of societies which had to stay above what was, before draining, a large expanse of swampy jungle.

The other great house of the area is **Florence Court**, six miles south of Enniskillen, by a right turn off the A32. It is the seat of the Coles, original settlers of Enniskillen and since the late eighteenth century Earls of Enniskillen. The family provided the borough MPs for generations. They still live in the house but it is now the property of the National Trust. Nothing is known of the architect, nor of the exact date of building, probably the middle of the eighteenth century, though the arcaded wings with their terminating pavilions are thought to be by Davis Ducart, and date from about 1767. The main east front is distinguished by a good deal of detail – deep rustication of the masonry, scrolls, projecting architraves, heavy keystones, niches, a central Venetian window on the first floor and door and window pediments – that suggest the strong influence of Gibbs, and in the case of the second floor, of Hawksmoor. The two sides and back of the house are plain by comparison, and it is said that the builder, in the manner of the times, ran out of money before he could match them to the front. Inside there is magnificent plasterwork (most of it restored since a bad fire in 1955), a lot of it best seen from the staircase, and a rich collection of pictures and furniture. The gardens are delightfully wooded and contain an upright or fastigiate Irish yew (*Taxus baccata fastigiata*), one of two specimens discovered in 1780 on a nearby hill by a farmer who gave one to Florence Court. From this have been taken – by cutting since, this being a lone female, sexual propagation is impossible – all known Irish yews everywhere. The area hereabouts is, like the Burren, of carboniferous limestone, and contains many caves, the result of water's action on the soluble rock. One of the finest and most readily accessible complexes is at **Marble Arch**, three and a half miles farther along the road on which Florence Court is, and signposted to the left. Marble Arch itself is a double natural arch about thirty feet high, at the head of a wooded glen. The ramifications of the caves extend four miles and are not yet fully charted. Organised visits, beginning at an informative exhibition hall, may be curtailed by sudden rises of water level following heavy rain, and involve descent and ascent of a hundred and fifty steps.

To return to Ballyshannon it is best to go almost all the way into Enniskillen again, then cut across to the A46 that goes along the south shore of Lower Lough Erne. Two and a half miles along we pass the old demesne of **Castle Hume**, the first Irish work of Richard Castle, done for Sir Gustavus Hume, who brought him from London in 1728. Only the stable block and a dovecote remain. There are several Plantation castles close to the road including **Monea Castle**, the most perfect of its kind in Ireland, rectangular in form with two Round Towers of typical Scottish flavour, three miles inland from Castle Hume. Many of these castles, combining spacious living accommodation with defensive exteriors, show clear influences of the Scottish styles from which they developed. For while Hugh O'Neill, Red Hugh O'Donnell and the other earls had sailed from Ireland in 1607, the native population remained hostile to new settlers and its grudges were later expressed in the 1641 rising. Defensive architecture was still essential. Lakeside **Tully Castle**, beside the lake six miles beyond Castle Hume, illustrates this well. Built in 1609, it was burned to more or less its present state in 1641. According to survivors they surrendered to Rory Maguire, the rebel chief, on the promise of safe passage, and most were then butchered. It was reports like this, perhaps inflated over the years, that incited the credulous Cromwell to his ruthless campaign. A mile or so later the road bends westward and the lake broadens to upwards of five miles. To the north, the mountains make a superb backdrop to the water. We carry on to Belleek, and thence, crossing the border, return to Ballyshannon.

16

Donegal

DONEGAL IS A political oddity. Like counties Cavan and Monaghan it belongs to the old nine-county province of Ulster; yet it is not partitioned off from republican Ireland as the other six counties are. The three are, all the same, closely tied to the six counties, and Donegal is only connected to the Republic by a thin neck on either side of Ballyshannon. They are linked to the north by history, trade, family ties, roads, and yet the men they vote into Parliament govern from Dublin. Edward Carson told Shane Leslie that during the First World War he had planned to include all Ulster in a separate British province. Later he saw his mistake. If his first wish had been granted Northern Ireland would have included a majority of Catholics who, in the course of time, would by democratic means have been able to vote themselves out of union with Britain and into the Republic. This might (or might not) have prevented the tragic conflicts of more recent times, but it would not have suited Carson and his Unionist successors. So Donegal and the other two were left on the outside. A recently published series of four books on the provinces of Ireland interpreted Ulster as 'the Six'. The three were not covered in any of the books, and that is the sort of humiliation they have to live with.

Donegal is one of Ireland's most beautiful counties and some insist it has no rivals. It owes its beauty to a characteristic west-coast landformation. The rock of the western half of its seaboard is granite, mixed on the edges with quartzite; and of the eastern half is mainly schists. Before most of the rest of the country's rocks had even begun to form, Donegal's western half crumbled in a north-east/south-west direction and formed a series of ridges, whose bottoms are still followed by the main inland roads. This took place four hundred or so million years ago and was caused by the slow, inexorable collision of the tectonic plates carrying America and Europe. The same process created the Caledonian mountains of Scotland.

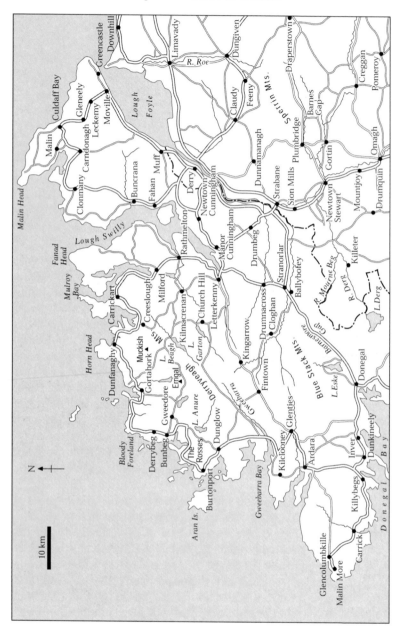

Donegal

Along the Atlantic coast the crumblings have formed into a long series of wild mountainous scarps and craggy inlets with rivers and lakes filling every channel and basin. There is little space for fields (though the Irish are adept at exploiting what space there is) and ocean storms prevent the growing of trees except in unusually protected spots.

But the climate is mild, almost as mild as Kerry's, and such vegetation as there is is luxuriant, and in some cases the rarities of Kerry are found here, too. In addition, the quartzite patches, as is their way, have resisted weathering and formed themselves into regularly shaped conical mountains that set off the wilderness of the glacial scene. In the eastern half of the county, and counties farther east, the schists have formed into hilly but less dramatic country. The west coast provides Donegal with her finest scenery, and it is to the coast we shall mainly keep. All this wilderness and rock have tended to keep the county to itself, since until people began to enjoy mountain scenery it was too remote or too easily defended by natives to bother with. So its history is peculiar to itself. In the later Middle Ages and up to the final conquest and plantation of Ulster, Donegal was the principality of the O'Donnells, who were created, in an early Tudor attempt to win their loyalty to England, Earls of Tyrconnell, the Irish name for their territory. Their eastern neighbours were the O'Neills (created Earls of Tyrone), whose lands included most of central Ulster and were bounded, on the east side, by that of the MacDonnells, Lords of the Isles.

The O'Donnells observed their obligations to writers and story-tellers. By the shore three miles north-west of Ballyshannon is Kilbarron, and the ruined castle they granted the O'Clerys, a family of historians and genealogists. Michael O'Clery, a Franciscan, was born here. He became chief of the group who in the 1630s compiled *The Annals of the Four Masters*, more correctly but rarely known as *Annals of the Kingdom of Ireland* and written in the 1630s in the fear that all knowledge of the Irish race might be expunged by English and Scottish occupation. Theirs was the first full account of Gaelic Ireland from what they took to be its birth through 4,500 years to its apparent death with the flight of the earls to the Continent, after Kinsale. They remain an invaluable source. Franciscans are conspicuous further up the coast, at Rossnowlagh, where the public is welcomed to walk or meditate at their Centre for Reconciliation. The walk leads to a summit with a fine sea view over a magnificent beach. Perhaps the place's most agreeable feature is an annual Orange Order march (for most visitors to the Republic a surprise in itself) which has throughout its hundred-year history been the nucleus of a carnival day – much music, food, great good humour – attended by locals and visitors of all religions.

The county town, and capital of Tyrconnell, Donegal, about ten miles on, is prettily set at the north-east corner of Donegal Bay. Fragments of the 1474 friary survive above a jetty on the estuary. It was blown up by Hugh Roe O'Donnell, besieging an English force, in 1601. The well-restored and very fine fortified house nearby, built in 1610 by Sir Basil Brooke, grantee of the land, has some good details – bartizan turrets, gables, mullioned windows and interior carvings – typical of the period. It now houses various historical exhibits. From Donegal the N15 leads north-east up to the Gap of Barnesmore, historically one of the principal links between the county and central Ulster, with excellent views to the rear over Donegal Bay. But we go north-west instead and follow the N56 round the coast to one of Ireland's wildest corners.

Inver, eight miles along, is a fishing village, in the cemetery of whose roofless, overgrown church is the tomb of Thomas Nesbit, to whom many Nordic countries owe the invention of the gun-harpoon for whaling. The road goes on tortuously through Dunkineely, at the head of a seven-mile-long narrow limestone promontory. At the end of this is a lighthouse, and views of mountains north, south and east, and a feeling of being a ship in mid-bay. Three miles beyond Dunkineely the road bends to reveal landlocked Killybegs Harbour, with its rocky coastline. **Killybegs** itself is a charming fishing port also known for its fish-processing and handwoven carpet factories, which since their founding in the nineteenth century have brought the name Donegal into the first league of carpet tradenames. The harbour itself is one of the best and busiest in Ireland. The mighty western peninsula we have reached is thickly mountainous, with attractive clefts in its perimeter sheltering small seaside communities. The cliffs are among the highest in Europe. About twelve miles beyond Killybegs we reach Carrick, with its colourful houses, standing at the head of long, thin, wooded Teelin Bay. Down the west side of this fjord-like creek a road runs for a while, then rises right to a commanding view of the concave, sheer, 1,800-foot sea face of **Slieve League**, and on a fine day the whole circuit of scenery round to north Mayo. Light plays subtle tricks with the varied striations of this three-mile rock façade, and numerous sea and land birds practise aerobatics in the mingling wind currents. The same and better views – as good as any in Ireland – are to be had from boats that can be hired from Teelin village itself. There is excellent walking country behind the peaks, though guides are advisable for ambitious tours.

From Carrick the road goes on to **Glencolumbkille** through a boggy plateau where turf is cut on a big scale. The village is beautifully set, spread across a valley that widens on its way down to sandy Malin Bay. Unexpectedly, the village adds to its busy turf industry a prolific output of home crafts and a fascinating folk museum, a collection of four cottages that illustrate the peasant way of life at different periods. On the outside is seen the authentic and very attractive Donegal manner of thatching: rounded at the ridge, with the securing ropes often fixed to stone pegs projecting from the walls. Both devices effectively increase the protection from the wind. (A hundred years ago the ropes used to be attached to boulders of sixty pounds' weight that hung below the thatch, keeping the whole roof tautly proof against winds.) Styles of thatchwork are no longer, as they once were, ways of identifying a region, any more than hayricks are. Anyhow, the emphasis in the museum is on interior furnishings and fixtures, and the scant comforts of the primitive life.

After the Second World War Glencolumbkille, like many western Irish communities, was dying. A Catholic priest, Father McDyer, came – some said from heaven. His worst enemies, he said, were 'indolence, emigration, cynicism, greed and individualism'. Only the very old and the very young stayed in the west – the rest migrated. In a survey of 1966 it was found that in one part of north Donegal thirty per cent of the farms in a given area were under thirty acres. That sort of size leaves little for one son, let alone two, to inherit. In Mayo, six hundred families a year were closing their farms altogether. Father McDyer's contention was that proper use of the land lying fallow in the west would vastly increase the already considerable contribution of the area to national income. His fight was to get enthusiasm from the people and grants from the government, and it saw steady results. He got piped water and electricity going, and helped create a weaving industry, a farming cooperative, the holiday village, a fish-processing plant and summer work for hundreds of young people drawn in from the area and beyond. Instead of dying, the place set a pace until Europe offered its chalice of panaceas. Father McDyer died here in 1987.

There is delightful scenery to the north, at Glen Head and Sturrall Head, and to the south, around the sandy flats of Malin Bay. A local legend says Bonnie Prince Charlie came here after Culloden and waited for a ship to take him to sanctuary in France. There is no apparent foundation for it. But Glencolumbkille is scattered with tangible memorials of St Columba, whose favourite retreat this was said to be, and an annual pilgrimage on 9 June brings the devout to follow a three-mile pattern round associated sites: House, Well, Chair and Bed on the Glen Head road.

A minor road to the east leads us through more of the boggy uplands of the promontory, then down by a series of hairpin bends to the fertile plain around Ardara (last syllable stressed), centre of the cottage industry of Donegal knitting. It is attractively situated by Loughros More Bay with mountain views to east and south. To the north the country becomes flatter inside its curtain of mountains, but walks along the coast or within the many promontories offer beautiful views, lakes, sandy beaches, dunes and frequent ancient remains. Five miles north-north-west of Ardara, immediately beyond Kilclooney, we can divert to the left to see the **Bawn**, a huge oval fortress with an eight-foot-wide walk at the top of its seventeen-foot walls. The rampart, waterbound in Lough Doon, can be reached by hire of a boat from a local cottage, or simply seen from the shore. Back on the R261 we keep close to the water past the Gweebarra estuary, cross the bridge, and stay with the N56 close to the coast. The Gweebarra River leads straight along the geological fault line to the Derryveagh Mountains and across them to a region of lakes to be visited later.

Dungloe (the 'g' not pronounced) nine miles farther on, is within the Gaeltacht, or Gaelic-speaking area, and populous for this part, with about eight hundred souls, a fishing port, and close to rivers and lakes well liked by anglers. To the north is a flattish area, several miles long and broad, known as the Rosses (Irish for promontories) and comprising windswept heathery gradients and small but dutifully cultivated fields in a region of innumerable little lakes. The coast road round the west side of this leads to Burtonport, with a fishing fleet and herring-curing station, and a quay from which boats leave for Aran Island or Aranmore (distinct of course from the better-known Aran Islands off the Galway coast), a pleasant island with a wild western seaboard. A prettier way lies north-east of Dungloe past rock-strewn watery terrain to Lough Anure, a glacial overflow both pretty and interesting to geologists for its rock-surrounds – mica slate with coarse granular dolomite – and the wealth of glacial remains including the most common sight hereabouts, moraine debris. Continuing through Creely we come next to

Gweedore, on the approach to which are good views, to the right, of Donegal's highest peak, the quartzite cone of Mt Errigal (2,466 feet).

Gweedore is a pleasant, unexpectedly cosy-looking village in the heart of this rugged north-western corner of Ireland. It and the land round about were, in the middle of the last century, one of the most backward parts of Ireland, still plagued by the wasteful practice of rundale, which along with the booley system had been the basis of all Irish peasant farming up to the early 1900s, and in parts far later. By rundale, each tenant was allotted small portions of land over the whole expanse of an estate, to make sure he had his fair share of good and bad, and of the different crops grown. But there was no boundary between each man's strips, and since any one tenant might have up to thirty separated plots (and one half acre could sometimes contain the plots of the same number of tenants) terrible confusion and apathy set in. This district was known as one of the poorest, roughest, and, in time of famine, most desperate in the country – hardly a man of the scores who published descriptions of their Irish tours allowed a word, or any time, to Donegal.

Then in 1838 a total of 23,000 acres around Gweedore was bought by Lord George Hill (1801–79), a man who besides possessing a decent level of humanity did the almost unheard-of thing and learned Irish, the better to tackle local problems. Gradually he improved the place out of all recognition, by redividing the land, fencing it, building stone houses, mills, shops, schools, a harbour at Bunbeg, offering premiums for the best crops, and a hundred other things that kept him tied full-time to the estate. Crabbed Carlyle, who came in 1849 and found nothing to admire in Donegal landscape nor most of the features of Irish life, still found in Hill a glint of hope. 'In all Ireland', he wrote in his economic prose, 'saw no such beautiful soul.' In the 1880s, after Hill's death, the place regressed, and the Plan of Campaign brought a trail of evictions in neighbouring estates. Maud Gonne was one who came to see the process, rebuilding cabins that the police and troops had battered down; and seeing mothers and babies sleeping under hedges or herded into workhouses, she here resolved 'It is the English who forced war on us, and the first principle of war is to kill the enemy.'

From Gweedore we can make a first venture into the awesome range of the Derryveagh Mountains. We drive east along the N56, moving right beside a power station on to the R251, staying beside Lough Nacung Upper, with the very mountain-shaped Mount Errigal ahead. Dunlewy has the impressive, quartzite-white shell of a Church of Ireland church dominating the lake which shares its name, and hidden among trees an old Guinness shooting lodge, still inhabited. To the south-east of the village a path leads into the steep-sided Poisoned Glen, named from the effect of Irish spurge (no longer present) on the fish in its waters, from where an adventurous walk can be done through the Ballaghgeeha Gap and down on to Glenveagh. To the east of the village the road ascends to the Gap of Dunlewy, from which there are dramatic views on both sides. They do not match the spectacle gained from climbing Mount Errigal, which takes a few hours but is not difficult as mountain-climbing goes. We return to the coast, via Gweedore, to continue our journey through the little ports of Bunbeg, Derrybeg – where the evictions of 1889 led to a famous murder of a police inspector – and on to Bloody Foreland.

This is best seen lit by a good sunset, which colours the mountains – along with the rock-strewn sea and islands – dramatically golden, if not red. The long island to the north is **Tory Island**, whose principal trade is lobsters, and which is rich in history and legend. In the days of Ireland's earliest occupation the Fomorians, sometimes described as one-legged, one-armed giants, lived here and from this base sallied out to destroy, plunder and exert an evil influence on the colonists. They were exterminated in the second Battle of Moytura, their king, Balor, coming to a horrible end beyond Gortahork, seven miles east of Bloody Foreland. The island has a population of 160 or so, from whom emerged a school of native naive painters whose attractive portrayals of the island's life and landscape have found markets far beyond their shores. Among the scanty remains of a monastery said to have been founded by the ubiquitous St Columba are a seven-foot so-called tau-cross, T-shaped, and a fifty-seven-foot Round Tower constructed of round pebbles gathered from beaches. There is a rich bird-life, including puffin colonies on the rocky heights at the eastern end.

Gortahork itself is a resort well placed for the whole north Donegal mountain complex and for the wealth of beaches along this northern coast. It is also a centre of the Donegal Gaeltacht and there is an Irish college nearby. Fomorian Balor's end came in the demesne of Ballyconnell House, three miles north-east. It had been forecast in a prophecy as the work of a grandson of Balor. Balor, having only one daughter, kept her virginally locked in a tor on the island. An old enemy renamed MacKineely came in disguise to Tory, slept with the girl and got her with child. In revenge, Balor caught MacKineely and chopped off his head. The 'stone of Kineely', a large boulder with red crystalline veins, in the demesne, is accounted the blood-stained table he used. Years later the grandson he had been unable to prevent grew up and, in revenge for his father's murder, pierced Balor's malignant eye with a red-hot iron.

Returning to the main road, we go on east by the N56. From Dunfanaghy, seven miles on, a minor road leads west and then north into the promontory of **Horn Head**, another beauty spot with cliffs at its north end supporting many varieties of sea-bird, some rare. On a clear day the Paps of Jura can be seen to the north-east. On the west coast, which is perforated with caves and tunnels, one called McSweeney's Gun has become well known. Into this the sea in rough weather is supposed to rush with such fury that it creates a bang loud enough to be heard at Derry. Dunfanaghy is a good starting point for climbing Muckish Mountain (2,187 feet) to the south. It has always been a favoured quiet resort, and 'AE' (George Russell, painter, mystic, poet, political writer and champion of the Gaelic League) used to come here for painting holidays. Five miles on, at Cashelmore (beside which is a nineteenth-century bell-tower, complete with huge bell, and lacking only a church), a lane leads left on to the **Ards Peninsula**, pushing into Sheep Haven. William Wray built Ards House here, in the eighteenth century, in what was described as 'the most beautiful private demesne in the country', but extravant road-building, always keeping twenty places ready at his table, and general living in pomp impoverished him at last. The house changed hands and was acquired in the twentieth century by Capuchin friars, who had it demolished in 1965. Creeslough is two miles farther along the main road, boasting a fine Catholic church of 1971, of simple design and economic line. A left turn here leads along a track two miles to **Doe Castle**, a ruined keep in a well-preserved bawn by the water's edge, restored and inhabited in the nineteenth century. It was originally a McSweeney stronghold. Red Hugh O'Donnell was fostered here, and though for a while it was granted to English planters it was restored to the Irish family before the Eleven Years War. Owen Roe O'Neill landed here to take a crucial part in the war, which in the north was, unlike elsewhere, a concerted effort to oust the Planters; but the place was taken by the Cromwellian General Coote in 1650. There are good views over the estuary from the top of the precarious steps.

A right turn two miles beyond Creeslough, followed by another right three miles further on, onto the R251, brings us to the entrance to the long drive of **Glenveagh Castle**, justifiably popular with tour-ists. The castle presents its nineteenth-century turrets and battlements to view on top of a rocky mound beside Lough Veagh, which is a widening of the straight geological fault slicing south-west to north-east from Gweebarra Bay to Sheep Haven; a film-set view, more folly than fortress, yet romantic and imposing with lake, mountains and deer-forest for background. The builder of the castle, John George Adair, was a loathed and ruthless landlord, and perpetrator of tragic evictions. After frequent changes of hand, the property was bought in 1933 by Henry McIlhenny, an amiable, aesthetic American, grandson of a Donegal native and heir to an industrial Philadelphian fortune, who in forty years gave the castle its present contents and character, created a series of gardens – Italian, walled, rhododendron, an orangery, whole hillsides of fine and rare trees and shrubs – enter-tained most of the Irish great and good, and many more besides, and bequeathed most of the property to the Irish people, but not sadly his paintings, which went back to Philadelphia. Recognisably American, spicker and spanner than is natural for a castle in such wild moorland, it is well worth the visit. There are good walks in the grounds and extensive deer-park.

From the entrance on the R251 we can go south-east to lovely Loughs Akibbon and Gartan, connected by a short channel. Above the west bank of the former is a ruined chapel, once an O'Donnell mausoleum and originally built, it is believed, on St Columba's birth-place. The saint's exact burial place is supposed to be under a flagstone some way south, on the hillside above Lough Gartan, marked by a modern High Cross. Columba is one of the best docu-mented men of his time, for his life was written – meticulously for the period – by Adamnan, abbot of the monastery on Iona which Columba himself founded. He comes over as a cold personality, self-righteous (as most of his saintly contemporaries are portrayed), and forcing on his monks the hardest of ascetic disciplines. His mission to Scotland was prompted by no less than a fierce battle caused by himself after he had refused to abide by a High King's judgment. He nevertheless was probably Scotland's most civilising influence in the Dark Ages. His exile, though nothing rare in a nation that sent hundreds of proselytising monks to Britain and the Continent in the wake of the barbarian invasions, caused him to become almost a patron saint of emigrants. Consequently, a night spent on the flag-stone where he was born is said to prevent homesickness, and has been resorted to by thousands of Irish, on the eve of departure to make new lives abroad. The area round about is thick with Columban associations.

Little more than a mile away, beside the shore of Lough Gartan, and close to the village of Church Hill, is the **Glebe House** and Gallery. This charming red-washed Georgian house, with its fanlight above the front door, set in a lush garden of trees and beds, was bought by the English artist Derek Hill in 1954, after he had stayed at Glenveagh. He decorated it deliciously and with a great gift for marrying works of art many might think incompatible. The walls are painted in deep pigments, or papered with Morris wallpapers, there are paintings from China, Japan, Europe, America, Ireland – not least Tory Island whose artistic school was nourished by Hill. There are fine and curious and colourful carpets, spreads and curtains, prints and pottery from many scattered sources. Though it must be wonderfully habitable, Hill nevertheless left it in 1981, making a present of it to the Irish nation, a warm enclave of art and cultivated good taste, regularly open to the public, in a stretch of country characterised for the most part by its rugged grandeur.

We can return to our coastal circuit along the N56, turning right before Creeslough on to the R245 towards the beautiful wild peninsula of Rosguill. We turn left at Carrickart to pass, on the west of the promontory's neck, **Rosapenna**, an 1893 hotel built by Lord Leitrim, with good beaches and an eighteen-hole golf-course among the sand dunes. The sand was a disastrous menace in the early part of the nineteenth century when Lord Boyne, having built himself a house here, complete with walled gardens, avenues and terraces, found it gradually piled up with sand-drifts. The desperate resistance of relays of workmen was of no avail and eventually the place was surrendered to the elements. In1843 the second Lord Leitrim bought the property and by planting bent-grass managed to stem the drifts. To the north, yet another superb view is to be had from the 682-foot hill of Ganiamore. Returning to Carrickart we drive on east, along the west side of narrow Mulroy Bay.

Two miles out of the village a lane leads left to Mulroy House, seat of the earls of Leitrim, a mid-nineteenth-century Tudor-revival house of little distinction. Continuing down the side of Mulroy Bay and past the village of Cranford, we come to Cratlagh Woods, where a cross, erected in 1960, commemorates the assassination in 1878 of the third and 'wicked' Earl of Leitrim. His estates hereabouts amounted to 57,000 acres. In the army he had been known for bravery and good discipline, but seems, on returning home, to have taken tenants for subordinate soldiers, to be ordered about at will. Petty and punitive, he deprived them of age-old rights in the land they worked, and when opposed quickly resorted to eviction or the courts. Having survived several attempts on his life, he was travelling, at the age of seventy-two, in the direction we are following, when he was ambushed from the woods. His clerk and car-driver were shot, then he himself was shot and battered to death. Occupants of a following carriage saw what happened but most evidence at the subsequent trial of three men was confused and contradictory and all were acquitted. 'One thing is certain,' wrote the novelist Stephen Gwynn twenty years later, 'every Irish-speaking person within five miles of Milford, and many others, could, and would not, tell you exactly who it was that killed Lord Leitrim.' The appearance on this memorial, a century later, of the names of the three men who here, it is claimed, 'ended the tyranny of landlordism in Ireland' suggests he was right.

Milford is the starting point for the circuit of the **Fanad Peninsula**, with a further succession of mountains, lakes, beaches and views. Attractions tend to concentrate on the eastern side. Fanad Head, at the end, offers predictably fine views of neighbouring coast and distant Hebrides. The return drive takes in the length of Lough Swilly, past Ballymastocker Bay, a two-mile crescent of golden sand and foam-flecked blue which officials with the soft task of judging such things have designated second best in Europe. Just inland, golfers follow their calling. **Rathmullan** is eight miles on, a trim little fishing harbour with beach, pier, handsome Georgian terrace, a picturesque ruined priory and a massive windowless fort displaying inside the sad story of the so-called Flight of the Earls in 1607.

With inexorable force, the armies sent by Elizabeth in the great grab of Munster had shot, hanged, tricked and exiled their prey (who themselves were well qualified in the tactics used). Submission was complete in all but the North. The opening years of the seventeenth century, following the decisive battle of Kinsale, saw the North's great leaders capitulate too. Hugh O'Neill renounced lands and titles at Mellifont in 1603. King James gave him and Rory O'Donnell, Red Hugh's younger brother and successor, new titles but power was now generated from England, and the stage set for the great Protestant plantations. Meanwhile O'Neill and O'Donnell, with a hundred or so kinsmen and allies, sailed from here with hopes of a triumphant return backed by Spain. It never came. All that awaited them was a stormy crossing, helpless shifting around the continent to suit the interests of France and Spain, the death of their hopes and soon of themselves.

The next seven miles take us close to mud-flats and intriguing creeks and a permanent shoreline shimmer of birdlife to Rathmelton (pronounced and sometimes spelt Ramelton), handsomely set at the mouth of the Glashagh River, its massive warehouses reminding of past prosperity. From here the R249 takes us to **Kilmacrenan**, two miles west of which is the holy well of Doon, still visited for its curative powers, and Doon Rock, where O'Donnell chieftains were inaugurated as Lords of Tyrconnell. Giraldus Cambrensis, who never came within a hundred miles of the place, left a vivid description of the inauguration rites – the gathering of the clan, the chief's embracing of a white mare, the killing of the mare and cutting its body in pieces, the chief's submersion in water used to boil the meat and the subsequent feasting on the meat, the chief remaining all the while in the water. Where alternatives offered, Giraldus was always on the side of the ghouls.

Just over six miles south of Kilmacrenan is **Letterkenny**, Donegal's largest town with a population approaching ten thousand, having doubled in twenty years. Its late-nineteenth-century Neo-Gothic-cum-Irish-Romanesque Catholic cathedral has several good windows by Michael Healy. Three miles south-west of the town, by Newmills, is the ford of Scarriffhollis, where in 1650 Sir Charles Coote, after several reverses in battle with the fighting Bishop MacMahon of Clogher, turned the tables on him and thoroughly routed his depleted forces. This was the end of the Royalist-Catholic cause in the north. To celebrate it, Coote had a son of Owen Roe O'Neill clubbed to death outside his tent and six months later hanged the bishop of Clogher at Enniskillen. The Newmills corn and flax mills remind how thoroughly the logical sequences of industrial processes have now been hidden behind chips and electronics. Water from the River Swilly enters a quarter-mile mill-race which feeds one flax mill and one grain mill (barley and oats), the huge wheel of the latter dating from 1867.

We round the head of Lough Swilly on the N14, and switch left on to the N13 to pass Manor Cunningham and Newtown Cunningham. The conspicuous silhouette on the left is sixteenth-century Burt Castle, an O'Doherty stronghold awarded, after it had been taken by the English following the capture of Derry, to Sir Arthur Chichester, first Baron of Belfast, and ancestor of the Marquesses of Donegal. Farther on to the right rises the hill of Greenan, on top of which is the remarkable **Grianan** (meaning 'sun-place') **of Aileach**, a concentric fort built as the royal seat of the O'Neills, lords of Tyrone and later much of Ulster. The fort, with walls over seventeen feet thick at the base, is itself enclosed by three rough earthen ramparts; but its defence was penetrated in 1101 when Murtagh O'Brien, King of Munster, came to force the submission of its king, Donal MacLochlann. The fort was badly restored in the 1870s. The views are superb, taking in the Benevenagh bluff to east-north-east, the snaking shape of Lough Foyle, the humped mass of the Inishowen Peninsula to the north, the busily indented outline of Lough Swilly, Fanad, the further promontories, capes and inlets, and to west and south the domes, cones and raggeder profiles of the distant mountains of Donegal, Sligo and Leitrim. And of course a confetti of bungalows carelessly sprinkled.

The **Inishowen Peninsula** is known, from the length of the road round it, as the 'Inishowen 100'. It has also been known in the past, like much of Donegal, as classic poteen country. Compared with some of the headlands to the west, it offers less return for more mileage, but it has attractive points and Malin Head is, if little else, the northernmost point of Ireland. The western coast road passes Inch Island – now an island no more, as a result of drainage – and approaches the waters of **Lough Swilly** at the pretty resort of Fahan. A holy well and a beautiful and important two-sided cross are all that remain of a seventh-century monastery founded by St Columba, demolished probably by Cromwellians. A bell named after the first abbot, St Mura, found its way to London's Wallace Collection, where it rests now. Lough Swilly witnessed the Flight of the Earls, as we saw at Rathmullan. It also saw Wolfe Tone's dreams destroyed. With the 1798 rebellion already quelled, he came with a French squadron to support Humbert's campaign, but the ship he was in was trapped by English frigates and he was arrested the moment he landed, either at Rathmullan or Buncrana. Sentenced to hang, he cut his throat with a penknife in his Dublin gaol.

The castle he was supposedly brought to survives as a solitary tower in Buncrana. Beyond, if we keep to the westward coast road, we cross hilly country and turn inland up the bleak Owenerk Valley. In this, a road to the left takes us across the steep Gap of Mamore, with brown barren mountains on each side, and marvellous views from the top. From Raghtin More, a cairn-topped peak to the right, the ubiquitous Finn McCool dispensed his laws. Carndonagh, ten miles on, is the marketing centre of the peninsula, and it has four worn but well-decorated early crosses on the roadside. An uninteresting road leads north to Malin Head, with good beaches and rock scenery and a deserted signal tower erected in Napoleonic times. There is a splendidly remote look about the farms in this northernmost corner of Ireland. We return to Malin village and a mile and a half beyond turn left, through plain boggy country, for Culdaff, where the road bends south and takes us past a circle of standing stones a mile south.

Moville, twelve miles farther, is a seaside resort that used to be a port of call for transatlantic liners, one of the valves through which Irish from this part of the country emigrated. Three miles east-north-east is Greencastle, with a fort erected against Napoleon's threatened invasion and now incorporated in a restaurant. Only fragments survive of the fourteenth-century castle, which passed to the O'Dohertys and in 1610 went, with the rest of the peninsula, to the planter, Sir Arthur Chichester. From this eastern coast-road there are good views across to the north Derry highlands and to the chimneys of Derry to the south. Just beyond Muff we cross the border between counties Donegal and Derry, and move into Northern Ireland.

17

Derry, West Tyrone and Antrim Coast

G LADSTONE, WHEN HE came to power in 1869, seeing that
the Protestant Church of Ireland embraced less than one eighth
of the Irish population and was unlikely ever to embrace any more,
disestablished it. Among those who thought this likely to bring about
the world's end was Cecil Frances, the poet wife of Dr William Alexander, Bishop of Derry and later Primate of Ireland. Her verse
includes the words of *Once in royal David's city* and *There is a green
hill far away*. At the Disestablishment she wrote a hymn which her
husband caused to be sung in the cathedral – 'Look down, Lord of
Heaven, on our desolation! /Fallen, fallen, fallen, is our country's
crown;/ Dimly dawns the new year on a churchless nation;/ – Amon
and Amaleck tread our borders down ...' It is in the light of that sort
of opposition that Gladstone's greatness shows up.

   Church and commerce have always figured large in **Derry's**, or
Londonderry's, history. St Columba founded a monastery in about
546, in a hilltop oak-grove (*daire*) that gave the town its name. In
1164 another famous foundation, Temple More, was built where the
Catholic church of St Columba now stands, which was probably the
original monastic site. This monastery was destroyed in 1566, in one
of the last battles fought by Shane O'Neill, the vain and refractory
Lord of Tyrone. A parson led the citizens through what Protestants
think of as Derry's finest hour, and a bishop several sizes larger than
life adorned the city and Irish history in general in the eighteenth
century. The latter, Frederick Augustus Hervey, fourth Earl of Bristol,
we shall come to at his home outside Derry. The parson comes at the
culmination of the city's seventeenth-century history, which opened
with the capture and fortifying of the place by Sir Henry Docwra for
the queen. A few years later the dispossessed O'Dohertys rebelled
and took it back. But the inexorable project of Plantation followed,
Derry was granted to the Irish Society, formed of citizens of London,
and her name combined with London's in a form – Londonderry –

which official Britain continues and Catholic Ireland ignores. (Either form is now officially correct but usage remains on the whole sectarian. Not the least hazard for citizens during the recent troubles – sometimes referred to by them as 'the bother' – was the dilemma that faced you if you were stopped by unidentifiable men blocking the road when you were driving back to the city, and asked your destination. To say 'Derry' pronounced a Catholic, 'Londonderry' a Protestant. Depending on the nature and intentions of the men, your answer might prove your death-sentence and on occasion undoubtedly did.) The town's walls went up between 1613 and 1618 and the original cathedral, now much altered, in 1633. Different parts of the country were entrusted to different London guilds and chartered companies, and the Grocers, Fishmongers, Clothworkers and others are still responsible for municipal buildings in some parts. Derry's citizens stayed staunchly Protestant, but the Corporation of London was wanting in efficiency. Lord Deputy Wentworth, as impatient with Protestant as with Catholic shortcomings, opened an inquiry and had the Corporation fined £70,000, so adding to the enemies who finally conspired to pull him down. In the Eleven Years War the city inevitably changed hands, at one point welcoming relief from Owen Roe O'Neill, the Catholic commander – such were the partisan confusions of the time.

In 1688, however, when Catholic James II and his Lord Lieutenant Tyrconnell (a Talbot, the O'Donnell earls of the same title having been attainted) were rallying Irish support, Derry pitched firmly for the Protestant, Williamite side. A critical moment came when one Jacobite regiment had left the city and its replacement had not arrived. There were plenty of Jacobite sympathisers and these included the governor, who was for letting the new force in. But he was expelled. To prevent further wavering, the town's apprentice boys seized the keys of the town and locked the Ferryquay Gate, towards which the troops were marching. (The gates are closed to this day in an annual ceremony, and the governor, Lundy, till recently burned in effigy.) The consequent siege by James's men began in April 1689, and lasted 105 days, being eventually broken by a Williamite ship sailing in the face of artillery up the Foyle, breaking the besiegers' boom, and bringing supplies to the townspeople. There had been great suffering. Almost all the children succumbed to disease. People ate dogs, cats, tallow. Rats changed hands for a shilling each, cats for five. The bulwark of the resistance was a forty-three-year-old clergyman from Tyrone, the Rev. George Walker, whose statue, bible in hand, used to stand high on the city walls. The fullest account of the siege, from which he emerges with heroic stature, is by himself. He also shows that the defenders kept their racial and religious priorities nicely distinct. When the enemy offered them terms, 'they unanimously resolved to eat the Irish and then one another rather than surrender to any but their own King William and Queen Mary'. Walker was killed the following year at the Battle of the Boyne. King James returned to France, consoled by an annual million-franc pension paid him for life by Louis XIV. Among Protestants, 'No Surrender' remains the motto to this day, and Derry, having repelled assault, is often known as the Maiden City.

Up to the end of the eighteenth century Derry had its being on the west bank of the Foyle. Indeed the first bridge across it was completed, by an American company, in 1791. Thereafter, Waterside developed on the east bank into what was in some ways a second town. But the heart of Derry remains on the hill that rises from the west bank, protected by a rough rectangle of city walls. In the nineteenth century it hurried into affluence, quadrupling its population of ten thousand before 1900, developing waterside quays and warehouses and a flourishing ship-building industry, trading with Scotland – from where the larger part of its population had come – and America, expanding west into what is now the Catholic Bogside and the Creggan beyond, and north into William Street, Clarendon Street, and the area about them, whose elegant Georgian terraces and bulky shirt factories are worthy subjects of conservation campaigns. The twentieth century brought decline in many respects, and thirty years of tragic confrontation. Yet it emerged from them a brighter, busier and cheerier town than the dull, somewhat killjoy and complacent place it had become.

The walls, a mile long and neatly enclosing the town centre, are the best preserved in the British Isles. A walk round the top gives glimpses of the river, the Diamond (a square at the old city's heart), the Church of Ireland cathedral, and of the spreading suburbs. Cannons from the great siege flank the walk. In the southern sector of the old city is a cluster of the more remarkable buildings. The **Church of Ireland Cathedral**, in a style sometimes called 'Planter's Gothic', contains many relics and some good monuments of the seventeenth century inside and incorporates nineteenth-century restoration work and early twentieth-century additions (the spire, like many in the county, was first erected by the Earl Bishop of Bristol; it fell down and was re-erected in 1823). The Bishop's Gate to the west, commemorating the siege, was built in 1788. In Bishop Street, the court-house of 1817 by John Bowden, has a portico modelled on the Erechtheum on the Acropolis, and there are several good Georgian houses nearby. Outside the walls, south-west of Bishop's Gate, is St Columb's Catholic church, on the supposed site of the saint's original foundation. The **Guildhall** (reached through the walled city along Bishop's Street, the Diamond, and Ship Quay Street, where the play-wright George Farquhar was born in 1679) dates from 1911, when it was rebuilt to the plans of its predecessor of 1890, which had burned down in 1908. One of the Victorian Gothic buildings in which Northern Irish cities abound, it contains many stained glass windows showing scenes from the glorious (Protestant) past, and various other relics. Half a mile north of the town is Foyle College, successor of the Free School founded by Planters in 1617. Its alumni include Sir John and Henry Lawrence, the first an enlightened Governor-General of India, the second Governor of Lucknow, killed in the Indian Mutiny in 1857; and the Victorian historian of Greece, Rome and ancient Ireland, John Bagenal Bury. Nearby is Magee University College, founded for the training of Presbyterian ministers in 1857, now part of the new University of Ulster based at Coleraine.

From Derry we cross the river (300 years ago Derry was almost surrounded by water, the Foyle creating watery bog in the lowlands) and follow the valley of the Foyle River south along the A5. On the left after a couple of miles we pass Prehen, a beautiful eighteenth-century house and scene of a tragic murder. In 1768 ardent John Macnaghten of Benvarden, near Coleraine, trying to abduct Mary Anne Knox, the fifteen-year-old daughter of the house, contrived to shoot her dead. He was tried, condemned and hanged. The rope broke, and spectators urged him to take the chance to escape. 'No,' he announced, 'I couldn't go about as half-hanged Macnaghten.' Though the new rope did its work, he has never been known as anything else.

To the south-east rise the Sperrin Mountains and some of the finest inland countryside of the Six Counties, A pleasant long diver-sion is to drive south-east from Derry, along the Faughan Valley by the A6, to Claudy and there to cross back south-west to **Strabane**, which, by whatever route, we come to next. It is a busy town with more a Scottish than an Irish look. Granted with 1,000 acres to James Hamilton, later first Earl of Abercorn, at the Plantation, it was besieged in 1641 by Sir Phelim O'Neill, who took the Hamilton castle and abducted the Hamilton Countess of Abercorn. Both were retrieved. A warehouse now covers the site of the castle, and there is little here of interest but associations. In Main Street is Gray's printing-works, with a pretty bow-window, still operating but now the property of the National Trust. Two of its employees helped to make American history. John Dunlap (1747–1812), who served his apprenticeship here, later issued America's first daily paper, the *Pennsylvania Packet*, and was the first printer of the Declaration of Independence (which was signed by five emigrant Scotch-Irish dele-gates and adopted by a Congress whose secretary was Scotch-Irish). The grandfather of President Woodrow Wilson also worked here, before emigrating in 1807. His home was at Dergault, two miles south-east of Strabane, where the thatched farmhouse in which he was born was owned by Wilsons till the National Trust acquired it. The Ulster contribution to American politics included no less than a quarter of America's presidents, some of whose birthplaces we shall come on in due course.

From Strabane the A5 continues south for eight miles to Newtown Stewart, prettily situated on a coil of the Mourne River and north of a wooded mountain, Bessy Bell (called, with nearby Mary Grey, after two Scottish plague victims of the seventeenth century who became subjects of a nursery rhyme). Running beside a lake west of the mountain is the Duke of Abercorn's demesne of **Baronscourt**, with one of Northern Ireland's best country houses, designed about 1750 by George Steuart, altered and added to by Sir John Soane in 1792, fully restored in the early nineteenth century by W.V. Morrison and partly pulled down in the twentieth. Individuals who were granted land in Ulster by James I undertook to fulfil certain conditions, and were known as undertakers. The first Hamilton undertaker acquired immense estates in Derry and Tyrone, and the ruin of his castle stands beside the largest of the three lakes. His grandson, fourth Earl of Abercorn, was aide to James II during his escape to France, and the anchor of the ship they sailed in is preserved on the estate. This earl fought for James at Aughrim in 1691. His successor switched to William's side in time to save family property and honours, and helped at the relief of Derry. The present house was built by the eighth earl. His heir, the first marquess, was a fastidious man. Housemaids had to wear gloves to make his bed. He tried three times to find happiness in marriage, but his first wife died young and his second, a cousin, eloped. He heard of her plans in advance and wrote one last plea – not that she should stay, but that she should leave in the family coach. It should never be said a Lady Abercorn left her husband's roof in a hack chaise. His grandson was created first duke in the 1860s, and was twice Lord Lieutenant. The third duke was Governor of Northern Ireland for twenty-three years after the state's inception in 1922. The formal gardens are set in a magnificently landscaped and maintained demesne, surrounded by forestry. The public are occasionally admitted. Regular access to the grounds is at present confined to golfers and clients shooting game.

On the return to **Newtown Stewart** we pass on the right the scant ruins of Harry Avery's Castle (half a mile west-south-west of the town), an O'Neill stronghold of the fourteenth century. The four-teenth-century builder is said to have had a sister with the head of a pig. Any man bold enough to marry her stood to receive a large dowry, but if his nerve failed him he would be hanged. She remained unwed and nineteen suitors went to the gallows. In the town itself are slight remains of a Plantation castle built by Sir Robert Newcomen in 1618. Sir William Stewart, who married Newcomen's daughter, was confirmed in the lands by Charles I and gave the place its name. He was tireless, at the outbreak of the 1641 rebellion, in organising rescuers of those settlers in danger of being butchered by deprived and oppressed natives across all the northern counties (the massacre for which Cromwell regarded his barbarities as holy recompense). James II was entertained at the castle on his way to and from the siege of Derry, and after the second visit perversely caused it to be burned down, and the town with it. The town was rebuilt by its Stewart owners in 1722.

Two miles south, off the Omagh road, is Camp Hill Cottage, from which in 1808 five year-old Thomas Mellon and his parents left for America, he to found a large family, a bank, and the Mellon fortunes. (Paul Getty and Alexander Brown, who founded the oldest American bank still existing, were also of Ulster stock.) The cottage is now contained within the remarkable Ulster-American Folk Park, Mellon-financed, which aims to show the enormous contribution people of the province made to the expansion of the United States, through an exhibition, covering several acres, of real and replica buildings from one or two centuries ago. There is a Presbyterian meeting-house and a Catholic mass-house of 1768, a wealthy family home, a weaver's cottage, a school house, a forge. Then come the stages of emigration: the harbour, ticket-office, quay, ship – life-size, with top deck and sleeping deck and the low stalls into which fami-lies squeezed, amid the reek (not reproduced, but imaginable) of unwashed bodies, excrement and death. Then America: shops, log cabin, frontier farm, smoke-house, spring-house, and families in a New York doss-house, with wheezings, coughs and snores. This is a good try at an impossibility: capturing reality.

Omagh, seven miles on, is the county town of Tyrone, dominated by a hilltop trio of big churches: the restored, double-spired Catholic cathedral of 1899, the dour Church of Ireland church and the dull, spireless Methodist church. Below them stands the grandly pedimented courthouse of 1820 at the head of the long High Street, part destroyed by the explosion of a bomb in 1998, probably by breakaway republicans. Twenty-eight were killed, two hundred injured: the direst and most undiscriminating act of terrorism of the period.

In the late fifteenth century, Omagh had a castle. The resident O'Neill's independent line provoked the Lord Deputy, who razed it to the ground. Its successor was taken in 1602 and garrisoned by Lord Mountjoy, squeezing the Earl of Tyrone – a falling star since the battle of Kinsale a few months before – out of his titular lands. But the place was of no great importance. A survey of 1666 showed it had twelve hearths, less than half the number in the O'Neill capital Dungannon. The whole county's population then was 12,000 but this northern and western part filled up in the increased confidence of the eighteenth century, and Omagh probably became the county town around 1786.

To return to the coast through some of the most attractive scenery in Derry and Tyrone we drive north-north-east along the B48. Somewhat less impressive than the American Folk Park is the Ulster History Park, another series of reproduction scenes and settings from the ancient to the recent past of the province. The adjacent Gortin Glen Forest Park offers good signposted walks in pretty country, rich in streams and woodland, and glimpses of sika deer and other wildlife in the mostly coniferous woodland. Passing through the great gorge known as Gortin Gap, we can turn right after one mile and left after another three to cross over Barnes Gap (*bearna* means gap), which has marvellous views over the Gleneely Valley to the mountains beyond. Coming down into the valley we turn right on to the B47 and keep going to **Draperstown**, rebuilt on its present spacious, slightly windswept scale, and named by its owners, the London Company of Drapers, in 1818. The Ulster History Centre here tells the fascinating story of the seventeenth-century colonisation of the province, mainly from south-west Scotland and the border country:

the remnant opposition; shortage of settlers meaning many Irish being taken on as tenants – an enemy within; the big figures of the settlement like Sir Arthur Chichester and Sir Thomas Phillips; the 1641 rising and massacres; the progressive policies of the Drapers in the nineteenth century; spreading education and habits of industry and thrift; the Famine and their response to it.

From here a fine stretch of road runs north-north-west to **Dungiven**, through vast lonely bog-lands. Then, a mile before reaching Dungiven, a track leads left to the old ruin of an Augustinian priory founded around 1100 and restored in the late fourteenth century after a fight of some kind of which no details are known. Thereafter it declined, though it was used for Church of Ireland services up to 1720. The tomb in the south wall of the chancel is the finest survival, with a beautiful traceried canopy covering the supposed effigy of an O'Cahan, the family which built and patronised the priory. This is one of the most beautiful tombs in the country. Outside, from a rocky promontory two hundred feet above the River Roe, there are fine views.

In the town the main landmark, more imposing from a distance than close to, is the ruinous, three-towered, 1839 castle, which incorporates part of an earlier structure granted to the London Company of Skinners. An interesting diversion is to **Banagher Old Church**, by a minor south-south-west road beside the castle grounds. The doorway of about 1100 is peculiar, squared off by a lintel outside but rounded inside, implying that the inner part was altered to suit a later rebuilding of the body of the church. The tiny steep-roofed building beside the church is thought to be the tomb of Muiredach O'Heney, a local saint and founder of the church, who may be represented by the little stone figure at the west end. Among his alleged gifts to his O'Heney posterity was making the sand hereabouts a talisman for winning all kinds of contest. It has at times been thrown at racehorses, in pious hopes.

The B192 north from **Dungiven** takes us nine miles down the Roe Valley to Limavady. Half a mile before turning right into the town, on the Derry–Coleraine road, we pass on the right **Roe Park**. This was the scene of a congress, the Convention of Drumceat, supposedly sited on the ridge called the Mullagh in the year 575, which was important enough to bring St Columba over from Iona to argue various causes. One of these was the preserving of the order of bards, a class firmly founded in the social system, but whose wit and satire made many enemies and brought about a demand for their complete suppression. Columba's pleas and prestige are supposed to have won the day against censorship. But there were also political matters for discussion, among them the status of the Scottish colony of Argyll, which was still forced to pay a tribute to its Ulster overlords. It was absentee landlordism, but not the familiar way round. Again Columba won, and brought back home rule for the Scots. An unlikely account tells that, having sworn when he left Ireland never to step on Irish soil again, he fastened clods of Scottish turf to his shoes to cover himself in this emergency. In the Middle Ages Roe Park was an O'Cahan stronghold, but their castle was destroyed in 1607. They clung to the ruins, however, and a later English visitor wrote that she found the dowager O'Cahan wrapped in a blanket in the draughts of a gutted hall, brushwood burning on the hearth where lordly logs had blazed. A museum in the park, with live demonstrations, shows how flax is grown and processed, through to the finished linen.

Limavady is a pleasant Georgian town, set in smoothly rounded farming country, rich in trees and pasture, officially called Newtown Limavady from the fact that it was bodily moved from the neighbourhood of the castle by an early Planter, Sir Thomas Phillips, to a more savoury distance. Thackeray came here and fell in love with the maid at the inn where he stayed ten minutes, composing later the long and delicate doggerel of *Peg of Limavaddy*. We leave it by the A2 to follow round the coast. Six miles along, at Tamlaghtard, a narrow lane on the right leads to an old church beside a modern one. In the graveyard is a humble ark-like structure of boulders, put up in the twelfth century but known as St Aodhan's, or Aidan's, Grave. Aidan was one of the most endearing and modest of the early travelling monks, and was appointed from Iona to be first abbot of the new monastery of Lindisfarne in Northumberland, where he died.

The next left turn leads through a duney nature reserve, past firing ranges and a prison, to Magilligan Point, at the neck of Lough Foyle, where stands a Martello tower. This was probably erected here, like its fellow at Greencastle, on the opposite shore, in 1812, against the possibility of French invasion. The great appeal here is to birdwatchers. The lough finds room in winter for a thousand whooper swans, six thousand Brent geese, over twenty thousand wigeon, two thousand oystercatchers, three thousand curlews, two thousand bartailed godwits, and hundreds of Bewick's swans, white-fronted and greylag geese, pintail, mallard, golden plover, dunlin, turnstone and others, including rarities like spotted redshank and curlew sandpiper. To the east of the point, a soft and sandy beach stretches several miles.

Back on the A2 we round the stepped end of Benevenagh, and after about eight miles come to **Downhill**. Of a very different ecclesiastical cast from the simply devout and disciplined St Aidan was Frederick Augustus Hervey (1730–1803), the fourth Earl of Bristol, and Bishop of Derry from 1768 to his death. Downhill, which we reach as the road bends east between the sea and the hills, was his home, begun in 1776 to be, as he put it, 'about the size of Blenheim'. Mussenden Temple, his classical library atop the precipitous cliffs north of the shell of Downhill Palace, is now the most beautiful reminder of his tastes. In his day he and his buildings adorned the province without rival. Everyone had an opinion of him – Fox thought him mad and dishonest, Voltaire brilliant, Boswell 'learned and ingenious', Lord Charlemont 'a bad father, worse husband', and Wesley, treated by him to roast beef and Yorkshire pudding at Derry, found him admirable. His influence was enormous; it was said 'the world consists of men, women and Herveys', and of his six children two became countesses, one a duchess and one, his heir, a marquess. From the job of chaplain to George III he became, thanks to his brother the Viceroy of Ireland, Bishop of Cloyne, then Bishop of Derry. Revising the lease system, he raised the episcopal revenue from £7,000 to near £20,000, and devoted almost all of it, and his other incomes, to buying up antiques and pictures on prolonged visits to Italy. Downhill was built, after consultation with Wyatt and Soane though the designs used were by Michael Shanahan, to be the treasure house that held works by Rubens, Tintoretto, Murillo, Correggio, Raphael, Perugino, Van Dyck and others. Outside, sixty acres of bog were transformed by two hundred workmen, landscaped to suit the dramatic setting, and planted with 200,000 trees. But Hervey was busy on other schemes, too. In Derry he repaired the Bishop's Palace, built a bridge over the Foyle, put up parsonage houses and here as elsewhere in the country clapped elegant spires on plain churches. He was concerned about social welfare and started several relief funds, gave numerous individual charities, and worked out a scheme to reform the tithe system (which was more or less adopted in 1838). He entertained his clergy at Downhill and made them race on horseback on the sands below, rewarding the winner with a fatter living. At night he is said to have scattered flour on the floor in the servants' quarters to see from the footprints in the morning who was sleeping with whom. He was a Juanesque lover himself.

He was all for Catholic emancipation, gave grants to Catholic churches and priests, and fought for their rights in Parliament. Politics brought out his megalomania, and when in true liberal form he put himself at the head of the Volunteers movement in the 1780s, he obviously saw a chance of becoming king in a newly independent Ireland. To this end he went to Dublin in 1783, toured streets lined with cheering volunteers in an open landau drawn by six horses, himself dressed in purple with gold tassels and diamond buckles, and surrounded by a squadron of dragoons and his own liveried servants. But he was beaten to the post of chairman of the Convention by Lord Charlemont, and subsequent reforms and government reaction took the life out of the movement. So he built another palace, Ballyscullion, beside Lough Beg just north of Lough Neagh, at a cost of £80,000 and partly modelled on the Pantheon; then another, Ickworth, on the same plan, at his family estate in Suffolk. In his last years he went more dangerously mad, was imprisoned in Italy as a spy by Napoleon's troops, and, released, died outside Rome in 1803.

Downhill, like Ballyscullion, lies in ruins, the first deroofed in 1950 – and twice badly burned in its previous history, the second deserted since his death. But the National Trust preserves **Mussenden Temple**, with its urn-topped dome, its handsome Corinthian pilasters linked by carved festoons, and interior stucco work, though its walls are no more lined with books for the earl's use when he sat here alone at night, working. Great ingenuity has been exercised by the experts of the National Trust in stabilising the cliffs, beside which the temple is perilously perched, by binding blocks of stone together. The Trust also maintains the attractive Portvantage Glen, to which the roadside Bishop's Gate leads. Close to the gate, on the left, is the Mausoleum, a memorial to the Earl Bishop's uncle, based on a Roman original.

We drive on to the east and come after six miles to **Coleraine**, a handsome harbour town which since 1968 has housed the University of Ulster on its north side. The Anglo-Normans had a settlement here and long before the English plantations there was a county of Coleraine extending from the Bann to the Glens of Antrim. As English power declined the MacQuillan family, albeit of Norman origin, rose to lead the Irish as 'Lords of the Route', and were allied for a while by marriage to the McDonnell Lords of the Isles. The old Anglo-Norman division of the land was forgotten. After the Plantations, Spenser's 'fishy, fruitful Bann' (still famous for salmon) was again the boundary of a shire that now extended to the east coast, but Coleraine and the land about it was merged with Derry. In the eighteenth century Coleraine was a thriving linen-manufacturing town, and the industry continues today. Mount Sandel Fort, beside the river on the south-west of the town, is the site of one of the two earliest known human settlements in Ireland, dated to about 7000 BC. It has yielded important mesolithic remains of habitations, food, and domestic bric-a-brac.

The A2 coast-road goes north from here through the popular, busy and bungalow-bound resorts of Portstewart and Portrush, with some good views west to Inishowen Head. It used to be said that Protestant fishermen put to sea at Portrush, Catholic fishermen at Bundoran. Certainly this coastline is within the heart of Scottish Presbyterian country, once known to Catholics as the Black North. An electric tramway used to run from Portrush to the Giant's Causeway, beside the sea and next to the golf-links; and there were frequent rumours that farmers with dying cows used to bring them here and prop them against the live wires, so that at least in their going they would bring compensation from the Tramways Board.

Three miles beyond Portrush on the left, perched precariously and romantically above sheer cliffs, is **Dunluce Castle**. The site has yielded traces of both early Christian and Viking occupation, but the first castle was built in the thirteenth century, later to become a MacQuillan stronghold, and finally headquarters of the immigrant McDonnells, after they had supplanted the MacQuillans at Ballycastle. It saw much action in Elizabethan times, and was forced to surrender to Shane O'Neill in his loyalist phase by his threat to starve Sorley Boy McDonnell, whom he held prisoner, to death. The castle reverted to the McDonnells after O'Neill's death and Sorley Boy's release in 1567, but was taken and held for a while by the English in 1584, after which the McDonnells came to terms with the Queen. However, Randal, Sorley Boy's third son and his successor, sided with Hugh O'Neill for a while at the turn of the century, before throwing in his lot with the English and being eventually created, in 1620, first Earl of Antrim.

In 1639 part of the cliff support at Dunluce gave way, carrying with it into the sea some of the living quarters and eight servants. Restored, it saw sporadic fighting in the Eleven Years War, and was damaged again. When the second Earl of Antrim, Randal's son, came back to his property at the Restoration, he built another (now ruined) house nearby and let the castle crumble. Its large rambling ruins, with barbican, tower and walls of the inner quarters, and even more its perilous position, have changed little since his day. Around it on the chalky ground clusters the pretty blue Meadow Cranesbill in late summer. Hereabouts it is known as the Flower of Dunluce.

Bushmills, a whiskey-distilling (licit) town, where the whole process can be visited and seen, is two and a half miles on. Here the road bends north to come after two miles to Causewayhead, from which the famous **Giant's Causeway** extends two miles towards Benbane Head. Its reputation was born in the eighteenth century after the Dublin Society and the Royal Society had issued illustrated reports of its wonders. Later the Earl Bishop of Derry returned from Italy with a mania for geology – he had seen Vesuvius in eruption, and been hurt in the arm by a steaming stone. He commissioned an artist to paint all aspects of the scene, and began the Causeway's great popularity. Soon various reports, popular and scientific, were being promulgated. One Englishman tried to show the causeway to be the work of Carthaginians. It was the time when the painting of wild landscapes first became popular, and people started to look on mountains and seas as places respectively to climb and bathe in, not fear and avoid. A few years before, Dr Johnson decided that, while the causeway might be 'worth seeing', it was not 'worth going to see'. (He was squashing Boswell's suggestion that they should tour Ireland – 'the last place where I should wish to travel'.) The discovery of wild scenery, and the embryonic Romantic Movement, went all against him. Of the causeway, a contemporary wrote: 'Here is the temple and altar of Nature, devised by her own ingenuity, and executed with a symmetry and grace, a grandeur and a boldness which Nature alone could accomplish. Those cliffs faced with magnificent columns; those broken precipices of vermilion-coloured rock; yon insulated pillars, obelisks erected before Greece boasted of her architectural skill, or Egypt laid the foundations of her Pyramids, proclaim the power and wisdom of their creator.' And in 1811 the Reverend William Drummond began a poem on the causeway: 'Ye cliffs and grots where boiling tempests wail,/Ye terraced capes, ye rocks, ye billows, hail!' and continued for a further 1,998 lines. More and more flocked to see the place. Scotland's Fingal's Cave, being a bother to get to, remained relatively untroubled. The causeway was often alive with sightseers, and the trend continues.

Whether myth or geology is applied, the Fingal's Cave connection is complex. Fingal is the old Irish hero Finn McCool, and it was Finn who, according to legend, built the causeway in the first place in order to be able to walk to Scotland. Geologists see the connection in basalt, a lava rock which, after it pours out from a volcanic eruption, cools slowly in the strange columnar forms seen here. The nature of this rock was the subject of a furious controversy between two scientific schools in the eighteenth century. Neptunists held, claiming the Old Testament as their support, that volcanoes are a modern phenomenon; and that basalts, or dolerites, which are certainly ancient, could not possibly have been formed from them. No, basalts must have been formed by chemical precipitation within the sea. Wanting to square their theories with the bible, they stated further that all fossils were formed by water action and could be traced – all of them – to one universal cataclysm, the Flood. Vulcanites or Plutonians, on the other hand, insisted that volcanoes had been going roughly as long as the earth, and that basalts could well have been thrown up in a molten state. Much of the argument centred on the nature of basalt, and therefore on the formations of this coast, to which partisans of either side came in large numbers. Among the features that prolonged the argument was an outcrop of basalt at Portrush that had got almost inextricably mixed with a layer of the prevailing lias beds. The lias was, as everyone agreed, thick with fossils. The confusion made it seem that basalt was, too, in which case basalt would be proved to be a sedimentary, not an igneous, rock. This was fine fuel for the Neptunists, reassured in the conviction of their Irish leader, Richard Kirwan, that 'sound geology graduates into religion', and they hammered home their accusations of blasphemy and atheism. In the end the Vulcanists won the day, after a campaign against the fundamentalists that was later to help Darwin considerably.

The extent of the causeway is posted with maps and explanations of the fanciful names given to individual sights: Giant's Chair, Ladies' Fan, Giant's Organ, Coffin and so on. About halfway to Benbane Head is **Spaniards Bay**, a semi-circle of 300-foot vertical cliffs which watched the destruction, in 1588, of the Armada's flagship *Girona*. About twenty Armada vessels were wrecked off Ireland's coasts. The survivors of several had boarded the *Girona* in Donegal and were making their way to Scotland in expectation of Stuart hospitality. At midnight on 26 October a storm dashed her to pieces here. It was not until July 1967, that Robert Stenuit traced the wreck and began a unique work of salvage, bringing from a depth of thirty feet a priceless collection of coins, jewellery and weapons. After years of research he had succeeded where others failed by disbelieving contemporary reports of the exact location, which he guessed were put about by local Irish to prevent the English from finding any treasure. This is the most important Armada find to date, and many of the best discoveries are displayed in the Ulster Museum in Belfast.

It is possible to walk several miles round Benbane Head to **Dunseverick Castle**, all on National Trust property. Somewhere above the track – the exact spot is secret – a pair of golden eagles nest. They have, moreover, been seen to do much of their hunting in Scotland.

Whichever way we go, by coast path or road, we come to Dunseverick Castle next, a ruined tower on a sheer and narrow headland, site of a castle since Christ's time when its owner, Conal Cearnach, a great Ulster hero and foster-brother of Cuchulain, travelled to Rome (as the story goes), joined the Roman army in Palestine, and helped his weakling comrades move the stone from the sepulchre after Christ's crucifixion. The existing ruin may have been built by Anglo-Normans first, and is known to have changed hands later, from MacQuillan to O'Cahan to O'Donnell. It was gutted by Cromwellians. A curious discovery made nearby was of the bones of great auks and reindeer amid evidence of a large-scale Bronze Age settlement, showing that both creatures featured in our ancestors' diet. A mile on we turn left on to the B15 and shortly after come on the entrance to **White Park Bay**, a strange, quiet, sandy contrast to the Giant's Causeway. The mile-long beach of white sand, backed by dunes and a sweeping hill, is maintained by the National Trust, whose contribution to the attraction of Ulster is incalculable. From the top there are views over Rathlin Island and beyond to the Mull of Kintyre (right) and Islay (left), and along the first part of the magnificent coastline that lies between here and Benbane.

Continuing on the road, we pass more ruined cliff-top castles, and at **Carrick-a-rede**, less than a mile east of Ballintoy, can walk down to the headland to look at the gigantic rock beyond, separated from the mainland by a sixty-foot-wide chasm hung with a rope swing-bridge (available to the public), from which fishermen hang large nets to trap salmon. Five miles more brings us to **Ballycastle**, the limit of the MacQuillans' Route – an old Gaelic territory – and the start of the Glens; Glenshesk to the south is the first. The town also marks the border between Ireland's north-east coast of sedimentary carboniferous limestone and the igneous basalt that adjoins it. Ballycastle is a pretty and popular resort, with a handsome Church of Ireland church of 1756, and a good local choice for the holidaymaker of fishing, beaches, hills, antiquities and other sights. From a house on the harbour Marconi transmitted the first wireless signals in 1905, and there is a memorial to him here. The destination of the signals was the lighthouse on Rathlin Island, four miles north. The race in between can be rough and dangerous: Niall of the Nine Hostages lost a son and fifty curraghs in a storm here.

William Petty, in his seventeenth-century survey of Ireland, described **Rathlin's** shape as like 'an Irish stockinge, the toe of which pointeth to the main lande'. It was in a cave on the east coast of the island that the lately crowned king of Scotland, Robert Bruce, rested in hiding in 1306, following one defeat at the hands of England's Edward I and another inflicted by Scottish enemies. Here on Rathlin he was inspired, by the famous spider that failed five times with a daring web-swing and succeeded at the sixth try, to make the resolves that led to Bannockburn. Rathlin was the first conquest from the English made by Sorley Boy McDonnell, who in 1573 sent here the women and children of the Glens for safety during the first Desmond Rebellion. For his part, the elder Earl of Essex sent a force of three ships, one captained by Drake, to take the island, which they achieved with little trouble. Everyone, to a total of six hundred, was butchered. Powerless to help, Sorley looked across from the mainland, 'likely to run mad from sorrow' as Essex reported to the Queen, who congratulated him and his troops for their bravery. In 1642 the McDonnells here were massacred again, this time by the Campbells, come for the purpose from Scotland on the king's orders. The island is rich in bird life, and the cliffs and stacks under the lighthouse at the west end are covered by several varieties of breeding sea-bird in spring.

This north-eastern corner of Ulster – the Route and the Glens – was all McDonnell territory in the late sixteenth century. They were a Scottish family, an offshoot of the MacDonalds, claiming the Lordship of the Isles, and first acquired Irish lands through marriage to the heiress to the Glens of Antrim in 1399. Their loyalty was mercurial, the bane both of the English and of resolute rebels like Hugh O'Neill, who led the last great native rising – the Nine Years' War – towards the end of the sixteenth century. Once that was over they bowed to the rising sun and swore fealty to the crown. As a result, 300,000 acres of the Route and the Glens came their way, as well as the earldom of Antrim, a title which (by a second creation) they still hold. There is a McDonnell mausoleum at the good and interesting ruins of **Bonamargy Franciscan Friary**, a mile east of Ballycastle. Here are tombs of Sorley Boy himself, and of his son and grandson, first and second Earls of Antrim. Sorley Boy died at Dunanynie, the now ruinous castle on the cliffs on the far side of the town, which may have been the McDonnells' first residence in Ireland. There is a grand MacNaghten tomb in the nave, not far from the supposed tomb of the nun Julia MacQuillan, who chose the spot for the additional abasement of being trodden by people walking along the nave.

To the south of the town is the conical basaltic mountain of Knocklayd, 1,695 feet high. In 1788 someone sent a stream of letters to Dublin newspapers, duly printed and taken seriously, about an eruption from the mountain, with detailed circumstantial evidence on the route of the lava, and the people and cattle killed. Though mention was made of the eruption, in print, as late as 1846, the report had no truth in it at all.

From the A2 going east from Ballycastle a lane leads off to the left after nearly three miles to **Fair Head**, a fantastic sight from the sea and providing excellent scenic walks on land. The headland itself consists of slopes of debris running down to the sea and, above them, sheer basaltic cliffs rising to a peak of 636 feet. To a landing place on Carrig Uisneach, the name given to the black rocks at the foot of the cliffs, came Deirdre 'of the Sorrows' with her lover Naoise and his brothers, the sons of Uisneach. They had been in Scotland (easily visible from here, as from most of the Antrim coast), escaping the wrath of aged king Conchobar, who had determined the girl should be his bride. He had lured them all back with promise of forgiveness, and sent the honourable knight Fergus to escort them to his palace at Emain Macha. Fergus had been misled, and so were they. Naoise and his brothers were murdered, and Deirdre forced into a marriage that repelled her. After much suffering she stabbed herself. This is one of the three sorrowful tales of Ireland, as old bards called it. Another is also connected with this place. The sea below the cliffs is known as the Waters of Moyle, on which the children of Lir, turned into swans by the magic of their jealous stepmother, and condemned to spend three phases of three hundred years on different Irish waters, passed the chill middle period. The first was spent on Lough Derravaragh in county Longford, the last on the sea off the west coast of Mayo (where we saw their harrowing end). A few hundred yards behind the headland is Lough na Cranagh, one of two lakes in the vicinity. In the middle is what appears to be an oddly oval island, which is, in fact, a man-made crannog, a type of Bronze Age habitation common in Ireland and parts of Scotland, but of which few good examples remain. Crannogs were made by stacking peat, stones and anything else available inside a wall of, in this case, stone, but in others of stakes.

Returning to the lane, we drive for several miles by a long, steeply rising, steeply falling, winding and wonderfully dramatic route, passing Torr Head, only thirteen miles from Scotland, until we descend gradually on the little village of **Cushendun**. From here to the west runs Glendun, which like most of the glens to the south makes a very pleasant drive or walk. The village is close to an excellent beach backed by a green, and the whole is owned by the National Trust. Most of the well-spaced, rather coy village cottages were designed by Clough Williams-Ellis, creator of the exotic enclave of Portmeirion in north Wales. Moira O'Neill, poet of the pious and patriotic *Songs of the Glens of Antrim*, and mother of the novelist Molly Keane, lived at Rockport Lodge, an 1815 house at the north end of the strand, and John Masefield met his future wife at Cave House, now a religious retreat. Charles Lanyon designed in 1839 the viaduct that takes the main road over the River Glendun, a river which further up provides some of the finest and wildest Glens scenery.

Shane O'Neill, who in his short life, 1530 to 1567, almost rolled up the province into his power, moving in and out of favour with the English, brought here in 1567 his prisoner and hostage, Sorley Boy McDonnell, hoping to trounce English ambitions through alliance with the McDonnell clan. In the old McDonnell castle, whose stumpy ruins lie beside Rockport, a row flared and O'Neill was stabbed to death. His head soon graced the gate of Dublin castle, sent there pickled in a pipkin. As in Norse and Anglo-Norman days, the Irish themselves were the invaders' best ally.

Four miles south, keeping again to the high road nearer the coast, we pass medieval Layd church, beautifully set, and containing several interesting McDonnell tombs. This was formerly the parish church of **Cushendall**, a sizeable resort with a number of hotels, which may well grow bigger still if a proposed ferry service to Scotland is introduced. The 1809 lock-up tower at the crossroads is built of old red sandstone. A coastal strip of this rock has become apparent already from the road, in long exposed flanks. Two miles south it edges the attractive Red Bay whose many caves were inhabited from neolithic to modern times, at the foot of one of the most beautiful of Antrim's glens, **Glenariff**. This runs inland five miles through a heavily wooded valley whose sides flicker with the froth of waterfalls and streams. A fenced-in area near the top (open to the public) contains many waterfalls and trees and is laid out with paths and viewpoints.

We can go on above the glen in order to see some of Antrim's interior, ascending the A43 to a rather featureless landscape swelling here and there into gentle green bulges, then through the rich valley of the River Main to **Ballymena**, the county town, famous in its day for the

manufacture, bleaching and dyeing of linen, and still a busy and prosperous town with weekly livestock and general markets. Two miles
west on the A42 is Galgorm Castle, built in the 1640s and much
altered since, whose grounds now form a golf course. Beyond that, on
the left, is the winsome village of **Gracehill**, a neat, clean Moravian
settlement of 1746 with church, irregular terraces, a square of
hawthorn-hedged lawn and many trees. The church contains Baroque
decoration. Behind, sexes segregated, is the graveyard. Moravian
ethics, piety and evangelical fervour, a mix of Calvinism and methodism, swept through Ireland at this time, and took root especially in
Antrim, where more than two hundred societies were formed. John
Cennick (1718–55), commemorated by a plaque, was its chief
promoter, and its vigour waned after his early death. The village of
Cullybackey is three miles north (passing the park of Italianate
Fenaghy House), and a little to the west of this, just off the B96, is the
ancestral home of Chester Alan Arthur, US president from 1881 to
1885, where demonstrations of traditional cooking and crafts are
given by women in period costume; a place remarkable less for itself
than as representing one of ten presidents of Scotch-Irish stock who
between them occupied the White House for almost half the nineteenth century and (Woodrow Wilson) eight years of the twentieth.
Six miles west is Portglenone. The river Bann, running from Lough
Neagh to the sea, is for most of its length the boundary between counties Antrim and Derry. Till the middle of the eighteenth century,
Portglenone had the only bridge over the river, and a drawbridge
would be raised at night to keep out disruptive bandits from the
wilder west. Portglenone Forest nearby offers some pleasant riverside
walks and rather too many commercial conifers. The big house was
for two centuries home of the Alexanders, one of Ulster's prominent
families.

Broughshane is four miles to the east of Ballymena, known for
distinguished breeders of narcissi, much in evidence locally in spring.
But the abiding presence throughout this detour is the rugged outcrop
of once volcanic Slemish Mountain (1,437 feet), to the east. Tradition
has it that St Patrick, captured as a boy by pirates on the British coast,
was put to minding sheep on the slopes of Slemish. Six years later,
instructed by a dream, he escaped, to return years later as Ireland's
apostle. A pilgrimage takes place on the saint's day, 17 March.

We can return to the coast by the A42 and B97, down **Glenarm** to
the town of that name. Or we can cut north from Broughshane to the
A43 and return by the way we came, down Glenariff. Either way, it

would be a pity to miss the coast road between the mouths of the two glens. From Glenariff, the road rounds Garron Point to the east on a splendid corniche. A turn to the right leads past **Garron Tower**, a school now, formerly a hotel and originally an Irish home, built 1848 to 1850, of the third Marquess of Londonderry and Frances, his second wife. The land – ten thousand acres of it – was hers, inherited from her mother, born a McDonnell, who became Countess of Antrim in her own right and caused her own family home, Glenarm Castle, six miles south of here, to be transformed into an impressive example of the Tudor Revival. Frances, a forceful character who once had a tender liaison with the Tsar of Russia – 'I can only wonder and rejoice', she wrote, 'that we came out of the ordeal innocent of guilt' – intended Garron, its design loosely based on a castle overhanging the Rhine, to surpass her mother's Glenarm. But it does no such thing, being rather bland in style. The marchioness passed off the work as 'famine relief' and had an inscription engraved in rock commemorating what she hopes will be 'an imperishable memorial of Ireland's affliction and England's generosity ... unparalleled in the annals of human suffering'. The inscription remains, but with the words 'and England's generosity' rubbed out by unknown hands.

A mile or two further, we come to the pleasant resort of **Carnlough** with its castellated railway bridge which well after the Second World War was carrying limestone from the quarries above, now worked out, to the harbour. Bridge, clocktower, courthouse and the fine Londonderry Arms hotel were all the achievement of the marchioness. Three miles later, along the coast-road, we reach Glenarm, a packed and pretty village with the quarrying of limestone proceeding to the south. The Church of Ireland church, with its neat spire, is beside the site of a fifteenth-century friary in whose grounds the murdered Shane O'Neill was buried. The glen here comprises the picturesque demesne of the McDonnell Earls of Antrim, and the florid, fanciful, Neo-Tudor castle incorporates part of that erected by Randal, the first earl, in 1636, when Dunluce, the seabound first family home, began to show alarming signs of structural weakness. The castle is private, but can be well seen from inside the gateway at the head of the town.

Eight miles from Glenarm we round Ballygally Head, near the village of Ballygally, whose castle, probably the best example of a Scottish Planter's castle of the early seventeenth century, was converted into a luxury hotel by the Earl of Antrim in the 1930s. It has changed hands more than once, and belonged for a while to an ill-starred speculator, Cyril Lord, but remains a hotel.

A four-mile drive brings us to the busy port of **Larne**, terminal of the ferry which brings shiploads of tourists from Cairnryan. Larne has seen more momentous arrivals in the past. Edward Bruce, having fought, together with his brother Robert, for Scottish independence, landed here in 1315, to accept the crown offered him by the Ulster chieftains, and begin a campaign which ended with his defeat at Dundalk three years later. In April 1914, as the likelihood of Home Rule drew nearer, Edward Carson's Ulster Volunteers ran a cargo of 20,000 German rifles and much ammunition into the harbour to help ensure that this province, at least, would remain British. In a token show of authority, some British destroyers appeared off the coast, but this was a rebellion the politicians were not, by and large, unhappy to see. Apart from the Round Tower memorial to James Chaine, who introduced the Stranraer steamer service, Larne is notable for the quantity of mesolithic flints and other artifacts found on the Curran, a spit of land to the town's south. These have been so prolific that the word Larnian is used to describe the Irish culture of the period.

From Whitehead, nine miles south-south-east, there is an interesting diversion into the narrow, misnamed peninsula, **Island Magee**. The cliffs on the east side, known as the Gobbins, make splendid scenery. The woods used to be renowned for the goshawks that bred there, and a Tudor tenant paid a certain number to Queen Elizabeth as his annual rent. At the opening of the Eleven Years War in 1641, the Protestants of this part were said to have been massacred by rebel Catholics and thrown over these cliffs, but the truth of the accounts has been disputed ever since. Contemporary depositions filled fourteen volumes, now in Trinity College, Dublin. The peninsula was often noted for witchcraft, the last trial for which in Ireland took place in 1711, after a local girl, Mary Dunbar, plagued by evil spirits, gave descriptions of several women alleged to be causing the trouble. These, accused, pleaded innocent throughout a trial full of ghoulish detail and were eventually imprisoned for a year. One of them, pilloried, had her eye knocked out by missiles thrown by the crowd. In 1808 a certain Mary Butters was charged with the same crime, but was discharged. Then in 1961 some hikers exploring a cave in the Gobbins cliffs came on a cache of cloaks, candles, decanters and the wooden effigy of a snake's head, as well as several documents suggesting the modern existence of a Black Magic cult. But nothing more than speculation about a 'Brotherhood of the Lefthand Path' came to light. A drive round the peninsula brings good views of sea and land, and some good but not unknown beaches at the northern end before the road descends steeply to an industrial area.

We return to the A2 and carry on in the Carrickfergus direction for four miles. On the right is the massive, tree-rich demesne of Castle Dobbs, built in 1730 by Arthur Dobbs, surveyor-general, governor of North Carolina, a worthy polymath who never paused to doubt his own theories; when he asserted after much study of the flimsy evidence about tides, ice-floes, previous explorers and so on, that the North-West passage – a sought-after, hypothetical short cut over the top of Canada to the Pacific, which might give Britain the trading edge to China over Spain – must begin within Hudson's Bay, he set the search back by about two hundred years. Sure knowledge of the passage's existence was to wait for the probings of two other Irishmen, McClure and McClintock, in the middle of the nineteenth century, and it was not till the twentieth that Norwegian Amundsen achieved the first through-journey in a single ship.

Down a lane on the left of the A2 is Kilroot, where in 1694 a disconsolate Jonathan Swift, aged twenty-seven, fresh from London and passed over for better jobs, held his first Irish living, worth an annual £100. His church and oval cottage are both gone, and the area is dominated by a business park and power station. Here he wrote *The Tale of a Tub*, and letters (still preserved) to Miss Waring of Belfast, sister of an old friend. The courtship lasted four years, but she refused his proposal of marriage. **Carrickfergus** itself once had an importance much greater than that of Belfast. After the Anglo-Normans had completed their conquest of Down in 1177 they picked on the pear-shaped rock promontory here as their base for expansion into Antrim. The magnificent castle, with its vast keep and four defensive D-shaped towers, was built about 1200, the first of its kind in Ireland. A century later it was forced, after a year-long siege, to capitulate to Edward Bruce, helped by reinforcements brought by his brother Robert. With the recovery of Gaelic power in the fifteenth century, it fell into disuse, and as that power waned in the sixteenth and seventeenth centuries, recovered in its turn. In the late seventeenth century it was the largest town in Ulster. William III landed here on his way to the Boyne at a spot now marked by a tablet. In 1760 the town was taken in an unlikely episode of the Seven Years' War by a French raiding party, who were shortly afterwards ousted. It saw another encounter in the American War of Independence when the Scottish captain of the American (and later Russian) navy, Paul Jones, in one of a series of dashing exploits, took on and captured an English ship before the castle. Thereafter, the castle, after use as a prison, and till 1928 as an English barracks, was allowed the dignity of an ancient monument and kept in good order. A good museum of various antiquities and reconstructions is within.

Over the way is the Church of Ireland church of St Nicholas. Parts are as old as the castle, but most is the result of a 1640 restoration. Inside, the nave's stained glass on the south and west sides came in 1800 from Dangan, the Duke of Wellington's ancestral home, the family having fallen on hard times. In the north transept are the stately monuments in marble and alabaster of Sir Arthur Chichester and his family. Chichester, whose impact on seventeenth-century Ireland matched Wentworth's and Cromwell's, is far less known. A Devonian and veteran of Drake's last voyage and various continental campaigns, he became Lord Deputy in 1604 and carried out his policies with the fashionable savagery and rare genius for twelve years. In the wake of the Gunpowder Plot he reversed his predecessor Mountjoy's liberal policy towards Catholics. He then turned to Ulster, where his exertions secured three million acres out of a total three and a half to Protestant immigrants within thirty years, though he himself retired in 1616, created Baron of Belfast. He died in 1625 without heir, but from his brother Edward descend the present Marquess of Donegall and, through the female line, Lord O'Neill (the name was adopted) of Shane's Castle. If any one man deserves the name, he was the founder of Ulster. His forty-room mansion, Joymount (an inversion of his patron Mountjoy's name), stood in lavish grounds near the church, but fell to ruins in the eighteenth century.

18

Belfast, Armagh, Lough Neagh and Surrounds

I N 1603 **BELFAST** hardly existed. Carrickfergus was the important town of the area. Belfast's history before that had been of
repeated attempts to grow, thwarted by Edward Bruce (1315), the
Lord Deputy Earl of Kildare (1503 and again 1512), by war, rebellion
and fire. (Well into the seventeenth century, chimneys were still made
of wood.) After the demise of the local O'Neills of Clandeboye, Sir
Arthur Chichester, granted the land, built the original city and 'a
dainty, stately palace' for himself that used 1,200,000 bricks. The
town grew from a nucleus, either side of what are now Castle Street
and High Street, flavoured Presbyterian by, among others, large
numbers of Cromwellian troops garrisoned here. Trade expanded. By
1700 the port was reckoned the second biggest in the country.
   In 1708 a fire engulfed the castle, killing several Chichesters and
servants. The countess, a widow, moved her young family out, and
left Belfast to stagnate for half a century. Her son, fourth earl of
Donegall, was feeble-minded and childless. He died in 1757 and his
nephew became fifth earl – later first marquess – a bright and enterprising improver in spite of being a chronic absentee landlord.
Terraces of handsome brick houses and many public buildings went
up, and the population more than doubled. Textiles, ship-building and
linen manufacture became the basis of the Belfast economy, long to
remain so. Unfortunately the second marquess, who inherited Belfast
– for that is what the family property was, that and nearly 90,000
more acres in Antrim, 11,000 in Wexford, 160,000 in Donegal and an
unspecified acreage in county Down – was a spendthrift nincompoop
who had passed most of his twenties in and out of debtors' prisons.
To subsidise his gambling and racing manias, he leased away chunks
of development land, losing all his father's control over quality and
appearance. He built a new house to the Tudor-revival designs of
William Vitruvius Morrison at Ormeau, to the south of the city, and at
his death left debts of nearly half a million. Ormeau Park remains, but

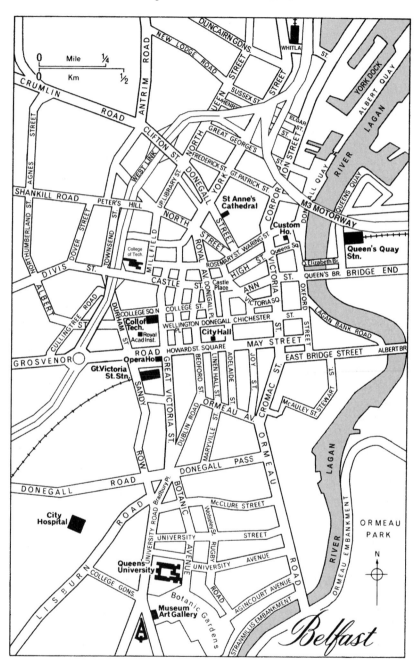

Belfast

the house is long gone. The third marquess built Belfast Castle on Cave Hill in 1870, Scottish baronial with a strong ring of Balmoral to it, but by now the important family ties with the city were severed.

Despite wayward proprietors, Belfast had prospered. Already in 1790 it was described as 'one of the most trading towns in Ireland'. A Belfast lady wrote to a Dublin doctor: 'You talk of a Dublin merchant paying 1,000 guineas for furnishing a house. I heard a Belfast one's wife say she could not fit up her drawing room for less.' With a population of 20,000, Belfast was in the first league. Its wealth was based mainly on linen, in the production of which in the course of the century it outdistanced Dublin. Bleach fields surrounded the city, and by 1801 it made £21 million from linen exports. Though even then it was a place of tensions. The predominant nonconformist Protestants suffered the same formal exclusions from public life and promotion as Catholics, and it was in Belfast that Wolfe Tone and others held the first meeting of the radical Society of United Irishmen. In the nineteenth century, during which the population of the rest of Ireland was reduced by three quarters, Belfast saw as high a rise in prosperity as in any British city and its population multiplied by over ten, reaching 438,000 by the time of the Second World War. Murray's *Handbook* a century ago listed the town's sights with admiring records of the cost of each major building, most of which was covered by the enormous profits of indefatigable, Protestant industrialists.

Everything changed in the twentieth century. Belfast became capital of a little, mainly Protestant province that clung to mainly Protestant Britain while the rest of the country broke away. World wars sealed bonds. Five thousand Ulstermen died in the first two days of the Somme. In 1941, in the Second World War, nearly 750 people were killed by a hundred tons of bombs in a single night. Another night ninety-five thousand incendiary devices raining down on the shipyards killed a hundred and fifty. Independent Ireland, neutral, sent the Dublin fire brigade to help but otherwise sustained no loss. Yet, in the North, a complacent staleness was setting in too. Harland & Wolff and other great firms were too often managed by old self-righteous men who wanted nothing changed, least of all the dominance of Orange Protestantism. The century opened with the sinking of the *Titanic*, and ended with the sinking of the firm that built it. Much of such industry as remained moved out to the new town of Craigavon. It is true that Short Brothers, whose long record boasts the development of the Sunderland flying boat and the first vertical take-off jet, remains crucial to the economy, employing thousands in the manufacture of aircraft and weapons systems on the east side of the Lagan. All the same, unemployment and urban poverty have risen. And of course for the last thirty years of the twentieth century there was a background of vicious, ruthless sectarian strife: thousands of murders and maimings and the seeming impossibility of reconciliation. Belfast remains a divided city, with Catholics occupying the south-western districts – Sandy Row and Lower Falls out to Bally-murphy and Andersonstown – and Protestants the rest. But as the millennium closed a new optimism was in the Belfast air, substantiated by foreign investment, central redevelopment, new road and rail bridges, a grand hotel and an exciting new concert hall. Self-government showed signs of a faltering return. Old enemies sat down together and talked. And Belfast emerged – what, in spite of the smugly respectable Presbyterian façade, the stupendous Victorian buildings, the stern loyalty (whether wanted or not) to king and country, Protestant resentment at Catholic advancement, Catholic resentment of continuing Protestant privilege – what it had never stopped being: an extraordinarily and paradoxically cheerful, spirited and, on the surface anyway, friendly city.

Belfast is infused by two royal ghosts. The first is of William III, whose image on a white charger is a familiar painting on the sides of Protestant houses, and whose colour – orange – was till recently the ubiquitous symbol of Protestantism and authority. (In fact the Pope of the day was delighted by William's victory, being seriously at odds with James's main allies, the French.) The second ghost is Queen Victoria. She haunts in attitudes, statues, and the styles of many buildings. A peak of municipal history was reached in 1849 when she came on a visit. The royal boat was greeted at the quay by thousands cheering. 'A very fine landing place was arranged', wrote the queen in her diary; 'Lord Londonderry came on board and *numerous* deputations with addresses, including the Mayor (whom I knighted), the Protestant Bishop of Down and clergy, the Catholic Bishop (an excellent and modest man), the Sheriff and Members for the County, with Lord Donegall (to whom the greater part of Belfast belongs), Doctor Henry from the new college, and the Presbyterians (of whom there are a *great many* here) ... the people are a mixture of nations ... It is really very interesting.'

The plan of the city's central streets and squares is a grid, first put into effect in the late eighteenth century. But in buildings it is Victorian and modern styles which predominate. John Betjeman once indulged his enthusiasm for Victoriana by placing a chair on the pavement in view of the nineteenth-century gasworks offices in Ormeau Road, by John Lanyon, and next door Meter House, his favourite building, and contemplating their magnificence. The dominating building in the middle of Donegall Square, the **City Hall**, is not quite Victorian – it was built in 1906 – but looks it; and a statue of Victoria stands imperiously in front of it. A sumptuous pseudo-Renaissance building (here and there quaintly known as Edwardian Baroque), capped by a massive dome, all to the design of Brumwell Thomas (who was knighted for it; and also did the extravagant Stockport Town Hall), it cannot fail to impress outside, but could be thought short on inspiration within. Among statues of mayors and other worthies outside the hall is one of Sir Edward Harland, Yorkshireman and founder of the famous Belfast shipyard Harland & Wolff, and on the west side a grandly set representation of the Marquess of Dufferin and Ava who became viceroy of India. Facing him, across the road, is the Scottish Provident building, a riot of multifarious stone decoration – animals, gods, distinguished people and countless artifacts; while on the north side is Belfast's oldest library, the famous Linenhall Library, originally, in 1788, housed in the White Linen Hall, which stood where the City Hall is now. Further east on the same side, Marks & Spencer are the unlikely occupants of a fine pinkish Italianate building of 1869, once the Water Office.

South-west of Donegal Square runs Bedford Street, thick with Victorian offices, and containing W.J. Barre's Ulster Hall of 1860. A little to the west in Great Victoria Street is the Crown Liquor Saloon, a working pub owned by the National Trust, its Victorian decor and panelled snugs well restored; and on the far side of the road the splendid **Grand Opera House** and the Europa Hotel, for long Belfast's biggest, which remained bravely open throughout the Troubles except when the often repeated explosion of bombs dictated closure for repair. The reopening of the sumptuously restored opera house in 1980 had the salutary effect of drawing a nervous public back into the city centre at night, though further dangerous times lay ahead. Any of the streets west from Donegall Square leads to College Square East, dominated by the heavy Presbyterian Church House and Assembly Hall, with the College of Technology built in the early 1900s on the other side. Behind this, and sadly hidden by it, is the **Royal Academical Institution**, always known as 'Inst', and one of the handsomest buildings in Belfast. Completed in 1814, it owed its design to Sir John Soane, although the present building is not much like his extant plans. In College Square North are other buildings of the same period or a little later, including the Old Museum, the first museum building in Ireland, and now, as then, headquarters of the Belfast Natural History and Philosophical Society. It was built in 1831, in Greek-revival style.

Donegall Place runs north from Donegall Square to Castle Junction, the city's focal centre and site of the original seventeenth-century development. A hundred yards to the left is a well known musical pub, Kelly's Cellars, frequented by United Irishmen over two centuries ago. Royal Avenue leads north from this for six hundred yards. In Rosemary Street, a right turn a third of the way along, is the Old Presbyterian **Oval Church**, with a most beautiful interior of 1783 (the outside was badly reconstructed in 1833) by Roger Mulholland, who was mainly responsible for the regular grid layout of the central city. Castle Court, on the other side of Royal Avenue, was the first new office and shop complex, completed in 1990, stuck like a shiny plaster where the city's old skin had been peeled away. Much more of the kind has followed, and a lot of slowly evolved intimacy, oddity and charm has gone, loving detail replaced by bland and glossy symmetries. But that is the modern replacing the old, and for the time being it suits a buoyant, optimistic citizenry. A quarter of a mile north, past the central library and offices of the Belfast *Telegraph*, at the junction of Clifton Street with Donegall Street, is Clifton House or the **Old Charitable Institution**, arguably the best piece of Georgian work in Belfast. Thomas Cooley was consulted over the design, and it opened in 1774, five years after the Belfast Bank building began life as a market-house. Its Palladian central block and low wings, pedimented at the ends, survive almost as they first appeared.

There is much admirable preservation too. Back on Royal Avenue, the domed and brightly panelled interior of Tesco, formerly the Provincial Bank and designed by Barre, is worth a visit. So too are the so-called **Entries**, between High Street and Ann Street, a tangle of old alleys replete with pubs of character, including Belfast's oldest, White's Tavern in Winecellar Entry. Farther north, the granite façade of the 1822 Commercial Building faces up Donegall Street, on the right of which, three hundred yards along, is **St Anne's Cathedral**, begun in 1899. Sir Thomas Drew designed it in Romanesque style, and in spite of many good details it is a prosy building, rather hollowly grand. In the floor of the nave, which contains a stone from every county of Ireland, is the grave of Edward, Lord Carson (1854–

1935). It was Carson who as a barrister acting for the defence brilliantly demolished his fellow Irishman Oscar Wilde's libel case against the Marquess of Queensberry, so in effect ruining his life. In 1910 he became leader of the Unionists, helped form the paramilitary Ulster Volunteers, and was the main source of pressure, both legal and otherwise, to give the Six Counties their own government in 1921 rather than come under Dublin's dominion. Nearby is the College of Art, one of the better post-war buildings in the city.

South-east of the cathedral, Hill Street leads to Waring Street, in which the Northern (formerly Belfast) Bank's head office is the oldest, though much altered, public building in Belfast. Much that was good in this street has been allowed to decay, with redevelopment in mind. We can walk through, glimpsing on the left the brash reflecting block, with its red lines and silver windows, of the Royal Mail buildings, to reach the Gothick Albert Memorial, 'admitted', Queen Victoria wrote, 'by competent judges to be one of the most graceful monumental erections in the kingdom', and designed by William Barre, whose work abounds in the city. The **Custom House**, to the east of it and towards the river, dates from 1857, and has a fine E-shaped exterior in palazzo style. In High Street, leading south-west off Queen's Square, is **St George's Church**, whose interior Barre remodelled. It was built in 1816 by John Bowden, but its best feature is the portico, removed from the Earl Bishop of Derry's redundant palace of Ballyscullion.

A stroll northward, under the sweep of the raised M3 motorway, brings us to the Clarendon Dock area, recently furbished, like much of the Lagan bankside, with modern buildings of great interest. Among older ones is the Sinclair Seamen's Church, in Corporation Street, opened in 1857, and designed internally with much nautical detail, including a ship's prow for a pulpit, port and starboard lights on the organ, and a binnacle for font. Continuing south we pass the Lagan Weir Lookout of 1994, beside the weir constructed to remove flood danger. Then, beyond the Queen Elizabeth bridge (eastbound traffic) and the Queen's bridge (westbound; the original of this was designed by Lanyon in 1843) we reach the pride and joy, justified or not, of recent Belfast architecture, the **Waterfront Concert Hall** by Robinson and McIlwaine, circular – though with extruding bumps and tangents – and with room for 2,250 in the auditorium. Sharing Lanyon Place in this lively Laganside site is the Hilton Hotel.

Over the bridges, on Queen's Island, are the severely depleted Harland & Wolff shipbuilding works, founded in 1859 and once employing 11,000 men, making them the largest of their kind in the world. The yards headed the world's list of tonnage output in no less than twenty-four different years. The ill-starred *Titanic* was built here in 1912, the *Canberra* in 1960 and what was, when launched in 1967, the largest vessel ever built in Europe, the oil tanker *Myrina*.

From Lanyon Place we can return to the City Hall past or close to the Royal Courts of Justice, some pleasant Georgian terraces, and in Alfred Street the Catholic church of St Malachy, designed by Thomas Jackson and completed in 1848. An oddity of gables, battlements and turrets outside, it has a breathtakingly sumptuous interior, the main feature being the elaborate fan-vaulted ceiling.

On the south side of the city, beyond Donegall Square and along Bedford Street and Dublin Road, is the **Queen's University**, independent since 1908, and up to 1879 one of the three 'godless colleges' designed to be open to all religions. The central red-brick Tudor-revival building, 600 feet long, was designed by Charles Lanyon, whose work dominated the architectural scene in mid-century; but it is now pressed at the back and sides by later buildings. Connected with the university grounds, to the south, are those of the **Botanic Gardens** and **Ulster Museum**. The gardens were first opened in 1827 and contain the Palm House, one of the world's first structures of curved iron and glass. The museum's collections are rich and of general Irish interest, with archaeology, geology, natural history, social and industrial history well represented. There is a fine display of effects salvaged from the *Girona*, the Spanish Armada vessel that went down off the Giant's Causeway. The art collection is a fine one, including works by Breughel, Turner, Morland, Lawrence, Sickert, Jack Yeats, Paul Henry, Louis le Brocquy, Belfast-born Sir John Lavery, and the great and lesser-known moderns – for the time is long gone when the city turned down the gift offered by Hugh Lane of a distinguished Renaissance *Mother and Child* on the grounds that the mother appeared not to be wearing a wedding ring.

Already the sectarian horrors of the late twentieth century have become history (though this is history whose tensions still hang in the air, perhaps to return in some form, as history so often does) and visitors show a perfectly legitimate interest in them. Bus tours bookable at tourist offices take in the once avoided, now legendary working-class areas of west Belfast. Catholic 'black taxis' and Protestant taxis operate openly from Castle Street, North Street and elsewhere, and the central tourist office nearby will tell of their tours and rates (though not perhaps where the profits go). The Westlink motorway is no barrier, although it marks the boundary between the city centre and the Catholic west, and was of considerable value to army and police – some say planned – in their efforts to monitor and curtail movements between the one and the other. There is no reason nowadays not to walk. Irish friendliness operates here as much as elsewhere, though as a rule night-time walks, pubs at any time and getting into arguments might be avoided. There is still plenty to see: the vivid murals, among them one of Bobby Sands in the (Catholic) Falls Road and triumphant King Billy in the (Protestant) Shankill Road; official buildings thickly clad in wire and concrete and snooping cameras; black flags marking the sites of killings; preserved bullet marks and bomb damage; a few remnants of the Dickensian nineteenth-century scene; bright new redbrick housing; and seen sporadically between the two roads the Peace Line, a wall of corrugated iron sheeting with gates now usually open. Here and there are signs that the present territorial divisions were not always in place. Lower Falls was a mixed area. There was an Orange hall and a Methodist church in the Falls road. Thousands have been displaced in vicious bouts of segregation since the present Troubles began. On the left, two miles down the Falls Road, is Milltown cemetery, where numerous Republican victims lie buried.

North of Belfast is **Cave Hill**, a landmark of 1,182 feet, and a popular resort of Belfast people at weekends. It contains Bellevue Zoo and Pleasure Gardens, and incorporates the grounds of Belfast Castle, built in 1867 for the Marquess of Donegall: an impressive baronial pile presented to the city in 1934. Of several dolmens and other prehistoric remains in the Belfast area, one fine dolmen with five supports is enclosed in an enormous seven-acre circular earthwork, 600 feet in diameter. It is five miles south of the city centre and a mile south of Shaw's Bridge, at Ballynahatty and is known as the Giant's Ring.

To Armagh and Lough Neagh

The A1 and the M1 motorway both run south-west from the suburbs of Belfast to Lisburn, six miles up the river Lagan. A mile before is the hamlet of Lambeg, where painted lambegs – drums weighing thirty pounds or more – are made. Introduced by William III's army, they have been used by Protestant and Catholic for their various marches, and before 1970 both would often use the same drum.

Lisburn is a neat town built round a triangular market place with a statue of General John Nicholson (1821–57), who was killed in Delhi at the head of a storming-party during the Indian Mutiny. 'The type of the conquering race', explains his memorial in the cathedral. But corporation flower-beds preclude inspection of some of the graphic relief panels on the plinth. The town was laid out on its present lines and settled by Sir Fulke Conway, of Conway Castle in Wales. Part of the castle walls he built stands in Castle Gardens, east of the market-place, and between the two is Protestant **Christ Church Cathedral**, built in 1625 and a good example of so-called Planter's Gothic. The spire was added in 1807. For the last few years of his life, Jeremy Taylor (1613–67), by then bishop of Down and Connor, lived here. In spite of the pleas for tolerance in his many poetically eloquent sermons and other writings (most written when, as a royalist in England and Ulster, he was hunted and sometimes imprisoned), he loathed the Presbyterians by whom he was surrounded (he called them 'Scotch spiders'; Milton's label for them was 'the blockish pres-byters of Claneboye'), imposed church rituals much too high for their taste, and replaced thirty-six of their ministers with Anglicans. They in turn had him charged with using the sign of the cross during serv-ices, thought by them to be papist sorcery. He died here, longing for England. There is a memorial to him, though he was buried at Dromore. Before he died he had all available copies of his chief work in favour of tolerance publicly burned.

But linen was the making of Lisburn. It lies well within the so-called Linen Triangle, bounded by Armagh, Dungannon and Belfast, from which came over half of Ulster's nineteenth-century linen output. Buried at the south-east end of the churchyard is Louis Crommelin, a native of Picardy, who in 1698 brought a colony of French Huguenots to the town, imported a thousand looms from the Netherlands, and founded a thriving linen business. (William III, while unfairly protecting the English wool industry, had made compensatory conces-sions to Irish linen production.) Twelve years after Crommelin's arrival, despite a fire that destroyed most of the town in 1707, income from production of Irish linen, till then a small cottage industry, was reckoned to account for a fifth of the whole Irish revenue.

At the centre of the town is the **Old Market House**, successor to the seventeenth-century arcaded market building, and now the town museum and Irish Linen Centre. Excellent exhibits and practical demonstrations carried out by lifelong masters of the various skills display all the stages of linen making. A good final film shows how refinements in manufacture, ingenious advances in loom design, the huge spaces given over to bleach greens, the broad flax fields, employment of women and children in their own homes as well as factories, the pride and pleasure often taken by workers and the exhaustion and sickness they often in consequence suffered, turned life into linen and linen into life in this heartland of Ulster for more than two centuries. It did not beautify it. 'I see [Lisburn]', wrote the fourth Marquess of Hertford in 1845, owner of much of the land and absentee beneficiary, on the grand scale, of the linen explosion: 'I see it for the first time ... and pray God for the last time.'

Another native of Lisburn, not commemorated by the diocesan authorities, was Laura Bell. She moved to London, grew rich as a courtesan and 'Queen of Whoredom', and possibly, through an affaire with a prince of Nepal, did more to end the Indian mutiny than her heroic townsman Nicholson. Then she saw God. Calling herself 'God's Ambassadress', she drew crowds to prayer meetings. In the end, Gladstone himself would attend. The present Technical College used to be the home of Sir Richard Wallace, local MP, connoisseur, collector, probably illegitimate half-brother of the fourth Marquess of Hertford and certainly heir to his paintings and his £50,000 annual rents, whose own collection in Hertford House, London, was given to the nation by his widow as the Wallace Collection. The plan of this building was based on that of Hertford House.

Continuing along the M1, we pass near and see the Maze prison, or Long Kesh, scene of much horror and unhappiness and in particular the 1981 hunger strikes in which Republican Bobby Sands and nine others starved themselves to death. **Hillsborough**, four miles south-west of Lisburn, is a pretty little hillside town with odd streets and nice terraces and several grand buildings. It was founded in the 1650s by Sir Arthur Hill, a shrewd Planter who kept friendly both with the Cromwellians and the Restoration government. His descendants grew in wealth and influence till much of the land between Lisburn and Newry was theirs. William III granted them leave, after staying at their castle, to own a private army and the present Marquess of Downshire is still Commander-in-Chief of the only constitutionally recognised private army in the United Kingdom, consisting until 1977 of one veteran bugler, who still wore the uniform of the old Dutch Guard. The first marquess was Wills Hill (1719–93), obstinate and disastrous Secretary of State for the Colonies under George III, and sponsor of Goldsmith's *Deserted Village*. It was he who caused the building of the cupola-topped market-house, now the courthouse,

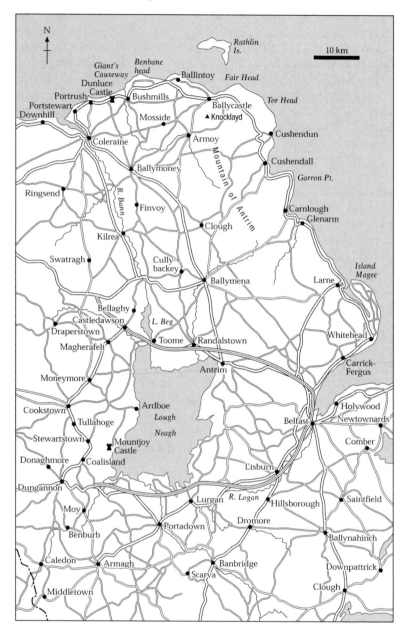

of **Hillsborough Castle**, a long low eighteenth-century mansion much restored and added to in the nineteenth century, formerly official residence of the governor of Northern Ireland and of handsome Church of Ireland St Malachy's, rich in monuments and set low down in its leafy glen. The marquess's unfulfilled ambition was that the church should become the cathedral of Down diocese. It was much altered by Sir Thomas Drew and others in the nineteenth and twentieth centuries. Among several points of interest inside and out are the grave and memorial to the composer Sir Hamilton Harty (1880–1941), born in Ballynahinch Street, whose father was church organist for forty years, and the Leslie memorial by Nollekens. The original seventeenth-century fort has been much altered, especially by charming eighteenth-century additions – a Strawberry Hill Gothic gazebo above the entrance, and a Gothic gatehouse. The third marquess is commemorated on a hilltop obelisk overlooking the town. The present one lives in England. As traditional tribute, the town was till recently sending him a pair of rather toy-like white doves every year.

From Hillsborough a minor road leads west to **Moira**. The battle of Mag Rath, or Moira, was fought in the year 637 between the armies of the king of eastern Ulster, the Ulaid, and Domnall king of Ireland. Domnall won. The unhappiest victim was Suibne, or Sweeney, the local king who was sent mad by the sight of battle and wandered Ireland reciting beautiful sad lines which appear in a long poem translated by Seamus Heaney as *Sweeney Astray*. The town was built in 1649 by Sir George Rawdon, later made a baronet, and filled by him with 'conformable Protestants'. His son Arthur built the first hothouse in Ireland and sent a skilled gardener to Jamaica to collect plants. His gardens are gone. Five miles north, at Upper Ballinderry, is the simple church, much restored, Jeremy Taylor built from 1664 on. It contains some original wooden fittings.

The prosperity of **Lurgan**, five miles west of Moira, dates from the introduction of damask weaving in 1691. George Russell (1867–1935), known as 'AE', an oracle to most of the distinguished literary and artistic figures of his day, was born and educated here. The demesne of the original settlers, the Brownlows, is on the east side of the town and is now a public park. The house, built in Tudor style in 1836, to the designs of William Playfair, is a lodge of a fellowship closely connected with the Orange order. The A26 leads two miles south of Lurgan to **Waringstown**. William Waring, a linen manufacturer, had Waringstown House built in 1667 and the church in 1681.

The three-storeyed house was one of the first unfortified houses in Ireland (the two terminal pavilions were added in the eighteenth century). James Robb, chief mason of the King's Works in Ireland, designed both buildings. Lord Lurgan owned the peerless racing greyhound Master McGrath, which is commemorated by a statue at Craigavon civic centre, a stained glass window in the parish church and in the town's arms.

Lough Neagh lies a few miles north of Lurgan, and a short drive brings us to **Oxford Island** National Nature Reserve, with bird-watching hides, walks, a large visitors' centre and, especially in winter, huge visible populations of duck, geese, waders and three kinds of swan.

Lurgan and Portadown, five miles south-west, are gradually being fused in a new city, Craigavon, which will reach north to Lough Neagh. At present **Portadown** is an industrial town, product of the nineteenth century, but famous above all for its roses. The mayor's chain is made of linked gold medals won in rose competitions, mostly by Sam McGredy, best known of Ulster's rose-growers. At an important junction of road, railway, river and canal, the town is one of Ulster's most prosperous. Its citizens are supposed to be close with their money and have been called 'the Aberdonians of Ireland', a judgment that may have more to do with outside envy than inner character. Government refusal, fuelled by Catholic objections, to allow a traditional Orange order march from Drumcree to the north of Portadown, through the wholly Catholic Garvaghy Road led to sustained tensions in the late 1990s. In a village called The Diamond, four miles west, in 1795, there was a battle between members of two secret societies, the Protestant Peep of Day Boys and the Catholic Defenders, in which the latter, attacking, were beaten off with the loss of thirty or so lives. The victorious Protestants marched to an inn at the nearby village of Loughgall and founded the Orange order. Intensely loyal to the king, but opposed to union with Britain (which was to come about in 1800) the order began, as it was to continue, a deep embarrassment to the objects of its loyalty.

The main road A3 leads direct from Portadown to **Armagh**, the ecclesiastical capital of Ireland since its early connection with St Patrick, and one of the most beautiful cities. Most of its old building goes back no farther than Georgian times, and that is what is most visually striking about the place. To Victorians, for whom Georgian was simply old-fashioned, Armagh was disappointing. 'No city is so rich in historical associations, and yet has so little to show and tell', wrote the antiquary Bishop William Reeves. Thackeray, who was immensely cheered by the 'wonderful circumstance of the sermon in the cathedral lasting no more than twenty minutes', summed up the place as having 'the aspect of a good stout old English town'. It is true that little is left to recall the older past, which comes into our knowledge with the first few centuries AD when King Conchobar and his Red Branch Knights held sway in their capital of **Emain Macha**, or Navan Fort, a well-preserved rath just over a mile west of the town. The best-known figures of that court, the most powerful in Ireland – petulant Conchobar, his perfidious wife Maeve, brave Cuchulain, beautiful Deirdre and the sad sons of Uisneach – went to make one of the most evocative story-cycles that have come down from ancient times (James Stephens's *Deirdre* is the most entertaining version, a very free modern adaptation). The site is visited by many, though some clearly get no further than the heritage centre, whose turfed dome perhaps suggests to them it is the real rath, a late Bronze Age site on which was built in the first century AD a large wooden structure, subsequently burned.

To Armagh came Patrick in the fifth century and, converting the king, was given land by him and founded Ireland's first diocese. Some centuries later the magnificent *Book of Armagh* (now in Trinity College, Dublin), containing a life of the saint and rivalling in its production the *Book of Kells*, was written and illuminated here. This was a time of monastic prosperity, and the town soon attracted ravaging Danes, based at Carlingford Lough and Lough Neagh. Burned several times, it became by 989 'the most melancholy spot in the kingdom'. But its prestige remained supreme and Brian Boru, by order of his will, lay in state and was buried here in 1014. After the Conquest it came under the Anglo-Norman mantle and a fourteenth-century decree ruled that Irishmen were not to be raised to the primacy. (A Florentine was appointed in 1478, and was horrified at his savage surroundings.) But as the Pale shrank in the fourteenth and fifteenth centuries, Armagh's position became less and less secure and archbishops prudently lived at Termonfeckin, in County Louth and better protected. Wisely, for in the sixteenth century, after the Reformation had in Catholic eyes annulled the place's sanctity, the town was destroyed by Shane O'Neill in his attempt to control all Ulster, and again in the 1641 uprising of Phelim O'Neill. By the middle of the eighteenth century it was little more than a village of mud-and-thatch houses (the material of the majority of Irish houses till far into the nineteenth century).

Then came Archbishop Richard Robinson (1709–94), a wealthy prelate whose autocratic ways and generous spending made him almost the match of his contemporary the Earl Bishop of Derry. Already in 1776 he had spent £30,000 on the beautifying of Armagh. He used Thomas Cooley for some of the buildings and put young Francis Johnston (1761–1829) – a native of the town – to work under him. He built as first priority a splendid episcopal palace, restored the historic cathedral, erected a public library (and gave it a valuable collection of books), the Royal School (founded on a different site by Charles II), a public infirmary, gaol and barracks. In 1793 he founded the Observatory. The town's streets were lit and paved, trees planted, and new three-storey houses built. The remarkable Robinson, who was created Baron Rokeby of Armagh in 1777 (his family was from Rokeby in Yorkshire), intended that Armagh should become capital of Ulster and seat of a university. It had to be content with the status of a county town and Ireland's best Georgian treasury outside Dublin. Robinson died respected by all (including his brother, Sir William, who out of deference had his shoes made on the same last, ate the same diet and always took the same medicines as his brother) though Wesley feared that 'in lieu of preparing for Heaven he had given too much time to works of public utility'. The adornment went on, but nothing that came later was an improvement, except for some constructions by Francis Johnston – the Courthouse, Market House and present Bank of Ireland building, originally a private house. Primate Lord John Beresford (1773–1862), brother of the second Marquess of Waterford, spent £20,000 of his own money, mainly on a complete, clinical and unfortunate overhaul of the Protestant cathedral carried out by Lewis Cottingham, who did similar work at Hereford Cathedral. (Much of the work was undone in the 1880s but the decoration that Cottingham cleared was irreplaceable.) Building the Catholic Cathedral occupied the years 1840–1875. But the town remained, above all, Georgian.

Like Rome, the city is built on several hills. On the highest of these is the Church of Ireland **Cathedral of St Patrick**, incorporating sections from the thirteenth century on, but virtually the nineteenth-century concept of Cottingham. It is on the site of St Patrick's original church, and of a later monastery, and at the centre of an ancient hill-fort, whose defensive earthworks can be seen in part still. Outside the west wall of the north transept is the alleged grave of Brian Boru. There are a few more ancient remains in the north transept including a small female statue which, an old guidebook explains, 'is naked, except for a girdle, and is therefore probably not of Christian origin'. The chancel is very slightly out of line with the nave, which may be for technical reasons but has been explained as symbolising the inclination of Christ's head on the cross. The memorials are a treasury of the work of great sculptors, including a statue, by the west door, of Sir Thomas Molyneux, physician and zoologist, by Roubiliac; a magnificent seventeenth-century likeness of Dean Drelincourt, by Rysbrack; Sir Francis Chantrey's statue of Primate Stuart; and a bust, by the amiable Nollekens, of the greatest benefactor, Archbishop Robinson, Baron Rokeby; besides effigies of Archbishop Lord John George Beresford, and his cousin Marcus, who succeeded him in 1862; and, in the north transept, seventeenth-century memorials to the Caulfeilds, Earls of Charlemont. North-west of the cathedral, beside the eighteenth-century houses of Vicar's Hill, is the **Public Library**, designed for Robinson by Cooley in 1771 and extended in 1820, containing 20,000 valuable books and manuscripts. George Ensor's Infirmary of 1774 stands behind it to the right.

The so-called St Patrick's Trian (pronounced tree-an, and meaning a third part) beside the tourist office offers reconstructions of the early city, of St Patrick's life and an ingenious presentation of the story of Jonathan Swift's *Gulliver's Travels*.

The handsome, Church of Ireland **Archbishops' Palace** is on the south side of the hill, beyond the bypass. The work of Ducart, Cooley and, later, of Johnston, who added the unadorned second floor almost identical to the first, it has been turned into office space by the local council in recent years. A little removed from the palace is its chapel of 1783, also by Cooley, and with a remarkable interior added by Johnston, who did some of his best work for his native town. The eighteenth-century stable block, set about a cobbled courtyard, houses a less than convincing reconstruction of daily life in the 1770s. In the demesne, part of which is now a golf-course, are remains of a thirteenth-century Franciscan friary, the only medieval ruin in the city.

A few yards from Dobbin Street's east end is the Bank of Ireland office, built by Johnston as a family house for the Dobbins. To the right the **Mall** opens up, once a racecourse, now a mostly elegant square (there are hideous modern additions on the west side) with its green, walks, lime-trees and differently designed Georgian terraces, and Johnston's court-house at the far end, badly damaged by a bomb in 1993 but completely restored. On the Mall's east side is the well-arranged **County Museum** of 1833, with good archaeological displays, stuffed wild animals, and some interesting Irish art, notably by George Russell ('AE'). The Royal School (founded in 1608, though the main building is of 1774) and Observatory, both by Cooley, are on College Hill, off to the right at the Mall's north end. The imposing Gothic **Catholic Cathedral**, with its landmark twin spires, is on the city's north-west side, standing on its own hill, with wonderful views of town and country. The process of building, to the designs mainly of J.J. McCarthy, alternated with Europe-wide fund-raising over twenty-five years; and the sumptuous interior, bright with stained glass, mosaics, gilt and paintwork, was not finished till the early twentieth century.

From Armagh we can do a small eastward tour to Tandragee, Scarva, Markethill, Gosford and back. The A51 takes us through Hamilton's Bawn, the eponymous walled enclosure of which has vanished, past Marlacoo lake, where in 1595 the Earl of Tyrone, Hugh O'Neill, secreted his family and valuables on an islet. On the right, a mile or so before **Tandragee** (the name, from the Irish for back, or bottom, to the wind, denotes the place's exposure to the elements) the demesne wall of the castle begins with a much restored gate-lodge. The nineteenth-century baronial-style castle, built by the future Duke of Manchester in 1837, has suffered an unlikely status drop to become an admirably run potato-crisp factory. It opens for public tours. An earlier castle belonged – till Cromwell dispersed them – to the O'Hanlons, of whom the outlawed Count Redmond (not to be confused with the living Redmond O'Hanlon, a distinguished and entertaining travel writer), as head of a band of 'tories', levied tribute from everyone he could from his stronghold on Slieve Gullion. Eventually his foster-brother shot him dead for a government reward.

We turn right on to the A27 and come after two miles to **Scarva**, a charming village inside county Down and beside the canal linking the Bann with the Newry canal. Here King William's forces mustered prior to the battle of the Boyne, and every 13 July, in a two hundred-year-old sham reenactment of the battle, two kings mount horse and joust, with much banging of lambeg drums and with predictable outcome. Scarva House, built about 1717 but much remodelled, has in its grounds a section of the Dane's Cast, a patchily surviving bank-and-ditch earthwork which marked the boundary of Ulaid (Ulster-to-be) as it was two thousand years ago. We drive parallel to the canal to **Poyntz Pass**, named after an engagement of about 1590 in which Lieutenant Poyntz and his men fought through a narrow path over what were then treacherous boglands, evading the rebel Earl of

Tyrone's forces. From here the B114 takes us west to Markethill, north of which lies the vast former demesne of Gosford Castle, now the Gosford Forest Park. The castle, a forbidding, massive jumble of towers round and square, arched doorways and windows, turrets and battlements, was built in 1819 and 1820 and represents the first revival of Norman styles in either Ireland or Britain. The interior was delicately and intricately done, rich in plasterwork and other decoration. Over a couple of years, Swift often stayed in the eighteenth-century house which preceded the castle, with the Achesons, later Earls of Gosford. He even bought some land nearby from his host, intending to build, but the plan and friendship both faded, as Swift's often did. What he did leave behind were two public lavatories. One earl, in the raffish and extravagant circle round the Prince of Wales who became Edward VII, overspent and had to sell his unique library and much fine furniture. With the estate sold off, the castle has been successively home to a circus, a Second World War army base (earning a place in Anthony Powell's *The Valley of Bones*) and a public records office. At present it is part lived in and mostly empty and dilapidated, with plants sprouting from chimneys. Eight miles westward along the A28 returns us to Armagh.

Another excursion from Armagh takes us fourteen miles south-west by the A3 main road, crossing the border into County Monaghan (in Ulster, but like Cavan and Donegal not one of the Six Counties). Half a mile beyond the border we turn right for the charming village of **Glaslough**, whose manorial demesne, Castle Leslie, is a massive Victorian pile in grey stone, with a strong Scottish baronial flavour, fussy external decoration, and a curious part-replica of a Renaissance Roman cloister attached. The contents are rich and fascinating: marble columns, Della Robbia chimneypiece, wooden panelling, mosaic floor, paintings, library, rare furniture, mostly fine but looking (and being) lived-in. This has for three and a half centuries been the home of the Leslie family. The first of the line in Ireland was a Protestant rector who, unable to reconcile fighting his king (James) with his principles, went on later to visit the Old Pretender in exile and to try and convert him. The previous house on the demesne was Georgian but the ruling Leslie of the 1870s, granted a baronetcy by Disraeli, built the present extravagant baronial mansion in honour of his elevation, and filled it with a magnificent collection of Italian paintings and *objets d'art*, styling part of the house and garden in the Italian manner. Sir Shane Leslie, who died in 1970, was a cousin and boyhood friend of Winston Churchill, some relics of whom are preserved in the house. His younger brother Norman was the last serving officer in the British army to fight a duel. He spent the summer of 1910 practising his sword-play on the lawn here, then went to Paris and honourably allowed himself to be wounded by Ysoury Pasha, a relative of the Egyptian khedive, whose wife he had seduced. Sir Shane himself was in his time an old-school eccentric, an IRA sympathiser, a Catholic convert and a prolific and witty writer with a special interest in ghosts. The public who come to this remote part to take advantage of the house's opening hours are quite likely to be shown round by a member of the family. Besides being a home, the house now functions as a hotel and conference centre.

Recrossing the state border (we must return by the way we came, as that is the nearest 'approved road') we reach **Caledon**, in County Tyrone, a model village beside the grand demesne of the same name. Originally known as Kenard, it was an O'Neill headquarters till the war of the 1640s. After the Ulster rising of 1641 which he led, and having put himself at the head of the royalist forces by virtue of a forged commission from the king, Phelim O'Neill brought Lord Caulfeild here a prisoner and killed him. In 1747 the castle and demesne came to John Boyle, fifth Earl of Orrery (1707–62), descendant of the Earl of Cork and friend and biographer of Swift, through his second wife, a Hamilton. 'Caledon has changed me into a Hibernian,' he wrote, and created a magnificent garden with all the new features William Kent (protégé of his kinsman the fourth earl, also Earl of Burlington) was advocating to create romantic effect. These included a hermit's cell made from tree roots, a popular device of the time, complete with matting couch, stools, table with manuscript on it, pair of spectacles, leathern bottle, bowls, hourglass, books and mathematical instruments – everything but a hermit, though some landowners went so far as to hire one. He also put up Latin tags on the rustic buildings which, in combination with naked classical statues, roused suspicion of paganism in the Presbyterian peasants; but he told them all the tags were different phrases of welcome, and all was well. The seventh earl sold this and other lands for £600,000 to James Alexander, soon to become Earl of Caledon, a merchant returned with a fortune from the East Indies. It remains in his family. The present house (not open to the public) was the work of Thomas Cooley, but was considerably revised in 1812 by John Nash who added wings, Ionic portico and colonnades outside and created one of his masterpieces, the oval drawing-room, within. The grounds, too, are magnificent, and include a large herd of deer, introduced by James Alexander, fourth Earl of Caledon along with wapiti and small black bears (no longer present). The park is also noted for its avenue of monkey-puzzle trees, a curiosity that became wildly popular after 1844 when William Lobb sent back seeds from Chile. Field-Marshal Earl Alexander of Tunis, younger brother of the fifth Earl of Caledon, was born here in 1891.

Eight miles north-east of Caledon (by the B45 then the B128) is **Benburb**, on the river Blackwater, where, under the uninspiring red-brick sprawl of the 1887 manor house, now a Servite priory, and hanging over a 200-foot cliff above the dashing river and the massed greenery on its banks, stands the fort built in 1615 by Sir Richard Wingfield. It consisted of four towers, of which one is still lived in, joined by curtain walls. In this vicinity two battles took place in two different wars, both briefly bringing exultation and hope to the native Irish. The battle of the Yellow Ford, on 14 August 1598, followed an ambush by Hugh O'Neill of a British force taking supplies to its beleaguered fort at Blackwatertown, two miles east of our present position. Eight hundred English soldiers were killed and O'Neill, by now known as the Prince of Ireland, was able to move south to try to reverse the English plantation of Munster. Forty-eight years later, on 5 June 1646, during the Confederate war, Hugh's nephew Owen Roe O'Neill, champion of Ulster and of Catholics, smashed an army of Scots parliamentarians here at Benburb, killing between two and three thousand. It was the only Irish victory in pitched battle ever, and it panicked settlers for miles around. Its effect was vitiated by the bickering of the Confederate Council, which should have consolidated Irish interests. From this time on, the Irish forces, under whatever guise, began to decline, and the death of O'Neill himself three years later combined with Cromwell's arrival to wipe out their hopes.

Three miles north-east is Moy, usually known as **The Moy**, a model village laid out by the cultivated patriot and Volunteer James Caulfeild, first Earl of Charlemont (1728–99) in 1754, on a plan close to that of Marengo in Lombardy. It used to be famous for a horse fair. Between this and Charlemont, just to the south-east, run the county boundary and the Blackwater River, overlooked by the remains of a fort of 1602 which, though demolished in the 1920s, still shows clearly, through surviving earthworks, the defensive arrangements of a Plantation stronghold. The British housed a garrison here till 1858. In the Roxborough demesne to the north of the village there stood the grandiose nineteenth-century mansion – massive, mansard-roofed, rather Ritz-like – that had been the home of the successors of Lord Charlemont. Although its entrance gates and a good iron screen survive, the house itself was burned down in 1922. A left turn off the B28, followed by another on to the Derrycaw road, leads to **The Argory**, a handsome, classical, 1820 house, well set among gardens, 315 acres of parkland and woods, administered by the National Trust. It maintains splendid historic amenities in working order, including gas lighting provided by a private acetylene gas plant in the stable yard.

Four miles east of Charlemont on the B28 is **Ardress House**, originally a farmhouse of Restoration times, and remodelled and transformed into a modestly elegant country house in the 1770s by its architect-owner, George Ensor. He worked at Armagh for Archbishop Robinson, and his brother was Richard Castle's assistant. Some gables and other features belong to the original building and give it a seventeenth-century look. But its greatest feature, the drawing-room, is very much of the eighteenth century. Michael Stapleton, whose work still abounds in Dublin, did the superb plasterwork of the ceiling which shows the influence of Italian stuccodores as well as of Adam. The house is owned by the National Trust which took it over in 1960 and restored it from an advanced state of decay. Behind it is a working eighteenth-century farmyard, with several rare farm breeds.

Returning to Moy, we drive due north-west to Dungannon, a characteristic hilltop Planters' town which had been till the end of the sixteenth century a principal seat of the O'Neills. Though it has a number of buildings of various periods, none of them is of great distinction. Hugh Roe O'Neill, Earl of Tyrone, preparing his long and vigorous campaign against Queen Elizabeth's army, professed to be improving his ancestral home here by reroofing it with lead. The English later learned the lead was in fact for making bullets. Nothing of the old castle survives. Some buildings of the Royal School, an early-eighteenth-century foundation, date from 1786, when their construction was funded by Archbishop Robinson, benefactor of Armagh. The statue in front, of former pupil General John Nicholson, hero of the siege of Delhi, (also figured beside Lisburn's market building) was returned from its original site by the Kashmir Gate in Delhi in 1960. Dungannon's most memorable year was 1782, when the Volunteers, mostly middle-class and Protestant patriots, formed to defend the peace while the British army was heavily engaged in the American war, met here at two conventions to press for a degree of independence for Ireland. This was granted, and exercised (till the

Act of Union cut it off in 1800) by Grattan's parliament. Lord Charlemont was leader of the Volunteers.

Donaghmore, three miles north-west of Dungannon, was the parish of the Rev. George Walker before Derry called him to immortality. From 1818 to 1821 Charles Wolfe, poet of the *Burial of Sir John Moore after Corunna*, was rector. (The poem was acclaimed, and credited to Byron and others, before its real author was known.) The church was at **Castle Caulfeild**, two miles south-west, and preserves good seventeenth-century details, though it was much altered in 1838. South of the village are the remains of a castle erected by Sir Toby Caulfeild, later Lord Charlemont, in 1619 and burned down in the 1641 rebellion. A few good mullioned windows and chimneys remain.

The A29 out of Dungannon leads north to Coalisland, centre of the Tyrone coalfield which, in spite of holding an estimated thirty million tons of coal, has never, because of technical difficulties and distribution costs, been profitably mined. An eighteenth-century canal links the town with Lough Neagh on the south-east, but the railways that came later brought English coal at less cost to the region. Two miles north-west of Coalisland is Roughan Lough, with a ruined Plantation castle of 1618 beside it. We take the B161 eastward and nearing Lough Neagh pass **Mountjoy Castle** on the left. Built by Sir Francis Roe, a Tyrone undertaker, or colonist, in 1602, it changed hands several times in the wars of the 1640s and was eventually dismantled by Parliamentarians in 1648. In spite of long neglect, it still shows well the ground plan and brick construction of a Tudor castle.

Lough Neagh, which we skirt for a while now and see from different angles, has been the biggest single natural influence on the way Ulster has developed, a vast sheet of water – 153 square miles and the biggest in the British Isles – abutting on five of the present six counties. Ten rivers flow into it but only one out – the Bann, that reaches the sea below Coleraine, due north. The edge on all sides slopes gently to a depth of a few feet, then drops abruptly to a uniform depth of forty or fifty feet, except for a narrow basin in the north-west which goes down 120 feet. In the past, before drainage, its periodic floods would cover up to 30,000 acres all round its shores. In legend, it began as a simple stream – the Bann – and people could jump from one side to the other. The stream's flow was controlled by a lid over the source which always had to be watched. One day, the watcher left her task. The spring overflowed, and filled the valley. All the houses and villages around were flooded, and ever since Round

Towers and other buildings have been seen by fishermen, Abu-Simbel-like, beneath the water. Giraldus Cambrensis, who took old tales seriously, supplied the crucial reason; bestiality among the peasants. 'It looked,' he wrote, 'as if the author of nature had judged that a land which had known such filthy crimes against nature was not worthy, not only of its first inhabitants, but of any others for the future.' Another account ascribed it to the hero Finn McCool, who, chasing a Scottish giant away from Ireland, picked up a lump of earth and threw it after him. The lump left a hole which is the lake's basin. The mud itself missed its target, landed in the sea, and formed the Isle of Man.

In more recent years scientists and locals, including the eminent botanist R. Lloyd Praeger, have heard loud bangs that continue, sometimes for hours, coming from the lake with no normal explanation. Biologists in search of diatoms and more conspicuous rarities like the American *Spiranthes stricta*, a species of Lady's Tresses known elsewhere in only one part of Scotland, find them on the shore. The lake supports up to 100,000 wildfowl in the winter, and there is a period in late autumn when hundreds of whooper swans, after a direct 800-mile flight from their Icelandic breeding lakes, fly in and remain till they split into smaller groups and disperse to smaller lakes. It abounds in salmon, trout and eels, and affords the biggest annual catch of eels in western Europe: up to seven hundred tonnes. Mile-long thousand-hook lines are used by fishermen to catch them off the west and north-west coasts of the lough. There are also large reserves of lignite to be exploited for fuel. Yet for all its curiosities and beneficence to humans, Lough Neagh is the least picturesque of Irish lakes, has almost no islands, and need not hold us long.

After Mountjoy Castle we take the first left turn, pass Stuart Hall, the Irish seat of Lord Castlestewart, turn left again for Stewartstown, then right for Cookstown. Two miles south of the town, on the right of the road beyond **Tullaghoge**, is a hilltop ring-fort mostly covered with trees. This prehistoric sanctuary used to have a stone on it which was used as the inauguration throne of the O'Neills, all of whom up to the great Hugh O'Neill, Earl of Tyrone, in 1593, were sworn in as chieftains. (As a ruling royal family the O'Neills lasted seven centuries, longer than any other family in Europe except the Wittelsbachs of Bavaria.) In 1602 Lord Mountjoy destroyed the chair. His successors destroyed and exiled the family. A right turn into a lane just after we enter Cookstown leads to **Killymoon** castle (private, but occasionally opened to the public), a bulky, castellated Gothic building consisting of towers big and small, round, square and octagonal, designed for Colonel William Stewart in 1807 by the versatile John Nash who, like most successful practitioners of his period, moved from classical styles (Rockingham and Caledon) to Gothic (here and Lough Cutra) and back with great facility. This designer of one of the five longest lists of English houses and public buildings in the record of distinguished English architects also planned the delightful Italianate rectory of Lissan, two miles north-east of the town. Killymoon once belonged to the Prince Regent, who won it in a game of cards. It is beautifully set over the river Ballinderry, but much of the old demesne is a golf-course now. **Cookstown** itself is built along a nondescript, forty-yard wide, mile-long main street, laid out by William Stewart, ancestor of the original Killymoon Stewart, in 1724. It is an early model village on a very large scale, but the width of the road was not designed for traffic – more as an elegant promenade.

On the otherwise featureless flat shore of the big lough ten miles to the east, via Coagh, the High Cross of Ardboe, of the ninth or tenth century and decorated with carved bible scenes, stands on a mound near a later, ruined church and other remains. Life hereabouts a generation or so ago, beside 'the dead-end of the graveyard and the vast soughing of the water ... out of kilter with the century' is made vivid in Polly Devlin's *All of Us There* and her stories of childhood – a time made hard to imagine by the ubiquitous sprawl, since then, of bungalow and carport. Three miles north-west of Cookstown is Lissan House, product of innumerable changes of design down the years, home of the Staples family for 350 years and thirteen generations. The present owner, granddaughter of a well-known society artist, Ponsonby Staples, who was always 'Ponsy' to the Prince of Wales, plans to turn the house into an arts centre. The gardens were laid out in the eighteenth century by Davis Ducart. There are fine park trees as old as the house, and Lissan rectory, close by, was designed by Nash for a member of the family in 1807.

Four miles north-east of Cookstown by the A29, and the same distance north-west of Coagh, is Moneymore, a town founded in James I's reign by the London Draper's Company, and elegantly redeveloped by them about 1840. A mile south-east of it, off the Coagh road, is the delightfully simple late-seventeenth-century (probably) house, **Springhill**, now owned by the National Trust. It used to belong to the Conynghams, an Ayrshire family later to spread its interests over all Ireland. From the beech avenue at the front it looks like a doll's house with a façade of large plain windows and one central gable window in the roof. The two wings were added in the eighteenth century by the builder's great-nephew, William, who made other additions and renovated the original house. This contains a good collection of furniture, in an arrangement and on a scale that put comfort before spectacle. There are some interesting portraits, including two of William III and Queen Mary presented by the king for loyal Protestant service. The outbuildings include a barn that now houses a collection of carriages, a model traditional Irish cottage and several rooms given over to a collection of old costumes. The gardens contain a circular dovecote rather like a stunted Round Tower. Beyond are some easy walks on woodland paths.

Midway between Slieve Gallion and Lough Neagh the A31 takes us to Magherafelt, a small village where anglers like to stay, then continues past Castledawson to **Bellaghy**. To the east of this small village, and within private grounds, is the diminished ruin of Bally-scullion, Earl Bishop Hervey's greatest Irish building, conceived on a heroic scale, and left to crumble as soon as he died. There is little to see here, but two miles south, on peninsular Church Island, are remains of a fourteenth-century church, with spire and tower added, as frequently in the region, on orders of the Earl Bishop; in this case to furnish an eye-catcher for the view from his new mansion.

Rich, undulating land, with the haunting silhouette of Slieve Gallion to the west, this valley of the river Moyola is modest country: it takes a little time to make its impression, but slowly works magic. This, and the fertile soil, are presumably why Hervey chose to build here, or why, upstream, Moyola Park is home to Chichester-Clarks, descended from a Planter pioneer and including a prime minister of Northern Ireland along the way – an Ascendancy family with the means to choose. It is traditional O'Heney territory, and one of that tribe, the poet Seamus Heaney, born in 1939 at Mossbawn, his family's farm, has added a new layer of attraction: so many of the landscape's features figuring in his work – Gallion, St Patrick's Slemish, the fields that Heaney the boy worked beside his father, and that his father had worked beside his own uncle. The Bellaghy Bawn, square, and with a circular tower at its south-east corner, built for the Vintners' Company of London before 1620, before the plantation of the county of Derry, contains the Heaney archive, available for scholars, and exhibitions of local interest with a film about the area presented by the poet himself (after the simple sincerity of which most such productions are seen to rattle hollowly with cliché and overstatement).

Coming down to the north-west corner of Lough Neagh we turn left and cross the Bann, the lough's only considerable outlet, at Toome Bridge, mentioned in a famous 1798 rebel song – 'there's never a tear in the blue, blue eyes; both glad and bright are they/As Roddy McCorley goes to die on the Bridge of Toome today'. Randalstown, six miles east, stands inland from the old lakeside demesne of the O'Neills. On the southern side of the romantically decaying demesne is **Shane's Castle** on its rocky foundations, accidentally destroyed in an 1816 fire but leaving a picturesque lakeside ruin which survives. The castle took its name from Shane MacBrian O'Neill, one-time comrade of the rebel Earl of Tyrone, but later pledged and loyal to the English crown. He died in 1619. From him descend the present Barons O'Neill, though the male succession was broken when an only surviving daughter in the eighteenth century married a Chichester, a family to whom O'Neills had once been implacably hostile. The present O'Neills live in a modern (1964) classical house near the cleared site of a Victorian mansion burned in the 1920s. For the time being there is no public access to the demesne, except for certain specific events.

Antrim is six miles south-east. Like many towns in the interior of the county its wealth was based mainly on linen, but it is one of the oldest religious sites in the province, and possesses one of Ulster's two near-perfect Round Towers (the other is on Devenish Island). From the name given to this one by original English settlers comes the name of the local townland, 'the Steeple'. A walk round the town might take in the fine 1726 courthouse, the Round Tower close to the 1827 Steeple House, in which the borough council has its being, and Pogue's Entry, two joined cottages in one of which was born Alexander Irvine, author of *My Lady of the Chimney Corner*, an enchanting picture of the life of the poor in nineteenth-century Antrim. A Tudor gateway at the west end of Market Square leads into the demesne of Antrim Castle, built in the early 1600s, enlarged in 1662 by Sir John Clotworthy, created Viscount Massereene by Charles II, and since 1922 a hollow shell surrounded by its once magnificent gardens – much restored – and park, now kept up by the local authority. The curved-gable stables are an arts centre. The wars of the seventeenth century brought action here, and there was even a naval battle on the lough in 1642. The 1798 rebellion saw a nearly successful move here by 3,500 insurgents, when they assaulted the town from three angles and almost had the dragoons and yeomen worsted before lack of communication between the various parties led to panic and flight. Henry Joy McCracken led the first attack. He was one of many Presbyterians who, downtrodden as much as the Catholics by laws that gave all preference to the Church of Ireland, conceived and carried through the rising, often in liaison with Catholic allies in the south. McCracken was later caught and hanged in Belfast.

From Antrim the M2 motorway or A6 to Belfast takes us after five miles past **Castle Upton**, seat of the Upton family, Viscounts Templetown since 1776. The house, which incorporates a refectory dating from the twelfth century, was built in 1611. In 1793 Robert Adam came to do one of his few Irish works, refurnishing the house inside and out and adding extensions. Little of this was appreciated in the nineteenth century when Victorian fireplaces replaced Adam ones. Early last century the place fell into decay, was sold to a farmer who replaced the crenellated top floor with a plain one, used the rubble to fill the lake and filled Adam's courtyard with styes for 1,000 pigs. New owners saved what could be saved and carried out extensive rebuilding on the eighteenth-century pattern. Adam's beautiful Upton Mausoleum adjoining the demesne is in the hands of the National Trust, and is the only building on the estate regularly open to the public. The house's gardens sometimes are. The return to Belfast from here is about eleven miles

19

Down

THE SOUTH SIDE of Belfast Lough is a long stretch of resorts, with most of the amenities resorts should have. But before getting on to the coast road (A2) we can take an eastward trip along the A20 to visit **Stormont**, a bright, white, Neo-classical building that looks as if it has been unrolled from the long straight avenue leading to it from the massive piers of the gateway. For nearly a century Stormont has lurched in and out of Northern Ireland's history, spasmodic home of the province's parliament. It was built between 1928 and 1932 to the imperially grandiose designs of Sir Arnold Thorneley, and a statue of modern Unionism's uncompromising godfather Sir Edward Carson stands above the many visitors who come to walk the sweeping parklands, freely open, that stretch around the buildings.

Holywood, five miles north-east of the capital, preserves, apart from Ireland's only maypole, in the main street, some remains of a sixteenth-century Franciscan friary. It was also the home of General Stonewall Jackson's ancestors, who emigrated in 1748. **Cultra**, to the north-east again, is the site of the magnificent **Ulster Folk and Transport Museum**, comprising outdoor and indoor exhibitions of past ways of life: buildings, machinery, furniture, horse-drawn and mechanical transport, aeroplanes, shipping, a Titanic exhibition, a miniature railway and much more. The spacious grounds comprise a convincing layout of historical buildings, brought brick by brick or stone by stone from all over the province: cottages, houses, whole terraces, churches, mills, schools, towers, farmhouses, shops, banks, re-erected among the abundant greenery, lakes, woods and looping lanes of the demense of Cultra Manor, a bulky mansion of 1904.

On the right of the main road four miles on is **Clandeboye**, seat of the former Marquesses of Dufferin and Ava, who trace their descent to an unscrupulous Scottish settler of the time of James I. The eighteenth-century house was enlarged in 1820 by Sir Richard Morrison; but the

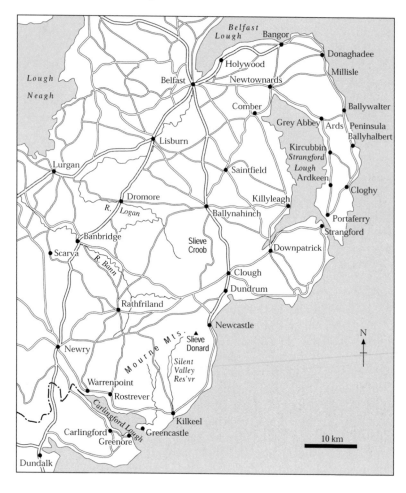

first Marquess (1826–1902), who was to be successively Governor-General of Canada and Viceroy of India (Ava is the name of the ancient capital of Burma) altered the interior and the grounds in the 1850s, until his money ran out. He was thus prevented from executing plans for a grandiose conversion to turn the surrounding fields into magnificent parkland with fine trees, lake, follies to Gothic towers, battlements and pinnacles, but was able to build, in 1861, the so-called Helen's Tower, in memory of his mother, on whom he doted. She, an early widow, was one of the three beautiful granddaughters of Sheridan, and only eighteen years older than her devoted son. 'My mother and I shared our youth', he was to say. Their story is told in *Helen's Tower* by Harold Nicolson, who was a kinsman. There is one room on each of three floors and a roof-bastion on top. The middle room is hung with golden tablets on which poems written to order by Tennyson, Browning and others are engraved. From the top there are superb views of the loughs, sea and Scotland beyond. North of the main road is the Marquess's baronial railway station of 1865, with a private waiting-room for the family. The estate's income has been raised by the creation on it of golf courses and other leisure amenities. To the north is Crawfordsburn, a pretty resort with a sandy beach and kempt glen which was part of the old Crawford demesne. C.S. Lewis, Oxford don, author of *The Screwtape Letters*, the Narnia novels and much else, brought up in East Belfast and educated at Campbell College nearby, brought to the Old Inn here his American bride Joy Davidman for their honeymoon. Their short marriage, and the brief reprieve it brought her from the grip of cancer, form the subject of the film *Shadowlands*.

The next town, **Bangor**, is a popular seaside resort on the site of one of the most famous early Irish monasteries – 'the nursery of the saints', St Bernard called it – founded in 559 by St Comgall, a saint said to have been graced with miraculous saliva. His spit could shatter a rock, and more than once a gobbet turned to gold. His greatest pupil here was St Columbanus, who like others left to preach on the Continent. His oak-like obstinacy earned him much praise and many memories, and he left behind him at least three monastic foundations in France and one, Bobbio, which still exists, near Milan. St Gall, his companion, also Bangor-trained, was too weak to cross the Alps with him and remained on the north side to found the Swiss monastery of St Gall. Nothing remains of Comgall's or the medieval house which was left to decay at the Dissolution. A bell and altar cross are displayed in the museum, housed, like the town hall, in the Tudor-revival Bangor Castle, designed by William Burn in 1847. A couple of miles east, Groomsport has the usual sandy beaches and also a harbour where Marshal Schomberg landed in 1789 with ten thousand of King William's soldiers, before the battle of the Boyne. Beyond Bangor, long stretches of attractive coastline as far as Bally-macormack Point and Orlock Point are owned by the National Trust, as is Lighthouse Island, three miles offshore, with its bird observatory, which can be visited by arrangement. One ageing layer of paint on the lighthouse in question was applied by the writer Brendan Behan, still unknown, earning his living after World War Two.

Rounding the headland we come after four miles to **Donaghadee**, another resort town with an attractive harbour from and to which the Scottish packet-boat crossed from Portpatrick in the eighteenth and nineteenth centuries. Scotland is visible from here in good weather, and it was from Scotland that John Keats arrived with his friend Charles Brown in 1818, intending to visit the Giant's Causeway, which he had been advised was forty-eight miles of walking. But, as he wrote, living in Ireland was 'thrice the expense of Scotland ... Moreover we found those 48 miles to be Irish ones which reach to 70 English. So having walked to Belfast on one day and back to Dona-ghadee the next we left Ireland with a fair breeze.' To the south from here stretches the **Ards Peninsula**, enfolding Strangford Lough down to Portaferry and the lough's narrow outlet to the sea.

We can start by crossing the peninsula to **Newtownards**, standing a little inland from the lake's head, and dating from the thirteenth century when a Dominican priory, some ruins of which remain, was founded here. All other traces of the old town whose existence is implied by the name seem to have vanished. The priory, parts of which were refurbished early in the seventeenth century, incorporates the family vault of the Stewarts, marquesses of Londonderry. There is a pleasant town hall, originally market-house, of 1765, with cupola and pedimented entrance. A mile north-east of the town are the few remains of **Moville Abbey**, which in the sixth century flowering of Irish monasticism, and like Bangor a few miles away, towered above most others in scholarship. Finnian, its founder, had studied in Scotland, acquired biblical manuscripts in Rome and here ruled his monks with an iron hand. At his first foundation seven monks died of hunger and cold. But Moville attracted novices from all over Ireland and often abroad, and many of its alumni were effective missionaries to countries where barbarians had suppressed the Christian practices.

Three miles west of Newtownards is the **Scrabo Tower** (pronounced 'scrabbo'), seen for miles around, set within a country park the underlying sandstone of which has been used for buildings in Dublin, New York and elsewhere. The tower commemorates the third Marquess of Londonderry and his care of his tenants during the great famine. His son had it put up. We now take the A20 down the eastern shore of the lough and come after six miles to **Mount Stewart**, home of Vane-Tempest-Stewarts whose titles include

Marquess of Londonderry. The land was bought in 1744 by the grandfather of Lord Castlereagh (courtesy title of the heir to the marquessate), who was born here in 1769, and became in 1797 Pitt's Chief Secretary for Ireland and a reviled architect of union with Britain. As a brilliant, commanding foreign secretary after Napoleon's final defeat, he with Metternich drew anew the political map of Europe. Then, a year after succeeding his father to the marquessate in 1821, he cut his own jugular vein, possibly after being framed as a homosexual by intending blackmailers. His half-brother and successor was married to the heiress to county Durham estates rich in coal, and the house here was much enlarged, though the façade of George Dance's 1803 to 1806 designs remains in place. There was money now for the palatial Londonderry House in Park Lane and more mansions in the English countryside. Mount Stewart's many treasures include the twenty-two chairs used by the delegates to the Congress of Vienna in 1815.

Because of the sheltered position and high humidity, the gardens almost match Kerry in the profusion of fuchsia, tree-sized heathers, eucalyptus, mimosa palms, bottle-brushes and other lovers of warmth and damp. There are several different kinds of garden. The wall of the Italian is lined with conspicuous, whimsical stone figures. On the same side of the road a short way south is the Temple of the Winds, a lovely octagonal garden house overlooking the lough (in which Castlereagh when a boy was nearly drowned) which was designed by James 'Athenian' Stuart and built in 1780.

In a pleasant garden beside the village of **Grey Abbey**, two miles south, are the remains of the abbey itself – an aisleless church, with interesting medieval and seventeenth-century Montgomery monuments, and a refectory building, in Early English style. It was founded in 1193 by Affreca, daughter of the King of Man, under her husband John de Courcy's patronage. Dissolved in 1537, it was burned by the O'Neills later in the century, to prevent its becoming a shelter to English settlers. It was re-roofed in the seventeenth century and used as a parish church till 1778. One of the effigies is thought to represent the foundress, it being unlikely any other woman would be buried here at that date. From the abbey grounds the house called Grey Abbey can be glimpsed, a good eighteenth-century Georgian house with ogee windows on the ground floor of the garden front. It is still occupied by the Montgomery family.

After Grey Abbey we can take the inland B5 and cross to the east side of the peninsula, reaching the coast at Ballywalter. Ballywalter

Park, an Italianate house designed with dash, sometimes compared to a London clubhouse, the work of Charles Lanyon in the 1840s, stands among good gardens which are occasionally opened on application. Further along the A2 coast road is the important fishing village of Portavogie, with a modern harbour and good fish for sale in the village, which is known also for being entirely Protestant and letting this be known at times by painting its kerbstones red, white and blue. Three miles on, at Cloghy, we can turn off left to see Kearney, a neat National Trust village which once made a good living from sea-fishing. From here we can cross back to Portaferry, and Strangford Lough's Narrows – the neck through which sea water daily passes.

Portaferry is a neat little town with a sixteenth-century tower house in ruins, close to the ferry terminal that gives the place its name. It was meant at first to guard this side of the Narrows, as the tower house at Strangford did on the other side. There is a handsome, classical Presbyterian church. If animals have to be put in unnatural captivity to amuse humans, the Exploris Centre is well designed, informative and often exciting, with tanks of various sharks, rays and more mundane species, and touch-tanks where, supervised, you can handle sea-urchins, hermit crabs, starfish, thornback ray and others, some of which seem no less curious about you than you about them. There is also a colony of seals being treated and convalescing after injury in the lough.

Strangford Lough would be an inland lake were it not for the twice-daily tide of four hundred million tons of sea water flowing back and forth through the Narrows, the five-mile long, barely five-hundred-yard-wide channel on which Portaferry is situated. The relative narrowness of this neck considerably slows the water, with the result that half the time the lough's water level is lower than the sea, exposing two fifths of the mud-flats that make up the lough's floor, and half the time higher. Either way the pressure on the tide to draw level is immense. The water rushes through at high speeds, slowing gradually as it proceeds down the lough's fifteen or so miles. This often reversing flow, and the hundred and twenty drumlin islands, along with rocks, creeks and bays, and neighbouring saltmarshes and freshwater lakes all make for an interesting ecology, with frequent changes of prevalent plant and animal species. There are rare species of seaweed, mollusc, crustacean and vertebrate fish. Most of the world's pale-bellied brent geese – about twelve thousand of them – stop over on their migrations. Four species of tern, perhaps the world's most graceful birds, albeit with their fishwife voices, breed here. Forty-five thousand waders spike the uncovered mud to capture burrowing shellfish and worms, though all of these are put at risk by mechanical harvesting. Bird hides, books, guides and explanations and all imaginable facilities are available at the Quoile Pondage in the lough's south-west corner and at Castle Espie in the north-west, both managed by the Department of the Environment.

We take the ferry over the water to the little town of Strangford, on what is known as the Lecale Peninsula, with its trim triangle, cafés and curios, and move on a mile and a half west to **Castleward House**, one of the best-preserved Georgian houses in Ulster, in the keeping of the National Trust. Built between 1760 and 1780, it is the result of a compromise between Bernard Ward, Lord Bangor, an admirer of the Palladian style of architecture, and his wife Anne, daughter of the first Lord Darnley, whose taste was for Strawberry Hill Gothic. The house combines both styles, the south-west front following Lord Bangor's preference – classical, with a pillared, pedimented portico – and the north east his wife's – Gothic, with seven bays of ogee windows under a row of battlements. Both are exceptional of their kinds, and the interior, which contains some fine and curious plaster-work, also reflects the two styles, though the central staircase tips the balance with classical. In the grounds, which stretch down to the shore of Strangford Lough, are an early canal, a Palladian garden temple and near the water a neat little Plantation tower-house of about 1610, and a mill which uses the incoming tide for power. In spite of their architectural compromise, the Bangors could not get on, and parted. Audley's Tower, another Plantation castle at the end of a two-mile cul-de-sac north of Castleward, set at the lake's edge in finely wood-rimmed pasture, looks across the Narrows to Portaferry.

Returning to Strangford, we continue on the A2 along the Lecale coast, opposite the southern tip of the Ards, past the long spread of Cloghy Rocks national nature reserve, where a colony of common seal breeds, past Kilclief Plantation tower-house, and turn left to see Killard Point, another national nature reserve famous for rare wild plants and the assertion that, some time about 432 AD, St Patrick preached a sermon to the fishes here. **Ardglass**, five miles ahead, was Ulster's busiest seaport in the Middle Ages and was taken over early in the fifteenth century by English traders who ringed it with forts and other battlemented defences. Jordan's Castle survives, as does a terraced row of these buildings, converted in the eighteenth century into a house and occupied by Emily, Duchess of Leinster, and her second husband and children's tutor, William Ogilvie. After her death, he helped to develop the town into a seaside resort. The couple's curiously contrived house is now the golf club. The fishing harbour remains a busy one, while Killough's, two miles on, can seem pleasantly forgotten, more or less a product of the eighteenth century. There are good walks along the coast beyond.

The inland road, B176, takes us eight miles across the peninsula to **Downpatrick**, a town rich in ancient associations, amid countryside full of prehistoric remains. In 1177, in what amounted to a Norman Conquest of his own, the freebooter John de Courcy, without licence from the king, took the then kingdom of Down in a rapid, skilful campaign. His first target was Downpatrick, which he surprised, took, and made the site of his principal castle. A few years later he decided to excavate three famous tombs, those of St Patrick, St Brigid and St Columba. They were found, according to Giraldus Cambrensis, 'through divine revelation', but there is room for doubt. St Patrick's tomb has also been claimed by Glastonbury, St Brigid's by Kildare, and St Columba's by Iona, and other parts of Ireland. Holy bones were a good bait for pilgrims, who brought money to spend on and around the shrines; and claims were sometimes made lightly. Nevertheless the town is forever linked with the name of St Patrick, who may well have founded a church and diocese here. An early monastery certainly existed, and de Courcy's action enabled him to invoke the church's blessing on his transfer of the see of the diocese from Bangor. He also built an abbey for Benedictines. This and most of the subsequent buildings were destroyed by an earthquake in 1245, again by Edward Bruce in 1316, and once more by the English in 1538. They lay in ruins for centuries, but with the town's considerable expansion in the eighteenth century the need for a restoration became urgent. Between 1790 and 1826 most of the old ruins were swept away irrevocably, the Round Tower being used to provide masonry for the new church tower. Part of the body of the Benedictine church survives in Charles Lilly's restoration of the cathedral, with a few fragments set into the wall. But the stone outside, inscribed with the letters PATRIC to mark his alleged grave, was made to order in 1900. The town, pleasantly set in hilly surrounds (with the dun or fortified hill sixty feet high to the north – hence the names of town and county) has good Georgian houses and Southwell, or Bluecoat, School, an almshouse and school of 1733, possibly designed by Edward Lovett Pearce. All these are in English Street, as is the old county gaol, now turned into a museum and visitor centre. The cathedral stands at the end of English Street, its sharp corner pinnacles piercing the sky. There are other good Georgian houses in Saul Street.

Saul, where St Patrick arrived on his mission to Ireland (though the same is said of Carlingford) twenty years after escaping from slavery in it, is two miles north-east. It preserves a few remains of a twelfth-century abbey, supposedly on the site of his first foundation, given to him by his first Irish convert. It was here that he died. A small, rather dubious replica of an early Irish church was built here in 1932, to mark the fifteen-hundredth anniversary of his arrival. Across the valley to the south are the holy and curative wells of Struel, with ruins of a chapel and various medieval buildings covering a drinking well, an eye well and tanks for the total immersion of men and women. To the hilltop statue of him dating from the same period, pilgrims still come on the night of 23 June. The wells owe their powers, naturally, to St Patrick.

South-west of Downpatrick, the A25 takes us seven miles to Clough, with motte and bailey and remains of a square castle dating from the twelfth century. A mile north, along the A24, is Seaforde, where an impressive pedimented Grecian arch leads to the large demesne of rather forbidding, three-storey, 1820-ish Seaforde House, home of the Forde family and a long line, mainly of soldiers, who have inhabited the place since Charles I's time. The interior is praised for its Greek-revival magnificence, above all in the library, which retains its original decorations. At present, however, the public is not permitted the slightest glimpse of the house, inside or out, though it is invited to negotiate a long bumpy drive for the dubious pleasures offered by a garden centre, a maze and a collection of captive butterflies.

Dundrum, three miles south of Clough, possesses the greatest of county Down's castles. Well placed by road and navigable water, and overlooking Dundrum Inner Bay, it was built about 1230 by John de Courcy on the site of an older fortification, and was intended by him to play the same part in Down as Carrickfergus in Antrim. It had a not unusual turbulent history, changing hands and burning many times. 'I assure your lordship,' Lord Deputy Grey wrote in 1553 to the Lord Privy Seal, 'as yt standeth, ys one of the strongyst holtes that ever I sawe in Irelande, and moost commodios for defence in the hole countre, both by see and lande.' In view of which, Cromwellians dismantled it in 1652. It had probably, before that, served as quarry for the construction of an Elizabethan mansion nearer the shore. Now it stands as a majestic ruin, surrounded by its moat cut in the rock.

We can cut along the coast to Newcastle from here, or return to the A25 first, to ascend to the striking, high and airy country about Castlewellan, a town with spacious layout, wonderful views and, close by, the fine forest park, from the early seventeenth century to after the Second World War, part of the demesne of the Annesley family's exuberant baronial-style castle – now a conference centre. Here is one of the country's finest tree collections, begun in 1874 and now the national arboretum, spread over 111 acres, set amid stately parkland, wooded slopes, lakes and mountain ponds. The family's career in Ireland began with aplomb. Sir Francis Annesley became secretary of state under James I and managed to avert a sentence of death put on him out of spite by Lord Deputy Strafford. His son Arthur, first earl of Anglesey, was commisioner for Ireland, known for integrity, and the first nobleman in Ireland to collect a good library – an activity till then considered the preserve of churchmen. But this Arthur's son squandered his fortune. A grandson of the first earl, another Arthur, skipped from wife to mistress so rapidly that his son James's legitimacy could not be established. Arthur's brother Richard (1694–1761) packed the boy, his nephew, off as a slave to America and later tried to have him hanged for murder. Richard's own marital life was volatile too, and doubts now rose over the legitimacy of his own claimed son, another Arthur (1744–1816). Eventually the Irish House of Lords found the son legitimate and confirmed his Irish titles (some of which continue to this day). The English House of Lords created an interesting tangle by declaring him a bastard and revoking his right to the Anglesey earldom. Meanwhile, back in 1720, confiscation of a tenant's land had led to the Sherlock v Annesley case, the consequence of which was a severe limitation of the Irish parliament's jurisdiction. Having thus twice strained the kingdom's legal systems, the family subsided in the nineteenth century into patrician respectability. They sold the Castlewellan estate to the Department of Agriculture in 1967.

Newcastle, five miles away by the sea, and with fine beaches and the bird-rich Murlough nature reserve (Ireland's first) stretching along its sand-duney peninsula to the north, is the gateway to the Mourne Mountains, which well deserve the reputation they have all over the world. The coast road, the northern road that borders them, and the steep curving road that slices them in two between Newcastle and Kilkeel, are all equally good ways to see them, but the best views are obtained by walking. From Newcastle the ascent of Slieve Donard on foot up the Glen River takes an able-bodied climber two hours or less.

From this the broadest views can be had. The northern fringe of Slieve Bearnagh is contained in the **Tollymore Forest Park**, a forestry area which, as elsewhere in Northern Ireland, provides various amenities for tourists as well as getting on with the business of growing and cutting wood. From a fine old arboretum, centre of the former demesne of the Earls of Roden, marked paths go in various directions, past streams and waterfalls and through woods and nicely sited, mostly Gothic, towers, hermitage, mock-church, arches and bridges. There are also camping and caravan sites, discreetly placed so as not to spoil the natural scene. The house of the Jocelyn family, earls of Roden, who owned nine thousand acres in county Down, four thousand in Louth and many more in Hertfordshire and Essex, had grown to enormous size over the centuries, but was demolished in 1952.

We carry on westward and after three miles turn left to cross the mountains, by the pass between Pigeon Rock Mountain and Slieve Muck, close to which is the source of the River Bann. The highest of the range, Slieve Donard, 2,796 feet, overlooking the sea, is five miles to the left. On the far side the road leads down to **Kilkeel**, a pleasant seaside resort with a good beach and pretty fishing-fleet harbour. An alternative on the descent is to turn left, pass close to the Silent Valley reservoir which supplies Belfast's water, and follow down the reservoir's outflow, the River Kilkeel. Seven miles south-west of Kilkeel is Greencastle, with an impressively sited ruin of a fourteenth-century English fortress. The road west from Kilkeel goes close to the steep south-western slopes of the mountains on the edge of Carlingford Lough. After five miles it crosses Causeway Water, on whose right bank, 500 yards from the road, is the Kilfeaghan Dolmen, its 35-ton capstone supported by two stones. **Rostrevor**, with its statue of General Robert Ross who died of wounds after commanding the British capture of Washington and burning of the White House in 1812, and Warrenpoint two miles farther, are very attractive resorts; Warrenpoint the more so, being bigger and more colourful, with a broad and busy square and Edwardian houses originally built for middle-class holidaying families. Half a mile on, with Narrow Waters Castle on the sea side and the Neo-Tudor extravaganza of Narrow Waters House on the landward side, there is little to suggest the death by IRA bomb of sixteen British soldiers in 1979. We continue along the A2, beside the creek of the Newry River which is succeeded by two miles of the Newry canal, the first inland canal completed in these islands – in 1742; it was extended to take ships to and from Lough Neagh in 1761.

Newry, almost on the border between the Republic and the Six Counties, and placed strategically and very vulnerably within the pass known as the Gap of the North, came into Hugh de Lacy's territories in the early thirteenth century. It was an ancient foundation and had at the time a large Cistercian abbey. But it was subject to a full list of medieval setbacks, being destroyed by Edward Bruce in 1315 and again by Shane O'Neill in 1566. It changed hands twice in the Eleven Years War and was burned down by the Jacobites, retreating after the arrival near Donaghadee of William's General Schomberg. When Swift saw it a few years later, the steeple of St Patrick's church (the first Church of Ireland church built as such in Ireland), was all that was left, and it was of Newry he wrote the lines, 'High church, low steeple,/Dirty town, proud people'. Later buildings have not much enhanced the town and St Colman's Cathedral, despite the stained glass and mosaics inside, is an uninspired pseudo-Gothic work. John Mitchell (1815–75), a recruit to the Young Irelanders, whose advocacy of force to effect complete separation revived a tradition forgotten since Emmet's day, is buried in the Unitarian churchyard, off High Street to the east of the town's centre. Two and a half miles west-north-west of the town is **Derrymore**, a charming thatched mansion preserved by the National Trust. A one-storey house formed around a courtyard, it is of a type often constructed by minor eighteenth-century gentry, but of which no others survive. It was built by Isaac Corry, Chancellor of the Irish Exchequer, in the 1770s. Here the Earl of Charlemont, Henry Grattan, Lord Castlereagh and others are supposed to have gathered to sign the Act of Union, though this is little more than an arguable tradition.

Newry is surrounded by delightful hilly countryside, the Mourne Mountains to the east and Slieve Gullion to the west, all of them worth a good deal of time and scrutiny. But to complete the round tour from Belfast we keep to the valley of the canal which connects Carlingford Lough with Lough Neagh. At Scarva we turn right and cross the river. Scarva House is the scene of an annual charade on 13 July, when a mock battle is staged to commemorate the Boyne. It was here that King William's forces rallied on their way to the battle in 1689. Also in the demesne is the best-surviving stretch of the Dane's Cast, a prehistoric dyke that marked off the ancient Ulster kingdom, more or less confined to Down. Eleven miles north-east is the cathedral town of **Dromore**, seat of a small Church of Ireland bishopric, and heart of the Magennis country, an old Irish clan of which the famous Guinness family may be a branch. Jeremy Taylor was administrator of the diocese (besides being bishop of Down and Connor) here from 1661 to his death in 1667. He built the core of the present cathedral, for the old one had been in ruins since the town was burned in the 1641 rising. Thomas Percy, editor of the *Reliques of Ancient English Poetry*, whose ballads were a seminal influence on Scott and the whole romantic movement, became bishop in 1781 and in 1808 carried out a major restoration of the cathedral. Both Percy and Taylor are buried here. Three miles west of Dromore, on the left of the B2 and in rich farmland, is the long demesne wall, the trees, fields and at present padlocked gates of Gill Hall, one among many big estates hereabouts. Gill Hall, however, is gone. Abandoned in 1909 because its several ghosts would pester family and guests, it was left to decay until the Irish Georgian Society patched it up, hoping a beneficent buyer would come along. None did, and not long afterwards, in the 1970s, it burned down.

East from Dromore, the straight B2 goes direct to Ballynahinch, a neat town with wide streets laid out by the Rawdon family in 1640, passing on the right the attractive range of Slieve Croob, whose sides contain many prehistoric remains. From Ballynahinch the A21 goes north-north-east to Saintfield, a mile before which is **Rowallane House**, a National Trust property with one of the finest gardens in the country. A hundred years ago it was rocky scrubland. Then Hugh Armytage Moore, brother-in-law of the song-writer Percy French, created between 1903 and 1955 a series of self-contained gardens spread over a fifty-acre estate. There are exotic Chilean and Chinese shrubs, and a large and varied collection of rhododendrons, magnolias, cherries and wall plants, as well as expanses of lawn and woodland.

A dozen or so miles to the east, back on the shore of Strangford Lough, is **Killyleagh** where, as at Clandeboye, a house was built by Sir James Hamilton in the early seventeenth century. It was, he wrote, 'ane vera strong castle; the lyk is not in the northe'. His grandson, something of an imbecile, married the first Earl of Drogheda's daughter, a lady who, determined to annexe the property for her own family, poisoned her husband and destroyed his will. After a long lawsuit the estate was divided between two branches of Hamiltons, and remained so until the Marquess of Dufferin, inheriting both Clandeboye and half Killyleagh in 1841, gave the latter to the owner of the other half in return for an annual tribute – he was a great lover of Walter Scott – of gold spurs and roses. The solid castle, with pointed pinnacle-roofs on each tower, still bulks impressively over the village and lough beyond. It was thoroughly restored and enlarged around 1850 by Sir Charles Lanyon. Sir Hans Sloane (1660–1753), who after a lifetime of collecting gave his collection of 50,000 volumes, 3,560 manuscripts and scientific items to be the nucleus of the British Museum, was a native of the village. The return to Belfast can be fast and direct on the A7 from Crossgar, or a lakeside dawdle taking in the very organised Wildfowl and Wetlands Trust reserve at Castle Espie.

20

Carlingford Peninsula, Dundalk, County Monaghan

THE STRATEGIC ROUTE between the richest part of Ulster and the rest of Ireland has always been through Newry. But a line of mountains lies south and west of the town and in the past only a few valleys, or the long, easily guarded way round the Carlingford peninsula, allowed reasonable access. When Hugh O'Neill, Earl of Tyrone, came out in full rebellion against the English at the end of the sixteenth century, he was wise enough to block the Moyry Pass, where the railway and main Dublin to Belfast road now go, so holding up his enemies for five years. Three hundred years before, Edward Bruce, recently crowned in Dundalk, and a serious threat to Norman Ireland, was killed by Sir John Bermingham just to the south of the pass. A thousand years before that, the long struggles between Ulster and Connacht reached their climax in the legendary cattle-raid of Cooley (or Cuailgne), in the epic account of which (Thomas Kinsella's translation from the Gaelic is perhaps the finest) old Irish literature also climbed to a peak. The Ulster hero of the campaign was Cuchulain. Cooley was the Carlingford Peninsula. Throughout it, names and relics recall that seminal struggle.

We drive south from Newry along the west side, first of the Newry Canal, then of Carlingford Lough, and cross the Six Counties border after seven miles. The water is said to be a good medium for the smuggling that goes on, a practice thriving on variant fluctuations of price and tax either side of the border. **Carlingford** itself is a much diminished town, overtaken long ago by Newry, but it keeps several remains, and a character created by streets of old houses and walls. It claims, as does Saul in county Down, the arrival of St Patrick in 432. Its main feature is massive King John's Castle, built in the shape of a D by John de Courcy about 1210, recently refurbished and impressively overhanging the sheer rock drop of the harbour wall. There are superb views from here of the Mourne Mountains over the water. Because of the town's position, the burghers who later built their houses here made them tough to resist attack, and several have survived. Taaffe's Castle is one, best seen from the shore. Beyond is the old Tholsel, once a town gate. The Mint, of the fifteenth century, has interesting interlacing patterns round the windows. The parish church has a medieval tower, once part of the walls; while the ruinous Dominican abbey, built in 1305, preserves a scant tower and turrets.

Above the town rises the steep slope of Slieve Foye, almost two thousand feet high, with superb views from its summit; it is better seen from Greenore, two miles south-east, a resort with a golf-links, shingle beach and busy harbour. Three miles south, off one of a complex of lanes in the extremity of the peninsula, is the old Bagenal stronghold of Ballug, but only the walls remain from the fifteenth century, when that minor colonist family encroached on the ancestral lands of the O'Neills, later to be horrified and implacable when Hugh O'Neill won and married a Bagenal daughter, and took her to what they considered the barbarities of his fortress at Dungannon. To judge, however, from modern genealogies, the Bagenals learned to take pride in the connection, even though it did not last.

The mountain shows up well from the main road on the west which takes us back to wealthier land. We pass the huge Proleek dolmen, with its forty-six-ton capstone, behind the Ballymascanlan House hotel, a Tudor-revival pile fouled by modern accretions, and a little later the Armagh Diocesan Pastoral Centre in a house modelled on Washington's White House. A few miles later we reach **Dundalk**, a big, solid, prosperous town with a good scatter of handsome buildings, built on flat marshy ground at the head of Dundalk Bay, which provides it with a harbour. Its history is a long catalogue of attacks and sieges, mounted in every century to get command of its dominating position on the road to Ulster. The Protestant church of St Nicholas has a fourteenth-century tower and some windows of a century later, but the Georgian character of Francis Johnston's renovations dominate. There is a memorial to Robert Burns's eldest sister, Agnes Galt, whose husband was steward to the Fortescues of Stephenstown, a few miles south. She is buried in the graveyard. The town possesses two interesting examples of architectural pastiche. The Catholic church of St Patrick owes its inspiration, loosely but recognisably, to the design of King's College chapel, Cambridge, though nobody would fancy himself in the university at sight of it. (After emancipation in 1829, Europe was combed for models for the vast programme of Catholic church building now permitted.) There is

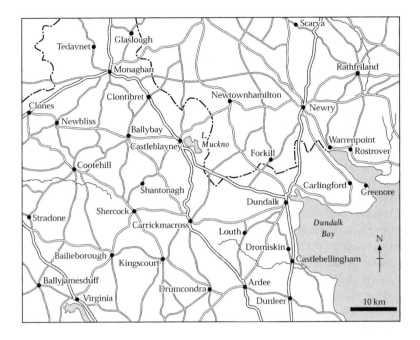

also the dignified, austere courthouse built in granite in 1818, whose portico is modelled on an end of the Theseum temple at Athens, best preserved of all ancient Greek buildings. There are also some remains of a medieval Augustinian friary.

To the north lies the southern bulge of county Armagh and those hills which made Dundalk in medieval times the extreme limit of the Pale. Over the border is the battle site mentioned above – the **Moyry**, where in 1601 the soon to be victorious Mountjoy erected a still extant castle to guard the pass. Three miles west is Forkill, outside which the house of one John Morgan illustrated till recently a familiar border anomaly. The boundary line cut through the middle of it, and he got Republic mail through the back door, Six Counties mail through the front. Officially he was in neither country. There have been many like him. A house at Ballyconnell got electricity from the Republic and water from the north. More seriously, many people have been cut off by the border from their natural markets and have to travel miles to another.

Between Forkill and Dundalk, a mile south of the border, is the village of **Faughart**. St Brigid, most revered of the saints of Ireland, the 'Mary of the Gael', was supposedly born here in 450, and Catholic hagiolatry rises to the heights in marking the link by means of the modern shrine, the smart auditorium, the glass-sheltered dais, electronic aids and facilities, grotto, statuary and unrestrained use of gold and other colours to welcome pilgrims at the beginning of February, on the saint's day, and at other times. Within the graveyard on the hill of Faughart above is the marked grave of Edward Bruce, brother of Robert and an almost equal menace to the Plantagenets. Edward's attempt to raise the Irish in support of the Scots reached its climax in his crowning at Dundalk, then collapsed in 1318 with his defeat and death here. It was a heroic failure, and Edward deserves better than to be eclipsed by his brother's reputation. This lichened slab hardly does him justice. Much of north Leinster lies visible below, like a chart of his campaigns.

A mile west of Dundalk, south of the N53 which we now follow into the county of Monaghan, is Castletown, in which **Dun Dealgan** – Delga's Fort – from which name Dundalk derives, is supposedly the birthplace of Cuchulain. Somewhere hereabouts this mythical hero died in battle, as always defending Ulster and its king, Conchobar, and the Red Branch Knights from invasion by the malevolent queen of Connacht, Maeve. Wounded, he bound himself to a pillar-stone in order to die standing. His horse, the Grey of Macha, in a final fury killed fifty men who came to finish him off. But the hero's face turned pale as 'a one-night's snow' and he died, and the importance of Ulster with him; for the time being, it has to be said. The extant motte and bailey go back to the Norman Bertram de Verdon, while the castle whose remains stand on the motte was built in the eighteenth century by Patrick Byrne, a pirate captain. In the school grounds to the north-east are the ruins of fifteenth-century Bellew's Castle, with its elegant parapets. Kilcurry Catholic church, two miles north, has two windows by Sarah Purser and guards a piece of skull bone, a relic of St Brigid.

Three miles west is Roche Castle, a very imposing, almost triangular ruin from the thirteenth century. The then owner, Rohesia de Verdon, promised herself in marriage to the builder on condition that his work pleased her. It failed to, and she had him tossed to his death out of a window, still indicated. Two miles to the south, the N53 takes us west for a hurried inland tour. Without ceremony it crosses into and out of the North, and south county Armagh where Crossmaglen,

Newtownhamilton and other places recall the gruesome Republican warfare of the 1980s and 1990s, and into county Monaghan. The name Monaghan means 'little shrubbery' or 'little thicket', which, though originally applied to the town alone, is apt for a generally unexciting, quietly agreeable county character. Patrick Kavanagh, who knew the county well, wrote of the farmers of Monaghan 'with their watery little hills that would physic a snipe'. The north, edged by the desolate boglands of Slieve Beagh, is hardly worth a visit, and we keep to the centre and south, which has some pretty lakes and undulations. Castleblayney, sixteen miles from Dundalk, is named after a settler of James I's time. His castle was succeeded by a Georgian mansion, extended and heightened in the nineteenth century. Now a restaurant with bars, Hope Castle is superbly sited on an eminence overlooking Lough Muckno. The lake, the county's longest and prettiest, offers good fishing for brown trout, pike, perch and rudd.

Monaghan itself is twelve miles on by the N2. Halfway there we pass through the little village of Clontibret, where in 1595, early in his rebellion, Hugh O'Neill ambushed an English force under his reluctant brother-in-law, Sir Henry Bagenal, and roundly defeated them. Monaghan is a busy and attractive, rather Scottish (they say the Scottish accent is still detectable under the brogue here) county town built round a central diamond. James I incorporated the town in 1614 but it has few historic relics. The market-house of 1792 is an elegant building and the Catholic cathedral of St MacCartan is a good Gothic-revival building of the last half of the nineteenth century, by Pugin's devoted disciple, J.J. McCarthy. Much of the town's building, including the market-house, is due to the patronage of the Westenra family, Barons Rossmore since the eighteenth century, who originally settled in Ireland from the Netherlands in the time of Charles II. Their demesne, Rossmore, was a mile or so south of the town, but the house, lately an imposing Gothic ruin, has been flattened. It is surrounded by an estate now given over to forestry.

West of Monaghan, the N54 gives us a pretty drive to Newbliss, where we can turn right for Clones. Annaghmakerrig House, two miles south of Newbliss, was the home, till his death in 1971, of Sir Tyrone Guthrie, the theatrical director. Descended, like the film-star Tyrone Power, from a famous Waterford actor of the eighteenth century, he put most of his money and enthusiasm in his last years into a jam factory established by him in the village. It went out of business a month before his death. The house with four hundred acres is now, as Guthrie intended, a residential centre for artists, writers and musicians.

Clones is a busy little agricultural centre on a steep slope rising to the Protestant church of 1822, puncturing the sky with the points of steeple and pinnacles. Its history goes back at least to sixth-century St Tigernach, first bishop and founder of a monastery here, who died of the plague in 549. The place grew in importance and an Augustinian abbey was built in the twelfth century. A topless Round Tower and some church ruins containing a church-shaped tomb survive from this. In the Diamond is a weathered High Cross, probably comprising bits of two tenth-century crosses.

Before crossing the state and county boundary into Fermanagh, we can drive four miles south to visit the handsome, heavy pile of Hilton Park, whose fine gardens, with mellowed terraces, wooded slopes and lake – but not the house, which offers a rather grand bed-and-breakfast – are open daily. The eighteenth-century building was financed by a mortgage to the Madden family from Trinity College, Dublin. Present in these parts since the early 1600s, the family still lives here.

Returning to Clones, we can cross the national border at Clontivrin, a mile west of the town, and make for Newtown Butler, in a part of county Fermanagh that Upper Lough Erne and its liquid outposts make more water than land. On the outskirts of the town in 1690 an Irish army on King James's side was defeated by a force from Enniskillen supporting King William. A hundred years before, the land to the north, which had for centuries belonged to the Maguires and which guarded one of the main approaches to Ulster from Connacht, was the scene of repeated attempts by that callous hothead, Sir Richard Bingham, to break into the last enclave of native Irish power. The Maguires held on till the 1590s. When they broke, the crafty Earl of Tyrone showed his hand fully on the side of the Irish, and raised the last and most critical of Gaelic rebellions. Maguire's Bridge, twelve miles north, recalls the old lords of Fermanagh. Lisnaskea, two miles this side of it, was another Maguire centre, and on a nearby rath, Cornashee Moat, half a mile north, they were inaugurated as princes by the O'Neill, their overlord. Aghalurcher church, a mile and a half south of Lisnaskea is where, in 1484, one Maguire killed another, at the altar, in a clannish feud. The ruin, the yews, and the macabre, untidy graves give it a haunting air.

Crom Castle, four miles south-west of **Newtown Butler**, is magnificently sited in the Earl of Erne's wooded 1,350-acre demesne by Upper Lough Erne. The earl's seat is a grandly battlemented Tudor-revival castle of the 1830s, designed by Scott's friend Edward Blore. In the grounds, which flank one of the hundreds of inlets of the lough, is old **Crom Castle**, the quintessence of a romantic ivy-covered ruin, built in 1611, scene of Jacobite assaults in 1689, and gutted by fire in 1764. At Belturbet, due south of Newtown Butler in county Cavan, we are back in the Republic. It is a pretty village on the River Erne, important once for holding an important pass between myriad lakes. As so often in Plantation towns, the sandstone Planter's Gothic Church of Ireland church dominates the main street, while the later, Italianate, Catholic church provides a more ebullient silhouette. Keeping to the R201 we next come to Milltown. Off a lane half a mile south of the village, beside Derrybrick Lough, are the attractive remains of a medieval church and Round Tower, built on the site of a monastery founded in the sixth century by St Mogue, a disciple of Wales's St David. From Milltown we round Lough Oughter, turning left on to the R199 at Killashandra (close to the Killysheen Forest Park, with good woodland and lakeside walking, and some scattered ancient remains) and left again on to the R198 at Crossdoney. Here and there are glimpses of the lake itself, a mazy complex of channels, islands, and peninsulas extending from the channel of the River Erne. Like all the lakeland complex of county Cavan, this inland archipelago draws many anglers, often coming regularly to their favourite spots.

Three miles before reaching the county town we pass on the left **Kilmore** Church of Ireland cathedral, a Neo-Gothic building that incorporates a Romanesque vestry doorway. Cathedral and attendant buildings can seem alone and forgotten. Bishop William Bedell (1571–1642), buried in the churchyard, was the first translator of the Bible into Irish. He also contended bravely for gentler official policies towards Catholics, but this did not stop his imprisonment in 1641 in Lough Oughter Castle by Catholic confederates, or his death from a fever while held there. In **Cavan** itself is the imposing and elaborate Catholic cathedral, completed in 1942. Beside it is the heavily classical courthouse built in the early nineteenth century by John Bowden. The ground rises just north of the town, and we get delightful views over the watery patchwork, interspersed with woods and fields and the odd spire piercing the horizon. Almost due west, and reached by a road off the R198, which skirts the lakeside demesne of the Maxwells, Lords Farnham, is the circular fourteenth-century tower of **Clough Oughter**, one of the best preserved of its kind in the country and fruitfully excavated in 1987. Well set on a small crannog, or prehistoric artificial island, it was scene of the short imprisonment of the above translator Bishop Bedell in 1641, and eight years later of the death of Owen Roe O'Neill, last and greatest hope of the Confederate Catholics.

Cavan's new cathedral replaces a Neo-Gothic one. This old building was transported to **Ballyhaise** and most of it re-erected as the parish church. We reach Ballyhaise by driving five miles north of Cavan along the R212. North of the village is a fine house built by Richard Castle in about 1732 – an attractive combination of red brick and stone. It is now an agricultural college, and around the building are some inept additions.

We now swing to the east, first driving two miles south-east to rejoin the R188, and coming in another ten miles to **Cootehill**, a neat Planters' town set up by the Coote family in the mid-seventeenth century in territory which had previously belonged to O'Reillys. Thomas Coote married in 1697 Ann Lovett, aunt of the architect Edward Lovett Pearce, which is how the exquisite Palladian villa, **Bellamont Forest**, came to be built a mile north of the town, in about 1730. Nearly square, and in red brick, with a massive Doric pedimented portico, it contains rooms of beautiful proportions and superb coffered plasterwork ceilings. The name Bellamont, with the ring of Italy in it, is artfully derived from Ballymount. The Coote family produced several generals, among them Sir Eyre, Clive's comrade and successor in India, and another whose dealings with boys of Christ's Hospital led to a public scandal in 1815 and his retirement as colonel of his regiment. Another soldiering Coote, who lived at Bellamont, became Earl of Bellamont in 1767, by which time he was father of innumerable illegitimate children. But he wanted a legal heir, the likelihood of which was not enhanced, it was thought, by a wound in the groin received in a duel with the ex-Viceroy of Ireland, Lord Townshend, in 1772. Two years later, however, he married Emily, daughter of the first Duke and Duchess of Leinster; but since the Duchess, by this time a widow, was rumoured to be secretly married to Mr Ogilvie, her children's tutor and an unredeemed commoner, the earl refused to speak to her at the wedding. The marriage produced an heir, but he died young. The distraught father had his body brought back to Bellamont, where it lay in state for three full days, and was then buried in the church, an enormous procession being arranged to follow the hearse. The earl maintained his eccentric ways – calling the Irish 'Hottentots', making his maiden speech in the Irish House of

Commons in his favourite language, French – until his death in 1800. The house remained in the hands of his illegitimate family till 1874, when poverty forced them to sell up. It is still privately owned and well maintained, but its small ration of parkland is at present belted in by a broad dark monotone girdle of conifers.

A mile north is the **Dartrey** demesne – also now state forest – whose Tudor-revival house has been completely demolished. However, a mausoleum by James Wyatt still stands among the fir trees, half a mile beyond the isolated redbrick Protestant church. It contains a beautiful monument to Lady Anne Dawson in a niche, erected after 1770 by her husband, the first Lord Dartrey. The statues – of Lord Dartrey and his young son looking up at an angel guarding a funeral urn – are the work of Joseph Wilton, a protégé of Lord Charlemont.

From Cootehill we drive south-east on the R190 and R192 to Shercock, passing on the left after three miles the ancient burial cairn known as the Cohaw Giants Grave, a well-preserved example of a double court tomb. Shercock itself, and Bailieborough to the south, and Ballybay seven miles north-east, are famous centres of fishing, as is **Carrickmacross**, ten miles east of Shercock on the R178. The Earl of Essex, granted lands by Queen Elizabeth, built a castle here, but the materials were used for a market-house in 1780. There is a steepled Church of Ireland church of the same period, and the Roman Catholic church has ten good lights by Harry Clarke, pupil of Sarah Purser at her Tower of Glass studio. The road continues direct to Dundalk, but a short digression to the north a few miles along takes us to Inishkeen, possessor of some desultory monastic remains, a folk museum in a deconsecrated church, and numerous associations with one of Ireland's important twentieth-century poets, the grumpy, grudging, humpy, cynical, self-made, drunken, fearlessly interfering, quintessentially Irish master of lyrical poetry and prose of telling simplicity, Patrick Kavanagh. He was born, brought up and buried here, and he often looked back on his migration to Dublin as a bad move. The village boasts a Kavanagh archive and Kavanagh trail, which he would probably have despised, or at least said he did. A few miles south of Dundalk itself, at Castlebellingham, we rejoin the route described in Chapter 2.

Appendices

History

Ancient Ireland was rich, from gold and other assets, and remote: almost the end of the known world. Its richness brought it trade and other contacts with Europe, while isolation spared it Roman invasion. The most enduring import from the continent was Christianity, of a mainly monastic kind which well suited the structure of Irish society. From the fifth century on, the Church grew in influence and for a time, after the barbarian invasions, carried the lamp of civilisation back to Europe. Nevertheless it remained, like the society around it, fragmented. Chief fought chief, abbot fought abbot, and all movement towards feudal unity was halted by rivalries and quarrels. High Kings were sovereign in name only, and even the Norse settlers of the ninth and tenth centuries, while building the country's first cities and promoting trade around the coasts, gave up trying to run the inland Irish. These, God-fearing as they were, still proved an administrative and doctrinal bane to their spiritual head, the Pope.

An Irish prince invited the Anglo-Normans to Ireland in 1169. A pope, the Anglo-Saxon Hadrian IV, gave the invaders his blessing. Seven hundred years of Irish history follow directly from that partially successful campaign. Beyond the Pale, an area around Dublin which stayed in English hands, a consistent pattern lasted for three centuries. Almost as fast as they were given lands and built their castles, Norman and English settlers adopted the ways and loyalties of their new surroundings and turned on their old masters; and native chiefs who were persuaded to pledge loyalty to the king redeemed the pledge whenever it suited them. Until the Tudors came, England's foothold was shaky.

The Tudors saw Ireland's potential value to an enemy, especially Spain. That being so, the Irish stood no chance of being free. Colonisation was more ruthless and resolute, and it was not just English grandees who were given land, but retiring soldiers, artisans, merchants and adventurers. Natives were eliminated, absorbed, or

467

forced to the far west, and Elizabeth's reign ended with the last mass Irish rising. The result was a vast exodus of Gaelic aristocrats, and the virtual end of the old Gaelic order.

Rebellion had been stiffest in the North, and to remedy this James I allocated all the best land of Ulster to Scottish settlers whose tenacious hold on their grants has lasted among their descendants. These new Presbyterian Scottish-Irish were soon protesting against laws which discriminated against them as much as they did against Catholics, and which boosted British farming and industry at the expense of their own. Many of them went to America. At home, a Republican tradition grew strong, and much subsequent rebellion has been conceived in the North. Elsewhere in the seventeenth century, Cromwell's campaign of 1649, the most vicious the country saw, left enduring scars and resentment. But it was no more than a continuation of Tudor policy, and in its own terms it succeeded. After a final Catholic rallying to James II's tattered flag in 1690, the country settled into what Yeats called 'the one Irish century that escaped from darkness and confusion'. The Catholics and poor, shackled by the Penal Laws, would not have agreed.

The eighteenth was the century of the Ascendancy, when the Anglo-Irish could not only dominate but – rebellion being dormant – build beautiful houses all over the country. Industry, agriculture and foreign trade boomed, roads and canals opened up the country. Money was made – fortunes by many – and society glittered. Dublin, Kilkenny, Limerick, Armagh, Birr and other towns were virtually built anew. Then once again the English in Ireland, resenting oppressive interference from Westminster, called for greater independence. In 1782 they were given a measure of it, but that little succeeded only in raising the hopes of radical reformers. These were soon fomented by the spirit of the French Revolution. When these hopes were expressed in the rising of 1798, England, fearing as always that an independent Ireland could make friends of England's enemies, brought all power back to London.

After coming to a peak in the early nineteenth century, the country's prosperity ebbed away, and many English left for good. The labouring classes, which had gained least from previous riches, now worked, when there *was* work, for landlords they seldom even saw. Work or no work, they were expected, for the most part, to pay rents. A blight in successive years on their staple food, the potato, worsened their plight. Five years of death and emigration during the 1840s reduced the population by two million from its all-time peak of eight and a half. By 1901 it was under four and a half million.

Concessions arrived during the century; Catholic emancipation (already under way in the eighteenth century), extended suffrage, repeal of the Corn Laws, the spread of education, and at last the right of tenants to buy the land they worked with money borrowed from the government. But now the call for Home Rule was loud at all levels. It might in the end have been given, but too many English promises had been false. Between 1916, the year of the Easter Rising, and 1921 the Irish snatched power by force.

The six counties of the new Northern Ireland, still one-third Presbyterian, were the exception. With no cause to love the English, whose laws had acted against non-conformists as much as Catholics, the majority liked popery still less. Discarding the three mainly Catholic counties of the province, a diminished Ulster stayed united with Britain, though it, too, had to use force to do so. It was a precarious basis for lasting union.

In the so-called South of Ireland – then the Irish Free State, and since 1949 the Republic of Ireland – civil war broke out, immediately after Independence, between those who accepted the Anglo-Irish Treaty and the island's partition and those, led by Eamonn de Valera, who rejected it. For two years there were fighting, ambushes, murders, executions sanctioned by law and many more not, destruction of buildings. At last de Valera and his Republicans gave up the armed struggle and formed the political party Fianna Fail. They won office in 1932. There followed a crippling economic war with England, and after that the privations – felt despite the South's neutral status – of World War Two.

De Valera's regime was very Catholic, nationalist, authoritarian. It heavily censored the arts, distrusted novelty, preferred cottage crafts to science and technology. Emigration continued to sap the country of its young people. Well into the 1960s the Republic was a picturesque backwater, rich in the charms of old ways and manners, desperately poor in economic terms. But younger leaders were by then forcing change. Reforms in education would produce in time graduates as adept at electronics and other disciplines as any in Europe. Spectacularly, material benefits of membership of the European Union began to transform the whole face of Ireland.

Change accelerated in the last decade of the twentieth century. Everywhere new roads, houses, industries sprang up. The tide of emigration turned, and exiles came back in their thousands. English and other foreigners came to seek jobs and homes in this buoyant expansion.

469

In places a price has been paid. Ireland followed the path England took a generation before. Efficient farming tended to uglify the countryside. Conspicuous bungalows tamed to drabness some of Europe's wildest landscapes. Roads ceased to be empty, or almost so. European subventions enabled farmers to wire off huge tracts of land where travellers were once welcome to walk. Amid all the prosperity, all too little was spent on preserving one of the country's inheritances – the houses, parks and public buildings, predominantly Georgian, erected by the old Ascendancy. All the same, change is the catchword of modern Ireland. For many years trends of all kinds will career ahead, reverse, skid, stall and start again. Ireland is a country with a new-found confidence, great gifts and resources and potential. It will certainly continue to fascinate.

Language

All the conquests, plantations and settlements – Norse, Norman, English, Scottish – and many smaller immigrations of Spanish, Huguenots, Swiss and Germans have so deeply diluted Celtic blood that there is probably none of the pure liquid left. This has not prevented – has possibly caused – a nostalgic move, before and after independence, towards a Celtic culture, and in particular the revival of the Irish language, still spoken early in the nineteenth century by over half the population, but dead by the end, except in outlying parts of the country and among the rather academic Gaelic League. The 1937 Irish Constitution declared Irish to be the first official language of a people most of whom knew hardly a word of it. Now it is taught in all schools and used widely on the radio and television, on bus and street signs, in government and other official papers, and so on.

There is, however, no denying that English remains the language of the people, and very little doubt that it always will. Even patriots like O'Connell saw it as the language of progress and urged people to speak it. In the Gaeltacht, the areas scattered round the south and west coasts where Irish has always been first language, it is now bolstered by a system of grants, so that students from other parts may come and learn it. It has to be subsidised. The language, like primitive farming methods, has been isolated in areas of traditional poverty.

The tourist needs no Irish at all. Those who speak it normally – scarcely 30,000 of them – switch politely to English when one of the company does not understand it. Even if he took the trouble to learn it, the visitor would find that Waterford Irish is substantially different from Kerry Irish, Kerry from Galway, and the official language a modern hybrid. He would find, too, that large numbers of people have no time for it, and sympathise with the member of the Dáil who once said its revival would make most people illiterate in two languages. And it may surprise him to find that, before leaving school to forget it, many Irish children not only learn Irish, but also do some of their

471

other lessons through the medium of the language. Nevertheless, its revival has been deeply bound up with the earnest search of a new state for its own identity. It has, moreover, an old and vivid literature of its own which nobody wants to see buried for ever in musty libraries.

The language was probably introduced into the country by the Goidels, Gaelic settlers of the last few centuries BC, though no writing survives from before the sixth century AD, and the earliest which does uses the Roman alphabet. The only exception is the curious ogham script, whose letters, in the form of notches on memorial stones, itself derives from the Roman alphabet. In time this Gaelic language evolved and modern scholars classify it into periods: Old Irish (which stands to Modern much as Latin to French) gave way in the tenth century to Middle Irish; Middle to Early Modern in the thirteenth century, and that to Late Modern in the seventeenth.

Until recently it had a written alphabet, of only eighteen letters, formed by symbols different from English ones. Though still found here and there, Irish script is disappearing after an official decision to adopt normal Roman letters. It is, in fact, an old decorative script known as uncial, and was used a lot in medieval monasteries.

Irish is an extremely difficult language. Like Latin and German it is inflected, its nouns and adjectives changing their endings, and sometimes other parts, depending on the case or number being used. *Fir*, for instance, means 'men' (it is often seen in public places), but its singular, 'man', is *fear.* English has similar irregularities – 'man' and 'men' is an example – but not nearly so many. Verbs are also complicated; and while there are two meaning 'to be' there is none meaning 'to have', so that possession is often indicated by what seems to others to be circumlocution. 'I have a dog' is expressed in Irish 'a dog is at me'.

Nor are there words with the range of meanings of our 'yes' and 'no'. This lack leads the Irish to express a positive or negative in English as they once did in Irish. A question opening 'Will you ...?' gets the English answer 'I will not' or 'I will', seldom 'no' or 'yes'. Other idioms spring from the same cause. 'After' doing something always means a temporal 'after', never a statement of intent. The existence in the Irish verb 'to be' of a 'habitual' tense leads to such phrases (they are very common) as Synge's 'the like of the holy prophets, do be straining the bars of paradise to lay eyes on the Lady Helen'. Which is to say they they are not simply straining now, but make a habit of it.

There are other problems. Aspiration, as long as Irish script was used, was shown by a dot over the letter in question (instead of the English habit of inserting an *h*). Then the official decision to replace Irish letters with Roman led to the adoption of the English practice, which in turn caused clumsy letter-sequences like *seachtmhain*, meaning 'week'. In 1948 a reformed spelling was introduced, which simplified the same word to *seachtain* (pronounced 'shochdin').

Eclipsis, in which the sound of the first letter of a word is eclipsed in certain contexts by one placed before it, this alone being pronounced, has no parallel in English and would take too long to explain. Among the many causes of eclipsis is when the word in question follows any of the numerals seven to ten, but does not follow the numerals three to six, unless in the genitive case. From things like this, opposition to revival gets much of its armour.

Pronunciation varies in the different Irish-speaking areas. Many difficult cases are explained where they occur in this book.

Over the centuries, English and Irish have left marks on each other. Plenty of what appear to be cryptic and complicated Irish spellings conceal ordinary English words, and several Gaelic words, like 'poteen', have been absorbed into English. Sometimes transference has led to confusion, as when people sought for some mythical explanation of the phoenix of Phoenix Park, when in fact the word is an English approximation to the original Irish *fionn uisge,* meaning 'clear water'. Sometimes, too, a word may seem to have three alternative spellings: Irish, an English approximation to the Irish pronunciation, and an English version pronounced differently. The word *ruadh* (red) might be spelt 'roo-a' to show how roughly it is pronounced. At the same time it has been absorbed into English as 'roe'. So *ruadh,* roo-a, roe and red all mean the same.

There are also words which, while not Gaelic, are not strictly the English of England either. Expressions like jackeen, shoneen, and gossoon (a boy-servant, from the French *garçon)* are really Anglo-Irish. Other words – strand, demesne, undertaker, tinker, turf – while being thoroughly English, have either changed their meaning minutely in Irish use, or are used more commonly there than anywhere else.

All these fluid processes at times make the spelling of place-names confusing. Old Irish, Norse, Norman, and various English versions of these have resulted sometimes in alternative modern spellings of the same name (Navan and An Uaimh are examples) which do not seem to represent the same sound at all. In looking for a standard, people usually go to the Ordnance Survey maps, but there are cases where common or local usage is different. The pioneer researchers of the Ordnance Survey in the early nineteenth century did a great deal of anglicising and so obscured a huge rich legacy of Irish place-names. But for want of a better, the rule in this book has been to follow the Ordnance Survey except in cases which would sound wrong to most Irish ears. There are necessarily examples which leave room for argument.

More confusion stems from the gradual change, over the centuries, of family names and titles from each other, and from the names of places from which they derive. Kinsale becomes Kingsale, Palmers-town Palmerston, Clonmel Clonmell, and so on. Different branches of families use different spellings: Plunket or Plunkett, McDonnell or MacDonnell, Power or Le Poer. Even standard reference books, not to mention other sources, occasionally contradict each other. This insouciance towards spelling is tied to the importance, in Ireland, of the spoken word in relation to the written. It should dismay only the literally literal mind.

Climate

No one season is clearly better than all others for going to Ireland. On average, its climate is warmer than Britain's, and it hardly ever sees settled snow. The south-east gets most warmth and sunshine; the mountainous west is rainiest. July and August tend to be best for warmth and beaches, but there are more tourists about. There can be serious crowds in and around Dublin, but the worst effect in most other parts (except at festival times) is that long stretches of beach have to be shared with a few others. September and October choke the hedges and moors with berries and greenery. But late spring is prettiest, and on average May and June have more sunshine than other months.

The main blight at any time can be rain or drizzle, especially in the west. But rain is not what it is elsewhere. It is soft, as the Irish say, and often dries quickly in sun and winds. It adds a blueness to distant hills and a richness to all natural colours. The clouds that bring it, endlessly changing the greater part of any landscape, are one of the finest sights of the country. On arrival it is worth making a mental note to watch clouds.

Food and Drink

Ireland's best restaurants and hotels provide as good wine and food as is to be found in the world. But they offer little that is especially Irish because Ireland had no tradition of gastronomy of its own; though native beef, lamb, pork, salmon, trout, eels and Dublin Bay prawns are superb raw materials .

The 1840s famines had the curious effect of making people associate free or cheap country food with poverty. They tried to get away from them, and now things like vegetables and salads that can be grown for almost nothing, and others that are free – blackberries, whortleberries, wild raspberries and strawberries – are astonishingly rare in middle- and lower-range restaurants. For the same reason, some Irish seem to find it incredible that visitors should want traditional cottage fare. You are more likely to be offered fried fish or scampi or chicken and chips, or the universal and so-called Limerick ham (which *can* be very good) with a pittance of salad, than Irish stew which, with its base of mutton neck, potatoes and onions, can when properly cooked be delicious.

The Irish eat rather fewer potatoes per head than the English, but in country districts they eat them differently, boiled and served – often as a separate course – in their skins, sometimes with butter. Bacon and cabbage, boiled together, make another traditional dish. You can still get soda bread, made with sour milk and raised with bread soda. Oysters, a poor man's food until disease killed the oyster beds of Wexford and Carlingford early last century, have returned. The largest beds are in Galway and in Carlingford Lough. Oysters with Guinness are a delight.

Most of the traditional milk products are made no more. There used to be a vast range of curds, butter and cream – 'whitemeats' they were sometimes called – but the home dairy has gone the way of the domestic bread oven. Cheese was hardly eaten. It was looked on askance as a kind of tallow. But it has made a good come-back; excellent cheeses are made and many more imported.

Irish drinks are well enough known. People say that Guinness, the most popular dark stout, tastes better in Ireland than anywhere else, and offer Liffey water as explanation, but its qualities vary widely from pub to pub (and the Liffey was never the source of the water anyway), as do those of Murphy's, its closest rival. At its creamy best Guinness can be as great as a great wine. Irish whiskey (usually spelt with the 'e') is made mainly from malted barley, like Scotch, but in a pot-still to which heat is applied directly by anthracite, as opposed to the Scotch patent-still (invented by an Irishman, Aeneas Coffey), in which the direct heat is provided by steam. Few people dispute the superiority of Scotch single-malt whiskies, but these apart the differences are matters for taste. Irish whiskies vary as much as Scotch, and Paddy or Northern Ireland's Bushmills may suit many whom Jameson does not.

Scotch's world-wide reputation is something new. In Victorian times (and Trollope's novels) and much later, gentlemen took a drop of Irish. Irish whiskey is always used in Irish coffee, a beverage drunk more by tourists than natives. It is made by pouring into a pre-heated glass first a measure of whiskey, then one or two teaspoons of sugar, then hot black coffee. The mixture is stirred before whipped cream, poured on over the back of a spoon, tops the whole with a layer of white.

Glossary

Adventurer	One who subscribed money to Parliament for the reduction of Ireland from 1642 onward, and stood to gain lands confiscated from rebels.
Antae	Short projections of walls beyond the corner of a building. Singular, anta, is rare.
Árd Rí	(pron. 'Aurd ree') High King, a title claimed and disputed by ruling Irish families from the fifth to the twelfth centuries.
Ascendancy	The Anglo-Irish ruling class in Ireland from the seventeenth to nineteenth centuries.
Bailey	Enclosed courtyard of a Norman or later castle, beside the keep or motte.
Bally	(from Irish *baile*). Settlement, town.
Bartizan	Small turret projecting from the angle of a parapet or tower, or half-way up it.
Bawn	Fortified enclosure of a castle.
Beg	(Irish *beag*) Small.
Beehive hut	Small circular structure, made in early Christian times from rough stones and by corbelling, q.v. Clochán.
Bivallate	Enclosed by two concentric banks.
Bohreen	Country path, usually flanked by stone walls, originally for driving cows through.
Bord Fáilte	Irish for 'Board of the Welcomes'; Irish Tourist Board.
Bull, Irish	Proposition whose comic inconsistency is not seen by the speaker, e.g. 'I must stop making resolutions'; 'Posterity never did anything for me'.
Bullaun	Stone, often found in early monasteries, with smooth depression in the side, used as a mortar.
Cahir	A fort of dry masonry.

478

Glossary

Carrig/Carrick	Rock.
Cashel	Stone-walled enclosure, round a fort, church or monastery.
Cheval-de-frise	Irregular, defensive arrangement of sharp stones or stakes in front of a fortress. (First used in Frisia.)
Clochán	Beehive hut q.v.
Coade Stone	A very hard patent composition made in London from 1769 to 1836, and used for architectural mouldings and sculptures.
Corbel	A stone projecting from a wall as a support. Beehive huts and other buildings were built by corbelling, each course of masonry projecting over that below until the walls met at the top.
Crannóg	A usually artificial island in a lake or marsh, belted by a ring of stakes or stones, and sometimes having a causeway to the land, just below water level.
Currach/Coracle	Keelless small boat made by stretching tarred canvas – in ancient times hide – over a framework of laths.
Dáil Éireann	(pron. 'Dau-il airan') The lower house, or House of Representatives, in the Irish Parliament (*Oireachtas*) .
Derg	(Irish *dearg)* Red.
Demesne	The word usually used for the enclosed park round a big house; from the Latin *Dominicus,* 'belonging to a lord'.
Derry	(Irish *doire*) Tree or wood of oak.
Diamond	The word used in Ulster for a town's central square.
Dolmen	Stone chamber of a neolithic tomb, usually consisting of a capstone supported on vertical stones, originally covered by a mound of earth.
Drum	(Irish *druim*) Ridge.
Dub, or Doo	(Irish *dubh*) Black.
Dun	Fort.
Ennis	(Irish *inis*) Island.
Esker	Long ridge of gravel, sand and other alluvial deposits, formed by movements of the ice-sheet.
Eye-catcher	Tower, obelisk or folly designed simply to catch the eye in a landscaped garden.
Féis	(pron. 'fesh') Festival.

Fianna Fáil	(pron. 'fee-anna fau-il') 'Sons of destiny', name of one of the Republic's two main political parties.
Fine Gael	(pron. 'finna gale') 'Race of the Irish', name of one of the Republic's two main political parties.
Finial	Stone ornament at the top of a spire, pinnacle, gable or other similar feature.
Fir	Men (indicating public lavatories).
Gaeltacht	Area in which Irish is the vernacular language.
Gallaun	Standing stone, usually isolated.
Gallery grave	Megalithic chamber tomb, either rectangular or wedge-shaped, sometimes divided into compartments by stones.
Gallowglass	Mercenary soldier from Scotland, used in Ireland from the thirteenth to the fifteenth centuries.
Garda	(pron. 'gorda'; plural 'gordee') Guard; policeman.
Grianan	(pron. 'greenan') Palace.
High Cross	Tall, stone (usually Celtic) cross, dating from the early tenth to the thirteenth century, generally with carvings.
Inch, or Innis	(Irish *inis*) Island.
Jackeen	Useless braggart.
Kill	(Irish *cill*) Small church or cell.
Knock	(Irish *cnoc*) Hill.
Liberty	Urban district which was not under the jurisdiction of the mayor.
Lis	(Irish lios) Earthen fort, or enclosure.
Mná	Women (indicating public lavatories).
Mor, More	Big, great.
Og	Young.
Ogee	Double-curve, as in the letter '*s*'.
Ogham	A script formed of lines representing twenty letters of the Latin alphabet, used around the fifth century AD to notch memorial inscriptions on standing stones; the earliest known Irish script.
Oireachtas	Irish national parliament, comprising the President, Dáil and Seanad.
Pale	The area, spreading to a variable distance from Dublin, to which effective English control was confined from the twelfth to sixteenth centuries.
Passage-grave	Megalithic grave in which a passage leads to the tomb-chamber.

Glossary

Pattern	Festival commemorating a local saint, in which indulgences can be won by various acts of worship and endurance.
Pillarstone	Megalithic standing stone.
Plantation	Used to describe effects of the colonising of Ulster in James I's reign, especially architectural styles which introduced many features from Scotland.
Poteen	Illicitly distilled Irish whiskey.
Quadrant	Curved connection, in the shape of a quarter-circle, between the main block of a Palladian house and its wings or pavilions.
Rath	Earthen fort or enclosure.
Scoil	Irish word for 'school'.
Seanad Éireann	Senate, or Upper House, of the Irish Parliament, or *Oireachtas*.
Sedilia	Seats, generally three and built into the wall, for clergy, situated on the south side of the chancel.
Sept	A large family grouping, comprising people who lived in one area, had the same surname, and traced their descent to common ancestors.
Shanachie	Genealogist, or story-teller.
Sheila-na-gig	Carving of a – usually grotesque and naked – woman in religious or secular buildings, generally thought to be connected with a fertility rite.
Shoneen	Fraterniser with the British (a 'little John').
Sinn Féin	(pron. 'Shin fane') 'We Ourselves', political party founded in 1905 for the furtherance of Home Rule.
Skerry	Rock.
Slieve	(Irish *sliabh*) Mountain.
Souterrain	Underground series of chambers, found often in ring-forts, whose purpose is unknown, but was probably storage and perhaps sometimes refuge.
Strand	Word most commonly used in Ireland for beach.
Tanist	Heir of a chieftain, elected by his sept. The *Tánaiste* today is the Deputy Taoiseach, or Prime Minister.
Taoiseach	(pron. 'Tee-shook') Prime Minister.
Teachta Dála	Member of the Dáil, usually abbreviated TD.
Tholsel	Town hall.
Tra, or Tráigh	(pron. 'traw') Beach.

Turf	Word normally used where peat or peat-fuel would be used in Britain.
Uachtarán	President of the Republic of Ireland.
Undertaker	Mainly Scottish colonists of Ulster in James I's time, who agreed to observe certain conditions in accepting land-grants.

Further Reading

Beckett, J.C.: *The Making of Modern Ireland*. Faber,1966.

Behan, Brendan: *Brendan Behan's Island*. Hutchinson, 1962.

Bence-Jones, Mark: *Burke's Guide to Country Houses, Volume 1: Ireland*. Burke's Peerage, 1978.

Bence-Jones, Mark: *Twilight of the Ascendancy*. Constable, 1987.

Berresford Ellis, Peter: *Hell or Connaught*. Blackstaff, 1975.

Boylan, Henry: *A Dictionary of Irish Biography*. Gill and Macmillan, 3rd edition, 1998.

Brown, Terence: *Ireland, A Social and Cultural History 1922–1985*. Fontana, 1981.

Carty, James: *Ireland, A Documentary Record* (3 vols). Fallon, Dublin, 1951 and 1952.

Caulfield, Max: *The Easter Rebellion*. Muller, 1964.

Chart, D.A.: *The Story of Dublin*. Dent, 1932.

Clarke, Desmond: *Dublin*. Batsford, 1977.

Connolly, S.J. (ed): *The Oxford Companion to Ireland*. OUP, 1998.

Coogan, Tim Pat: *The Troubles: Ireland's Ordeal 1966–1995*. Hutchinson, 1996.

Corkery, Daniel: *The Hidden Ireland*. Gill, Dublin, 3rd edition, 1941.

Craig, Maurice: *Dublin 1660–1860*. Hodges, Figgis, Dublin; Cresset Press, London, 1952.

Craig, Maurice, and the Knight of Glin: *Ireland Observed*. Mercier Press, Cork, 1970.

Craig, Maurice: *The Architecture of Ireland*. Batsford, 1982.

Craig, Patricia (ed): *The Oxford Book of Ireland*. OUP, 1998.

Crookshank, Anne, and the Knight of Glin: *The Painters of Ireland*. Barrie and Jenkins, 1978.

Curran, C.P.: *Dublin Decorative Plasterwork*. Tiranti, 1967.

Danaher, Kevin: *In Ireland Long Ago*. Mercier Press, Cork, 1962.

Dillon, Myles: *The Cycle of the Kings*. OUP, 1946.

Dillon, Myles, and Nora Chadwick: *The Celtic Realms*. Weidenfeld and Nicolson, 1967.

Dudley Edwards, Ruth: *An Atlas of Irish History*. Methuen, 2nd edition, 1981.

Ellmann, Richard: *James Joyce*. OUP, 1959.

Evans, Estyn: *Irish Folk Ways*. Routledge and Kegan Paul, 1957.

Evans, Estyn: *The Irish Heritage*. Dundalgan Press, 1942.

Flower, Robin: *The Irish Tradition*. OUP, 1947.

Foster, R.F.: *Modern Ireland*. Allen Lane, 1988.

Gibbings, Robert: *Lovely is the Lee*. Dent, 1949.

Gibbings, Robert: *Sweet Cork of Thee*. Dent, 1951.

Giraldus Cambrensis: *The Topography of Ireland*. Dundalgan Press, Dundalk, 1951.

Gogarty, Oliver St John: *As I Was Going Down Sackville Street*. Sphere, 1968.

Guinness, Hon. Desmond and William Ryan: *Irish Houses and Castles*. Weidenfeld and Nicolson, 1971.

Guinness, Desmond: *Georgian Dublin*. Batsford, 1982.

Harbison, Peter, Homer Potterton and Jeanne Sheehy: *Irish Art and Architecture*. Thames and Hudson, 1978.

Henry, Françoise: *Irish Art in the Early Christian Period*. Methuen, 1965.

Kavanagh, P.J.: *Voices in Ireland*. Murray, 1994.

Kee, Robert: *The Green Flag*. Weidenfeld, 1972.

Kee, Robert: *The Laurel and the Ivy*. Hamish Hamilton, 1992.

Kennelly, Brendan (ed): *The Penguin Book of Irish Verse*. Penguin, 1970.

Killanin, Lord, and Michael V. Duignan: *Shell Guide to Ireland*. Ebury Press, revised edition, 1989.

Lecky, W.E.H.: *A History of Ireland in the Eighteenth Century* (5 vols). Longmans, 1895.

Lehane, Brendan: *The Quest of Three Abbots*. John Murray, 1968.

Lehane, Brendan: *Dublin*. Time-Life, 1979.

Lehane, Brendan: *Wild Ireland*. Sheldrake Press, 1995.

Lydon, James, and Margaret MacCurtain, (eds): *The Gill History of Ireland* (11 vols). Gill and Macmillan, 1972–1975.

Lyons, F.S.L.: *Ireland since the Famine*. Collins, 1973.

Macardle, Dorothy: *The Irish Republic*. Irish Press, Dublin, 4th edition, 1951.

MacLysaght, Edward: *Irish Life in the Seventeenth Century*. Talbot Press, Dublin, 2nd edition, 1950.

Further Reading

Macrory, Patrick: *The Siege of Derry*. Hodder, 1980.

Magan, William: *Umma-More*. Element Books, 1983.

Malins, Edward, and Patrick Bower: *Irish Gardens and Demesnes from 1830*. Barrie and Jenkins, 1980.

Malins, Edward, and the Knight of Glin: *Lost Demesnes*. Barrie and Jenkins, 1976.

Mason, T.H.: *Islands of Ireland*. Mercier Press, Cork, paperback, 1967.

Maxwell, Constantia: *Dublin under the Georges*. Harrap, 3rd edition, 1946.

Maxwell, Constantia: *Country and Town in Ireland under the Georges*. Dundalk, new edition, 1950.

Mills, Stephen: *Nature in its Place*. Bodley Head, 1988.

Mitchell, Frank: *The Irish Landscape*. Collins, 1976.

Moody, T.W. and F.X. Martin: *The Course of Irish History*. Mercier Press, Cork, 1967.

Moriarty, Christopher: *A Guide to Irish Birds*. Mercier Press, Cork, 1967.

Murphy, Dervla: *A Place Apart*. Murray, 1978.

O'Connor, Ulick: *Oliver St John Gogarty*. Cape, 1964.

O'Faolain, Sean: *The Great O'Neill*. Longmans, 1942.

O'Faolain, Sean: *The Irish*. Penguin, 1947.

O'Sullivan, Maurice: *Twenty Years A-growing*. OUP (World's Classics edition), 1953.

Pakenham, Thomas: *The Year of Liberty*. Hodder, 1969.

Pochin Mould, Daphne D.C.: *The Irish Saints*. Burns and Oates, 1964.

Praeger, Robert Lloyd: *The Way that I Went*. Allen Figgis, Dublin, paperback edition, 1959.

Praeger, Robert Lloyd: *The Natural History of Ireland*. Collins, 1950.

Ranelagh, J.O'B.: *Short History of Ireland*. Cambridge, 2nd edition, 1994.

Rolt, L.T.C.: *Green and Silver*. Allen and Unwin, 1949.

Somerville-Large, Peter: *The Coast of West Cork*. Gollancz, 1974.

Somerville-Large, Peter: *Irish Eccentrics*. Hamish Hamilton, 1975.

Somerville-Large, Peter: *The Irish Grand Tour*. Hamish Hamilton, 1982.

Taylor, Geoffrey: *The Emerald Isle*. Evans Bros, 1952.

Thackeray, W.M.: *Irish Sketch Book*. London, 1842.

Thomson, David: *Woodbrook*. Penguin, 1976.

Walsh, Caroline: *The Homes of Irish Writers*. Anvil Books, 1982.

Companion Guide to Ireland

Welch, Robert (ed): *Oxford Companion to Irish Literature*. OUP, 1998.

White, Terence de Vere: *The Parents of Oscar Wilde*. Hodder and Stoughton, 1967.

White, Terence de Vere: *A Fretful Midge*. Routledge and Kegan Paul, 1957.

Wilde, William R.: *Beauties of the Boyne and Blackwater*. Sign of the Three Candles, Dublin, new edition, 1949.

Wilde, William R.: *Loch Coirib*. Three Candles, Dublin, new edition, 1955.

Woodham-Smith, Cecil: *The Great Hunger*. Hamish Hamilton, 1962.

Houses, Castles and Gardens Regularly
Open to the Public

Note: Dates of opening, particularly of private properties, are very approximate and liable to change. They should always be checked with the property itself or the local tourist office.

Antrim

Antrim Castle, Antrim	Gardens only, all year
Benvarden, Dervock, Ballymoney	Gardens only, June to August
Carrickfergus Castle, Carrickfergus	All year
Templetown mausoleum, Templepatrick	All year

Armagh

Ardress House	April to September
The Argory	April to September
Derrymore House, Bessbrook	Easter; May to August

Carlow

Altamont, Ballon	Gardens only, April to October
Lisnavagh, Rathvilly	Gardens only, May to July

Clare

Bunratty Castle, Bunratty	All year
Cratloe Woods House	June to September
Knappogue Castle, Quin	April to October

Cork

Annesgrove, Castletownroche	Gardens only, Easter to September
Ballymaloe Cookery School Gardens	Gardens only, all year

Bantry House, Bantry	March to October
Barryscourt Castle, north of Cobh	All year
Blarney Castle, Blarney	All year
Castle Gardens, Timoleague	June to August
Creagh, Skibbereen	Gardens only, Easter to October
Desmond Castle, Kinsale	April to October
Fota, Carrigtwohill	House being restored; arboretum March to October
Riverstown, Glanmire	May to September

Derry

Bellaghy Bawn, Bellaghy	All year
Hezlett House, Coleraine	April to September
Mussenden Temple, Downhill	April to September
Springhill, Moneymore	April to September

Donegal

Ardnamona, west of Lough Eske	Gardens only, all year
Glebe House and Gallery, Church Hill	Easter; May to September
Glenveagh Castle, Church Hill	Easter to early November

Down

Ballywalter Park, near Newtownards	Being restored
Castle Ward, Strangford	House: Easter; May to October Gardens: all year
Mount Stewart, Newtownards	April to October
Rowallane, Saintfield	Gardens only, April to October
Seaforde Gardens, Seaforde	Easter to September

Dublin

The Dillon Garden, 45 Sandford Road, Ranelagh	Gardens only, March to September
Drimnagh Castle, Drimnagh	All year
Howth Castle, Howth	All year
James Joyce Tower, Sandycove	April to October
Malahide Castle, Malahide	All year
Marino, Casino	June to September

Houses, Castles and Gardens Regularly Open to the Public

National Botanic Gardens, Glasnevin	All year
Newbridge House, Donabate	All year
Powerscourt Town House, South William Street	All year
Rathfarnham Castle, Rathfarnham	Easter; June to October
Shaw's birthplace, 33 Synge Street	May to October

Fermanagh

Castle Coole, Enniskillen	April to September
Crom estate, Newtownbutler	April to September
Enniskillen Castle	All year
Florence Court	All year

Galway

Ashford Castle Hotel, Cong	Grounds only, all year
Athenry Castle, Athenry	June to September
Dunguaire Castle, Kinvara	May to October
Kylemore Abbey, Letterfrack	All year
Nora Barnacle House Museum, Galway	May to September
Patrick Pearse's Cottage, 10 miles north of Kilkieran	June to September
Thoor Ballylee, Gort	April to September

Kerry

Derreen, Lauragh	Gardens only, April to September
Derrynane, Caherdaniel	All year
Dunloe Castle Hotel, Dunloe	Gardens only, April to October
Muckross House, Killarney	House and garden, all year

Kildare

Castletown, Celbridge	All year
Japanese Gardens, Tully	February to November
Larchill, Kilcock	Gardens and park only, May to September
Straffan Walled Gardens and Steam Museum, Straffan	April to September

Kilkenny

Kilfane Glen, Thomastown	Gardens only, April to September
Kilkenny Castle	All year
Rothe House, Kilkenny	All year

Laois

Belvedere House, south of Mullingar	June to October
Emo Court, Emo	House: June to September Gardens: all year
Heywood, Ballinakill	Gardens only, all year

Leitrim

Lough Rynn	House and grounds, May to September

Limerick

Castle Matrix, Rathkeale	June to September
Glin Castle	House and grounds, May to June

Longford

Carrigglas Manor	House: June to August Gardens: May to September

Mayo

Westport House	Easter to September

Meath

Butterstream Garden, Trim	Gardens only, April to September

Monaghan

Hilton Park, Clones	May to September

Offaly

Birr Castle, Birr	Gardens only, all year
Cloghan Castle, Banagher	May to September

Roscommon

Clonalis, Castlerea	June to September
Frybrook House, Boyle	June to September

Houses, Castles and Gardens Regularly Open to the Public

King House, Boyle   April to October
Strokestown Park House
   and Famine Museum   May to September

Sligo
Lissadell, Carney   June to September
Parke's Castle, on north coast of
   Lough Gill   April to October

Tipperary
Cahir Castle, Cahir   April to October
Damer House, Roscrea   June to October
Ormond Castle, Carrick-on-Suir June to September
Roscrea Castle   June to October
Swiss Cottage, south of Cahir   March to November

Tyrone
Wilson House, Dergalt, Strabane All year

Waterford
Curraghmore, Portlaw   Gardens and shell grotto only,
                                     Easter to October
Lismore Castle, Lismore   Gardens only, April to September

Westmeath
Ballinlough Castle, Clonmellon Gardens only, May to September
Tullynally Castle, Castlepollard House: June to August
                                     Gardens: May to September

Wexford
Johnstown Castle, near Wexford Gardens only, all year.

Wicklow
Avondale, Rathdrum   All year
Kilruddery   Gardens only, April to September
Mount Usher gardens, Ashford   Gardens only, March to October
Powerscourt, Enniskerry   Gardens only, all year.
Russborough, Blessington   June to August

Some Regular Events

March: St Patrick's Day (17th)

April: Irish Grand National, Fairyhouse
              Dublin International Film Festival
              Final of Gaelic Football League, Croke Park, Dublin

May: Cork International Choral and Folk Dance Festival
              2,000 and 1,000 Guineas, Curragh
              Kilkenny Beer Festival
              Galway Arts Festival

June: An Fleadh Nua. Traditional music; varying sites
              Festival of Music in Great Irish Houses
              Listowel Writers' Week
              Bloomsday, day of Joyce's *Ulysses*; Dublin (16th)
              Festival of Tipperary
              Dublin Organ Festival
              Lough Derg pilgrimages begin, county Donegal (1st)
              Irish Derby, Curragh

July: Battle of Boyne anniversary (12th)
              Irish Oaks, Curragh
              Wexford Strawberry Fair
              Fleadh Cheoil na hEireann, varying sites
              Croagh Patrick pilgrimage, county Mayo
              Open Tennis Championships of Ireland, Dublin
              James Joyce summer school, Dublin
              Galway Races

Some Regular Events

August: Robertstown Grand Canal Fiesta, county Kildare
                 Lough Derg pilgrimages end, county Donegal (15th)
                 Galway Hookers' Regatta, Kinvarra, county Galway
                 Steam Rally, Stradbally, county Laois
                 Dublin Horse Show
                 Puck Fair, Killorglin, county Kerry
                 Yeats Summer School, Sligo
                 Connemara Pony Show, Clifden, county Galway

September: Rose of Tralee Festival, county Kerry
                 Irish St Leger, Curragh
                 Oyster Festival, Clarinbridge, county Galway
                 International Festival of Light Opera, Waterford
                 All-Ireland Hurling Final, Croke Park, Dublin
                 All-Ireland Football Final, Croke Park, Dublin

October: Horse Fair, Ballinasloe, county Galway
                 Wexford Opera Festival
                 Cork Jazz Festival
                 Cork Film Festival
                 Dublin Theatre Festival

November: Belfast Festival: arts

Index

Index

Santry (Dub.) 58
Sarsfield, Patrick 117, 144, 290
Saul (Down) 449
Scariff (Clare) 301
Scarriffhollis (Don.) 387
Scarva (Down) 430, 452
Scattery Island (Clare) 310
Scheemakers, Peter 58, 186
Schomberg, Marshall 34, 443, 452
Scone, Stone of 89
Scota 282
Scott, John, Earl of Clonmell 21, 61
Scott, Michael 38, 237
Scott, Sir Walter 244, 453
Scrabo Tower (Down) 444
Screeb (Gal.) 332
Scullabogue (Wex.) 170
Seaforde House (Down) 449
Seefin (Cork) 297
Selskar Abbey (Wex.) 161, 163
Semple, George 32
Semple, John 134
Shackleton, Sir E. 175
Shanagarry (Cork) 229
Shanagolden (Lim.) 286
Shanahan, Michael 399
Shanahoe (Laois) 133
Shanbally (Tip.) 217
Shandon (Cork) 236
Shane's Castle (Ant.) 439
Shanid (Lim.) 286
Shannon, Earl of 229
Shannon, River 105, 111
Shannon Airport (Clare) 307
Shannonbridge (Off.) 114
Shannongrove House (Lim.) 287
Shannon Harbour (Off.) 114–115
Shannon Pot (Cavan) 359, 364
Shaw, G.B. 11, 38, 62, 164, 254, 270, 313
Shawe-Taylor, John 318
Sheares, J. and H. 47
Sheila-na-gig 113, 370
Shelley, P.B. 18
Shelton Abbey (Wick.) 150
Sheppard, Oliver 163, 178
Shercock (Cavan) 463
Sheridan, R.B. 22, 82, 443
Sheridan, Thomas 82

Sherkin Island (Cork) 257
Shillelagh (Wick.) 176
Shrule (Mayo) 328
Siddons, Mrs. 23
Sidney, Sir Philip 245
Silken Thomas 94, 174
Silvermines Mts. (Tip.) 129
Simnel, Lambert 27f, 203
Sixmilebridge (Clare) 308
Skelligs (Kerry) 271f
Skerries (Dub.) 64
Skibbereen (Cork) 256, 257
Skreen (Meath) 89
Skull (Cork) 258
Slade Castle (Wex.) 167
Slane (Meath) 78f
Slaney River 177f
Sleator, James 42, 238
Slemish Mt. (Ant.) 408, 438
Slieve Anierin (Leit.) 364
Slieve Bloom (Laois) 125f
Slieve Donard (Down) 450
Slieve Felim (Lim.) 129
Slieve Gallion (Derry) 430, 438
Slieve League (Don.) 378f
Slieve Mish (Kerry) 276
Slievenamon (Tip.) 194, 198
Sligo (Sligo) 354f
Sloane, Sir Hans 454
Slyne Head (Gal.) 334
Smeaton, J. 114
Smerwick (Kerry) 280
Smith-Barry, A. 219, 230
Smyth, Edward 47
Smyth, John 9, 30
Sneem (Kerry) 270
Soane, Sir John 394, 399, 417
Somerville, Edith 35, 253, 255, 320
Southwell family 296
Spaniards Bay (Ant.) 493
Spenser, Edmund 170, 178, 210, 213, 222, 236, 238, 245, 246, 247, 280, 349, 400
Spiddal (Gal.) 332
Springhill (Derry) 437
Staigue Fort (Kerry) 270f
Stapleton, Michael 19, 22, 43, 44, 434
Stephens, James 242, 427

Index

Yeats, Jack B. 12, 238
Yeats, John B. 12
Yeats, W. B. 10, 12, 18, 19, 271,
317f, 364, 365
Yellow Ford, Battle of the (Arm.)
433

Youghal (Cork) 211f
Young, Arthur 221, 244, 265, 368,
372

Zucchi, Antonio 202

The Companion Guide to Rome
GEORGINA MASSON, revised by TIM JEPSON

The Companion Guide to Paris
ANTHONY GLYN, revised by SUSAN GLYN

An exuberant performance by a man thoroughly at ease in the subject. – THE TIMES

Writes about Paris with love... so well that he is a genuine companion guide in himself – DAILY TELEGRAPH

I stumbled upon this gem when buying six guidebooks to Paris for a) a long flight and b) a week of business in France. This Anthony Glyn publication significantly outdid the others. It was insightful, and USEFUL, and, best of all, quite humourous. I liked it so much, I bought one dozen as Christmas presents for co-workers with future stints in Paris. – Customer review, amazon.com

The Companion Guide to Florence
EVE BORSOOK

This is a book to read before you go, to carry with you and to re-read on your return. – THE SPECTATOR

A sure and illuminating guide – SUNDAY TIMES

Eve Borsook's The Companion Guide to Florence *is the key to the city. In addition to all the names, dates, places of history, Borsook skillfully weaves in meaning and context. You can go to Florence to shop for many beautiful Italian creations. But with this book, you can gain a clear appreciation about why the names, images and achievements from this amazing city's glorious past still resonate in our lives today.* – Customer review, amazon.com

The Companion Guide to London
DAVID PIPER, revised by FIONNUALA JERVIS

It is surely remarkable to write of a guidebook that it is difficult to put down. But it is certainly true of this one. – ECONOMIST

Calls our attention to everything beautiful, historical or curious left in the heart of London. – SUNDAY TIMES

Many guidebooks are long on information and short on readability. This book... is both erudite and witty. He covers all the essentials but puts on a gloss of wit and lards his facts with stories and comments which complement the text. There are some very fine guide books on London but this is among the best. – Customer review, amazon.com